V&R

Ellert R. S. Nijenhuis

The Trinity of Trauma: Ignorance, Fragility, and Control

Enactive Trauma Therapy

Vandenhoeck & Ruprecht

With 26 figures and 7 tables

Bibliographical information published by the Deutsche Nationalbibliothek

The Deutsche Nationalbibliothek lists this publication in the Deutsche Nationalbibliografie; detailed bibliographic data available online: http://dnb.d-nb.de.

ISBN 978-3-525-40268-9
You can find alternative editions of this book and additional material on our website: www.v-r.de

Cover image: Anatoli Styf/shutterstock.com

Printed in Germany.
Typesetting: Satzspiegel, Nörten-Hardenberg
Managing Editor: Joseph A. Smith
Cover: SchwabScantechnik, Göttingen
Printed and bound in Germany by ⊕ Hubert & Co., Göttingen

Printed on non-aging paper.

Table of Contents

Volume III

Enactive Trauma Therapy

Preface

It is impossible for man not to be a part of Nature and not to follow the common order of Nature. But if he lives among such individuals as agree with his nature, his power of acting will thereby be aided and encouraged. On the other hand, if he is among men who do not agree at all with his nature, he will hardly be able to accommodate himself to them without greatly changing himself.
Baruch Spinoza (1677a, Part IV, Appendix VII, p. 156)

Human action is the process of the intertwining of the body and the environment in cooperation with other people, and the results of human action are an inseparable part of this process. The human being belongs together with the other human beings and may only in this context have his own existence. Individuality is possible only in a social system.
Timo Järvilehto (2000a, p. 53)

Interpersonal neglect, maltreatment, and abuse can cut deep wounds, particularly when the misery commences in early childhood and lasts for years and years. Healing[1] the visible and invisible injuries in a later phase of life constitutes a profound challenge. Regaining wholeness without any aid from supportive others may be exceptionally difficult if not in fact impossible. A little help from friends rarely suffices to get by, and not even a lot of help from one's allies may do. Some individuals have not or scarcely experienced that other people can be caring and loving. If life has been this harsh to them, they may have major difficulty establishing or maintaining close relationships at all.

Strictly speaking, it is not within the power of clinicians to heal someone else's injuries. In principle, only the injured individuals themselves can heal their own wounds. However, professional assistance can be a crucial ingredient to their recovery. Clinicians can serve

1 Healing means to 'make whole' and thus clearly relates to health. The word 'health' can be traced back to the old English term *hælτ*, which stood for 'wholeness, a being whole, sound or well.' *Hælτ* in turn can be traced to the Proto-Germanic '*hailitho*' and to the Proto-Indo-European *kailo-*, which means 'whole, uninjured, of good omen.' Old English also has *hælan* for 'to heal.' In Middle English health meant physical health as well as 'prosperity, happiness, welfare, preservation, and safety.' When I use the terms healing, health, and wholeness, I intend each of these meanings.

as effective coaches inasmuch as they understand chronic trauma, know the do's and don'ts of trauma therapy, and possess the required clinical skills.

Ignorance, Fragility, and Control versus Realization

To fulfill their coaching role, clinicians also need professional, societal, and financial contexts that allow them to contribute to the recovery of traumatized individuals. Yet such environmental criteria are not easily met. One major obstacle is that society as well as psychology and psychiatry are not eager to invest in the prevention, education, treatment, and study of chronic traumatization and dissociation. History testifies to this (see Volume I and Chapter 20 of this series; Nijenhuis, 2015a, 2015b). Many families in which emotional, physical, and sexual horrors have occurred prefer denial to realization. Per definitionem perpetrators disregard their victims' interests. The common social pattern is to *ignore* the involved children's *fragility* and pain. Trying to *control* the immense problem of chronic interpersonal traumatization, many individuals and groups turn a blind eye to the outright cruel ways in which a substantial proportion of children are raised. It is a sad fact that many societal echelons prefer to discount rather than acknowledge the suffering of the involved children and the multiple effects of the horrors they are forced to live with. Most peoples, families, and perpetrators as well as mainstream psychology and psychiatry pay little heed to the effects on the health and welfare of abused, maltreated, and neglected children. There are, of course, many fine exceptions. But exceptions are not the rule.

Dramatic cases may serve to disrupt the sweet personal and societal ignorance, at least for some time. Individuals, families, and communities are bound to feel pained and fragile when the reality of chronic childhood traumatization strikes home. Emotionally affected in one way or another, they start engaging in more active ways of controlling the painful situation. Some blame others for failing to serve the best interests of the child. Others disbelieve or discredit the facts of the traumatization. Perpetrators bluntly deny even undeniable facts – or counterattack victims who won't be silenced anymore. Psychology and psychiatry slowly awake from their trauma-ignoring and trauma-ignorant swoon. Society cries out. But when the storm that some dramatic case stirs is over, and when the news of the day leads people's minds in different directions, the soothing veil of ignorance is spread once more.

Ignoring realities is a simple way to control them. Almost by definition it involves only a low to modest level of consciousness. Domineering others is an equally shortsighted means of controlling the complexities of one's world, including one's own fragility. Ignorance and totalitarian attitudes, however, come at a major price: The direct and indirect emotional and economic costs of chronic childhood traumatization are *huge*. The challenge, then, is to realize that this traumatization constitutes a major personal, familial, clinical, and societal problem that defies simple solutions.

Becoming aware of chronic childhood traumatization is a difficult action. Acting responsibly on the basis of this knowledge is even harder. This realization means enduring high levels of consciousness, intense communication, coordination, and cooperation. It demands a major desire to act as well as a major power of action. It also takes a lot of courage since full realization of chronic childhood traumatization means *taking lasting complex action*. Serious consideration of the existence and high prevalence of chronic childhood abuse, maltreatment and neglect means personally and socially rethinking how every child can be raised in safety. It means being open to a critical analysis and perhaps even a creative reformulation of some basic social structures. This examination necessarily includes a reconsideration of parent's rights and obligations as well as societal responsibilities regarding every new and every evolving human life (see Volume II, Chapter 20, of this series). These personal, familial, professional, and societal actions demand a lasting high level of consciousness as well as tremendous dedication and courage.

So social action is called for, but how social are we at heart? Our essence is our longing and striving to preserve our own being. We have no clue where the will to persevere in nature including ourselves comes from, but it is there, always and everywhere. Acting from virtue, however, is far more complicated. It takes reason: "*Acting absolutely from virtue is nothing else in us but acting, living, and preserving our being (these three signify the same thing) by the guidance of reason, from the foundation of seeking one's own advantage*" (Spinoza, 1677a, Part IV, Proposition 24). Reason tells us that coordinating our actions with those of other individuals, as well as cooperating and communicating with them, is more useful than ignoring or harming them. Hence, according to Spinoza, it is more useful (within limits) to surrender our natural right (i.e., the longing and striving to preserve our being) for the better sake of all than to only consider our own immediate narrow profits. But acting from reason is difficult. It takes a level of consciousness that far exceeds the interests and scope of the present moment. It takes an ability to contemplate life under what Spinoza calls a species of eternity (i.e., from the perspective of the eternal, the perspective of what seems to be universally and eternally true[2]): "*Whatever the mind understands under a species [aspect, perspective] of eternity, it understands not from the fact that it conceives the body's actual existence, but from the fact that it conceives the body's essence under a species of eternity*" (Spinoza, 1677a, Part V, Proposition 29). Despite appearances, understanding realities under an aspect of eternity is not primarily a cognitive act; it is basically affective in that it concerns a love of nature and a love of understanding nature. This perspective, this level of consciousness and its implied perfection provide us with a better chance of overcoming the bondage by our more primitive affects. The challenge we

2 Thomas Nagel wrote in *The Absurd* (1971, p. 720): "Each of us lives his own life – lives with himself twenty-four hours a day. What else is he supposed to do – live someone else's life? Yet humans have the special capacity to step back and survey themselves, and the lives to which they are committed … Without developing the illusion that they are able to escape from their highly specific and idiosyncratic position, they can view it *sub specie aeternitatis* – and the view is at once sobering and comical."

all face to realize chronic childhood traumatization and its implied hate, then, is to develop a will, dedication, courage and ability to acknowledge its existence, prevalence, and harmful present and future consequences. The challenge is to generate and maintain a deep and lasting understanding that overcoming this traumatization, as difficult as it may be, is inherently useful-and hence good–to all.

The efforts of chronically traumatized individuals to heal as well as the efforts of friends and clinicians to support and guide their recovery demand a steadily high level of consciousness. Inasmuch as the societal frame is geared toward ignorance and domineering control rather than toward realization (i.e., knowing facts and taking heed of the consequences of the facts involved), a clash of interests and levels of consciousness will result. Increasing levels of consciousness in chronically traumatized individuals are prone to encounter motivated low levels of consciousness in perpetrators, their partners in crime as well as in psychology, psychiatry and larger societal structures. In light of Buddha's wisdom that *"[t]he darkest night is ignorance,"* trauma healing seems more than a personal venture: It is also a political action. The more traumatized individuals and their bystanders overcome their own recurring alterations of ignorance, fragility and control, the more pressure builds toward a societal realization and limitation of the classic trinity of trauma. The more these individuals speak out, the less society can proceed with blunt ignorance and vicious control.

Theory: A Navigational Instrument

Assisting chronically traumatized individuals is an inspiring and important clinical work. As any clinician knows, it is also emotionally, practically, and intellectually demanding. For example, what to do when a patient presents with an eating disorder, multiple phobias, major depression, suicidality, self-mutilation, nightmares, amnesias, anesthesias, panic attacks, concentration problems or even occasional loss of consciousness, relational troubles, and other symptoms, too? How do I begin to understand the complexity? What are the various symptoms *of*? Do they perhaps relate to each other – and how? And what if the patient, as is so often the case, is seeking emotional and relational proximity, while at the same time fighting this closeness the very moment it materializes? What to do? Where to start?

Clinicians may further have difficulty coping with their patients' recurrent suicidality and acts of self-mutilation as well as with the intensity of their fear, rage, shame, disgust, neediness, and mistrust of others and themselves alike. They must also navigate their patients' tendency to reenact traumatizing relationships in the framework of the therapeutic relationship. Their patients' projective identifications tend to entail another considerable personal test.

The more clinical realities that pose a challenge, the more practical a good theory becomes. Let there be no misunderstanding: Theories are tools, nothing more and nothing less. They can support, but they are no substitute for real life. Like other navigational instruments, they ascertain a traveler's present position, propose a direction, and suggest a particular speed of traveling. They warn about obstacles and suggest detours. Theories are clearly useful inasmuch as one does not know the way. But who needs them when you've become your own effective and efficient guide? Only fools consult navigational systems to find a route they know well. But the harder it is to find one's way, the more convenient and important such a supportive guide becomes.

Yet, users know that navigational systems (or well-meaning advisors) are not flawless. The machines may stubbornly announce nonexistent delays or fail to report real traffic jams. When their software is out of date, 'navis' may in fact not find the best available route. They sometimes suggest a road that is blocked or that does not (or no longer) exist at all.

Like other navigational systems, theories are imperfect tools. No matter how helpful they may be in many regards and in numerous situations, even the best of theories err at least some of the time. They do not replace common sense, and they do not obviate the need for occasional experiments to enrich or modify former formulations. Theory and practice as well as solid received ideas and new experimental findings ideally crossfertilize each other and progress together.

Theories describe and try to explain a part of the world that an individual or a group of individuals experience and know. The formulations do not exist separate from this environment. Rather, one's personal, clinical and scientific theories constitute an inherent part of one's world. They are influenced by and in turn influence one's experiences and actions. Moreover, patients tend to have ideas of their own regarding the causes of their troubles and any possible routes to recovery.

A Player and a Coach: Two Organism-Environment Systems Enacting a Common World

Overall, the *Trinity of Trauma* presents a particular understanding of trauma and the practice of trauma treatment. This, the third volume describes enactive trauma therapy both theoretically and practically. Enactive trauma therapy does not involve a strict protocol or set of protocols. It does not prescribe a fixed set of interventions that can be used in a cookbook fashion. Nor does it provide more or less authoritarian recipes or manuals. Rather, the goal is to offer and illustrate an approach to trauma therapy which is broadly applicable and which deeply respects and values autonomy of traumatized individuals and their natural capacity for self-organization.

In enactive trauma therapy, patients are encountered and conceived of as individuals who wish to enhance their power of action, their power of healing a major injury that has life inflicted and that only they can heal with consistent support and coaching from others. Trained in psychology, psychiatry, and psychotherapy, trauma clinicians are seen as professionals who can serve as coaches to traumatized individuals. Inasmuch as they have been traumatized themselves, they have developed and executed the actions required to resolve their injuries and pain sufficiently in order to fulfill this task.

As coaches, enactive trauma clinicians do not dictate to the patient what the treatment entails. Instead, they flexibly meet their patients 'where they are' at any given point in time. From 'there,' they invite and encourage patients to engage in new viable and creative actions. These actions are the ones that their patients desire to develop or improve, that are within their reach, and that constitute steps on the way to recovery – on the path to wholeness.

This 'whole' constitutes a new organization. Some patients have never existed as a phenomenal whole prior to successful treatment of their dissociative condition. Some have been operating in a dissociative fashion for as long as they can remember. And the full recovery of individuals who existed as a phenomenal whole prior to the traumatization does not comprise a reinstitution of this unity. Life is dynamic. Everything that exists is in constant motion. In this sense there is no former phenomenal whole there to be reinstituted. Mending a dissociative disorder is not like pasting the pieces of a broken cup back together.

To reiterate, one of the basic insights of enactive trauma therapy is that clinicians or clinical interventions do not in fact cause a change in patients. As self-organizing systems, only patients themselves can effect change. This does not mean that patients and other individuals exist apart from the rest of the world. On the contrary, like any organism, patients comprise an inherent part of their immediate world. In this sense they are necessarily organism-environment systems (Järvilehto, 1998a, 1998b, 1999a, 2000a, 2000b). Clinicians are clearly also organism-environment systems. This common feature allows patients and clinicians, at least in principle, to form a common environment. The vehicle of change, then, is the *encounter* between the patient and the clinician. Engaging in an ongoing dance of coordination, cooperation, and communication, patients and clinicians can create a common environment that, in the sense of Gibson (1977, 1979), *affords* change. This enacted common environment or *umwelt* allows the patient and the clinician to strive for a common result: an increase in the patient's power of action to overcome his or her trauma, and, thereby, to enhance his or her ability to engage in new and useful actions.

Like any living organism, traumatized individuals primarily strive to persevere in their existence. Any form of life constitutes an operationally autonomous, primordially affective, and goal-oriented system. Such systems can be stimulated to reorganize themselves when existing actions are or have become useless or harmful. In the service of self-reorganization, enactive trauma clinicians sometimes challenge the unduly fixed action patterns that maintain or even worsen the patient's problems. In order to create something new, it can be helpful, if not necessary, to destabilize the old, albeit not too much but just enough. This challenge is metaphorically referred to as 'throwing a little sand in a well-oiled pathology machine.' As Milton Erickson powerfully put it, "enlightenment is always preceded by confusion" and "until you are willing to be confused about what you already know, what you know will never grow bigger, better, or more useful[3]." In this sense, "change will lead to insight far more often than insight will lead to change." These aphorisms beautifully express that in many cases benign, well-timed, and well-dosed experiential destabilization prompts individuals to reorganize themselves more than rational understanding[4].

Rather than prescribe them, enactive trauma clinicians more generally *propose*, *invite*, and *encourage* new actions. To repeat, individuals who have been deeply and recurrently hurt by domineering others are sick and tired of authoritarian instructions. Gentle enactive therapeutic stimulation does not come out of the blue, but rather generally follows small steps of attunement and consensus building. To refurbish an interior design, one needs to first secure access to the house.

One of the most desirable side effects of the therapeutic collaboration is that it tends to increase the clinician's power of action. Clinicians can acquaint themselves with theories of therapy and therapeutic techniques through books, including books such as the present work, that offer transcripts of therapy sessions. They can learn from videos of therapy sessions and from taking part in therapy sessions. This is all true, but there is no substitute for their learning by doing, for working directly with patients, for struggling with complex therapeutic challenges, for discovering new terrain. In order to increase your power of action, you have to seek out your limits and push yourself beyond. One does not learn to climb a mountain by staying in the valley.

The Trinity of Trauma and The Haunted Self

The understanding and practice that *The Trinity of Trauma* presents does not intend to replace the theory of structural dissociation and the phase-oriented treatment described in *The Haunted Self* (Van der Hart, Nijenhuis, & Steele, 2006). On the contrary, the theories and practices involved belong together and complement each other: I experience and regard them as a unity. For example, *The Haunted Self* and *The Trinity of Trauma* both present action psychologies that are related and largely compatible, and both comprise a phase-oriented approach to trauma treatment.

Whereas *The Haunted Self* embraces many Janetian ideas, the present trilogy was, among many things, inspired by contemporary enactivism and by Spinoza's work, which constitutes an early and powerful form of enactivism. While writing Volume I and II, I

3 The reverse, however, does not work. That is, confusion may not lead to enlightenment, but cause a decomposition. Extremely adverse events tend to destabilize living systems as well as provoke a new organization. Dissociation of the personality can be understood in this sense. It follows a decomposition of the personality and comprises a new viable composition of this living system. Enactive trauma therapy is the recomposition of a trauma-related composition that has lost its viability.

4 In my experience, this principle commonly also applies to clinicians who wish to develop new skills and understanding. I have often noticed this mild destabilization and creative reorganization in classes, and I have experienced it myself. For example, I started to learn about trauma and dissociative disorders following mild experiential shocks of my own; see Chapter 30.

concentrated on Spinoza's contributions in his *Ethics* Part I (*Of God*) and *Ethics* Part II (*Of the Mind*). At the time I had not expected that the present Volume III would become to be written partly in the spirit of *Ethics* Part III (*Of the Affects*), *Ethics* Part IV (*Of Human Bondage*), and *Ethics* Part V (*Of Human Freedom*). However, while reviewing the drafts of the first chapters of the present volume and searching for a deeper understanding of trauma and trauma treatment, I read and reread these three last parts. Grasping Spinoza's dense language and depth of thought was most rewarding, albeit not always easily achieved. The venture was not a goal in itself, let alone a romantic flight in history. Rather, it was guided by the growing realization how wisely *Ethics* speaks to human confusion, conflicts, and trauma–as well as to a possible liberation from human bondage by passions. The endeavor was also compelled by a growing insight into how several 'new' and contemporary psychological insights, theories, and approaches to treatment strongly appear to be Spinoza's original thoughts in disguise. Honor to whom honor is due.

Enactivism emphasizes that in order to experience and know themselves, other selves, and the material world, individuals must *act*. They must *do* something. Enactivism essentially proposes that *organisms bring forth a self in action as well as a world and the relationship of this self and this world.* It holds that 'subjects' and their 'objects' (including other 'subjects') constitute and depend on each other, and that they always occur together (Järvilehto, 1998a, 1998b, 1999a, 2000a; Northoff, 2003, 2014a, 2014b; Schopenhauer, 1819, 1844; Spinoza, 1677a). That is, there is an *intrinsic* relationship between subjects and their perceived and conceived material and social world (or *umwelt*). Practically speaking, no world exists without an experiencing and knowing subject, just as all subjects exist, mature, and develop in virtue of a material and social *umwelt.* Subjects and their material and social objects exist in virtue of their coupling. They exist and can only be known relative to each other.

It is, however, quite common in psychology and psychiatry to regard and treat organisms and the world they experience and know as two separate systems. For example, by assuming that individuals and their environment constitute two systems, many neuroscientists look for normal and abnormal consciousness in the brain. In this sense, trauma means there is something wrong 'in' the individual. *The Trinity of Trauma*, however, rejects the dissociation of organisms and their environment. I understand trauma to be a feature of an *organism-environment system*.

Traumatized individuals are host to more than one conception of who they are and what the world is like, and how they relate to this experienced and conceived world. Confronted with a violating reality, their personality as a whole organism-environment system has become divided into two or more dissociative organism-environment subsystems or parts. As each dissociative part they enact, that is, they bring forth in action a particular phenomenal self, a particular phenomenal *umwelt,* and a particular set of relationships between this self and umwelt. For example, some dissociative parts mainly bring forth a phenomenal self that experiences a traumatizing *umwelt* without realizing that this self and this *umwelt* in fact belong to past realities. Traumatologists describe this constellation of actions as a reenactment of traumatic experiences and a reenactment of traumatic relationships. Other dissociative parts in turn enact a phenomenal self that does not or not sufficiently integrate and realize this traumatized phenomenal self and this traumatic phenomenal *umwelt*.

The Haunted Self and *The Trinity of Trauma* are more generally attempts to integrate particular insights stemming from, among others, learning theory, including classical, operant, and evaluative conditioning, dynamic systems theory (Thelen & Smith, 1994), attachment theories (Bowlby, 1969, 1973, 1980; Fonagy, Gergely, Jurist, & Target, 2002; Liotti, 1999, 2004, 2006), and affective neuroscience (Panksepp, 1998; Panksepp & Biven, 2012). The two works also integrate ideas on transference and countertransference (Dalenberg, 2000), particularly but not exclusively with regards to interpersonal reenactments of traumatizing relationships.

Accepting and integrating components of these various theories does not mean accepting and integrating all of the elements they encompass. Nor does it necessarily imply adherence to the background (i.e., the philosophical) assumptions that drive these models. As detailed in Volumes I and II, and as also discussed in the present volume, *The Trinity of Trauma* rejects philosophical dualism, materialism, epiphenomenalism, realism, and representationalism. For example, it assumes that matter and mind are two properties of one system that may include many more properties (that we are not aware of) (Spinoza, 1677a). The brain/body and the mind are thus not regarded and treated as different substances or systems. And they are not seen as causes. For example, the brain is not seen to cause the mind, and the mind is not considered the cause of its objects. Mind and matter are rather conceived of as different attributes, properties, or appearances of one system: nature.

Like *The Haunted Self, The Trinity of Trauma* considers the dissociation of the personality. But, given the above considerations, *The Trinity of Trauma* explicitly regards 'personality' as an intrinsic component of an organism-environment system. Another difference between *The Haunted Self* and *The Trinity of Trauma* is that the present work uses the term controlling emotional parts, whereas *The Haunted Self* prefers the term perpetrator imitating emotional parts. The term controlling emotional parts in my view captures *the goal* or *final cause* for imitating perpetrators in some regards. Any organism strives to control its one's fate as much as possible, and children learn an immense amount by imitating others. As William Wordsworth (1770–1850) observed, every young child goes through a phase in which he or she is "as if his whole vocation were endless imitation" (1807). What else is there for chronically traumatized children to imitate than the negative kinds of control that perpetrators and their accomplices enact? In this light, clinicians are challenged to model positive ways of influencing one's self and one's world.

The Trinity of Trauma: A Trilogy

The current third volume of *The Trinity of Trauma* offers clinicians, to use a Beatles phrase, a little help to get by[5]. It builds on Volumes I and II, which provide, define, and ground basic concepts. These include trauma, event, traumatizing event, traumatic event, traumatic experience, dissociation, personality as major features of an organism-environment system, dissociative subsystems or parts of the personality, and more. As mentioned above, the formulations are grounded in a monistic philosophical framework that strives to avoid and overcome the major problems of philosophical dualism, idealism, materialism, and realism. Volumes I and II also present empirical findings, including the results of functional and structural biopsychosocial research of trauma-related dissociation of the personality.

The opening theoretical chapters of the present volume look at enactivism and enactive trauma therapy. The practical chapters describe how the philosophical, conceptual, and theoretical formulations and empirical insights can assist clinicians in their practical work with chronically traumatized individuals. Whereas in some respects the trilogy begins at a rather abstract level of analysis, it culminates in transcripts of actual therapy sessions. These records are complemented with my technical and personal comments and, in two cases, with posthoc comments from the involved patient. The comments are not meant to be exhaustive, which would only serve to exhaust the reader. Rather, they illustrate some of the major feelings, thoughts, and dynamics regarding both the patient's and the clinician's efforts to achieve a common result: the healing of the patient.

The *Trinity of Trauma* addresses several aspects of the philosophy of mind. Any psychological theory and practice is grounded in philosophical assumptions and reflections regarding mind, matter, and more. It is important to be explicit about this foundation. Volume III thus reiterates some of the philosophical problems discussed in some more detail in Volumes I and II. While overall the *Trinity of Trauma* covers some of the major issues from the philosophy of mind, it is not an exhaustive treatise in this regard. An excellent, more complete, and quite accessible account may be found in Northoff's *Minding the Brain* (2014a).

Readers with limited interest in theoretical issues or those with a touch of 'philosophy and theory phobia' may prefer to begin reading with Chapter 30. As they go along, however, they may have the experience that philosophical and theoretical reflections are not completely irrelevant to the practice of psychotraumatology. They may actually detect that these considerations are indispensable.

To emphasize that *The Trinity of Trauma* constitutes a unity, Volume III starts where Volume II left off. The first chapter of the present volume is thus numbered 22. This system serves to invite readers unfamiliar with Volume I and II to explore the preceding texts. Volume III picks up on but does not fully reintroduce the contents of the first two volumes. However, the major, rather complex insights of the prior works are taken up again–and several are elaborated on. A certain redundancy and frequent references to pre-

5 From the song "With a Little Help from my Friends" on the album *Sgt. Pepper's Lonely Hearts Club Band* (1967). George, John, and Paul sing "*What do you see when you turn out the light?*" Ringo answers "*I can't tell you, but I know it's mine.*" This is a good example of how we cannot experience someone else's experiences, but we can empathize with them.

vious chapters are intended to orient readers who are not or not completely familiar with Volumes I and II.

Clinicians and Therapists

Clinicians need not also be psychotherapists or other therapists. However, like therapists, clinicians who are not also therapists have as their goal to assist and hence affect their patients. Whether and how a clinician or a therapist exerts influence on the patient depends on the actions and passions of both parties. The ambition of the present volume is to inspire the actions of clinicians and therapists alike. It therefore seemed best to generally address the general class (i.e., 'clinicians'), even if, in many instances, the text speaks to therapists more than to clinicians who are not also therapists.

Gratitude

The Trinity of Trauma is a work that stands on the shoulders of many giants. To name a few major inspirations: Aristotle, Baruch Spinoza, Arthur Schopenhauer, Pierre Janet, Charles Myers, Ludwig Wittgenstein, Francisco Varela, Andreas Weber, Evan Thompson, Stephen Braude, Timo Järvilehto, Georg Northoff, Thomas Metzinger, Frank Putnam, Richard Kluft, Onno van der Hart, Giovanni Liotti, Bessel van der Kolk, and more. I am also indebted to several colleagues who attended my classes and to other colleagues who thought along with me. To keep the list short, I shall restrict myself to expressly naming only Arne Blindheim, Raimund Dörr, Peter Heinz, Gabriele Heyers, Hanne Hummel, Astrid Lampe, Isabel Lopez-Fiestas, Sebastian Lorenz, Winja Lutz, Andrew Moskowitz, Olivier Piedfort-Marin, Julia Michel, Henk Otten, Siegfried Rathner, Thomas Renz, Stella Sadowsky, Harald Schickedanz, Manfred Stelzig, Steinar Svoren, Ingrid Wild-Lüffe, Dominik Schönborn, Rainer Schwing, Sander van Straten, Fabian Wilmers, and Eva Zimmermann. I am indebted to all of them. Timo Järvilehto's comments on a previous version of the present text were most helpful, as were our continuing discussions. Highly appreciated, Timo, there is so much to learn from you! Peter Ward brought several most worthwhile papers to my attention. Much appreciated, Peter! I am no less grateful to the many helpful colleagues whose names are not mentioned here. Joe Smith, your linguistic corrections and other editing have been vital. My sincere thanks go to you.

No matter how much I learned from historical heroes, contemporary masters, and acquainted colleagues, *The Trinity of Trauma* primarily rests on the many encounters with the many traumatized individuals who were willing to engage in a therapeutic dance with me. A few of them appear in this book. It is an exceptional privilege that they allowed me to use their therapy sessions verbatim along with more general descriptions of their personality and painful history. 'Ineke' and 'Sonja' deserve a very special place among them.

They were willing to watch and comment on the videos of therapy sessions contained verbatim in this volume. As mentioned above, their comments on *what it was like for them* to be in these sessions are also included in the present volume. Their courage provides readers with intimate access to the first-person and quasi-second perspectives of these traumatized but now fully healed individuals as well as to their second-person perspective regarding me as their former coach. In closing, I express my deep gratitude to my near family members for their continuing love, support, and understanding, especially the straightforward honesty of children: Our eldest grandchild, Asia, told her mother that it was better to return the first two volumes of *The Trinity* to granddad. Moving to a new home, she was concerned that such a heavy book without any pictures would overload their car.

We are all organism-environment systems. No one exists, feels, thinks, and moves in solitude. Blossoming is infinitely easier in a benign, sympathetic, and loving *umwelt*.

Westerbork, The Netherlands; Ciudad Quesada, Rojales, Spain
April 2015–February 2016

Introduction

Volume III in Brief

> *The striving by which each thing strives to persevere in its being is nothing but the actual essence of the thing.*
> Baruch Spinoza (1677a, Part III, Proposition 7)

> *. . . the decisions of the mind are nothing but the appetites themselves, which therefore vary as the disposition of the body varies. For each governs everything from his affects; those who are torn by contrary affects do not know what they want, and those who are not moved by any affect are very easily driven here and there.*
> Baruch Spinoza (1677a, p. 73)

In order to orient readers to what is to come, I would first like to present an overview of the structure and contents of this text. It starts with a number of theoretical chapters and continues with eight practical chapters.

Theoretical Basis

The problems of trauma and dissociation are largely problems of consciousness and self-consciousness. The initial Chapter 22 is therefore concerned with self-consciousness and world-consciousness in general as well as in trauma and enactive trauma therapy. In Chapter 12 of *The Trinity of Trauma* (hereinafter referred to as ToT), it was stated that self-consciousness, our 'I,' involves our phenomenal conception of self (for a clarification of the term 'phenomenal,' see below). Generated in our ongoing action, it tells us who we are. As Metzinger (2003, p. 1) put it, a phenomenal conception of self is "a wonderfully efficient two-way window that allows an organism to conceive of itself as a whole, and thereby to causally interact with its inner and external environment in an entirely new, integrated, and intelligent manner." This self, the inner world, and the external world are not pregiven but involve our phenomenal conception of them.

Chapter 22 provides an additional perspective to the effect that (self-)consciousness evolved as an efficient means of supporting relationships between individuals (Järvilehto, 2000b). Simple relational forms demand little coordination, cooperation, and communication, whereas the more complex the tasks organisms face, the more they are challenged to coordinate their actions – and to cooperate and communicate with each another. Interpersonal traumatization involves a totalitarian relationship of 'dictators' and 'slaves,' and totalitarian relationships comprise relatively low forms and degrees of consciousness. In contrast, healing trauma demands high forms and degrees of consciousness and self-consciousness. This healing challenges the patient and the clinician to generate and maintain intense coordination, cooperation, and communication.

Trauma and dissociation of the personality pose a number of intricate part-whole problems. The thrust of Chapter 23 is that a deep understanding of traumatized individuals and individuals in general cannot be found in parts of them (e.g., in genes, cells, parts of the brain, the entire brain, or any other parts of the body). Such comprehension takes an even wider perspective than that of the (traumatized) individual, because no one exists or could exist in an environmental void. Living organisms and their environment constitute each other (i.e., they exist and are known only relative to each other), depend on each other, and at all times occur together (see ToT Volumes I & II). Individuals enact a self, a world as well as the relationships between this self and this world. Like all living organisms, we are organism-environment systems (Järvilehto, 1998a, 1998b, 1999a, 1999b, 2000a, 2000b). The best methodological principle is thus to analyze trauma and trauma therapy as problems of organism-environment systems. And it often makes the best sense to study these systems from combined material, phenomenal, subjective, and social perspectives (ToT Volumes I & II).

Chapters 24 and 25 discuss in more detail that living organisms are primarily affective creatures. Whatever else they need and desire, they primarily strive to persevere in their existence. They are primarily interested in themselves. In this frame, they mentally and behaviorally enact a self and a world (Colombetti, 2014; Varela, 1991, 1997; Weber, 2002a, 2002b). This world – their environment or *umwelt* – is a world of personal and affective significance (Di Paolo, De Jaegher, & Rohde, 2010; Thompson, 2007; Varela et al., 1991). All living organisms continually evaluate themselves and the world they bring forth in action relative to their desires and goals. This view is clearly very different from the idea that organisms interact with an external world that exists by itself.

These two chapters thus make the point that all living organisms *feel* (Weber, 2014). They *are primarily affective, self-oriented, goal-oriented, and oriented toward their personal world of meaning. Traumatized individuals and clinicians are such feeling and sense-making systems with a point of view.* Their primal point of view is their first-person perspective on which all other person-perspectives they may have depend. The third-person human clinical or scientific perspective is one of these. Like scientists, clinicians are not knowers of objective truths. They basically experience and know everything, including themselves, traumatized individuals, trauma, and the world at large, from their affectively charged first-person position.

All living systems strive to achieve results that are advantageous to them. This takes power of action. When they achieve a goal, they experience joy and gain more power of action. When they fail to achieve a goal, they experience sorrow and lose power of action. Enactive trauma therapy, then, is the endeavor to increase traumatized individuals' power of action that they lost or were unable to develop as the traumatization proceeded. Enactive trauma therapy is the striving to increase their joy and reduce their sorrow by inviting and encouraging new actions that replace their painful passions.

Chapter 25 further states that trauma involves a particular decomposition of the personality. This view is extended and detailed in Chapter 26. It analyzes three prototypical conscious and self-conscious dissociative subsystems or 'parts.' Each strives to persevere in their existence in their own way. 'Apparently normal parts' (ANPs) primarily aim to achieve the goals of common life. 'Fragile emotional parts' (fragile EPs) primarily defend the basic integrity of life amid a devastating *umwelt*. 'Controlling emotional parts' (controlling EPs) primarily strive to generate and maintain a sense of personal power, of shining autonomy. To achieve their aims ANPs strive to ignore the phenomenal selves and worlds of the EPs. They strive to feel, know, and/or realize it as little as possible. In the attempt to delimit their fragility, ignoring (e.g., mentally avoiding) EPs is a form of control. Although fragile EPs feel and know themselves to be fragile, they long and strive to defend their very existence. Their defensive actions or passions involve a form of control. Stuck in the dreadful past, however, they remain more or less ignorant of the actual present in terms of the third-person's conception of chronological time, place, and the unity the fragile EPs are a part of. Controlling EPs share this ignorance and try to ignore their fragility. They strive to control their life and their *umwelt*. Being prototypes, traumatized individuals can encompass both mixtures and variations of these three prototypes.

Chapter 26 also proposes that most, if not basically all, dissociative parts include more than one mental and behavioral state. These 'states' are described as 'modes of longing and striving.' It also makes the point that there are important differences between modes of longing and striving some authors refer to as 'ego-states' and dissociative parts. These differences are clinically as well as scientifically relevant.

Chapter 27 proposes that, like traumatized individuals as a unity, dissociative parts constitute operationally autonomous systems. Operationally autonomous systems are constantly being challenged to engage in a variety of actions (and passions) to continue their existence. This striving is their primary urge. In this context, these systems generate and signify a self, a world, as well as intrinsic relationships of this self and this *umwelt*. No matter how simple or complex, autonomous systems operate under precarious conditions: They perish if they fail to engage in the actions that generate and maintain their self, their world, and their dialectical self-world relationships. Dissociative parts, then, continuously bring forth, that is, enact and reenact, their particular self, *umwelt* and dialectical self-*umwelt* relationships. Enactive trauma therapy is the endeavor to invite and encourage traumatized individuals at large as well as each of their dissociative parts to substitute their problematic or harmful actions and passions for more useful actions. Among other things, enactive trauma clinicians thus stimulate them to exchange such passions as reenactments of traumatizing events and relationships for more profitable actions. The most profitable action would be the full (re)integration of the personality. This "work" (Janet) implies the fusion of the operationally autonomous, self-centered dissociative parts into one single new operationally autonomous self-centered *unity*: a whole, healthy individual.

While traumatized individuals, like any one of us, constitute a self-centered system (because we primarily strive to keep ourselves alive), this does not mean that we are not also social, or even *very* social. On the contrary, as Chapter 28 points out, we achieve more, indeed far more, when we cooperate and communicate with other individuals and coordinate our various actions (cf. Chapter 22). We often long and strive to achieve common results simply because together we can achieve more. Our other-directedness starts prenatally and only ends when we die. Being social, then, turns out to be useful. The implied collaboration, however, is complex. We consist of many different needs (unconscious) and desires (consciously known), so that we struggle to find a consistent path in life. What is more, different individuals have, at least to some degree, different needs and desires. Social affects, cognitions, and behaviors, however, arise because we human beings have particular needs and desires in common, and because we may also have complementary longings and strivings (as in child-mother and mother-child attachment). It is evident that social coordination, cooperation, and communication become deeply problematic particularly in chronic interpersonal traumatization. For some individuals, the injuries go back to prenatal life. However, trauma therapy is a thoroughly social endeavor. This creates two major paradoxes: First, that healing takes a social relationship and its implied trust in others, but others have deeply compromised social trust. Second, that increasing coordination, cooperation, and communication implies an increase of consciousness. But increasing levels of fields of consciousness imply more feeling, knowing, and realizing trauma. And this pain is antithetical to the good-old attempt to control one's fragility by *ignoring* hurting feelings and realities as much as possible.

We are not bodiless minds or mindless bodies. Life rather encompasses the mental and the physical as two different properties of one system that some call Nature, others call God, and others, including Spinoza, regard as one entity. As detailed in Chapter 29 Spinoza was the first to grasp our essential embodiment. He proposed a most important view of how *our mind implies our body as well as our brain and an environment that affects us.* Trauma, then, is an injury to the body as much as an injury to the mind. One implication is that enactive trauma therapy is not restricted to mental coordination and communication. Rather, it is an *embodied pas de deux.* Psychotherapy is a form of participatory sense-making that equally comprises the mind and the body. Indeed, it could not be otherwise.

The power of scientific terms to hint at the primordial affectivity, embodiment, and environmental embedment of organisms is limited. Poetic words may intimate this experiential and perspectival quality more directly or more effectively. But even poetry is restricted in its ability to capture experience. Words may point to experience, but they cannot be substitutes for it. The point is that there is no intrinsic connection between a word and what a word alludes to (ToT Volume I, Chapter 9). Words and other symbols necessarily have a gap between themselves and what they are trying to express, be it experiences or something else.

This gap is clearly a limitation *and* an asset. A limitation in that science can never become a complete theory and practice of life: Not even the most sensitive and artful literature can ever replace experience. However, there is an advantage to words and other symbols: Symbolized traumatization can be endured better than reenacted traumatic experiences since symbolization creates an affective distance between unbearable past experience and present existence.

Unable to be the master of their own life, traumatized individuals engage in recurrent and passionate reenactments of the toxic events and relationships that have harmed them. By implication, enactive trauma therapy involves moving away from these sensorimotor and commonly (but not necessarily highly) affectively charged reenactments. The venture is geared toward new viable and creative enactments of a phenomenal self, phenomenal world, and this self as an inherent part of this personal world of significance. In other words, enactive trauma therapy is the progression from passions to actions – or the evolution from being strongly affected by external causes to becoming an agent whose life is guided more by own causes. Important actions include putting the past in symbols such as drawings, paintings, or music[1], and subsequently in words, sentences, paragraphs, and chapters. Eventually, the past should become a whole story. Following this path, the sensorimotor and often strongly affectively charged traumatic memories can become lived narrative memories of a terrible past.

The Practice of Enactive Trauma Therapy

Chapter 30 presents detailed case presentations that illustrate the practice of enactive trauma therapy. This chapter describes my first encounter with a dissociative individual, at least the first I came to diagnose. It also portrays me as a primarily affective individual who is embodied, embrained, and environmentally embedded.

Chapter 31 introduces a clinical style and several techniques that the hypnotherapist Milton Erickson developed which closely fit the thinking and practice of enactive trauma therapy. In this context, the text introduces three permanently ongoing clinical actions: attunement, consensus building, and gentle leading toward patients' goals. Such leading is basically grounded in utilizing the actions, passions, and affective interests patients bring to the clinical situation. One complication in the treatment of dissociative individuals is that this three-step approach needs to recognize the different interests and views of every dissociative part a patient may encompass. At the same time, clinicians should be oriented to the patient as a whole person.

The next chapter, Chapter 32, focuses on common enactive trauma assessment, illustrating the principles of Chapter 31 as well as the interwoven nature of assessment and therapy. To this end it includes a transcript of the second assessment session with Ineke, a patient with dissociative identity disorder, DID (American Psychiatric Association, APA, 2013). The transcript is complemented with comments that flow from my own personal perspectives on the work. A unique feature of the chapter is that it includes Ineke's

1 For example, Johann Sebastian Bach, who suffered several losses, composed the impressive "Ich hatte viel Bekümmernis."

posthoc comments on the videorecorded session. Fully healed, she was recently able to watch the video and provide explanations that would be enlightening to every clinician.

Chapter 33 comprises two examples of uncommon enactive assessment of trauma and trauma-related dissociation. Like the previous chapter, it illustrates that the traditional distinction between assessment and therapy is highly artificial. It also exemplifies that the road to a diagnosis is not always smooth. Assessment may take the creation of an original clinical track – which apart from other things keeps clinicians from boredom.

Many things can be said in a straightforward way. However, there can be good reasons to apply a more indirect communicative style and/or to use metaphors. Chapter 34 makes these points.

Chapter 35 exemplifies what I call 'the therapeutic internet: *www*,' where www stands for the quest of '*who does what and why*.' Dissociative parts are not split off from each other; they often communicate with or intrude on each other. One dissociative part, say an ANP, may be affected by one or more other dissociative parts without any conscious awareness of who is intruding, and why. In this case, the dissociative part that is intruded on experiences and knows the '*what*.' However, he or she cannot answer the question '*who* does it?' or the question '*why?*' And he or she may not be happy to know the answers. The chapter provides a transcript of a complex session with Ineke in which she slowly and with major effort approached a most painful truth.

As mentioned above, and given our essential embodiment, enactive trauma therapy cannot remain limited to the mental domain. Verbal therapeutic communications may be inefficient or may completely fail to engender more viable and creative actions. Chapter 36 illustrates the therapeutic use of occasional and prudent, albeit quite restricted forms of physical contact between traumatized individuals and clinicians. If embedded in a verbal discourse, they can bring forth what words alone cannot achieve or only with much more difficulty.

Clinicians tend to find working with controlling EPs exceptionally challenging. These dissociative parts can be controlling and most intense indeed. They tend to be energetic, impulsive, wary of attachment. It is important to realize that controlling EPs also tend to secretly feel fragile, and that there is a lot they are ignorant of. Beset by negative power models, controlling EPs are in need of more positive ways of self-determination. Scared clinicians do not meet the need for positive power models. Clinicians who feel that controlling dissociative parts should just quit their 'manipulative' passions and who tend to end up in a power struggle with them will also fail to model positive power. Chapter 37 considers these issues and illustrates an egalitarian approach to controlling EPs. This action is grounded in a deep respect for these brave parts and in the realization that their energy and striving for self-determination are major assets. It also relies on the recurrent experience that clinicians can help these parts to achieve higher levels of mental and behavioral efficiency.

Chapter 38 summarizes the major points of the present volume in the form of concise propositions on enactivism and enactive trauma therapy.

The book includes six appendices. The first involves some notes on the efficacy of trauma treatment and its measurement. The second details why it is useful to constrain the concept of a dissociative part of the personality. The others concern two self-report questionnaires, the Somatoform Dissociation Questionnaire (SDQ-20 and SDQ-5) and the Traumatic Experiences Checklist (TEC).

Chapter 22

Consciousness in Trauma

Axioma 2: Man thinks . . . or to put it differently we know that we think.
Axioma 3: There are no modes of thinking, such as love, desire, or whatever is designated by the word affects of the mind, unless there is in the same individual the idea of the thing loved, desired, and the like.
Baruch Spinoza (1677a, Part II, p. 32)

It is just because the individual finds himself taking the attitudes of the others who are involved in his conduct that he becomes an object for himself.
George Herbert Mead (1968, p. 57)

Many problems of traumatized individuals involve problems of integration and consciousness. The core of the injury that trauma is involves a lack of integration of the personality. The division ensues when individuals are unable to integrate horrible experiences in full or in part. This lack of integration often, though not always, takes the form of a dissociation of the personality as a whole system in two or more dissociative subsystems. A distinguishing feature of dissociative subsystems (or 'parts') is that they are conscious and self-conscious. Each includes his or her own experience and idea of self, of their world, and of relationships of this experienced and known self as a part and this experienced and known world.

Trauma may also comprise a lack of integration of various modes of functioning. These modes are to be distinguished from dissociative parts of the personality. As detailed in Chapter 26, the modes of functioning involved more specifically include *modes of longing and striving* to achieve a particular result. These modes of longing and striving do not qualify as dissociative parts because they do not include their own phenomenal ideas of their self, their world, and their self as a part of this world.

A Trinity of Prototypical Dissociative Subsystems of the Personality

As described in ToT Volumes I and II, there exists a trinity of prototypical dissociative parts in trauma: apparently normal parts (ANPs), fragile emotional parts (fragile EPs), and controlling emotional parts (controlling EPs). These prototypes essentially include their own affective interests. ANPs primarily long and strive to live daily life. They desire to eat, sleep, relax, explore, work, attach, have children and care for them, meet friends, etc. Stuck in traumatic experiences that ANPs have been and still are unable or unwilling to integrate, fragile EPs primarily long and strive to defend their physical existence when they feel threatened or in fact are threatened. They can startle, flee, freeze, or try to ward off threatening subjects and objects. Apart from these hyperaroused fragile EPs, there are hypoaroused fragile EPs, who tend to play dead when they are or feel threatened. Controlling EPs most of all long and strive to be in charge rather than to be controlled by overpowering interoceptive or exteroceptive causes.

While trying to fulfill needs and desires of daily life, ANPs avoid the fragile and controlling EPs and the feelings and memories of the perpetration wherever they can. They try to ignore the EPs in order to protect their own fragility. The ignorance of ANPs is greatest when they succeed in being completely amnestic of the existence of EPs, their memories, feelings, thoughts, and behaviors. Such ignorance involves a lack of realization when they know the EPs but do not experience or heed their fragility and control.

Fragile EPs carry the load of the traumatization, so to speak. They may feel fragile, but they long to control the overwhelming situations they find themselves in. Their method of control lies in their mammalian defensive actions or in their cry for attachment – in their cry to be protected or saved by others. Part of the threat they experience, perceive, and conceive pertains to ANPs inasmuch as these dissociative parts negate, reject, or neglect them. When controlling EPs threaten or actually hurt them, fragile EPs also fear and despise these dissociative parts. For example, controlling EPs may call them names or cut "their body." Fragile EPs are generally ignorant of the actual time and place, the patient's identity at large, as well as the status of other persons and objects. They may misperceive clinicians or interpret other individuals as perpetrators. To them, a household knife or piece of wood may be a dangerous weapon.

Controlling EPs present themselves as strong, powerful, courageous, and uncaring. To some degree, this presentation fits the facts. However, below the veil of power and control they also tend to feel quite fragile. They may feel less powerful than they claim to be, and silently they may find it difficult to hurt other dissociative parts. Moreover, they may feel hurt themselves by the abuse, maltreatment, and neglect far more than they like to or allow themselves to admit to themselves or to others. Controlling EPs are also ignorant in several important regards. Like fragile EPs, they tend to be disoriented to place, time, and the patient's identity as well as that of others. Many controlling EPs are oriented toward the third-person past they experience as their own first-person present. What is more, they may more or less successfully ignore their own fragility and ignorance.

A dissociation of the personality in trauma manifests in dissociative symptoms or phenomena (ToT Volume II, Chapter 12 and 13). In other words, a symptom or a phenomenon qualifies as dissociative when it relates to the existence of dissociative parts. Some dissociative symptoms and phenomena can be described as negative (something fails to be sensed, perceived, conceived, recalled, or done). Others in turn are positive (something is sensed, perceived, etc.). Yet the two categories tend to be intertwined. For example, forgetfulness involves dissociative amnesia when one dissociative part does not recollect what another dissociative part remembers very well or all too well. And an inability to feel or see a body part is dissociative only if the phenomenon pertains to one or more dissociative parts, but not to one or more other conscious dissociative subsystems. A general lowering of consciousness (e.g., general forgetfulness, general numbing, or absent-mindedness) or a general narrowing of consciousness (e.g., concentration on a limited set of signals) does not meet these criteria. Such symptoms and phenomena would thus better not be classified as dissociative (for a discussion and debate, see ToT Volume II, Chapters 13 and 14).

Some dissociative symptoms can be classified as *sensorimotor* or somatoform, and others as *cognitive-emotional* or psychoform (Nijenhuis, 1999/2004, 2015a, 2015b; Nijenhuis, Spinhoven, Van Dyck, Van der Hart, & Vanderlinden, 1996, Nijenhuis & Van der Hart, 2011a, 2011b; Van der Hart & Nijenhuis, 2008; see also ToT Volume I, Chapter 4, pp. 80–81, ToT Volume II, Chapter 12 and 13). *Negative sensorimotor symptoms* include analgesia, various kinds of anesthesia (e.g., auditory, visual, kinesthetic, genital), loss of consciousness, and motor inhibitions such as stiffening or paralysis or one or more parts of the body. *Positive sensorimotor symptoms* are, for example, pain or other aversive sensations that fragile EPs experience and that intrude on an ANP. *Negative cognitive-emotional dissociative symptoms* include dissociative amnesia, dissociative depersonalization, dissociative derealization, and dissociative affective numbing. *Positive cognitive-emotional dissociative symptoms* pertain to intrusions such as often trauma-related images, emotions, thoughts, voices, and memories. These memories include more or less complete reenactments of traumatic experiences. For example, one dissociative part may hear another dissociative part speak or cry as this part reenacts traumatic experiences (e.g., see Chapter 32).

The actions or passions of traumatized individuals (see Chapters 25 and 27) include lack of synthesis, personification, presentification, and realization. *Lack of synthesis* involves insufficient integration of various components of experience causing phenomena such as analgesia as well as bodily and affective anesthesia; *lack of personification* manifests in depersonalization symptoms. Saying that a traumatized individual does not 'presentify' a particular experience means, among other things, that he or she experiences a past event as if it were a present event. More formally, a *lack of presentification* stands for insufficient integration of one's past, present, and future experiences in a coherent, cohesive, and fitting framework of time, place, and identity. Another trouble is *lack of realization*, that is, misjudgment of the degree of reality of one's experiences and failure to take heed of the implications of the injuries. For example, traumatized individuals may (re)experience traumatic memories in a dreamlike fashion. It may also escape them how strongly the traumatic experiences have affected their past, or how they continue to influence their present and future life.

Knowing facts is not identical to realizing them. Knowing that smoking and taking drugs is dangerous does not equal realizing these facts. Societies may more or less know the reality of child abuse and neglect and yet, as was remarked on in the Preface, this knowledge has no practical meaning if societies do not take action upon that knowledge, if they do not delimit its occurrence, mend its consequences, and discuss how every child can grow up in safety. In contrast, the realization of the fact that approximately one in ten children is raised in terror means taking every measure imaginable to help endangered and hurt children and to prevent more injuries (ToT Volume II, Chapter 20).

Consciousness: Cooperation, Coordination, Communication

Given the problems of consciousness in trauma, we need to consider ideas regarding the origins and nature of consciousness. An important and compelling view is that consciousness is a property that developed in evolution on the basis of mental activity. Once it had appeared, it provided the life process of those organisms that possessed it clear advantages (Järvilehto, 2000a, 2000b; Metzinger, 2003).

All living systems are mental systems. They are *mental* because they must know what is useful, poisonous, or insignificant to them (see Chapters 24 and 25). But not all living systems are also conscious or *phenomenal* systems. Järvilehto (2000a, 2000b) holds that the more organisms became dependent on cooperation to achieve results that are useful to all, the more they became conscious systems. His idea is that consciousness was not a disposable luxury to them, not an epiphenomenal fringe. It was *a necessity*. Had the involved organisms remained mental but not phenomenal systems, they would not have been able to achieve the common results that conscious organisms can achieve. They would not have accomplished what organisms can achieve only in close and intense cooperation with each other.

Consciousness is not 'one thing.' The required form of consciousness may well be relative to the degree to which different individuals must communicate and coordinate their actions to attain a result that they can only achieve in virtue of their cooperation and reciprocal coordination. Social activity as such may not be enough for the development of a more than rudimentary form of consciousness . The more the achievement of a common result depends on the cooperation of various individuals, the more each individual must coordinate his or her actions (operations) with those of others. Rudimentary forms of cooperation demand only rudimentary levels of consciousness; complex forms of cooperation demand highly evolved levels. Simple ventures only take simple communication, quite limited coordination, and quite restricted cooperation, whereas complex projects take intense communication, delicate coordination, and major cooperation. This high level of coordination and cooperation would not function without intense and fine-tuned nonverbal, linguistic, and paralinguistic communication.

In sum, Järvilehto's (2000a, 2000b) appealing hypothesis is that there is a family of actions that can generate consciousness. They are actions that particular species developed in evolution in order to foster the achievement of common results. More specifically, the species involved needed a particular kind of consciousness that was relative to the degree to which they attempted to achieve common results. The more organisms started to cooperate in order to achieve ever more intricate common results, the more advanced their level of consciousness had to become.

Achieving a common result is not a goal in itself but allows new actions. Life and the development of life do not stop when a particular goal has been attained. Success is only a stepping stone to the next endeavor. One action predicates another.

Our species became particularly dependent on profound and lasting cooperation. As Järvilehto (2000a, p. 46) details:

> The conditions of the achievement of common results in human social action are extremely complicated. For example, lifting a stone together presupposes may coordinated and integrated actions whose temporal and spatial dynamics must be exact. If lifting is asynchronous then the individual efforts do not join as a common force; the same is true of spatial organization. In order to create a common organization the participants must be able to influence each other, indicate their intentions, and the purpose of the common action. The common result could be achieved when every participating individual plastically changed his organization such that it fitted the organization necessary for the result. Such a process of fitting was possible through the simultaneous influence of one participant on another other and on himself through a gesture or sound that both participants could follow (cf. Mead, 1934). One individual has to be able somehow to indicate to the other his place in the organization and the instant action so that the individual forces could be joined in a simultaneous effort, lifting or moving a stone to protect the camp, for example. Such influencing was the beginning of communication that later developed into the use of language.
>
> ... In this process it is possible to see through the other participants what the relation is of one's own action to the common result as well as to the efforts of the other participants. This was the beginning of human consciousness.

We are a species that cannot survive on our own (see also Chapter 28). Our existence, maturation, development, and projects depend crucially on the existence and actions of other individuals. For example, babies, toddlers, and even somewhat older children could not survive without parents or other primary caretakers. If caretaking is to work, these adults should consciously sense and empathize with the children's needs. They should care about them, appreciate their abilities, and accept their limitations. Primary caretakers and children should intensely communicate and sensitively coordinate their actions. They should persistently cooperate to achieve a common result: the sound stepwise and ongoing development of the child.

Many human endeavors demand the ongoing presence and efforts of significant others. An essential venture is the ongoing composition of our personality, but there are a host of others as well. Cultures are clearly thoroughly social. Societies need politicians and politicians need voting citizens. Architects, builders, investors, and banks are no less dependent on each other. Actors, musicians, painters and sculptors seek an audience, and audiences wish to be entertained. And many traumas are inflicted and can only heal in a social framework.

General, Personal, and Subjective (Phenomenal) Consciousness

The term consciousness is a *cluster concept* (see ToT Volume II, Chapter 12). It has various meanings. Three of these are general, personal, and phenomenal consciousness (Järvilehto, 2000a). These concepts comprise the answers to the questions of who experiences and knows what. *General consciousness* captures common knowledge of a whole social organization as a cooperating system. *Personal consciousness* denotes this general consciousness as realized from the perspective of a participating embodied individual. Consciousness can further stand for subjective and phenomenal experience.

Personal consciousness presupposes a bodily point of view (see ToT Volume II, Chapter 12, as well as Chapter 29 below). This perspective provides a relative constancy in that the body provides a rather stable point of reference. It entails appreciation of 'I' as related to 'not I,' inasmuch as individuals synthesize and personify their phenomenal experiences (perceptions, affects, thoughts, memories, and movements) in the framework of their phenomenal bodily feelings.

Traumatized individuals may not or not sufficiently engage in the actions of synthesis and personification. This deficit may generate experiences and symptoms such as 'out of the body' experiences, and phenomena of depersonalization, analgesia, and bodily anesthesia. However, if all goes well, individuals connect their phenomenal "I" to the phenomenal body of this "I" and the embodied actions of this "I." The actions of synthesis and personification imply experiences such as "I and my sensations," "I and my body," "I and my movement," "I and my action." Connectivity to a body also offers a "here" and thereby a "not here," that is, a "there." Synthesizing and personifying their body, individuals situate themselves in space (here, there) and person (me, not me).

This does not mean that personal consciousness is situated 'in' the body. Rather, it addresses a *set of relations* (see Chapter 23). It comprises "I and objects," "I and other subjects," "I as embedded in situations." "I's" do not and could not exist in a vacuum. Personal consciousness is embedded in general consciousness and social consciousness. As one recovering traumatized patient put it, "I am here because you are here with me; my ability to be with me depends on your ability to be with me." According to Hurley (1998) and Järvilehto (2000a), the 'I' is not to be found in a neural network or in the body more generally. Rather, it is a point of intersection in a network of relationships (e.g., 'I-You,' 'I-They,' 'I-thing,' 'I-event'). Not a piece of flesh among other physical phenomena, an individual's 'I' is part of a system of social relations and embodied and world-embedded actions (ToT Volume II, Chapter 12).

Language serves an important function in the achievement of common human results (Järvilehto, 2000a). In this sphere, words are less symbolic representations of 'some thing' (e.g., an object, a situation, a person, an understanding, a feeling) than proposals for common actions and indications of common results. However, language cannot fully replace actions and their results (see Volume I, Chapter 9). They point to actions and their results, but they cannot fully capture them. Words hint at, but cannot take the place of life. And words separate what does not exist in separation. For example, words separate 'I' from 'You' and these from an action such as 'telling.' But in life, 'I,' 'You,' and the act of 'telling' constitute a unity. Telling demands a speaker, someone spoken to as well as something that the speaker communicates and that the addressed listener can understand.

Totalitarian, Corporative, and Communicative Cooperation

Järvilehto (2000a) relates consciousness to three prototypical forms of cooperation: *totalitarian*, *corporative*, and *communicative*. He suggests that these prototypes involve three developmental phases of consciousness. They may also pertain to three probable phases of human phylogenesis. This distinction is most helpful in developing an understanding of interpersonal (and other) traumatization, and thereby of traumatized individuals and their dissociative parts.

- *Totalitarian:* At this level, there are fixed roles or specializations. The common result is not preset but rather emerges when the involved individuals rigidly stick to their roles in the organization. Mead (1934) referred to this organization as physiological. Indeed, it involves general consciousness, not personal consciousness, and communication is quite limited.
- *Corporative:* Corporative consciousness is based in the relative specialization of participants. In contrast to a totalitarian organization, the common result to be achieved at this level is preset by goals or laws. It includes personal consciousness, albeit not at a high level. There is communication and there is a degree of cooperation. The various contributors to the common result must coordinate their respective actions more than at the totalitarian level of organization. For example, they ideally communicate more and agree that everyone does his or her job in the interest of a common result. However, participants may resist the formation of the common result or they may not authentically join the project.
- *Communicative:* A communicative organization involves participants who do not fulfill specialized roles. Participants can take on each other's roles. Further, the common result is not predetermined. It is achieved through intense communication in the collective and coordinated action of fitting together the organizations of the participating individuals (Järvilehto, 2000a, pp. 50–51). The common result emerges when participants closely communicate, cooperate, and coordinate their actions. Dialog is the main type of communication at this level. The realization of a new, often surprising common result raises the level of conscious of the participants, because they get acquainted with new aspects of themselves and the world they are a part of.

Interpersonal Traumatization as a Totalitarian Organization

Generally speaking, totalitarian organizations do not demand more than relatively simple communications, simple coordination, and simple forms of consciousness (Järvilehto, 2000a). The roles are fixed and specialized, and their communication is simple: There are those who command and those who (are forced to) obey. There are leaders and followers.

This organization can be viable. For example, it makes sense to adhere to a strong hierarchy of power in situations of need. Immediate threat to the survival of a nation, a group, or an individual may demand firm hierarchically organized defense. Group discussions are useless when lions attack or bombs explode. In these circumstances, there is striving toward one common result: basic survival. To achieve their common results, generals, officers, and soldiers use straightforward communication lines (top-down orders) and simple coordination (strict rules). Their cooperation involves a rigid hierarchical structure involving well-defined functions and limited roles. Leaders command and their followers execute the orders. Leaders and followers need each other.

This organization demands a degree of consciousness. For example, leaders must be consciously aware that their orders need to be understandable to the followers, and that followers need to be equipped with an ability to understand the orders. Furthermore, hierarchical organizations must allow followers to inform their leaders about local conditions. Efficient and effective leaders consciously integrate these local conditions and other general considerations.

The consciousness of participants must and indeed will rise when the achievement of common results requires a higher level of communication, coordination, and cooperation. Under these circumstances a totalitarian organization may become a corporate structure. A corporate structure may, among other things, be better suited to formulating laws and rules that participants follow. For example, rules guide traffic, and in traffic most drivers abide by these rules to achieve relative safety for all. Strict rules and boundaries in trauma therapy ascertain that the venture can be safe for both the patient and the clinician. Trespassers in traffic and trauma therapy are held responsible for their actions – and are penalized for infractions.

Totalitarian organizations can also be vicious. This is the case when they do not serve a group's common interests, but only the commanders' singular needs and desires. Under such circumstances, the leaders become dictators and the followers become slaves. The simple communicative and instrumental format is that dictators command slaves behaviorally, verbally, and paralinguistically to do whatever serves the involved dictators' urges. Driven by extreme narcissism, totalitarian commanders leave their slaves no chance to counter, at least not effectively. Slaves are bluntly forced to obey and have nothing to gain but to secure their very existence.

Like viable totalitarian organizations, vicious totalitarian structures have no preset common results: They are guided by some individuals' personal hunger for power and control. However, vicious patterns of commanding and obeying still bring forth a social organization as a common result: a dyad, a family, a firm, a subculture, a culture, or a nation. Dictators and slaves play their fixed roles and thereby constitute and maintain the existence of the organization. After all, dictators are dictators only when they successfully enslave others. And slaves are slaves only inasmuch as they accept their enslavement and embrace their roles. Consciously aware of their fragility and guided by their will to survive, they adapt.

Narcissism is not restricted to individuals. Whole groups can become totalitarian. As Geoff Mulgan (2006) put it, "[a] modest dose of self-love is entirely healthy – who would want to live in a world where everyone hated themselves? But taken too far, it soon becomes poisonous." As Mulgan also asserted, "[a]ll of nationalism can be understood as a kind of collective narcissism." History clearly shows where nationalism and religion can lead. Whole nations and religions can become dictators who enslave other nations or belief systems. Narcissism at the personal and social level involves low levels of consciousness. Their implications can be unspeakable, as both past and present wars demonstrate.

Dictators tend to have a low level of consciousness in at least some crucial regards. For example, they do not consider and empathize with the fate of their slaves. They mostly or completely ignore the destiny of their slaves inasmuch as it is insignificant to the pursuit of their unbounded lust for control. Or they in fact enjoy their slaves' fragility if it serves to increase their sense of power. They generally experience and regard their slaves as their instruments – as things, not as persons. Dictators are further not highly aware of the eventual consequences of their actions. It escapes them that they sooner or later will provoke a revolution against them. Had they achieved a higher level of consciousness, the Caligulas, Napoleons, Stalins, Hitlers, Maos, and Idi Amins of this world could have anticipated their fate. They need only to have been more engaged in the action of presentification. While it is easy for most to see that history repeats itself, dictators, totalitarian groups, and whole cultures choose to ignore this fact. Blinded by their lust for control and feelings of omnipotence, they ignore their fragility. But each dictator crumbles one day.

Struggling to survive, many enslaved individuals attempt to lead a life "at the surface of consciousness" (Appelfeld, 1994, p. 18). They feel forced to ignore their sad reality as much as possible. They adapt in order to save their skin. Restricting the level of consciousness is one form of control. However, low degrees of synthesis, personification, presentification, and realization also contribute to maintaining a status quo. Survival of terror does not mean having a life. Erich Marie Remarque (1929/1982, p. 165) put the need to remain relatively ignorant of inflicted and inflicting terror in clear words:

> . . . I cannot get along with the people. My mother is the only one who asks no questions. Not so my father. He wants me to tell him about the front; he is curious in a way that I find stupid and distressing; I no longer have any real contact with him. There is nothing he likes more than just hearing about it. I realize he does not know that a man cannot talk of such things; I would do it willingly, but it is too dangerous for me to put these things into words. I am afraid they might become gigantic and I be no longer able to master them. What would become of us if everything that happens out there were quite clear to us?

Totalitarian organizations do not end because dictators change their mind and course of action. They basically become decomposed when slaves decide that risking their life in an effort to end their misery is more useful to them than maintaining their existence at all cost. Sooner or later all systems of slavery ends when the slaves, despite their fragility, abandon their ignorance and strive to achieve a new form of control.

Järvilehto (personal communication, September 2015) agrees that interpersonal abuse and neglect are totalitarian. Perpetrators are like dictators. They command their immediate victims such as the children they abuse, maltreat, and neglect. They also attempt to rule over their somewhat more peripheral victims such as their families. Perpetrators do not consider their victims as subjects but as objects. They more or less regard them as toys or as some other kind of instruments that exist solely to serve their ill needs.

Societal and other perpetrators require accomplices. Their accomplices or partners in crime are individuals who decide that allowing perpetrators to continue their vicious actions and passions, and that playing a supportive role is more useful to them than opposing them. They may feel that opposing perpetrators damages them more than allowing these individuals to maintain their abusive behaviors. Choosing the side of the powerful means ignoring the interests of the powerless. Accomplices in crime must ignore the interests of those who are abused, maltreated, and neglected – or else they would suffer, too. For example, how could a mother leave her fragile child unprotected in the hands of an abusive father if she were fully conscious of the child's suffering and her role in the drama? Fearing the perpetrator's repercussions, her love of herself causes her to overrule her empathy for the child.

Some totalitarian organizations include corporative elements. For example, family members and other members of society that allow child abusers to rule particular quarters of society may expect others to take charge of a problem they cannot deal with or that they do not wish to handle. These others typically include law enforcement officers, social workers, psychologists, physicians, and psychiatrists. Another corporative element within a totalitarian organization is a father who is an accomplice to his wife's sexual abuse of their daughters but who takes care of his daughters in other regards. For example, he may assist them with their homework from school or support their ambitions in sports. The level of consciousness of both the father and his abused daughters will probably be higher with regards to these activities than his and their level of consciousness regarding the abuse and its immediate and eventual consequences.

Dissociative Parts of the Personality in Trauma: Totalitarian and Corporative

Dissociation of the personality in the context of chronic interpersonal traumatization tends to include elements of totalitarian and corporative consciousness. For example, controlling EPs strive to command and control other dissociative parts (see, e.g., Chapters

31, 35, and 37). They feel, think, and behave first and foremost totalitarian. Given the low level of consciousness and the restricted field of consciousness that totalitarian positions imply, these EPs tend to more or less successfully ignore or cover up their own fragility and ignorance.

Dominated by their perpetrators, fragile EPs are and feel enslaved. To save their skin, they may obey totalitarian commands. Perhaps even more so than controlling EPs, they operate at relatively low levels of consciousness, and their field of consciousness is commonly very restricted. In this sense fragile EPs are typically ignorant of the third-person perspective on space, time, the whole individual's identity, and the identity of many other individuals.

Many ANPs can operate at a corporate level of consciousness when they feel relatively safe. For example, they manage to hold a job, take care of their children, or engage in voluntary work. In these cases, they can focus on their tasks and recognize what the adequate execution of these tasks demands of them. At times, some ANPs reach a communicative level, for example, when they manage to discuss complicated emotional issues with a partner, child, or friend, or take part in meetings at work.

However, when ANPs feel threatened by other individuals, other dissociative parts, or objects, their field of consciousness may retract considerably and their level of consciousness may decrease significantly. For example, when ANPs feel threatened by EPs, they tend to lose appreciation of the involved EPs' interests and their other important features; they may come to regard them as dangerous subjects or even as scary objects. They may also lose the capacity to talk to them. Some start to act like dictators who only want the intrusive parts to obey: "Leave me alone, back off!" When this happens, ANPs regress to totalitarian actions. Fragile EPs, on the other hand, may obey for a while. Actions driven by basic needs and desires are not that sensitive to punishment (see Chapter 35). Hitting crying toddlers makes them cry louder. Some may stop crying for a while, only to start again in an instant. Controlling EPs are more inclined to fight for totalitarian control: They are ready for war.

When dissociative parts know each other and agree on a division of tasks, they operate like two divisions in a company, each with their own assignments. This division of labor takes on a corporative kind of communication and coordination. In this sense, dissociative parts operate like a corporate entity whose divisions communicate poorly with each other: Each dissociative part exerts its own function or set of functions. Communications between them remain restricted to simple exchanges, as several transcripts of therapy sessions illustrate (e.g., Chapter 32).

Overcoming a dissociation of the personality, however, demands *intense* communication, coordination, and cooperation among the various dissociative parts. It commonly also demands profound and recurrent communication, coordination, and cooperation between them and the clinician. Enactive trauma therapy is the realization of this insight.

Enactive Trauma Clinicians: Corporative and Communicative

Because chronically traumatized individuals are being or have been raised in a totalitarian world, and because dissociation of the personality at best operates at a corporative level ("You do this, he does that, and I'll do still something else" and "First do this, then do that, etc."), they need better, more viable interpersonal models. And because overcoming traumatization takes higher levels of consciousness, clinicians need to engage in and thereby also model high levels of empathy, compassion, coordination, and communication. They show a deep interest in the patient's needs, desires, and interests. They are clearly also focused on the achievement of the common results defined by the patient's wish to heal. Clinicians, then, foster, among other things, increasing levels of coordination and communication among the various dissociative parts. The objective is for these parts to experience that cooperation is ultimately more useful than ignoring, controlling, or hurting each other. This approach generally takes a high level of consciousness. In any case it takes a higher level of consciousness than the level required at the corporate level of consciousness, which is commonly sufficient to understand and apply therapeutic manuals.

The paradox of enactive trauma therapy is that higher levels of consciousness and relatedness – including relatedness with the clinician – imply more intense affects, bodily feelings (sensations), and emotions. These affects, sensations, and emotions are precisely the experiences that the ignoring and controlling parts of the personality fear, detest, and preferably avoid. In a word, traumatized individuals tend to fear, despise, and avoid the very actions and the implied higher levels of consciousness that could heal their injuries.

The paradox also affects clinicians. Ideally they develop a high level of consciousness regarding both traumatized individuals and themselves. But this intense empathy and clear understanding implies a fierce and rather direct confrontation with the adverse and traumatizing features of the world. It can be most difficult to tolerate this experience and knowledge. It is a small wonder that clinicians can feel fragile, can get hurt, may want to hide in ignorance, or can become fixed in anger while attempting to assist traumatized individuals.

Enactive trauma therapy is the sensitive and dedicated effort to raise consciousness to levels of corporation and communication that allow the emergence of new, benevolent, and healing actions and experiences in the steps that patients can manage. This wound healing is possible only when traumatized individuals and their dissociative parts become embedded in an interpersonal frame that helps them to integrate and realize their traumatic past and the consequences this past had and continues to have. This work also assumes that clinicians are highly consciously aware of, and integrate, their own person perspectives (first, quasi-second, second, and third) and those of the patient (first, quasi-second, second, and third).

These various person perspectives are discussed in ToT Volumes I and II, particularly in Chapter 5; they are presented again in Chapter 27. Let it briefly be said here that the first-person perspective denotes the phenomenal experience of being someone, more specifically an 'I' with a point of view (the term 'phenomenal' is explained below). This 'I' is the cornerstone of all other person perspectives. The quasi-second person perspective in turn concerns the phenomenal relationship of this 'I' with 'me,' 'myself,' 'mine,' 'my (features, possessions, and the like).' It includes the phenomenal experience (e.g., "feeling; feeling one's hand"), as well as the phenomenal judgment of this experience (e.g., "The hand I feel is my hand"). The second-person perspective involves phenomenal 'I-You' relationships, experiences, and judgments. Finally, the third-person perspective concerns physical or technical 'I-object' relationships, experiences, and judgments.

Being Sentient and Being Conscious

All organisms are sentient beings. In this sense all are mental. However, there is a difference between being sentient (being mentally active) and being conscious. A host of organismic operations proceed (or can proceed) without conscious awareness. Some are unconscious in the absolute sense of the term. For example, we are absolutely unable to take a direct look into our brain to see how it takes part in the generation of our conscious existence. Other operations are unconscious in a more relative sense. As described before and to illustrate, a particular ANP may not recollect an experience, whereas a fragile EP is consciously aware of it. Depending on the nature and the mental state of the system or organism, some actions and their results are clearly conscious, whereas other actions are preconscious (e.g., ToT Volume II, Chapter 19).

Access Consciousness and Phenomenal Consciousness

The term 'consciousness' carries with it various meanings. One distinction, according to Block (1996, 2005, 2007), may be made between access consciousness and phenomenal consciousness. Various authors have defined and use the two concepts in somewhat different ways. However, access consciousness generally pertains to the mental content that an individual can access consciously. For example, the person may explicitly see a knife on the table or hear the voice of a dissociative part.

The adjective 'phenomenal' in phrases like 'phenomenal consciousness' and 'phenomenal action' does not express that the mental content or the action is fantastic or outstanding. Rather, it stands for 'consciously experienced,' i.e., 'known or derived through the senses' (ToT Volume II, Chapter 12). This use of the term 'phenomenal' is directly derived from the term 'phenomenon' which stems from the Greek substantive *phainomenon* and the verb *phainein,* meaning 'to appear, to shine, to show, to be manifest, or to manifest itself.'

Basically comprehended as 'appearances' or 'experiences,' phenomena are related to observables and to what some describe as 'qualia.' The rather vague plural term 'qualia' stems from the Latin adverb *quâlis* that means 'what sort' or 'what kind' (the singular form is "quale"). As Dennett (1988, p. 381) gracefully put it, it is "an unfamiliar term for something that could not be more familiar to each of us: the ways things seem to us."

Qualia, for example, pertain to *what is it like* for a particular person to consume an omelet, to enjoy a glass of Amarone, a sunset, a painting by one's child or a Modigliani, to watch a tedious movie, to experience or observe an accident, an assault, or some other adverse event.

The term 'phenomenal consciousness' thus designates mental states that include a subjective and experiential character (Merleau-Ponty, 1945/1962; Thompson, Lutz, & Cosmelli, 2005). It does not denote the content of a conscious mental state as such, but rather signifies *experiencing* this content. It denotes what kind of experience it is to see a knife on the table, to notice it is a red knife, not a blue one, to experience it is blunt, to be interested in sharpening it, or to be deadly scared of the knife. Phenomenal consciousness similarly captures what it is like to hear voices of hurting children or controlling voices that other persons do not (and cannot) hear, what it is like to reenact a traumatizing event with its implied sensations, motions, and emotions; and what it is like to feel that no one can be trusted. Phenomenal consciousness further addresses experiencing what it is like to be 'I,' to be the one who has these experiences and perceptions, and who evaluates them. In other words, phenomenality corresponds to the qualitative appearance of one's self, world, and self-world relationships for consciousness.

Phenomenal consciousness evidently presupposes access consciousness. Conscious sensorimotor and emotional states feel a certain way, and conscious thoughts or episodes of conscious thought are commonly experiential as well (Husserl, 2000). Whereas perceptions, beliefs, thoughts, memories, dreams, fantasies, and so on, tend to include a feeling about what it is like to live that mental state (Nagel, 1979; Thompson & Zahavi, 2007), access consciousness does not imply phenomenal consciousness.

The distinction between access consciousness and phenomenal consciousness is clinically and scientifically useful. For example, depersonalized individuals have access to the fact that they exist. However, they may feel like a robot, like an automaton (e.g., Chapter 32). They know their relatives and interact with them, but may feel disconnected from them. Like depersonalization, derealization involves a lack of phenomenality. Further, dissociative parts may know each other, though they typically do not experience or know what it is like to be that other part (see e.g., Chapters 35 and 37). Some dissociative parts sometimes experience sensations and emotions of one or more other dissociative parts. Or they remember what another part remembers. This does not imply that these sensations, emotions, or memories have meaning to them, or have the same or a similar meaning. Some dissociative patients know they cannot move or otherwise control a part of their body. However, they do not seem to care. They display 'belle indifference.'

To illustrate, we can revisit Sonja's case (introduced in ToT Volume II, Chapter 12, p. 317). At some point in her therapy, Sonja as the main ANP had learned that she had a daughter of 22 years. She had not known this reality before, even though the daughter had been living with the patient for most of her life. She had known that there was a child around, but she had not experienced or known that this child was *hers*. That is, she had had conscious access to the physical fact that there was a child in her house, but experiencing that this child was her child had not been part of her phenomenal consciousness. With therapeutic progression, Sonja as the main ANP became consciously aware that the child was *her* child. However, this knowledge remained a mere fact for her. In this phase, she reported knowing that the by then 22-year-old daughter was her child (access consciousness). However, that fact did not imply phenomenal consciousness. As she put it, knowing that the young woman was her daughter "did not feel real." As therapy progressed further, she became more intimately connected with The Helper, the dissociative part who experienced and acknowledged that she was the mother of the child. The Helper also encompassed the traumatic rapes of her stepfather, the traumatic pregnancy, and the traumatic childbirth. When Sonja as the main ANP and The Helper shared these traumatic memories in a therapeutic session, not as mere facts but as sensorimotor and emotional experiences, Sonja as the main ANP realized with a shock that the daughter was *her* child. A physical fact became a phenomenal reality. The session will be detailed more in Chapter 37, along with the immediate consequences of this profound realization for Sonja's external and inner worlds.

Phenomenal and Subjective

It may at first sight be tempting to think that the adjective 'phenomenal' is a synonym of the adjective 'subjective.' Phenomenologists, however, explain that there are differences between the two concepts. Whereas the term 'phenomenal' stands for the way things feel or appear to a particular person, the concept of subjectivity signifies that experiences are given and can only be given from the person's first-person experience. This givenness pertains to the first-person inasmuch as access consciousness includes at least some self-reference, at least a primitive degree of experiential self-referentiality (Thompson & Zahavi, 2007). To attain experiential self-referentiality, individuals must engage in the act of personification. The more they engage in this action, the more they will experience and appreciate that they are subjects – real persons with their own experiences.

Individuals do not have direct access to each other's feelings. That is why experience is subjective. It is not in the nature of things that John can feel what Mary feels and vice versa, or that trauma clinicians can feel what traumatized individuals feel. However, one person can feel into and along with another person. Empathy, sympathy, and other forms of phenomenal nearness to someone else's experiences require more than engagement in the first-person perspective. It also takes engagement in the second-person perspective that involves a phenomenal relationship between 'I' and 'You.' Clinicians therefore strive to maximize their ability and skills to engage in this perspective. They aim to be very good at attuning to traumatized individual's subjectively given experiences and to the way it must be like to be traumatized and to have all symptoms of trauma. At the same time, they are aware that in doing so they should not lose track of themselves, neither personally nor professionally.

Clinicians clearly also need a solid third-person understanding of trauma, and they need to combine this technical judgment with their phenomenal experience and judgment in the second-person perspective. The upcoming theoretical chapters intend to deepen the third-person perspective on trauma, dissociation, enactivism, and enactive trauma therapy. The practical chapters indicate how clinicians are challenged to integrate the second-person and third-person person-perspective. But not even this perspectival integration suffices. All person perspectives are grounded in the first-person and quasi-second person perspective. That is why clinicians are summoned to integrate their second-person and third-person perspectives regarding the traumatized individuals they assist and coach with their first-person and quasi-second perspective regarding themselves. A challenge indeed!

Chapter 23

Enlightenment, Enlivenment, Enactivism

> *A path is made by walking on it.*
> Zhuang Zi (ca. 369–286 BC)

> *The basic unit of psychological investigation is not a psychological process within the organism, but a process in the whole organism-environment system. This is the system in which "psyche" is realized and if this system is divided into smaller parts, we lose the psychological object of study.*
> Timo Järvilehto (2001b, p. 3)

Trauma is an injury, and trauma treatment a striving to heal the wound. But what has become damaged, what is in need of repair, and what or who can cure the harm? As described in the first volume of this trilogy, one idea is that, apart from harmful environmental conditions, the problem and its solution are a matter of the *brain*. This idea emerged during the 17th century and has been around ever since. It currently even seems to be spreading and intensifying. Particularly, but not only, since commencement of the human genome project, another inkling is that the disturbance relates to abnormal or 'unlucky' *genes*. If so, can genetic engineering mend the defect? Or is trauma perhaps a physiological problem? As ancient and contemporary intuitions tell, emotional shocks can cause an unbalance of *body fluids* that medication can mend. These two hunches were to become the stronger the more the human body was explored. Some maintained that, in a more general sense, the body keeps score. Is it, then, this material structure that is in need of healing?

Still another take on the matter is that not the body but the *mind* is the cause of the suffering and of the physical features of trauma – and that therefore the mind should be the target of restoration. For example, some claim that trauma involves faulty beliefs, most of all the idea that traumatic memories are dangerous where in fact they are innocuous. Some feel that the remedy would, at least in principle, be as simple and straightforward as the theory: Expose individuals to their traumatic memories and *voilà*, confrontations with the 'objective reality' correct the mistaken idea on their own (see Chapter 37 on exposure). Others feel that in trauma the metaphorical *heart* is broken, or that, particularly in chronic traumatization, the problem lies in conflicted *interpersonal relationships*, in deep problems of attachment and attachment loss. What else, then, than a sound and solid therapeutic relationship could mend relational tragedies?

Enlightenment

Putting the question aside where one situates the injury – in the brain, the body, or the mind – there is a potent tendency in psychiatry and psychology to regard the human body and the human mind as complex *machines* of some sort. In this light, trauma is essentially a sort of mechanical defect. This view constitutes the core of the Enlightenment, a philosophical and scientific movement that originated in the 17th century and that basically stretches to the present. Hopes were and continue to be that pure, dispassionate human reason will triumph in the end. Its assumptions are that human experience, thought, and behavior will prove to be fully explicable in mechanical processes that are amenable to human understanding. In this frame of mind, effective body-oriented approaches to trauma and/or mind-oriented treatment methods would involve 'rational' and technical refitting.

For example, and as described in ToT Volume I, in the 17th century the physician Thomas Willis (1612–1673) and others performed autopsies on the bodies of deceased hysterical women to arrive at a better understanding of the disorder. Was hysteria due to a 'wandering womb' as had been suspected for ages? Or were the bodies and minds of hysterical women perhaps haunted by wandering metaphysical forces? The postmortems revealed neither displaced, suffocated wombs nor any evil spirits. Willis felt that the secret to hysteria lay in the motions and proportions in mixtures of the five principles of the chemist: spirit, sulphur, salt, water, and earth. He first allocated the disease in the body, but later asserted that the disorder is seated in the brain. His colleague Thomas Sydenham (1624–1689) suspected that, in addition to abnormal material compositions, hysteria comprised an affliction of the mind. More specifically he held that hysteria was a *disorder of the whole person* stemming from a merger of the mind and nerves under the influence of '*animal* spirits.' These spirits involved exceptionally subtle matter distilled from arterial blood in the cerebral cortex which link the body and the mind. This link became necessary in accordance with René Descartes' (1596–1650) distinction between *res extensa* (the extended thing, i.e., matter), *res cogitans* (the thinking thing, i.e., mind), and *God.* The philosopher, mathematician, and scientist conceived res extensa and res cogitans as two different substances, and speculated that the pineal gland is the locus of body-mind interaction. But how can the body and the mind interact at all if matter and mind are different substances?

Given his understanding that hysteria pertains to a physically unbalanced human body that somehow disturbs the hysterical individual's mind, Willis prescribed medications. Many physicians followed this type of treatment in the ages to come, and many physicians and psychiatrists continue to follow it now. The psychopharmaceutical industry has actually grown to huge proportions, and it has become a major power structure. Sydenham emphasized the emotional nature of hysteria, though he also asserted that its cause was in part physical. Suggesting that hysteria is related to a constitutional weakness of the nerves that particularly, though not exclusively, characterized the female body, he applied body-oriented treatments such as soothing medication, iron supplements, blood-letting, and vigorous exercise. Both physicians suspected that emotional upsets could disturb the animal spirits, a derangement that manifested in both somatic and mental symptoms.

Willis and Sydenham's views, hopes, and approaches to treatment may sound quite reasonable to some ears. While the terms and metaphors have changed over the ages, the materialistic and mechanical ideas they denote have not. However, as discussed in ToT Volumes I & II, there are good reasons to suspect that the notions involved are, at least in part, if not more profoundly, misleading. They might even be like the Sirens that crossed Odysseus and his crew's course.

Advised by Circe, a minor Goddess of magic, Odysseus ordered his men to plug their ears with beeswax and to tie him to the mast of the ship. The sailors were even instructed to tighten the ropes more firmly should the half women/half birds' fabulous voices, melodies, and words entice and delude their leader. The measures enacted by Circe and Odysseus' saved the ship and the men from shipwreck on the rocky shores of the island where the mysterious vocalists dwelled.

Is it, so to speak, the chanting of the Siren of Particles which the brain – or perhaps even some particular part of the brain – emits that fully explains trauma? Does this Siren perhaps entice the field to accept that trauma is basically reducible to the prefrontal cortex, which in turn fails to control the emotional brain? Or is it the constant bleeping of the Siren of Cybernetics, that the brain does not adequately process information? Is there a Siren of Matter proclaiming that the trouble lies in body stuff? Is there a fourth Siren of Thought, i.e., does the problem involve a mind that can no longer think straight? Would the Siren of Objectivity hum the tune that trauma is an objectively existing external event? And do they, like the Siren of Mechanics, in concert voice the idea that traumatized individuals are best seen as disrupted machines, be it brain, body, or mind machines? Who is right and who is wrong?

No matter how exceptionally impressive the achievements of Enlightenment are, where do we find *life* amid the material and mental machinery? Were Odysseus and the crew of the endangered ship mere aimless, affectionless puppets on the strings of eternal mechanistic laws? Is there any trace of life, any feeling, any compassion in the Sirens? Or are they merely heartless machines themselves, zombies in effect? What luminosity does the Enlightenment bring to life itself?

Songs Beyond the Siren of Mechanics

There are several important differences between living organisms and machines. Organisms, including scientists who study matter, are not zombies. They are not objective. They *feel*, and they are all subjective. All life forms have an affective *interest* in themselves and their world. Among all affective interests, life most of all longs and strives to preserve itself. Intimately related to this primary affectivity, life encompasses a subjective *point of view*. Machines do not include these twins, primary affective interest and first-person perspectivalness.

Physical structures do not reveal mental actions or contents. No one has seen the mind in the brain (or elsewhere) and no one ever will. Brain matter does not speak to us. Structures such as the brain or parts of the brain only make sense to observers who comprehend their observations in a particular way. This way is made possible as well as curtailed by the way in which they are 'constructed.' Observers include and are constrained by their interests, body, brain, eyes and other senses; their intellect; their developmental history as well as scientific or cultural paradigms. Their structural and functional features allow certain perceptions and conceptions while excluding others. What is more, their measuring instruments such as microscopes, EEG machines, and structural and functional MRI affect what they see or fail to see.

Although life involves stable features such as primary affectivity and a first-person perspective, it is also dynamic. Organisms and their environment are in constant flux. They are ever changing – unlike mechanical devices, which are in principle static. Conceived parts of a machine such as nuts and bolts, pistons, valves, pumps, wheels, and gears are unchanging. Kept in a vacuum, anorganic structures can exist forever.

Related to this, inanimate structures can exist and remain even perfectly maintained in an utter void. Machines and isolation are splendid friends. Not so living organisms. They do not and cannot exist by themselves. All life forms are *utterly* dependent on their environment. Short of a livable environment they perish soon. Isolation is the deathly foe of all life.

There is yet another difference between organisms and apparatuses: As discussed in detail later, life does not meet a pregiven, objectively existing world that is meaningful in and of itself. A computer is programmed. It runs on software that involves pregiven information and pregiven rules about how this information is to be operated on. But to live is to make meaning in an intimate and ongoing organism-environment dance.

Songs Beyond the Siren of Matter

Philosophical materialists as well as scientists who adhere to this doctrine basically assume two separated systems: an 'objectively existing' world and 'subjective' individuals. Trying to resolve the Cartesian body-mind divide, they hold to, or at least hope that the mind can in principle be completely analyzed in terms of matter. Within this framework, materialists claim that the mind *is* the living brain[1].

1 A common tendency in psychotraumatology and in psychology in general is to assume that physical processes cause the division of the mind into unconscious and conscious parts. For example, Chefetz (2015, pp. 155–156) asserts that, "affects are nonconscious, protosensations arising from visceral and neuromuscular tensions that reflect an overarching summation vector of the moment-to-moment equilibrium of the physiological state of a human being." He continues: "[A] feeling is a sensed accumulation of nonconscious somatically generated affects that crosses over an imagined threshold of intensity to reach a level of consciousness." These formulations follow Tomkins' theory of affects (see Demos, 1995, p. 86): "... (1) by the terms 'affect' or innate 'affect,' we reference a group of nine highly

They basically regard the brain as an extremely complex machine and assume that some parts of the brain generate consciousness and self-consciousness. When trying to unveil the 'mental secrets' of this apparatus, the common strategy is thus to look for the parts of the brain that would generate (self-)consciousness. Materialists are then faced with all the problems that analytical machine metaphors pose.

Assuming that matter is all that matters, philosophical and scientific materialists ignore the fact that consciousness cannot be reduced to anything else. The bottom line is that their projects hang on the thread of consciousness. Science is an intentional human affair guided by the conscious and unconscious interests and abilities of scientists. It does not involve a blind view from nowhere. For example, neuroscience *presupposes* consciousness and affective interest; it presumes there are individuals with an interest in and ability to examine and understand the brain and mental functions in a certain way. Put differently: It presupposes what it tries to explain. The neuroscientific study of normal and abnormal consciousness involves a third-person perspective. However, the project is essentially grounded in the experiential existence of the scientists involved, in their first-person perspective and subjectivity.

Whereas living systems include physical and mental features, their physical features do not, indeed *cannot,* capture their experiential nature. Physical structures are unable to tell what it is like to have a particular experience or experiences in general. They are also unable to reveal what it is like to have a point of view. Neuroscience is fascinating and clearly important. However, the attempt to reduce consciousness and self-consciousness to brain structures and processes, or more generally to matter, is futile if matter and mind are different attributes or properties of the same substance or system. One can relate two or more properties to each other, but efforts to explain one property in terms of another property are doomed to fail[2] (see ToT Volumes I & II).

---

specific unmodulated physiological reactions from birth. (2) We use the term 'feeling' to describe our awareness that an affect has been triggered ..." Chefetz and Tomkins are philosophical materialists inasmuch as they assume that physiological states cause mental states. However, if I understand their writings correctly, they also claim that mental states can influence physiological states. Hence, they are philosophical dualists. But no one knows or has the slightest idea how a certain level of physiological activity causes a mental or phenomenal state – or how a certain phenomenal state causes a physiological state. Following Spinoza (ToT Volumes I & II, and below), I maintain that physiological processes and ideas involve different appearances of one substance or system. In this light, the physical does not *cause* the mental (unconscious mind) and the phenomenal (conscious mind) or vice versa. Rather, "unmodulated physiological reactions" and "feelings" are the appearances of one substance or system. Unmodulated and modulated physiological reactions are also mental, just as feelings are also physiological.

2 Leading neuroscientists with an interest in consciousness and self-consciousness began following Varela's (1996) integrative proposal to explore indirect links between neurological and phenomenological features. A good example of this methodology is the work of the neuroscientist and philosopher Georg Northoff (2003, 2014a, 2014b). His nonreductive neurophenomenological approach considers the brain and the mind to be properties of a whole and claims that individuals are intrinsically environmentally embedded (ToT Volumes I & II). This is a most interesting and viable approach.

The division of 'subjective' individuals and an 'objectively existing' world also entails serious problems. One major issue relates to what was said above: Any claim about what exists relies on what a particular individual feels, believes, and thinks from his or her particular point of view and under the strong influence of his or her interests. 'Views from nowhere' and disinterested views simply do not exist (see ToT Volume I; Chapter 24 and 25). There is no observer-independent 'objective reality.'

Proclaiming that trauma involves brain matter that has become disturbed by matter external to the traumatized, that is, the injured individual may sound very scientific, but there a painful truth haunts the materialist: No one has a clue as to how disturbing and disturbed matter would generate hurt and hurting minds.

To sum up, consciousness and self-consciousness (and hence trauma) cannot become fully 'naturalized.' The Sirens of the Enlightenment are silent regarding the essential first-person perspective. They also seem to overlook or ignore the libretto expressing that consciousness and self-consciousness cannot be reduced to anything else (see ToT Volumes I & II).

Songs Beyond the Siren of Thought

Like philosophical materials, philosophical idealism also longs and strives to repair the gap between the individual and the world – between mind and matter – which philosophical dualism brought forth. Idealism proposes that the mind generates ideas, both ideas of the mind's owner as well as (constellations of) of other subjects and (constellations of) of objects. Taken to its extreme, this entails the idea that the ideas of the experiencing and knowing individual are *nothing but* his or her ideas. Matter, then, would be an organism's idea or construction. But as mentioned above, living organisms do not and cannot possibly exist in emptiness. Philosophical idealism further comprises an omnipotent view of mind: "The world is my idea and I am my idea as well." This view is also deeply masochistic inasmuch as it holds that trauma only exists in the mind and is crafted solely by the mind.

Adverse Life: Coincidental Suffering?

Some philosophical materialists also adhere to philosophical epiphenomenalism, meaning the mind is a mere epiphenomenon. This position seems to entail a further masochistic view of mind and nature. What is the point of personal suffering if suffering is an insignificant and meaningless coincidence of matter? Is trauma a mere cruel concomitance of material forces? What survival value can malevolent epiphenomena possibly have?

Enlivenment and Enactivism

The ambition of enactivism and enactive trauma therapy lies in safely guiding psychology and biology's ships past seductive voices and perilous rocks. One important striving is to save lives by bringing life back to these disciplines (Varela, 1979, 1997; Varela, Thompson, & Rosch, 1991; Weber, 2010, 2014; Weber & Varela, 2002). As the biologist and philosopher Andreas Weber (2010, 2014) puts it, enlightenment needs to be complemented with "enlivenment." This occurs when it is realized that organisms *want* to live, that they *feel*, and that in one way or another they *make sense of themselves and their world* within this framework.

In order to get a deeper feel for the enactive perspective, examining the historical roots of enactivism may be a good start (see also ToT Volumes I & II).

Spinoza: A Father of Enactivism

The roots of enactivism lie in a distant past. Several date back to the 17th century, and a few involve ideas that emerged in even more remote times. Probably unaware of Willis, Sydenham, and others' 17th-century British medical and psychological ventures to comprehend and mend hysteria, Baruch d'Espinoza (1632–1677) set an even higher goal for himself: His ambition was to investigate how the sane and the insane would best *live*, how they could achieve joy, come to terms with sorrow, and moderate their naturally given, practically insatiable needs and desires. Torn by powerful, enduring, and contrary affects, what are our best options? And how can individuals come to terms with a devastating life, with a life that dramatically disagrees with their very being?

Part of Spinoza's brilliance was to avoid philosophical materialistic and idealistic traps. As described in ToT Volumes I and II, he did not succumb to his colleague Descartes' philosophical dualism, in which matter and mind are seen as two substances that, nonetheless, as if by magic, influence each other. Spinoza (1677a) countered that substances *cannot* possibly affect each other, or else they are not different substances. The body cannot get the mind to work, and the mind cannot affect the body if they reside in quarters of their own and have nothing in common.

Had Spinoza known Willis and Sydenham's understanding of hysteria, he would have told them that their own as well as hysterical individuals' thinking and body constitute a unity. This whole, he would have continued, includes material and mental *properties*, not different substances. How then, the physicians might have asked the philosopher, how can the body and the mind that strike us as so very different be *one*? Spinoza would have responded most carefully, and *sub rosa*[3]. Speaking his mind freely and openly might have

3 This Latin phrase means "under the rose." The rose has several symbolic meanings. One of its ancient meanings is secrecy or confidentiality. As Runes (1951, Introduction) reminds us, Spinoza was "a much watched man in a very watchful time." This is why most of his work remained *sub rosa* during his lifetime, including *Ethics*.

inspired the Inquisition to decompose his body and mind alike. He would have softly, yet steadfastly confided that God or Nature is one, that being part of Nature any organism is one, and that body and mind are one as well. No dualism. No mind-body divide. No philosophical materialism, no philosophical idealism.

Surpassing divides of matter and mind, Spinoza composed a philosophical monism in which mind and matter are seen as two *attributes* (i.e., properties or appearances) of one substance[4]. Being different properties or appearances of one thing, they are not each other's cause. And each property or appearance must be analyzed and understood through itself. This monism entails that no one in the 17th century could tell, that no one knows to date, and that nobody will ever succeed in explaining how the mind gets the body to work or the body the mind. Spinoza asserted there is no answer to these enigmas. He felt that the core problem lay in the misguided and misguiding questions, not in difficulty to find solid answers.

To detail Spinoza's monism a bit more, by substance Spinoza (1677a, Part I, Definition 3) understood "what is in itself and what is conceived through itself." In other words, substance cannot be reduced to anything else. This singular existing substance, this "infinite and eternal being which we call God or Nature" (1677a, Preface Part IV, p. 114) – comprises "an infinity of attributes of which each one expresses an eternal and infinite essence" (Part I, Definition 6). Of this infinity, man only knows two: mind or thought, and matter or extension.

Spinoza (1677a, p. 1) defined attribute (or property) as "what the intellect perceives of a substance, as constituting its essence" and 'mode' as "the affections of a substance, *or* that which is in another through which it is also conceived." An attribute, that is, must be understood in and through itself, that is, within its own domain. Therefore, "singular thoughts ... are modes which express ... nature in a certain and determinate way ... Therefore ... there belongs to [nature] an attribute whose concept all singular thoughts

4 Substance would be better called 'ipstance,' as Adriaan Koerbagh (1633–1669) proposed (Leeuwenburg, 2013; Wielema, 2003). The term 'substance' literally means something that stands *under* something else on which it is dependent. But in philosophy, the term substance intends something that is ontologically independent, something that must be understood through itself. The Dutch term 'zelfstandigheid' and the German equivalent 'Selbstständigkeit' effectively express this meaning: something that stands by itself. The Latin word 'ipse' means himself, herself, or itself. Hence, Koerbagh's neologism ipstance. I concur with Koerbagh's terminological precision, but in ToT can only somewhat reluctantly conform to the common practice to use the term substance when actually a 'zelfstandigheid' is intended. Belonging to the circle of Spinoza, an even more radical and outspoken freethinker Koerbagh composed a lexicon demolishing the dogmas of the reformed and other churches. For example, he concluded that the Bible and dogmas like the Holy Trinity and the divine nature of Christ involve human ideas. Betrayed by the printer who knew the contents of his new book *A light shining in dark places, to shed light on matters of theology and religion* (1668/2011), the authorities arrested him in 1668. Koerbagh was found guilty of blasphemy and was sentenced to no less than 10 years in the Rasphuis jail at Amsterdam as well as to a serious fine. He died a couple of months later from hard forced labor and the harsh prison life. See also Leeuwenburg, 2013.

involve, and through which they are also conceived ..." Hence, thought is a property of nature, and nature "*is a thinking thing*" (Part II, Proposition 1[5]). By the same reasoning, extension or something that has volume, is also a property or appearance of Nature. Hence, Spinoza wrote, God or "*Nature is an extended thing*" (Part II, Proposition 2).

It is important to grasp that Spinoza did not hold that mind and matter exist and operate in parallel, as it is sometimes erroneously stated (see Van Reijen, 2013). He rather stated that they are ontologically and functionally *one*,[6] so that "*[t]he body cannot determine the mind to thinking, and the mind cannot determine the body to motion, to rest, or to anything else (if there is anything else)*" (Spinoza, 1677a, Part III, Proposition 2, italics in original). For example, considered under the attribute of matter, the whole personality and various dissociative parts include gray and white cells, networks of these cells, neurotransmitters, and many more material 'bodies.' Considered under the attribute of mind, they have their phenomenological, psychological, and psychosocial features. But being attributes or properties of a singular substance, matter and mind cannot possibly cause each other or run in parallel as two independent but perfectly correlated substances.

However tempting it may be, however sweet particular Sirens may sing, according to Spinoza it is false to think that the brain generates mind, or that thought can cause the brain and body to move (see also ToT Volumes I & II). Traumatized individuals are not scared *because* their amygdalar cells fire, *because* their locus coeruleus excretes a massive amount of noradrenaline, or *because* their heart beats fast and their heart rate variability is low. And their

---

5 In the 1996 reprint of Spinoza's Ethics, the propositions are in italics. I retain this style.

6 For example, in her otherwise excellent and important book on enactivism and primordial affectivity, Colombetti (2014) interprets Spinoza's ontology as a form of parallelism. But this is a *profound misunderstanding*. His radical ontology did not hold that mind and matter, so to speak, run parallel courses. Rather, Spinoza asserted that being manifestations of one substance, they do not operate next to each other. They do *not* cause each other, and they *cannot* be fully understood in each other's terms. He famously wrote, "*[t]he order and connection of ideas is the same as the order and connection of things*" (1677a, Part II, Proposition 7). To grasp the point, it might be helpful to consider that any material object has a certain weight and a certain shape, but that the weight and the shape of the object cannot be explained in each other's terms. The object's weight and shape do not run in parallel, but concern two distinct properties or appearances of one thing. In another most important contribution, George Herbert Mead (1968, originally published in 1925) also rejected Spinoza's philosophy on the false grounds that it would comprise parallelism of mind and matter. The implication of Spinoza's metaphysics is that trying to understand the mind by studying the brain in isolation of the mind, in isolation of the first-person perspective, will dramatically fail. The brain does not reveal what it is like to have experiences, to feel, to know indeed. Actually only conscious minds can study the brain, only to conscious minds does this venture make sense, and only conscious minds can experience what it is like to be conscious. Any study and understanding of the brain thus presupposes mind (e.g., Husserl, 1954/1970; Varela, 1996). Brainstuff and mind can, however, be *indirectly* linked, as Varela (1996) and Bitbol (2008) have detailed. They claim that their *methodological* approach does not resolve the hard problem of consciousness, i.e., the problem of explaining how we can be the subject of phenomenal experiences, how we can have visual, auditory, and other sensory experiences, but rather *dissolves* it. See ToT Volume I, Chapter 8.

medial prefrontal brain structures do not inhibit their amygdalar cells *because* their owner engages in the act of presentification of traumatic memories and realizes that the horrors happened in the past, not now. Or, vice versa, this realization or any other feeling and thought do not cause particular patterns of brain activity. The phenomena of thought and extension are two sides of a 'coin' (Nature) – a 'coin' that probably entails far more properties than man knows and can know (Spinoza, 1677a, Part I, Definition 6).

Spinoza's position implies that mind is not exclusive to human beings, but constitutes a continuous feature of all life. The human mind has a number of properties such as the ability to reason, to reflect, and to report mental states that do not seem to characterize the minds of other organisms (or not as much). However, this does not mean that other organisms are mindless, as Spinoza taught us, and as several contemporary authors now agree (Colombetti, 2014; Jonas, 1966; Thompson, 2007; Weber & Varela, 2002; see Chapters 25, 27, and 29).

Building on his impressive philosophical monism, he formulated in the remainder of his *Ethics,* his magnum opus, what an ethical life entails. Far more than a philosophy, the book includes a most inspiring affect-oriented and action-oriented psychology. Few psychologists seem to be aware of this. Yet many later philosophers and psychologists, some wittingly and others unwittingly, stood and continue to stand on the shoulders of this tormented giant, of this frail man who was excommunicated by his Jewish kin in Amsterdam, whose works were banned by the Jewish, Catholic, and Protestant Churches alike, who survived an attack on his life, and who decided to reside in relative solitude, but not without friends, grinding lenses to earn a very modest income. Indeed, "[n]o philosopher was ever more worthy, but neither was any philosopher more maligned and hated" (Deleuze, 1988, p. 3). Spinoza chose a life with few possessions apart from his parental bed, his books, and his quill. Professionally, he sought, found, and maintained complete professional autonomy, implying a career without academic positions. He lived for his philosophy and psychology, and he lived them. As Bertrand Russell asserted, "ethically he is supreme" (see the 1996 reprint of Spinoza 1677a).

More Fathers of Enactivism

Enactivism explicitly acknowledges and uses Spinoza's philosophy and psychology. The persuasion also includes Buddhistic insights and attitudes as well as several of Lao Tze and Zhuang Zi's thoughts. There are in fact significant parallels between these ancient Eastern ideas and Spinoza's work. The commonality is quite remarkable because, to the best of my knowledge, there is no evidence that Spinoza was even familiar with Buddhism, Lao Tze's, or Zhuang Zi's ideas. His library did not include these early sources, and he certainly did not refer to them.

Two common elements of Zhuang Zi, Spinoza, and enactivism are the idea that need and desire are man's essence, and the insight that these cannot be reduced to anything else. As Zhuang Zi (ca. 369–286 BC; 2008), the great successor to Lao Tzu (2009), wrote

> For whether the soul is locked in sleep or whether in waking hours the body moves, we are striving and struggling with the immediate circumstances. Some are easy-going and leisurely, some are deep and cunning, and some are secretive. Now we are frightened over petty fears, now disheartened and dismayed over some great terror. Now the mind flies forth like an arrow from a cross-bow, to be the arbiter of right and wrong. Now it stays behind as if sworn to an oath, to hold on to what it has secured. Then, as under autumn and winter's blight, comes gradual decay, and submerged in its own occupations, it keeps on running its course, never to return. Finally, worn out and imprisoned, it is choked up like an old drain, and the failing mind shall not see light again.
>
> Joy and anger, sorrow and happiness, worries and regrets, indecision and fears, come upon us by turns, with ever-changing moods, like music from the hollows, or like mushrooms from damp. Day and night they alternate within us, but we cannot tell whence they spring. Alas! Alas! Could we for a moment lay our finger upon their very Cause?
>
> But for these emotions I should not be. Yet but for me, there would be no one to feel them. So far we can go; but we do not know by whose order they come into play. It would seem there was a soul; but the clue to its existence is wanting. That it functions is credible enough, though we cannot see its form. Perhaps it has inner reality without outward form. (cited in Wu-Chi, 1990, p. 42)

Spinoza (1677a, p. 76) likewise stated that "appetite is nothing but the essence of man, from whose nature there necessarily follow those things that promote his preservation." Whereas individuals are to some degree conscious of their actions, passions, and appetites, they are"not aware of the causes by which they are determined to want something." Schopenhauer (1819, 1844) would agree: Existence is will, and while we experience and know will in ourselves and in nature, we are ignorant of its cause.

There are still other insights of enactivism that can be traced back to Buddhism, Zhuang Zi, Spinoza, and Schopenhauer. One postulate is that dissociating the brain, the body, and the mind, or dividing 'rational thought,' affect, and behavior is basically nonsensical, hence useless. Another understanding they have in common is the idea that it is erratic to divide organisms and 'the world.' Subjects and objects do not and could not occur or exist in isolation of each other. They are all entangled, as Zhuang Zi already knew: "Heaven and earth are produced at the same time with my being born; all things are in oneness with me." This insight is consistent with the Upanishadic *tat tvam asi*, 'thou are that': all is one; subjects and objects – that include other subjects – are essentially the same.

Parts and Wholes

It is not easy for us to grasp this oneness. We feel far more comfortable taking things apart. We love to hear the Siren of Particles sing. As mentioned above and as described in more detail in ToT Volume I, the tempting inclination to divide up wholes started (but did not end) with the philosophical and scientific Enlightenment in the 17th century. It actually continues to be the predominant approach in science and clinical practice to this very day[7]. It may therefore not be completely superfluous or terribly tedious to reiterate, albeit in a slightly different form, what was already said in ToT Volumes I and II.

Common Dissociations in Science and Clinical Practice

Common parsings and metaphors of life include the following:
- individual and world;
- inside (intrapersonal) and outside (extrapersonal);
- subject and object;
- subjectivity and objectivity;
- response and stimulus;
- idea and event;
- representation [Latin: representandum] and the represented [Latin: representatum];
- mind [mental structures] and matter [physical structures];
- psyche and soma;
- psychology and biology;
- brain and [the rest of the] body;
- brain/body and environment;
- parts and wholes.

Each of these conceptual dissociations poses the problem of the relatedness or connectivity of the divided parts (e.g., the brain and the mind; the individual and the individual's environment). It is therefore valuable to briefly consider some of the issues that concern part-part, part-whole, and whole-whole relationships. These problems constitute the subject matter of mereology, the theory of parthood relations. It should be rather obvious that the business of mereology is of major relevance to the theme of trauma and trauma-related dissociation.

The Contrast Between Machines and Life Revisited

As noted above, many philosophical materialists, including scientists and clinicians following a materialistic trail, regard organisms as more or less complex machines. Like

7 Dividing wholes into parts is clearly also a problem at the scale of politics. Divide the world in individuals, groups, and nations and then rate the interests of some higher than the interests of others leads sooner or later to suffering. See George Orwell, *Animal Farm*. National and international conflicts as well as the immense resistance to develop international environment protection programs testify to this. Basically ignoring childhood abuse and neglect to protect the interests of adults fits this dissociative frame.

philosophical dualists, they are also confronted with part-whole riddles. Their material and mechanistic view prompts them to divide the machine into pieces (molecules, genes, cells, cell assemblies, brain structures, the brain, etc.). Knowing the parts can certainly be very useful, as the exceptionally impressive successes of the Enlightenment demonstrated beyond any measure of doubt. However, the machine metaphor of life includes serious limitations.

One limitation is of a very general nature: The parts of a machine do not explain the whole artifact. For example, the steering of a car does not lie in the wheels. Steering cannot be derived from a steering wheel or any other part alone. Not even the whole collection of tires, chains, brakes, and other components explain the bicycle.

This fact is intimately related to another limitation of machine metaphors: An artifact does not exist and is neither useful nor harmful in and of itself. The existence and meaning of a machine lies not somewhere hidden 'in' the device, but rather in a source beyond the material structure. Its existence and meaning are felt and known by the designer who designs it and by the user who uses the appliance to achieve some result. A machine exists only in their imagination, and it only makes sense to them. And what goes for the whole machine goes for its conceived parts.

There are no naturally existing rules that dictate what constitutes parts and what constitutes wholes. Nature does not come to us as pregiven parts and wholes, but allows us to create particular divisions and collections according to our concepts, perspectives, and interests.

Like machines, life is not a collection of elements that can be dismantled and screwed back together again without some idea of the (point of the) whole. However, while we can analyze a machine, because we exist outside and beyond it, we cannot step out of ourselves to detect the meaning of our existence and life more generally. Like all other species, we cannot consult a source beyond ourselves. Anything we experience, know, and imagine is something *we* bring forth. We enact a phenomenal self, world, and self as a part of this world.

Like other parts and wholes, our self, our world, and the coupling of ourselves to our world are not pregiven. And opposed to philosophical idealism and constructivism, neither we nor other organisms generate sensations, feelings, perceptions, and conceptions (thoughts) out of the blue. Rather, they emerge from self-engaged and world-engaged actions. From our conception to our death, mental and phenomenal realities are generated in an entangled *pas de deux* of an organism and its environment.

Järvilehto (1999b) put it like this:

> I agree that [man] will never know in any absolute sense this 'outside world,' but in all his actions he concretizes some aspects of this 'objective reality.' His perceptions or ideas are not 'constructs,' but some ways how the reality may be used. Because of its infinity this reality may have any properties depending on beings which live in it. Hence, there is probably an infinite amount of possible parallel descriptions of the reality. However, the order of the universe (cf. Bohm and Hiley, 1993) for the human being is the order of the human body in its environment,

> i.e., it is determined by the fit between the parts of his body and specific parts of the environment ..., creating a system (organism-environment system) directed toward the results of behavior. If there was in the universe a time when there were no living systems then it means that there was a time of a universe without properties, because only living organisms made possible the existence of its definable properties.

In other words, organisms do not develop and entertain 'constructs,' but rather generate, maintain, and develop *conceptions* (ToT Volumes I & II). They conceive of themselves, their world, and themselves as a part of this world in their own particular ways. Living systems, that is, intrinsically couple themselves to their *umwelt* – to their surrounding world as experienced and lived from their perspective (Von Uexküll, 1934). Organisms are *environmentally embedded* in an ontological and epistemological sense. They exist and can exist only relative to this world, just as this world is in any case epistemologically and practically relative to them. This implies that the question "What exists?" is identical to the question "What can we know?" (Järvilehto, 2004, entry 51). In this sense, there is no difference between ontology (i.e., the logos or principles of what exists) and epistemology (i.e., the logos or principles of what can be known) (see also ToT Volumes I & II).

Is Small the Fairest?

Small things entice. Molecules, atoms, quantum particles, neurons, receptors, genes, alleles, etc., fascinate both scientists and the public. While small can be beautiful (Schumacher, 1973, 1999), it can also be tricky! Conceptions that pertain to larger components of animate wholes can be as appealing and devious as the tiny parts. They must also be handled with caution since they are parts of living wholes too. Parts such as 'genes,' 'cells,' 'cell assemblies,' 'brain structures,' 'neural networks,' 'the brain,' 'the body,' and even 'individuals' and 'the environment' constitute components of the whole living system they are parts of. Like tiny parts, they cannot exist and cannot be fully understood in isolation of other parts of the animate whole. Love of one part easily blinds the importance of the other parts and mystifies the whole.

What Constitutes a Part?

The material, personal, and social world can be parsed in an endless number of ways, and there are no pregiven principles that define how these worlds are best parsed (Braude, 1995). And what applies to 'parts' applies to 'wholes' as well. What is more, relationships between parts and relationships between wholes are also not pregiven. Parts and wholes can be related to each other in an infinite number of ways, and there is no pregiven principle that defines what kind of relationship is preferable. To reiterate, parts, wholes, and relationships among them are an organism's conceptions. They are in the eye of the beholder. How organisms parse and unite their particular self and world depends on them – more specifically, on their current and more general interests. Living organisms must and do long and strive to *make meaning from their particular perspective and affectively charged interest.*

Parts and Wholes as Metaphors

It is easily overlooked that parts and wholes can be metaphors, not objects or collections of objects that exist separate from perceivers. As Järvilehto (2004, entry 34) explains with respect to parts,

> [m]easurement is the only possibility to 'observe' a photon, because we cannot join this micro part directly into our macro system. With the measurement we relate the photon to the human world and culture, and we may conclude from the result that there must be certain kinds of material elements, elementary particles, in order to make the result of measurement understandable. These particles, however, have no such properties as the things around us. They are not 'balls' or 'colored,' they are not even 'particles,' because these descriptions are metaphors borrowed from our ordinary world.

Parts Are Parts of Wholes, and Wholes Are Part of Other Wholes

The contemplation of parts of nature such as matter and mind can be a very valuable and important endeavor. But when parts of nature are unduly dissociated from each other, problems ensue that cannot be solved at the level of the parts. For example, and as alluded to above, delving deeper and deeper in the brain does not reveal consciousness, and the hunt for ever smaller and elementary particles does not uncover the essence of matter (Järvilehto, 2004).

Problems of parts can eventually be solved only when whole systems are contemplated. To reiterate, it is risky to regard parts of whole living systems as *separate systems that could, in principle, exist and be fully known in isolation of whatever they are a part of.* Parts of living wholes do not and cannot exist and operate in solitude. Living parts relate to other animate and inanimate parts. Together they constitute the whole on which each single part depends. If the whole ceases to be, so do its parts. If an organism's environment collapses, so does the organism that inhabits it. And when (all) organisms die the (total) reportable world dies with them. It is as dramatic and simple as that.

Further, it should be realized that, like parts, wholes too are not pregiven. A major problem of psychology, and hence of psychotherapy and trauma treatment, lies in the conundrum: What can be best seen as parts and wholes? The brain, the body, the individual, anything else?

Dividing Individuals and the World

The rather common conception in psychology, psychiatry, and most societies is that the individual and his or her environment constitute two interacting but separate systems (wholes). For example, as Järvilehto (2000a, p. 35) asserts,

> in most explanations of human behavior ... behavior and psychological processes are conceived as processes belonging to the organism, and the environment is seen as something that either triggers or modulates these processes. This leads psychological and psychophysiological research to search for the structure of psychological processes (mental activity and consciousness) in the organism and their neural correlates in the brain, which eventually ends with identification of psychological processes with some characteristics of neural activity.

Many if not most psychologists (and clinicians) tend to divide up nature in individuals as one system and their environment as another system as if the two could exist separately from each other. For example, they talk about traumatizing events as one system (the environment) that can hurt an individual (the other system). Dualists further divide individuals into a mind and a material body. Whatever the virtues of these dissociations may be in some contexts, they unavoidably raise the question of how the various conceived parts relate to each other and to the conceived whole.

Enactivism: A Viable One System Approach to Life

As a whole, *The Trinity of Trauma* is grounded in the view that the above-mentioned or other dissociations in our culture, science, and clinical models and practices (e.g., individual–world, subject–object, and mind–matter divides) are in want of (re-)integration. This (re-)integration cannot be achieved by adjusting two systems views (individual–world, mind–matter, etc.), or by reverting to problematic monistic views such as philosophical materialism or idealism. This integration takes the development of a different scientific and clinical paradigm (e.g., Colombetti, 2014; Di Paolo, 2009; Di Paolo et al., 2010; Järvilehto, 1998a, 1998b; 1999a, 2000a, 2000b, 2004; Overton, 2015; Thompson, 2007, 2011a, 2011b; Schopenhauer, 1819, 1844; Spinoza, 1677; Varela, 1988, 1992, 1996, 1997; Weber, 2002, 2010, 2014; Weber & Varela, 2002). As was discussed in ToT Volumes I and II, and as is more detailed in the present Volume III, this evolving paradigm is, among others, philosophically monistic (though not philosophically materialistic or idealistic), holistic, relativistic, relational, dynamical, integrative, and action-based as well as affect-based.

Enactivism fits this emerging alternative paradigm. As a whole, *The Trinity of Trauma* is influenced by the original enactive perspective of Varela et al. (1991). It is also guided by elaborations that Thompson (2007, 2011a, 2011b) and others have crafted (e.g., Colombetti, 2014; De Jaegher & Di Paolo, 2007; Järvilehto, 1998a, 1998b, 1999a, 1999b,

2000a, 2000b, 2001a, 2001c). Their joint formulations are not totally new, but rather comprise a synthesis of new and (age) old themes. For example, the roots include the shining ideas of several classic authors introduced in ToT Volumes I and II (and above). They include the philosopher and psychologist Spinoza (1677a) and the philosopher Arthur Schopenhauer (1819, 1844), as well as the phenomenologists Husserl (1954) and Merleau-Ponty (1945). The formulations also include insights from ecological psychology and dynamic systems theory.

Enactivism in a Nutshell

Enactivism is a combined philosophical, biological, and psychological perspective that places affectivity and sense-making at the heart of organic life, including human emotion, cognition, and behavior. The term 'enaction' is currently used in different ways, and there are various accounts that their creators call 'enactive' (Colombetti, 2014; De Jaegher & Di Paolo, 2007; Hutto & Myin, 2013). Amid this variability, the verb 'to enact' and the adjective 'enactive' basically express that what organisms experience and know is deeply influenced by how they act (Protevi, 2006). The terms convey the idea that experience and knowledge of self and world are the result of couplings of a subject and its objects. These comprise couplings of an organism's affective, sensorimotor and cognitive capacities and interests, and its environment (Thompson, 2007).

In this light, "cognition is not the representation of a pregiven world by a pregiven mind but is rather the enactment of a world and a mind on the basis of a history of the variety of actions that a being in the world performs" (Varela et al., 1991, p. 9). In other words, cognition arises from ongoing dynamic couplings of an acting organism with its environment. This environment does not involve an 'objective' reality 'out there.' It is a living organism's niche or *umwelt.* It is a world of significance that they selectively and creatively bring forth through their capacities to generate couplings with their environment. It is a meaningful domain that subject and object engender and maintain in a co-constitutive, co-dependent, and co-occurrent dance (ToT Volume I, Chapters 6, 8, and 10).

Most trauma clinicians are acquainted with the substantive 'reenactment' and the verb 'to reenact.' The terms 'reenactment' and 'to reenact' and the meaning thereof may serve as aids in grasping the meaning of the terms 'enactment,' 'to enact,' 'enaction,' and 'enactive.' Trauma clinicians appreciate that a reenactment of a traumatic experience involves a sensorimotor, and in many cases highly affective, way of bringing forth a painful past, which, however, is experienced as if happening here and now (but note that it may also involve degrees of hypoarousal, sensory and emotional anesthesia and motor weakness or paralysis). Clearly, reenactment needs a subject who reenacts. 'To reenact' stands for bringing forth a former reality. 'To enact' communicates the notion that living organisms bring forth a self and a world of affective significance through ongoing sensorimotor and affectively charged engagement with themselves and the world that they find and create in a relativity of subject and object.

In part introduced in ToT Volumes I and II, in an enactive perspective, living systems or organisms comprise several key properties:

- Living systems are *enactive.* Being centers of mental and behavioral action, they bring forth a self, a world, and a self as a part of this world.
- Living systems are *primary affective.* More specifically, they long and strive to persevere in their existence and to achieve results that meet their particular needs and desires. Spinoza referred to this property as *conatus.*
- Living systems, in this frame, strive to *make sense* of themselves and of the situation in which they find themselves (Colombetti, 2014; De Jaegher & Paolo, 2007). They thus have an interest-based point of view regarding themselves and their world – behaviorally, cognitively, and affectively (Colombetti, 2014; Spinoza, 1677a). That is, they engage in ongoing *signification.*
- Living systems are intrinsically coupled to their *umwelt*, that is, to their surrounding world as experienced and lived from their perspective *environmentally embedded.*
- Living systems are autonomous in the sense that they are
  - self-constitutive;
  - operationally closed;
  - minded, i.e., they include mind, a property that cannot be reduced to matter. Some organisms are also phenomenal systems, that is, systems that are conscious and self-conscious.
  - *embrained* and *embodied.*

Formatting the text given above necessitates a more or less sequential presentation; yet the involved principles stated there are intrinsically (and not sequentially) related. That is, the one exists and can only exist within the framework of the others.

Enactivism fits Spinoza's philosophical monism that also constitutes the philosophical foundation *The Trinity of Trauma.* To reiterate, this philosophy holds that mind and matter constitute two appearances of one substance or system called Nature or God. Matter includes the brain, the body, and the material environment; mind comprises unconscious and conscious mental actions and their contents. They are properties of this single system: The mind does not cause matter and matter does not cause the mind. The mind cannot be reduced to the brain and the brain cannot be reduced to the mind. Each property or appearance is to examined and comprehended on its own. Nevertheless, the mind and the brain can be indirectly linked to one another. In the following chapters the various pillars of enactivism are presented in greater detail. From Chapter 30 onward they are applied to the treatment of traumatized individuals as whole organism-environment systems and to dissociative parts that involve organism-environment systems any less.

Chapter 24

Embedment, Entanglement, and Conatus

> *The human body, to be preserved, requires a great many other bodies, by which it is, as it were, continually regenerated.*
> Baruch Spinoza (1677a, Part II, Postulate IV)

> *The idea of any mode in which the human body is affected by external causes must involve the nature of the human body and at the same time the nature of the external body.*
> Baruch Spinoza (1677a, Part II, Proposition 16)

> *Quantum entanglement is a physical phenomenon that occurs when pairs or groups of particles are generated or interact in ways such that the quantum state of each particle cannot be described independently – instead, a quantum state may be given for the system as a whole.*
> Wikipedia

Chapter 23 explained that the proper unit of analysis in psychology and biology cannot be an isolated gene, cell, organ, etc. None of these can exist and do exist in isolation of the wider context, and a mere collection of parts does not reflect the whole. An analysis of conceived parts of the world means nothing if the parts are not understood in their intrinsic connectivity with each other and with the conceived whole that they are parts of. Life and our understanding of life demand an appreciation of *relationships*. But what relationships are of primary concern to psychology and biology – and hence for an understanding of trauma and trauma therapy?

A Knotty Ontological Dialectic

Organisms consist of parts (e.g., elements such as cells and organs) that exist for the whole and by means of the whole. Immanuel Kant formulated this core circular and dynamical feature of life as follows:

> In such a product of nature every part, as existing through all other parts, is also thought as existing for the sake of the others and that of the whole, i.e., as a tool (organ); ... an organ bringing forth the other parts (and hence everyone bringing forth one another) ...; and only then and because of this such a product as an *organized* and *self-organizing* being can be called

> a *natural* purpose. (Kritik der Urteilskraft 65, 373, 1910, with Kant's emphasis. Translated by Weber & Varela, 2002, p. 106)

Organisms combine this ongoing self-organization with the ongoing generation of a border between themselves and their stable or changeable environment. That is, they bring forth their structure as well as their own border, their own literal and metaphorical "skin" that sets them apart from their environment with which they are nonetheless coupled (Varela, 1997; Weber, 2002a). By creating themselves in a process of unfolding identity, organisms indeed bring forth their

> ... surrounding world as the 'other' of its self. Between the organism and the world thus brought forth exists a certain paradox. The living creates its surroundings and consequently is rather autonomous. However, at the same time it is still depending on these surroundings as a material source of its real existence. (Weber, 2002a, p. 16)

Varela (1991, p. 79) formulated the paradox by saying that an

> [o]rganism connotes a knotty dialectic: a living system makes itself into an entity distinct from its environment through a process that brings forth, through that very process, a world proper to the organism.

To the extent that organisms are, apart from material structures, also social operationally autonomous systems, the dialectic is that the subject becomes a subject distinct from other subjects through the subject's actions. Those very actions bring forth a social world proper to the subject. The paradox is that the subject and its objects, which include other subjects, exist relative to each other (ToT Volumes I & II). No object, no subject; no subject, no object. The organism and its material and social environment are different but intrinsically coupled structures. This ontological relativity implies a phenomenal relativity:

> If the process of life is already a dialectical, not substantial, but rather relational affair, then this is the case far more prominently for the resulting phenomenology, which is brought forth by the living: Inside and outside are not really separated, only in relation to the process of self-establishment. Subject and object are not 'really' separated but become so only in the process of constitution of a subject vis-à-vis to its substrate. (Weber, 2001, p. 8)

Organisms and their environment thus exist and can only be known and understood relative to each other[1] (Schopenhauer, 1819, 1844, 1889; Spinoza, 1677a; Järvilehto, 1998a, 1998b, 1999, 2000; Northoff, 2003, 2014a, 2014b). The implication of this relativity is that subjects do not interact with their environment as a collection of objects and other sub-

1 One implication of Spinoza's original insight, and one that was evident to him, is that the social and natural sciences should become merged. It is interesting that quantum mechanics includes the realization that a measuring subject and a measured object are relative to each other. The point is that the observer's type of measurement of a system affects the end state of that system. *An observer, then, is not a mere observer, but an influence upon what is being observed.* This effect is not exclusive to quantum mechanics. Many domains of physics, psychology, and psychiatry include such 'observer effects.'

jects. Rather, they enact a self, a world, and a self as a part of that world. In the words of Colombetti (2014, p. 101),

> ... as the organism maintains itself via self-organization and self-regulation, it enacts a specific world of significance (an *umwelt*). Otherwise put, normativity is intrinsic to the organization of living systems. This view also implies that the activity or behavior of the organism is constitutive of the activity of appraising (in the sense that it enacts or performs it) and does not merely 'interact' with it as an extrinsic phenomenon (see also Di Paolo et al., 2010).

Living beings evidently do not stand by themselves. No matter how simple or complex they may be, they are an inherent part *of* their world. There can only be subjects because there are objects, and this *umwelt* (Von Uexküll, 1934) has properties only if it is connected to the organism. All forms of life, from single cells to the most complex multicellular organisms, more than being intrinsically embedded in their environment, are totally dependent on it. As noted before, living organisms that fail to establish viable couplings between themselves and their *umwelt* do not remain living organisms for long.

A Knotty Epistemic Dialectic

There is also an epistemic relativity of subject and object. Although this relativity is not commonly realized in psychology and biology, the idea is not new. For example, one of the mottos of the present chapter says, "*[t]he idea of any mode in which the human body is affected by external bodies must involve the nature of the human body and at the same time the nature of the external body*" (Spinoza, 1677a, Part II, Proposition 16). "From this it follows, first, that the human mind perceives the nature of a great many bodies together with the nature of his own body" (p. 45). Further, "... notions by which ordinary people are accustomed to explain Nature are only modes of imagining, and do not indicate the nature of anything, only the constitution of the imagination" (p. 30). Hence, "... the ideas we have of external bodies indicate the condition of our own body more than the nature of the external bodies" (p. 45).

An important condition of our own body is defined by our needs and desires, by what we *wish* to achieve: "... men act always on account of an end, namely, on account of their own advantage, which they want" (p. 26). Hence, the way in which we conceive of ourselves and our environment is strongly influenced by the nature and present state of our body. This present state commonly reflects our interest in future goal-fulfilling actions.

Several centuries later, Henri Bergson (1911) similarly pointed out that the percept is relative to the perceiving individual as well as relative to the active interest that lies in his or her future actions. In this regard, George Herbert Mead (1968, p. 53) said the following about Bergson's ideas:

> [a] particular organism would become conscious from his standpoint, that is, there would be a world that would exist for the organism, when the organism marked or plotted out or, to use

> Bergson's term, canalized its environment in terms of its future conduct. For Bergson, a percept is an object of possible action for an organism, and it is the active relationship of the organism to the distant object that constitutes it as an object. . . . consciousness of the organism consists in the fact that its future conduct outlines and defines its objects.

The Ontological and Epistemic Relativity and Entanglement of Subjects and Objects

Mead thus agreed that "[t]here is a relativity of the living individual and its environment, both as to form and content" (p. 55). In any practical sense objects and events therefore only exist inasmuch as an individual perceives and conceives them. Talking about objects and events as if they (could) exist independent of perceivers separates organisms and their environment. But individuals are an embedded part of the world, something they can know only according to their particular epistemic abilities and limitations. Individuals and their world are, thus, ontologically and epistemically *intertwined* – or rather *entangled.*

Because they rise, stand, and fall together, living organisms and their *umwelt* constitute and depend on each other. They always co-occur (Järvilehto, 1998a, 1998b, 1999a, 1999b, 2000a, 2000b, 2000c, 2001a, 2001c; Northoff, 2003, 2014a, 2014b; Spinoza, 1677a; ToT Volumes I & II). In this sense, Järvilehto (1998a, p. 317) asserts that, "[o]rganisms and their environment are in any functional sense inseparable and form one unitary system."

The conceived functional unity of organisms and their environments reflects a deep appreciation of the ontological and epistemic relativity of subjects and objects. If we consider that, like modern physics, psychology and biology constitute domains of subject-object relativity, possibility, and probability, the classic or 'Newtonian psychology' would better be known as 'Einsteinian psychology' and 'quantum psychology.' Grasping relativity may not be easily achieved; it seems to take a very high-level action tendency that Pierre Janet once described as a progressive action tendency (see Chapter 33).

The realization that subjects and objects are ontologically as well as epistemically related has important consequences. One of these is that normal and abnormal forms of experience, perceiving, thinking, and behaving cannot be situated 'in' the individual, 'in' the brain, or 'in' some part(s) of the brain. They rather involve particular *systems of relations.* That is, they comprise and depend on the intrinsic relations of the brain, body, and the environment. Mind and behavior are of the world (Noë, 2009). And so is trauma.

Embedment and Subject-Object Relativity in Trauma

Like all organisms, traumatized individuals as a whole as well as any dissociative part they may encompass are, in an ontological sense, organism-environment systems that generate and strive to maintain themselves. In doing so, they generate and maintain ontological and epistemological boundaries between their inner and external domains, between their self and nonself, that is, their objects and other subjects.

Ontological: From the third-person perspective, traumatized individuals and dissociative parts exist because they generate and maintain themselves in a world in which they are intrinsically embedded. They must continuously enact their internal structure, borders, and environment. If they cease to engage in these actions, they perish as an individual, or they dissolve as a dissociative part. (The dissolution of two or more dissociative parts can be a therapeutic goal; it generally goes along with the formation of a new, more complex dissociative part or else with the fusion of all dissociative parts that an individual with a dissociative disorder may encompass.) Dissociative parts are in ontological regard also embedded in the individual's body, as well as in their *umwelt.* This *umwelt* is not restricted to an 'outer' domain inasmuch as the *umwelt* also includes other dissociative parts.

Epistemological/phenomenal: Engaging in these ongoing self-constitutive and self-preservative actions, traumatized individuals – as whatever dissociative part – actively bring forth a phenomenal self and a phenomenal world as well as phenomenal couplings between this phenomenal self and *umwelt.* In other words, traumatized individuals and their dissociative parts are, to a greater or lesser extent, consciously aware of themselves and at least some aspects of their environment. Dreamless sleep and other unconscious states aside, they enact and continue to enact their own *phenomenal conception of self* (PCS; ToT Volume II, Chapter 12) and nonself, their phenomenal conception of what is internal (e.g., "my inner feelings and thoughts") and external (i.e., objects, other subjects, events). Thus, they also enact phenomenal couplings between their phenomenal self and each phenomenal object or other subject. To a certain degree they tend to consciously grasp these intentional couplings as well. As detailed in ToT Volume II, Chapter 12, the coupling of subject and 'object' (a thing, another subject) can be described as the phenomenal conception of an intentionality relationship (PCIR). The term 'intentionality' in this phrase expresses that consciousness intrinsically involves being conscious *of* something. It is intrinsic because consciousness *implies* being conscious of something.

As noted above, the environment that a dissociative part phenomenally experiences and knows may encompass or exclude one or more other dissociative parts. One or more other dissociative parts may intrude on another dissociative part that does not experience or know the origin of the intrusion. When this happens, the dissociative part that is intruded on only experiences and knows the influences, but not their source and reason (e.g., pain, fear, disgust, visual images, or voice of one or more intruding dissociative parts). This phenomenon can be referred to as 'dissociative source amnesia.' Some dissociative parts lack the mental level to appreciate that they are components of a singular organism; other dissociative parts recognize but resist acknowledging this third-person truth.

In some cases, the phenomenal self-conception of a traumatized individual or dissociative part includes components that, from an observer's third-person perspective, belong to the external world. For example, some fragile EPs believe that they are 'bad' (even if they cannot tell in what sense they would be bad), that others had to 'punish' them for that reason, and that they should be deeply ashamed of themselves. This is one way in which some fragile EPs try to make sense of what is happening to them. In their view, it does not count much that they were neglected, maltreated, and/or abused, mostly because they cannot and do not allow themselves to comprehend that significant others are 'bad.'

Particularly controlling EPs may have difficulty generating a fitting distinction between themselves and (features of) a perpetrator. Looking for a sense of control, they may start to indulge in the fantasy that they are as powerful and mean as the perpetrators. In this frame, they tend to uncritically adopt the perpetrators' points of view and behaviors. The point of controlling EPs, then, becomes that fragile EPs and ANPs deserved what came to them.

Conatus or Will

As Spinoza (1677a), later Schopenhauer (1819, 1844, 1889), and much later others (e.g., Barbaras, 1999; Kull, 2000) clearly recognized, organisms are basically unconscious and conscious 'appetite'[2] or will: "Desire is man's very essence, inasmuch as it is conceived to be determined, from any given affection of it, to do something" (Spinoza, 1677a, Part III, Definition of the Affects, Definition I; p. 104). And what man primarily does is engage in actions and passions that promote his preservation (Spinoza, 1677a, p. 76).

No matter how clever our intellect may be, our energetic desires will beat it. In the words of Schopenhauer (1844), "[t]he intellect grows tired, the will is untiring" (p. 211; see ToT Volume II). He emphasized that the will "gives all things, whatever they may be, the power to exist and to act" (Schopenhauer, 1889, p. 217; see ToT Volume II). Spinoza aptly called this unceasing longing and striving *conatus,* a term derived from the Latin *conari,* which means 'to try.'[3]

Polyvalences

Conatus characterizes every form of life. In Schopenhauer's words, "[l]onging, craving, willing, or aversion, shunning, and not-willing, are peculiar to every consciousness; man has them in common with the polyp. Accordingly, this is the essential and the basis of

2 As mentioned in Volume I, p. 68, Spinoza described the strivings of organisms as 'appetites' or needs. He stressed that the appetites can be unconscious or conscious. But apart from the fact that some appetites are conscious and that others remain unconscious, there is no difference between them. Spinoza referred to appetites together with the consciousness of them as 'desires.' Since in our time appetite has received a more restricted meaning, I use the term 'need' for unconscious appetites or urges, and the term 'desire' for conscious ones.

3 Garrett (1999) defends an Aristotelian interpretation of Spinoza's theory of teleology. Garrett (2002) involves an influential defense of the validity of Spinoza's ideas on conatus.

every consciousness" (1844, p. 204). We may be exceptionally proud of our intellect, but "in all animal beings the *will* is the primary and substantial thing; the *intellect,* on the other hand, is something secondary and additional, in fact, it is a mere tool in the service of the will" (p. 205).

Particularly in humans, conatus has become highly differentiated. To quote Schopenhauer again,

> the more complicated the organization becomes in the ascending series of animals, the more manifold do its needs become, and the more varied and specially determined the objects capable of satisfying them, consequently the more tortuous and lengthy the paths for arriving at these, which must now all be known and found.

Having many different affectively charged interests, we can enjoy and suffer life in many different ways. But it also implies that we are stuffed with ambivalences, or rather *polyvalences.* In Spinoza's (1677a, p. 104) poignant words,

> . . . by the word *desire* I understand any of man's strivings, impulses, needs, and volitions, which vary as the man's constitution varies, and which are not infrequently so opposed to one another that the man is pulled in different directions and knows not where to turn.

The Primacy of Affect

The principles of conatus and primordial affectivity are incompatible with views that primarily regard human beings as cognitive beings that once in a while have emotions, and that these emotions are basically a kind of nuisance. With Spinoza (1677a) and Jonas (1973), *feeling is the first unfolding of a subject and its objects, of a self and a world.* In this context, enactivism claims that affect, cognition, and behavior are intrinsically coupled phenomena. This view implies that cognition does not guide or define affect, but rather that needs and desires, together with their implied goal orientation organize and guide sense-making. In this framework, needs and desires organize perception, conception, affects (moods, emotions), thoughts, and behaviors; in the enactive perspective, these different components (i.e., perception, emotions, etc.) are not comprehended as sequentially organized phenomena or actions. They are rather seen as intimately coupled components of life that are guided by the goals of the organisms (Hurley, 1998), that is, by their final causes (ToT Volumes I & II, Chapters 10–12).

Dynamic Causality

Spinoza (1677a) postulated that *Nature conceived of as matter* can in principle be fully understood in terms of material (the existence of matter) and efficient causality (mechanical causes) (ToT Volume I). Any change in a material structure (e.g., a nerve cell) is efficiently caused by a change in material structures that are internal or external to that structure. A change in the state of a material structure is in turn efficiently caused by a change in the state of another material structures that influence it, and so on. As Schopenhauer (1889) said, objects do not cause a change in other objects; rather, changes in the state of one object cause changes in the state of another object:

> Every effect, at the time it takes place, is a *change* and, precisely by not having occurred sooner, infallibly indicates some other *change* by which it has been preceded. That other *change* takes the name of a cause, when referred to the following one – of *effect,* when referred to a third necessarily preceding *change.* This is the chain of causality. (Schopenhauer, 1889, p. 38)

There is backward and forward in time no end to efficient causation. Moreover, efficient causes depend on each other, so that there is circular causality. For example,

> [i]n general, nucleotide triplets are capable of predictably specifying an amino acid if and only if they are properly embedded in the cell's metabolism, that is, in a multitude of enzymatic regulations in a complex biochemical network. This network has a chicken-and-egg character at several levels. First, proteins can arise only from a DNA/RNA "reading" process, but this process cannot happen without proteins. Second, the DNA "writing" and "reading" processes must be properly situated within the intracellular environment, but this environment is a result of those very processes. Finally, the entire cell is an autopoietic system – that is, an autonomous system defined by an operationally closed network of molecular processes that simultaneously both produces and realizes the cell concretely in the physical space of its biochemical components. (Thompson, 2007, p. 55–56)

Nature conceived of as mind, however, cannot be satisfactorily understood in terms of material causes and efficient causes. As remarked below, explanations in terms of material, efficient, and circular causality do not tell why and how particular compositions of matter generate experience and thought. They do not show why or how matter generates and influences consciousness and self-consciousness. Moreover, matter does not unveil what it is like to experience, feel, think, want, or move something. These types of causation also are unable to explain why organisms have first-person, quasi-second person, second-person, and third-person perspectives.

The principle of the primordial affectivity or conatus of organisms pertains to their private final causes. Need and desire are all about an organism trying to achieve some goal. They are about gaining the useful, ignoring the useless, and trying to avoid or getting rid of the harmful (see also Chapter 25). Conatus indeed points to the basic fact of life, which is that organisms, clearly including traumatized organisms, organize themselves and strive to sustain their existence. As Spinoza (1677a, Part III, Proposition 9) asserted, "*[t]he mind, both in so far as it has clear and distinct ideas, and also in so far as it has confused ideas, endeavours to persist in its being for an indefinite period, and of this endeavour it is conscious.*" He added that

> [e]very man exists by the highest right of Nature, and consequently, everyone by the highest right of Nature does those things which follow from the necessity of his own nature. So every-

> one, by the highest right of nature, judges what is good and what is evil, considers his own advantage according to his own temperament . . ., avenges himself . . ., and strives to preserve what he loves and destroys what he hates . . . (Part IV, Note II to Proposition 37, p. 135)

Implying goal-orientation (longing) and goal-directed action (striving), unconscious conatus (need) and conscious conatus (desire) involve teleology or final causality. Varela (1991) initially resisted teleological explanations of human experience, affect, thought, and behavior although he prudently agreed that

> [w]hatever is encountered must be valued one way or another – like, dislike, ignore – and acted on some way or another – attraction, rejection, neutrality. This basic assessment is inseparable from the way in which the coupling event encounters a functioning perceptual-motor unit, and it gives rise to an intention (I am tempted to say "desire"), that unique quality of living cognition. (p. 97)

In a most important article with Weber (Weber & Varela, 2002), Varela, however, had become completely convinced that organisms are guided by internal final causes. As he and Weber wrote,

> an integration of teleological descriptions [in science] can only be possible by taking them seriously: by accepting that organisms are subjects having purposes according to values encountered in the making of their living. This means clearly to reintroduce value and subjectivity as indispensable organic phenomena, a theory of the organism as the dynamics of establishing an identity and, hence, as a process of creating a materially embodied, individual perspective. (p. 102)

Weber and Varela's emphasis on value and subjectivity clearly dovetails with Spinoza's conatus. It also roots in and agrees with Jonas' perspective that "[t]heories about the living can only be conceived from the fragile and concerned perspective of the living itself" (Jonas, 1973, p. 91, cited in Weber & Varela, 2002, p. 110). Material and mechanical (efficient) causes cannot do the work by themselves, because "... life can only be known by life" (Jonas, 1973, p. 91). Living organisms are not machines, but active sense-making agents. They do not passively meet a world, but actively constitute themselves and strive to maintain their self-generated existence (Jonas, 1992). Thus,

> ... the very ground of our existence is originally teleological and as such, in the ongoing coupling with the world brings forth meaning and categories. Teleology thus is not only a necessary mode to think the living; the "teleological circle" is a real mode of being and is the only possible way for organic life to exist. (Weber & Varela, 2002, p. 111)

It should be clear that a full understanding of world-embedded organisms entails more than a formulation of their material and efficient causes. There is more that defines them than the material 'stuff' that composes them (material causality). And more changes and moves them than changes in the state of things that affect them (efficient causality). Living organisms also include a structure, that is, an organization of elements such that the whole is more than the sum of its parts (formal causality). An example is the organization of an individual's personality.

Guided by their unconsciously given, and perhaps consciously experienced, aspirations (final causality), living organism-environment systems include self-organizing and intrinsically related structures and functions. These systems' structures, functions, and goals continuously affect each other. Whereas structures, functions, goals, and actions can be distinguished, they cannot be separated. They go together (cf. Järvilehto, 2000a). ToT Volumes I and II thus detailed that living organisms comprise the intrinsic composition of the four Aristotelian causes or explanations – material, efficient, formal, and final. This composition can be described as the system's *dynamic causality* (Northoff, 2003; Overton, 2015).

Summary

Subjects and their objects (e.g., 'things,' 'events,' other individuals) do not exist separately from each other; they constitute and depend on each other, and necessarily occur together. Entangled organisms and their *umwelt* are best seen as one system.

Embedded in their *umwelt*, organisms act to realize their goals. Their essential, natural action is to persevere in their organic and implied mental integrity, that is, their very existence. The effort is through and through *affective* and *basic*, because existence is, "meaningful, relevant, or salient for the agent at stake – without or before being bounded into distinct emotions; in addition, this [affective] dimension grounds other forms of mentality, namely, it makes them possible" (Colombetti, 2014, p. 15). In this sense, they include the capacity and striving to enact a meaningful world from a particular point of view (Colombetti, 2014, p. 15; Maturana, 1980; Maturana & Varela, 1987; Weber, 2002a, 2002b). The next chapter focuses on this affect-driven meaning making.

Chapter 25

Desire, Joy, and Sadness

Desire is man's very essence, insofar as it is conceived to be determined, from any given affection of it, to do something.
Joy is a man's passage from a lesser to a greater perfection.
Sadness is a man's passage from a greater to a lesser perfection.
Baruch Spinoza (1677a, p. 104)

Living organisms try to make sense of the world as they find it. Being the outcome of eons of evolution, and guided by the prime interest of survival, they generate meaning. They most of all conceive what is 'good' and 'bad,' what enhances their existence, and what obliterates it. Good is what increases their power of action or force of existing; what decreases this ability is bad. This does not mean that organisms feel or judge that good things are useful and bad things are worthless. Nature works the other way around: To them useful objects, events, or persons are good, and harmful, injurious ones are bad (Spinoza, 1677a). And what organisms cannot use and what does not harm them is merely insignificant to them. Morality does not cause but *follows* the judgment of what is useful (significant-good), harmful (significant-bad), and useless (insignificant-meaningless).

Evaluation as Signification

Organisms do not passively wait for the good to come, and they do not merely hope that the bad and the ugly will not materialize. On the contrary, they frantically work to attain what they need and desire – what is useful to them – just as they can go to great lengths to avoid what they fear, hate, and despise – what harms them. They also recurrently sense and judge what is useless or insignificant to them. This ongoing, affectively charged evaluation keeps them from investing time, energy, and interest in things that do not increase their power of action. In this fashion organisms – from the simplest (see Figure 25.1) to the most complex – *signify* the world and themselves as a part of it (for the epistemic consequences of this insight, see the section on panpsychism in Chapter 27). In *signification* (Varela, 1992; Weber, 2002a, 2002b), they intrinsically couple themselves to their environment.

Their signification indicates directions in which they move best, and specifies which directions they were better to avoid. And in moving, organisms adapt to their environ-

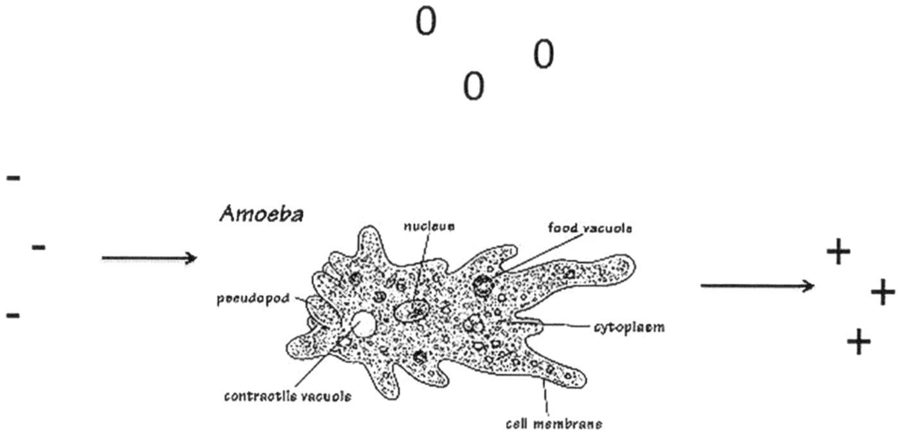

Figure 25.1. Signification in amoebas. *Note:* Single-cell organisms move away from what they perceive, and hence conceive of, as harmful, move toward what they regard as useful, and neither move away from nor move toward what they perceive as neither strengthening nor harming their inner relationships. Movement is enabled by the cell's temporary generation of pseudopods. The involved perception and conception are understandings in terms of Nature conceived of as mind.

ment, as well as shape the world they find to serve their wants within the limits of their abilities. More than adapt, organisms generate and maintain themselves as well as modify themselves and their world. More than being dynamic, life is creative.

Given conatus, organisms explore their environment to find what is significant to them. They seek food, consume, and digest it. They may rest to regain energy, as well as attach to and love each other. All species procreate, and many care for their offspring. And, clearly, all hate pain and hate what causes this sadness. To that end they try to avoid, or escape from, threat to their personal existence and perhaps also to that of their kin. For example, mammals are equipped with an ingenious immune system and encompass various defensive actions to threats from predators and conspecifics to their physical integrity. When threatened or attacked, they swiftly startle, flight, or freeze. When attack is near, they may try to ward off the adversary, or they feign being dead. Some strive to befriend their foes, and some produce disgusting odors to spoil their opponent's appetite. Moreover, prey can abruptly change tactics when the situation in their estimation so demands. For example, their freezing may explode in flight, and their efforts to befriend the enemy in one way or another may suddenly switch to defensive fight or some other defensive strategy.

From the simplest to the most complex, living systems strive to increase their *power to exist*, which prevents losses in this regard. Bacteria that thrive on sugar will move toward places offering this commodity, just as they will move away from places that contain less sugar or that hold substances that are toxic to them. Bees seek pollen and defend against wasps. Cats chase mice, but are wary of owls and hawks. Thirsty babies seek a full breast and cry when left alone too long. Any child desires a loving, supportive parent, and fears aggressive and rejecting individuals. Adolescents strive to increase their independence and may therefore resist parental advice. Many young adults wish to raise a family, but find it hard to balance this interest with other desires such as having a career or enjoying a bachelor's life.

The *umwelt* that an organism lives in and signifies may be benign, supporting their survival and other affective interests. It may also challenge their striving to survive, to achieve joy and to evade sorrow. Or worse: it may be harsh and violent, obstructing these desires. Commonly, of course, an individual's *umwelt* comprises a blend of the useful, the useless, and the harmful. Life generally brings forth a mix of joy and sorrow, an amalgam of pleasure and pain.

Signs and Sense Making

The meaning of the world is not pregiven but depends on the organism-environment system that co-constitutes and evaluates it (Maturana & Varela, 1987; Peirce, 1978; Spinoza, 1677a). For example, 'stimuli' (or 'triggers') do not exist independent of experiencing and knowing individuals, and actions cannot be adequately understood as 'responses' to an independently existing 'reality.' Hence, neither organism-independent 'stimuli' or 'events' nor organism-independent 'information'[1] exists (Merleau-Ponty, 1945; ToT Volume I, Chapter 8). In an epistemological and pragmatic sense, a stimulus or event is only a stimulus or event when it exists and carries meaning for an organism.

The present view also denies that man involves an exceptionally complex machine, a kind of supercomputer that 'processes' (pregiven) 'information.' Since the world is a largely unlabeled place, individuals cannot passively follow pregiven algorithms. Very little has meaning for them in and of itself. They do not find pregiven 'information,' but rather must give meaning. Living organisms, thus, generally engage in *wahrnehmung* (German. Literally: taking something to be true) or rather *wahrheitsgebung* (literally: the action of giving truth to something). Whereas this action clearly involves unconscious (mental) and perhaps also in part conscious (phenomenal) cognitive actions, the current view denies that cognition precedes affect. It rather holds that needs and desires are primary, and that cognition helps organisms to fulfill their strivings. Cognition is only meaningful in this context.

Signs can bring about a *perturbation* (Maturana & Varela, 1987), a temporary change in environmental conditions, which causes a change in the organism that experiences the environmental alteration involved. This description clearly reflects the relativity of subject

---

1 To speak with Thompson (2007, p. 57), "[i]nformation is formed within a context rather than imposed from without." Gregory Bateson used to say, "information is a difference that makes a difference" (Bateson 1972, p. 315). We could elaborate this insight by saying that information, dynamically conceived, is the making of a difference that makes a difference for some*body* somewhere (see Oyama 2000). Information here is understood in the sense of *informare,* to form within (Varela 1979, p. 266). An autonomous system becomes informed by virtue of the meaning formation in which it participates, and this meaning formation depends on the way its endogenous dynamics specifies things that make a difference to it (Kelso & Kay, 1987; Turvey & Shaw, 1999).

and object: A perturbation exists and receives its meaning and value in virtue of a particular coupling that an organism generates between its inner and external world. A sign, then, can be seen as an invitation to further action (cf. Järvilehto, 2000a).

The term 'sign' expresses this relativity, since *a sign is only a sign when it signifies something to or for another* (Peirce, 1978). In this spirit, and "[i]n a pragmatic sense, the only reality is signification" (Weber, 2002a, p. 24). Or, to speak with Kant's metaphors (1781/1998), we – and organisms more generally – do not know the 'thing in itself.'[2] The only thing that can be experienced and known is 'the thing for me.'

Organisms must experience and assign a particular meaning to a sign or a series of signs, otherwise they would not be signs. They must experience these signs (such as an inner feeling, an external change, a word, a term, or a concept) as otherwise they cannot and would not be affected by them in any significant way, either positively or negatively. And experience, meaning, and life in general are based on primordial affectivity. For example, the sentence "shall we play a little game?" will make any child happy who has learned that this constellation of words promises 'fun.' The same words, however, may upset an abused child if a sexual offender refers or has referred to the perpetration as a 'little game. ' As Weber (2002a, p. 22) put it, "[t]he world without living agents would be a completely neutral place. Only after life has come into it, the world becomes real in prospering and pain, joy and misery. Only the living is interested in its life as continuity."

Sense-making can, but need not, include a conscious awareness or an understanding of language. It is clear that spoken words as such do not mean anything to preverbal children. However, the way in which they are uttered (gently, softly, loudly, angrily) can make all the difference to them. When children have experienced that a delicate tone of voice goes along with tender care, they feel fine; when it signifies a prelude to sexual transgressions, their alarms go off.

Insignification

To live life efficiently, it is not enough to engage in signification, that is, to 'decide' what is significant-good and what is significant-bad. Rather, organisms must also 'decide' which phenomena are in fact *insignificant* for them. Some things will be more significant,

2 Kant realized that no one can say anything about things 'in themselves.' There is no view from nowhere. Spinoza's take on the issue was to formulate that God or Nature comprises endless attributes or properties, and that man only knows two of these, matter and mind. Realizing that we cannot rise beyond our human limitations, Schopenhauer intuited that the general will in Nature might be the thing in itself. My reading of Kant's terms 'thing in itself' and 'thing for me' is that any species', any individual's, and any dissociative part's cognition is subject to absolute and relative limitations, and that any view is someone's view. Enactive trauma therapy is concerned with overcoming traumatized individuals' relative limitations. With every new viable and creative action, their perspectival (affective, experiential, cognitive) scope widens, meaning that their power of action has increased.

more meaningful for them than others, and many things will be insignificant for them. Misjudging the degree of (personal) significance entails a major loss of energy and efficiency. For example, some people fret over matters that others regard as 'nonsensical,' whereas other individuals are deeply concerned with other people's problems they cannot possibly resolve, while avoid addressing their own urgent personal troubles. Individuals with obsessive-compulsive disorder are in the grip of useless mental and behavioral actions. Individuals who have been sexually abused by several men may believe that all men are sexual predators and organize their life around this idea. Efficient living requires the ongoing actions of signification (judging something is useful/good, or harmful/bad) as well as insignification (judging something is useless, irrelevant, or unimportant).

Signification is Species-Dependent

Different species enact their own *umwelt*, as do different members of one species. All organisms are part of the world, but an ant will never regard what in our view constitutes a 'table' as a 'table.' What one person may regard as a thing of beauty and value may be seen by someone else as ugly and worthless. Truth is indeed in the eye of the beholder. Zhuang Zi put this principle in clear and poetic words: "Mao Qiang and Xi Shi were beauties by our standards. When fish saw them, they swam to the bottom. When birds saw them, they flew high above. When the tailed deer saw them, they quickly ran away. Which one of these four knows the beauty standards of the world?" (Zhuang Zi, 2008, p. 49.)

The Power of Action

To live life efficiently and effectively, organisms must appreciate which environmental bodies and ideas tend to promote their power of action and their power of existing, that is, their power to preserve their existence. In this sense they must also reach a conclusion as to which other bodies and ideas might endanger them, that is, diminish, if not ruin, these powers. Organisms strive to enrich their body and their ideas by entering in particular composition of relationships with other bodies and ideas, while avoiding entering into compositions of relationships with physical and mental components of their *umwelt* which will harm them (i.e., decompose them to a greater or lesser extent). In Deleuze's clear phrasing of Spinoza's insights,

> [t]he order of causes is defined by this: each body in extension, each idea or each mind in thought are constituted by the characteristic relations that subsume the parts of that body, the parts of that idea. When a body "encounters" another body, or an idea another idea, it happens that the two relations sometimes combine to form a more powerful whole, and sometimes one decomposes the other, destroying the cohesion of its parts. And this is what is prodigious in the body and the mind alike, these sets of living parts that enter into composition with and

decompose one another according to complex laws (Spinoza, 1677a, Part II, Proposition 15). The order of causes is therefore an order of composition and decomposition of relations, which infinitely affects all of nature. But as conscious beings, we never apprehend anything but the *effects* of these compositions and decompositions: we experience *joy* when a body encounters ours and enters into composition with it, and *sadness* when, on the contrary, a body or an idea threatens our own coherence.

Affections and Affects

When organisms achieve something by their own doing and realize they have achieved a goal as a result of this effort, they experience joy, and this joy increases their power of action, their degree of "perfection[3]." According to Part IV's Proposition 11, joy, then, is the *passion by which the mind passes* [from a lesser] *to a greater perfection*. When organisms fail to attain a goal (e.g., to accomplish a task, to be and feel secure), they become sad. As Spinoza out it, sadness is the *passion by which the mind passes* [from a higher] *to a lower perfection*. Sorrow lessens an individual's power of action.

Spinoza calls "the *affect of joy which is related to the mind and body at once ... pleasure* or *cheerfulness*, and that of *sadness pain* or *melancholy*" (1677a, p. 77). Further, "pleasure and pain are ascribed to a man when one part of him is affected more than the rest, whereas cheerfulness and melancholy are ascribed to him when all are equally affected" (p. 77). Because all other affects arise from joy, sadness, and desire, for Spinoza these three are primary.

Many years after Spinoza, Pierre Janet reached the same conclusions regarding the importance of joy and triumph (see Van der Hart et al., 2006). As the 19th century French proverb intimates, "rien ne réussit comme le success" ("Nothing succeeds like success").[4] And probably nothing fails like consistent and enduring failure, no matter what one does to bring about a better outcome.

Joy and sadness: Because they are interested in the generation and continuation of their existence, all organisms are essentially *affective* beings. But what exactly are 'affects'? The term 'affect' relates to 'affection,' which stands for 'acting on organisms' actual mode of existence.' (Spinoza defines 'mode (of existence)' in Spinoza 1677a, Part I, Definition 5; see footnote 21 below.) Here Spinoza links 'affect' to 'affections of the body' to 'the body's power of acting' and 'the ideas of these affections.'): "By affect I understand affections of the body by which the body's power of acting is increased or diminished, aided or restrained, and at the same time, the ideas of these affections" (Spinoza, 1677a, Part III, Definition 3).

Affections can, of course, pertain to external powers acting on organisms; they can also denote features of the organisms themselves, including, for example, their own needs and

3 Spinoza considered 'reality' and 'perfection' to be the same thing (1677a, Part II, D5).
4 The saying was used by Sir Alfred Helps in his book *Realmah* from 1868.

desires, the implied action tendencies, and their current or past bodily condition and mental state (e.g., their present ideas).

Internal affections and external affections can agree or disagree with each other. What is more, affections are manifold. Life would be simple if all external forces were to 'push' or 'pull' an organism in one profitable direction. But the more complex an organism's *umwelt* becomes, the more this umwelt entails disparate affections. And the more complex an organism is, the more the organism entails incongruent internal affections. Some affections 'invite' it to move in one way, others 'prompt' it to take a different track, and still others 'summon' it to move in still other directions. Quo vadis? Left or right, forward or backward, up or down?

Spinoza's definition of affects indicates that affects have physical and mental properties. His emphasis on the body (e.g., "the body's power of acting") may sound curious to some readers. Are affects not emotions, and are emotions not basically mental phenomena? These questions obviously address the body-mind problem and the brain-mind problem (Northoff, 2003). The role of the body and the body's intimate relationship with the mind were already discussed in ToT Volumes I and II. This role will become clearer below, when we turn to the theoretical level in Chapter 29 and to the practical level in later chapters. For the time being, let it be said that "the order of actions and passions of our body is, by nature, at one with the order of actions and passions of the mind" (Spinoza, 1677a, Part III, Scholium to Proposition 2, p. 71: see also pp. 71–74 more generally). This statement derives from the view that the body and the mind are two attributes of one substance. This is why, when defining affects, Spinoza wrote that they equally concern the body's power of acting and the ideas of these affections.

Affects further comprise actions and passions. Affects that are actions, Spinoza asserted, increase the organism's power of action, whereas affects that are passions lower this capacity. In the first case individuals act on their own behalf, and in the second they are rather acted on, that is, they undergo something: "*. . . if we can be the adequate cause of any of these affections, I understand by the affect an action, otherwise, a passion*" (Spinoza, 1677a, Part III, Definition 3, italics in the original text). According to Spinoza's definitions, which I basically[5] adopt,

> . . . we act when something happens, in us or outside us, of which we are the adequate cause, that is . . ., when something in us or outside us follows from our nature, which can be clearly and distinctly understood through it alone. On the other hand, I say that we are acted on when something happens in us, or something follows from our nature, of which we are only a partial cause (Part III, Definition 2).

5 I write 'basically' because passions and actions are not completely distinct categories. In fact, they are not distinct categories at all. Categories are artificial: As Zhuang Zi already taught us, they are human constructions (Zhuang Zi, 2008). See also Wittgenstein, 1953. In particular contexts it may be helpful to use more refined groupings.

Actions, Passions, and *Umwelt*

It can be hard to obtain joy, to avoid sadness, and to dispense with the insignificant. Part of the problem is that the power of organisms, including human power, "is very limited and infinitely surpassed by the power of external causes" (Spinoza, 1667a, p. 160). Yet organisms basically try to prevail under all circumstances. Whatever organisms do and can do, they strive to serve their self-interest in the best possible way. In this sense, phenomena that from a third-person perspective may be seen as 'symptoms' of a 'mental' or 'behavioral disorder' can also be considered optimal for an organism given its current state, power of action, and living conditions.

The human power of action is influenced by many causes. Inasmuch as a probability of decomposition is concerned, the term 'risk factors' can be used. Risk factors include but are not limited to the following (ToT Volume I, Chapter 6):

- developmental phase
- genetic make-up
- temperament
- attachment patterns
- incongruent internal affections (e.g., emotional conflicts)
- incongruent external affections
- the nature, duration, and intensity of constructive events
- the nature, duration, and intensity of destructive events
- previous and current environmental conditions
- relationships to individuals involved in events
- availability of social support during or following previous harmful life events
- availability of social support during or following current harmful life events.

The power of action of organisms is also defined by their present organismic state or, as Spinoza put it, their 'mode.'[6] For example, an exhausted organism is capable of less than a vivacious one; a worried mind can endure less than a free spirit.

6 Spinoza (1677a, Part I, Definition 5): "By mode I understand the affections of a substance, *or* that which is in another through which it is also conceived." This "another" is Nature, the only existing substance. Modes, thus, are modifications of attributes of one substance called Nature. Since we humans know two of these properties—matter and mind—we know modes of matter and modes of mind. The singular existing substance is eternal and infinite: Its existence is necessary. In contrast to this substance, the modes of its attributes include duration. Beyond that, modes need not exist. They may exist, presently, in former days, or in future times. Spinoza (1677a, p. 32) highlights that "[m]an thinks ... or, to put it differently, we know that we think." Man is conscious. Spinoza continues, "[t]here are no modes of thinking, such as love, desire, or whatever is designated by the words affects of the mind, unless there is in the same individual the idea of the thing loved, desires, and the like" (p. 32). Being conscious thus implies being conscious *of something*. Modes of thinking or 'mental states' imply thoughts, affects, wishes, memories, etc. They imply 'mental contents.' A feeling, thought, or memory exists inasmuch as there is an organism that feels, thinks, and remembers. Given

Confrontations with trying events test the viable and creative abilities of organisms to make sense of their *umwelt* and of themselves as part of this world of meaning. Challenging events are bound to intensify their emotionality. Intense affects do not necessarily elicit inadequate or confused actions, affects, and ideas. In other words, these affects need not involve passions. Trying circumstances may even lift some individuals' viable and creative abilities. Life may rise to the occasion.

Adverse events imply even stronger affects; otherwise, they would not be detrimental to the organisms that experience them in the first place. The degree of adversity of an event is defined by the combination of the subject's present and potential power of action and the particular features of the object (here, the perceived and conceived event). In other words, adversity is defined by the degree to which the subject and the object agree or disagree. The quality and meaning of an event are relative to the properties of both the subject and the object.

Even under very difficult circumstances (such as war) some exceptional subjects may reach more power of action. Other individuals may manage to more or less deal with a particular adverse event, whereas still others can barely cope or fail to handle the situation completely. In other words, when entangled with events – the subject and the object are entangled because they constitute and depend on each other; see Chapters 24 and 27, as well as ToT Volumes I & II – some individuals become injured, whereas others handle them more favorably.

Still, there are limits to everyone's abilities to survive a dark world unscathed. Particularly when the harmful aspects are intense and lasting and the useful aspects are largely lacking is our capacity to continue enacting a meaningful phenomenal self, world, and self-of-the-world tried to the extreme. A trying or adverse event becomes an injurious or traumatizing event to such an individual when it demands more complex actions than the individual who is experiencing it can come up with – when it demands more power of action than they currently possess (cf. ToT Volume I, Chapter 11). How adverse an event is then matches the degree to which the event decomposes the individual who experiences it.

Passions and Substitute Actions

The less organisms are able to achieve optimal or at least sufficient adaptation and creativity, the more they engage in passions rather than in actions. Passions and actions are not completely distinct categories. When organisms' affects involve mild passions, they are acted on while also acting. Milder passions thus have features of actions inasmuch as organisms are an influential cause, albeit not the *only* cause of their experiences, body

their relevance for the discussion on consciousness, the involved axioms were used already as the motto for Chapter 22. The term 'mode' is detailed more in Chapter 26.

sensations, emotions, thoughts, memories, and behaviors. However, the more organisms are acted on, the less they tend to act; the more external affections and disparate inner affections determine their experiences, sensations, affects, cognitions, and behaviors, the more intense their passions become.

The category of passions includes 'substitute actions.'[7] Substitute actions are compositions of lesser complexity and power that take the place of more efficient, viable, and creative actions that lie beyond an organism's present reach (Janet, 1903, 1909, 1928b; Spinoza, 1677a; Van der Hart et al., 2006). All substitute actions imply gains and losses. They are meaningful, albeit confused efforts to organize and sustain life. An organism's efforts to maintain itself in the face of many (in part) divergent internal and external influences affect the mind as much as they do the body. It therefore holds that: "... [the mind] strives to persevere in its being both insofar as it has inadequate ideas and insofar as it has adequate ideas ..." (Spinoza, 1677a, p. 76).

Some substitute actions in trauma are of a lower quality than others. Engaging in low-quality substitute actions or intense passions, traumatized individuals may faint or panic and act chaotically. They may also seriously injure themselves, engage in suicidal acts, or intensely and recurrently reenact traumatizing events. Other substitute actions such as relational reenactments may involve less severe degrees of decomposition and confusion, but they are nonetheless problematic. By way of illustration, patients may perceive, conceive, and relate to clinicians as if they were a potential or actual perpetrator. Examples of other substitute actions that are not of an excessively low quality are avoiding bodily feelings or recollecting traumatic experiences, operating on impulse in situations that demand reflection, or engaging in overeating as a means to avoid distressing emotions.

Whereas some substitute actions (such as trauma-related obsessions) may be specific to humans, many others also appear in animals. Homo sapiens are far less unique than they tend to think they are. For example, following traumatization human beings – and other animal species as well – may freeze in situations in which defensive or other actions would in fact be more useful. Pavlov's dogs that became traumatized during a flood thereafter engaged in freezing when confronted with even small amounts of water (see ToT Volume I, p. 206–207). Traumatized individuals may also engage in freezing when they are confronted with signs that remind them of traumatizing events in which they displayed this type (or another type) of mammalian defense. Many substitute actions therefore involve regressions to simpler actions. For example, trauma often entails a loss of the human symbolic ability and implies a loss of language and a loss of the ability to reflect.

The distinction drawn between actions and passions is theoretically clear. However, there are clearly some borderline cases between (efficient and/or high-level) actions and passions. Also numerous fuzzy boundaries exist between mild passions (or intermediate-

---

7 It would be more precise to write 'passionate substitutes for actions,' but for the sake of consistency I adhere to the terminology from *The Haunted Self* (Van der Hart et al., 2006).

level substitute actions) and deep passions (or low-level substitute actions[8]). In fact, it makes sense to say that there is a dimension of mental and behavioral efficiency. Just as some actions are extremely efficient and others less efficient, some substitute actions are more efficient than others.

Adverse, Traumatizing, and Traumatic Events

Given the entanglement and relativity of subjects and objects, a particular event cannot be said to be traumatizing *per se* (say, an accident or an assault). Any judgment must necessarily also take the experiencing subject into account. This is why it is important to make a distinction between adverse events and traumatizing events or traumatic events (ToT Volume I; see also below): Adverse events can be defined as events that are generally detrimental to a species, but that do not necessarily hinder any particular member of the species from experiencing it. Traumatizing or traumatic are events that have truly injured an individual who experienced them. Generally whether or not, and if so to what degree, an event has been traumatizing or traumatic to an individual can be made only *de post facto*.

In ToT Volume I, Chapter 11, I tied the concept of 'traumatizing events' to the third-person perspective. In this case, an observer technically judges that an event has been injurious. For example, a clinician may technically judge that a particular event has been a major cause of a particular patient's disorder. The concept of 'traumatic events' was defined as the phenomenal, that is, experience-based judgment that an event was injurious. In this case, the individual who experienced the event in question experiences it from the first-person perspective and on the basis of that experience phenomenally judges from the quasi-second-person perspective that the event has wounded him or her. An individual who can 'feel with' the exposed individual may, on the basis of this empathy, also phenomenally judge from the second-person perspective that the event was 'traumatic' for the individual who actually experienced it.

Decomposition and (Re)Composition of the Personality in Trauma

Depending on the degree to which their *umwelt* has turned dark, and depending on the degree to which they can cope with such adversity, individuals become decomposed to a greater or lesser degree: The relationships among some of the many components of their personality as a whole organism-environment system can become loose or even be destroyed. Because matter and mind constitute two attributes of Nature as a singular sub-

8 Consistent with his definitions, Spinoza would certainly have categorized substitute actions as passions.

stance, this system includes the body and the unconscious as well as conscious mind. In other words, events that strongly disagree with the involved individual's nature can provoke an inferior cohesion within an individual's personality, including that person's phenomenal self, world, and self-of-the-world. To quote again from Deleuze's (1988) exposition of Spinoza's philosophy and psychology, "[t]he object that does not agree with me jeopardizes my cohesion, and tends to divide me into subsets, which, in the extreme case, enter into relations that are incompatible with my constitutive relation *(death)*" (p. 21).

What has become decomposed in trauma is not the *possibility* of the relationships among components of an individual's personality as it exists in nature, but rather the *actual* relationships of these elements. Like a physical decomposition, say, a cut or a broken leg, traumatizing events do not destroy all vital relationships among the elements of an individual's personality (when the individual was not killed). At its core trauma is a more or less profound decomposition of particular relationships within an individual's personality as a whole organism-environment system (ToT Volumes I & II).

Moreover, trauma also comprises a particular new composition of conscious and self-conscious 'subsets' or subsystems. These subsets, subsystems, or 'parts' of the personality are not static structures: They exist in virtue of their ongoing actions and more or less intense passions. That is, dissociative parts exist in virtue of their ongoing constitution of relationships among their vital inner elements. They also exist in virtue of relationships among themselves and relationships with their *umwelt.*

Dissociative parts of the personality are subsets of actions and passions. They are self-generating, self-maintaining subsystems within the confines of a traumatized individual's personality as a complete organism-environment system. These subsets, subsystems, or parts are and continue to be dissociative inasmuch as they do not or not sufficiently agree with each other.

In order to avoid misunderstandings regarding the term dissociative 'parts,'[9] let me emphasize once again that the metaphor is not to be understood in the sense of parts or pieces of a cake or some other static object. Rather, dissociative parts are living and dynamic *divisions* in a wider living organization (ToT Volume II, Chapter 12).

The internal and external relationships that dissociative parts generate and maintain can, at least in principle, be described and analyzed in biological, psychological, and social terms. However, because they involve different properties of the same substance (Nature), these various analyses cannot be directly linked to each other, and the brain/body and the mind do not cause or explain each other. However, indirect links between the body, the brain, the mind, and the material and social *umwelt* are within reach (see ToT Volumes I & II). *Dissociative parts, then, are biopsychosocial subsystems of an individual's personality as a whole biopsychosocial organism-environment system.*

9 The term 'part' stems from the Latin *partem* (nominative *pars*) which stands for "a part, piece, a share, a division; a party or faction; a part of the body; a fraction; a function, office." The verb 'to part' stems from the Latin *partere, partire* which means "to share, part, distribute, divide." See The Online Etymology Dictionary.

The decomposition and the re-composition of the personality in trauma are like a physical injury and its consequences. Just as the physical skin can resist incision by an object up to a point, individuals (a whole system) manage to cope with life within limits, including situations adverse to them. At a certain, critical degree of 'pressure,' however, the 'skin' of their personality becomes divided (inasmuch as the personality was previously integrated). Like a cut, traumatizing events do not necessarily destroy all vital relationships among the elements of an individual's personality. But there is 'blood,' there are 'immune reactions,' there is 'pain' involved, and in some phases perhaps a degree of 'analgesia' and 'anesthesia.' In due course the tendency arises to 'close the gap,' to 'heal the wound.' This organismic repair may succeed, but 'infections' may also ensure which hinder recovery. For example, dissociative subsystems or parts of the personality can 'infect,' that is, reject and aversively intrude on, each other. Severe wounds can even be lethal. Some dissociative parts can turn suicidal and engage in suicidal acts that sometimes succeed.

Reenactment of Traumatic Memories and Relationships: Seeking Joy, Remaining Stuck in Sadness, Suffocating in Hate

"Man is affected with the same affect of joy or sadness from the image of a past or future thing as from the image of the present thing" (Spinoza, 1667a, Part III, Proposition 18). Spinoza demonstrates this proposition by saying that "[s]o long as a man is affected by the image of a thing, he will regard the thing as present, even if it does not exist . . .; he images it as a past or future only inasmuch as its image is joined to the image of a past or future time." This second image – the result of the mind's action of time-designation – can be lacking. When it is absent,

> the image of a thing, considered only in itself, is the same, whether it is related to time past or future, or to the present, that is . . . the constitution of the body, *or* affect, is the same, whether the image is of a thing past or future, or of a present thing. And so, the affect of joy or sadness is the same, whether the image is of a thing past or future, or of a present thing. (p. 80)

This proposition is of major relevance for trauma. Among other things it speaks to reenactments of traumatic memories including their essential sensorimotor, perceptual, and affect-laden features. In the third-person perspective, these reenactments of prior injurious experiences and relationships are substitute actions that generate confused images and ideas. In the first-person perspective of reenacting individuals, however, they comprise *current* events. The confusion of reenacting individuals exists inasmuch as they do not engage in the actions of imagining a past time – and inasmuch as they do not synthesize their current experience with this image of a past time. However, once they start engaging in these integrative actions, traumatic reenactments become enacted memories of traumatizing events.

More than 200 years later, Janet described this fourfold action as *presentification* (see Van der Hart et al., 2006). It includes the following:

1) experiencing an event or relational pattern;
2) imagining a past;
3) synthesizing the experience ("1) and the image of the relevant past ("2) in the framework of one's present existence and present phenomenal reality;
4) assigning more reality to one's present existence than to one's past existence.

When these various actions succeed, individuals experience and assume that the (actual) present is *more real* than the image of the past.

Spinoza's Proposition 18 of Part III (1667a) and presentification pertain to a variety of affects. Some of these abundant and dominant in trauma: hope, fear, despair, and remorse:

> For *hope* is nothing but *an inconstant joy which has arisen from the image of a future or past thing whose outcome we doubt; fear,* on the other hand, is *an inconstant sadness, which has also arisen from the image of a doubtful thing.* Next, if the doubt involved in these affects is removed, hope becomes *confidence*, and fear, *despair* – namely, *a joy or sadness which has arisen from the image of a past thing we feared or hoped for.* Finally, *gladness is a joy which has arisen form the image of a past thing whose outcome we doubted,* while *remorse is a sadness which is opposite to gladness.* (p. 81)

Some dissociative parts fear significant others as a result of their dreadful experiences with them. Lacking presentification, they tend to recurrently reenact the traumatizing events involved. Their images of these events and the implied experiences are in fact *too real* (Van der Hart et al., 2006). Their fearful and horrible past remains their fearful and horrible present.

One of the hopes of individuals who have been chronically traumatized by their father, mother, or other primary caretakers is that one day these persons will eventually love, or at least accept, them. Although they are uncertain as to whether in fact this will ever happen, many of them keep up this hope ("If I try harder, my mother will appreciate, perhaps even love me one day"). A complication in dissociative disorders is that some dissociative parts recurrently imagine that this acceptance and love will come. In this spirit they go to great lengths to realize their hopes, even though they also continually experience that their 'positive' images of the future fail to match reality. For them, relational disappointment does not cause relational disentanglement.

Children phenomenally experience and perceive that they have the right to exist, and that they are good when their parents or other caretakers love them. But what if these individuals recurrently abuse, maltreat, neglect, and chronically hate them? The children can hardly afford the realization they are living with criminals, both now and in the future (child abuse, maltreatment, and neglect are crimes). It certainly helps when the traumatizing individuals admit their crimes at some point and ask the ones they hurt so much for forgiveness (see the cases of Ineke, Chapters 32 and 35, Martha, Chapter 33, and Sonja, Chapter 37). But confessions of this nature are rare (Martha), and waiting for a confession and excuse puts victims in a passionate position (Ineke).

In their attempts to cope with the situation at hand, some children (or dissociative parts of them) fantasize that their parents or other caretakers actually love them. It is not hard to comprehend how useful this confused and stubborn idea can be. Some children continue to cling to the fantasy even after having grown up: another ongoing reenactment. While believing in their fantasies of the love and goodness of primary caretakers can be helpful at times, there is a serious price to pay: "If my parents and other family members are *good*, then I must be *bad*. I deserve punishment." Controlling EPs that reenact (i.e., mirror) perpetrators' deeds typically reinforce these ideas.

Individuals or dissociative parts of them entertaining the hopes and fantasies of acceptance and love must at some point come to terms with the naked reality of hate and rejection. But such realization that their hopes were and continue to be empty is exceptionally painful and commonly takes consistent emotional support from benign individuals. The insight that their belief in such a sweet fairytale has allowed them to survive otherwise unbearable terror may also help alleviate the pain. Affectively comprehending the point of these relational reenactments is a liberating enactment.

Other chronically traumatized individuals or dissociative parts of them despair at the thought that significant others will ever accept and love them ("No one is to be trusted"). They imagine a past without acceptance, recognition, secure attachment, and love. They cannot imagine, or resist imagining, a brighter future. They may even feel remorse at having the involved needs and desires ("It was so stupid of me to believe that one day love would come. It is bad to have needs"). This sorrow leads them to deny their needs entirely and to replace them with a hate of the dissociative parts that live in hope or that are stuck in fear. And hate entails the desire to put an end to the objects of their hate: *He who imagines that what he hates is destroyed will rejoice* (Spinoza, 1667a, Part III, Proposition 20). When acceptance- and love-seeking dissociative parts fail – usually ANPs – and when scared dissociative parts remain stuck in fear – commonly fragile EPs – the controlling EPs that hate the ANPs and fragile EPs are pleased.

However, hopeful dissociative parts may eventually gain friendship and understanding in common life and therapy. Fearful parts may gain power of action and become courageous. These developments conflict with the interests of hateful controlling parts, which are terribly scared that other individuals will again betray them. They therefore typically forbid secure attachment to significant others. They feel a need to counter the promise of acceptance and love as well as the evolution of further hope. These urges can and often do affect the therapeutic dyad:

> *If we imagine someone to affect with joy a thing we hate, we shall be affected with hate toward him also. On the other hand, if we imagine him to affect the same thing with sadness, we shall be affected with love toward him* (Spinoza, 1667a, Part III, Proposition 24).

And: *We strive to affirm, concerning what we hate, whatever we imagine to affect it with sadness, and on the other hand, to deny whatever we imagine to affect it with joy* (Spinoza, 1667a, Part III, Proposition 26). Controlling EPs therefore tend to hate clinicians who accept, recognize, understand, and assist hopeful ANPs and scared fragile EPs. They are inclined to attack clinicians and their therapeutic interventions, just as they attack ANPs and fragile EPs. For example, controlling EPs may forbid ANPs and fragile EPs to come to the therapy sessions. They may ridicule clinicians or even sabotage their therapeutic interventions. When controlling EPs succeed in bringing forth these effects, they rejoice. In the same spirit, controlling EPs love individuals who cause ANPs and fragile EPs to feel sorrow. This means they love and identify with perpetrators, their partners in crime, and other controllers in society.

This said, it must be added that the reenactments and dynamics of ANPs, fragile EPs, and controlling EPs can be more complex than this sketch might suggest. The deeper layers of dissociative parts and the interactions among them are detailed later in Chapters 35 and 37. For now, the above descriptions must suffice to illustrate that inconstant affects in (chronic) trauma can lead to a distribution of affects and images among dissociative parts as well as to an implied distribution and opposition of various kinds of reenactment. Generally speaking, ANPs tend to reenact hope and love, fragile EPs fear and sadness, and controlling EPs remorse, rejection, rage, and hate.

Dissociative Intrusions

Inasmuch as dissociative intrusions (e.g., intruding trauma-related affects, bodily feelings, images, motor actions) are intensely affect-laden, for the intruded dissociative part they qualify as passions (see also Chapter 27). Intruded parts experience and think that something or someone is *acting on* them. In their perception and conception, this something or someone is external to them. Although some dissociative parts experience or know that the cause of the intrusions exists within their own body, they disregard this source as a part of *their* being.

Intruding dissociative parts can be the proximate cause of what intrudes on the intruded dissociative parts. This is the case when the intrusions pertain to *actions* of the intruding parts. For example, a controlling EP that calls other dissociative parts names engages in a self-initiated and goal-directed action (e.g., Chapter 37) – as does an intruding fragile EP that tries to get an ANP's attention and help (e.g., Chapter 32).

Such intrusions may also pertain to *passions* rather than to actions of the intruding parts. For example, an ANP can be intruded on by a fragile EP that unwillingly relives a physical or sexual assault and that screams at a perpetrator "Stop, don't do it" (see Chapter 32). In this case the EP does not willingly self-initiate the reliving; rather, the reenactment is afforded by confrontations with potent reminders of traumatic experiences and events that the involved EP signifies.

Demoralization: Power of Action Lost

In the current enactive perspective, being traumatized means acting in particular ways, both mentally and behaviorally. It basically entails affect-laden efforts to make sense of a hurtful world and to nevertheless preserve life. These substitute actions and passions imply manifold mental and physical complaints that clinicians comprehend as symptoms of a mental disorder. For example, traumatized individuals reenact their horrors from time to time, by day and by night. They tend to have various phobias, find it hard to concentrate, mysteriously lose track of time and place, act like a robot, feel dirty, or cut themselves. Some cannot stay away from alcohol or drugs for very long. Particularly chronically traumatized individuals struggle to comprehend their hard, almost incomprehensible life.

As Martha (Chapter 33) wondered, “Why me? Why did my parents beat, blame, abuse, and hate me? What did I do wrong that kept them from loving me? They loved my sister, right? Why? I just don’t understand it.” Ineke (Chapters 32 and 35) went to great lengths to please her mother, who sometimes was “normal,” but then, “out of the blue,” threw her down the stairs in anger or locked her in a cellar for days on end. When she was 6 years old, Ineke basically did all the cooking, cleaned the house, and took care of the laundry. Yet her sacrifice was to no avail: Her mother rejected her no matter what she did. When her mother had hit her hard, her father would sometimes console her. However, his concept of consolation entailed rape (Chapter 35). The whole family knew that her father was obsessed with sex, and, still, no one rescued Ineke from her disturbed parents. Like Martha, Ineke did not comprehend what might be wrong with her that she should deserve such endless neglect, maltreatment, and abuse. She eventually became convinced that she was an exceptionally bad, horrible person.

These and other troubles and riddles generally beset in particular chronically traumatized individuals over long periods of time, perhaps even decades. It is therefore quite unlikely that these problems in themselves prompt them to eventually seek professional help. Why, then, do they present themselves for treatment at some point? Like many other individuals with serious mental troubles, individuals who have lived through such horrific events generally request treatment when they have lost all hope, when they have lost the confidence that they can manage, let alone resolve, their problems on their own, with or without help from their families or friends. They seek help when they do not know what to do anymore, when they cannot discover any good in life, cannot get rid of the bad, and no longer know how to change their fate. Indeed, having lost hope means a major loss of power of action. The longer individuals are unable to cope, the more they are bound to feel helpless, hopeless, and incompetent. Their self-esteem suffers greatly and may eventually crumble, and their world is certain to lose ever more positive meaning. Disheartened and demoralized (Clarke & Kissane, 2002; Frank, 1968), traumatized individuals just want clinicians to ‘do something’ that will alleviate or resolve their suffering.

Enactivism and Participatory Sense Making

Trauma clinicians 'do' something, for sure. But they do not do something independent of their patients. Rather, they aspire to do something *with* them, in the sense that enactive trauma therapy is essentially about a wounded individual ('the patient') striving to make new sense in life in close collaboration with a less unfortunate individual ('the clinician') as a consistent guide or coach. Trauma entails reducing an individual's power of action. In full contrast, enactive repair is about finding new meaning in life. This healing is about developing new mental and behavioral actions that increase injured individuals' power of action in viable and creative ways (Janet, 1925; Spinoza, 1677a; Van der Hart et al., 2006). The conjoint action-focused adventure of this therapy involves a kind of autonomy that can be described as 'participatory sense-making' (cf. De Jaegher & Di Paolo, 2007; De Jaegher, Di Paolo, & Gallagher, 2010). It is like engaging in a creative dance together that builds on the interests, ideas, and skills the two partners bring to the situation. As the saying goes, it takes two to tango. In fact, any human sense-making is basically an interpersonal action. More than anything else, man is indeed a social creature.

Healing trauma involves making available and replacing the passions that trauma comprises – its unchecked, intense affects as well as its implied confused ideas – by more adequate achievements. It demands a composition consisting of new actions and associated "clear and distinct ideas," that is, lucid understanding (Spinoza, 1677a, particularly Part V). And because organisms (including humans) are affective, this understanding is not anything like a matter of 'pure reason.' It is ever so important to grasp that 'pure reason' cannot restrain affect: *"No affect can be restrained by the true knowledge of good and evil insofar as it is true, but only insofar as it is considered as an affect"* (1677a; Part IV, Proposition 14). Any trauma clinician knows that *"[a]n affect cannot be constrained or taken away except by an affect opposite to, and stronger than, the affect to be restrained"* (Part IV, Proposition 7). Healing trauma demands affects that are opposite to, and indeed stronger than, the traumatic passions. These stronger affects affect the body more than the traumatic affections of the body. Inasmuch as it takes reason, it takes an *affect-laden understanding that flows from love of God or Nature* (Spinoza equated the concepts of God and Nature).

In this light, enactive trauma therapy entails progressing from reenactments, substitute actions, and passions to new, more viable, and creative enactments of a self, a world, and a self as a part of this world. To be clear, I am not claiming that the actions and passions of traumatized individuals are not creative in some way. On the contrary (see Chapter 26), enactivism contains the idea that creativity is an inherent feature of life. Traumatized individuals, however, recurrently engage in actions and passions that are overly rigid – and psychopathology in general involves overly inflexible actions or passions. They bring forth a phenomenal self, a phenomenal world, and phenomenal relationships between this self and world that in at least some crucial regards are problematic. This rigidity captures the meaning of the term "trauma-related pathology." Enactive trauma therapy invites and assists traumatized individuals to increase their power of action, to engage in actions that bring forth more joy in their lives, and that lessen their sorrow. Such progression is possible, at least in principle, inasmuch as the traumatized individual decides to strive for this development despite the temporary sorrow the venture sometimes entails.

Chapter 26

Dissociative Parts of the Personality and Modes of Longing and Striving

> *Whatever so disposes the human body that it can be affected in a great many ways, or renders it capable of affecting external bodies in a great many ways, is useful to man; the more it renders the body capable of being affected in a great many ways, or of affecting other bodies, the more useful it is; on the other hand, what renders the body less capable of these things is harmful.*
> Baruch Spinoza (1667a, Part IV, Proposition 38)

Enactivism holds that all living systems are sense-making systems because they are autonomous, viable, and creative (Colombetti, 2014; Thompson, 2007; Varela, 1979). Traumatized individuals are not any different in these regards. Being autonomous centers of operation or action and passion (see Chapter 27), they strive to cope with a world that, among other things, has been or continues to be threatening, hurting, and devastating. They make every effort to survive in viable and creative ways the overpowering world they encountered.

Some individuals experience an extremely adverse *umwelt* and lack the capacity and support to integrate their horrific experiences. Moreover, traumatizing families may instruct the children they abuse and neglect to ignore or 'forget about' the inflicted horrors. Under these circumstances, developing a more or less complex dissociation of the personality may be the victims' best option. Of course, such a division is only a substitute for achieving or maintaining an integrated personality, and it generally entails tormenting consequences in the short and long run. But it is a creative action. Keeping this intricate system up and working for a longer period of time, sometimes even for decades or a whole lifetime, constitutes no less than an impressive work of art.

Dissociative Parts and Action Systems

The dissociative subsystems or parts that traumatized individuals generate and maintain in *ongoing enaction* essentially include one or more prototypical ANPs as well as one or more prototypical EPs (Nijenhuis, Van der Hart, & Steele, 2002; Van der Hart et al., 2006; ToT Volumes I & II; Chapters 22 and 26). It is hypothesized that each prototype is primarily mediated by quite particular evolutionary-derived actions systems (Nijenhuis & Den Boer, 2009; Nijenhuis et al., 2002; Panksepp, 1998; Panksepp & Biven, 2012; Van der

Hart et al., 2006; ToT Volumes I & II). Action or will systems involve basic needs and desires that guide what an organism senses, perceives, thinks, feels, remembers, and does. They guide the system's mode of action. These wills, the implied goal orientation, and the action systems that they belong to are integrative because the particular form that will takes integrates sensations, emotions, perceptions, cognitions, and behaviors relevant to it. Action systems also guide what an organism does *not* tend to sense, perceive, think, feel, remember, and do. Thus, so to speak, they open and close the doors to particular kinds of actions and passions – and thereby to their implied mental and behavioral contents.

Action systems should thus not be seen as systems subservient to psychological 'functions' such as perception, emotion, and memory. Rather, they are systems that integrate all actions (e.g., perceiving, feeling, thinking, moving) in the service of goal attainment (Järvilehto, 2001a) – goals that pertain what the organism needs and desires: getting something useful and avoiding or getting rid of something harmful. Action systems thus constitute systems that serve the achievement of particular results. To this end, they guide and integrate what an organism perceives and fails to perceive, feel, think, and do: They influence the actions of signification and insignification.

Action Systems that Mediate Apparently Normal Parts of the Personality

To recapitulate, prototypical ANPs desire and strive to experience daily life. They want to eat, sleep, relax, explore, love, play, provide care, make money, and enjoy friends when they can. These parts of traumatized individuals are, hypothetically speaking, primarily mediated by action or will systems to function in daily life. The ones that seem to guide them most include energy management, exploration, caregiving, procreation/sexuality, attachment, play, and social engagement.

To handle daily life to the best of their abilities, ANPs consciously and preconsciously avoid if at all possible reminders of any traumatizing events, inasmuch as confrontations with these reminders in their estimation would decompose them. To navigate their phenomenal and perhaps also actual *fragility* in this regard, ANPs try to *ignore* or otherwise evade physical sensations, thoughts, and behaviors implying such confrontations. This ignorance constitutes in part their effort to hide their fragility from themselves as well as from other individuals. Because EPs are directly associated with traumatizing events, ANPs also try to *ignore* or otherwise avoid EPs as much as possible. Ignoring interoceptive[1]

1 What we commonly call 'internal' and 'external' is what we consider relative to ourselves, i.e., what we perceive and conceive as something that exists internally and externally *to us*. English verbs with '-ceive' and nouns with '-ception' stem from the Latin *capere*, which means 'to take onto oneself.' Given the intrinsic relationships of our brain, body, and *umwelt*, what we from the first-person, quasi-second-person, and second-person perspective call inner or internal and outer or external is in the third-person perspective actually as much internal as external. This third-person view is reflected in the terms 'interoception'/'interoceptive,'and 'exteroception'/'exteroceptive.'

('internal') and exteroceptive ('external') trauma-related cues through mental and behavioral avoidance is an effort at *control.* This control may be mediated by action systems of daily life inhibiting incompatible interests. The efforts of ANPs to ignore EPs, however, may also be guided by derivates of the action system of mammalian defense. It is at least conceivable that mental defenses evolved from physical defenses.

Inasmuch as this avoidant control succeeds, ANPs remain *ignorant* of traumatic memories, EPs, and (trauma-related) physical and emotional affections. As ANP, traumatized individuals recurrently *reenact* the fragility and their means of controlling this vulnerability that has developed since the actual traumatization. As a consequence, they leave traumatic memories and dissociative parts associated with these memories at least insufficiently integrated. The continuing avoidant control of ANPs thus maintains the dissociation of the personality.

Action Systems that Guide Fragile Emotional Parts of the Personality

Mediated by the action system of mammalian defense, fragile EPs phenomenally experience and judge that they are acutely endangered and *fragile.* Trying to *control* (or at least influence) the danger so as to persevere in their existence, fragile EPs engage in defensive actions such as startle, flight, freeze, fight, or passive immobility. Some may also apply interpersonal defensive actions described as 'tend and befriend.' Another defensive social action lies in 'attachment cry' (a mode of the attachment action system). Fragile EPs are primarily stuck in a traumatic *umwelt.* As they experience and see it, this *umwelt* does not age, just as they themselves do not seem to age. They maintain this phenomenal *ignorance* by recurrently reenacting the actual past; ANPs or other individuals leave EPs to their own devices.

Action Systems that Influence Controlling Emotional Parts of the Personality

Living as ANPs and fragile EPs, chronically traumatized children or older individuals have only a restricted sense of control. To the extent to which they experience self-control, this is mostly of a *negative* kind, in the sense that at best it curtails harm. It is not about the power of getting something positive; it is not about gaining something useful. The method of control ANPs prefer is this: Do not sense sensory and emotional affections, do not remember dread and do not contact EPs. The control mechanism of fragile EPs is: Prevent or curtail any (further) harm to the integrity of the body as much as possible.

Positive control fosters power of action. Eventually, it is more rewarding to achieve something useful, something significant-good than to evade something harmful – no matter how important it may be to evade or curtail the significant-bad. Mediated by the action system of social dominance, controlling EPs seek a *positive* sense of power. This urge emanates from their need and desire to achieve a positive sense of power for the whole individual. As much as they can they act brave and resist perpetrators.

However, chronic traumatization actually leaves ANPs, fragile EPs, and controlling EPs rather powerless. Despite their best efforts, controlling EPs cannot change this reality. The power wielded by external injurious causes exceeds the power of action of the whole traumatized individual by far. They thus engage in passions more than in actions.

Controlling EPs are confronted with their failure and their own *fragility*. These features are antithetical to their need and desire to be in charge of things and of themselves. The best they can do is to hide this vulnerability from themselves, other dissociative parts, and other individuals. Longing to save face and to gain or restore a positive sense of power, controlling EPs may start to imitate the appalling power displays of individuals they are all too familiar with: their perpetrators. Children learn a lot by imitating others.

This imitation of *destructive control* models implies a rather low level of consciousness as well as a quite retracted field of consciousness (Chapter 22). These features hinder controlling EPs, who notice that ANPs grow up and that the traumatization stops at some point (assuming it does). And there is another reason why they remain more or less *ignorant* of the third-person understanding of time and place as well as of the individual's actual age, developmental phase, and circumstances of life: They resist integrating traumatic memories associated with fragile EPs. They also resist entering into intimate contact with the involved "weak and despicable" boys or girls and with the "worthless" ANPs (see Chapter 37). Controlling EPs do not wish to be hit, kicked, and raped. And they have no interest in "mere babbling." They want to hit and kick themselves. That feels far better! Vice versa, ANPs and fragile EPs avoid relationships with the controlling EPs, whom they truly fear. This dynamic keeps them from joining forces.

At some point controlling EPs may want to get rid of the fragile EPs and the feeble ANPs. Some think they can kill them without dying themselves in the act. However, these wishes conflict with their original task of "saving the weak ones" and with their hidden feelings of sympathy for them. This old task and the will that drives it prompt controlling EPs to continue engaging in relationships with these other prototypical parts, at least to some extent.

In conclusion, the present view does not regard controlling EPs as 'perpetrator introjects.' They do not comprise some kind of twin perpetrator. Rather, they imitate one or more perpetrators and that only to some degree. This imitation provides them with a sense of control. But they are also fragile and remain ignorant in important regards (e.g., time, place, identity, status of other individuals). Showing a mighty face, controlling EPs hide their fragile and in part ignorant existence. Their hope is to persuade themselves, other dissociative parts, and other individuals that they are most powerful.

ANPs with 'EP-like' Features and EPs with 'ANP-like' Features

It may be said that some ANPs include 'EP-like' features and some EPs 'ANP-like' features. That is, some ANPs can be quite emotional at times, and some EPs can also pursue interests of daily life. These facts do not reveal a weakness of the core concepts of ANP and EP or more generally a basic flaw in the theory of trauma-related dissociation of the personality. To provide an analogy, the fact that there are many shades of primary colors and many mixtures of primary colors does not mean that it is useless to distinguish the primary colors. Quite on the contrary, knowing the primary colors allows us to know and appreciate the many mixtures of primary colors. Similarly, it becomes possible to comprehend fog when one can perceive and conceive water as a fluid and water as a gas. The fact that some ANPs can have some 'EP-like' features, and that some EPs can have some 'ANP-like' features thus strengthens rather than weakens the concepts of ANP and EP. This circumstance should not prompt us to abandon or alter the theory; rather, the task is *to formulate the distinctive features of these dissociative subsystems of the personality.*

In our search for clarity, the first step is to grasp that dissociative parts can include various needs and desires. Whereas prototypical ANPs are *primarily* mediated by interests and action systems for functioning in daily life, in this framework they are *also* mediated by the need and desire for safety. For example, and as asserted above, they try to ignore or otherwise avoid traumatic memories and the associated traumatic memories. This method of evasion can be a conscious, preconscious, or unconscious act (ToT Volume II, Chapters 17–18). Prototypical ANPs are motivated to avoid feeling, knowing, or realizing the traumatization as much as possible, because they are or feel too fragile to integrate their horrible experiences. The ignoring or other avoidant actions involve a certain degree of defensive control. Further, most ANPs are comediated by the action system of mammalian defense. This proposition seems warranted since they generally strive to secure the integrity of their body. They avoid subjects, objects, and events they associate with danger to their physical existence. For example, most people drive responsibly, cross a busy street carefully, and avoid places of ill repute. Not all ANPs, however, consistently operate this wisely.

Feeling fragile and threatened, and in the attempt to protect themselves as much as possible (which concerns an effort at control), prototypical fragile EPs are *primarily* mediated by the action system of mammalian defense and/or attachment cry. However, they are not strangers to the needs and desires for fluids, food, sleep, play, and the like. For example, once a very scared fragile EP started to trust me as her clinician, she liked to play around when she presented herself in therapy sessions. This play can be seen as an expression of the action system of play (Panksepp, 1998). The EP involved thus encompassed various longings and strivings even if the need and desire to protect herself from further harm were dominant.

Controlling EPs display power, though they may actually feel quite fragile. However, and as noted above, these dissociative parts commonly forbid themselves to exhibit vulnerability. By covering up their fragility, they present themselves as exceptionally powerful; they display a high degree of (attempted) control. Within this framework, controlling EPs tend to remain quite ignorant of the present state of affairs, including the patient's present age and life experiences. However, instances occur both in real life and in therapy in which they can nevertheless reveal their fear and/or sadness.

For example, one male controlling EP of a female patient with DID recounted that several perpetrators had viciously laughed at him when he showed fear and shed some tears. Since that time he had forced himself to mask his fear and sorrow as he tried to resist the abusers. I praised him for his tremendous courage and endurance and invited him to explore what horrors the "weak girls" (several fragile EPs) experienced whom he had tried to protect. This recognition reassured him. Thereupon, I challenged him by asking whether he would also be courageous enough to engage in some brief crying. He consented under the condition that I would not laugh at him as he cried. "I'm not a sissy, you know." I promised him that I would not do that, and that I would be most impressed if he dared to hold the hands of "the ridiculous girls" for a minute while sharing the emotions that belonged to a traumatizing episode. Once he had cried for a minute he was much surprised that the fragile EPs he had depreciated so much were not angry with him or disappointed in him. In fact, they were happy and expressed their joy that he, like them, was able to experience and express fear and sadness.

Dissociative parts of the personality, then, tend to comprise several longings and associated strivings. Exceptions aside, they do not comprise a single biopsychosocial state but several states. Some even comprise multiple actual and possible states. Inasmuch as dissociative parts comprise more than one biopsychosocial state, it makes no sense to describe dissociative parts as 'dissociative states.' While 'dissociative state' is a common term in traumatology, it is actually quite imprecise and confusing.

Modes of Longing and Striving

Mental and behavioral states can also be described as *modes*. Since states (or modes) are guided by primary affectivity, they involve *modes of longing and striving*. 'Longing' stands for manifest needs and desires; 'striving' captures actions or passions to fulfill these longings. A mode of longing and striving, then, can be defined as an integrated, cohesive way of sensing, perceiving, feeling, thinking, remembering, and moving oriented toward the fulfillment of a particular need or desire, or constellation of various longings. (How [in]coherent and [in]efficient the involved actions are is a different matter.) Since mental and behavioral actions imply mental and behavioral contents (see footnote 13 in Chapter 24), modes of longing and striving imply particular feelings, desires, affects, perceptions, conceptions (thoughts, ideas), memories, and behaviors (see Figure 26.1).

Organisms can engage in different modes of longing and striving, sequentially or in parallel. Compatible urges generate synergistic modes of longing and striving (e.g., earning an income and play when work is playful) (see Figure 26.2). They imply harmonious perceptions, sensations, feelings, thoughts, memories, and behaviors. Ambivalences and polyvalences, however, entail contrary modes of longing and striving (Figure 26.3), hence conflicted mental and behavioral contents.

Figure 26.1. A visual metaphor for an organism's unambiguous mode of longing and striving.

Top area of the cone: The cone captures the idea that the actions of organisms are guided and coordinated by particular needs and desires. Such longing guides the organism's way and constitutes its systemic attractor (see text). The arrow indicates the direction of the organism's striving.
Contents of the cone: The organism's mental and behavioral 'contents': perceptions, physical and emotional affections, thoughts, memories, goal-directed movements.
Bottom of the cone: Actions guided by a particular need/desire. This includes the actions of perceiving, sensing physical and emotional affections, thinking, recalling, fantasizing, and moving in a goal-directed fashion (including speaking). The various actions form a synergetic cluster. Actions and contents are two aspects of the same thing (see footnote 17). For example, perceiving and perceptions are two sides of a coin.

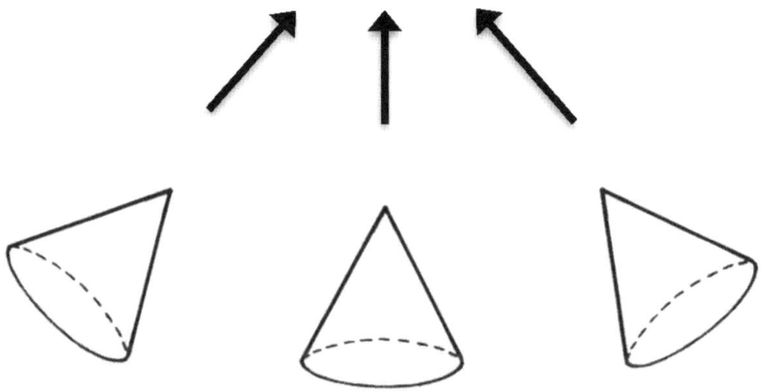

Figure 26.2. Synergistic modes of longing and striving.

Each cone represents a particular mode of striving in an organism-environment system. The top area of each cone represents a need/desire that guides the rest of the mode. The need/desire operates as a systemic attractor (see text). The bottom stands for the various integrative, cohesive actions that this need/desire brings forth (a cluster of actions involving perceiving, feeling, emoting, thinking, recalling, goal-oriented movement in the framework of the occurrent need/desire). The 'filling' of the cone stands for the mental and behavioral 'contents' (the perceptions, feelings, affects, thoughts, memories, and movements that the actions bring forth). The three cones are directed toward each other to depict three synergetic needs and desires, that is, synergetic modes of longing and striving. This organization (or an organization with some synergy and some counteraction) can pertain to an individual as a whole organism-environment system. It can also pertain to a dissociative part of this system.

In terms of dynamic systems theory (Colombetti, 2014; Thelen, 2005; Thelen & Smith, 1994), our various affective interests in ourselves and in our world operate as systemic attractors and repellers. Dynamic systems are systems that change the mode or phase they are in over time. They continuously shift between a limited number of phases that together constitute the system's *phase space.* The shifts from one phase to the next are not ran-

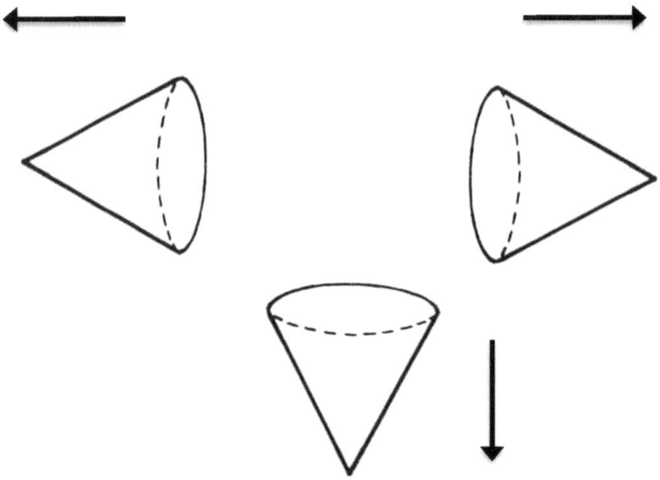

Figure 26.3. Counteracting modes of longing and striving.

The cones represent three contrary modes of longing and striving of an organism-environment system. The upper area of each cone represents a particular need/desire that guides the rest of the mode of functioning in the indicated direction. The organism's needs and desires operate as systemic attractors (see text). The bottom stands for the various integrative, cohesive actions that a particular need/desire brings forth (a cluster of actions involving perceiving, feeling, emoting, thinking, recalling, goal-directed movement in the framework of the need /desire). The 'filling' represents the mental and behavioral 'contents' (the perceptions, feelings, affects, thoughts, memories, and movements that the actions bring forth). The three cones point away from each other. This divergence depicts counteractive needs and desires, hence counteractive modes of longing and striving. Overall, the figure thus portrays a conflict among three needs and desires, a conflict between three different systemic attractors. The more powerful the conflict is, the more the individual will feel torn, will be desperate, will not know where to go. This organization (or an organization with some synergy and some counteraction) can pertain to an individual as a whole organism-environment system. It can also pertain to a dissociative part of this system.

dom, but rather tend to follow one or more *phase trajectories.* Together these different trajectories constitute the system's *phase portrait.* For the sake of consistency, I use the term 'mode' rather than the term 'phase,' so that the important terms here are *mode space, mode trajectory,* and *mode portrait.*

Attractors and Repellers

The system's mode space is guided by a smaller or larger set of mode variables, which essentially include one or more systemic *attractors* and *repellers* that powerfully influence the mode trajectories of a dynamic system. The singular or multiple attractors of a system are points or regions of the mode space toward which the system's mode trajectories tend to converge. Points or regions from which the system's mode trajectories are deflected are known as its repellers. Expressed in affective language, one might conveniently say that attractors are the modes that a dynamic system finds 'useful' – that it 'likes and seeks'; repellers are the modes a dynamic system tends to regard as useless or harmful – that it

Figure 26.4. Three examples of attractors and mode trajectories.

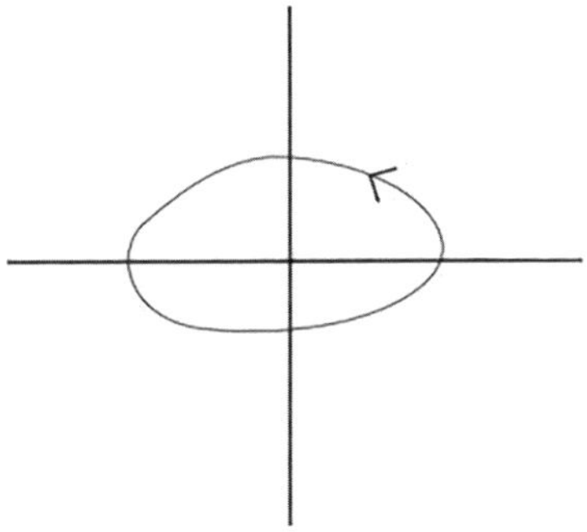

Figure 26.4.1. A mode trajectory perfectly following a limit-cycle attractor.

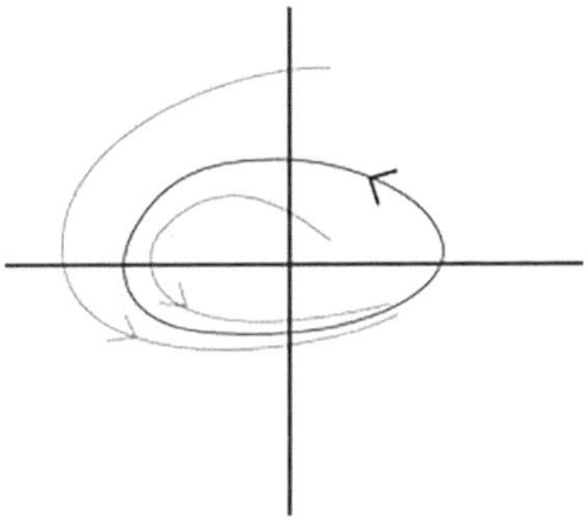

Figure 26.4.2. Two mode trajectories strongly influenced by a limit-cycle attractor.

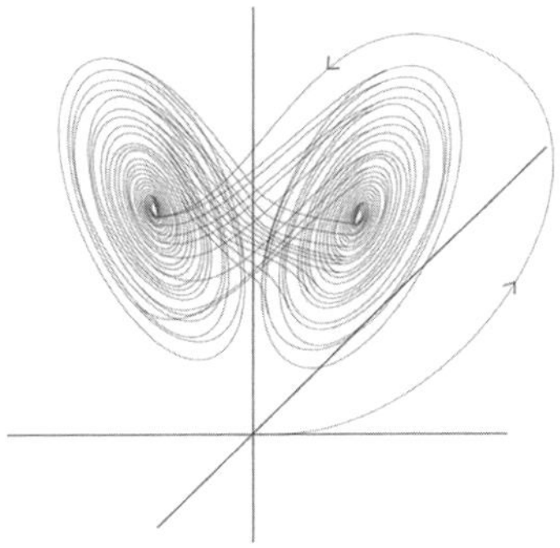

Figure 26.4.3. A mode trajectory guided by a strange attractor.

'dislikes and avoids.' What dynamic systems 'like and seek' is 'significant-good' to them; what they 'dislike and avoid' is 'insignificant-worthless' to them at its best and at worst 'significant-bad.'

There are various types of attractors and repellers. A fixed-point attractor is a point in a mode toward which any mode trajectory sooner or later (re)turns. For example, no matter where and how forcefully one thrusts a metal ball that hangs at the end of a rope, it will always return to the single deepest point as defined by gravity. In this case, the mode trajectory always leads to the same mode inasmuch as other forces do not affect it. This is the system's 'preferred mode' or final mode. A limit-cycle attractor is a recurrent mode trajectory encompassing two or more different points or regions of a dynamic system's mode space. Figure 26.4.1 shows a perfect limit-cycle attractor and Figure 26.4.2 mode trajectories that approach this perfection. The four seasons constitute a well-known meteorological example of a limit-cycle attractor. Systems may also go through a more complex series of modes such as the metabolism of a cell. Some systems comprise a wide set of modes that become manifest along a highly complex mode trajectory in their occurrent mode space. Mathematically these systems are guided by 'strange' attractors and have a fractal structure (i.e., a structure that displays self-similarity on all scales of its manifestation; see http:/en.wikipedia.org/wiki/Attractor). Figure 26.4.3 provides an example of a system guided by a strange attractor.

Mode Trajectories

The living system's mode portrait entails an 'endless' mode trajectory or succession of systemic states. The involved modes and trajectories may, at first sight, appear random, but in fact they entail a particular pattern within a particular mode space. Further, the modes and trajectories are similar yet never quite the same. This variability is expressed in the term 'dynamic.' As Thelen (2005, p. 262) puts it, "dynamic means that the state of the system at any time depends on its previous states and is the starting point for future states." Qualitative changes of a system's mode portrait are described as *bifurcations* or *mode transitions.* They may evolve following smaller or larger changes in the value of the variables that guide the system and its modes of longing and striving.

While organisms are in constant flux, they also include a degree of dynamic stability. For example, walking and speaking are relatively stable features of healthy persons. Many forms of psychopathology include undue stability (and dominance) of at least some modes of longing and striving as well as of at least some mode trajectories. For example, phobic individuals consistently fear and avoid particular signs. ANPs consistently fear and avoid EPs, traumatic memories, and other trauma-related signs. Controlling EPs consistently seek power and strive to avoid feelings of helplessness. This stability becomes pathological when it does not serve the patient's best interests and options. In this sense, enactive trauma therapy is the effort to destabilize unduly stable modes and mode trajectories in order to invite and encourage patients to reorganize themselves. This self-reorganization relates to the therapeutic development of new actions (including skills).

Thelen (2005, p. 259–260) offers a beautiful metaphor for human experience, behavior, and development which conveys the above abstract ideas in a more tangible and accessible form. I quote her at length:

> I suggest [a] metaphor for human behavior: a mountain stream. This is an apt comparison to keep in mind because a stream is moving all the time in a continuous flow and continuous change. Development is continuous – whatever has happened in the past influences what happens in the future. But the stream also has patterns. We can see whirlpools, eddies, and water-

falls, places where the water is moving rapidly and places where it is still. Like the stream, development also has recognizable patterns: milestones and plateaus and ages and stages at which behavior is quite predictable. In the mountain stream, there are no programs or instructions constructing those patterns. Just water and the streambed lie under it. The patterns arise from the water and natural parts of the stream and the environment, such as the streambed, the rocks, the flow of the water, the current temperature and wind. The patterns reflect not just the immediate conditions of the stream, however; they also reflect the history of the whole system, including the snowfall on the mountain last winter, the conditions on the mountain last summer, and indeed the entire geological history of the region, which determined the incline of the stream and its path through the mountain. In addition, the stream also carves the rocks and the soil and creates its own environment, which then constrains and directs the water. It is not possible to say what directly causes what because the whole system is so mutually embedded and interdependent. Development also has these system properties. How a child behaves depends not only on the immediate current situation but also on his or her continuous short- and longer-term history of acting, the social situation, and the biological constraints he or she was born with. Every action has within it the traces of previous behavior. The child's behavior, in turn, sculpts his or her environment, creating new opportunities and constraints.

Dissociative Parts Include Various Modes of Longing and Striving

The way enactivism and dynamic system theory views 'normal' and 'abnormal' human experience, thought, behavior, and development offers a perspective that leads psychology away from stimulus-response or information-processing models of mind – or, for that matter, away from gene-ruled, materialistic perspectives[2]. The core idea is that healthy individuals flexibly enact meaning under the influence of a complex set of attractors, repellers, and other systemic features (e.g., their history, *umwelt*, body, genes). Healthy individuals enact a self, a world, and a self as an intrinsic part of this world that maximize the reception of what is useful (significant-good) to them, and that minimize the reception of what is harmful (significant-bad) or useless (insignificant) to them. On the contrary, individuals with trauma-related disorders and mentally ill individuals in general enact a self, a world, and a self as an intrinsic part of this world that unduly limit their profits, unduly increase their losses, and lead them to invest time and effort in something useless.

The mode space of traumatized individuals is too limited and their mode trajectories are too inflexible. Guided by conflicting attractors and repellers, these individuals are unable to integrate; they recurrently jump from one nonintegrated mode to the next. Each

---

2 Organisms including man require genes, but environmentally isolated genes are unable to work in any way. They can only exert their effects as inherent parts of an organism-environment system. A meta-analysis of twin studies suggests that the influence from genes and environment ('nature-nurture') lies at about 50%–50% (Polderman et al., 2015). Moreover, there is no one-to-one relationship between single genes or even groups of genes and the human mind, human behavior, and human dispositions. For a discussion, see Ross, 2014b, 2014c.

of these modes encompasses its particular kind of rather integrated and hence cohesive perceptions, sensations, feelings, emotions, thoughts, memories, and behaviors. Moreover, dissociative parts enact their own phenomenal idea of who they are. Traumatized individuals alternate between a variety of modes of longing and striving within dissociative parts as well as between the dissociative parts of their personality. These shifts or bifurcations among dissociative parts involve more than mode transitions: They concern transitions of the very ideas of who and what they are, what the world is like, and how they relate to this world.

As mentioned above, prototypical dissociative parts are strongly influenced by particular interests and the associated action systems. The core attractors of ANPs concern the pursuit of the 'goodies' of daily life. The main attractor of fragile EPs is to defend their physical existence in one way or another. They may also cry for individuals to whom they feel attached. Controlling EPs are attracted to control beyond anything else and wish to dominate in the service of self-determination.

However, these various prototypical dissociative parts can also comprise other needs and desires, hence other modes of longing and striving. Some of these modes may be synergetic. For example, the needs and desires of ANPs to eat can (but need not) be synergistic with their need and desire for social contact. Their pursuit of interests of daily life generally combines well with their striving to evade EPs, traumatic memories, and other trauma-related signals that are repellers for them. The mode space of ANPs may include these various *synergistic modes of longing and striving.*

Dissociative parts can also encompass *contrary modes of longing and striving.* They can include ambivalences (two contrasting needs and desires) or even polyvalences (more than two opposing needs and desires). As Spinoza (1677a, Part III, Proposition 17) proposed, "[i]f we image a thing which usually affects us with an affect of sadness is like another which usually affects us with an equally great affect of joy, we shall hate it and at the same time love it." For example, guided by a need for attachment (one attractor), as an ANP abused and maltreated children may experience an urge to approach a perpetrating parent. However, guided by the need of physical and psychological safety (another attractor), they tend to avoid that very individual when he or she constitutes a repeller. These two needs of the child – feeling attracted to the parent and being repelled by the parent – are incompatible and counteracting. Together, they constitute a deep approach – avoidance conflict that can also be described as an attractor (attachment)-attractor (safety) conflict. Often described as 'disorganized attachment,' this alternating of longing and striving for attachment and longing and striving for detachment actually involves *an organization* of contrary needs and desires regarding adults who, for whatever reason, fail to meet the child's essential longing for secure caretaking, guidance to navigate intense affects, and love (see also Liotti, in press a, in press b). These conflicting modes of longing and striving can (but need not) exist within one dissociative part.

By way of illustration, it may be helpful to reiterate what happened to Ineke, a 50-year-old woman with DID when she wanted to say farewell to her dying father (ToT Volume

II, Chapter 20, p. 523; Ineke also features in Chapters 31 and 35). By this time, she had already been in treatment with me for 5 years. Among other things, the therapy had addressed chronic interfamilial emotional neglect, emotional abuse, physical maltreatment, and bizarre punishment as well as extrafamilial sexual abuse. In full contrast to several EPs, as the main ANP Ineke had no recollection of, and indeed long did not want to recollect, that her father had sexually abused her for many years. More recently, however, she had started to recognize and acknowledge this component of her traumatization.

Severely emotionally and physically neglected and abused by her mother (see Chapters 32 and 35), as the main ANP Ineke badly needed her father's acceptance of her as a good person (an attractor in the framework of attachment). This acceptance would give her "the right to exist." She also hoped that he would acknowledge what several EPs kept telling and showing her – something she had slowly started to acknowledge herself after decades of motivated ignorance: frequent incestuous abuse that had started when she was four and that had lasted until she was 17.

Her father recurrently ignored Ineke's careful attempts to bring up the subject, or he quickly changed the topic of their conversation. As this pattern continued, Ineke became ever more confused and despondent. She had to run from the agonizing situation (an attractor in the framework of defense). The best solution she could think of was to kiss her father on his forehead before fleeing. The action was an effort to coordinate the need for attachment and the urge to defend herself from further harm. But when she bent forward to do this, her father took her head, kissed her fully on the mouth, and worked his tongue inside. As ANP and with several EPs, Ineke ran from the hospital. After several desperate hours, she managed to call me for help. It took considerable effort to prevent a(nother) dissociative psychotic episode, that is, an episode in which one or more bewildered fragile EPs become totally dominant for several days or an even longer stretch of time. One of these dissociative psychotic phases had followed when her mother had died without any reconciliation.

A Common Mode Trajectory of ANPs

The case example above illustrates that the mode space of an ANP can include emotional, mental, and behavioral modes of longing and striving. This emotionality of ANPs is not exceptional. A common mode trajectory is that a more or less depersonalized and numb ANP is sometimes intruded on by modes of longing and striving of one or more fragile and/or controlling EPs. The intrusions may be such that the ANP involved becomes emotional, which happens when the ANP is scared of, detested by, or angry at voices, utterances, and images of the EPs. It also happens that the ANP, along with one or more EPs, reenacts a traumatic memory. The ANP commonly does not long and strive to integrate the EPs and their sensations, perceptions, emotions, thoughts, fantasies, memories, and behaviors. His or her next common mode of longing and striving is thus to get rid of and forget about the intrusions as soon as possible. Inasmuch as this passionate action succeeds, the ANP reverts to the modes of longing and striving that concern the dissociative part's interests of daily life.

Schematically, a common mode trajectory of prototypical ANPs and its limit cycle attractors and repellers runs as follows:

1. Prototypical ANPs prefer to engage in modes of longing and striving that concern functioning in daily life (sleep, eat, drink, play, explore, etc.).
2. These 'daily life' modes are intimately associated with the synergistic mode of longing and striving to avoid EPs and their mental and behavioral contents.
3. When EPs nonetheless intrude on ANPs, ANPs engage in a mode of desperate longing and striving to escape these EPs and their mental and behavioral contents. The intrusion may occur when the mental energy and mental efficiency of ANPs are too low to ignore or otherwise avoid the EPs, and/or when the ANPs are not sufficiently distracted by work, raising children, social engagements, and the like. Intrusions, for example, are more likely when the ANP is tired at night from work and the ongoing effort to evade EPs. The risk of intrusions also increases when one or more EPs perceive powerful reminders (signs) of traumatic memories and become strongly (re-)activated.
4. Avoidance on the part of the ANPs may include substitute actions such as drinking, using medications or other drugs, self-mutilation, or loss of consciousness. An extreme evasion lies in the full or nearly full deactivation of the ANP (see Chapter 33).
5. When one or more EPs intrude on ANPs and the involved ANPs mental avoidance falters, the ANPs become emotional and may join the emotionality of the intruding EPs. This emotionality can involve or include the reenactment of one or more traumatic memories.
6. When the substitute actions are successful and/or when the emotionality/reenactment of traumatic memories is over, prototypical ANPs revert to interests of daily life described in #1. They also revert to #2. The implication is that they do not integrate the EPs and the heavy load these dissociative parts include.

Possible Emotional Features of ANP

Even though prototypical ANPs are more or less depersonalized and emotionally numbed, they can sometimes be emotional. ANPs may be scared, irritated, frustrated, angry, ashamed, disgusted, or jealous. They may also reenact traumatic relationships. These mood shifts and emotionally charged reenactments do not define them as EPs or as 'mixtures of ANPs and EPs.' What defines ANPs as ANPs is that their *primary* affectivity, their *primary* attractors concern the needs and desires of daily life. In this context, their *primary* repellers are EPs, traumatic memories, and other trauma-related signs. The *primary* affectivity of EPs concerns efforts to survive traumatizing events by engaging in mammalian defenses including attachment cry (fragile EPs) or by engaging in interpersonal control (controlling EPs).

One or more fragile EPs, controlling EPs, other ANPs, or still other kinds of dissociative parts (e.g., suicidal ones) can intrude on a particular ANP, just as this ANP can intrude on these other dissociative parts. A general description of dissociative intrusions is that they involve modes of longing and striving of one or more dissociative parts that consciously or subconsciously affect one or more other dissociative parts. Intrusions thus imply a mode transition for the ANP that is intruded on. The transition runs:

1. from being focused on daily life concern and simultaneous effortful avoidance of trauma-related experiences and conceptions,
2. to being intruded on and reenacting,
3. and then back to #1.

This mode trajectory can perhaps be captured in terms of the strange attractor pattern depicted in Figure 26.4.3. Inasmuch as intruded ANPs are consciously aware of the intrusions, they may not only experience and conceive of the contents of the intrusive modes; they may also experience and conceive of them as phenomena belonging to "someone" or "something" else. Relating to "someone else that intruded on me" involves a second-person perspective ("I – other subject" relationship). Relating to "something that intrudes on me" comprises a third-person perspective ("I – object" relationship). The experienced and known "someone else" or "something else" commonly concern one or more EPs. (In the observer's eye the intrusions evidently belong to the whole patient as a first-person.)

Under the influence of powerful intrusions, ANPs may join EPs to reenact traumatic memories or relationships. In this case, they phenomenally experience and conceive of traumatic memories and relational reenactments in the first-person perspective. This emotional commonality need not, and often does not, lead to a permanent integration of ANPs (i.e., synthesis, personification, presentification, symbolization, and realization) of the traumatic memory, the involved EPs, or the traumatizing relational pattern[3]. In this case, the ANP(s) and EP(s) only have a mode of longing and striving in common for a restricted period of time. Following the intrusions – as indicated above – ANPs commonly engage in another profound mode transition that includes a redissociation of the traumatic memory and the associated EPs.

The theoretical claim (or fact) that ANPs have dissociated particular traumatic memories and relational patterns does not imply the claim (or fact) that they have dissociated *all* memories of terrible experiences. ANPs may include modes in which they recollect memories of terrible events they have never dissociated or no longer dissociate. This applies inasmuch as they consistently experience and conceive these modes as their own.

Further, recollecting adverse experiences and facts can move ANPs. Whereas the memory can be emotional for them, this emotionality need not be abnormal. Anyone can become emotional when recollecting painful life events.

---

3 The more ANPs engage in these integrative actions (synthesis, personification, etc.), the less they qualify as an ANP – and the more the patient becomes a healthy personality.

Some mentally healthy individuals or psychiatric patients readily talk about 'a part of them.' This does not mean that they experience, perceive, and conceive of this 'part' as a dissociative part of their personality. Rather, they may use the term 'part' as a figure of speech or as a synonym for a particular mood or interest. When the issue is explored, it commonly becomes obvious that the involved individuals experience and conceive of the 'part' as an inherent 'part' of their first-person perspective.

In such cases, the phrase 'part of me' pertains to a particular mode of longing and striving. It does not reflect any *serious* sense of the word '(dissociative) part.' Real dissociative parts are defined as subsystems of an individual's personality which essentially include their own phenomenal experiences and conceptions of self, world, and their self as a part of this world (Nijenhuis & Van der Hart, 2011a, 2011b; ToT Volume II, Chapter 12 and 13; Chapter 21, Propositions 119–127. See also Appendix 2). Modes of longing and striving need not be associated with dissociative parts, and thus defined, at all.

To prevent confusion, clinicians and researchers should also better avoid talking about '(dissociative) parts' when they actually do not have real dissociative parts in mind but (perhaps contrary) modes of longing and striving. They should also better avoid using phrases like 'ANP and EP mixtures' when they mean to express that an ANP includes quite emotional modes of longing and striving, or that an EP includes modes of longing and striving that pertain to daily life interests.

In conclusion, ANPs and EPs may and often do include and alternate between different modes of longing and striving (e.g., moods, emotions, and relational patterns) which they experience and regard as their own. In the case of ANPs, the modes involved may include emotional feelings or emotional memories. These emotions may pertain to a variety of events, including adverse life events. In the case of EPs, the modes may concern interests of daily life. The modes of longing and striving involved do not qualify as dissociative parts inasmuch as they do not involve their own phenomenal conception of self and world. Further, ANPs and EPs can have modes of longing and striving in common, either temporarily or permanently. Temporary intrusions of an EP on an ANP (or an ANP on an EP) should not lead clinicians to say that the ANP has features of an EP (or the EP features of an ANP).

A case example may better clarify the issue of ANPs with emotional features. Chronically traumatized by her mother and many men from her early childhood onward, Sonja developed DID. Her case was described in ToT Volume II, Chapter 12, p. 317, and briefly reintroduced in Chapter 22. It is detailed more in Chapters 33 and 37. Sonja became pregnant from her stepfather when she was 15 years old. She included a strong-willed ANP. However, the pregnancy, traumatic childbirth, and daily confrontations with her daughter implied more suffering than this courageous ANP could take. In this context, the patient developed a dissociative part that referred to herself as The Helper.

The Helper grew to become the mother of the child in the common sense of the word. She primarily encompassed several daily life modes of longing and striving that included attachment to her daughter. But whereas she positively cared for the daughter, The Helper was physically rather anesthetic. Her touch was not delicate, and she moved briskly. The Helper's proprioceptive and kinesthetic anesthesia negatively affected the mother-daughter relationship. The anesthesias related to the fact that this brave ANP also carried the load and memories of the stepfather's rapes, the pregnancy, and the childbirth. She recollected these events and could talk about them in an organized way. Whereas The Helper had clear emotional features, she did not constitute an EP. For example, she did not reenact the rapes, pregnancy, and traumatic childbirth. Calling The Helper a mixture of ANP and EP would therefore be a mistake. She was a brave and emotionally sensitive helping ANP with several physical anesthesias. She had integrated horrible events within her autonomous existence which Sonja as ANP, the dissociative part that The Helper strongly supported, had yet to integrate (see Chapter 37).

To sum up, dissociative parts of the personality may and commonly do encompass several needs and desires. Each need and desire entails a particular mode of longing and striving, that is, each includes a particular cohesive cluster of perceptions, physical and affective feelings, thoughts, memories, and movements (behaviors). Inasmuch as dissociative parts personify these modes, they experience them as their own. Some of their modes of longing and striving may be more dominant than others, and dissociative parts can alternate between their various modes. This alternation can be viable and creative. However, dissociative parts can be in conflict with themselves inasmuch as two or more different needs and desires are contrary and strong. In this case, they experience ambivalences or polyvalences and comprise a lack of integration of different modes of longing and striving.

This integrative deficit does meet the criteria for dissociation. 'Integrative deficits' and 'dissociation' are not synonyms.

Lack of Integration and Dissociation: Related but Different Concepts

Dissociation of the personality involves a lack of integration, though not all kinds of integrative deficiency constitute a form of dissociation[4]. The following conceptualization may be helpful to develop a clear understanding of the matter:

---

4 Many authors on trauma-related dissociation do not define the concept or regard a confusingly large variety of phenomena as dissociative. This liberal understanding entails conceptual inconsistencies. Overly broad concepts are useless, and internal consistency is a prominent requirement of a good theory (see ToT Volume II, Chapters 12 and 13). Ross (2014a) as well as Schimmenti and Caretti (2014) formulated several comments on what Ross regards as unresolved problems of the theory of structural dissociation. Ross feels that it makes no sense to formulate minimal constraints on the concept of dissociation. In the light of the above and because is clear from the present section and from ToT as a whole, I respectfully disagree. My specific rejoinder to Ross' objection (Nijenhuis, 2015) is included as Appendix 2. My full rebuttal can be freely accessed at http://www.fioriti.it/riviste/pdf/1/Ellert.pdf

It can be said that *God or Nature* constitutes a perfect integration of every possible mode of matter, mind, or any other attribute of this singular existing substance. (Nature is likely to include many other attributes than mankind knows, Spinoza [1677a] intuited.) *Human mental health* does not come anywhere close to this perfection. Every individual encompasses a multitude of modes of longing and striving, and in this sense conflicting needs and desires. And everyone fails to integrate these at times. However, mentally healthy individuals more or less manage to navigate or resolve these kinds of conflicts, which do not cause major suffering and/or significant dysfunction. As a result, their actions are largely viable and creative.

In *common forms of psychopathology* such as phobias (which are not part and parcel of a dissociative disorder), interest in defense has become unduly dominant. Under the influence of the defense action system, phobic individuals fear and avoid situations that they would in fact love to enter into. For example, individuals with agoraphobia would love to go shopping or meet friends – if they only weren't so scared. Attachment-phobic individuals long to have a secure relationship, but are too scared to commit themselves. Conflicting needs and desires usually belong to different action systems. In agoraphobia, there is a conflict between defense and social engagement (social contacts) and play (going out to have fun) or exploration ("How is this year's fashion?"). In attachment phobia, the conflict is basically between the action system of defense (avoidance of intimate relationships) and the attachment action system (engagement in intimate relationships). These conflicts do not involve conflicts between dissociative parts inasmuch as there are no different phenomenal selves that personify the involved pathological or other modes of longing and striving. In other words, individuals who alternate between pathological and other modes of longing and striving do not have a dissociative disorder when these modes are associated with one overarching phenomenal sense and conception of self. Rather, individuals have a dissociative disorder when they consist of modes or clusters of modes that include their own phenomenal sense and conception of self, world, and self as a part of this world. The distinction follows from the definition of dissociation (Nijenhuis & Van der Hart, 2011a, 2011b; ToT Volume II, Chapters 12–14).

Failing to make this distinction means *practically any form of psychopathology could be a dissociative disorder.* This practice would empty the dissociation concept of any meaning. It is thus important to adhere to a concept of dissociation that is clear and distinct, and that is not a huge transcendental concept "like Being, Thing, and Something" (Spinoza, 1677, p. 56). As Spinoza explained, transcendental terms

> arise from the fact that the human body, being limited, is capable of forming distinctly only a certain number of images at the same time . . . If that number is exceeded, the images will begin to be confused, and if the number of images the body is capable of forming distinctly in itself at once is greatly exceeded, they will all be completely confused with one another. (p. 56)

Max Weber (1904/1949, pp. 72–80; cited in Hodgson and Knudson, 2010) similarly held that "the most general laws" are "the least valuable." "The more comprehensive the validity – or scope – of a term, the more it leads us away from the richness of reality . . ." and from the task of explaining the phenomenon in question. Oliver Williamson (1995, p. 33) put it like this: "There is . . . a grave problem with broad, elastic and plausible concepts . . . Concepts that explain everything explain nothing."

In what are often called '*ego-state disorders*,' there are recurrent conflicts between two or more opposing needs and desires, the implied contrary action systems and modes of longing and striving. The term 'ego-state' is not satisfactory. For one, it is unclear what exactly the term 'ego' stands for. Second, 'ego-states' as presented in the literature include far more than a phenomenal conception of self (if that is what 'ego' is supposed to mean). Third, an 'ego-state' in fact commonly comprises several 'states.' The term is better abandoned.

According to the present analysis, an 'ego-state' concerns an insufficiently integrated mode of longing and striving of an organism-environment system that nonetheless experiences and conceives *one single* phenomenal self. That is, an individual (say his name is Peter) remains Peter in his own eyes despite his profoundly shifting moods and interests. In the light of these concerns, a more precise and fitting term for 'ego-state' is 'nonintegrated mode of longing and striving.' Disorders of this nature involve two or more dominant, but recurrently opposing modes of longing and striving. Shifts between them involve mode transitions, not transitions between different dissociative parts.

In the present analysis, those dissociative disorders that include posttraumatic stress disorder (PTSD; American Psychiatric Association, 2013; see ToT Volumes I and II) are disorders comprising two or more dissociative parts of the personality. To repeat, dissociative parts are *per definitionem* conscious and self-conscious subsystems of an individual's personality as a whole organism-environment system (see ToT Volume II, Chapters 12 and 13).

The order of integration and lack of integration can briefly be portrayed as follows (Table 26.1):

Table 26.1. Degrees of separation.

Phenomenon	Degree of integration
1. God or Nature.	Perfect integration.
2. Mental health.	Largely integrated modes of longing and striving. One phenomenal conception of self.
3. Common forms of psychopathology that do not meet the criteria for a dissociative disorder.	Undue dominance of one need and desire (or constellation of these), its implied mode(s) of longing and striving, and its implied action system or constellation of action systems. This dominance occurs at the expense of other modes longing and striving and the implied interests of action systems. Examples include phobias, obsessive-compulsive disorders, and eating disorders. One phenomenal conception of self.

4. Forms of psychopathology that involve recurrent conflicts between different needs and desires.	Recurrent conflicts between two or more contrary powerful modes of longing and striving. One phenomenal conception of self.
5. Dissociative disorders.	Division of the personality into two or more dissociative parts. Each of these parts can include problems at the level of #2, #3, and #4. Each dissociative part includes his or her own phenomenal conceptions of self, world, and self as related to this world.

Chapter 27

Traumatized Individuals and Their Dissociative Parts: Autonomous Centers of Action and Passion

> *... besides characterizing the nervous system's operation as a closed network, we need to characterize its performance in its structural coupling with the rest of the body (and the environment). Similarly, to characterize the organism as a finite cellular or multicellular entity, we need to characterize it as an organizationally and operationally closed system. At the same time, we need to characterize the organism's performance or behavior in its structural coupling with the environment.*
> *... there is no inconsistency between characterizing the nervous system and organism as autonomous and emphasizing their somatic and environmental embeddedness.*
> Evan Thompson (2007, p. 51)

Traumatized individuals and dissociative parts of their personality meet the criteria for and operate[1] as *autonomous systems.* This feature further distinguishes dissociative parts from 'modes of longing and striving.' The distinction is theoretically, scientifically, and clinically useful.

Autonomous Systems

Systems are autonomous when their constituent operations or actions "(i) recursively depend on each other for their generation and their realization as a network, (ii) constitute a system as a unity in whatever domain they exist, and (iii) determine a domain of possible interactions with the environment" (Thompson, 2007, p. 44; Varela, 1979, p. 55; see also Thompson et al., 2005).

ad (i). Autonomous systems are *operational unities.* They include a network of constitutive and self-maintaining operations that are heavily dependent on each other. Each constitu-

1 In the present text, the term 'operation' denotes mental or behavioral goal-oriented endeavors that organisms unconsciously, preconsciously, or consciously engage in. A synonym of 'operation' is 'action.' I frequently use the latter term, particularly but not exclusively when the operation includes conscious awareness. In this spirit, the verb 'to act' stands for an organism's mental and behavioral endeavor to achieve a particular goal or set of related and convergent goals.

tive operation is a component of a network of such operations; otherwise, it would become extinguished, just as without this network the system as a whole could not constitute and maintain itself (Di Paolo, 2009, p. 16; Varela, 1997). That is, autonomous systems and their various elements operate under fragile, *precarious conditions* (Colombetti, 2014, p. 16; Di Paolo, 2009, p. 16). This characteristic is intimately linked with the second characteristic of such systems.

ad (ii). Autonomous systems are *operational unities across environmental domains, time, and place*. Examples include living singular cells and multicellular organisms, nervous systems as well as entire ecosystems (Varela, 1979; Varela & Bourgine, 1991). These systems generate and regenerate the unity they are irrespective of internal variations (e.g., state shifts) and external alterations (e.g., changes of temperature, time, place, social conditions). This certainly does not mean that they comprise a network of fixed operations. On the contrary, they are viable and creative dynamic centers of self-generating and self-maintaining action.

As Varela (1997) put it, autonomous systems fundamentally involve the action of constituting an *identity*. The terms 'self' and 'identity' are intended here in a general sense and do not refer to an individual's personal identity. Rather, Varela wished to express that the systems involved operate as a unity *despite* changing internal and external conditions. This general identity, thus, does not denote a static entity but a dynamic structure. The classic analogy of a river, introduced in the previous chapter, may help: Although each river and its environment are in continuous flux, a river still preserves its general identity. Otherwise, it becomes a different thing, say, a lake, a part of a desert, or a perpetual glacier. In many cases, the continued existence of an organism as an identity, 'self,' or 'subject' is actually dependent on recurrent change: *Plus ça change, plus c'est la même chose.*

Identity exists at different levels of organization and development. At some level, it begins to include a phenomenal 'I' that can be verbalized (cf. ToT Volume II, Chapter 12). The levels that Varela (1991, p. 80) distinguished include

> (1) a minimal or cellular unity; (2) a bodily self in its immunological foundations; (3) a cognitive perceptuo-motor self; associated to animal behaviour; (4) a socio-linguistic 'I' of subjectivity, and (5) the collective social multi-individual totality. In all these regions we are dealing with levels and processes where an identity comes about not as substance but as movement and whose fabric of organisation is the organism.

With respect to (4) and (5) in this quote, Jonas (1966, 1973) like Varela argues that "even the paradoxes of human existence, which oscillates between autonomy and necessity, stem from the making up of organic identity by metabolism" (Weber, 2002, p. 17). There may thus be a continuity of 'self' in the sense of general identity from the simplest to the most complex organism-*umwelt*[2] systems.

---

2 I use the terms 'organism-environment system' and 'organism-*umwelt* system' synonymously.

Generating and maintaining themselves in action as a subject, autonomous systems generate and sustain borders as well as links between themselves and their environment on which they are co-dependent as their object. They thus generate and maintain an identity as well as dialogical couplings with their *umwelt*. This *umwelt* is the world as they experience and know it from their perspective. It is the world that is of significance and value to them (see iii below). Their identity and dialogical couplings with this *umwelt* entail a point of reference for autonomous systems' other actions (Weber & Varela, 2002).

ad (iii) As Weber (2002, p. 25) puts it, "[t]he living body in its existential concerns is the interpretant of the *umwelt*'s signs." This dense statement expresses that autonomous systems constitute organism-environment systems involving a relativity of subject and object. As autonomous systems, organisms are the source of their own activity, and their actions are primarily guided by their interest in their own existence and survival. In this sense, they *lay down their own affect-laden cognitive domains as well as their domains of possible mental and behavioral interaction with the environment.* Autonomous organism-environment systems specify their *umwelt* – their world of significance; they interpret what components of their environment are useful (significant-good), useless (insignificant), or harmful (significant-bad) to them (Chapter 25). By coupling themselves with this *umwelt* on which they are co-dependent, they make meaning. Merleau-Ponty (1966, p. 377) thus asserted the following:

> [a]n object ... is not really *given* in perception, but experienced and internally constructed insofar as it belongs to a world, whose basal structures we find in ourselves and of which it represents only one of the possible concretations.

Meaning-making is not a fixed action: It is dynamic, multifaceted, selective, and context-dependent. Nature, 'the world' of which any form of life is an inherent part, includes endless features and properties (Spinoza, 1677a). As autonomous systems, living organisms only experience, know, and show an affective interest in some of these features and properties, and not in a host of others.

Apart from this restriction, their interest is not static. It shifts in at least some regards as they change their state or mode of longing and striving, as they mature and develop. For example, thirsty infants interpret themselves and their environment in other ways than sleepy infants or infants who are eager to play. And what attracts an infant may be insignificant to a toddler. It may even repel an adolescent.

This biopsychosocial and developmental semiotic[3] perspective is very different from the idea that organisms (including animals and human beings) operate "as transducers of inputs or functions for converting input instructions into output products" (Thompson et al., 2005, p. 43–44). Being autonomous systems, organisms do not react to 'inputs'

3 Semiotics is the philosophy and science of signs and symbols, the discipline that studies meaning making. See ToT Volume I, Chapter 9.

or 'process information.' Led by their very nature, they in fact generate, sustain, and modify their *umwelt* even as they generate, maintain, and modify themselves. In their ongoing signification they specify a self, a world as well as couplings between the two, allowing and supporting possible and worthwhile couplings.

This does not mean that autonomous systems 'invent' the world. Different from philosophical idealism and constructivism, the world is not merely their idea, because autonomous systems do not and could not exist in environmental emptiness (cf. Chapters 23, 27, and 28 as well as ToT Volumes I & II). Autonomous systems exist as part of nature. As discussed above, subjects and their objects, which clearly includes other subjects, are co-constitutive. The two are also co-dependent. How the world is and how it appears to them is defined by the subject and the object alike. Objects are in any practical and empirical sense constituted by subjects, and subjects can only exist because there is a wider world that affects them (Northoff, 2003; ToT Volumes I & II). Objects exist for a subject, just as a subject exists in virtue of a relationship to objects. Further, both change all the time. In perpetual movement, subjects and their objects are dynamic, and so are their couplings. Finally, subjects and their objects are co-occurrent in that they necessarily occur together.

In this framework of subject-object co-occurrence, co-dependency, and co-constitution, autonomous systems *specify a domain of possible couplings with themselves and their umwelt.* In Maturana's (1980, p. 11) words, "for every living system its organization implies a prediction of a niche, and the niche thus predicted as a domain of classes of interaction constitutes its entire cognitive reality." This world comprises "... all the interactions[4] in which an [autonomic] system can enter without loss of identity ..." (Maturana & Varela, 1980, p. 136).

---

4 It might have been better to use the term 'coupling' here. An organism-environment system does not comprise an interacting individual and an organism that exist or could exist separate from each other. It seems quite probable that Varela would have rejected the idea of the interaction of subjects and objects as if they were separate systems from the time he started to regard what he called the knotty dialectic of subjects and objects, of individuals and their *umwelt* (see Chapter 24). To further elucidate the point, it can be helpful to compare two statements, one by Weber and one by Järvilehto. Weber (2002, p. 16) writes, "[a]s a visible expression of this dialectical linkage (or 'coupling'), organisms are contained within a material border: a cuticle, a skin, a shell etc., which is at the same time a product of the organism and its limit to the exterior. One could nearly say: Organisms are prima facie an act of constant self-separation from the surroundings." Järvilehto (2000a, p. 38–39) replies, "It is precisely here that we come to the basic difference between the inanimate and living systems: A cell as a system is not limited to its membrane, the border between the cell and environment, but it extends as a functional unit into the environment. The membrane of the living system is not a line of separation, but rather connects the inner parts of the cell with selected parts of the environment. The membrane is an organ of connection, not just a cover as in the case of the surface of the watch. The cell is, in fact, bound to its environment, to its indefinite and changing parts, in such a complex way that we may no more see these connections, and the cell therefore seems to be independent, separated from the environment. However, the cell is continuously growing into the environment and connects to constantly new environmental parts." In my view, the membrane constraints autonomous systems from their *umwelt* as well as connects autonomous systems and their *umwelt* without which not a

As autonomous systems, the actions of organisms encompass more than mere signification; they also engage and must engage in the action of 'insignification' (see also Chapter 25), which, as discussed above, is as important as the action of signification, because there exist a host of 'things' that for a particular organism are generally – or for its present state or context – insignificant (i.e., useless, inconsequential, irrelevant). For example, when individuals concentrate, they assign real meaning to some phenomena and simultaneously less meaning (or no meaning at all) to many other phenomena. Their ability to discriminate between what counts, what counts less, and what does not count at all is highly viable. The reverse also holds: The inability to make these distinctions is maladaptive. For example, individuals with obsessions and compulsive behaviors have major troubles in this regard: They signify the insignificant, engaging in useless thoughts and behaviors while neglecting matters that are in fact of real importance to them.

Traumatized Individuals and Their Dissociative Parts: Autonomous Systems

Traumatized individuals as well as the dissociative parts they consist of meet the three criteria for autonomous systems formulated above.

ad (i). They meet the first criterion of autonomous systems in that their ongoing constituent operations recursively depend on each other for their generation and their realization as a network of actions (or substitute actions) and passions. Being interested in themselves, traumatized individuals as whole systems and as each of their conscious and self-conscious dissociative parts entertain a repertoire of recurrent, related actions and passions. These actions and passions serve to constitute and maintain themselves as well as their *umwelt* – their world of significance – across time, place, and situations. Traumatized individuals and their dissociative parts signify their world, they determine what is and is not useful to them, and they assess how they can best interact with their environment, including its harshness. Traumatized individuals and conscious and self-conscious dissociative subsystems generate meaning.

Both as a whole system and as dissociative parts traumatized individuals operate under precarious conditions. Their existence depends on this coherent network of unconscious, preconscious, and conscious actions and passions that are minimally required to preserve

single creature exists or could exist. Autonomous systems are operationally closed, and they are also *necessarily* open to their environment. I thus concur with Thompson (see the motto of the present chapter) that there is no inconsistency. When living organisms are seen as a system, it makes sense to say that this system interacts with the environment as a different system. However, that is not the end of the story. Autonomous systems are embedded in the environment which they co-constitute and on which they are co-dependent. In the sense of this embedment, it is better to speak of and consider the organism-environment system.

their existence as an identity in the general and personal sense of the word. They exist in virtue of this ongoing work of codependent actions and passions.

Without this network, dissociative parts and traumatized individuals as whole systems would be extinguished or in any case cease to exist in their present form. For example, two dissociative parts can become ever more alike during therapy. This effect occurs when they gradually (or rapidly) stop engaging in their respective self-constituent[5] and self-sustaining actions, and instead start enacting new networks of self-generating and self-maintaining actions. Through the generation of new actions, they elaborate their mode space. This elaboration relates to a change of their mode trajectories: As they heal, the respective dissociative parts attract each other ever more and repel each other ever less. They start to regard their respective modes ever more as significant-good, as useful, and ever less as significant-bad or insignificant.

The 'fusion' (i.e., total integration) of two or more dissociative parts involves more than the elaboration of a dynamic subsystem with a new mode. It constitutes a systemic transition; it comprises a profound reorganization of the individual's personality. The actions of the newly created autonomous system commonly include many but not all former actions of the involved dissociative parts as well as several new actions. If all goes well, this evolving repertoire of actions exclude at least several, and preferably many (if not all) maladaptive actions (passions) that characterized the previously dissociated parts.

The integrative development of the involved dissociative subsystems of the personalities thus finds its summit in their eventual fusion. Such a fusion is a relative progression inasmuch as it involves two or more but not all previously dissociated parts. The advancement is absolute when all dissociative parts have become combined into a whole, integrated system.

Of course, dissociative parts can resist this integrative advancement. They may be too scared to embark on this road toward a higher level of integration. They may resist walking down this new path[6] when they still have difficulty imagining or believing that there is a life after their divided existence, as long as they still doubt that there is even a real possibility of new self-constituting and self-maintaining actions. One component of enactive trauma therapy is, therefore, to stimulate and coach dissociative parts to enlarge their repertoires of common actions and the implied new modes of operation (i.e., modes of longing and striving). These new actions may include moves that some parts may initially regard as nothing less than 'suicidal' acts. These parts are beset by the vague idea that these communal steps will sooner or later annihilate them.

---

5 'Self' in these phrases stands for 'identity' in both the general and personal sense of the word.

6 The idea of enacting a self and a world is beautifully reflected in Antonio Machado's (2003; Spanish poet, 1875–1939) words: "Wanderer, your footsteps are the road, and nothing more; wanderer, there is no road, the road is made by walking. By walking one makes the road, and upon glancing behind one sees the path that never will be trod again. Wanderer, there is no road – Only wakes upon the sea." The metaphor, however, stems from Zhuang Zi; see the motto of Chapter 23.

ad (ii) Traumatized individuals and their dissociative parts also qualify as autonomous systems because they are operational unities across environmental domains, time, and place. They maintain their general as well as their personal or phenomenal identities. Prototypical ANPs, fragile EPs, controlling EPs, and other kinds of dissociative parts do not cease to be the operational unities they are when they find themselves in different places or times. On the contrary, dissociative subsystems of the personality and traumatized individuals more generally tend to be unduly inflexible in at least some crucial regards. As detailed above, each recurrently enacts a rather fixed set of modes of longing and striving, and follows a rather fixed set of mode trajectories. Their mode portrait is unduly restricted. Their predominant fixed actions were probably the best they could bring to a life that was chronically traumatizing (or else they would have acted differently). But this rigidity may not fit the fact that the individual has developed and matured and/or that his or her environmental conditions have changed for the better.

Dissociative parts tend to lack sensitivity to the context in which they find themselves. Particularly EPs continue to generate a phenomenal conception of their *umwelt* that, from the third-person perspective, concerns the past. In close relationship with this anachronism, they also keep up an outdated phenomenal conception of self (ToT Volume II, Chapter 12). For example, the phenomenal self of a fragile EP may be "I'm a schoolgirl living with my parents, whom I need as much as I fear." But the actual person may be an adult who has been living in her own house for many years. Continuing to enact and reenact this EP may not be the patient's best option, inasmuch as she would, in fact, be able to integrate the memories of her traumatic encounters with her parents. This integration could succeed once the traumatization has come to an end, and once the dissociative parts involved and the traumatized individual as a whole have reached a mental level that allows them to integrate realities they could not experience, know, and realize previously.

This insensitivity regarding time, place, and personal identity applies to individuals with any kind of dissociative disorder, including those with PTSD (ToT Volume II, e.g., Chapter 18; Nijenhuis, 2014a, 2014b). Whatever the degree of complexity of the dissociative disorder, reenactments of traumatizing events include these confused, passionate ideas. When traumatized individuals engage in reenactments, they situate themselves in phenomenal conceptions of self, world, and self-of-this-world that do not match the third-person, technical, or physical judgment of who they currently are, where they are, what hour and day it is, who other individuals are or their intentions.

Traumatized individuals thus comprise more than one general identity and more than one phenomenal identity, however rudimentary some of these general and personal identities may be (ToT Volume II, Chapter 12). The phenomenal conception of self of most dissociative parts lies at a sociolinguistic level of identity (Varela, 1991), meaning that these dissociative subsystems can, at least in principle, talk to other dissociative parts and other individuals. For example, as ANPs most traumatized individuals can verbalize their phenomenal conceptions of self and can talk about them to other persons. ANPs may even manage to operate as a member of a community, and thereby reach the level of Varela's collective social multi-individual totality (see above). In terms of Järvilehto's levels of consciousness, they may achieve a corporative form of cooperation and coordination in particular regards (see Chapter 22). At some point in therapy, they may also learn to relate, or at least to relate more intensely, to the patient's other dissociative parts, thereby promoting an inner community of dissociative parts. This level involves Järvilehto's communicative form of cooperation and coordination (see Chapter 22).

EPs generally have far less social ties than ANPs. However, many EPs can express their personal identity – their phenomenal conception of self – in a more or less refined sociolinguistic form. They can tell other individuals and other dissociative parts who they feel and believe they are. The identity of some EPs as an autonomous system remains limited to a cognitive perceptuomotor, nonverbal, and perhaps even nonsocial level. These dissociative parts can feel, think, and engage in motor action, but they have very limited linguistic skills or even completely lack language. EPs may further be too scared to engage in social relationships or have a limited or minimal interest in these dealings.

Whatever level of identity dissociative parts in Varela's (1991) general and personal sense they may attain, they are very stable (actually, far too stable) across the various domains in which they operate. They remain unities across shifts in environmental domains, time, and place – which corresponds to the second criterion for autonomous systems.

ad (iii) Traumatized individuals and their dissociative parts also fulfill the third criterion for autonomous systems because they determine their respective domains of possible mental and behavioral interaction with the environment. Generating and maintaining themselves as an identity in the general and personal sense of these terms, they also generate and sustain borders and links between themselves and their environment as the object of their interest. This environment is their world of significance. It is the *umwelt* they co-constitute in a relativity of themselves as the subject and their *umwelt* as their object. It is also the niche on which they are co-dependent.

As autonomous systems, traumatized individuals and their dissociative parts must discriminate between what counts, what counts less, and what does not count at all for them. But they may signify something they would better regard as insignificant (useless, inconsequential, irrelevant); they may also fail to signify what actually counts. For example, a dissociative part may feel and think that "all men are dangerous," or that "the little one [a fragile EP] seduced father." However, it may well be that many men in the environment of this part are safe, and that "the little one" did not even know what seduction entails. Taking the reenactments of traumatic experiences for current events means assigning too much significance, too much reality, to past traumatizing events (Janet, 1903, 1928a, 1932; Van der Hart et al., 2006).

Traumatized individuals and the dissociative parts thus generate, uphold, and sometimes elaborate (Van der Hart et al., 2006) their own domains of action and environmental interaction. Engaging in these domains, their phenomenal self, their 'I,' constitutes a core point of reference for their relationships with themselves, with other persons, and with their *umwelt* in general. It comprises their first-person perspective (see below). The most important component of the phenomenal (conception of) self as a point of reference is their body, which does not mean the material organism (in German, *körper*) but their lived body (in German, *leib*). Their embodiment is discussed in Chapter 29.

The phenomenal self and its implied first-person perspective constitute the cornerstone of the quasi-second-person perspective of dissociative parts (phenomenal 'I-me, myself, mine' relationships, experiences, and judgments). They also comprise the foundation of their second-person perspective (phenomenal 'I-You' relationships, experiences, and judgments) and third-person perspective (physical 'I-object' relationships, experiences, and judgments) (see ToT Volumes I & II).

Dissociative parts include their own phenomenal conceptions of self, *umwelt*, and their phenomenal self's relationship with this phenomenal *umwelt* (ToT Volume II, Chapter 12; Chapter 25). That is, they signify themselves, their perceived and conceived phenomenal *umwelt* as well as their relationship to this *umwelt*. For example, as an ANP, a particular patient may like the clinician, whereas as a fragile EP the same individual may be scared of the clinician – and as a controlling EP the person may judge the clinician to be a powerless softy. Hence, the slogan: different dissociative parts, different sense-making, different meanings.

The 'skin' that dissociative parts erect and that delimits them from other dissociative parts is a special biopsychosocial kind (ToT Volume II, Chapters 16–18). The phenomenal self and *umwelt* of each part can include as well as exclude elements of the domains of other dissociative parts. For example, different dissociative parts may have particular ideas (e.g., sensations, perceptions, feelings, conceptions, memories, fantasies, dispositions) in common. They may also perceive and conceive of components of other dissociative parts' self and world. However, they tend to perceive and conceive of these components from a different perspective. For example, they may not phenomenally experience the sensations, perceptions, affects, etc., of other dissociative parts in the first-person perspective (e.g., "She is scared, I feel fine"). Or they may not regard a thought or emotion as a personal thought or emotion, but rather as a thought or emotion of another part (e.g., "He put his thoughts in my head"; "I feel her anger, but I am not angry"). These are confusions between the second-person perspective or even the third-person perspective (e.g., "The urges and thoughts of that other part are not my own") and the quasi-second-person perspective (e.g., "The [involved] urges and thoughts are [also] mine").

Dissociative parts typically sustain their phenomenal (mis)conceptions when third persons explain to them that what they (i.e., the involved dissociative parts) experience and know as someone else's mental and behavioral domains are in fact realms to which they themselves belong. Detailing to dissociative parts that the "others" and they themselves in fact constitute components of a single person may not persuade them by any means. For example, many controlling EPs regard themselves and some or all other dissociative parts as separately existing individuals. They may not conceive of themselves and other dissociative parts as the 'dividuals,' that is, as the parts of a whole they in fact are in the eye of third persons (ToT Volume II, p. 279). They may believe that they have a body of their own, that they can hurt or kill the "others" without being hurt or killed themselves. Some dissociative parts cling to these beliefs despite powerful contradictory third-person evidence. Their stubbornness does not flow from stupidity, some whimsical idea, or an oppositional or some other negative mood, but from their very reason of existence.

Whereas the various dissociative parts generate and maintain particular borders between themselves, these borders are not impenetrable, and in many cases they are actually quite permeable. Dissociative subsystems of the personality tend to influence each other, wittingly and/or unwittingly. They tend to experience these influences as intrusions on their respective experiential, perceptual, cognitive, and behavioral domains. And these intrusions are often quite unsettling to the dissociative parts being intruded on. Formally speaking, positive dissociative symptoms are nothing else than the successful influence(s) of some dissociative part(s) on the experiential, sensory, perceptual, emotional, cognitive, and behavioral domain of another dissociative part. The phenomena include hearing voices of other dissociative parts, experiencing their physical aches, becoming exposed to their emotional turmoil, and moving in ways that other dissociative parts initiate and control. Apart from these upsetting influences, there can also be pleasant inspirations. For example, some dissociative parts are quite supportive or knowledgeable and give wise advice; others may feel strong and help to handle difficult situations. Positive dissociative symptoms also include "switches" between different dissociative parts, where one dissociative part takes over executive control from another dissociative part.

The existence of semipermeable borders between the various dissociative parts is also useful at a more general level. Without particular reciprocal dynamical relationships among dissociative parts, these subsystems would not last very long. For example, dissociative parts that refrain from eating survive in part thanks to the fact that one or more other dissociative parts continue to eat. And particular EPs can only eat and live in a house because ANP earns or receives an income. And without controlling EPs, ANPs, and fragile EPs may lack any sense of significant power.

The *umwelt*-engaged actions and passions of dissociative parts cannot be fully understood in terms of material and efficient causality (ToT Volumes I & II). A complete understanding of human traumatic or other experience, thought, and behavior – including full comprehension of these features in dissociative parts – requires understanding that actions are purposeful efforts that serve actual and phenomenal self-interests. Like any other organism, traumatized individuals and their dissociative parts have *affective interests in themselves and their umwelt without which they could not exist.* Their actions and interactions are goal-oriented or teleological (see Chapters 24 and 25). Traumatized individuals and their dissociative parts are guided by their needs and desires that operate as *final causes.*

Autonomous Systems: Operationally Closed, Environmentally Open

An autonomous and viable system is *operationally closed*, because the fruits of the operations performed by the constituents of the system stay within the system itself (Colombetti, 2014). Concerned with itself (Weber, 2002), in this sense and only in this sense is an operationally closed system self-enclosed. However, *it is certainly not environmentally isolated*. It must actually couple itself in suitable ways with its environment or else it would perish[7]. While operationally closed, an autonomous system is thermodynamically open. As Colombetti (2014, p. 15–16) explains,

> ... for the physical realization of autonomy, the operationally closed network needs to be *thermodynamically open*, namely, able to continuously swap matter and energy with the environment, to regulate its self-generating activity as well as its exchanges with the environment. Operational closure ... thus refers not to material or energetic isolation but to a specific mode of functional relatedness among the components of a system that makes the system autonomous.

By the same token, social beings tend to be and must be positively open to each other to the benefit of each and all; the issue is taken up again in Chapter 28. A deeper and far more common appreciation and realization of the latter fact would turn the world in a far grander place. This truth woefully escapes those who emotionally neglect or abuse, viciously dominate, physically maltreat, and sexually persecute or abuse other individuals – as well as those who know the facts but fail to act responsibly (ToT Volume II, Chapter 20).

Traumatized Individuals and Dissociative Parts as Operationally Closed Systems

Like any organism, traumatized individuals constitute operationally closed systems. They basically strive to preserve their own existence and try to realize their particular

---

7 Part of an organism's environment is not external to the organism's body, but exists internal to this structure. For example, the human body includes at least as many bacterial cells as human cells (Sender, Fuchs, & Milo, 2016). The human body constantly takes in matter stemming from its environment as well as excretes matter to the environment (e.g., food, oxygen, waste products of the human body). The same continuous dynamic exchange exists with respect to ideas. Moreover, it is not always clear what belongs and what does not belong to the human body and mind. For example, one would be tempted to say that inhaled oxygen does not 'belong' to the human body. But what about oxygen and sugar circulating in the brain? How much sense does it make to say that these substances do not constitute an inherent, albeit temporary, part of the living human brain/body? How many ideas are actually internal to the individual human mind? According to the present analysis, the human body and mind can best be conceived as organism-environment systems involving fuzzy boundaries between what is internal and external. In many cases, strictly speaking it would be better to speak of 'interoception' and 'exteroception.' It is always important to see *who* experiences and conceived *what* as internal or external. 'Internal' and 'external' are relative to the properties and interests of an experiential and knowing system.

goals. They work for themselves. This self-centeredness also applies to dissociative parts.

The pursuit of goals of daily life in prototypical ANPs is not a luxury, but a deep need. They must attend school, concentrate on the lessons, sleep, eat, engage with the other children, and more. And given the individual's inability to integrate traumatic life, ANPs must avoid realizing the truth of their current and future situation, or else the person might collapse. As prototypical fragile EPs traumatized individuals may cry for attachment or defend the integrity of the body in one or more ways that evolution has prepared them for; as prototypical controlling EPs, they strive for positive power. Apart from these prototypes, there can be still other kinds of dissociative parts involving goals of their own. But whatever goals they may wish to attain, dissociative parts essentially work for their own sake.

This even applies to dissociative parts that aim to support one or more other dissociative parts. For example, and as illustrated in Chapter 37, some ANPs receive support from one or more benign 'helpers,' who feel better when they can effectively assist other dissociative parts and who enjoy their success in this regard. Some controlling EPs may even have obedient 'assistants' whom they instruct to do 'jobs' for them. These assistants feel better when they manage to execute these commands rather than when they fail. Even suicidal dissociative parts may wish to keep up their existence: What they basically seek is not death, but calm and peace. It, therefore, seems justified to say that all traumatized individuals and all dissociative parts serve their own needs and desires.

This operational self-enclosure, however, is also what strongly contributes to the maintenance of a dissociative personality. While some dissociative parts may have evolved as an effort to live the unlivable, once they have become settled or more elaborated, they basically work for themselves and not for the whole. They primarily or exclusively serve their own needs and desires, not those of the other dissociative parts.

However, inasmuch as the traumatization has stopped and the individual both as a whole and as the various dissociative parts has gained the power of action, dissociative parts achieve more when they cooperate. Enactive trauma therapy of dissociative disorders, then, reflects the effort to 'open up' operationally closed subsystems of the personality, to foster collaboration between them, and eventually to generate an integrated personality. The best result of enactive trauma therapy would be the generation of a new, autonomous, viable, and creative organism-environment system that maximizes joy and minimizes sorrow.

Autonomous Systems: Minded

Enactivism regards the unconscious and conscious mind as a continuous feature of organic life (Thompson, 2007). This panpsychistic view can be traced back to Spinoza (1677), who held that the mind is not exclusive to human beings, but constitutes a continuous feature of life.

Panpsychism

Signification is an affectively charged cognitive act. But can cellular systems (single-cell organisms) be usefully described as cognitive systems? Must we accept that all organisms are cognitive and hence mental systems? By taking a panpsychistic position of life, my position is, following Spinoza: *Yes, organic life is mental throughout, just as it is physical throughout.* Besides agreeing that all organisms involve needs, and that they are basically guided by their particular needs, I also fully concur with the following words of Varela (1992, p. 8):

> The reader may balk at my use of the term cognitive for cellular systems, and my cavalier sliding into intentionality. As I said above, one of my main points here is that we gain by seeing the continuity between this fundamental level of self and the other regional selves, including the neural and linguistic where we would not hesitate to use the word cognitive. I suppose others would prefer to introduce the word "information" instead. Well, there are reasons why I believe this even more problematic. Although it is clear that we describe an X that perturbs from the organism's exteriority, X is not information. In fact, for the organism only is a that, a something, a basic stuff to in-form from its own perspective. In physical terms there is stuff, but it is for nobody. Once there is body – even in this minimal form – it becomes in-formed for a self, in the reciprocal dialectics I have just explicated. Such information is never a phantom signification or information bits, waiting to be harvested by a system. It is a presentation, an occasion for coupling, and it is in this entre-deux that signification arises (Varela, 1979, 1988; Castoriadis, 1987). Thus the term cognitive has two constitutive dimensions: first its coupling dimension, that is, a link with its environment allowing for its continuity as individual entity; second – by stretching language, I admit – its imaginary dimension, that is, the surplus of significance a physical interaction acquires due to the perspective provided by the global action of the organism."

Saying that life is *mental* does not imply that life is necessarily *phenomenal.* Not all mental systems are also phenomenal (i.e., conscious and self-conscious) systems. Moreover, phenomenality is not one thing. There are many different kinds and degrees of mentality and consciousness. They probably relate to the complexity of the system (e.g., Spät, 2009–2010). In this sphere, the various forms and 'levels' of consciousness that exist in Nature involve 'emergent properties.'[8]

Even in the simplest living systems, mind as affectivity and cognition manifests itself in two ways: mind as conatus – as affective interest – and mind as perspectivalness.

Mind and Conatus

First, and as discussed above, organisms are *affectively interested* in themselves and thereby in the continuance of their own existence (Jonas, 1966; Spinoza, 1677a; Weber & Varela,

8 The term 'emergence' has been understood and defined in various and quite different ways (e.g., Bedau, 1997; Chalmers, 2008; Clark, 2001). The present text adheres to the view that mind and matter cannot be reduced to each other (Bitbol, 2008; Spinoza, 1677a; Varela, 1996; see also ToT Volume I, Chapter 8, and footnote 10 in the present volume). Consciousness is a property of Nature that cannot be reduced to anything else.

2002). They 'care' about themselves, and, in this light, their *umwelt* also matters to them (Colombetti, 2014). All living organisms display this sensitivity to themselves and their surroundings. They show an interest in their world, perceive and conceive it in a particular species-dependent and often also subject-dependent way, adapt to this world, and may also creatively modify their environment to some degree. This conatus or primordial affectivity, as Colombetti (2014) calls it, also forms the grounds for more differentiated forms of affect-laden sense-making that more complex organisms (can) engage in.

Mind and Perspectivalness

A second and related way in which even very simple organisms constitute mental systems is that they generate an asymmetrical relationship with their environment. The idea is that "living systems realize a perspective or point of view from which the world acquires meaning for them, and not vice versa" (Colombetti, 2014, p. 20). This perspectivalness comprises an epistemic distinction between an organism and its environment, between the living system as a primordial subject and the object(s) it perceives and evaluates. That is, all organisms 'feel' and 'know' they are different from the object(s) of their affectively charged 'attention.' However, all organisms also couple themselves to the object(s), epistemically, practically, and, above all, affectively. They 'feel' and 'know' their objects – which involves two epistemic subject-object relationships. This experiencing and knowing are grounds for handling them in one or more particular ways – which is a practical relationship. And the actions are guided by the organisms' needs and desires – which is an affective subject-object relationship.

Being situated in a world and perspectivalness are core features of consciousness (ToT Volume II, Chapter 12). Consciousness means being conscious *of* something: It is intentional. The adjective 'intentional' stems from the Latin expression '*intendere arcum in*,' which means 'to aim a bow and arrow at.' The existence of a primordial point of view regarding something that the organism regards and treats as 'not self' thus involves a basic form of mind. A 'not-self' appears when organisms organize themselves and bring forth a boundary that generates an inner domain ('self') as well as an external domain.

As has been mentioned several times before, individuals engage in various points of view: the first-person, quasi-second-person, second-person, and third-person perspective. These four perspectives were extensively discussed in ToT Volume I (Chapters 5 and 10) and ToT Volume II (Chapter 12). Given the importance of the theme of person perspectives, however, some basics are reiterated here.

The first-person perspective is all about prereflectively experiencing oneself as a subject. As I wrote in ToT Volume I (p. 237),

> [T]he first-person perspective concerns subjective, phenomenal experience: our 'raw' or prereflective sensations and other feelings that are experienced as subjective, private, and internal. It includes our body as our spatial center and our 'I' as the center of our existence. In other

> words, the first-person perspective pertains to the subjective feeling of being someone with a point of view, that is, of being an acting and experiencing self with a subjectively experienced outward perspective on one's perceived environment, and a subjectively experienced inward perspective regarding oneself (Metzinger, 2003). This someone involves our 'I' or our 'self.' The first-person perspective thus subserves living present events (Northoff, 2003) and, as it were, answers the question: What it is like to be an 'I,' to be a subject, to have experiences, to be an agent, and to have a personal point of view?

The fact that our first-person experiences are phenomenal does not mean that we have access to the actions involved in generating a phenomenal conception of self. Rather, we experience that our 'I' is a given:

> We can *contemplate* that consciousness and self-consciousness are not givens, but concern the mental contents we generate as organisms in action. However, we cannot *experience* that our 'I' and the feelings, perceptions, etc., are continuously generated conceptions. (ToT Volume II, Chapter 12, p. 237)

A subject may phenomenally relate to and judge himself or herself. This is the quasi-second-person perspective, which involves phenomenal I-me, myself, mine relationships, and implied judgments. With the generation of this person perspective, there will be an 'I' who experiences, knows, and evaluates himself or herself, thus relates to something that belongs to this 'I' and that is the object of this 'I': me, my, myself, mine. For example, "This hurts *me*," "I feel *my* hand," "I am ashamed of *myself*," "The idea was *mine*." When individuals engage in the quasi-second person perspective they generate a phenomenal relationship with themselves. To illustrate, an individual's phenomenal, immediate first-person feeling of being scared of the dark becomes more personified when the person also phenomenally judges in the quasi-second-person perspective that *(s)he* is afraid (e.g., "I feel someone is threatening *me*; he is after *my* body.").

In many cases, phenomenal judgment in the quasi-second-person perspective does not require much reflection. An individual does not commonly first feel pain and then, upon reflection, conclude that the pain is his or her own pain. However, whereas phenomenal judgment in the quasi-second-person perspective is often experienced as a given (e.g., "clearly this is *my* hand," "of course that is me in the mirror"), it still takes a synthetic mental action: the action of synthesizing phenomenal experiences with a phenomenal judgment of agency (e.g., "*I* condemn *myself*") and ownership (e.g., "This is *my* book"). It takes a synchronic synthesis of 'I' and 'hand' as well as a phenomenal judgment of a relationship between the two. It also includes an appreciation of the short span of time. The phenomenal 'now' approximately lasts 2 to 3 seconds. Phenomenal judgments commonly also take a diachronic synthesis 'I and my hand across time.' Without this diachronic synthesis, there would not be any enduring phenomenal (experience and conception of) self.

As a phenomenal 'I' an individual may phenomenally relate to and judge another subject. For example, he or she can feel, love, long for, care for, pity, despise, hate, or be ashamed of someone else; and (s)he may phenomenally judge that the other person is sensitive, kind, adorable, in need, helpless, strong, rude, sneaky, or mean. In this second-person perspective, a subject or first-person engages in a phenomenal relationship with a 'not-self' that (s)he phenomenally experiences and judges to be a different 'I,' hence a phenomenal '*You*.' As 'I' engage in this perspective, '*I*' can more or less intensely and completely feel into and hence co-experience '*your*' desires, physical and emotional feelings, and affect-laden thoughts, hopes, and memories – or at least subjectively believe '*I*' can (e.g., "I can feel how his words really hurt you"). As applies to the quasi-second person perspective, the second-person perspective also includes synchronic synthesis (the phenomenal conception of an 'I-You' relationship in the framework of a phenomenal now) and diachronic synthesis (the phenomenal conception of an 'I-You' relationship across time).

A subject generates a third-person perspective when (s)he knows and relates to something that, or someone who, is 'not-self' in a way that can be described as 'physical.' For example, '*I*' may know, relate to, and judge a house as a physical *object*, as a *thing* with physical features (an object with three-dimensional spatial features, a composition of various materials [stone, wood, metal], each with its own texture, color, weight, age, etc.). Such knowing involves a third-person physical or technical judgment; it involves a relationship of a judging 'I' and the physical house, its parts, and its physical features. In the quasi-second-person perspective, the house may be phenomenally experienced, known, and judged with a feeling of warmth, as '*my* home.' Clinicians may similarly assess their patients' mental disorder in the third-person perspective. They may technically judge that "patient X has a major depression." What they actually should say is that something like "'*I*' technically judge that person X meets the formal criteria for 'major depression." At the same time, clinicians may like, dislike, fear, pity, or condemn the individual in the second-person perspective. This evaluation is not physical or technical but phenomenal.

As with the quasi-second person perspective and the second-person perspective, in order to achieve constancy, the third-person perspective must include more than synchronic synthesis ('I-object' *now*). Without the additional action of diachronic synthesis ('I-object' relationship *across time*), 'I,' 'You,' and 'thing' would not exist for us as relatively stable phenomena. For example, without it, we would not be able to develop and maintain a general and personal identity, and we would not have a phenomenal conception of our past. Phenomenal identity, thus, can exist even if the experienced and judged subject or object actually 'physically' changes to a lesser or larger degree. To illustrate, according to a third-person analysis, my friend Arne 'physically' changes (e.g., by growing older), but in my phenomenal experience and judgment in the second-person perspective he remains the same person.

Diachronic synthesis is much more than linking historical experiences and facts. It must include the action of presentification. As mentioned before, presentification involved two actions: One action is bringing what was or what will be to the phenomenal present; the second action is experiencing and judging that the phenomenal present (phenomenal judgment in quasi-second-person perspective, second-person perspective) or physical present (physical judgment in third-person perspective) is *more real* than the phenomenal or physical past or anticipated future. When they do not engage in presentification, individuals will not know what constitutes the past, the present, and the anticipated future (Van der Hart et al., 2006).

All person perspectives, thus, involve their own kind of sense-making, and all involve synchronic and diachronic synthesis – when all goes well, that is. This sense-making is ongoing because phenomenal reality and physical truths are seldom if at all static: 'Panta rhei,' (everything flows, Heraclitus). These realities depend on an individual's ongoing epistemic actions. In other words, any (kind of) person perspective results from the ongoing action of generating, maintaining, or changing a (particular kind of) point of view.

Whereas the quasi-second-person, second-person, and third-person perspectives entail their own types of relationships and judgments, all presuppose and involve an 'I,' a subject who experiences that (s)he is someone. This is the first-person perspective. One straightforward implication is that clinicians' and scientists' physical judgments regarding patients are not 'objective,' but 'subjective' (ToT Volume I). When clinicians and scientists fail to realize this fact, they may be fooled into thinking that they can assess an 'objectively existing reality,' an 'objectively existing mental disorder,' an 'objectively existing dependency problem,' an 'objectively existing mother transference,' etc. Realization of our principled subjectivity serves our modesty.

Mind, Affectivity, and Perspectivalness in Trauma

Given the view that all organic life is minded, traumatized individuals are minded autonomous systems, as are their dissociative parts, no matter how rudimentary some of these parts may be. As whole persons and as their dissociative parts, they are also affective (see below). The various person perspectives in traumatized individuals and in their dissociative parts were discussed in Volumes I and II. Their troubles regarding the person perspectives of the dissociative parts as well as their implied different synchronic syntheses, diachronic syntheses, personification, presentification, and realization, and the consequences thereof, need not be reiterated here. However, these features and problems remain a frequent theme in the practical chapters of the present volume.

Conatus and Passions

Our affects can exist as 'passions' (Spinoza, 1677a; the topic was introduced in Chapter 25), as unchecked, intense physical affections, emotions, and confused ideas. Passions lower our power of action, including our power to make sense of ourselves and of our world in a consistent and clear way. Passions, thus, involve a limitation of our power to act efficiently. Beset by two or more contrary passions simultaneously, we become volatile creatures: "*Men can disagree in nature insofar as they are torn by affects which are passions; and to that extent also one and the same man is changeable and inconstant*" (Spinoza, 1677a, Proposition 33, p. 131). Struggling with intense ambivalences (or polyvalences), we know not where to go. This all-too-human condition led the Danish philosopher Søren Kierkegaard (1843/1987, p. 159) to conclude that, whatever one chooses, one will always regret it: "... I see it all perfectly; there are two possible situations – one can either do this or that. My honest opinion and my friendly advice is this: do it or do not do it – you will regret both." There is no escape, choosing one thing implies losing, not getting, or not achieving another.

"[T]he force of each affect is defined by the power of the external cause compared with our own. The power of the mind is defined by knowledge alone, whereas lack of power, *or* passion, is judged solely by the privation of knowledge, that is, by that through which ideas are called inadequate" (Spinoza, 1677a, p. 170–171). Inadequate, confused ideas decrease the power of action, and adequate ideas increase it. It is, therefore, useful to replace inadequate ideas by "clear and distinct" alternatives, and it is harmful to regard them as thoughts of no concern that can be left intact. However, developing clear and distinct ideas – looking reality into the face – can be a major struggle. Guided by passions, we may not welcome certain facts of nature. As Spinoza (1677a, p. 171) observed,

> sickness of the mind and misfortunes take their origin especially from too much love toward a thing which is liable to many variations and which we can never fully possess. For no one is disturbed or anxious concerning anything unless he loves it, nor do wrongs, suspicions, and enmities arise except from love for a thing which no one can really fully possess.

We cannot dictate Nature. We cannot make individuals love us when in fact they hate us. For example, as the practical chapters in this volume demonstrate, it can be a tremendous waste of time and energy for daughters and sons to continue seeking parental love when their parents hate them and feel contempt for them. On the other hand, children are more or less forced to engage in this search of parental recognition and love when realizing that their love-seeking efforts are in vain would be more harmful than continuing their passion. As mentioned before, *how can children progress when the reality of such hate is completely clear to them*? When this rejection is massive and enduring, it constitutes an external cause that is far more powerful than children's power to change their parents' passions. The need and desire of children to receive the parental love that remains beyond reach, that they will never possess, may easily generate intense passions in them. It produces confused ideas such as perpetual denial and distortion ("They will love me if I try harder." "It's my fault that they don't love me." "I must be deeply ashamed of myself"). To prevent or overcome this inadequacy, rejected (neglected, maltreated, abused) children must come to terms with reality when they have grown older and have become less dependent on their family of origin. At some point they must clearly and distinctly understand that regardless of the fact that their wishes are natural, their fulfillment will remain painfully elusive. As *The Rolling Stones* realize "You can't always get what you want." One's power of action can be overruled by the power of external causes. It is often important but painful to realize this.

By the same reasoning, perpetrators can never fully possess the ones they haunt and torture inasmuch as the objects of their passions refuse to comply. For example, maltreating and abusive family members strive to fully possess and completely dictate the objects of their ill needs and desires (e.g., lust). They strive to have that power but lose it when their victims sooner or later realize that

> mind is most acted on, of which inadequate ideas constitute the greatest part, so that it is distinguished more by what it undergoes than by what it does. On the other hand, that mind acts most, of which adequate ideas constitute the greatest part, so that though it may have as many inadequate ideas as the other, it is still distinguished more by those which are attributed to human virtue than by those which betray man's lack of power. (Spinoza, 1677a, p. 171)

However, the more organisms include different needs and desires, and the more these urges are contrary, the harder it becomes to agree with all of them, to bring them into one solid and sound composition of self, world, and self as an intrinsic part of that world.

One day 3-year-old Asia noticed there were some not-so-nice tracks of a marker on her table.

> "You don't like them?"
> "No."
> "Who did it?"
> " . . . mmm . . . errr . . . *Baby Asia!*"
> "Hmm, Baby Asia did it."
> Asia nodded decidedly, looking quite relieved.
> "And where is Baby Asia now?"

The unexpected and somewhat strange question invited reflection. After a while, the little girl's face turned uncomfortable. Laughing out the wrong side of her mouth, and pointing at her chest, she whispered, '*here* . . ."

Conatus and Passion in Trauma

It is difficult for everyone to integrate the mixture of various and in some cases quite opposite needs and desires we carry as our evolutionary inheritance. Nobody is a miracle of perfect integration. We all struggle with polyvalences, with battles among our various urges. In trauma, the difficulty is to integrate one or more terrible experiences in the story of one's life, experiences one in fact would prefer not to include in this narrative. Everyone wants to become a success, and this interest clashes with shocking and painful events that jeopardize this ideal. Depending on the severity of the event in relation to one's capacity to come to terms with it and depending on the event's consequences, the skin of one's personality becomes scratched – or worse, ruptured. The injury that may ensue basically involves a conflict between the needs and desires of daily life, those of biopsychosocial preservation under attack, and those of self-respect and self-determination. Attack readily evokes fear and rage, whereas shame, disgust, and loss of self-respect and confidence are released by damage to one's self-esteem, pride, and power.

Foremost chronic traumatization by caretakers presents an exceptional integrative challenge. It is the major difficulty to navigate contrary wills regarding the same individual(s): various interests of daily life (nourishment, sleep, a partner, friends, work, play), active and passive defense, attachment, power, and still more. The devilish complexity is to somehow integrate opposite wants regarding abusive others on which one is dependent, notably parents and other close relatives or otherwise significant others. As described before, a profound division of the personality may be the best option of the developing abused, maltreated, and neglected child, despite the fervent passions it entails.

Like anyone else, traumatized individuals – as a whole and as the dissociative subsystem(s) they encompass – are primarily affective and teleological. We all possess specific needs and desires, and we all strive to fulfill these as much and as good as possible. As autonomous systems, their common and primary goal is to persevere in their existence. Like anyone else, individuals who are confronted with adverse events want to continue their existence. In this context and in this spirit they may generate two or more dissociative parts, each guided by a selection of the needs and desires of the whole individual. *From that moment onward their personality does not constitute and operate as one autonomous system anymore but as two or more.* From the moment of their creation, from their self-generation and starting self-organization, all dissociative parts, no matter how rudimentary they may be, will strive to maintain their own existence. From the moment of their constitution as autonomous systems, *different dissociative parts of a traumatized individual's personality are more interested in extending their own existence than in the extension of the existence of the other dissociative parts or in that of the individual as a whole.*

A related complication of dissociation in trauma is that different (types of) dissociative parts will try to achieve their affect-laden goals in their own style. Prototypical ANPs, fragile EPs, controlling EPs, and other kinds of dissociative parts essentially include their own needs and desires and their own ways of achieving their urges. *Dissociative parts consist basically of will, but none includes the full gamut of needs and desires of the overarching autonomous system to which they belong – to the individual's personality as a whole.* And the more their conatus is contrary, the more dissociative parts sooner or later become trapped in enduring conflicts with one another.

The power of action of dissociative parts is not only limited by these conflicts; their power also lessens the more they become isolated and traumatized, and the less other individuals and other dissociative parts recognize, validate, and support them. Trauma-related structural brain damage (ToT Volume II, Chapter 19) lessens their power of action as well. Dissociative parts thus tend to become ever more acted on, rather than act. Sooner or later, even their better actions and substitute actions may also become debilitating passions.

A Recapitulation

A division between prototypical ANPs, fragile EPs, and controlling EPs – each of which is teleologically guided by one horn of a basic triple lemma – may be the best adaptation a maturing chronically traumatized child can raise: (1) one or more ANPs, primarily entailing major desires and needs of daily life; (2) one or more fragile EPs, primarily involving sympathetically mediated mammalian defense (startle, freeze, flight, circa-strike defense/fight) and/or dorsal vagal parasympathetically mediated defense (tonic immobility as it is sometimes called, perhaps better described as "playing dead"), and possibly attachment cry; and (3) one or more controlling EPs, primarily striving for the power to influence fate, to develop and maintain a sense of autonomy despite all actual vicious domination by perpetrators (self-determination, social dominance).

ANPs

Functioning in daily life, no matter how adverse this life may be, is the prototypical *raison d'être* of ANPs. As these conscious subsystems, traumatized individuals primarily wish to eat, sleep, explore their environment, play, earn an income, attach to and take care of their children and other significant others they love, socially engage with friends, and more. In this context, they consciously or unconsciously feel that they must evade traumatic memories and the associated EPs as much as they can. But their passionate and ongoing efforts at mental avoidance take incessant energy. Apart from this energetic waste, the price of successful evasion is emotional and physical numbing as well as depersonalization that restrict if not obstruct the ability to experience joy. The avoidance generates a normality that is only apparent.

Fragile EPs

The more and the more effective ANPs ignore fragile EPs, the more the latter remain stuck in a traumatic past that to them constitutes the present. That is, fragile EPs enact a phenomenal self, world, and self-of-the-world that should have become part of the involved individual's personal and personalized history. In this sense, they are prone to perceive hazards that, in the third-person perspective of observers, do not exist or no longer exist. Fragile EPs encompass many inadequate ideas indeed.

When they feel endangered, fragile EPs try to defend themselves against all perils, particularly (though perhaps not exclusively) by engaging in mammalian defenses. Their defensive maneuvers clearly involve conatus, that is, the need and desire to persevere in their existence. However, even if their defensive actions are at target – the individual may also presently be truly endangered – the type and quality of their defense may not meet the demands of the situation.

The entrapment of fragile EPs in a former reality and identity is revealed in a variety of ways. These include reenactments of the traumatic experiences once experienced. Mostly sensorimotor, highly emotional, and reflexive[9] as well as largely or completely non-symbolized, these reenactments involve a rather low level of functioning. While some re-enactments of traumatic memories include a few words, these are generally little more than exclamations (e.g., "It hurts!") or brief emotional and reflexive statements ("Please, don't hit me! Please stop it!"). Some reenactments do not take the form of active defenses but involve hypoaroused tonic immobility including a degree of psychophysiological hypoarousal, emotional, and physical anesthesia, and muscle weakness or paralysis (ToT Volumes I & II).

According to some fragile EPs, certain needs and desires must be inhibited. For example, they may feel that it is too scary to eat, relax, and sleep, or to trust other individuals. They fear they might miss danger signals if they were to grant themselves these favors. One problem with this strategy is that they spend too much time and energy on their defensive actions. Another downside of their excessive defenses is that they do not learn to reduce their passions through rest, trust, and the like. The avoidance and lack of realization of traumatic memories in ANPs further implies continued sorrow and fear for EPs: The more ANPs manage to evade fragile EPs and the traumatic memories of these EPs, the more fragile EPs are bound to remain stuck in their terrible life.

Controlling EPs

Controlling EPs seek ways to influence their own fate. They desire such power. Many controlling EPs evolved out of the individual's wish to gain sovereignty. Being either ignorant and ignoring, or injured and fragile, is a poor foundation for independence. In due course, however, pristine controlling EPs tend to lose track of their original desire to complement ANPs and fragile EPs, to compensate for the absent or weakly developed sense of self-determination of these parts. As they come to see it, the desperate longing for attachment, acceptance, love, and a better future is hopelessly idle. Because in the view of controlling EPs these passions lie at odds with self-determination and independence, they simply ban them. Observing that perpetrators are in charge, controlling EPs gradually find their way to power by imitating the vicious actions of perpetrators. This leads them to vehemently attack other dissociative parts and sometimes other individuals as well.

---

9 In the present text, the adjective 'reflexive' stands for a 'reflex-like,' impulsive quality of action. It is used as an antonym of 'reflective,' which in this context means deliberate, thoughtful.

Dissociative Part-Dependent Signification

Traumatized individuals as a whole system and as their dissociative parts conceive and evaluate themselves, other parts, other individuals, objects, and events in their own affect-laden idiosyncratic context. Their sense-making or signification is highly distinctive. For example, what scares one traumatized individual most may not mean much to another. As an ANP a traumatized individual may regard something as useful which as a fragile EP (s)he may regard as dangerous, as a controlling EP as useless.

Traumatized individuals and dissociative parts constitute and maintain their own phenomenal conceptions of self, world, and self-of-the-world. They generate and uphold their own distinct inner and external realities. Their ongoing signification and insignification are intimately related to their needs and desires, their major traumatizing and other significant life events, the context in which these events happened, and probably several other 'risk factors' such as their sex, temperament, and intelligence (see Volume II, Chapter 6).

In this sense, at least initially, they tend to perceive, conceive, and relate to the clinician in ways they have learned to perceive, conceive, and relate to adults who are of significance to them. In other words, they are inclined to reenact former significant interpersonal relationships. These commonly include, or at least concern, traumatic bonds (in the second-person perspective) and traumatizing ties (in the third-person perspective). For example, individuals who experienced emotional neglect may, as an ANP, regard the clinician as a person who is not really interested in them ("You don't care about me"). ANPs who have tried to persevere by trying to please traumatizing family members may wish above all to please the clinician ("Tell me what you want, I'll do it"; "I'll do whatever you want me to do"). The clinician, however, serves as a different sign for a fragile EP who engages in attachment cry ("Help me!" "Stay with me!"). And a fragile EP who engages in active or passive mammalian defense may see the clinician as a dangerous individual by ("You want to get me"; "Sooner or later you will hurt me as well"). Controlling EPs may think the clinician wishes to curtail if not annihilate their power and prohibit all hope ("There is no hope, hope must be banned"). They also tend to ban attachment ("You want them [the other dissociative parts] to trust you; they are so stupid and fall into that trap; trusting and binding to others is the most foolish thing one can do; I am my own boss, and that's how it's going to stay; I will punish the others for their folly").

From Survival to Confusion and Decompensation

Trauma-related dissociation of the personality evolves and operates as a survival strategy in the framework of the limited integrative ability of that autonomous system. Its implied urge to maintain itself brought forth the self-generation in the first place as well as subsequently the self-maintenance of two or more dissociative subsystems. These subsystems comprise their own needs, desires, and phenomenal conception of self, world, and self-of-the-world. Being autonomous systems, they too strive to sustain their very existence. However, guided by their own conatus, they do not (or insufficiently) experience, know, and acknowledge the interests that steer the other dissociative parts – and that are the very reason for their existence. Dissociation of the personality, then, becomes a battlefield of largely contrary needs, desires, and phenomenal conceptions. It grows to be an arena of conflicted autonomous conscious and self-conscious organism-*umwelt* systems. The structural and dynamical make-up of an individual's personality entails the continued existence of intense passions. These notably include recurrently reenacted traumatic memories.

The implication is that the injury that trauma represents fully heals only if the individual begins to operate as a whole personality and as *one* autonomous organism-environment system, as one dynamic structure that encompasses and efficiently navigates all contrary needs and desires. For example, rather than believing (as a controlling EP) that the woman who abused and neglected the involved patient "is not my mother," the patient may accept and realize clearly and distinctly that his or her mother is "a very disturbed woman, who sadly is my biological mother, but who did not behave like a good mother" (see Chapter 37).

The repertoire of actual and possible actions of dissociative parts are thus mostly guided and limited by the very needs and desires that are their prime reason for existence. The dissociative, part-dependent, primordial, affective, goal-orientation or conatus involved is intimately associated with the equally dissociative part-dependent signification and in-signification. This dependency may be clinically observed and empirically discovered (see ToT Volume II, particularly Chapters 12, and 16–18). Given their integrative limitations, individuals may promote their ability to sustain their difficult life by dividing their personality. Under these circumstances, dividing this singular, operationally closed autonomous system into two or more operationally closed, autonomous systems may be a useful act. This applies particularly when the life of the person comprises chronic and multiple forms of traumatization by significant others such as parents or other close relatives. However, dividing the personality also constitutes the very core of the biopsychosocial injury that trauma is. Dissociative parts are essentially interested in maintaining their existence. As conscious and self-conscious, autonomous systems, dissociative parts perceive, conceive, and evaluate themselves from their restricted person perspectives and their life experiences. To the degree that they wholeheartedly disagree what needs, desires, and goals are significant and insignificant in life, they have trouble appreciating and understanding each other, let alone assisting, cooperating, intensely communicating, and eventually fusing with one another.

Dissociation of the personality thus begins as the creative attempt to sustain life – and ends as a major struggle to live it. Torn by contradictory needs and desires that lie at the very root of their dissociative parts – as autonomous centers of action – traumatized individuals are deeply confused about what to feel, think, believe, remember, and do.

Chapter 28

Ego and Socius

Nothing can agree more with the nature of any thing than other individuals of the same species.
Baruch Spinoza (1677a, Part IV, Appendix IX)

Each to each a looking-glass
Reflects the other that doth pass.
Charles Horton Cooley (1968, p. 90)

... selves only exist in relation to other selves.
George Herbert Mead (1968, p. 56)

Like all organisms, humans are guided by the prime interest of survival: "*Each thing, as far as it can by its own power, strives to persevere in its being*" (Spinoza, 1677a, Part III, Proposition 6), because "*[t]he striving by which each thing strives to persevere in its being is nothing but the actual essence of the thing*" (Part III, Proposition 7). Like any autonomous system, we are self-centered creatures by our very nature. We strive to gain as much of the useful ('good') as we can, and try to avoid or get rid of as much of the useless ('bad') within the limits of our abilities. We thus make every effort to maximize our gain and to minimize our losses:

> Everyone exists by the highest right of Nature, and, consequently everyone, by the highest right of Nature does those things which follow from the necessity of his own nature. So everyone, by the highest right of Nature, judges what is good and what is evil, considers his own advantage according to his own temperament ..., avenges himself ..., and strives to preserve what he loves and destroy what he hates ... (Spinoza, 1677a, p. 135)

It is a principle from which Nature allows us no escape.

Ego as Socius

One might fear and protest that our primordial affectivity and self-interest obliterate any chance of building harmonious social ties and societies. But that is just not the case, because,

> [t]hough men ... generally direct everything according to their own lust, nevertheless, more advantages than disadvantages follow from their forming a common society. So it is better to

> bear men's wrongs calmly, and apply one's zeal to those things which help to bring men together in harmony and friendship. (Spinoza, 1677a, Part IV, Appendix XIV)

And,

> [i]t is especially useful to men to form associations, to bind themselves by those bonds most apt to make people of them, and absolutely, to do those things which serve to strengthen friendships. But skill and alertness are required for this. For men vary – there being few who live according to the rule of reason – and yet generally they are envious, and more inclined to vengeance than to compassion. So it requires a singular power of mind to bear with each one according to his understanding, and to restrain oneself from imitating their affects. (Spinoza, 1677a, p. 156–157)

How different this world would be if we, as individuals, could consistently achieve the required mental level to appreciate and to enact that each one of us achieves more when we cooperate with each other:

> If men lived according to the guidance of reason, everyone would possess this right of his … without any injury to anyone else. But because they are subject to the affects … which far surpass men's power, *or* virtue, they are often drawn in different directions … and are contrary to one another …, while they require another's aid … In order, therefore, that men may be able to live harmoniously, and be of assistance to one another, it is necessary for them to give up their natural right, and to make one another confident that they will do nothing which could harm others. (Spinoza, 1677a, p. 136)

How does it happen that humans, who are necessarily subject to variable and changeable affects, should nevertheless be able to make one another confident and have trust in one another becomes clear in Part IV, Proposition 7 and Part III, Proposition 39: "*No affect can be restrained except by an affect stronger than and contrary to the affect to be restrained,*"[1] and "*everyone refrains from doing harm out of timidity regarding a greater harm.*" The important point for anyone to feel, see, and realize is that *social harmony is useful to everyone*, hence a good thing:

> Part IV, Proposition 40: *Things which are of assistance to the common society of men* or *which bring about that men live harmoniously, are useful; those, on the other hand are evil which bring about discord to the state.*

---

1 Spinoza's insights with respect to emotions and emotion regulation — the substance of *Ethic*'s Parts III, IV, and V — antedated the contemporary principles of 'desensitization,' 'countercondition,' 'mindfulness,' and 'acceptance and commitment,' some of which are also part of the far older doctrine of Buddhism. History reveals that some wheels can be discovered 'for the first time' more than once. That is why it is useful to be acquainted with our evolutionary and cultural history – and to learn from it – even if learning from history is as difficult and rare as realizing that everyone wins by self-moderating their natural, sovereign right of self-interest. The history of trauma testifies to the fact that little is forgotten or ignored so quickly and effectively as the lessons of the past. The sad truth is, however, that striving to control our essential fragility by ignoring yesterday's wounds and their dynamic causes is guaranteed to precipitate further personal and societal injuries.

However, when concluding *Ethics* (p. 180–181) Spinoza expresses the difficulty humans have to realize the truth:

> ... not only is the ignorant man troubled in many ways by external causes, and unable ever to possess true peace of mind, but he also lives as if he knew neither himself, nor God, nor things; and as soon as he ceases to be acted on, he ceases to be. On the other hand, the wise man, insofar as he is considered as such, is hardly troubled in spirit, but being, by a certain eternal necessity, conscious of himself, and of God, and of things, he never ceases to be, but always possesses true peace of mind.
> If the way I have shown to lead to these things now seems very hard, still, it can be found. And, of course, what is found so rarely must be hard. For if salvation were at hand, and could be found without great effort, how could nearly everyone neglect it? But all things excellent are as difficult as they are rare.

As autonomous systems, organisms are basically driven by self-interest. Other interests, prominently including social interests, exist in the framework and service of the primordial self-interest to persevere in their existence. However, social interests are primordial affective interests as well: Animals who live in groups and who are dependent on each other and the welfare of the group express social interests that remain with them practically from their first to their last breath. No other mammal is as intensely and pervasively dependent on caretakers as homo sapiens. Given our general social nature and given our long-term dependency on parents or other caretakers as we develop and mature, we foster social needs and desires in our urge to persevere in our existence. Under the influence of evolutionarily derived needs and desires for attachment, social engagement, and play, and the respective action systems (Panksepp, 1998; Panksepp & Biven, 2012), maturing babies, toddlers, and younger as well as older children are inherently social beings. Social interests stay with us for the rest of our lives. Even newborns look at faces more than at objects, and they soon imitate facial expressions and movements such as protruding the tongue.

Some Perspectival Features of Prenatal Development

Perspectivalness and social life, in fact, do not wait until birth to become active, as they are already enacted in the womb. In the interest of understanding enactivism more, it may be helpful to dwell a bit on the life of the fetus, which is a self-concerned *and* a social existence. For example, at 22 weeks of gestation fetuses can touch their own eyes and mouth (Zoia et al., 2007). They are goal-directed, and their movements are not coincidental or suffer from a lack of intrauterine space, but clearly involve a remarkably advanced level of motor planning regarding the self. These actions comprise a pristine form of phenomenal I-me, myself relationship (quasi-second-person perspective). Furthermore, fetuses respond with heart-rate acceleration and motor response to both music and (human) voices, albeit not to sham noises (Al-Qahtani, 2005). Also, fetuses between 33 and 34 weeks of gestation start to recognize their mother's voice (Jardri et al., 2012). In one study fetuses reacted to both their mother's and father's voice with an increase of heart rate, and once born, they showed a preference for their mother's voice over their father's voice (Lee & Kisilevsky, 2014). This finding suggests the existence of *distinct, affect-laden*, fetal, second-person perspective regarding the mother and the father in that preferences are grounded in affect. Preterm newborns responded to maternal sounds with decreased heart rate throughout the first month of life (Piccioloni et al., 2014; Rand & Lahav, 2014). Early exposure to their mother's voice exerted a favorable effect on both their autonomic and neurobehavioral development (Picciolini et al., 2014). But how fetuses' heart rate and motility respond to their mother's voice seem to be affected by both maternal and fetal state (Voegtline, Costigan, Pater, & DiPietro, 2013).

The social nature of fetuses may have been best demonstrated in an intrauterine twin study (Castiello et al., 2010). Twin fetuses engage in self-directed movements and movements directed at the uterine wall – again, not accidentally because of limited space, but quite intentionally. However, more than enacting a quasi-second-person perspective and an elementary I–Object relationship, from the 14th week of gestation on they also reached deliberately toward their twin. This finding might point to a primordial second-person perspective. In the weeks thereafter they even tended to move toward themselves less and to reach more often toward their twin. By the 18th week, they were stroking their uterine partner's head or back more than touching the uterine wall or touching themselves, suggesting distinct perceptions of self, objects, and especially the twin. Another remarkable finding was that their twin-directed movements seemed to be more accurate than their self-directed motor actions. Gallese, one of the authors of the study, suggested, "[t]he womb is probably a crucial starting point to develop a sense of self and a sense of others" (see Weaver, 2011).[2]

Turning to the developmental social path of the developing (born) child, based on Tronick et al.'s (Tronick, 1989, 2006; Tronick & Beeghly, 2011; Tronick & Cohn, 1989; Weinberg & Tronick, 1996) most important studies of early mother-child interactions, Krueger (2010, p. 70; already quoted in ToT Volume I, p. 192) concluded that "... the self arises within a sympathetic context of sharing, that is, an affective ethos of bodily relatedness that confers phenomenally new (i.e., enriched) experiences of the world-as-shared."

How developing children feel and think about themselves, behave, recollect their past, experience their present, and look forward to the future depends heavily on how they are received in their world, on how they are treated and seen by their caretakers: the ones whom they desire and need, to whom they need to attach, and with whom they mentally and physically interact on a daily basis. Mutual sympathy does not mean that parents and their children are always perfectly mentally, physically, and physiologically attuned to each other. Such an ideal biopsychosocial dance is repeatedly interrupted by phases of misattunement (Brazelton, Tronick, Adamson, Als, & Wise, 1975). However, benign and healthy

2 On touching after premature birth, see https://www.facebook.com/photo.php?fbid=10156466774055252&set=pcb.10156466775205252&type=3

early relationships include consistent and recurrent efforts at relational repair. In this fashion developing infants and children experience that the world is basically 'good,' that it sometimes can and will turn 'bad,' but that the 'bad' is followed up by their caretakers' reparatory actions, so that the brighter world reappears. According to Tronick, this repetitive pattern of relational synchrony and desynchrony is what helps children grow up healthily: They learn that neither the 'good' nor the 'bad' lasts forever. They also experience and trust that the occasional 'bad' becomes associated with an expectation that the 'good' will eventually resurface. They learn there is *reason for hope* (Hart, 2011). Learning how to deal with daily life stress in this fashion teaches them how to be better prepared to cope with life's deeper disappointments, including outright adverse events (Tronick, 2006).

However, maternal psychopathology may have a negative impact on the affective state of the infant and on the capacity for repairing states of miscoordination (Tronick & Reck, 2009). Parental depression and anxiety as well as infant medical, behavioral, and temperamental problems can in fact precipitate protracted episodes of dyadic disorganization and maladaptive infant outcomes (Beeghly & Tronick, 2011). Infant sense-making actions may thus govern typical and pathological outcomes (Tronick & Beeghly, 2011). In Tronick and Beeghly's words that (in part[3]) fit the enactive perspective,

> [i]nfants, as open dynamic systems, must constantly garner information to increase their complexity and coherence. They fulfill this demand by making nonverbal "meaning"-affects, movements, representations about themselves in relation to the world and themselves into a "biopsychosocial state of consciousness," which shapes their ongoing engagement with the world. ... infant mental health problems emerge when the meanings infants make in the moment, which increase their complexity and coherence and may be adaptive in the short run, selectively limit their subsequent engagement with the world and, in turn, the growth of their state of consciousness in the long run. When chronic and iterative, these altered meanings can interfere with infants' successful development and heighten their vulnerability to pathological outcomes. (p. 107)

Ego and Socius in Prenatal and Postnatal Trauma

Because even very simple organisms know what is useful, useless, and detrimental to them, sensu Spinoza enactivism regards mind as a core feature of life. It is generally assumed that relatively few species are consciously (i.e., reflectively and reportedly) aware of what they want, feel, perceive, conceive (think), and do. And relatively little of what those species who are endowed with such properties want, signify, and do seems to be

3 I would have avoided the terms 'information' and 'representation' for the reasons given in ToT Volumes I and II as well as in the present Volume III. While I have deep respect for Tronick's excellent work, in my view the terms 'signs' and 'conception' could better replace the terms 'information' and 'representation,' respectively.

accessible to their conscious awareness and experience. However, as described in previous chapters, all species experience longing, feeling, signification, and striving – and these are *mental properties*.

One implication is that fetuses are more than just evolving living matter. They also encompass mind. Newborns do not suddenly become mental and (partly) phenomenal systems the moment they are born. As indicated above, fetuses are essentially mental from the moment of their conception, and they rapidly gain mental complexity from that pristine constitutive event onward. They develop an interest in themselves and their world, that is, an interest in and perspective toward themselves and the objects of their interest (which can include other subjects as well). Fetuses assess what is useful, useless, or harmful for them, and they work to get what they want and to get rid of anything useless and harmful. Another implication is that the developing mind, brain, and body of the fetus can become injured during gestation by external adverse causes. Traumatization may start in the womb.

Prenatal Trauma

Since the topic of prenatal traumatization was not covered in ToT Volumes I and II, I would like to discuss the issue briefly here[4]. By its very nature, human gestation is a period of intense body/brain development, laying the groundwork for all future, postnatal bio-psychosocial development (Anderson & Thomason, 2013; Trevarthen & Aitken, 2001). Nine months is a relatively brief phase for the tremendous development of the mind, the body, and the brain. This development cannot and does not proceed in an environmental void. Connected with the mother through the placenta, the fetus is from the very beginning an organism-environment system. An amazing organ, the placenta supplies the fetus with adequate nutrition and oxygen as well as disposing of carbon dioxide from the fetus. It also serves as a filter between the blood of the fetus and the mother, thereby helping to protect the fetus from infections. The placenta thus constitutes one way in which the fetus and the mother are intimately connected in various regards and are, at the same time, divided in different regards.

The placenta's protective capacity, however, has its limitations. Despite challenging methodological difficulties of the involved research (risk factors tend to cluster together and interact; Monk, Georgieff, & Osterholm, 2013; Williams & Ross, 2007), it is safe to say that the placenta cannot – or at least not completely – protect the developing fetus

4 Postnatal adverse ego-socius interactions and relationships and their consequences were presented in ToT Volumes I and II, so that these topics need not be reiterated in the present chapter. However, the themes of *traumatic* (a term that fits the *second-person* perspective) and *traumatizing* (a term that fits the *third-person* perspective) interpersonal events and relationships remain a general, recurrent, and essential concern in the chapters to come, as does the theme of therapeutic relationships (see Volume I, Chapter 11 for refined definitions of the terms 'traumatic' and 'traumatizing').

from a variety of harmful environmental influences. These include smoking and alcohol (Williams & Ross, 2007), particular medications (El Marroun, White, Verhulst, & Tiemeier, 2014), pesticides (Gonzalez-Alzaga et al., 2014), recreational drugs such as cocaine (Bhide, 2009) as well as maternal unhealthy diet (Monk et al., 2013) and eating disorders (Micali & Treasure, 2009).

Whereas these influences on the fetus are basically physical in nature, the developing prenatal baby's environment is also deeply psychosocial (Pisoni et al., 2014). The fetus is subject to the mother's states of mind, for better or worse. Moreover, physical and psychosocial risk factors can interact (e.g., Monk et al., 2013), and the placenta is not the only means of communication the fetus possesses with the mother and the broader environment. For example, using their haptic and mechanic skin-receptors, fetuses can perceive amniotic fluid pressure waves generated by intrauterine sounds (Vas, 2013). The evolving baby starts to hear sounds between 23 to 27 weeks of gestation. These obviously include nearby sounds such as those of the mother's heart, streaming blood, breathing, and gurgling tummy as well as sufficiently loud sounds stemming from the external world. To illustrate, loud sounds can cause changes in the fetus' heart rate and movements (Brezinka, Lechner, & Stephan, 1997; Johansson, Wedenberg, & Westin, 1992).

Fetuses may be aware of their body, may perceive pain, and react to touch, smell, and sound as well as show facial expressions when responding to external stimuli (Lagercrantz & Changeux, 2009). Touching and hearing might play an important role in the mother-fetus attunement and in the development of the fetal nervous system (Vas, 2013). Given this openness to the intrauterine and extrauterine world, we may wonder what happens to a fetus if the mother and/or father do not want the child? Or if a mother is severely stressed or deeply depressed during gestation? Or using drugs? What if the fetus must recurrently hear angry voices such as parents fighting? What if the mother is maltreated or sexually abused during the pregnancy, or if she was incidentally or chronically traumatized before conceiving? And what if several (or all) of these and perhaps still other conditions apply (e.g., smoking, alcohol and drug abuse, self-mutilation)?

Researchers have addressed some of these and related questions. One finding is that unwanted and mistimed pregnancies were associated with unhealthy perinatal maternal behaviors (Cheng, Schwarz, Douglas, & Horon, 2009). Unintended pregnancy was associated with women who smoked in the third trimester, received delayed or no prenatal care, did not breast-feed, were physically abused during pregnancy, said their partner had not wanted a pregnancy, or had a low-birth-weight infant (D'Angelo, Gilbert, Rochat, Santelli, & Herold, 2004). The size of these various links depended on whether the mother had not wanted or had mistimed her pregnancy.

Low birth weight is associated with various risk factors. They include young age, multiple pregnancies, previous low birth weight infants, poor nutrition, heart disease, hypertension, substance abuse, smoking, and poor prenatal care (Zhou, Rosenthal, Sherman, Zelikoff, Gordon, & Weitzman, 2014). Physical environmental risk factors include air pollution (e.g., by lead; Cleveland et al., 2008). Some important social risk factors are maternal depression, domestic and intimate partner violence (e.g., Abdollahi, Abhari, Delavar, & Charati, 2015; Alhusen, Ray, Sharps, & Bullock, 2015; Han & Stewart, 2014), low maternal education, and low socioeconomic status. Several studies concluded that violence against women exposes them to poor reproductive health, infant and child mortality, and poor infant and child health (e.g., Asling-Monemi, Naved, & Persson, 2009; Taft, Powell, & Watson, 2015). Negative outcomes of verbal and emotional abuse (i.e., being threatened, screamed at, insulted) have also been documented (Gentry & Bailey, 2014). For example, being threatened was associated with adverse birth outcomes. Women reporting any instance of this type of abuse during pregnancy were twice as likely to deliver a low birth weight baby.

Low birth weight can be associated with serious consequences. It is linked with newborn health and survival, higher risk of infant and childhood mortality, and smaller brain volume (e.g., Schlotz, Godfrey, & Phillips, 2014). Very low birth weight is correlated with small hippocampal volume, which in turn is associated with inferior memory function, particularly with respect to working memory (e.g., Aanes, Bjuland, Skranes, & Lohaugen, 2015).

Mild to moderate maternal 'stress' during pregnancy need not be harmful to the developing fetus. While more research is needed, some studies indicate that a limited degree of stress may actually stimulate the fetus to develop a healthier immune system and better motor capacities. The placenta, however, has a restricted capacity to protect the fetus from severe maternal psychosocial stress. The implication is that too much stress is too much: Excessive maternal stress can harm the fetus. Maternal psychosocial stress is associated with the stress hormone cortisol (Entringer, Buss, Andersen, Chicz-Demet, & Wadhwa, 2011), and higher circulating levels of C-reactive protein, a marker of inflammation. It is also linked with proinflammatory cytokines and lower circulating levels of an anti-inflammatory cytokine (Christian, Franco, Glaser, & Iams, 2009; Coussons-Read, Okun, Schmitt, & Giese, 2005). A review of the literature suggests that, along with elevated cortisol, imbalances in pro- and anti-inflammatory cytokines can distort fetal brain and body development (Buss, Entringer, Swanson, & Wadhwa, 2012). These distortions may cause negative effects. They include long-term sequelae such as neurodevelopmental disorders and psychopathology (Swanson & Wadhwa, 2008) as well as impaired fetal maturation, infant mental and motor development, infant temperament, and infant cognitive development (e.g., Davis & Sandman, 2010).

One important finding is that prenatal cortisol exposure may predict hypothalamus-pituitary-adrenal (HPA-) axis[5] functioning in the child in response to separation-reunion stress (O'Connor, Bergman, Sarkar, & Glover, 2013). Other studies suggest that the effects

---

5 Including three endocrine glands, this axis is an important component of the neuroendocrine system. It influences human reactions to events we experience and perceive as stressful. The HPA axis is also involved in the regulation of moods, emotions, and sexuality as well as in digestion, energy storage and expenditure, and the immune system.

of abnormal maternal cortisol can stretch beyond the attachment system. For example, excessive maternal stress during pregnancy, high placental corticotrophin-releasing hormone (CRH), and maternal cortisol were associated with impaired fetal maturation, infant mental and motor development as well as infant temperament (Bergman, Sarkar, Glover, & O'Connor, 2010; Class et al., 2008; Davis, Glynn, Dunkel Schetter, Hobel, Chicz-Demet, & Sandman, 2005; Davis, Glynn, Schetter, Hobel, Chicz-Demet, & Sandman, 2007; Entringer et al., 2011; Entringer et al., 2013; Pechtel & Pizzagalli, 2011; Sandman, Davis, Buss, & Glynn, 2011). Maternal exposure to excessive psychosocial stressors during pregnancy, such as domestic violence or the death or serious illness of a loved one, can thus have negative effects on fetal and infant neurodevelopment (Buss et al., 2012).

These effects, which probably relate to stress-related alterations in brain structure, connectivity, and function, include delayed mental and motor development, difficult temperament, and impaired cognitive performance (Pechtel & Pizzagalli, 2011; Sandman et al., 2011). For example, leukocyte telomere length, a predictor of age-related diseases and mortality, is related to cumulative psychosocial stress exposure in adults. It has been documented that exposure to maternal psychosocial stress during intrauterine life is associated with leukocyte telomere length in young adulthood (Entringer et al., 2013). Further, children born to mothers who experienced high levels of anxiety in the early second trimester of pregnancy had region-specific reductions in gray matter volume (Buss, Davis, Muftuler, Head, & Sandman, 2010) as well as impaired executive function (Buss, Davis, Hobel, & Sandman, 2011).

Abnormal brain structures and functions that evolved as a result of the gestational environment may be helpful in some contexts – and problematic in others (Andrews, Gangestad, & Matthews, 2002; Buss et al., 2012; Del Giudice, Ellis, & Shirtcliff, 2011; Flinn, Nepomnaschy, Muehlenbein, & Ponzi, 2011; Pluess & Belsky, 2011). The brain abnormalities involved, for example, might improve the ability of children to detect and avoid predators, thus preparing them for and allowing them to deal with adverse social life (Flinn et al., 2011). However, these abnormalities may also constitute a risk factor for posttraumatic stress disorder (PTSD), depression, and perhaps dissociative disorders beyond PTSD as well (cf. ToT Volume II, Chapter 19). It can thus be difficult to distinguish adaptation from insult, and beneficial and detrimental effects of brain abnormalities may be context specific (Andrews et al., 2002).

In sum, the studies quoted above and other related studies document that exposure to (the consequences of) maternal stress can have harmful short-term and long-term effects on fetuses relative to its timing, duration, and intensity (Buss et al., 2012). The inversion is also true: The development of a secure parent-infant attachment relationship and an enriched environment can protect the developing child from these injuries or perhaps repair them (Buss et al., 2012). This attachment pattern, for example, can modify the effects of prenatal maternal stress on infant temperament (Bergman, Sarkar, Glover, & O'Connor, 2008) as well as the effects of prenatal maternal cortisol on infant cognitive development (Bergman et al., 2010).

Postnatal Trauma

The development of a secure attachment relationship after prenatal as well as postnatal injurious interpersonal events can be healing. But what happens to the emerging wounded infant/child/adolescent/adult if this biopsychological protection and repair do not ensue? What if postnatal life continues – or commences – to be bad and ugly? What if parents or other family members do not assist developing children in regulating their affects? What if these affects are exceptionally intense because of recurrent emotional neglect, physical maltreatment, and sexual abuse? We are faced with a multitude of open questions:

- How should these children make sense of their world?
- What meaning will life have for them?
- How should they come to feel worthwhile, loved, and respected?
- How can they ever love and value themselves, learn to love and trust others, and dare to love and trust others again who have severely neglected, maltreated, and abused them?
- How will they know what safe and delicate touch is like?
- How will they know how to sensitively touch others?
- Who will teach them about healthy relationships and how can they experience what it is like to be in a healthy relationship?
- Who will teach them to relate to others in adequate and effective ways?
- How can they learn to be positively intimate and sexual?
- How can they detect healthy sexuality?
- How can they integrate and live a past, present, and anticipated future filled with horror?
- How can they concentrate in school and work (or elsewhere)?
- How will they learn how to play, sleep, and live in peace?

Infants and children who grow up within a recurrent antipathetic relational context involving emotional neglect and abuse, physical maltreatment, and sexual abuse tend to develop negative feelings and ideas about themselves, significant others, and the world in general if that world turns them a blind eye. Trusting and attaching to others as well as cherishing the hope of a brighter future become dangerous and despicable actions, as particularly controlling EP realize and broadcast, both internally and externally (e.g., in therapy).

In this light, enactive therapeutic understanding and assistance for individuals who have encountered this dark world and who live with its consequences take a meticulous third-person and empathic second-person analysis of the patterns of physical, affective, and cognitive exchanges among the hurt child and the perpetrator(s). It also takes a deep analysis of the role of insiders who knew (and maybe know) or who at least can suspect or could have strongly suspected what has happened or is happening to the child – but who simply let it be.

The sense-making activities of perpetrators involved and their accomplices often turn out to be as vicious as the neglect, maltreatment, and abuse were in the first place. For example, and as mentioned in ToT Volume II, Chapter 20, particularly high-risk sex offenders have severe cognitive distortions (Coxe & Holmes, 2009) related to the denial or minimization of their guilt, responsibility, deviance, the harm they inflicted on their victims, and their own need for treatment (Nunes & Jung, 2012). Denial was also associated with increased sexual recidivism for perpetrators of incest but not for other sex offender populations (Nunes et al., 2007; see also Harkins, Howard, Barnett, Wakeling, & Miles, 2015). A meta-analysis suggested that the major predictors of sexual recidivism for both adult and adolescent sexual offenders are not denial but deviant sexual preferences and antisocial orientation (Hanson & Morton-Bourgon, 2005). Antisocial orientation was, in fact, the major predictor of violent recidivism and general recidivism.

Under the influence of these and related perpetrator characteristics, traumatized children may come to believe that *they* are the guilty, bad, and undeserving ones, that all fathers engage in sexual relationships with their child, or that they are simply "sluts" or "sissies." Further, many perpetrators forbid a child to talk about the traumatization with others (e.g., other children or families, physicians, child protective services, police) or to seek help from anybody more generally (e.g., Crowley & Seery, 2001; Donalek, 2001) (see also Chapters 35 and 37). Some tell the child that nobody will believe them anyway when they speak out, a prediction that all too often proves to be true. Depth interviews with incestuously abused individuals regarding the termination of the involved incestuous relationship revealed that their feeling of being a victim lasted long after the abuse stopped (Lorentzen, Nilsen, & Traeen, 2008). They also reported that lack of support from family, friends, and healthcare personnel as well as the psychological power that the offender exerted were important themes in this respect.

Many perpetrators and families tend to show the external world an apparently normal face. And "normal" society all too often uncritically accepts this presentation. It likes to uphold the illusion that families are largely safe, loving, and caring. The idyllic vision is that children enjoy happy times by day and sweet dreams at night (see ToT Volume II, Chapter 20). Anyone who tells neglected, maltreated, and abused children this wishful fable contributes to their confusion, to the fierce contradictions that rage between intrafamilial reality and extrafamilial tales. This conflict only reinforces the tendency of chronically traumatized children to develop and maintain the division between ANPs and EPs. It also deepens their overall mistrust in adults, particularly caretakers, including clinicians.

In short, social cooperation and secure attachment become most difficult actions after interpersonal traumatization and chronic childhood traumatization. This development particularly applies when significant others (e.g., parents) were, and perhaps still are, the main offenders. In some cases, this traumatization may have already started prenatally. The paradox is that overcoming the injuries inflicted by interpersonal life through therapy takes much trust, attachment, and cooperation with one or more other adults in the form of the clinician or the therapeutic team. How patients and clinicians can best create a world of growing trust, attachment, and cooperation despite this paradoxical situation is a major concern of enactive trauma therapy.

Chapter 29

Conatus, Cognition, and the Body

Every true act of [a subject's] will is also at once and inevitably a movement of his body; he cannot actually will the act without at the same time being aware that it appears as a movement of the body. The act of will and the action of the body are ... one and the same thing, though given in two entirely different ways, first quite directly, and then in perception for the understanding. The action of the body is nothing but the act of will objectified, i.e., translated into perception.

... the knowledge I have of my will, although an immediate knowledge, cannot be separated from that of my body. I know my will not as a whole, not as a unity, not completely according to its nature, but only in its individual acts, and hence in time, which is the form of my body's appearing, as it is of every body.
Arthur Schopenhauer (1819, Book II, Section 18, pp. 101–102)

There is no such thing as affect-barren cognition. There is no "pure reason" (cf. Kant, 1781/1998). Realizing that cognition is no stranger to conatus, Spinoza spoke of an intellectual love of God or Nature[1]: *"He who understands himself and his affects clearly and distinctly loves God, and does so the more he understands himself and his affects"* (1677a; Part V, Proposition 15). He continued: *"This love of God must engage the mind most"* (Proposition 16), "[f]or this love is joined to all the affections of the body ... which encourage it ..." (p. 169). The intellectual love of God or Nature is thus intimately related to physical affections: "By affect I understand affections of the body by which the body's power of acting is increased or diminished, aided or restrained, and at the same time the ideas of these affections" (Part III, Definition 3). Higher human cognitive functions remain in concrete and abstract touch with the physical affections.

The principles of conatus and primordial affectivity are also more generally incompatible with views that primarily regard human beings as cognitive beings who once in a while have emotions, and that these emotions are basically a kind of nuisance compro-

---

1 Spinoza is often seen as an important philosopher of the Enlightenment, a 17th- and 18th-century philosophical movement that emphasized intellect and reason (see Chapter 23); other major representatives are Voltaire, Hume, and Kant. However, this understanding overlooks that Spinoza did not regard reason as 'pure reason,' as 'nonemotional.' In fact, he emphasized that cognition is affect-laden, and that affect cannot be controlled by mere thinking: We can only restrain or overcome one (problematic) affect by developing or activating an affect that is opposite to and stronger than the affect to be restrained or taken away (see Spinoza, 1677a, Part IV, Proposition 7).

mising rational thought, judgment, and behavior. In the enactive perspective, affect, cognition, and behavior are intrinsically coupled phenomena. Not the cognitions of organisms but their affect-laden strivings primarily guide their sense-making, and these goal orientations, not their cognitions, primarily organize their affects, thoughts, and behaviors (Colombetti, 2014). In other words, perception, affect, cognition (including memory), and behavior exist as dynamic clusters that serve the involved conatus or will of an organism (Schopenhauer, 1819, 1844).

If we consider that living organisms continuously evaluate the world they bring forward – relative to their needs, desires, and goals – cognition is affective to its very bones. Any appraisal – any thought – includes and is influenced by affect. Neuroscientific data also suggest that cognition and emotion are not distinct faculties. It appears that affective and cognitive functions are not associated with mutually exclusive neural structures. For example, long portrayed as exclusively involved in emotion (e.g., Öhman & Mineka, 2001), the amygdala and the limbic system more generally also fulfill critical roles in cognitive actions such as attention, associative learning, values, and decision-making (Gallagher & Chiba, 1996; Lewis, 2005; Pessoa, 2008, 2010, 2012). And brain structures traditionally believed to be exclusively or primarily involved in cognition now appear to have important roles in emotional life as well (e.g., the anterior cingulate as well as the orbitofrontal, ventromedial, and lateral prefrontal cortices; see Davidson, Jackson, & Kalin, 2000). In this light, Lewis (2005, p. 182) concluded that "many neural systems that become activated in appraisal also take part in emotional functions, and systems that generate emotional responses may also serve appraisal functions." Further, traditional motor brain areas are intimately involved in emotion and cognition (Rizzolatti, Cattaneo, Fabbri-Destro, & Rozzi, 2014; Schutter & Van Honk, 2005, 2006, 2009). The motor system does not merely produce movements, it is crucially involved in goal-directed action and in our understanding of other individuals' intentions (Rizzolatti et al., 2014). Finally, there is no evidence that discrete emotions are consistently and specifically associated with distinct brain regions (Lindquist, Wager, Kober, Bliss-Moreau, & Barrett, 2012).

Consistent with a psychological constructionist view of mind, Lindquist et al. (2012, p. 121) concluded that "[a] set of interacting brain regions commonly involved in basic psychological operations of both an emotional and nonemotional nature are active during emotion experience and perception across a range of discrete emotion categories." To illustrate, the insula is quite consistently activated when we perceive and experience disgust, though the structure is not preferentially associated with this emotion (Colombetti, 2014, p. 212). Yet some areas of the brain are more commonly activated than others when we perceive and experience a particular emotion. For example, the amygdala is more consistently associated with fear perception and experiencing disgust (Colombetti, 2014; Lindquist et al., 2012).

To sum up, cognition does not constitute the *cause* of individuals' emotional and behavioral troubles. Rather, perception, emotion, cognition, and behavior are inherently and intricately interwoven components of organic life. These dynamic clusters are all organized and guided by the desires and needs of organisms (see Figures 29.1. and 29.2.). Will, and not

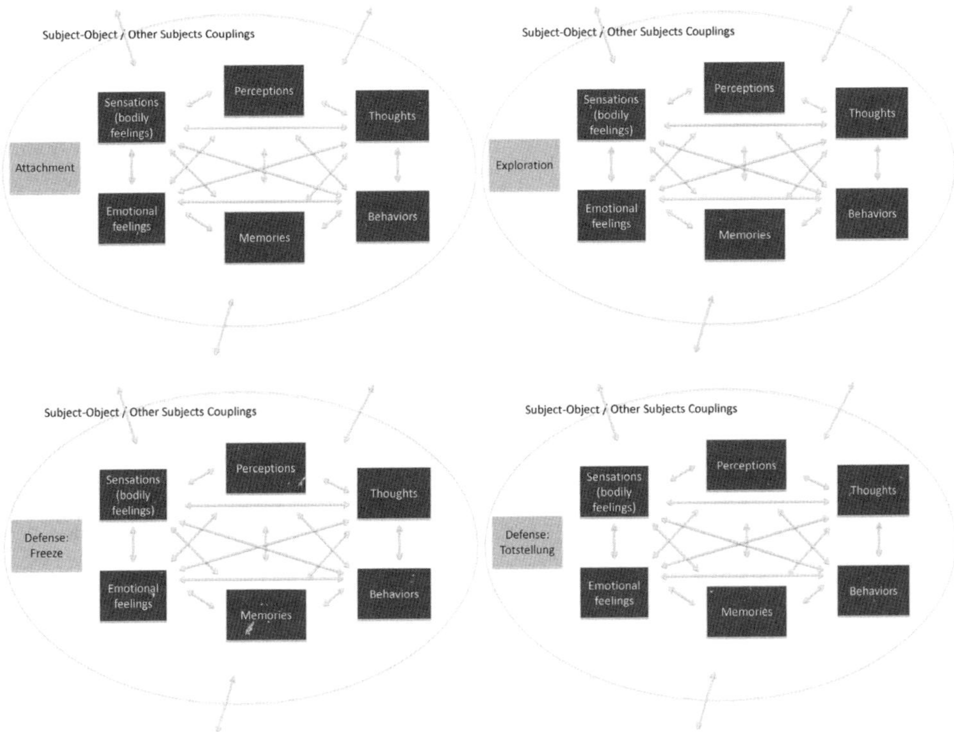

Figure 29.1. Needs and desires guiding dynamic clusters of sensations, emotional feelings, perceptions, memories, thoughts (conceptions), and behaviors.

Note: Various needs and desires guide dynamic clusters actions (i.e., particular ways of sensing the body, having emotional feelings, perceiving in the environment, thinking, remembering, and moving). It is easier to integrate components of a particular dynamic cluster than to integrate various needs and desires. On the other hand, some needs and desires are easier to integrate than others. For example, a securely attached child finds it easier to integrate needs and desires for attachment and those for exploring the environment than to integrate attachment-related actions and defense-related actions, particularly when the 'subject' of attachment (say, the child's mother) is also a most dangerous 'object' for the child (see also Figure 29.3). The uninterrupted ovals do not suggest that individuals and their environment are isolated from each other or interact with each other; rather, they are intrinsically related: Subjects are environmentally embedded. The individual must be seen as an organism-environment system.

cognition, is basic to life. In this order of things, mind – in the sense of appreciating, however unconsciously, what is useful, useless, and harmful – follows like the shadow of will.

Conatus and Cognition in Trauma

Given conatus and primordial affectivity, enactive trauma clinicians (and scientists) understand trauma as a biopsychosocial injury, implying a person's tremendous difficulty to make sense of a horrific world. The injury includes the inability to engage in integrative

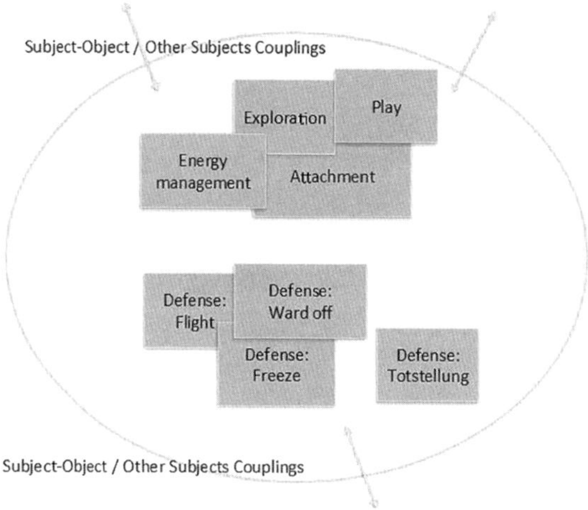

Figure 29.2. A space of needs and desires.

Note: Largely compatible needs and desires – each with its implied dynamic cluster of actions – are easier to integrate than less compatible or incompatible needs and desires. The uninterrupted oval does not suggest that individuals and their environment are isolated from each other or interact with each other; rather, they are intrinsically related: Subjects are environmentally embedded. The individual must be seen as an organism-environment system.

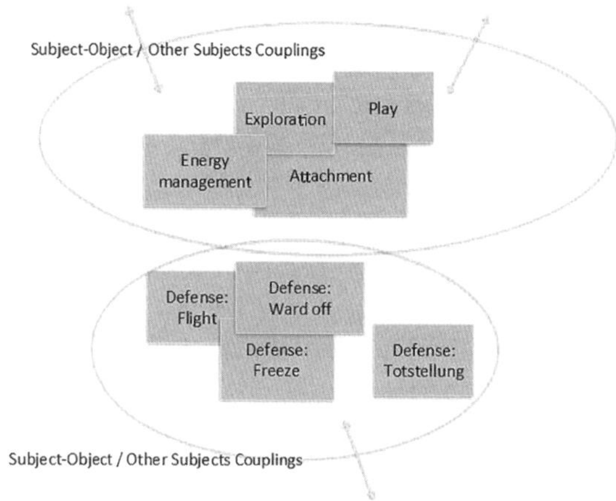

Figure 29.3. Division of the personality in trauma.

Note: When an individual's various needs and desires pertain to a parent or other primary caretaker who is the subject of one's attachment needs and the object of one's defensive urges, dissociation of the personality becomes particularly likely. In its simplest form, the division includes one ANP and one EP. The uninterrupted oval does not suggest that individuals and their environment are isolated from each other or interact with each other; rather, they are intrinsically related: Subjects are environmentally embedded. The individual must be seen as an organism-environment system.

actions regarding traumatic experiences, dissociative parts, trauma-related emotional and physical feelings, and more. Low integrative capacity relates to a variety of causal factors. A major hindrance to this integration is the difficulty encountered in integrating contrary interests in one's phenomenal self and in integrating a phenomenal world that critically involves those individuals who have hurt or continue to wound them deeply (see Figure 29.3). Since the issue was extensively discussed in Volumes I and II, it need not be reiterated here completely. However, the relationship between conatus and cognition in trauma remains a recurring theme in the later chapters.

Mind, Brain, and Body

The mind does not float in a physical vacuum. Many organisms are *embrained,* and all are *embodied.* This means that mind is intrinsically physical, just as, given conatus, everything that is alive (i.e., all organic matter) is intrinsically mental. This does not imply, Spinoza emphasized, that the mental can be reduced to the physical, or the physical to the mental. As explained above, they are better comprehended as different attributes of a single substance. Spinoza explicitly asserted that each attribute has to be understood on its own terms. For example, consciousness cannot be reduced to anything else, because any reduction, any understanding, presupposes consciousness, and because consciousness is absolute (e.g., feeling warm is what it is). Yet this does not exclude the possibility of studying the mind and the brain in proximate indirect relationship to each other. As mentioned above, they can be indirectly linked (ToT Volume I, Chapter 8; see also Northoff, 2003, 2014a, 2014b; Varela, 1996).

When considered under the attribute of matter, many organisms include a primitive or more advanced nervous system. However, because the brain cannot exist by itself, it cannot be seen as the minimally sufficient physical ground for an organism. Some simple organisms do not even have or require a central nervous system, but rather are guided by biochemical metabolic operations. Organisms comprise a (wider) body as well. For example, vertebrates also consist of a body with its interacting fluids, cells, organs, muscles and bones, with central and peripheral nervous systems, and with circulatory, endocrine, and immune systems.

This embodiment is curiously overlooked in many scientific and clinical accounts of human experience, emotions, thought, and behavior, in the sense that it is not, or only insufficiently, realized that being embodied deeply influences an organism's brain, mind, and behavior. Enactivism stresses that the embodiment is a crucial component of individuals as conscious, living, moving, and goal-oriented organisms. In this regard enactivism is also deeply indebted to Spinoza: Several of his propositions express just how central the body is to the mind.

The Object of the Idea Constituting the Human Mind is the Body

Part II of *Ethics* (1677a) is called *Of the Nature and Origin of the Mind.* In this part, Spinoza states that: "*[t]he first thing which constitutes the actual being of a human mind is nothing but the idea of a singular thing which actually exists*" (Part II, Proposition 11; italicized in the original text). In order to understand this proposition and what follows, it is important to realize that Spinoza's concept of 'idea' includes far more than what is presently called a thought or 'cognition.' He defines 'idea' as "... a concept of the mind which the mind forms because it is a thinking thing" (1677a, Part II, Definition 3). The definition is immediately followed by the explanation that "I say concept rather than perception, because the word perception seems to indicate that the mind is acted on by the object. But concept seems to express an action of the mind" (p. 32). An idea is dependent on a mental action, on "thinking," on conceiving "a singular thing which actually exists" (Part II, p. 38). To think is to act, and in the sense of a concept of the mind idea constitutes its implied result.

As mentioned in ToT Volume I (p. 68) and footnote 20, the term 'conceive' stems from the Latin verb *capere,* meaning 'to take something onto oneself.' The mind, thus, develops ideas, and ideas are concepts that the mind forms, not out of the blue, but of things that "actually exist." These existing things do not work on a passively receptive (or, rather, passively perceptive) mind. Quite the contrary, the mind must *work* to know objects; it must actively take objects onto itself; it must actively conceive, not passively receive or perceive. With Spinoza, the human mind and its concepts ("ideas") and objects ("things") are deeply relative to each other (ToT Volumes I & II).

Reading Spinoza's second axiom of Part II "Man thinks,"[2] one might nonetheless come to the conclusion that 'thinking' is limited to developing or having thoughts. But this is not what Spinoza had in mind. The third axiom of this part of *Ethics* reveals that his concepts of 'thinking' and 'idea' extend much further. As he states, "[t]here are no modes of thinking, such as love, desire, or whatever is designated by the word affects of mind, unless there is in the same individual the idea of the thing loved, desired and the like ..." (p. 32). (This axiom was used as a motto for Chapter 22, which addresses consciousness.) "Thinking" comprises many modes, including the mental actions of generating feelings and emotions, so that "idea" includes having self-related and object-related desires, affects, emotions, and feelings. In short, thinking is a mental action that implies being conscious, and being conscious implies being conscious *of* something. Brentano (1838–1917) was not the first to say that consciousness is intentional.

Ideas of the Affections of the Body

Following the proposition that: "*[t]he first thing which constitutes the actual being of a human mind is nothing but the idea of a singular thing which actually exists,*" Spinoza links the mind and the body: "*The object of the idea constituting the human mind is the body, or a certain mode of extension which actually exists, and nothing else*" (1677, Part II, Proposition 13). He comments: "From these [propositions] we understand not only that the human mind is related to the body, but also what should be understood by the union of the mind and the body" (p. 40). The phrase "*singular thing which actually exists*" is thus the human body. In other words, "*[t]he first thing that constitutes the actual being of a human Mind is nothing but the idea of a human body which actually exists*" (Part II, Proposition 11). In this sense, the human mind is inseparably and intrinsically coupled to the human body.

In Proposition 19 (1677a, Part II) Spinoza further posits the epistemological linkage of mind and body: "*The human mind does not know the human body itself, nor does it know that it exists, except through the ideas of affections by which the body is affected.*" For the

2 In the *De Nagelate Schriften van B.d.S.* (1677b), Spinoza elaborated this axioma with the following statement: "Man thinks, or to put it differently, we know that we think" (see Spinoza, 1677a, p. 32). The axioma contrasts with and avoids the problems of Descartes' axioma "I think, therefore I am."

mind to know that the body exists, the body must be affected in one way or another. It must be alive – its heart must beat, its blood must stream, its parts must move, its nervous system must be awake. The affections also stem from the body's environment with which it is coupled in conatus and its implied primordial affectivity. Through the affections of its body by light, earth, wind, rain, sounds, plants, and a host of other bodies, some of which are alive, the human mind can know the human body and through this body other, external bodies. But in order to know the human body, the mere existence of physical affections is not enough. The crucial point is that human mind only knows the human body when it notices and generates ideas of these affections. Therefore, "*[t]he human mind does not perceive any external body as actually existing except through the ideas of the affections of its own body*" (Part II, Proposition 26).

Limited Conscious Knowledge of the Body and Mind

The existence of ideas of the physical affections does not imply that the human mind consciously knows itself. When the mind does not engage in further work, it remains unconscious of its own existence. Self-consciousness takes further action: "*The mind does not know itself, except insofar as it perceives the ideas of the affections of the body*" (Part II, Proposition 23). The mind only becomes conscious of itself when it perceives its own ideas or conceptions of the affections that have affected the body. And to become conscious of its own existence, the mind must "think" (see above): It must notice that the body is affected in one way or another, develop ideas of these affections, and then perceive these ideas. With these actions, individuals can feel the "sunlight warming my face, wind playing with my hair, sand moving under my bare feet, and being delighted." Or, they can experience that "my brother is laughing at me," "my mother is shouting in my ears," "my father slaps me in the face," or "my heart aches and races."

As indicated above, the mind's noticing and perceiving of the affections of the body is not passive but creative. Noticing and perceiving something does not mean passively receiving an inner or external affection; rather, it takes the active development of an idea of the involved affection. To feel the human body, the human mind must engage in the action of feeling it. How the mind feels the body, how that feeling is, depends on the way it 'takes' the affection of the body 'onto itself' (the literal meaning of the Latin word *capere*). These mental actions do not and cannot proceed apart from the body, because each act of thinking as well as the feeling, thought, memory, or another idea this action generates *implies* the very embrained and thinking body: "*The order and connection of ideas is the same as the order and connection of things*" (Part II, Proposition 7).

There are serious limitations to the conscious mind's ability to know itself. These constraints are implied by several propositions. First, remember that "the order of actions and passions of our body is, by nature, at one with the order of actions and passions of the mind" (Part III, Scholium to Proposition 2, p. 71: see also pp. 71–74 more generally).

This statement clearly flows from the view that the body and the mind are two attributes of one substance. The implication is that if we do not have a complete understanding of our body, we do not (indeed, cannot) have a complete understanding of our mind.

In order to explain that there are serious limitations to the conscious mind's ability to know itself, first remember that "*[t]he object of the idea constituting the human mind is the body ...*" (1677a, Part II, Proposition 13). However, "*[t]he ideas of the affections of the human body, insofar as they are related only to the human mind, are not clear and distinct, but confused*" (Part II, Proposition 28). This lack of clarity exists because "*[t]he idea of any affection of the human body does not involve adequate knowledge of the body itself*" (Part II, Proposition 27). Our body includes countless parts and particles that we do not know. For example, as first persons, we do not know our brain cells, blood cells, hormones, neurotransmitters, etc. And no one knows the ultimate nature of matter (Järvilehto, 2004). Apart from this fact, we do not know all objects or the parts or particles of the external objects that affect our body. Further, "*[t]he idea of the idea of any affection of the human body does not involve adequate knowledge of the human mind*" (Part II, Proposition 29). This limitation exists because "*[t]he mind does not know itself except insofar as it perceives ideas of the affections of the body*" (Part II, Proposition 23). Because the mind's ideas of the affections of the body are so profoundly limited, and because the mind and the body are different attributes of the same substance, it follows that the total mind surpasses the conscious mind by far. The unconscious mind was not discovered in the 19th century, and not in Vienna.

In sum, for Spinoza consciousness is primarily affect-laden body awareness of an environmentally embedded (or *umwelt*-embedded) organism that longs and strives to satisfy its need and desires. Enactivism takes this embodiment very seriously.

More Than a Brain

Currently, there is a tremendous interest in the brain. Some authors even curiously claim that we *are* our synapses (LeDoux, 2002) or more generally: our brain (Swaab, 2010). However, it is crucial to realize that "[t]he presence of a nervous system inside the organism does not make sense-making suddenly 'shrink' to it (and correlatively, it does not relegate the rest of the organism to a mere interactant that provides inputs to the nervous system and receives outputs from it)" (Colombetti, 2014, p. 102). The brain cannot even exist without a body, just as the body cannot exist without the brain. They continuously regulate each other (Cosmelli & Thompson, 2010; also see http://espra.scicog.fr/Thompson_Cosmelli_BrainBody.pdf). What is more, the brain and the body of organisms do not just interact: They constitute intrinsically related components of one organism-environment system. In this sense,

> [t]he brain isn't a reflex machine whose activity is externally controllable through input instructions. Rather, it's a highly nonlinear and self-organizing dynamical system ... Inputs per-

> turb such complex systems but don't specify particular outcomes. Furthermore, most inputs arise as a consequence of the system's own intrinsic activity. (Cosmelli & Thompson, 2010; cited in Colombetti, 2014, p. 102–103)

This is why Susan Hurley (1998, p. 333–334) regarded an organism as a 'dynamic singularity,' as a mixture of recurrent and reentrant operations encompassing the brain, the entire body, and the environment. There is a world that affects the body, but these affections as such do not determine what meaning they have for the affected organism – and how the organism reacts.

This perspective is very different from classical learning theory in which organisms are seen as more or less complex collections of stimulus-response and stimulus-stimulus associations (for more critique of this psychology, see ToT Volume I, specifically the works of Bolles and Fanselow, 1980; Garcia, 1981; Timberlake & Lucas, 1989). Indeed, traumatized individuals do not respond to 'conditioned stimuli' or 'triggers' in mechanical, fixed ways. They signify affections in context-dependent and interest-dependent manners. The meaning that a 'stimulus' (or a mixture of 'stimuli') has for an organism depends on its relevance for the organism as defined by, among other things, its present state (e.g., current needs, desires, emotions, mood, energy level). That is why we should stop using terms such as 'inputs' and 'outputs,' 'stimuli' and 'reactions,' and speak of 'signs,' 'perturbations,' 'operations' (unconscious), 'actions' (conscious), and 'passions.'

In the same spirit, Overton recently suggested that

> ... an active organism (system of organized processes) approach should avoid, except in very limited cases, the terms stimulus, reinforcement, response, elicit, and evoke. Affordance (opportunity to act), resources, and asset should be substituted for both stimulus and reinforcement, and activity (at the biological level) and action or act (applied to the psychological level, entailing intention or goal-directedness) should be used to replace response and behavior. As also described earlier, the term interaction should be eliminated from our scientific vocabulary – again, except in very limited cases – and replaced with coaction. (2015, p. 46)

Motricity

In the perspective of enactivism, consciousness and cognition are phenomena that emerge through our recurrent patterns of world-engaged perception, conception, and (motor/behavioral) action (Fuchs & De Jaegher, 2010; Krueger, 2010; Thompson, 2007). Thinking does not *cause* motor action or behavior (as cognitivists claim); rather, as pointed out above, cognitive acts and structures – including the cognitive capacities at the root of our social interactions – are grounded in ongoing, affect-laden, embodied patterns of environment-oriented action (cf. Figure 29.1.) In this sense, motor action is far more than a mere movement to achieve a set goal. *Goal-oriented movement brings forth a world.* We seek, notice, and move toward other subjects and toward objects we desire, and we move away from individuals and objects we fear or hate. We also tend to grasp, touch, hold, cuddle, stroke, kiss, tickle, explore, feel, smell, taste, look at, drink, eat, chew on, or create what we like and find useful. And we run from, ward off, destroy, or depreciate what interferes with our interests.

Any act or (en)action essentially includes motricity. Like Spinoza and others who – knowingly or unknowingly – followed in his footsteps, Llinas (2001; Llinas & Roy, 2009) regards mind as a continuous feature of mobile forms of life and stresses the primordial importance of sensorimotor subject-object couplings. Mobile species may have developed a brain and an implied mind in the first place to predict the outcome of their *umwelt*-engaged motor actions (Llinas, 2001; Llinas & Roy, 2009). To that end, they must generate couplings between their significant sensory perceptions, their impending motor action(s), and the probable consequences of their world-engaged motricity.

Since plants are spatially fixed, they do not require a central nervous or another biochemical system that enables them to make such predictions. To illustrate the point, Llinas (2001) describes how in its larval form the sea squirt includes a brain-like ganglion, the simple animal's equivalent of the human brain. Being a sensorimotor system, it permits the mobile creature to navigate its *umwelt* and hence to support the animal's survival. As an adult, the sea squirt becomes a sessile[3] animal, attaching itself to a rock or some other hard surface on the ocean floor and staying there for the rest of its life. This immobile existence would seem to render the animal's brain/mind superfluous if it is the core business of the brain/mind to predict the consequences of goal-directed actions (which concern the prediction of the consequences of goal-directed actions). Consistently, the sea squirt undergoes a metamorphosis once it has found a definitive place to stay, essentially including the reduction of its cerebral ganglion. In this sense the settled animal is said to 'consume' most of its own brain/mind.

Like (far) more primitive mobile organisms, human beings enact a world of personal significance, and this enactment crucially includes goal-oriented mental and behavioral movement, that is, *action*. From the very beginning of our existence as a fetus, we actively explore our own body. Even in the womb, we move our emerging mouth, arms, hands, fingers, and legs in a goal-directed fashion. Even in this early developmental phase, we open our mouth *before* moving our hand toward or in it. As newborn babies, we also explore our body and our environment and thereby affect them. As we mature, we strive to distinguish ourselves from other individuals and other worldly objects we find and create. From our early days onward, we react to and may even imitate the facial expressions and other actions of other individuals. We also generate ever more movements, sounds, and still other 'productions' that influence our world. Our conceptions of ourselves and of our *umwelt* are strongly shaped by our embodied actions (ToT Volume I, Chapter 10) – for better or worse. Infants and children who are physically and emotionally caressed – that is, loved – and positively encouraged are furthered in their development

3 Sessile animals such as sea squirts and sponges are unable to move about once they have become settled adults. However, they typically go through a motile larval phase.

of a positive sense of themselves, their bodies, their capabilities, and their entire world. They generally feel at home in their bodies and in the world they experience and know. They move about freely. Hated children, on the other hand, tend to hate themselves, including their bodies. They may engage in repulsive, frustrated movements, and they tend to despise the world they experience and know. Intensely depersonalized as well as emotionally and physically numb, some neglected children may in fact hardly sense they really and truly exist. They may have tremendous difficulty experiencing and believing they are *entitled* to exist.

Chapter 30

Participatory Sense-Making

Minds . . . are conquered not by arms, but by love and nobility.
Baruch Spinoza (Part IV, Appendix XI)

. . . every description of life is a metaphor created by human beings, and it touches only some aspect of life . . . Life cannot be exhaustively described, and even if it could this description is not identical with life. We cannot create life by following linguistic descriptions. Life can be created only by living, not by imitating life.
Timo Järvilehto (2001b, p. 10)

The goal of enactive trauma therapy is to increase the power of action of traumatized individuals. This progression ensures that they become determined more by their own causes and be controlled less by external causes. In this sense, enactive trauma clinicians invite, encourage, and assist them to turn their traumatic and other passions into actions. A part of this work lies in helping traumatized individuals to enact a healthier phenomenal self, *umwelt*, and self as an inherent part of this *umwelt*. This health replaces their recurrent reenactments of traumatizing events and relationships, and the implied traumatized phenomenal conceptions of self and environment. Particularly following chronic and severe abuse, maltreatment, and neglect, enacting this curative path on one's own – in social isolation, that is – may be exceptionally difficult if not nearly impossible. Enactive trauma therapy is a joint enterprise of a hurt and hurting individual and a (psycho)therapeutically trained, less unfortunate individual to create a healthier path for walking together. This is the common result enactive trauma therapy aims to achieve.

The principles and ideas that ground enactive trauma therapy were in part nonexistent and in part forgotten when I first encountered – or recognized – traumatized individuals in the early 1980s. At that time the phenomena and terms 'trauma' and 'dissociation' were largely unfamiliar, or in any case largely meaningless, to me as significant terms in psychology when I commenced my university studies in 1972. And even when I finished my academic training in 1978 they had still not gained much meaning. It is ironic that my professional life was to become populated by these subjects. During my formative years they had not been mentioned once, let alone discussed. It is no less ironic that the two themes are of high relevance to the matters that started to occupy my mind from the formative years onward. So, what drove me to psychology?

Entering the World of Psychology

Passing through the entrance to the magnificent academic building at the University of Groningen for the first time, I felt ... elated. Ages of reflection on human experience, thought, and behavior were about to be unveiled to me. Conundrums that had occupied my mind from my early teenage years were to become clarified. For example, I wondered how the human mind is able to understand itself, its world, and its place in this world? Do humans truly grasp the world or only some version thereof – or is all that can possibly exist for us our constructed, all too human world? How can the human body know itself? Does the brain cause the mind? Or does nature work the other way around? Maybe the brain and the mind do not actually cause each other. So what is consciousness and what is self-consciousness? What is an 'I'?

In my juvenile simplicity, I trusted that the wise men and women would provide me with clear and definitive answers. After all, places of organized higher learning and reflection had already existed in ancient Greece, Persia, Rome, Byzantium, China, India, and the Muslim world. Founded in 1088, the Italian University of Bologna was the first university in the Western sense of the concept: a community of teachers and scholars. Situated in the northern part of The Netherlands, the University of Groningen had been established in 1614. From its very start, this academy included a Faculty of Philosophy, the discipline that included what was to become the science of the psyche from the 19th century. By 1846, the original academy building was in such a poor state that it had to be torn down, to be replaced by a larger construction that burned down in 1906. An impressive neo-classical edifice, the third academy building opened its grand doors 3 years later. These were the doors I walked through as a college freshman.

The puzzles that beset my adolescent mind included the mystery of the disturbed psyche. Unlike other puzzles, this particular problem had not dogged me primarily from any intellectual wonder: It was rooted in an emotional shock. The tiny rural community in which I had been raised constituted a largely predictable and mostly secure world. Sure, life had taught me that people differed from each other, and that not everyone is friendly, understanding, fair, and clever.

But a boy who suddenly showed up at my small combined kindergarten and primary school was very different from anyone else I had met before in my short life – I was perhaps 5 or 6 years old. Running across the playground, hissing and hiding, he would scream words in an unfamiliar tongue. He reminded me of the wild cat that had panicked when accidentally enclosed in the kitchen of my parent's farm. The boy's terror and rage were a mystery to me. He scared but intrigued me. And somehow I felt some of his pain. Why couldn't we talk, play, be friends? Why didn't he allow us, the other children, to come near him? Didn't he know he was safe with us? And what was he doing in our small and remote village anyway?

I bombarded my parents with questions. They talked about a revolt in Hungary, about Russians occupying the country, about a world of danger and injustice and refugees. I had seen pictures of Russian tanks in the streets of Budapest. Yet, I was too young to take this all in. But from that early time on I knew two things for certain: Some boys are like wild cats, and this fact somehow relates to fear, rage, pain, violence, and unfairness.

When I left the university, I had gained, among many other things, substantial knowledge of the behavior of especially cats and rats, prominently including those shocked and food-deprived or love-deprived. Learning theory and behavior therapy were popular in those days. But the professors had not spoken of shocked, unloved, and shattered people. They had not mentioned wild boys who were scared to death.

More generally, I learned that, according to the behaviorists, consciousness and self-consciousness were better left enclosed in a black box. But it seemed to me that the mind refuses to be incarcerated. Prisons neither erase nor prevent needs, desires, emotions, thoughts, and memories. As cognitivism gained dominance over behaviorism, over simple 'input' – 'output' models, consciousness started to reemerge from the methodological cage in which behaviorism had tried to lock it up. However, the thinking individual was basically portrayed as some kind of machine. Terms like 'cognitive mechanisms' and 'mental representations' became commonplace. In the emerging cognitive paradigm, some clinical psychologists focused on the 'irrational' thinking patterns of disturbed individuals and on ways to get them to think more 'rationally.' But why do some psychiatric patients comprehend themselves and their world in 'illogical' ways? Why are they so resistant to grasping the 'obvious' and to applying this common sense logic to themselves?[1] Can the human mind operate at all without interests? Does a rational mind even exist? These questions still stood out for me as my studies were formally 'completed.'

Knowing about the principles and practice of classical and operant conditioning, systematic desensitization, exposure, flooding, and the like proved to be vital when it came to comprehending and treating individuals with phobias and obsessive-compulsive disorders. There are indeed significant commonalities between humans and other mammals. Whereas efforts to bring individuals with a psychiatric disorder to logic sometimes worked, I was impressed by the ability of the human mind to cling to 'irrational' or otherwise 'maladaptive' ideas. These were the experiences I gained in my first years of working as a behavior therapist.

Paula

But then why did Paula[2] – briefly introduced in Volume I, p. 60–61 – not respond to these interventions? When I first met her in 1982, she presented with several phobias, including

1 For an impressive example of a sharp contrast between an exceptionally deep understanding of logic and the difficulty of applying logic to oneself, see Ray Monk's biography of Ludwig Wittgenstein (1991).

2 This name is a pseudonym, as are all the names of individuals with a dissociative disorder presented in this book. To protect their identity and privacy, I have modified the case presentations in some regards, though these modifications leave the points I wish to make fully intact. All patients generously granted me permission to use the presented material.

social phobia, as well as other serious troubles such as major depression, chronic relational and sexual problems. As I got to know her better, it also became obvious that she overprotected her children. Too scared that bad things might happen to them, she actually interfered with their normal desires to partake in social, extrafamilial life. It would be fair to say that she was deeply mistrustful of other people. It also became clearer that Paula was somehow not really 'present' in her daily life – or so it seemed to me. She adapted to other individuals' wishes, or at least to what she thought other people wanted from her; and she did not seem to know, value, or express her own needs and desires.

Other people's actual or presumed wishes included mine. For 2 years, I seriously applied the repertoire of known behavior therapeutic interventions, and Paula tried hard to respond. However, we achieved very little. My very experienced and able supervisor at that time strained himself to help me improve my 'behavioral analysis' of Paula's case as well as my treatment plan and my delivery of the implied therapeutic interventions. But regardless of what he and I came up with, our efforts remained fruitless. The continuing therapeutic failure drove my supervisor to utter the urgent advice, if not clear instruction, to end the useless struggle.

My head understood his view, and my heart fiercely protested against it. For one, I cared for Paula and felt great compassion for her. She was a very sympathetic, middle-aged woman, who, in contrast to her modest education, was bright and wise. Though filled with pain, sorrow, and loneliness, her brown eyes and soft facial features also expressed sincere warmth and kindness. Moreover, never missing a session, she was dedicated to overcoming her troubles. How could I simply leave her to her misery?

Apart from these reasons, there was also something secretive about her that my intuition traced and that my reason failed to grasp. Two or three times Paula had confused me in a way I could hardly put in words. On these rare occasions, her face and eyes grew hard for a second or two. Some words she spoke sounded unexpectedly tough. The episodes were so brief and out of context that I wondered whether what I saw or heard had really happened or if it had been a mere figment of my imagination. I did not know what to make of it, but there was just *something about her.* My mind is obsessive in certain regards. It tends to get hooked on things that it deems important but does not understand. A farmer's son, I was also raised to keep on trying when life gets rough.

This combination of circumstances made me resist my supervisor's suggestion to terminate the therapy. My will to obey my supervisor and leader was weaker than my will to understand and assist Paula. For 2 more years, Paula and I met once every other month. She felt grateful for my not giving her up, for my not abandoning her. She prudently started to share bits and pieces of her childhood, a topic she had previously sidestepped in our encounters, perhaps not – or not only – because she did not dare to really trust me, but also because she was too scared to admit the story of her life to herself. Today I would say it was a history of emotional neglect, emotional maltreatment, and physical abuse, a painful past that frightened her and that she was unable and unwilling to realize. She had a deep phobia of her own traumatic memories.

I clearly remember the day on which the nature and course of Paula's treatment underwent a dramatic shift. It was also the day that my professional life took a new and completely unexpected direction. A strange, scary, and confusing dream had come to Paula. The least disturbing part of it was that she was on her way to visit her parents.[3] It was bitterly cold when she undertook the long walk to their house. In the dream, the house was situated in an exceptionally remote area, and once inside the modest dwelling, the atmosphere was, as usual, uninviting. Her father and mother remained discontent no matter how hard Paula tried to please them or cheer them up. Growing ever more sad and despondent, she eventually had to take her leave. The long way home led through a desolate landscape. Following a path along an endless frozen canal, she saw in a flash what might be a corpse caught in the ice. The sight terrified her, and she awoke in a panic. The corpse or whatever it was had deeply upset her. Even sharing this phase of the dream with me gave her the creeps.

Listening to Paula, I got a general, rather intuitive idea of what her nightmare might mean. In order to understand my reasoning, it may be helpful to know some of the general history and culture of the province of Groningen, the part of The Netherlands where she was born and raised. It may also prove valuable to know that this northern province was my own native home turf as well. However, whereas she originated from the southeastern part of the province, my roots lie in the upper northern part. Because any individual is an organism-environment system, the patient and clinician's historical and cultural backgrounds constitute an integral part of the psychotherapeutic (ad)venture they engage in together. In this light, it can be helpful to describe the province and some of its history.

The Province of Groningen

The province of Groningen is, like most of The Netherlands, flat – very flat. Clay grounds in the northern and northeastern part, retaken from the sea, present an endless emptiness, wide skies, and distant sounds: waving golden wheat in the summer, straight dark furrows in the winter. Here, the green dikes defend the fertile grounds against a shallow sea. A national park, now included in the UNESCO World Heritage List, *The Wadden*[4] Sea is generally calm and peaceful. But its waters can occasionally rage. The waters have sometimes even reclaimed the rich soil the Dutch had slowly gained from it, cleverly using the

3 Her father was in fact deceased before she entered treatment, while her chronically dysphoric, self-centered, and attention-demanding mother was still alive. Paula felt an obligation and drive to take care of her, no matter how hard and unrewarding her efforts continued to be.

4 'Wad' (= 'mud flat') is the earliest written word in the Dutch language. It was first written down in a Latinized form as *vadam* by an ancient Roman, Publius Cornelius Tacitus, in the fifth book of his '*Histories*' in the year 107 AD. A *vada* is a fordable or wadeable place in a river. The word also gave its name to the Wadden sea and the Wadden Islands.

workings of the tides. Across the ages, occasional storm surges have thus broken the dikes, flooded the land and removed the former peat and sampled clay. More than that, they have taken many lives.

In the year 77 AD, the Roman author, naturalist, and natural philosopher Pliny the Elder published his encyclopedic *Naturalis Historia* (1949–1954), in which he reports on his travels. Describing *the Chauk*, who lived in Northwest Germany, an area very similar to the northeastern Dutch coastal region, Plinius wrote:

> There the ocean flows at two intervals, at day and at night, in a tremendous flood over an immense land. Because of this everlasting struggle with nature, it is doubtful whether the bottom is land or sea. In the area a miserable people live on high hills, or better on man-made mounds, just above the highest water level known by experience. On these mounds they have built their shacks, and when the water is high they are like sailors, but when the water is low they are more like shipwrecked sailors. Then they hunt for the fish that flee with the water around their huts. They don't have cattle, so they cannot feed on milk, like their neighboring people. Nor can they hunt for game, since the sea washes all brushes away. Out of reed and rush they make a sort of string, of which they knot fishing nets. They dry cloth of soil in the wind rather than in the sun, and burn them to cook their food and to warm their limbs that are chilled by the northern wind. (Plinius the Elder, Book XVI, section I, quoted in Bijker, 1996, p. 391)

But Plinius' impression of the poor living conditions of these people was not without flaw (Bijker, 1996). Archeological findings suggest that the inhabitants of the mounds were less miserable than suggested. They did possess cattle, made iron, and did other sorts of handicraft of a relatively high level. They even counted bronze-, silver-, and goldsmiths among their population. However, the age-old and incessant struggle with the waters of the sea may have provided some truth to the stereotype that people from the north are stubborn folks, individuals who do not give up easily. As the English say, "God created the world but the Dutch created Holland."

In the area immediately behind the northern and northeastern coastal ridge lies a layer of peat – partially decayed vegetable matter found in marshy or damp regions (Bijker, 1996). Whereas the Roman historian Tacitus depicted peat land as "land that cannot be treaded and water that cannot be sailed," probably around 600 AD the layer had become thick and high enough to permit modest habitation. From about 800 AD on the few inhabitants started to create primitive dikes to protect their land, cattle, and own life against the surrounding water. Since peat settles, they constantly had to raise the constructions. Their efforts were not in vain. At some point, the dikes were high enough to restrain the sea, the harbinger of food and dread, rather effectively. Well, that is, most of the time.

The peatland grew to be a vast area known as *The Bourtange Swamp*. Apart from its many troubles, the marshes provided two major assets: Water has been the Dutch's friend more than once in confrontations with its mortal foes[5]; and, once cut and dried, peat serves quite well as a fuel.

Peat as a Military Defense

During the 80 Years War between Spain and the evolving Dutch state (circa 1568–1648), Count Rennenberg, Stadhouder of Friesland, Groningen, Drenthe, and Overijssel, and along with him the city of Groningen, went over to the Spanish side in 1580. Supplies had to be secured using the only road between this city and Germany. The road followed the sandy ridge through the Bourtange Swamp ('tange' stands for sandy ridge). In order to control the connection, William of Orange instructed Diderick van Sonoy to construct a fort. The strategy worked. In 1594, the city of Groningen was reconquered, and Fort Bourtange became an important part of the fortifications on the border between Germany and the three northern provinces (Groningen, Friesland, and Drenthe).

Peat as Fuel

The earliest citations on the use of peat in Europe can be traced back to the time around 2000 years ago when Cajus Plinius Secundus, in *History of Natural Sciences*, noted the use of peat in the village of Delmenhorst in Germany. The way peat was used at that time was remarkably advanced. Extracted peat was mixed with a suitable amount of water after which the peat blocks were left to dry. In The Netherlands, cutting peat for fuel was initiated in connection with the establishment of monasteries some 1000 years ago.

Since the Middle Ages peat-cutters dug the huge moor off for the turf as fuel, until nothing was left. During the 17th century, the city of Groningen and its surroundings developed into a peat-cutting center, from where techniques spread over to Germany. The work then became a large-scale manual enterprise in this era. To transport the 'brown gold' as it was called, beginning in the 18th century several straight long canals were dug, by hand as well: hard work, low wages.[6] Many laborers and their families had to live under abominable circumstances, dwelling in moist sod huts infested with pests and vermin.[7]

When the peat land was used up, a sandy soil remained. Many people lost their job and hence their income. Less fertile than the northern clay, it was and is today mostly used for growing potatoes. Having yielded all its brown gold, the southeastern part of Groningen became one of the poorest areas in the country – and still is even today.

5 For example, in the 80 Years' War of Independence against Spain (1568–1648), the Dutch more than once flooded low-lying land. During the Siege of Leiden in 1574, *The Hollandic Water Line* proved to be an effective defense.

6 For an impression, see Vincent van Gogh's *Two women in the moor*, 1883.

7 For an impression, see Vincent van Gogh's *Huts*, 1885.

Defrosting a Frozen Lady

With this brief historical and cultural sketch in mind, it may become easier to picture and understand the probable symbolic meaning of the crucial elements of Paula's dream: the lonely house, the vast, sandy land, the infinite canals, the work-focused parents who lived a life of few words, limited education, rigid religious and cultural customs and ideas, and poverty. This characterization reflected Paula's descriptions of her family and broader environment, a world in which she was unable to thrive.

I also couldn't help but realize the contrast between her *umwelt*, the economically, psychologically, and socially deprived part of Groningen, and my own, the far more fertile and prosperous northern clay lands where I was born and raised and at the time still lived. She had been raised in an abusive and neglectful family, whereas I had enjoyed a happy childhood. Fortune and misfortune are clearly not evenly distributed. It was as if the dream spoke to this gloomy distinction as well. At the time, I actually commuted each working day between the two regions of the province, just as I, so to speak, moved back and forth between Paula's private world and my own.

Apart from this, however, the dream also suggested a path to Paula's healing. It seemed to say that it might be better to say goodbye to her deceased father and her unloving mother, to give up her righteous but hopeless hopes for parental acceptance, care, and love. Nothing she could ever do would trigger the fulfillment of her deepest needs and desires. The dream suggested it was time for Paula to engage an act of termination, more specifically in *l'action d'échec,* the act of 'misachievement' (Janet, 1927; Van der Hart et al., 2006).

But then why the frozen body? Was it metaphorically revealing Paula's fate – being caught in an icy world forever, being and remaining mentally dead? Did it show her destiny if she failed to overcome her longing for the impossible?

Although my first thoughts went in this direction, I certainly did not want to impose them on her. It would be better that she, the dreamer, would find her own meaning for her dream. But how to do this? Hadn't she fled from the body that might be a corpse?

In the early 1980s, the works of Milton Erickson (e.g., Haley, 1967; Erickson & Rossi, 1979) started to intrigue me. Having experienced psychiatric patients' 'resistance' to cease thinking 'irrationally' and to stop avoiding 'conditioned fear stimuli,' my simple thought was that well-meant and judicious therapeutic suggestions might sometimes be an effective means of promoting more viable thoughts and behaviors. Unduly simplistic or not, I started to attend classes on Ericksonian psychotherapy. One intervention I became acquainted with was to invite the dreamer to revisit an apparently uncompleted dream, if not by night then by day.

I thus remarked: "Paula, your dream presents a sad and lonely world. A world with parents who somehow cannot provide what you need and desire. What you need and desire is what everyone needs and desires. Having left the house, you were confronted with a body in the ice or whatever else the image may have been. It is no wonder you got scared stiff and ran off. Still, could the dream be telling you something of importance? How would you feel if the body or whatever else it was were to stay enclosed in the ice? Perhaps it would be wise to revisit the image?"

Paula nodded; she was apprehensive, but closed her eyes as she turned her attention 'inside.' The scary image popped up almost instantly. I kindly invited her to examine it.

> "It's a woman," she shivered.
> "A woman," I repeated. "The image seems to scare you."
> "Yes, it does."
> "Is she dead?"
> "I don't know, but it's an awful sight."
> "An awful sight."
> "Yes."
> "Even though it's an awful sight, do you feel like taking another look?"
> "She seems to be suffering."
> "Perhaps she's suffering like you do."
> "Hm."
> "Should she stay in the ice, or would you rather get her out of it?"

Being the caring, compassionate person she was, Paula felt, despite her fears, that it would be better to get the woman out of the frozen canal. I proposed she might want to use an ice saw or some other instrument she needed to do the job.

Paula did not tell me what she was doing, but her face and body expressed engagement in hard work. After a while she said, "She's ashore now."

> "You took her ashore. What a feat! Is she dead or what?"
> Paula did not know. The woman was still caught in a layer of ice.
> "Maybe it would be a good idea to hold her so that she can defrost?"
> "Should I?"
> "No, not necessarily, but it might be an idea ... How do you feel about it?"
> Paula's face grew even more bewildered. Still, she held and warmed the clump of ice.
> As the ice melted, she suddenly screamed, "She's starting to move!"

The next second Paula's eyes grew icy. Her face grew hard and her body stiffened. Looking me straight in the eye, her mouth spoke cold and angry: *"Well, that took you a long time!"*

I felt shocked, my heart raced, and my mind rushed to find some kind of understanding. What was this? *What* had taken me a long time?

> "Paula?" I asked.
> "I'm not Paula, that stupid patsy. I'm not her and I'm not like her. She's weak. She's a disaster. I'm in charge."
> Having never seen or heard anything like this before, I was flabbergasted. Or had I seen this face, these eyes, and this tone of voice in those prior confusing moments? Not Paula, she said. But Paula was sitting opposite me – wasn't she? Yet, her eyes, her face, her posture, and her words did not fit the Paula I had known for four years.

"Not Paula?"

"No, I'm not Paula. I'm different."

"And you're not weak, you say?"

"I know how to handle things. She doesn't. She tries to please anyone, and that includes you. But it leads nowhere."

I had many more questions, but the tough presence displayed her autonomy and power of action by leaving just as suddenly as she had emerged. There was more to come during that striking session. The Paula I knew resurfaced, but disappeared several more times with three other 'ways of being,' including two childlike 'existences' taking her place, one after the other.

What to think, what to do? That was my dilemma!

Paula somehow regained control after 30 minutes or so. Like me she did not understand what had precisely happened, or what the shifts and words meant. Feeling deeply ashamed, she apologized morc than once.

I shared with her what she had expressed and what I had observed. While she did not recollect all that had happened, she knew something "weird" had occurred. Like me, she too did not comprehend what it was about. Discussing the issue more, she volunteered for the first time that she had heard voices talking to her in the way I had been spoken to. She also shared that she recurrently lost episodes of time, and that things disappeared or changed in her house. She could not explain how or why. These experiences and phenomena had actually been with her for many years, she then admitted shamefully.

Although the condition had not been mentioned during my training as a psychologist and my ongoing training as a psychotherapist, I vaguely aware of multiple personality disorder (MPD), which had been introduced in DSM-III (American Psychiatric Association, 1980). But until the remarkable session with Paula, I had not even read the text. In fact, I did not have the faintest idea of what the disorder was like, what it precisely entailed, and how it could be mended, if at all. I asked Paula if she had heard about the condition. She had not. Like me, she was not aware of any popular or scientific articles or books on dissociative disorders. She had neither seen television programs on these conditions nor had she met other individuals diagnosed with a dissociative disorder. In fact, she had not been in close contact with any other psychiatric patient. In a word, her presentation was authentic and inexplicable in terms of the sociocognitive model of MPD or DID (see ToT Volume II), which claims that DID is a consequence of suggestibility, high fantasy proneness, suggestion, and role-playing.

I had no clue how to diagnose MPD, if that indeed was the accurate diagnosis, let alone how to treat it. Sharing my ignorance with Paula, I added that I did not know any expert on the condition, so that I did not know to whom I could refer her. After some discussion, we agreed that there was no other way open to us than to make the best of it together. I promised her to explore the available literature and to help her to the best of my poor knowledge and limited skills. I also told her that if she had MPD or something like it, I was, given my ignorance, bound to make many mistakes in treatment. "But," I tried to reassure her, "I am willing to learn and to keep an open mind as we confront the perplexing phenomena you present. I am willing to continue working with you if you are prepared to work as hard as I intend to do. If you so wish, we can cooperate on this basis." Paula needed little time to express her consent.

Making Meaning Together

Our endeavor was to become an instance of enactive trauma therapy *avant la lettre.* Since I knew close to nothing about dissociative disorders, and since Paula had her first-person experiences but no (third-person) understanding of her disorder, we had to make sense of her condition together as we moved forward. There had to be some meaning somewhere, and we had to find it. We had to pursue meaning, understanding, and healing in joint action.

There were many things to wonder about. Why did the icy lady and the other existences wait for 4 years before showing themselves beyond vague indications? Why did this lady present herself in the dream? If the frozen lady was as almighty as she seemed to suggest, then why and how had she become frozen? What apparently even more powerful force had entrapped her in the ice? And once she had escaped, why did she not use her authority to take full control continuously or leave the Paula she apparently despised? Why did she allow the childlike existences come forward for a period of time? And why did the other existences pop up in a more direct form? Had Paula known anything about them before? If so, why had she not talked about the frozen lady and the other appearances? Could there perhaps be more of them than I had met so far? Another core question was why Paula existed in a plural form in the first place. And why did some of her various existences appear childlike and others more mature? I also wondered why the defrosted woman despised Paula so intensely?

Where to begin, what to do? The least I could do was to carefully listen to Paula, to observe her closely, and to become attuned to her affectively in whatever way of being she presented herself. What I also did was to invite the icy lady and the other existences that had popped up in that remarkable and in part unnerving session to "talk to me more if they pleased."

The strategy appeared to work. In the course of our collaboration, I would get to know and better understand the various dissociative parts of Paula's personality, as Onno van der Hart, Kathy Steele, and I would later call these conscious and self-conscious structures (e.g., Van der Hart et al., 2006). Some presented themselves sooner and with more ease and clarity than others. It was not very difficult to get in touch with the two other ANPs that existed next to the Paula I knew and whom I for so long had seen as the complete person. Several of Paula's fragile EPs, on the other hand, were less communicative. Some commonly displayed low levels of consciousness and/or very restricted fields of consciousness. Her controlling EPs were strong. The icy lady was one of them. It was hard for me to achieve any degree of cooperation with these powerful parts. It proved equally hard to foster cooperation and coherence between the various dissociative parts. All EPs operated at low or moderately low levels of mental efficiency (Van der Hart et al., 2006). All dissociative parts of the entire Paula had a different understanding of what was useful, harmful, and useless; they seemed to need and desire different things. And all strove to persevere in their existence. Even the suicidal ones did not particularly want to die. They wanted to find rest. The various parts were not like islands of consciousness, but rather entertained relationships with each other. Over time and with great effort we started to develop an understanding of their inner and external dynamics.

As a whole organism-environment system, Paula comprised the trinity of dissociative parts: ANPs, fragile EPs, and controlling EPs. In addition to these prototypical parts, there were two suicidal parts, both with a teenage identity. The suicidal parts were more in touch and associated with the controlling EPs than with the ANPs and fragile EPs.

Inspired by the literature and sensing that integrative actions would best replace dissociative actions and passions, I promoted interactions among Paula's dissociative parts. Sometimes fostering these movements was possible, but at other times it was hard to create an integrative path in walking together.

Assessment

Diagnosing a disorder means in principle assessing symptoms, and comprehending a disorder means understanding what the symptoms are symptoms *of.* I did not know any dissociative symptoms, let alone know why they even exist and what they mean. My knowledge and understanding evolved through my work with Paula and several other individuals who appeared to have a complex dissociative disorder as well as through consultation of the sparse literature at the time. Meeting Paula's various dissociative parts acquainted me with a great variety of symptoms and phenomena I had previously been unfamiliar with. The encounters also helped me to grasp that the domain of dissociative symptoms was best delimited to phenomena that signal the existence of a dissociation of the personality[8]. These revelations and this understanding allowed me to make a definitive diagnosis in Paula's case: MPD or, as the disorder was later to be called, DID (American Psychiatric Association, 1994, 2013). The revelations would also be of major importance regarding the assessment and differential diagnostics in other cases.

8 As detailed in ToT Volumes I and II, Van der Hart, Steele, and I only regard symptoms as dissociative in nature when one or more parts have the symptoms but not one or more other dissociative parts. For example, phenomena such as depersonalization, emotional numbing, and forgetting are, in our opinion, not dissociative if an individual's personality does not include dissociative parts or if a phenomenon is common to all dissociative parts. For example, when none of the existing dissociative parts recalls a personal event, the event is forgotten, not dissociated. And features that all parts have in common are not dissociated from each other.

Starting with the session in which some of her other dissociative parts emerged, as the Paula I had already been familiar with and as various other dissociative parts of her, Paula started to share ever more symptoms. They involved dissociative symptoms that she had not mentioned to me or anyone else before, and that I had not formerly known as symptoms of dissociative disorders. She had been too scared to talk about the phenomenon, among others things because they pointed to the (other) dissociative parts (fragile and controlling EPs) she feared, rejected, and avoided. Moreover, commanding voices, which in hindsight prominently included the icy lady, had forbidden her to talk about the dissociative symptoms and the backgrounds of their emergence and continued existence. Paula also feared that these and other intrusion symptoms would prove that she was psychotic, and that she would have to be admitted to a mental hospital.

The full gamut of Paula's dissociative symptoms included positive and negative ones, some of which can be classified as cognitive-emotional, others as sensorimotor dissociative symptoms (Chapter 22). Her positive cognitive-emotional dissociative symptoms included dissociative parts hearing the voices of other dissociative parts. The childlike voices of the fragile EPs sounded childlike, whereas the voices of controlling EPs were far more powerful. Some voices spoke kinder or supportive words. The positive cognitive-emotional dissociative symptoms also included feeling influenced by 'inner forces' in a variety of other ways such as feeling intruded on by emotions and thoughts that she did not experience as *hers*, but that in fact belonged to or stemmed from other dissociative parts. The category also encompassed recurrent nightmares and other reenactments of toxic things that had happened to her, and that some of her dissociative parts reenacted. Paula's positive sensorimotor dissociative symptoms included experiencing intruding physical feelings such as being touched and physical pain in particular parts of her body as well as seemingly inexplicable, surprising, and uncontrollable physical movements. The phenomena came and went unsuspectedly and were beyond apparent understanding.

These symptoms, however, became explicable once Paula as ANP or as some other dissociative part of her personality and I came to understand that the intruding sensations, emotions, thoughts, memories, and behaviors stemmed from other dissociative parts of the complete Paula. Dissociative parts are not isolated from each other. They can and frequently do intrude on each other. Further, the dissociative part intruded on may or may not be consciously aware of the source of the intrusion and its reason(s). The part may or may not have dissociative source amnesia. For example, as ANP Paula first had not understood that the intrusive cold and hard voice was the icy lady speaking – who referred to herself as Sandra. And it took intense work for her to understand that Sandra, despite appearances, was trying to protect her. In the same fashion, ANPs can intrude on fragile EPs and controlling EPs, generating dissociative symptoms for these EPs which they may or may not comprehend. In dissociation, symptoms are relative to the 'receiving' and 'sending' dissociative parts.

The negative dissociative symptoms that Paula ventured included cognitive-emotional symptoms such as depersonalization, emotional numbing, and amnesia as well as sensorimotor symptoms such as analgesic or anesthetic body parts, and intermittent paralysis of a member. These symptoms constitute negative dissociative symptoms when a dissociative part (or parts) does not sense, feel, think, remember, or do what one or more other dissociative parts sense, feel, think, remember, or do. For example, as the therapy progressed, it became clearer that, as ANP, Paula sometimes did not remember what she had recently done. She experienced this amnesia as 'gaps in time,' and they counted as dissociative when one or more other dissociative parts of her *did* recollect the episode in question. At some point, as ANP, Paula shamefully confided she once in a while found herself bleeding from wounds she could not explain. The dissociative nature of this amnesia became clear when a dissociative part admitted having inflicted the wound and explained why.

Literature on Dissociative Symptoms and Disorders in the Early 1980s

The emergent literature on MPD in the early 1980s was valuable but quite limited, and there was very little research on this disorder and other dissociative disorders (e.g., Brende, 1984; Coons, 1984; Crisp, 1984; Gelinas, 1983; Kluft, 1984a, 1984b; Ludwig, 1983; Mesulam, 1981; Nemiah, 1981; Putnam, 1984a, 1984b; Rosenbaum & Weaver, 1980; Schenk & Bear, 1981; Spiegel, 1984; Steingard & Frankel, 1985). Most valuable and helpful contributions were yet to be written (e.g., Bliss, 1986; Kluft, 1990a; Putnam, 1989; Ross, 1989; Van der Hart & Friedman, 1989). However, Henri Ellenberger's (1970) brilliant book on *The Discovery of the Unconsciousness: The History and Evolution of Dynamic Psychiatry* with a superb chapter on the works of Pierre Janet had been available for over a decade. Ernest Hilgard's book on *Divided Consciousness: Multiple Controls in Human Thought and Action* had been published in 1977. In the 1970s Ludwig and colleagues (Ludwig, 1983; Ludwig, Brandsma, Wilbur, Bendtfelt, & Jameson, 1972) had embarked on the psychophysiological study of dissociation.

Moreover, there were excellent far earlier sources available. Under the label of hysteria, much on dissociation and dissociative disorders had been written in the second half of 19th century and in the beginning years of the 20th century (e.g., Briquet, 1859; Janet, 1889, 1893, 1901, 1907; for more references, see ToT Volume I). Particularly Janet's work – brought to my attention by Onno van der Hart – was a revelation. *The Mental State of Hystericals* (1893, 1901) as well as *The Major Symptoms of Hysteria* (1907) basically described Paula's dissociative symptoms and personality structure as well as the dissociative symptoms and personality organization of some other patients with a dissociative disorder whom I was soon to meet – or that I at least *recognized and valued*[9] for the first time.

9 It is well known that knowledge can guide perception, and that a lack of knowledge can prevent us from noticing what is obvious to the informed. Prairie Indians, for example, had a refined perception and understanding of a major variety of prairie grasses – that constituted a complex ecosystem –

Janet (1893, 1901, 1907) proposed that the major symptoms of hysteria included two categories, which he referred to as mental accidents and mental stigmata. The term 'stigmata' expressed that the involved symptoms were stable features of hysteria. The symptoms involved would appear in practically any individual with the disorder, and their form would be quite similar. It struck me that the mental stigmata pertained to phenomena of the undue absence of mental action and contents such as an inability to remember significant life events or to sense or move particular parts of the body. This is why we decided to refer to the mental stigmata as negative dissociative symptoms (Nijenhuis, 1999/2004; Nijenhuis & Van der Hart, 1999, 2011a, 2011b; Van der Hart, Van Dijke, Van Son, & Steele, 2000; ToT Volumes I & II).

According to Janet (1893, 1901, 1907), the mental accidents were more variable phenomena. They captured the uncalled-for presence of phenomena such as reenactments of traumatic memories. This inspired us to address them as positive dissociative symptoms (Nijenhuis, 1999/2004; Nijenhuis & Van der Hart, 1999, 2011a, 2011b; Van der Hart et al., 2000; ToT Volumes I & II). The mental accidents also comprised hearing voices and being intruded by thoughts that patient do not experience or regard as their own. I had been taught that these and still other intrusions constituted the first-rank symptoms of schizophrenia (Schneider, 1959). But Paula did not impress me as an individual with schizophrenia, and research would soon start to show that the first-rank symptoms of schizophrenia and psychotic symptoms more generally are not specific to schizophrenia (Allen & Coyne, 1995; Dorahy et al., 2009; Ellason & Ross, 1997; Foote & Park, 2008; Kluft, 1987; Laddis & Dell, 2012; Putnam, Guroff, Silbermann, Barban, & Post, 1986; Ross, Norton, & Wozney, 1989; Ross, Heber, & Anderson, 1990; Steinberg, Cicchetti, Buchanan, Rakfeldt, & Rounsaville, 1994). Moreover, since dissociative parts are not totally isolated from each other, it seemed only natural that they can affect one another.

Conceptual Confusion

Reading the recent literature on dissociative symptoms and disorders in the 1980s was in part helpful and in part confusing. It was a puzzling experience inasmuch as the definition of the domain of dissociative symptoms and the realm of dissociative disorders was concerned.[10] One perplexity was that the domain of dissociative symptoms had become far

---

where an ignorant observer would have seen mere "grass." Perceptual and conceptual refinement stems from need. The lives of Prairie Indians depended on having a keen appreciation of this ecosystem, whereas a casual observer did not need to see more than just "grass." The principle of knowledge-guided and interest-affected perception can also be applied to clinicians and scientists who say that they have never seen a case of DID or a similar condition. The world does not speak for itself. Everyone lives their own truth, not The Truth.

10 The literature on the domain of dissociation published in the 1990s and in the first decade of the 21st century only served to reinforce the confusion; see ToT Volumes I & II.

wider than Janet and other 19th-century authors on hysteria had proposed. Whereas the pioneers had limited the category to manifestations of the existence of a dissociation of the personality, contemporary authors had also begun including all sorts of other changes of consciousness such as absorption, selective attention, and low level of consciousness. However, it was not explained why these forms of altered consciousness would be *dissociative*. In any case, the elaboration did not strike me as meaningful or otherwise helpful.

A second confusion pertained to the understanding of the sensorimotor symptoms of individuals with more or less complex dissociative disorders. When I started working with Paula and individuals like her in the 1980s, I was surprised to read that the DSM-III (American Psychiatric Association, 1980) and DSM-III-R (American Psychiatric Association, 1987) defined and categorized the sensorimotor dissociative symptoms that Janet had so clearly described and recognized as major symptoms of hysteria as conversion symptoms and disorders. In particular, in his *The Mental State of Hystericals* Janet (1893/1901) articulated the sensorimotor dissociative phenomena that Paula reported and I observed.

Did Paula, in terms of the DSM-III system, have two major diagnoses, MPD *and* conversion disorder? Would the 'conversion' symptoms and disorders not be dissociative in nature? And were dissociation and conversion unrelated? Or, if they are related phenomena and constructs, how are they connected? The DSM-III did not provide answers in this regard. Assigning two main diagnoses did not seem to be an attractive option, particularly because the 19th-century logic behind dissociative symptoms, whether cognitive-emotional or sensorimotor phenomena, is convincing. The original logic was that a dissociative symptom is dissociative because it is a manifestation of the existence of a dissociation of the personality. That is, a symptom and disorder are dissociative, because one or more dissociative parts of the personality feel, know, remember, or do something that one or more other dissociative parts do not feel, know, remember, or do – whether in part or in full. Hence, it makes no sense to say that a particular anesthesia constitutes a conversion symptom, whereas a particular amnesia involves a dissociative symptom inasmuch as the anesthesia, just like the amnesia, applies to one or more dissociative parts but not to one or more other dissociative parts of the individual's personality.

The 19th-century logic applied to Paula as much as it had applied to Janet's hysterical patients. For example, as ANP Paula did not sense her body well. It sometimes appeared to her that some parts of her body were things that actually did not belong to her. She did not sense her pelvic area and genitals – and neither did Sandra, the part I came to classify as a prototypical controlling EP. However, as our therapy progressed, it became clear that several fragile EPs suffered intense pain in these and other body parts. These dissociative parts could occasionally intrude on Paula as an ANP, in which case the physical pain of the involved fragile EPs temporarily replaced Paula's anesthesia. At times particular dissociative parts of Paula were unable to move body parts, and at other times they experienced that body parts moved beyond their control. These intermittent motor problems might be related to freezing or to passive immobility and the implied paralysis of one or more fragile EPs (see ToT Volumes I & II). They might also pertain to willful, intentional actions or passions of dissociative parts that affected the ability of another dissociative part to move the body. For example, when one of Paula's dissociative parts wanted to go to somewhere one or more other dissociative parts of her feared or detested, the latter parts might block the former part's motor actions.

In this context, it was an intellectual and clinical relief to read that the category of dissociative disorders in the *International Classification of Diseases, ICD-10* (World Health Organization, 1992) included dissociative disorders of movement and sensation. In this regard, the ICD-10 made a lot of sense to me as well as to Paula and other individuals with sensorimotor dissociative symptoms. Consistent clinical observations of sensorimotor dissociative phenomena in individuals with complex dissociative disorder and the inconsistencies in the literature inspired my colleagues and me to empirically study the issues at stake. The findings of this work and that of other researchers of sensorimotor dissociative symptoms and disorders were reviewed in ToT Volumes I and II. Despite all excellent theoretical, clinical, and empirical grounds for saying that conversion symptoms and disorders are dissociative phenomena, later versions of the DSM (DSM-III-R, DSM-IV, DSM-5) would continue to regard sensorimotor dissociative symptoms and disorders as instances of 'conversion.' Sometimes meaning making is a struggle. Consistent with the principle of primordial affectivity, enactive meaning making is an affective affair, and at times the affects in science are more political than intellectual.

Dissociation and Traumatizing Events

Paula's positive dissociative symptoms often related to events that had been traumatic (in the first-person and quasi-second person perspective) and traumatizing (in the third-person perspective) to her as a whole individual. As mentioned above, my training as a psychologist and psychotherapist had left me as ignorant regarding trauma and traumatic/traumatizing events, just as it had left me unenlightened regarding the concept and facts of dissociation. Moreover, standard clinical assessment in the early 1980s did not include inquiring about terrifying or otherwise adverse life events or dissociative symptoms. Apart from this, scientifically tested instruments to assess adverse life events, the severity of dissociative symptoms, or the presence of a dissociative disorder were still unavailable.[11]

For the most part, I learned through my interactions with traumatized individuals what dissociation, a dissociative disorder, and a trauma are; I learned the difference between an adverse event and a traumatizing event, and how these various phenomena are connected.

---

11 There is evidence that still far too few colleagues and psychiatric institutes systematically assess adverse events and dissociative symptoms and disorders, even though good assessment tools are now available for this purpose. Most of these instruments can be freely used, and most of them are brief, easy to use, and simple to interpret. See Appendices 3–5.

(See the definitions provided and discussed in ToT Volumes I and II.) Working with Paula and other individuals with complex dissociative disorders educated me. The patients displayed their symptoms, and we attuned to them, discussed them, and tried to find ways to reduce or alter them; the patients presented their dissociative parts, and we worked with them. And the patients started to talk about horrors I did not even know existed. Together we tried to find meaning in their dreadful *umwelt*.

For example, across our sessions, Paula started to share with me in ever more detail how difficult it was for her to eat in company. She prepared the family meals, but she did not join her husband and children in consuming them. Even sitting at the family dining table while the other family members were eating was very difficult for her. Formal dinners were a tremendous struggle. She had to avoid them as much as possible.

Discussing the issue, as ANP and more so as several fragile EPs, Paula unveiled in a stepwise manner that in her family of origin it had been forbidden to talk over meals. The silence had been cold and full of tension. Everyone had had a fixed place at the dining table. The family rules had been as straight as the canals of the region, and the emotional familial soil as poor as the area's earth. Paula had been seated between her father and mother: Father to the right of her, and Mother to her left. Paula had been a metaphorical and literal go-between. The parents' relationship had been generally distant and icy, and at times explosively aggressive. A sensitive child, Paula could not bear this atmosphere.

When she once tried to break the ice by uttering a few kind words, her father's fork landed full force in her right hand. Since that time, eating in company had become practically impossible for Paula. But she had to eat nonetheless, since her parents also punished what they saw as her refusal to eat. Caught in opposite needs and desires of physical and emotional defense, of tending and befriending her parents, and of eating/refusing food, Paula ate only the smallest portions. In her own family, as ANP, Paula hardly ate at all. As one fragile EP, she ate at night once her husband and children were asleep.

During her later teenage years, Paula had felt strongly attracted to a French teacher. He was the first person ever who was kind to her. Appreciating her intelligence, he introduced her to literature. They had long talks together that both of them valued. And they fell in love. But he was her teacher, she was 17 at the time, and religion was still very strict. Some classmates and other individuals guessed what was going on, and some openly disapproved. Paula was once more caught between contradictory needs and desires: The relationship with the teacher was her refuge as well as the source of major conflicts.

During therapy, one fragile EP spoke French, enjoyed emotional intimacy, and had sexual feelings. She longed for attachment and longed for the teacher. Controlling EPs, on the other hand, had nothing good to say about this EP and this part's sensations and feelings: They punished her. Whereas as ANP Paula was sexually anesthetic, she valued the relationship she had had with the teacher – and she missed him as well.

The therapy and our therapeutic relationship included similar elements: long talks together on very personal topics, mutual sympathy and respect, and emotional acceptance. But there were also differences: Our venture was professional, open, and socially approved, even if her disorder was not generally accepted (e.g., not in my professional community of the time), but Paula's controlling EPs did not seem to appreciate these differences. They feared another impossible interpersonal relationship and another implied relational loss. They, therefore, had to restrain those dissociative parts that were open to therapy.

As ANP, Paula also feared relational losses. More than this, she actually feared a normal life for both herself and her children. Her phenomenal conceptions of herself and her *umwelt* were that life "is dangerous and that [interpersonal] relationships are damaging. There is little one can do about that. It is better to stay away from others." In this context, Paula felt a need to isolate herself socially and to protect her children from engaging in attachment relationships. The best protection was to keep them at home. Needless to say, this passionate reenactive approach conflicted with her children's natural desires to explore the world, including all the options for interpersonal relationships it offers.

Therapy, thus, was filled with contradictions and pitfalls. As ANP, Paula wanted change without risk-taking and emotional pain. As fragile EPs, she feared while also intensely longing for interpersonal recognition, acknowledgment, and acceptance. As controlling EPs, she strictly forbade hopes of a better personal future. The controlling EPs *claimed* total control of "Paula and the others." However, in fact they lacked this total control. For example, they had been unable to prevent the ANP and fragile EPs from attending therapy. Apart from this, it seemed that the controlling EPs were set not only on maximizing their power: They presented themselves in therapy although they would probably have retained more (negative) power if they had remained in the dark. Sandra, the icy lady, revealed her existence in a telling nightmare, and she entered into an explicit relationship with Paula as ANP, with me, and gradually with the various other dissociative parts as well. *Why did she do that if she was only interested in control?* Her actions and passions, and similar actions and passions of other controlling EPs, did not seem to make sense. But if enactivism is correct, there had to be a meaning despite all appearances.

Therapeutic Errors and Growing Understanding

As I told Paula from the start, I was bound to make errors given my original ignorance regarding trauma and dissociation. And I did err, though some faults proved to be more serious than others. The best that could be done was to learn from them. Milton Erickson once said how surprised he had been that his fellow medical students were trying so hard to avoid making mistakes. Realizing that people tend to learn the most from their blunders, he was more relaxed about the issue. While this perspective is helpful, I cannot say that recounting the following incident is a pleasure.

One day, Paula had risen to the point of realizing that she had not been a wicked child: The bad and the ugly had come from other agents, including her parents. Reviewing the evidence, I concluded, "it appears you were a good girl." Somewhat scared and nervous,

Paula prudently replied, "I guess I was a good child." Guided by my basic but shortsighted thought that she would learn to accept herself more, not just as a child, but also as a girl, I reiterated, "a good child and a good *girl*." Stupid me. I even missed the message when Paula stated again, now in an angry tone of voice, "I was a good *child*." Two days later, she cut her vagina with glass, and quite seriously at that. Now I understood she thought she was 'a bad girl,' revealing complex sexual issues that had previously remained hidden. A major lesson for me and indeed for any clinician was that we should be aware of *our* will and refrain from imposing it on patients. *As clinicians, we should want* ***nothing*** *from patients.*

A far better response would probably have been something like: "You were a good child, we agree ... [await her response, and attune to the reaction]. You may want to take that in ... [await her response, attune again]. What is it like to be a good child? ..." [await her response, including her physical reaction, attune again]. In any case, once Paula had stipulated that she was not a good girl, I could have remarked, "You were a good child. I've heard you say that. Would you feel like telling me, now or later perhaps, why you feel you were not a good girl?

Part of the problem was that Sandra, inspired by and imitating what perpetrators had been telling Paula, kept on reproaching Paula and fragile EPs that they had, in fact, seduced the men. That's why Paula was a bad girl. Sandra had "cut Paula" for having had the nerve to confirm that she had been a good child. I had the impression she also had punished me for thinking that Paula had been a good girl. Sandra's accepting Paula's innocent femininity would have implied that the perpetrators were bad. And realizing that fact was a bridge too far.

Another error on my behalf was thinking simplistically regarding the steps involved in healing. Sensing ever more that emotional neglect had been a major efficient cause of Paula's MPD, I guessed that setting up a caring relationship with her various dissociative parts (and thereby with her as a whole individual) would be welcome and curative. This relationship would entail 'corrective emotional experiences' – or so I hoped. Sure, some of Paula's dissociative parts, and primarily her fragile EPs, were happy to meet my concern, sympathy, and compassion. However, her controlling EPs fiercely objected to the development of joy and hope. They basically ruined the progression, time and again, causing major pain for the fragile EPs and the ANPs.

Their 'destructive' actions irritated me. Fooling myself into thinking that I could hide my annoyance and disappointment – my first-person experiences – I ran into relational troubles with the controlling EPs. Dissociative parts, and particularly EPs, need few signs to detect the clinician's true feelings. They are experts in tracing dishonesty in other people. The controlling EPs thus clearly sensed my negative feelings regarding them. They felt misunderstood and misjudged. Confused, at first I did not quite know what to do.

Through repeated struggles with controlling EPs and upon more reflection, I began to understand that, in their view, generating hope and positive relationships is an utterly dangerous proposition. Their life experiences – disappointment upon disappointment upon disappointment – had taught them that cherishing hope for better days is the worst possible plan. Those brighter days never came, and, as the controlling EPs repeated on end, they would never come. Controlling EPs see no reason for believing that things have changed just because some clinician 'acts nice.' It is better to expect the worst. Hope is for dummies. Hope must be banned. Clinicians promise the little ones (i.e., the childlike fragile EPs) the world, but clinicians are weaklings. They just talk, talk, talk. Who's taking care of the others (i.e., the other dissociative parts) when the sweet clinician goes home at night, leaves for a holiday, or moves on to some other job? No, a better tomorrow is a bitter dream. That's why clinicians should just back off.

Once I started to understand controlling EPs more, my therapeutic life with them became less complicated. It became easier to talk and relate to these powerful parts the more I grew to understand that they protect the whole person – of which they are a part. They do this by keeping up a sense of personal autonomy in a world in which the individual's factual autonomy was minimal (here I do not refer to the systemic autonomy discussed in Chapter 25). Controlling EPs balance the child's dependency on significant others who neglect, maltreat, and abuse them by imitating these very people. On the surface, it may appear that they have chosen the side of the perpetrators. However, they more essentially attempt to control needs and desires of recognition and acknowledgment from perpetrators. They also long and strive to navigate despondent attachment needs regarding significant others who are perpetrators. They know these deep wishes will remain unfulfilled. In this sense, controlling EPs must hide their own fragility, their own tears, and any perpetrator-directed rage as well as their shame from not being able to protect the fragile EPs and ANPs any better. They must also disregard the fact that their power is vastly exceeded by external causes: the power of perpetrators, of their partners in crime, of misunderstanding, rejecting, and controlling psychologists and psychiatrists, and of people who do not adequately protect or save chronically traumatized children. Controlling EPs must further ignore that their personal actions are mostly passions (see Chapters 25 and 27).

Another issue I learned is that, like fragile EPs, controlling EPs tend to live in the past, although some hide it. Whereas controlling EPs may present an adult-like identity, they may actually possess a younger personal identity. This also applied to Sandra: At first, she presented herself as an adult woman, but as I got to know her better, it became clear that she felt 18 or 19 years old. Apart from her adolescent phenomenal conception of self, her phenomenal conception of the world and her relationship to this world also pertained to Paula's adolescent existence.[12] Sandra, in fact, had evolved in the context of the broken relationship with her French teacher.

As I began understanding the above dynamics and features more, my discourse with controlling EPs as well as my communications with other dissociative parts regarding these heroic parts changed. The more Sandra and other controlling EPs felt I had grasped something of importance, the more they changed and the more therapeutic advance-

12 These various concepts are explained and discussed in ToT Volume II, Chapter 12.

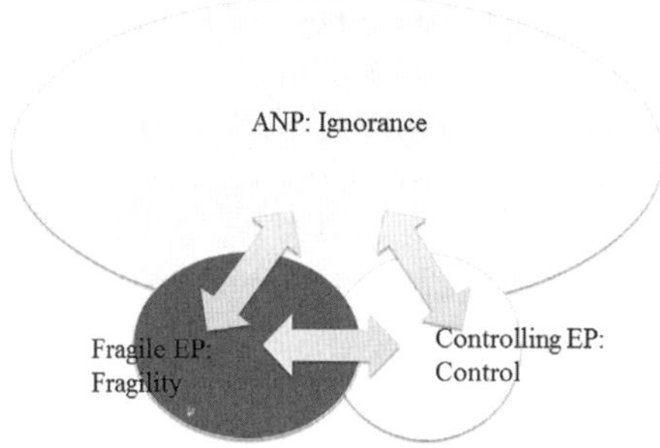

Figure 30.1. The predominant phenomenal features of the trinity of dissociative parts in trauma.

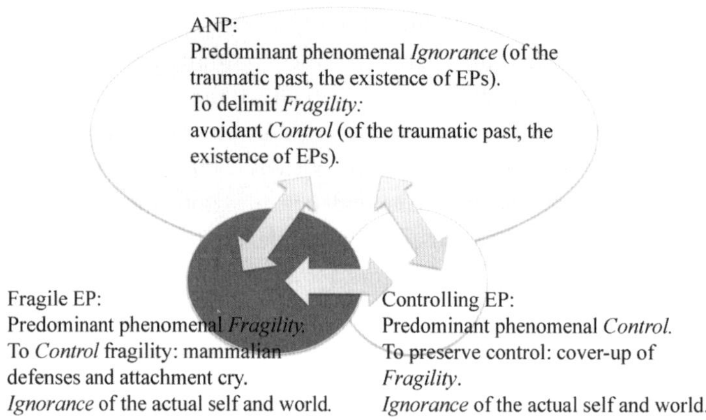

Figure 30.2. Ignorance, fragility, and control: Features of ANP, fragile EP, and controlling EP.

ments followed. At some point, controlling EPs started expressing their hidden fragility and displaying their ignorance. Many also began expressing sorrow that they had haunted or still had to haunt "the little ones" and the ANPs, and how hard it is to carry out that task. In this stage, they would also begin to unveil how sad they are themselves regarding the traumatic history and their inability to be of more help to "the others."

Developing More Power of Action in the Patient and in the Clinician

As ANP, Paula had great difficulty making personal choices and taking personal decisions. Her family of origin had not allowed her to have an opinion of her own. To the degree that she had a point of view and uttered it, she was punished or laughed at for her "stupid" ideas. In the end, she felt stupid and worthless and avoided sharing personal views. Paula's personal insecurity was not helpful to her fragile EPs, to say the least, and it was ridiculed by her controlling EPs. However, she did have strong opinions with respect to her children, and she lived these views in the form of obsessive concern and overprotection.

My efforts to correct her fixed fears and ideas through analysis and discussion of their backgrounds and their irrationality remained fruitless, though Paula had no trouble understanding and accepting the points I made. For example, she fully grasped the idea that past punishment and ridicule of her personal opinions do encompass personal views being met with such reactions from others in the present. But in the end, these and related cognitive insights did not change her affects and behaviors in any way. Different solutions were called for.

It appeared that, as ANP, Paula was physically, perceptually, and emotionally quite numbed. For example, she lacked many normal physical feelings, and she did not seem to have color or taste preferences. I attuned to and accepted her limited power of action in these regards by fully and recurrently agreeing that she experienced her body, affects, and perceptions of her *umwelt* in the ways she did. Having reached that consensus, its existence was affirmed several times in order to mirror and ratify my understanding of and compassion with Paula's realities.

Initially, more by means of trial and error than through rational planning on my behalf, the next move we practiced was tracing or developing and uttering personal preferences. We rehearsed sensing contrasting materials, fabrics, and textures (e.g., leather, cotton, steel, wood) by touching them, first with the eyes open and then with the eyes closed. We walked into the woods to touch and later hold different trees and plants, again first with open eyes and thereafter with closed eyes. I also invited her to listen to different tones, instruments, voices, and songs, and later to different renderings of the same song. Next, I asked her to experience and judge which material, texture, color, tone, or voice she liked more (e.g., "Do you prefer the red ball or the black one?"). When she had become able to make such choices, she learned to experience and phenomenally evaluate (i.e., judge) different tastes as well as different body postures (e.g., standing more erect), ways of moving (e.g., moving slowly or faster; taking lighter or more solid steps), and different degrees of eye contact.

Regarding the expression of her preferences, she was first invited to point to her preferences (e.g., the red ball) and then to express her choices in words. Next, she practiced defending her preferences against my role-played weaker or stronger silly opposition (e.g., "I think you're wrong, the black ball is much nicer" or "How can you be so stupid to like a red ball?"). Later, I voiced earnest opposition (e.g., "I like the black ball more"), and encouraged Paula to disagree with me in several regards (e.g., "You may like the black ball more, but I prefer the red one"). I also invited her to reject some of my statements (e.g., "You are rude and wrong to say that liking the red ball more is stupid"). We also ratified and amplified her newly won sensations, movements, preferences, and her courage to express her preferences and to stick to them in the face of opposition. For example, when Paula confided that she felt a weird urge to hold trees, I supported her doing so and joined her in the moving act.

In this stepwise fashion, as ANP Paula learned to develop stronger and more distinct phenomenal sensorimotor and affective experiences in the first-person perspective and phenomenal judgments in the quasi-second-person perspective. She also learned to voice her preferences in a second-person perspective, first in writing, then with discourse me, and later in chats with other individuals. Through increasing interaction with her fragile EPs, she could help them to embark on similar tracks to lift their power of action.

At each completed step, I stimulated Paula to realize, voice, and celebrate her success. Her habitual style was to nullify her advancements. She was afraid that others would squash her progress, so she crushed it herself. And she had to please the controlling EPs who laughed at her like her family of origin had laughed at her. They also forbade her to develop any hope that she might gain more power of action. They disliked her growing mental and behavioral efficiency.

In this and other contexts, I learned to treat Paula ever more as a whole person rather than as this or that particular part of her. Working with individual dissociative parts is generally valuable. It makes them feel heard, seen, and understood. However, the strategy has its limitations. One risk is that focusing too much on a particular dissociative part may generate problems with the other parts, which may feel neglected, excluded, or misunderstood. When this happens the problematic dynamic relationships among the various parts tends to remain intact. For example, ANPs may continue to avoid fragile and controlling EPs. Fragile EPs may continue to be scared of and rejected by ANPs and controlling EPs. And controlling EPs may continue to reject and despise ANPs and fragile EPs. Another risk is that increasing the power of action of one dissociative part may pose a threat to the position of one or more other dissociative parts in the individual's whole personality or organism-environment system. A change in one dissociative part directly or indirectly affects the other parts, for better or worse. As was noted before, these conscious living subsystems are not 'split off'; rather, they constitute parts of a dynamic organism-environment system that can affect each other to some degree.

Primarily Treat the Whole Organism-Environment System

Clinicians reduce the risk of treating dissociative parts when they continuously mind and recurrently address this whole dynamic system as much as possible. They consider the affective interests of *each* dissociative part, the first-person and other person perspectives as well as the phenomenal conception of self, world, and self of each part as related to that *umwelt*. Clinicians apply this principle even when only one or a few dissociative parts seem to be 'present' or when other dissociative parts are co-present but remain more in the background.

Therapists would do well to 'talk through' the dissociative part that exerts executive control as a means to address and include the dissociative part or parts that are active along with the dissociative part that stands in the foreground (Kluft, 1990b, 2013; Kluft & Fine, 1993; International Society for the Study of Trauma and Dissociation, ISST-D, 2011; Putnam, 1989). Clinicians better be inclusive in this regard. In short, they *consider and treat the individual as a whole system, not the individual parts*. This principle also holds when they sometimes talk to one or a few dissociative parts in particular.

Multispeak

Addressing all dissociative parts at a time requires a particular style and language I refer to as 'multispeak.'[13] This neologism expresses that the clinician speaks to multiple dissociative parts that are active in parallel. In doing so, the clinician realizes that (1) each dissociative part includes and is guided by his or her own affective interests, which essentially include the preservation of their existence. The clinician also heeds the fact that (2) each dissociative part entails his or her own first-person and other person perspectives, and that (3) each enacts his or her own phenomenal self, world, and self-of-that-world. The clinician further realizes (4) that the various dissociative parts entertain dynamic relationships with one another, and (5) that their affective interests tend to be contrary. In order to be effective and efficient, the clinicians at all times keeps in mind (6) that, in order to heal the injury that trauma is, the various dissociative parts must learn to communicate and cooperate with one another, and to coordinate their actions ever more. This healing happens only (7) when the various parts give up their longing and striving to preserve their existence as a dissociative part and substitute this desire for a higher aim which is the preservation of the whole they are a part of. However, (9) inasmuch as they remain ignorant of the fact that they constitute a part of a whole that can achieve more as an integrated whole than as a dissociative whole, the dissociative parts may not long and strive to become a more inclusive integrated whole. Clinicians also better realize that as first persons, dissociative parts may have a hard time experiencing, knowing, and realizing (10) that interpart cooperation and communication is more useful than splendid isolation and that interpart dissociation is harmful by involving a serious risk of decomposition of the whole.

Epilogue

The work with Paula and 'her team' proceeded in virtue of our common goals and our incessant investment of time and energy. Sometimes we stumbled and fell. More often, however, we advanced forward, grew wiser, and achieved a greater perfection. We struggled but survived: *Luctor et emergo*[14]. Slowly surviving a deplorable world became living a life worth living. Once Paula had succeeded in overcoming her traumatic passions, once

13 The term multispeak is also used in the domain of electronics. As Wikipedia states, "MultiSpeak is a specification/standard that defines standardized interfaces among software applications commonly used by electric utilities. It defines details of data that need to be exchanged between software applications in order to support different processes commonly applied at utilities." MultiSpeak was set up in 2000. I have used the term for clinical purposes from the early 1990s.

14 *Luctor et emergo* is the motto of the Dutch province of Zeeland, another part of the Netherlands that continuously battles with the sea. While at times, such as in 1953, the sea triumphs, Zeeland is still on the map, stronger than ever before.

she had integrated and realized her traumatic memories, her various dissociative parts were ready to fuse, one by one. As a result, she finally managed to enact a new composition, a new phenomenal self, a new world, and new and more viable relationships of this self and this *umwelt*. The work took over a decade. Its favorable results remained stable over the years. Paula felt much, much better, as did her family. The marriage remained intact, and the relationships with her children improved considerably. Paula recently peacefully died a loving grandmother.

Chapter 31

Attunement, Consensus Building, and Sensitive Leading by Utilization

> *You see, we don't know what our goals are. We learn our goals only in the process of getting there. You don't know what the baby is going to become. Therefore, you wait and take good care of it until it becomes what it will.*
> Milton H. Erickson

Particularly chronically traumatized individuals do not experience that significant others value and respect their interests and points of view. Perpetrators are clearly not attuned to their victims, at least not for their own sake (though they may groom them). Per definitionem, they do not seek consensus. Trauma therapy should strive to correct the idea that the needs and desires and views of traumatized individuals are insignificant, worthless, ridiculous, or sick. Clinicians carefully pace the affective and other interests of their patients as well as their various person perspectives (first-person, quasi-second-person, second-person, and third-person). They track their current verbal and nonverbal expressions and become attuned to their present and past phenomenal conceptions of self, world, and self-of-that-world. In this sense, they adapt to and in fact often utilize their patients' verbal and nonverbal language as well as their patients' level and field of consciousness. In brief, clinicians try to feel and think themselves into their patients' world.

Yet, the careful accommodation of clinicians to their patients' realities is not a goal in itself. Rather, it serves the enactment of a common world, a world the patient and the clinician enact together. The attunement of clinicians to their patients' world generates an *umwelt* in which the patients are sensed, felt, seen, and heard. The dyad generates a consensual reality when the patient expresses a feeling, a desire, an interest, a thought, a memory, a dream, or a fantasy, and when the clinician verbally and nonverbally affirms these mental contents. Consensus is achieved when the patient thoughtfully and wholeheartedly says, nods, or otherwise express "Yes," "Yes, that what it's like," "Yes, that's how I feel," "Yes, that's my concern," "Yes, that's what I would like." This common social reality supports the phenomenal self and world of the involved patient (or the dissociative part).

Effective attunement particularly concerns the achievement of a consensual understanding, acceptance, and affirmation of the patients' core wishes. Accordingly, patients may be more open to engaging in more efficient but perhaps also more demanding actions. Clinicians may even propose some of these, whereas others flow from the increasing power of action of patients. The new actions need not be revolutionary, but they will be new nonetheless. They often comprise smaller or bigger steps along an evolving therapeutic path patients and clinicians enact as they proceed toward common objectives.

Attuning, building consensus, affirming wishes, and proposing and encouraging new actions are not four sequential therapeutic phases. They occur recurrently over the duration of the clinical venture, not in a serial or circular movement, but rather as steps along an enacted helix. This helix does not preexist but is created continually. This consensual development, this joint movement, resembles dancing. The dance partners wish to attain the pleasing motions and feelings these motions create. In order to achieve this mutual agreement in action, they must feel each other's movements and intentions, adapt to them, and, regardless of whatever movement they engage in, find balance. This attunement and balancing are dynamic, ongoing, effortful. Sometimes, of course, they move too quickly, too slowly, too prudently, too wildly; sometimes they inadvertently step on each other's toes; sometimes they even stumble and fall. But, rather than accusing each other of erring, they best analyze what went wrong and how to prevent or at least delimit future failure.

And then there is that occasional flow, that enjoyable success in action that fosters growth. Such achievement invites continued practice and dedication to more complicated moves. The metaphor of *therapeutic dancing* reflects the fact that (psycho)therapy is far more than just a verbal exchange. When words are the lyrics, dancing to the song entails taking in the words, feeling their meaning, going with the rhythm, and sensitively moving together, mind and body united.

Pediatric Hypnotherapy as a Model of Any Form of Psychotherapy

Milton Erickson (1958a) described the phases of generating attunement, building a consensual understanding, affirmation of patients' wishes, and stimulation toward new, more efficient actions in a beautiful and most impressive four-page article entitled *Pediatric Hypnotherapy*. Given its major importance for an enactive approach to trauma therapy, I have taken the liberty of quoting the paper at length and putting some terms in **bold** to emphasize their close correspondence with the principles of enactivism and enactive trauma therapy. Although the document focuses on children and hypnotherapy, Erickson explicitly communicates that its contents actually apply to any patient and to any form of psychotherapy. He wrote the following:

> Of the utmost importance in the use of hypnosis is the fact that there governs the child, as a growing, developing **organism**, an **ever-present motivation** to seek for more and better understanding of all that is about him . . . He is willing to receive ideas, he enjoys responding to them, and there is only a need of presenting those ideas **in a manner comprehensible to him**. This, as in all forms of psychotherapy and for all types of patients, is a **crucial** consideration. (p. 418)

Erickson next explains that:

> [s]uch **presentation of ideas** should be in accordance with the **dignity of the patient's experiential background and life experiences** – there should **not be talking down to or over the head of the patient.** (p. 418)

Clinicians thus recognize, acknowledge, and adapt to the patient's past and present phenomenal worlds, to their past but uncompleted and current *umwelt* in an egalitarian style. In this sense, clinicians meet their patients at their level of action in order to establish a goal-oriented agreement and collaboration geared toward the need of the patient to be helped and progress, and the clinician's desire to be of help, to be useful:

> There needs to be the simple presentation of an **earnest, sincere idea** by one person to another for the purpose of achieving **a common understanding and a common goal and purpose.** The mother croons a lullaby to her nursing infant, not to give it an understanding of the words, but to convey a pleasing sense of sound and rhythm in association with pleasing physical sensations for both of them and for the achievement of a common goal. (p. 419)

Many chronically traumatized children have never heard such a lullaby and have had to grow up in the absence of pleasing physical sensations. What is more, development is not built on *occasional* pleasurable sensations; they need to be continuing experiences:

> ... it is not just a single touch or pat or caress, but a **continuity of stimulation** that allows the child, however short its span of attention, to give a continued response to the stimulus ... (p. 419)

This recurrent therapeutic stimulation or encouragement is best when kept as simple as possible. It is not about fancy interpretations made to please only the clinician's intellectual and affective needs; rather, it concerns signs and ideas that make sense to the patient or, more specifically, to the involved dissociative part of the patient, some of which operate at early developmental levels:

> Hypnosis, whether for adults or children, should derive from a willing **utilization** of **simple, good, and pleasing** stimuli that serve in everyday life to elicit normal behavior pleasing to all concerned. (p. 419)

Clinicians' language should preferably comprise simple words and short sentences, sensitively spoken in a rhythm, befitting and utilizing the patient's experiential and epistemic world.

The next interest is that clinicians refrain from displaying any air of authority and superiority:

> ... there should never be any threat to the child as a functioning unit of society. Adult physical strength, intellectual strength, force of authority, and weight of prestige are all so immeasurably greater to the child than his own attributes that any undue use constitutes a threat to his adequacy as an individual. Since hypnosis is dependent on a **cooperation in a common pur-**

> pose, a **feeling of goodness and adequacy is desirable for both participants.** That sense of goodness and adequacy is not to be based on a sense of superiority of one's own attributes, but upon a **respect for the self** as an individual dealing rightfully with another individual with **each contributing his full share** to **a joint activity of significance to both.** There is **a need,** because of the child's lack of experiential background and understanding, to work primarily ***with*** and not ***on*** the child. (p. 419)

Authority and superiority are *poison* to individuals who have been chronically traumatized by significant others. And whereas it may in some cases be true that "... the adult can better comprehend passive participation" (p. 419), this statement may not apply to seriously neglected, maltreated, and abused individuals. And it certainly does not apply to dissociative parts with the identity of a toddler, child, or adolescent. Also, more generally, adults may learn less from "passive participation" than from active engagement in new actions. In this sense, enactive trauma clinicians take it very seriously that

> ... there should be a **utilization of language, concepts, ideas and word pictures meaningful** to the child [adolescent, adult] ... (p. 419)

Further, the cognitive and affective capacities of patients should not be underestimated. They are to be respected and challenged within manageable limits:

> Similarly, respect must be given to the child's ideational comprehension with no effort to derogate or minimize the child's capacity to understand. It is better to expect too great a comprehension than to offend by implying a deficiency ... (p. 419). The child must be respected as a **thinking, feeling** creature possessed of a capacity to **formulate ideas and understandings** and **integrate them into his total of experiential comprehension**; but he must do this in accord with **the actual functioning processes** he himself possesses. **No adult can do this for him,** and **any approach to the child must be made with an awareness of this fact.** (p. 420)

Indeed, clinicians should cooperate with their patients, whatever their age. They attune themselves to them and strive to enact a common world in close collaboration and proximity with them. They also support, guide, and sometimes educate their patients. But no matter how helpful their actions may be, clinicians know and realize that only the traumatized individual as a whole organism-environment system can heal the injury that their trauma is.

Attuning to the Patient's Phenomenal Realities

Erickson's pediatric hypnotherapy encompasses four phases, alluded to above. The first phase concerns *attunement*. For example, when Erickson's 3-year-old son fell down the stairs, he split his lip, and an upper tooth was knocked back in the upper jawbone. Engulfed by a hurting, profusely bleeding body and a terrifying world he could not agree with, Robert screamed loudly. Instead of picking him up instantly, however, Erickson attuned to Robert's shattered phenomenal self and world by saying, the moment his son paused to take a breath for continued screaming, "That hurts awful, Robert. That hurts terribly."

As Erickson asserted, "Right then, without any doubt, my son knew that I knew what I was talking about. He could agree with me and he knew I was agreeing completely with him" (p. 420). His father's sympathy and empathy complemented Robert's enclosed first-person world of pain and fright with a second-person offer of sympathy, empathy, and understanding: He was no longer alone.

In terms of action systems, Robert's mammalian defense system (experiencing pain leads to screaming for help) became complemented with activation and utilization of the social engagement action system. As Erickson put it, "In pediatric hypnotherapy, there is no more important problem than so speaking with the patient that he can agree with you and respect your intelligent grasp of the situation as judged by him in terms of his own understandings" (p. 420). This agreement and understanding clearly do not pertain to a mere third-person technical judgment but crucially includes the patient's second-person phenomenal judgment that someone else empathically grasps what the situation is about.

Generating a Consensual Understanding

Hence, the *consensual* second step in which Erickson told his son, "[a]nd it will keep right on hurting" (p. 420). As he commented, "In this simple statement I named his own fear, confirmed his own judgment of the situation, demonstrated my good intelligent grasp of the entire matter and my entire agreement with him, since right then, he could foresee only a lifetime of pain and anguish for himself" (p. 420).

Like Robert, traumatized individuals commonly find themselves in a lonely, terrifying world. It is a horrible and confusing first-person world that goes without second-person acceptance and understanding. And this hurting world goes on and on. Like Robert, they need an empathic significant other to liberate them from this encapsulation; they need someone who can intellectually and affectively grasp the whole situation and who simply and directly says what's going on.

It is only too human that clinicians wish to save their patients from their frightening and agonizing worlds. However, it is often better that they withhold this personal need and desire. Traumatized patients, first of all, need the full acceptance and deep understanding of an emotionally clever clinician. Rushing saviors who almost enforce change generally do not thrill them. Rescuers who, perhaps for their own sake more than for the patient's good, hardly resonate with the patient's horrified phenomenal self and the horrific phenomenal world are of very little use. They are generally not very effective in bringing about the change they would much like to achieve and as quickly as possible. At times clinicians may not find it easy to sympathetically and empathically attune to traumatized patients' damaged selves and terrifying past and present worlds. But this is exactly the adjustment enactive trauma therapy takes. This therapy is about walking a painful path together.

Affirmation of a Wish for Change

Erickson's next move was to voice Robert's *wish for change* when his son was taking another breath: "And you really wish it would stop hurting" (p. 420). As he explained, "Again we were in full **agreement** and he was **ratified** and even **encouraged** in this wish. And it was ***his*** wish, deriving entirely from within him and constituting his own **urgent need**" (p. 420).

Enactive trauma therapy is likewise guided by the patients' needs and wishes. Before clinicians can fruitfully engage in therapeutic leading, they must first fully acknowledge, confirm, and encourage their patients' wishes. They must strive above all to achieve a common *umwelt* that opens the door to therapeutic change, to new viable and creative actions. This order of things becomes all the more important, the less the patients' wishes have been heard, accepted, and boosted in the past. Timing is everything.

Sensitive Leading and Utilization

Erickson felt that his last remark generated a situation that might allow Robert to accept a little, carefully formulated suggestive leading: "Maybe it will stop hurting in a little while, in just a minute or two" (p. 420). It was important to formulate "maybe it will stop" because this suggestion was in agreement with the child's needs and wishes and with his understanding of the situation. Erickson did not present himself as an authority endowed with any superior knowledge. He did not say, "it will stop hurting," but offered the idea that it *might* stop hurting. He modestly uttered a possibility that allowed Robert to respond freely on the basis of his own current frame of mind and his own interests.

Following the attunement to Robert's world, generation of a consensual world, affirmation of his wishes, and some gentle initial leading in the direction of change, Erickson utilized some of his son's other vibrant needs and wishes. He made use of Robert's urge to be a competent individual in an exceptionally trying situation. Recognizing and acknowledging the actual terrifying world once more he said, "That's an awful lot of blood on the pavement" (p. 421). This statement reflecting Robert's terror ("an awful lot") was immediately followed by a surprising shift from (the action system of) defense to (the action system of) exploration: "Is it good, red, strong blood?" Not just Robert and his father, but the boy's whole world of significance (Robert, Father, Mother) had to see that awful amount of blood – and they all had to check the quality of his blood: "Look carefully, Mother, and see. I think it is, but I want you to be sure" (p. 421). This shift also directed attention to the meaning of the event: "In a situation in which one feels seriously damaged there is an overwhelming need for a compensatory feeling of satisfying goodness" (p. 421). Absorbed in the problem of the quality of his blood, Robert stopped crying. The blood was scrutinized and its fine quality was ascertained. However, to be fully sure, it would be important to contrast the blood against the white of the bathroom sink. Mother took her son to the bathroom where she poured water over his face to check, as his father had wondered whether the blood would properly mix with the water and gave it a proper pink color.

The next topic of the joint investigation became the concern whether Robert's mouth was bleeding and swelling properly. The remark that his lip might need stitching was bound to trigger a negative reaction. Utilizing this framework of serious worry, Erickson expressed the concern whether Robert could have as many stitches as he could count. It seemed that no more than ten stitches would be needed, whereas Robert could count to twenty. Further,

> Regret was expressed that he could not have seventeen stitches, like Betty Alice, or twelve like Allen, but comfort was offered in the statement that he could have more stitches than his siblings Bert, Lance, or Carol. Thus the whole situation became transformed into one in which Robert could share with his older siblings a common experience with a comforting sense of equality and a touch of superiority. (p. 422)

Therapeutic utilization is the art of utilizing whatever patients bring to the situation. It is about utilizing what *they* have experienced, what *they* currently feel, think, can imagine, and certainly, need and desire in the shorter and longer run. It is one dancing partner suggesting a new move that employs the existing feelings, thoughts, images, needs, and wishes of the other dancing partner for the sake of their common goals. It is not a good idea to lead the partner to do a pirouette that will make her feel awfully dizzy. The partner who engages in this whirl has left the common path, stubbornly pursues own wishes, and creates chaos. It is better to feel into one's partner's abilities and wishes. It is far more useful to gracefully invite and support an achievable movement that both dancers fancy and enjoy.

The Dance of Enactive Trauma Therapy

Figure 31.1. depicts the general action model of

- the clinician's constant attunement to the patient's phenomenal experiences and conceptions of self, world, and self-of-that-world ('*attunement*'),
- the constant generation of a consensual phenomenal understanding of the state of affairs ('*consensus building*'), including constant affirmation of the patient's needs and desires ('goal-orientation'), and
- encouragement to engage in new, more efficient actions that lie within the patient's actual reach ('sensible leading by utilization'), and that fit the striving toward the patient's healing ('the common result' of the whole venture).

These three actions constitute a basic and general therapeutic *gestalt*: Effective therapeutic change takes each of these therapeutic actions, and each action is only meaningful, and hence useful, in the context of the other actions.

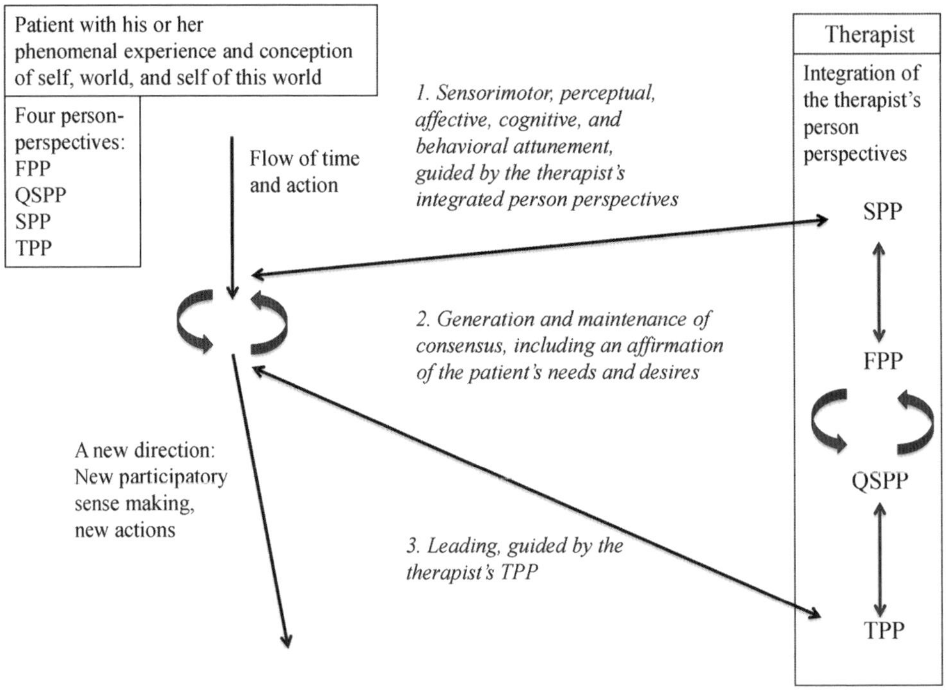

Figure 31.1. Therapeutic attunement, consensus building, and leading.

Note: FPP = first-person perspective; QSPP = quasi-second-person perspective; SPP = second-person perspective; TPP = third-person perspective. The clinician strives to attune to the patient's phenomenal experience (FPP), phenomenal conception of self (FPP and QSPP), phenomenal conception of other subjects (SPP), physical conception of objects or constellations of objects (TPP), and self as a part of this world (integration of the FPP, QSPP, SPP, and TPP). This attunement serves to generate and maintain consensus between the patient and the clinician regarding the contents of the patient's experiences and judgments of self, other subjects, and objects. Achieving attunement and a consensual world are therapeutic, though not mere goals in themselves. Rather, they serve to generate a solid therapeutic relationship and a sufficiently common world that affords the achievement of common results. They are steps toward the patient's eventual healing. The therapeutic relationship, the common environment, and the dedication to achieve common results allow a degree of therapeutic leading. This leading is not authoritarian but egalitarian and involves inviting and encouraging the patient to engage in new, more integrative actions. Attunement, generation of a consensual domain, and leading are ongoing actions in enactive trauma therapy. The success of the venture is dependent as well on the clinician's integration of his or her various person perspectives. Ideally, the endeavor is not guided by the clinician's personal conatus but is geared toward the patient's conatus, inasmuch as it is viable. That is, the actions of the clinician are guided by the patient's viable conatus and are influenced as little as possible by the clinician's personal needs and desires – which are irrelevant to the patient's steps toward healing. In other words, the clinician is ideally guided by his or her needs and desires *as a clinician*.

Attuning to Traumatized Individuals

Attunement occurs both verbally and nonverbally, and concerns clinicians' affective as well as cognitive adjustment to their patients' first-person, quasi-second-person, second-person, and third-person perspectives. Enactive trauma clinicians are deeply interested in, focus on, sensitively feel into, and carefully track their patients' phenomenal experiences and points of views. They regard them as primordially affective and operationally autonomous centers of action and passion. They thus wonder:

- What does the patient phenomenally experience? (interest in the patient's first-person perspective)
- What is it like to have these phenomenal experiences? (attunement to the patient's first-person perspective)
- How does the patient phenomenally conceive and judge him/herself? (attunement to the patient's quasi-second-person perspective)
- How does the patient phenomenally conceive and judge significant others, including the clinician? Who is useful, who is harmful, who is insignificant? (attunement to the patient's second-person perspectives)
- How does the patient, in a more physical or technical than experiential sense, conceive of objects, including subjects, and constellations of objects, including groups of other subjects? (attunement to the patient's third-person perspectives)

In other words, clinicians examine:

- What is it like to be the patient's 'I'? (the affective and operationally autonomous center of experience and action and passion)
- What is it like to phenomenally conceive and judge this 'I'? (experience-based 'I-me, myself, mine' relationships)
- What is it like to phenomenally conceive and judge this 'I' in a relationship with other individuals? (experience based 'I-You' relationship)
- What is it like to more technically or physically conceive and judge 'things of this world'? (physical or technical 'I-object' relationships)

Since life is historical and dynamic, clinicians also wonder: "What is it like to have lived, to live, and to continue living this patient's life?" For example, they may marvel, "What it was like to be a young neglected, maltreated, or abused girl? What was it like to meet these horrors, not once but each day anew? How did the patient manage to live this exceptionally difficult life? What was and is it like to receive no acceptance, no understanding, no help despite the fact that the world is full of other persons? What was and is it like to have met clinicians who did not show an interest in trauma and dissociation or who say that dissociation is due to suggestion and role-playing? What was and is it like to have met clinicians who misdiagnose and engage in a treatment that is ineffective or that makes things worse?"

Clinicians are not information-processing machines; they are feeling and willing persons; they are experiential and meaning-making operationally autonomous and self-organizing systems. And because any experience and judgment presupposes and flows from a first-person perspective, clinicians' interest in their patients is grounded in an interest in themselves. Clinicians thus also ask themselves: "How do I feel right here and now, and what do I currently feel? How do I presently and, more generally phenomenally and more technically, judge myself? How do I phenomenally relate to the patient today and to my significant others? And how do I technically judge the patient: What is the diagnosis, what is the current problem, what would I say and more generally do best to help the patient, what do my psychotherapeutic training and orientation and model of psychopathology tell me?"

The diagnostic and therapeutic enterprise exists in virtue of a relationship and a sound collaboration between the patient and the clinician. Since they are two operationally autonomous organism-environment systems that affect each other, clinicians must keep in mind how the patient affects them and how they seem to affect the patient. Clinicians are challenged to consider the affective dynamics going on between them, on the realization that – given their primordial affectivity and conatus – patients and clinicians are primarily interested in themselves. They thus wonder: "What does the patient need and desire, and what do I need and wish? What urges does the patient seem to experience and display, and what urges affect me? Do my needs and desires perhaps control what I am currently saying and doing more than my assessment of the patient's current modes of longings and strivings?"

In short, attunement demands a complex set of ongoing and related personal and interpersonal considerations. This set pertains to clinicians' phenomenal experiences and judgments in the framework of their primary interest in themselves and their secondary interest in their patients.

Generating a Consensus

But attunement is not a goal in itself; rather, it is geared toward the generation of a consensual *umwelt*, of a conceived self and world with which both the patient and the clinician can agree. This agreement can bring joy, the conscious awareness of a passage to a greater personal perfection. The consensus is achieved in a present moment when the patient and the clinician agree on what the patient is experiencing, perceiving, and conceiving, on what the patient feels, thinks, wishes, hopes, fears, fantasizes, dreams, remembers, anticipates, and does.

This agreement may be captured in a discourse or a longer sentence. However, it is more commonly and often more effectively cast in the form of a short statement and a nonverbal signal, or a series of such short communications. Short communications are particularly effective when the patient's mental efficiency[1] is low or moderate. Grasping long communications takes more working memory. It takes a synthesis of the various elements of the sentence or sentences, and more reflection. These abilities may be limited in traumatized individuals, particularly in EPs.

1 Levels of mental efficiency can be expressed in terms of a hierarchy of action tendencies. See Chapter 33.

The clinician's agreement need not be more than a simple and clearly affirmation of a patient's utterance, not seldom accompanied by some nodding, a brief lowering of the eyelids, an affirmative exhalation, or a more general affirmative movement. Clinicians can further ratify and thereby highlight the achievement of a consensus. For example, when the patient has affirmed the clinician's mirroring (e.g., "Yes, that's how it feels"), the clinician may want to reconfirm the consensual understanding, usually with a deepening tone of voice and some deceleration ("Hm, yes, . . . that is how it feels"). The clinician may also mirror the patient's intonation, in the understanding that it can make all the difference in the world whether, say, a patient says "*Yes*, that's how it feels" or "Yes, *that*'s how it feels" or "Yes, that's how it *feels*."

Clinicians may also want to emphasize patients' experiences and conceptions by formulating an appropriate hyperbole. For example, when a patient says, "I'm *scared*," the clinician can emphasize the fear, particularly when the patient looks very scared, by remarking, "You're *scared*. I get that. *Really* scared." A common result has been achieved when the patient agrees, "Yes," or "Yes, really scared."

Enactive trauma clinicians generally realize the major importance of attunement and the implied mirroring. Attunement and mirroring provide an affirmation of the other person's existence and value. They are commodities that parents of other primary caretakers who chronically neglect, maltreat, and abuse the children under their care rarely if ever grant. Thus, clinicians more carefully and more profoundly attune to and mirror their patients' phenomenal self, world, and self-of-this-world.

If all goes well, the generation and affirmation of consensus tend to be a mutual affair. For example, Chapter 36 includes the following transcript of a therapy session in which Agnes, a young EP of a patient with complex dissociative intrusion disorder (CDID)[2], was

2 This new term needs an explanation. 'Dissociative disorder not otherwise specified' in DSM-IV, example 1 (DDNOS-1, APA, 1994), and 'Chronic and recurrent syndromes of mixed dissociative symptoms' in DSM-5 (APA, 2013) involve NOS categories, that is, nonspecific diagnoses. However, evidence suggests that the condition involved may be the dissociative disorder with the highest prevalence. It is curious and indeed antithetical to clinical and scientific interests that the most common dissociative disorder – being similar to DID though less extremely developed – be classified as an NOS category. Classificatory systems should not include indistinct compartments for frequently occurring phenomena, or else they are of little use. These systems should classify the most common occurrences. The working group that was invited to propose a categorization for ICD-11 'Dissociative disorders' (Nijenhuis, Lewis-Fernandez, Moskowitz, & Moreira-Almeida, 2014) thus felt that the condition – DDNOS/chronic and recurrent syndromes of mixed dissociative symptoms – should become a *specific* dissociative disorder under the label CDID. In CDID, basically one major dissociative part of the personality primarily pursues appetites of common, daily life. This dissociative part is dominant most of the time, but becomes frequently intruded on by several emotional dissociative parts of the personality. In contrast to DID, these intruding dissociative parts do not, or only rarely, take full executive control. And in contrast to simple and complex PTSD, the intrusions tend to be more complex. Hence, the label 'complex dissociative intrusion disorder.' In ToT Volumes I & II, I referred to CDID as "minor DID." However, now that the proposal has been released, it is justified to use the better term CDID. When using the acronym CDID, it should be kept in mind that the "I" does not stand for

dominant (the actual transcript includes nonverbal elements not provided here). The EP held her hand and arm tight to her chest. At some point, I said:

E: You feel that removing your arm from [the rest of] your body leaves your body *unprotected*? [Attunement]
A: (nods several times) [Consensus]
E: . . . and then it feels that you will be in great *danger*. [Attunement]
A: (nods several times more; remains tense) [Consensus]
E: And now we want to *figure out* if that is *really* true or not.
A: If I do that it is as if my body is *naked*.
E: Yeah, as if it is *naked*. [Attunement]
A: (nods) [Consensus]
E: *Unprotected*. [Attunement and consensus]
A: (nods) Yes. [Consensus]
E: You have learned to keep your arm close to your body when you were with your father to *protect yourself*? [Attunement and consensus]
A: Yes. [Consensus]
E: Yes. [Reaffirmation of consensus] Have you *often* kept your arm and hand against your chest? (etc.)

A lack of consensus, that is, the existence of a lesser or more substantial disagreement, can be similarly expressed in several sentences, one sentence, a few words, or a clear and emphatic "no." Like everyone else, patients may also express disagreement by accompanying nonverbal means: They may shake their head, raise their eyebrows, open their eyes more, open their mouth in astonishment, wave or nervously move their hands, or withdraw their upper body, hands, or mouth. Clinicians pick up the disagreement with a simple "Aha, so that's *not* how it feels." When the patient affirms that this is the case, he or she may say something like "No, it's different." The clinician can thereupon simply reply, "It's different." The patient may next say, "Yes," which allows the clinician to agree, "Yes . . .," and then ask, "How *does* it feel?"

The consensus is not a simple or complex verbal and nonverbal statement; rather, it is *an affectively lived reality*. A quick, superficial affirmative "Yes" and jumping to the next issue does not suffice. However, analyses of the utterances of clinicians who are insufficiently aware of the importance of attuning to the patient, of the generation of a consensus, and of the affirmation of an achieved consensus often reveal such superficiality. This can also apply to clinicians who are just starting to practice this communicative style. Such shallowness is not meaningful to the patients, and the clinicians may not give themselves a chance to really feel into the patient. The achievement and realization of a consensus

---

"identity" but for "intrusion." An alternative name that would avoid this potential confusion would have been 'complex dissociative intrusion syndrome.' However, one limitation of this option is that none of the other dissociative disorders are described as 'syndromes.' In ToT Volumes I & II, I referred to CDID as "minor DID." Whereas 'minor' means 'a lesser form of,' the phrase may sound contemptuous in English. Clearly, nothing of the sort was intended.

take time and insistence. Achieving consensus is not so much about technical facts, although an agreement on such facts may be included; rather, it means achieving a common result. It is the realization of a common phenomenal state of affairs.

Affirming Traumatized Individuals' Desires for Change

For traumatized individuals a successful attunement that brings forth a consensual phenomenal state of affairs in the pursuit of common goals constitutes *change*. Most will not have previously experienced that interpersonal coordination, cooperation, and communication can take on this form. Even if clinicians do not necessarily engage in attunement and the creation of a consensual world to engender therapeutic change, simply taking ample time for the realization of these recurrent steps can and often does imply the achievement of something new. Achieving a consensual world through fine-tuned communication, coordination and cooperation raises consciousness; it builds and strengthens the therapeutic relationship, and it generates and supports trust. An accepting and nonjudgmental clinical attitude tends to open up patients more. It counters their feelings of shame, and it encourages them to speak out; it increases their power of action. Moreover, the achievement of these successes increases the clinician's power of action as well.

Sensitive Leading and Utilization in Trauma

Since therapeutic change involves new actions, clinicians may propose new actions inasmuch as patients do not spontaneously start to engage in new actions themselves. Following the generation of a substantial, consensual *umwelt*, clinicians may invite patients to experiment with new actions that have attracted their affective interest, and that seem to be within their current reach. Clinicians can obviously only propose a course of action when they have a solid idea about where the patient should best go. In this respect, their technical third-person perspective on the resolution of traumatization plays an important, albeit nonexclusive role. The venture is also strongly guided by the patient's wishes and ideas as well as by the ongoing assessment and evaluation of all other person perspectives, including those of the clinician.

It is generally good clinical practice to start proposing new actions that the patient can almost certainly accept, ones that he or she can almost certainly endeavor and complete. As mentioned above, nothing succeeds like success. Clinicians should thus often break down more demanding, more difficult, and more complex actions into less challenging components. This strategy reflects the application of a general educational principle: Parents applaud every new step along the way to independent walking, such as sitting with some aid, sitting unaided, crawling, standing with aid, standing with less support, standing without support, and, of course, the first step. They give toddlers crayons and some paper, celebrate a first 'drawing,' see to it that drawings are made on paper and not on furniture, and help their children at some point to draw lines that later constitute letters. The first time they write their name, the whole family is informed. They may even get a present. Parents may also help their children to engage in difficult actions such as bridging time. When our grandchild Asia became 4 1/2 years old and could not wait for her 5th birthday, her clever mother baked a *half* birthday cake. The compromise fully met Asia's needs and wishes.

Whatever a patient does in therapy, the direction of his or her actions or passions is the joint outcome of his or her needs, wishes, insights, wisdom, and developments – and the clinician's insights and encouragement. In this regard, too, clinicians are coaches, not dictators; they are partners in a dance inasmuch as the patient and the clinician have agreed to dance and to continue dancing and what kind of dance the venture is going to be. There are, of course, limits to what either partner can and wishes to accept. Patients are not forced to engage in actions proposed by the clinician, and clinicians are not obliged to accept their patients' initiatives they cannot or, a fortiori, should not accept. More on this later.

From Flatland to Spaceland

In the discussion of clinical work so far, it has been assumed that traumatized patients encompass one set of first-person, quasi-second-person, second-person, and third-person perspectives. In the case of dissociative disorders, however, these perspectives exist in a plural form. As detailed in the theoretical chapters of the present volume, dissociative parts of the personality constitute autonomous, conscious, self-conscious, primordially affective, and embodied subsystems of a wider organism-environment system. Semipermeable, they are embedded in and affected by their material and social world. This *umwelt* includes the existence of other dissociative parts that may and often do relate to each other in a dynamical fashion.

In dissociative disorders, there is no singular "I" but several "I's" to which clinicians attune to, which they strive to meet in a consensually enacted world, and which they encourage to experiment with new actions (see Figure 31.2). In fact, dissociative patients comprise as many sets of person perspectives as there are dissociative parts. Each dissociative part includes his or her own second-person perspective regarding other significant individuals. For example, one dissociative part may like a person whom another part fears. And inasmuch as dissociative parts are aware of one or more other dissociative parts, they include a second-person perspective or perhaps even a third-person perspective regarding these other dissociative parts. For example, some ANPs *phenomenally* experience and judge fragile EPs (e.g., "The little one scares me") and controlling EPs ("He's dangerous and mean"). Other ANPs may only *technically or physically* judge other dissociative parts in the context of a third-person perspective (e.g., "That little one is a stupid thing").

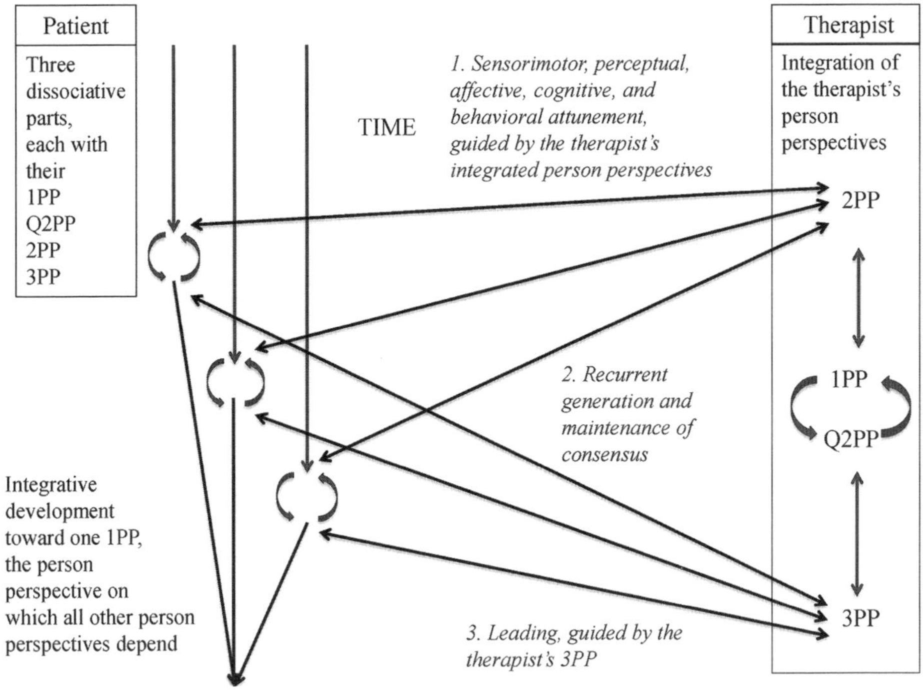

Figure 31.2. Therapeutic attunement, consensus building, and leading when there are two or more dissociative parts.

Note: FPP = first-person perspective, QSPP = quasi-second-person perspective, SPP = second-person perspective, TPP = third-person perspective. The clinician strives to attune to the patient's phenomenal experience (FPP), phenomenal conception of self (FPP and QSPP), phenomenal conception of other subjects (SPP), physical conception of objects or constellations of objects (TPP), and self as a part of this world (integration of the FPP, QSPP, SPP, and TPP). The clinician attunes to each dissociative part's self, world, and self of this world, and strives to achieve consensus, that is, a common world with an orientation toward the achievement of a final common result: the integration of the various dissociative parts and their attributes. Leading involves the clinician's invitation and encouragement of dissociative parts to engage in new actions. The clinician's leading is inspired by his or her various person perspectives, including his or her third-person perspective. This third-person perspective pertains to the clinician's understanding of human experience, thought, and behavior as well as the model of therapeutic change the clinician adopts. The success of the venture is codependent on the clinician's integration of his or her own various person perspectives regarding each and every dissociative part. Ideally, the endeavor is not guided by the clinician's personal conatus regarding the patient as a whole or regarding each dissociative part the patient includes. Rather, it is geared toward the needs and desires of the patient's dissociative parts – inasmuch as these are viable. They are influenced as little as possible by the clinician's personal needs and desires inasmuch as these are irrelevant to the steps toward the healing of the patient and each and every dissociative part. The clinician, thus, treats the various dissociative parts evenhandedly.

Inasmuch as dissociative parts do not engage in a second-person or third-person relationship with other dissociative parts, the other parts involved may still intrude on them. In this case, the dissociative parts are intruded on are phenomenally open to these influences in the first-person perspective and quasi-second-person perspective. For example, when a scared fragile EP intrudes on an ANP who does not know the EP, the ANP may feel scared without actually knowing the source (i.e., the fragile EP) and the reason for this fear (the EP's fear of a perpetrator). In this case, the ANP may feel that "there is some force inside that scares me." The ignorance or dissociative source amnesia ensues when the ANP does not engage in a second-person or third-person relationship with the EP as EP.

Dissociative parts tend to have an unduly restricted field of consciousness and understanding (Janet, 1907; Van der Hart et al., 2006). They perceive, feel, know, remember, and imagine some things, albeit in total too few. Another common feature is that their level of consciousness tends to be too low. In combination with each other, the restricted and low levels of consciousness manifest in phenomena such as depersonalization, derealization, a meager or distorted body image, physical anesthesias, absent-mindedness, lack of concentration, a weak sense of time and a reduced understanding of the past, present, and future.

To further clarify the issue, it may be metaphorically said that dissociative parts lack adequate "dimensionality." There are things they (can) sense, perceive, conceive, remember, and do. However, there are also important things they cannot or do not sense, perceive, conceive, remember, and do. They live, as it were, in "Flatland" (Abbott, 1884/1992). In his novella *Flatland: A romance in many dimensions*, Abbott presented a fictional two-dimensional world to comment on the hierarchy of Victorian culture. Flatland is occupied by geometrical two-dimensional figures such as modest squares and rectangles. For example, men are polygons with various numbers of sides. Circles, however, are obviously Flatland's perfect citizens. Women are only simple line segments.

Even simpler creatures than the two-dimensional figures that inhabit Flatland are the one-dimensional citizens of "Lineland." Lineland is a one-dimensional world whose population consists of many "lustrous points." Pointland has no points as this world consists of only a single point. Not endowed with a capacity to comprehend dimensionality, Point is unable to understand or relate to the collection of points that make up Lineland. Linelanders, in turn, have no clue about two-dimensional beings. Flatlanders are rather pleased with themselves since they have no trouble grasping the virtues and vices of Pointland *and* Lineland.

The deeper meaning and purpose of the novella is its explorations of dimensions, as well as its portrayal of the rather common human phobia of change and the ubiquitous phobia of truths that challenge cherished beliefs and ideas. Whereas human beings (can) know three spatial dimensions and a time dimension, there may actually be other dimensions out there, as advanced models in physics strongly suggest. It may be said that dissociative parts involve limited dimensionality, which limits their ability to appreciate and understand each other, their willingness to cooperate and communicate with each other as well as the courage to detect new truths and to abandon outdated personal realities.

The plot of the novella can be read in this light. One day, a Sphere, a representative of a three-dimensional world visits Square. Sphere speaks of Spaceland, his home. Now Square is terribly confused. Confined to two dimensions, Square fails to grasp Sphere's concepts and realities. His misery becomes resolved when Sphere takes Square to Spaceland. This opens Square's eyes and inspires him to educate his fellow Flatlanders. However, when Flatland's leaders get a glimpse of Spaceland, that utterly strange world, they get scared. The foundations of Flatland they have guarded for so long like good shepherds are shaken. To protect their power and to save face, they proclaim that Square's revelations are dangerous, confusing figments of the imagination. Anyone who shares the truth of Spaceland and the third-dimension, they declare, must be silenced. Spacelanders painfully observe how Flatlanders who have witnessed the third dimension get massacred or imprisoned.

Similarly, clinicians observe how dissociative parts that inhabit Flatland, Lineland, or Pointland have immense difficulty understanding each other as well as the truth and importance of the third dimension. They perceive how proud Circles denigrate lesser Circles or simple Squares, and how Big Circles, Edgy Pentagrams, and Square Squares ignore, hide, or otherwise control the scary Spacelandish truth when this truth starts to dawn on them. They also observe how these various Shapes entice or pressure them to accept their two-dimensional point of view. Clinicians may further meet an occasional Pointlander who feels and thinks he or she is the solely existing monarch of the country. When pressured or not at their best, clinicians may even become mesmerized, so that they themselves begin to feel, think, and act Flatlandish, perhaps even speak Linelandish, or, worse, retreat to Pointland.

Enactive trauma therapy is for patients who lack the dimensions to heal their injuries on their own, but who, like some Brave Squares, are sincerely open to broadening their scope. The venture also includes clinicians who observe the disruptions, who are brave enough to visit painful Flatland. Like Sphere, they attune to lower dimensional worlds and grasp that Flatland, Lineland, and even Pointland make enough sense given the dimensional limitations that characterize these domains. Moreover, the enterprise demands clinicians who strive to remain Spacelanders even as they visit these lower dimensional worlds. The success of the venture also depends on clinicians who are keen to notice a temporary personal loss of footing in Spaceland, yet who can find their way home when this confusion happens. The project further takes seasoned spacelandish travelers. Using their expertise, they coach other Spheres who explore or have become overly enmeshed with Flatlandish, Linelandish, or Pointlandish realities.

Figures 31.3 and 31.4. capture the main features of the involved complexity. The bottom symbolizes the patient as a whole organism-environment system. Its flatness reflects the idea that the system and its subsystems do not engage in the actions needed to overcome the individual's trauma(s). They do not or insufficiently synthesize, personify, presentify, symbolize and realize the traumatic past. The various shapes involve parts of this whole system, each with its own mental and phenomenal features. The depicted Flatlanders are a prototypical ANP (Circle), a prototypical Fragile EP (Oval), and a prototypical Controlling EP (Square). The Figure also includes another kind of dissociative part (Triangle). This might be a suicidal one, an ANP including quite emotional modes of longing and striving, or an EP including modes of longing and striving that fit daily life. Still other

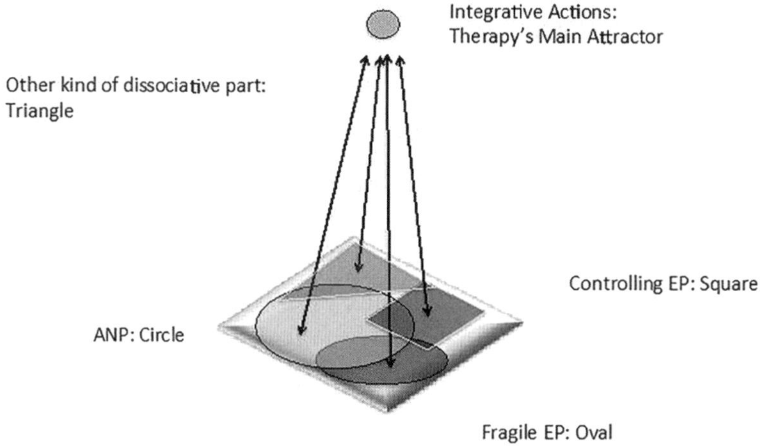

Figure 31.3. The therapeutic pyramid: Lifting Flatlanders to Spaceland.

dissociative parts may inhabit territories of even lesser complexity. These Linelanders or Pointlanders are not included in Figure 31.3. Each of the areas of the various shapes depicts the domain of manifest and latent biopsychosocial modes of longing and striving that a particular dissociative part can enact and reenact.

The four domains overlap to some degree. The overlapping areas express that the actions and contents of dissociative parts are not fully split but have common features. The involved areas comprise two phenomena: First, they symbolize common biopsychosocial states (e.g., the various dissociative parts speak one language, and all can walk and talk); second, they represent interactions among two or more dissociative parts. Confrontations of these Circles, Squares, Lines, or Points with themselves can involve close encounters of the first-person and quasi-second-person kind. The first kind is the part's first-person experience ('I'). Encounters of the quasi-second kind represent the encounters of a dissociative part with himself or herself. These meetings reflect a quasi-second person perspective ('I' – 'me, myself, mine' relationships). Confrontations of two or more dissociative parts with each other involve close encounters of the second-person kind (phenomenal 'I' – 'You' relationships). The black double arrowed lines symbolize interactions of a dissociative part with the clinician. The involved phenomenal 'I' – 'You' relationships also involve close encounters of the second-person kind. Technical or physical 'I – object' relationships constitute close encounters of the third-person kind.

As Spheres, competent clinicians have a grasp of the whole pyramid. That is, they are competent inasmuch as they do not lose touch with and the sight of the three-dimensional virtues of their Spaceland as they travel to Flatland (or Lineland, or Pointland). Such understanding is crucial because the added dimensions of Spaceland guide the way toward the (re)integration of the patient's divided personality. Spheres can introduce willing Circles and Squares to Space. They are careful to introduce Lines to Flatland and Points to Lineland first. The more the patient's personality becomes integrative, the more he or she

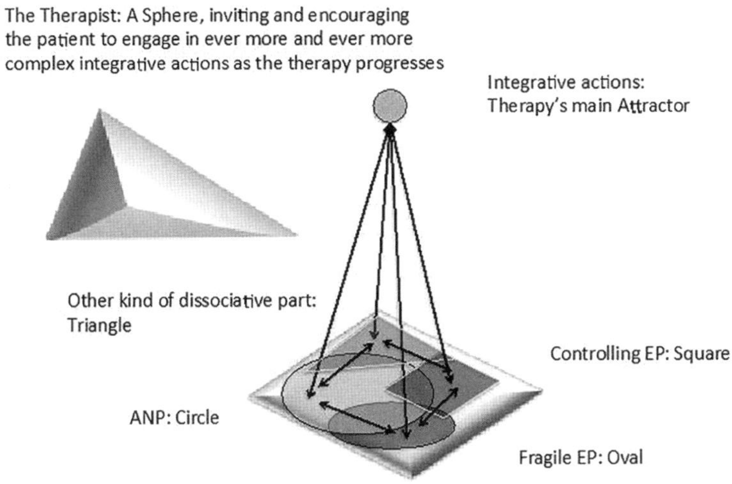

Figure 31.4. A Sphere meeting and influencing Flatlanders.

will become a Sphere, like the clinician. Spheres have more power of action than Flatlanders, Linelanders, or a Pointlander. The repertoire of mental and behavioral actions of Spheres is higher than that of creatures of lower complexity, and they tend to be mentally and behaviorally more efficient (Van der Hart et al., 2006). They achieve more common results by investing an equal amount of energy, or perhaps even less energy.

The top of the pyramid in Figure 31.4. reflects the clinician's ideal point of orientation. In terms of dynamic systems theory, the top operates as a systemic attractor, as a point of gravity guiding the therapy. The attractor comprises the interest of integration. Prompting the actions of synthesis, personification, presentification, symbolization, and realization, it 'pulls' or 'lifts' Flatlanders into Spaceland. Guided by this attractor, clinicians perceive and understand the pyramid their traumatized patients' personality can eventually become. In this sense, they invite and encourage their patients to add a third dimension to their two-dimensional world (inasmuch as it is limited to this two-dimensional world).

Traumatized individuals clearly do not operate in Flatland, Lineland, or Pointland at all times or in all regards. Some even operate at a high dimensional level in some domains of their life. However, with respect to their trauma(s), they lack the 'third dimension.' Some dissociative parts do not even seem to attain the virtues of sensing and knowing two dimensions.

The pyramid stands for the whole therapeutic venture. The slopes of the construction symbolize the dimensional 'downward' routes that clinicians travel in order to reach each of the dissociative parts in their domains. They may reach them directly or more indirectly. These gradients also represent the dimensional upward paths that each of the dissociative parts must climb to become an ever more inclusive or integrated organism-environment system. With each upward step, they gain the power of action and overcome their substitute actions or passions. However, the dissociative parts involved may stay put, mis-

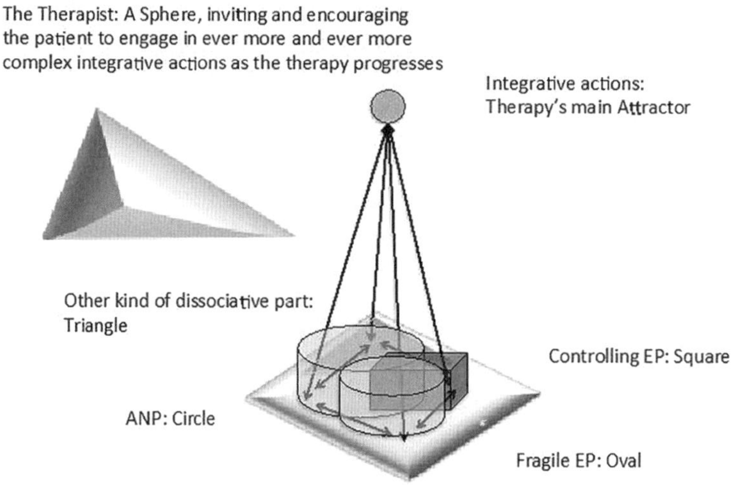

Figure 31.5. Dissociative parts gaining dimensionality through integrative actions.

understand, or punish these upward tendencies. Perils that threaten clinicians include conscious or unconscious loss of connectivity with the top as they sail down the slopes. For example, they may comprehend, value, and like some dissociative parts more than others; they may fight with, say, "the impossible" controlling EPs, pamper "the poor little" fragile EPs, side with ANPs who must "be stabilized," and ignore or ardently avoid travels to the "barren and outright dangerous" land of suicidal parts.

The whole pyramid presented in Figure 31.5. is the attempt to represent the increasingly integrative and integrated personality. It shows that the various dissociative parts do not get lost. The therapist strives rather to help them become integrated into the three-dimensional structure – into the pyramid that stands for an individual as a healthy, whole, and safe organism-environment system.

The pyramid does not reflect The Whole Truth. As Spinoza taught us, as a species we can only perceive and grasp some of Nature's infinite properties. Apart from this absolute dimensional restriction[3], clinicians are subject to their relative limitations. Whereas the ideal clinician is always three-dimensional or can embrace even more than three dimensions, real clinicians may lose access to Spaceland at times; sometimes they turn into Flatlanders, Linelanders, or Pointlanders. This happens when they fall prey to countertransferential passions, limited energy supplies, personal confusions, or negative moods, or when they are confronted with tasks that lie beyond their current levels of expertise and skills. This also occurs when they meet situations that do not accord well with their relative limitations, such as their selective interests, dispositions, capacities, and life experiences.

---

3 Some authors such as Jim Redfield (1993) and Carlos Castañeda (1970) speculated that our abilities as a species to experience, perceive, and conceive of attributes of nature may evolve, that they may not be limited for all eternity. Who knows?

Loss of Control in Trauma and Dissociation

Like other animals, humans have the urge to control their life circumstances whenever possible (Rofé & Rofé, 2013). Harmful cognitive, emotional, and physiological effects can ensue when this control is seriously compromised (Hofmann, 2005; Overmier, & Murison, 2005; Plumb, Cullen, & Minor, 2015; Pryce et al., 2011; Shvil, Rusch, Sullivan, & Neria, 2013; Wellman, Cullen, & Pelleymounter, 1998; White, Lehman, Hemphill, Mandel, & Lehman, 2006). Traumatization involves a profound loss of control regarding one's phenomenal self, *umwelt*, and self as a part of this *umwelt* per definition (ToT Volume I, Chapter 11).

Dissociation of the personality and its implied dissociative symptoms involve a major loss of control as well. True, dissociation is often comprehended as a survival strategy; it is in fact commonly seen as an effort to control and save what can be controlled and saved under harsh circumstances. This idea, however, makes sense only with respect to *negative* dissociative symptoms – and only when one regards the issue from the perspective of an ANP (see ToT Volume II, Chapter 13). There is nothing protective about *positive* dissociative symptoms, and dissociation of the personality is a curse rather than a blessing for fragile and controlling EPs. The striving of ANPs to keep their distance from agonizing sensations, feelings, thoughts, and memories wherever possible is an urge that EPs cannot control, and that keeps them encapsulated in these painful phenomenal realities. Inasmuch as ANPs do not have or use the power to integrate, symbolize, realize, and overcome the traumatization, EPs are bound to remain confined in this traumatic time-space *for life*. ANPs, in turn, suffer a lack of control regarding EPs. They cannot influence this emotionality inasmuch as they remain dissociated from EPs. EPs can and often do intrude on them, or even take full executive control at times. Fragile EPs and controlling EPs can and commonly do intrude on each other as well. Imitating the harmful power models that perpetrators display, controlling EPs strive to keep up at least some sense of control, however illusory it may be.

The development of dissociative parts within an individual entails still another type of phenomenal loss of control for that individual: First, dissociation of the personality need not commence as a more or less *conscious* substitute action or passion. For example, there is no evidence that PTSD is the result of a conscious decision to engender an ANP–EP division. An unconscious evolutionary influence may be that contrary action systems (Bolles, 1970; Bolles & Fanselow, 1980, Fanselow & Lester, 1988; Garcia[4], 1981; Nijenhuis & Den Boer, 2009; Nijenhuis et al., 2002; Timberlake, 1993; Timberlake & Lucas, 1989; Van der Hart et al., 1996; ToT Volumes I & II) tend to inhibit each other. This influence

4 John Garcia's career is an illuminating example of the affect-laden subjectivity of the third-person perspective in psychology (Lubek & Apfelbaum, 1987). Because he went against the basic claims of Skinnerian S-R psychology and provided consistent evidence that this psychology includes serious flaws, leading editors and reviewers rejected his papers wherever they could.

may unconsciously shape the basic ANP–fragile EP division: ANP guided by action systems for functioning in daily life, and fragile EP powerfully influenced by the action system of mammalian defense and/or attachment cry. This effect can be seen as an effect of mode-dependent learning (e.g., Eich, 1995; Eich, Macauley, & Ryan, 1994), or, more generally, what might be called 'action system-dependent' learning.

These unconscious affections do not exclude conscious actions or passions. Most traumatized individuals are at least initially consciously aware of the traumatizing events that happen/happened to them. Unable to integrate the experience, evolving ANPs may start to mentally avoid traumatic memories and other trauma-related signs, including the associated evolving EPs and interoceptive signs that point to these EPs. Evolving ANPs may also start to avoid exteroceptive signs that remind them of their unintegrated traumatic experiences and memories. An eye-tracking experiment demonstrated that, in contrast to fragile EPs, ANPs prefer to look at happy faces and avoid looking at sad and angry faces (Seidmann, Schlumpf, & Jäncke, 2014; see ToT Volume II, Chapter 18). The mental and behavioral avoidance of ANPs can encompass seeking out a variety of distractions. They can avoid feared persons, places, activities, films, books, discussions, thoughts, and physical as well as emotional feelings. ANPs can also focus on other persons, places, activities, etc., that they do not signify as dangerous, despicable, or disgusting. Further, they can cultivate physical and mental feelings that inhibit the feared, shameful, or otherwise despised ones. For example, they can start to engage in excessive work or sports. They may also start drinking or taking drugs. Some binge and purge or mutilate themselves. ANPs may also instruct themselves to forget traumatic experiences and events as well as the associated EPs. They may also attempt to suppress recollections of traumatic memories or other mental contents. Research has demonstrated that directed forgetting, retrieval suppression, and thought substitution are potentially effective mental actions (Anderson 2005; Anderson & Green, 2001; Anderson & Huddleston, 2012; Gottlob, Golding, & Hauselt, 2006; Sego, Golding, & Gottlob, 2006; Van Schie, Geraerts, & Anderson, 2013). However, there is also evidence that intentional forgetting becomes more difficult as we age (Anderson, Reinholz, Kuhl, & Mayr, 2011). As they age, then, ANPs too may experience growing difficulty keeping traumatic memories and the associated EPs at bay. At some point, their nonintegrated traumatic life and existence may start to intrude on them ever more and ever more intensely.

Before this decline sets in, it seems quite possible that the originally quite conscious actions and passions of ANPs to avoid trauma-related signs become so automatized that they phenomenally experience and conceive ever less of what they avoid. They may even become consciously unaware *that* they avoid something they fear and detest. Consistent with this hypothesis, using subliminal confrontations with trauma-related cues, we found that ANPs in adult women with DID *preconsciously* avoid focusing on neutral and angry faces, and that EPs are preoccupied with these faces (Schlumpf et al., 2013; ToT Volume II, Chapter 18). We also found that ANPs do not have phenomenal, psychophysiological, and neurobiological emotional reactions to audiotaped descriptions of the traumatic memories of EPs (Reinders et al., 2006, 2012, 2016), but cannot explain their reactions well. ANPs in DID can thus preconsciously avoid attending to signs they associate with traumatizing events, and EPs are clearly associated with these events.

These research findings are consistent with the clinical fact that the emergence, possible elaboration, and maintenance of fragile and controlling EPs can be more or less perplexing to ANPs, just as the emergence, possible elaboration, and maintenance of EPs is often puzzling to other prototypical dissociative parts. ANPs in individuals with complex dissociative disorders may not know EPs, at least not for what they are. Dissociative individuals do not tend to recollect *how* they generated EPs, just as fragile EPs do not commonly recall how they came into existence. At some point in therapy controlling EPs may explain that they tried to save fragile EPs, but they too cannot clarify exactly how they emerged. The fact that dissociative parts tend to be unaware how they are maintained could in part be due to preconscious substitute actions.

Chapter 32

Enactive Assessment of Dissociation and Traumatizing Events

Every person's map of the world is as unique as their thumbprint. There are no two people alike. No two people who understand the same sentence the same way . . . So in dealing with people, you try not to fit them to your concept of what they should be.
Milton H. Erickson

An investigation of the first-person perspective is of paramount importance not only for philosophy of mind, but also for a number of related disciplines including social philosophy, psychiatry, developmental psychology, and cognitive neuroscience.
Shaun Gallagher & Dan Zahavi (2008, pp. 221–222)

Although assessment and treatment mark different emphases, assessment affects and hence changes patients, while treatment of course includes ongoing assessment. If all goes well, patients meet up with interested, caring, knowledgeable, and skilled clinicians from the diagnostic phase onward. Ideally, they experience that clinicians do more than pose technical questions in the framework of a third-person perspective and draw technically correct conclusions. Apart from assuming their role as third-person professionals, clinicians also interact with their patients as second persons. They show a sincere affective interest in their patients' phenomenal experiences and judgments; they present themselves as feeling, empathizing, compassionate, and professional human beings – not as distant technocrats. That is, from the minute the two parties meet, clinicians strive to interact with their patients from a combined and coordinated second-person perspective and third-person perspective. Both of these perspectives are by their very nature grounded in their first-person perspective and quasi-second-person perspective. Like everyone, clinicians feel and know themselves, their world, and themselves as a part of this world from various standpoints. They include affective and epistemic plurality.

For example, clinicians do not just examine whether their patients hear voices and simply move on to the next question when patients provide an affirmative response. They also empathetically, compassionately, and nonjudgmentally ask what it is like to hear voices or to be confronted with commanding voices one cannot control. When these voices become activated during a diagnostic session, clinicians assist their patients in regaining control while also showing an affective and intellectual interest in and respect for "the voices" and whatever they may utter.

The implication is that assessment commonly includes some therapeutic interventions. On the other hand, therapy is also about the ongoing exploration and analysis of what happens during and around the sessions, both in terms of clinicians' third-person understanding as well as in terms of patients' and clinicians' conjoint second-person empathic angles. In other words, assessment and treatment can only be distinguished artificially, as both involve enactments of two phenomenal worlds – that of the patient and that of the clinician. These overlap in part, and, if all goes well, they increasingly overlap. This overlap is purposeful and utilized to achieve a common general goal: healing the patient's injuries.

Therapeutic Democracy and the Development of Positive Control

Since to live is to act, it can be generally said that traumatized individuals who present for assessment and therapy long to increase their power of action, providing them with a sense of positive control. New viable actions in this sphere replace their demoralization and the implied detrimental passions.

In this general atmosphere, enactive trauma clinicians adhere to egalitarianism and therapeutic democracy. One way in which they live their understanding and appreciation of their patients' affective core interests in the power of action is to grant the individuals who seek their assistance a relatively high degree of control regarding the clinical endeavor. For example, the moment therapists meet new patients, they invite them to pose any question *they* may have rather than to start asking questions themselves. Before patients decide to engage in a professional relationship with a particular clinician, they may want to know more about the setting, the organization of the practice, department, or clinic as well as its rules and methods. Fresh patients may have an interest in hearing their clinician's view on mental problems in general and in his or her basic method. And, of course, they may want to discern what kind of person the clinician is. In this democratic, egalitarian sphere clinicians convey to patients that they are free to leave the clinician's questions unanswered and to stop them from exploring any matters they – the patients – are not yet up to.

Enactive trauma assessment and therapy are democratic, collaborative ventures. Whereas patients and clinicians have different roles and responsibilities, their relationship should be symmetrical in terms of control in the therapeutic situation. Enactive trauma clinicians, therefore, adhere to Ferenczi's wise advice that therapists and other clinicians should not dominate their traumatized patients in one way or another (see ToT Volume I, Chapter 2). The dyad operates best in an egalitarian spirit of mutual respect, dedication, cooperation, and open communication.

Clinicians clearly have many diagnostic and other questions. But gathering all kinds of details regarding their patients' mental problems and life is authorized and relevant only within the framework of an evolving clinical collaboration. The point or final cause of the venture is, in principle, the patient's desire for a viable change. Therapy is not about a transformation aspired to by the clinician. Prior to asking diagnostic questions, clinicians therefore first ask their patients what *they* wish to change. And since changing oneself and one's world depends on one's actions, the more specific clinical interest lies in exploring what viable and creative goals patients may want to achieve, what actions on patients' behalf will likely be necessary to attain these goals, and why that power of action has to date been unavailable to them – or why they have not used the power of action they actually possess.

So what are the frequent goals of traumatized individuals? Generally, they want to get rid of their symptoms and do not know how to procure this relief. They want to sleep better and sleep undisturbed, achieve a permanent sense of time, become freed from reenactments of traumatic events and other intrusions, such as voices and horrible sensations. They may want to overcome their bingeing and throwing up food. They may desire to get rid of their fears, obsessions, addictions, their hate of their own body, and more. They may also long to end problematic relationships. Some may express a wish to achieve agreeable experiences such as more rewarding personal and professional relationships, and skills, such as an increased ability to take favorable decisions and to assert themselves more. And more than a few long to even feel they exist and have the right to exist as a subject. Before traumatized individuals decide to seek professional help, they may have tried long and hard to overcome these various troubles and to achieve these goals on their own, albeit to no avail.

Whereas some individuals can specify these goals, others may operate at a level of consciousness that seriously limits their ability to know or formulate viable therapeutic goals. Controlling EPs may forbid ANPs from having hope for a better future or from voicing a personal wish or opinion. And particularly those who have experienced chronic interpersonal traumatization may not feel they are individuals worthy of autonomy, choice, interest, and respect.

To use a political metaphor, these individuals have been raised in a harmful dictatorial world dedicated to erasing their personal autonomy (Chapter 22). Traumatizing relationships are power displays. They involve the power of perpetrators to satisfy their needs and desires at the expense of the needs and desires of the individuals they abuse, maltreat, and neglect. Patients who have been raised in these harmful relational frames may not be familiar with a lived democracy and the humane, mutually respectful interactions this societal structure encompasses. They may not know or trust that trauma therapy is the enactment of this egalitarian fairness and the implied deep respect for any individual's autonomy and worth.

If only because of this context, clinicians do not impose their needs, desires, and ideas on their patients or define specific therapeutic goals for them. If necessary, clinicians can carefully assist patients in restoring or developing a sense of personal value and identity what would allow them to make choices and take decisions in due course and for the exclusive sake of the patients' own interests. To this end, clinicians carefully mind that clinical and therapeutic relationships constitute the opposite of traumatizing, domineering relationships. They communicate and experience that, although clinicians, patients, and dissociative parts of patients' personality are not in equal positions, each deserves and should receive the proper recognition, acknowledgment, appreciation as well as a say. This is the lived principle of egalitarianism: Each individual – and for that matter, each dissociative 'dividual' – is fundamentally equal. This implies, among other things, that each has a vote when it comes to issues of common interest. Each has one vote, not some two votes, and others none. To use George Orwell, some pigs are not more equal than others.

Some clinicians may find this therapeutic democracy hard to live by. They may have been raised with models that hold them highly, if not unduly, responsible for the therapeutic project. For example, they may have been taught that clinicians actually better know what serves patients than patients themselves, or that therapy best involves the rigid administration of 'evidence-based' protocols. Clinicians may also be under the influence of personal limitations. They may struggle with an intolerance of uncertainty, an undue need to *know* a lot about the patient before being able to act therapeutically, a fear of strong affects, or an uncalled-for urge to stay in charge of the therapeutic venture.

Clinicians obviously do have their responsibilities, but responsibilities and decision power should not be confused with one another. Clinicians may know some things better than some patients do, but patients know many things better than their clinicians do. Protocols can be helpful, but one size does not fit all, and the rigid administration of protocols may not meet or honor a patient's needs, creativity, and more general power of action. Further, like everyone else, clinicians have their personal limitations. Nobody's perfect, and patients do not expect clinicians to be exceptions to the rule. Clinicians should know their limitations and be very honest about them while interacting with their patients. In sum, enactive trauma assessment and therapy crucially include clinical and more general egalitarianism.

Standard Assessment

When patients are ready to discuss their problems, clinicians may begin by posing diagnostic questions. Inasmuch as clinicians do not already know the nature of a patient's disorder beforehand, they may first want to scan a variety of symptoms such as symptoms of major depression, anxiety disorders, psychosis, and eating disorders. This examination should include some questions addressing dissociative symptoms.

When the patient's reactions suggest they may have dissociative symptoms, a useful and efficient next step is to administer self-report questionnaires that evaluate the presence and severity of dissociative symptoms. The Dissociative Experiences Scale (DES; Bernstein & Putnam, 1986) addresses cognitive-emotional dissociative symptoms, but also includes items addressing alterations of consciousness that need not be dissociative (see ToT Volume II). An instrument that assesses sensorimotor dissociative symptoms is the Somatoform Dissociation Questionnaire (SDQ-20; Nijenhuis et al., 1996; see Appendix 3). The Multidimensional Inventory of Dissociation (MID; Dell, 2006) addresses cognitive-emotional as well as sensorimotor dissociative symptoms. Dell (2006) found that the

MID's factor scales constitute one factor (see also Somer & Dell, 2005). Patients with scores for one or more of these instruments exceeding the cutoff value in the screening for dissociative disorders can be invited to give a few recent examples of some of the items they endorsed.

The commonly recommended cutoff for the DES is ≥ 30; the cutoff for the SDQ-20 is ≥ 29; the cutoff for the SDQ-5 is ≥ 8 (see Appendix 4). Scores at or beyond these values indicate that the patient may have a dissociative disorder. According to our research, approximately two-thirds of patients with a score at or beyond the SDQ-5 cutoff can be expected to have a dissociative disorder. The likelihood of a dissociative disorder increases with the score. Extreme scores may, but need not, indicate that the patient is a false positive case of dissociative disorder. Mean SDQ-20 scores for various diagnostic groups can be found in ToT Volume I, Chapter 6, pp. 134–135.

The administration of a diagnostic instrument should be considered when the descriptions patients provide continue to suggest the existence of a dissociative disorder. These instruments include the Structured Interview for DSM-IV Dissociative Disorders, SCID-D (Steinberg, 2000) or the Dissociative Disorders Interview Schedule, DDIS (Ross et al., 1990). Suzette Boon and Marjolein Runhaar (see http://www.suzetteboon.com/en/downloads-en/) are currently working on a new diagnostic interview to assess chronic trauma-related disorders, in particular dissociative disorders. Validation studies of this Trauma and Dissociation Symptoms Interview (TADS-I) are in progress.

Clinicians should be aware that these interviews can be demanding on the patient and consider whether the administration is clinically timely and wise. They should also deliberate whether all items of these tools are best employed in one lengthy session, or whether they are perhaps better distributed over a series of sessions. In my experience, a phasic approach is generally preferable, particularly in complex cases. When the patient encompasses these dissociative parts, structured interviews addressing dissociative symptoms may stir up one or more EPs as well as ANPs other than the ANP generally taking the questions. The latter ANPs may have a hard time handling the reactions of these other dissociative parts during and after the interview.

Assessment also includes asking patients about their significant life events, including adverse ones. Initial explorative and nonintrusive questions can be followed up by the administration of self-report instruments. One option is to use the Traumatic Experiences Checklist (TEC; Nijenhuis, Van der Hart, & Kruger, 2002; Schumacher et al., 2011; see Appendix 5). Because the items of this instrument address adverse or potentially traumatizing events in a general fashion, most patients do not experience the items as intrusive. They pertain to a rather broad variety of such life events, so using the TEC communicates the clinician's interest in each of them. If it seems clinically important and wise, clinicians can then ask the patient to say a bit more about (some of) their adverse life events. They can leave it up to the patient to decide which items they want to address in this phase of the treatment and which they may prefer discussing later. And, as always, clinicians should not probe into matters that patients are not able and ready to handle.

Stop Signals

The clinical questions and items on self-report questionnaires or diagnostic instruments which address dissociative phenomena can affect patients in a variety of ways.

If the phenomena the items describe are irrelevant to their condition, they typically and adequately phenomenally feel (in the first-person perspective) and phenomenally as well as physically or technically judge (in the quasi-second-person perspective and third-person perspective, respectively) that the described phenomena do not pertain to them. They are neither attracted to these questions nor repelled by them. For these reasons, they commonly engage in the action of insignificance.

Inasmuch as patients display an interest in having a dissociative disorder they actually do not have, they are engaging in the action of significance when clinicians examine dissociative symptoms and disorders. These patients are attracted to these questions, they value the clinician's effort to raise the issues, and they affirm their having the symptoms. However, such affirmative reactions are grounded in their physical or technical third-person judgment and are not based on their phenomenal first-person judgment. Because these individuals do not consist of dissociative parts, they do not actually experience dissociative symptoms. They are therefore not in a position to phenomenally judge that the items of questionnaires and interviews describe their authentic experiences. Their judgment is based rather on a technical judgment like "I believe I include dissociative parts."

False-positive cases of dissociative disorders do not include operationally autonomous conscious systems apart from themselves that affect them in one way or another, and this shows! For example, reading or hearing descriptions of dissociative symptoms and talking about them tends not to affect their body much. Their face, eyes, hands, and posture remain relatively calm, and the descriptions do not scare them. They do not include ANPs that are scared of EPs, no fragile EPs and controlling EPs that intrude on ANPs and on each other – and no controlling EPs that interfere with responses to the questions.

To the degree that 'false positives' show affective reactions, it is the affective interest of these individuals (i.e., of false positives) in having the symptom that guides their emotionality. This attraction may reveal itself in an investigate attitude, an eagerness to persuade clinicians that a particular symptom applies to them, an open face, a search for eye contact, forward body movements, or other explorative and social actions. When clinicians judge that they do not have a particular dissociative symptom or disorder, these patients tend to be disappointed or confused, and some may even get angry.

If the items of self-report questionnaires and structured or semistructured interviews address phenomena that do apply to patients, the items will significantly affect them. For this reason, patients tend to feel and judge that the items are useful and hence good. For example, patients with dissociative disorders tend to be glad that clinicians show an interest in their dissociative symptoms. Many have previously experienced clinicians who do not have this interest, do not know the symptoms, or do not even believe they are 'real.'

They may also have met up with clinicians who misinterpreted dissociative symptoms, for example, who took them for psychotic symptoms.

These patients may at the same time fear a deep examination of dissociative symptoms and disorders. Many ANPs are repelled by it because it can highlight and often trigger the phenomena under consideration – the very phenomena they fear and detest. For example, ANPs may be ashamed of dissociative amnesia, hearing voices, and being intruded on by forces beyond their control. They may also fear that the questions will trigger inner turmoil or inner reactions they fear and cannot fully control. This fear may become reinforced when during or after the interview voices start shouting when sensations and emotions intrude on them and traumatic memories get reactivated. ANPs may become confused or intimidated when they hear scared a fragile EP or receive ardent instructions of controlling EPs to "Shut up," "Go home," or "Keep your mouth shut."

Patients with dissociative disorders may also become apprehensive about how these professionals will interpret their responses to the questions and what decisions they will take based on the revelations. For example, they may wonder "Will he think I'm mad?" – "Will he prescribe antipsychotics?" – "Will he admit me to a mental hospital?" – "Will he believe me at all?" – "Will he think I am making things up?"

For these reasons, patients with dissociative disorders tend to experience and regard assessment (and treatment) as a mixed blessing. This makes it important to provide patients with a means of controlling the diagnostic situation. Clinicians should allow them to stop the interview if it becomes too dangerous or otherwise intolerable to them. Moreover, prior to asking any questions, they should invite patients to show how they can express their need for a pause or a longer interruption. They should further invite them to *practice* such signaling. The point of this rehearsal is that patients may have difficulty using a word like "stop," seeing that many perpetrators forbid their victims to set limits and even punish them when they nonetheless attempt to set boundaries – or they simply ignore their victims' wishes altogether. If saying "stop" is problematic, patients may be invited to choose a different word. And if uttering a verbal stop-signal still proves too difficult for them, showing a nonverbal stop-signal may be less threatening to them. An additional advantage of using nonverbal stop-signals is that dissociative parts that are subdominant but activated during the interview can also use them and thereby experience from the start that clinicians are interested in them as well. Nevertheless, clinicians do not want to suggest the presence of dissociative parts; the thoughtful wording of the invitation to use nonverbal stop-signals is required.

By practicing limit-setting in the clinical situation, patients start to experience that clinicians value and react favorably to their expressed wishes. The case example below details how this exercise can proceed, and how the patient actually used her verbal and nonverbal stop-signals during the SCID-D interview. The session also illustrates that assessment and therapy are to some degree intertwined. It more generally offers exemplifies an enactive diagnostic and therapeutic style.

Ineke

Diagnosed with complex PTSD and eating disorder, Ineke (43 years at the time of the assessment) had been receiving treatment for 5 years. Her treatment included daycare programs. She and the therapeutic team had given it their best, but no progress had materialized.

Ineke reported severe childhood emotional neglect, emotional abuse, and physical abuse by both her mother and father as well as several instances of sexual abuse by a physiotherapist during her adolescent years. Sometimes she seemed to vaguely suggest that her father had sexually abused her. However, each time she quickly withdrew her faint indications. At times Ineke even denied that she had touched on the subject of incest. The topic remained beyond discussion.

Ineke appeared to be very good at assisting other patients with eating disorders. While the women she helped improved, her own atypical bulimia (alternating episodes of fasting and bingeing with purging) grew worse. As an adolescent and young adult, she had struggled immensely with anorexia and was admitted to a psychiatric unit of a general hospital where she was isolated for 3 months. Ineke felt totally rejected and misunderstood by the staff. She eventually weighed only 26 kg. At some point, in fact, she was clinically dead.

With increasing recognition of dissociative symptoms, some team members had recently started to suspect that Ineke might have more dissociative symptoms than had been previously presumed. This inkling inspired them to request a thorough examination of the issue. Ineke consented to a referral to me and fully cooperated. She impressed me as a sympathetic and dedicated woman. She showed a rather happy face and displayed a good sense of humor. Now and then she even laughed happily. At times, however, her eyes turned sad and her body grew tense.

I first invited Ineke to pose any question she might have. She used the occasion to ask what the examination would entail, whether I thought she was responsible for the lack of treatment results, and whether there was any hope for improvement. I told that, in my view, a lack of treatment results can be due to many causes, including an incorrect or incomplete assessment or understanding of an individual's problems. I added that my experience with other patients had convinced me that years of unsuccessful treatment do not necessarily prove no treatment can be effective. Following a discussion of these themes, Ineke was ready to complete the DES, SDQ-20, and TEC. Her scores for the DES and SDQ-20 were in the range of individuals with CDID.

The First Session

Items addressing cognitive-emotional dissociative symptoms tend to distress patients with dissociative disorders more than a discussion of sensorimotor dissociative symptoms. They further generally find that items addressing positive dissociative symptoms may elicit more turmoil than an investigation of negative dissociative symptoms. For these two reasons, it is often wise to examine negative sensorimotor dissociative symptoms first. Depending on the patient's reactions, the assessment can then proceed with a discussion of negative cognitive-emotional dissociative symptoms or with a sensitive exploration of positive sensorimotor dissociative symptoms, provided it does not delve too deep. Positive cognitive-emotional dissociative symptoms are generally best held back until the patient has developed a working relationship with the clinician.

However, some dissociative parts may not want to wait that long. 'Smelling' that the clinician knows about dissociative problems, experiencing his or her interest in them, and stimulated by the items of the interview, they may start exerting their influences. For example, they may start to intrude on the ANP in executive control. The transcript of the second session testifies to this.

During the first session, Ineke described a wide range of negative and some positive dissociative symptoms. She reported various physical anesthesias. For example, she was hardly in touch with her lower body parts, particularly but not exclusively when she went to bed. She did not feel any pain when she cut herself at times. Ineke also experienced recurrent physical paralyses that were sometimes accompanied by fainting spells. Her positive sensorimotor dissociative included feeling touched even when no one else was present or near, and feeling physically influenced by inner forces. She also stated that her body sometimes moved in an apparently goal-directed manner beyond her control.

Addressing the topic of dissociative amnesia, Ineke shamefully confided that she recurrently lost touch with time. These episodes were generally relatively brief, but at times they lasted for several hours. When I, consistent with the SCID-D instructions, kindly asked her whether she was perhaps willing and able to provide an example, she shared the following: Not too long ago, she awoke in her car, whereas she thought that she had gone to sleep in her bed. Totally confused, she noticed that it was dark around her. The car was parked in the middle of nowhere. Once she was ready, she started driving to determine where she was. It appeared she was at about 25 km from home. Upon approaching her house, she had no clue as to why she was unable to park her car in front of it. Her arms and feet would simply not follow her intentions. The best she could do was to park her vehicle at a distance of some 400 m. But then she could not get out of her car. She could not even take her hands from the steering wheel.

At some point, her partner woke up to detect that Ineke had left the bed and the house. Her partner found a note written in adolescent-type handwriting that she did not want to live in the house anymore and said goodbye. When he then determined that Ineke's car was gone, he called the police. The policemen on duty found Ineke after several hours of searching. They invited Ineke to get out of her car, but it she could not. They would have had to break her fingers. Ineke was still in a panic when her physician arrived. She gave her a muscle-relaxation injection. When she and the policemen took Ineke home, she continued to scream that she did not want to enter the house ever again. Nobody had a clue as to what had caused her condition. Ineke herself told me she had not been screaming herself: She felt controlled by unknown forces.

But there was a perfect explanation. When Ineke's power of action as ANP had sufficiently increased, she became ready to increase her level and field of consciousness (see Chapter 22). At some point, she was willing and courageous enough to feel and know more. Provided the conditions, the timing, and the wider context are right, it makes considerable sense for hitherto ignorant dissociative parts and clinicians to inquire: "*Who* does *what* and *why?*" (This *www* action is further discussed in Chapter 35.) Given the dissociation of personality, intrusions always represent the actions or passions of some dissociative part or parts (Chapter 25). Given conatus (Chapters 24, 25, and 27), the involved actions or passions are always affect-laden and goal-oriented. And given dissociative part-dependent signification (Chapters 25 and 27), dissociative parts have their own ideas as to *who* they are, *what* the world is like and *how* they and this world are related.

At the proper point in therapy, Ineke and I thus were ready to detect that the amnestic episode involved an adolescent EP. This younger part believed Ineke was living with her family of origin. Unable and unwilling to endure any further horrors, she wrote the note that she had to leave the *parental home for good.* When Ineke regained consciousness as the prime ANP and drove home, the suicidal teenager made every effort to prevent further traumatization. At the time of the SCID-D interview, the leading ANP did not know the suicidal one, let alone her affectivity and goals. At this time, she was still in the dark about what exactly had happened and why.

The Second Session

At the beginning of the second SCID-D session, Ineke spontaneously reported that she had been struggling with her eating disorder more in the past week. We continued as follows:

*Table 32.1.*The second session with Ineke

Verbatim transcript with brief descriptions of nonverbal features in parentheses.	Nonexhaustive comments in terms of my various person perspectives. FPP: Occasional indications of my phenomenal experiences, that is, my first-person perspective. QSPP: Occasional indications of my phenomenal judgment of my phenomenal experiences, that is, my quasi-second-person perspective SPP: Indications of Ineke's and my phenomenal judgments as based on our phenomenal relational experiences, that is, our second-person perspectives TPP: My third-person perspective, that is, my technical ideas and judgments regarding Ineke's actions and passions.	Ineke's nonexhaustive comments while watching the video recording of the session in January 2016. The original session took place in December 2006. I invited Ineke to stop the tape when she wanted to comment or when watching the recording was too hard for her.

I: Since our previous session, I had new episodes of binging, and had to throw up more . . . er . . . purely to gain control in one way or another.	TPP: There must be a reason or final cause why Ineke needed more "control." Gaining control through bingeing and throwing up seem to be passionate substitute actions involving particular modes of longing and striving. These passions substitute for other, more efficient ways of affective control that she is unable to achieve so far. It is not clear *what* she needs to control.	
E: To gain *control.*	SPP: My attunement to Ineke's apparent final cause: "gaining control." Emphasis on control.	
I: Yes.	SPP: Consensus accomplished.	
E: Were your previous problems with eating also an effort to gain control over things that are not easy to manage?	TPP: Testing the hypothesis that Ineke's past and present eating problems are related. Repetition of the core phrase: "gain control."	
I: Yes . . ., yes, they were.	SPP: Consensus, based on Ineke's reflection. TPP: some confirmation that the hypothesis may be correct.	
E: An attempt to control things that you could not control in a different way?	TPP hypothesis: Could the control through eating be a substitute action?	
I: Yes.	SPP: Consensus.	
E: Yes.	SPP: Confirmation of the consensus.	
E: And if I had to guess, I would say that you experience the emotional things inside as a threat.	SPP: Attunement to and utilization of a statement Ineke had made in the first session.	I: (grimaces)
I: Yes, yes.	SPP: Consensus. TPP: Keep in mind that it is unclear so far what constitute "the emotional things inside."	I: Yes. (grimaces) I felt so caught. I clearly remember that feeling. (Uses her hands to express how she felt caught in a harness.) E: You remember the feeling? I: Sure.
E: I propose that we continue with the items of the interview (i.e., the SCID-D).	TPP: Continuation of the pursuit of a common goal: diagnostic clarity. SPP: "I propose" is an invitation, not a command.	
I: OK.	SPP: Acceptance, consensus.	
E: Before starting I'd like to remind you that you have a way to stop. You can say "stop" or signal "stop" with the movements of your hands and arms that you chose during our previous session. Do you recall them?	TPP: I remind Ineke that she has a means of controlling the situation, verbally and nonverbally. SPP: Meaning: We are partners in a joint venture, the clinician is not the boss.	
I: (nods)	SPP: Consensus.	

E: Fine, I will always respect your stop signals.	SPP: Reassurance that her wishes are important. I try to distinguish myself from perpetrators who typically do no ask for and respect stop signals of the ones they maltreat.	
I: Yes.	SPP: Consensus.	
E: We have been talking about bodily phenomena and about your memory.	TPP: Orienting Ineke to a common goal, linking the previous and the present session.	
I: Hmm.	SPP: Confirmation.	
E: I would now like to talk about the way you experience yourself. My first question is whether you sometimes feel unreal about yourself, whether you sometimes wonder if you really exist? Do you have these kinds of experiences?	TPP: Goal-orientation. Introduction of the theme of depersonalization.	
I: I believe anyone fulfills roles in life, but it is as if I only play roles. It is as if I am only in touch with myself when I am completely empty after vomiting or self-mutilation. Only then I experience who I really am.	TPP: If Ineke does not engage in other substitute actions, she feels depersonalized, which may well be the result of another substitute action. This passion is the mental avoidance of or escape from experienced and known threat or threat signals. Ignore to remain ignorant. Why can she only be in touch with herself when she has emptied or mutilated herself? FPP, QSPP, SPP: What would it be like to live like this? How does it feel? How would I feel, and judge myself if I would recurrently overeat, vomit, and mutilate myself?	I: (nods several times, looks sad) I: (nods again)
E: Do you start to get more in touch with yourself *as* you vomit or mutilate yourself, or does this feeling evolve *after* you have vomited or mutilated yourself?	TPP: Let's explore the issue a bit more. SPP: Utilization of Ineke's expression "in touch with myself."	
I: As I'm doing it. But once I've done it, I feel guilty.	TPP: Why would the effect already materialize when the substitute action is still going on? The execution of the substitute actions entails a conflict. The substitute actions are useful to her as well as harmful. The usefulness seems to win at times, but the harmfulness may prevent Ineke from engaging in the substitutes even more. FPP, QSPP, SPP: What would it be like to be in such conflicts?	I: (grimaces in confirmation, a faint smile)

E: And as you're doing it, what do you experience?	TPP and SPP: Based on all foregoing considerations, explore Ineke's experiential world a bit more. Stay with Ineke.	
I: Relief.		I: (nods)
E: Relief. Does it perhaps become calmer inside?	TPP: "Relief" may be a final cause of her substitute actions. What kind of relief, relief *from what*? Gentle suggestion that relief may involve a relief from emotional tension "inside." The gentleness is in the word "perhaps." SPP: Attunement and consensus through repetition of Ineke's term "relief." Communication that I understand that she wishes to achieve relief.	
I: Absolutely. Relief from tension.	TPP: My hypothesis seems to be on target. SPP: Ineke seems to feel understood.	
E: Before you start, is there a disturbing tension inside?	TPP: Since "tension" is a very general term, and since her measures to deal with it are passionate, using the term "disturbing" may communicate understanding. It may also invite her to elaborate on the nature of the tension. SPP: Feeling into Ineke's inner world of tension. FPP and QSPP: What would it be like to experience so much "tension" that Ineke has to engage in her substitute actions?	E: Was it helpful to you when I adopt your expressions, and sometimes use some more words as I try to grasp your feelings and thoughts? I: Oh, yes. I felt understood for the first time. What I expressed was so very much my process, and you tracked it. Sometimes I had used a half word but you got it. And you *posed questions*, you inquired whether your understanding was on target. This made me feel: "You get it, you really get it." You don't sound like someone who knows it better. *You check your understanding*. That is ever so helpful. It invites me to continue responding to your questions, and to open up more. Had you simply drawn your conclusions, then, already at this point, I would have started to withdraw myself. (giggles) Yes. E: In my view, clinicians better follow this communicative path (see Chapter 22). Clinicians may have an opinion, but ask if it fits. I: Yes, check it. E: Only the one who is concerned can feel and decide whether the clinician's understanding fits. I: Yes, yes.
I: Yes.	TPP: Support for the hypothesis. Ineke may be ready to say more about her "tension" and her ways of coping with it.	

E: A tension you do not know how to resolve in a different way?	SPP: Consensus. TPP: Testing the hypothesis that Ineke's passions (vomiting, self-mutilation) are indeed substitute actions or passions.	
I: That's how it is.	TPP: Confirmation. SPP: Affirmation.	
E: And then you overeat or mutilate yourself, and as you're doing it you calm down. How long does this reduction of tension last?	SPP: Summary, statement of the final cause. TPP: Exploration of the effectiveness of the substitute actions.	
I: It depends on the situation. Sometimes I only need to cut myself for a brief time; sometimes it takes longer. It depends on what happened before, on the kind of trigger. It also depends on my guilt feelings. When these are strong, when I tell myself, "This is not the way, this is not right," the tension mounts again.	TPP: Having been in therapy for 5 years, Ineke is familiar with the term "trigger," which suggests that there are particular inner of outer signs that generate "tension" that Ineke reduces through overeating, vomiting, and self-mutilation. Ineke distinguishes different kinds of triggers. Her guilt feelings also constitute a trigger. But these are not the primary triggers, but rather secondary emotions. The rapidly ensuing relief of tension reinforces the substitute actions, but the problem is that they are effective only for a short while. Apart from the tension relief, the feeling of being in touch with herself also reinforces the substitute actions. But her phenomenal self is never 'right,' because substitute actions are 'wrong.' Being alone is useful because the guilt feelings – guilt is a social emotion – are less intense. Hypothesis: Ineke engages in her substitute actions more often and perhaps also for a longer time when she is alone.	
E: The guilt spoils the calmness. I: Right. And when I'm with my partner, the guilt feelings are stronger. Then I feel more responsible. When I'm alone and the guilt feelings are less intense, I stay calmer for a longer time.		[We skipped the next couple of minutes.]
E: And then you feel more that you are actually *alive*?	SPP: Focus on the final cause, on her wish. Communicate that I understand that she has an excellent reason to engage in the substitute actions.	

I: Yes. It is as if I'm only allowed to live when I have pain, *real* pain, as if I'm only allow to feel sad when I am completely empty. E: Does it perhaps feel like you have a reason to be sad when you endure real pain?	TPP: "Allowed to live," "allowed to feel sad," and "*real* pain" are remarkable expressions. Ineke communicates that she "feels sad," but that she is only "allowed to feel sad" when she is "empty." The meaning of being in "touch with herself" seems at least in part to be "being allowed" to "feel sad." Where do these expressions stem from? Who has allowed or still allows her? Where and from whom did Ineke pick up the expression "*real* pain?" The pain that self-mutilation may comprise does not seem to qualify as real pain? SPP: Utilize her terms: "real pain," "sad." Be gentle in the expression, hence "perhaps." Communicate the understanding that substitute actions are goal-oriented and grounded in "reasons." "Reasons" communicates that her passions are not nonsensical, not a sign of madness, but in their own way "reasonable." FPP: An empathic feeling of pain while hearing Ineke say that her pain would not be seen as real, and that she must torture herself to gain allowance to exist. What horror!	
I: Yes, it might be that mutilating myself makes my [emotional] pain more tangible.	TPP: Ineke seems to be exploring herself. She is referring now to a different kind of pain, to her emotional pain that somehow does not seem to be "real."	
E: Do you generally feel that you're allowed to be sad, to be angry?	FPP: I feel increasingly in touch with Ineke's conflicts. I feel a desire to tell her that, from my affective perspective, her emotions are allowed to exist, and that she is allowed to exist because she exists, because she is worthwhile and totally acceptable. I also feel in SPP that it is better to communicate my view implicitly. An explicit statement would not seem to be fitting at this point, as it would probably intensify her conflicts.	

I: Hm, yes, rationally I say, yes, emotionally it feels like a no. My reason says there are worse things, and bla, bla, bla.	TPP: Ineke rationally knows that she is entitled to have her emotions. But her "reason" also tells her that "there are worse things," and this idea and probably more ideas like this tell her "emotionally" that her emotions are not real enough, not serious, not important. FPP, QSPP, SPP: I expect that the trouble will become clearer in due course. It feels better not to push the issue. Withhold personal opinions.	
E: Do you ever feel you are functioning like an automaton, like a robot?		[We picked the session up from here]
I: Yes.		
E: Can you give an example please?		
I: It happens a lot when I am among people. For example, when I'm going to the supermarket, I'm experiencing many impulses and do not feel that I am really there. Once back at home, I may wonder who I met, who was sitting behind the counter, how I came home, what route I took.	TPP: What "impulses?" Why would she not be "present" in the situation as she is undergoing "impulses."	
In this sense I have lost my way.		I: (sighs)
E: That must be confusing.	SPP: Expression of empathy, communicating acceptance of emotional confusion.	
I: Sure.	SPP: Consensus.	
E: Do you ever experience that you look at yourself from a distance?		
I: No, I only experienced that when I was clinically dead.		I: (presses her lips) E: I have never asked you about this. When was this and what happened? I: I was 21 years old or so. I had been admitted for a long time to a psychiatric department of a general hospital because of my anorexia. The treatment included 3 months of full isolation: no visitors, no mail. The door of my room was locked. I had feeding tubes. These measures made me feel I was a terribly bad person. It gave me another reason to tamper with the feeding tube. I did not gain weight and did not want to eat anymore. Thus at some point my weight had dropped to 26 kg. E: Only 26 kg?

		I: Yes, and only 21 years old. My heart received too little potassium. Then I turned clinically dead. I saw myself lying in my bed though, from above. I heard a voice saying "Come . . . come." I have never heard a sweeter voice. That warm and inviting. I was able to see the most beautiful colors. And there was a tunnel. Normally, I detest tunnels, but this was a magnificent experience. I was drawn to that voice and the colors. And then, all of a sudden, bright lights, signal-horns and bells. I recall I was extremely cold. As it all happened, I watched myself from above, everyone working on me. And I thought, you go ahead, I'll stay here, it's wonderful up here. So I was not at all happy when I came back. E: Did you return against your will? I: Yes, yes. E: Any idea what made you return? I: It seems I shouted, "Not yet, not yet!" Nurses told me this. I used the experience several times when life was completely unbearable, when I had no way out anymore. That voice . . . I am not at all afraid of dying. I also felt this when, at some point in the treatment, I told you I wanted to die. This was when the therapy became exceptionally burdensome. I now realize that dying may be different. But it remains a consoling experience. E: It was a terrible time, and it also was sometimes of immense value. I: Yes, and I also floated above my body during the rape in Morocco [Ineke had reached adulthood by then]. They could do anything to me, I had left.
E: Not in daily life?		
I: No.	SPP: Consensus.	
E: You're, so to speak, always "in" your body.		
I: Yes.		
E: And do you experience your body as your own?		
I: No.		
E: How do you experience your body?		

I: No . . .. That body feels big, huge, a thing I don't have a grip on . . . Sometimes it screams horribly inside me. And suddenly it is completely silent, which is also scary . . .	TPP: "That body" suggests that Ineke does not sufficiently personify her body. Why would it feel "big, huge?" She knows it is not big or huge. She does not have a "grip on that body." Could it be that these feelings and this lack of control constitute triggers that cause her to engage in her substitute actions? And then a new, scary element that describes what is happening "inside." "It screams." "It is suddenly completely silent." What is "it?" Why does "it" scream gigantically? FPP, QSPP: what would it be like to have these experiences? How would I phenomenally experience and judge myself if this screaming and all would be happening to me?	I: Hmm. Gulp. I: [grimaces]
E: Could you perhaps tell me what happens when it screams horribly inside you?	SPP: Gentle invitation to detail the issue. "Could you perhaps tell me?" is a question that Ineke can respond to by saying "No" or "Yes," and saying "Yes" does not imply that she *must* actually tell me or tell me *straightaway*. I copy her expression: "It screams gigantically inside" to attune to her phenomenal experience and understanding.	I: [grimaces again]

	TPP: It seems that a "screaming baby" is intruding on Ineke. She cannot control this baby. Could this screaming baby be a trigger to engage in her substitute actions? Why does this baby exist inside and why does the baby scream without end? FPP, QSPP: What would it be like to have a screaming baby inside me? What would I do? What would I think why it would be there and why it would be screaming? I guess it would also "drive me nuts." TPP: Mind that it is wrong to speak bad of "the baby." If the baby were a dissociative part related to the severe emotional neglect and physical abuse that Ineke experienced from her early childhood onward, than speaking bad of the baby might negatively affect the baby, and it might stimulate Ineke's depreciation of the baby. If so, I would side with Ineke (as an ANP) and turn myself against the baby as a fragile EP. This would be a grave therapeutic error. I would become a part of a potentially existing dissociative system, and thereby disappear in Ineke's "Flatland." I must stay at the top of the pyramid.	E: Could I ask you a kind of technical question? Did you notice I often repeat or use your words, your ways of saying things? What it was like for you? I: Wonderful. Really wonderful. What happened here was exceptionally emotional. I notice how very stressed I was, my face, and body like that. It was a huge step to start putting my experiences and secrets in words. And when you feed my words back to me, then they become . . . yeah . . . err . . . *my* experiences. They are my words, they fit how I have experienced things, and you use my words. And that helps me to return to my feelings and thoughts. I have carefully chosen my words. I have chosen them for a reason. I did not say "yelling". Had you said "yelling" instead of my word "screaming," then something gets blocked. When that happens, I lose my cooperation with you (cf. Chapter 22). Had you said "yelling," I would have thought, "OK, go ahead on your own track" but things between us would have become blocked. E: Had I used a different word, you would have had to backtranslate it in your own understanding? I: Yes, sure, and it took me so many years to express my experiences in the best possible words, to express my feelings in those particular words. So, what you're doing is so helpful, so comforting. E: I frequently notice that my colleagues and I myself when I'm not at it, reformulate what a patient says. Some colleagues who start using the patient's words more, say they feel like a parrot. I: It's not parroting at all. No it isn't. It's fine.
I: It is sooo exceptionally sensitive. It is a baby that doesn't stop screaming. It goes on and on and on. It drives me nuts.		I: Oohh, yes . . . (bites her lip)

E: As if there is a very young child screaming inside?	TPP: Avoid being unduly suggestive by phrasing "as if." "The truth" must come from Ineke, not from my ideas. SPP: Show an interest in the phenomenon, attune.	
I: Yes. And one that won't stop. For example, when I want to go to sleep at night – it can also happen during daytime – then I want to shake myself to get rid of it . . .	SPP: Consensus. TPP: Ineke wants to get rid of the screaming baby, but "shaking herself" does not seem to be effective.	
E: You hear it as a voice . . .?	SPP: Continued exploration. TPP: The phenomenal concept of a "screaming baby" implies the concept of "a voice." I say nothing new.	
I: (nods vigorously)	SPP: Consensus.	
E: It sounds like a very young child . . .?	SPP and TPP: ditto.	
I: (nods again)	SPP: More consensus.	
E: What age could it have?	TPP: Nonleading exploration.	
I: It's a real baby.	SPP: I communicate that the baby is not a figment of her imagination but phenomenally real. FPP, QSPP: What would it be like to have a phenomenally real screaming and uncontrollable baby inside?	E: Should I have said "baby" instead of "very young child"? I: No, it was OK. I was enraged with "that child." So your word "child" fit my rage at "that child."
E: A baby. And do you have any idea why it is screaming so loud?	TPP: Confirmation. SPP: Affirmation. TPP and SPP: Babies scream for a reason. The baby is guided by a need.	
I: (sighs, shakes her head). No. Well, yes, I could imagine why, but I don't know. (shrugs her shoulders)	SPP: Ineke tells me she "could imagine" a reason, but that she actually does not know the baby.	
E: Does it ever talk to you?	TPP: Does the baby sometimes manifest as a slightly older individual? Would the baby understand words?	
I: (shakes her head)		
E: Only screaming . . .		
I: (nods)	SPP: Consensus.	

E: Do you ever try to calm this baby-like voice inside? Or does it perhaps scare you and you prefer to stay away from it?	TPP: Avoidance of eagerness to interpret the baby as a dissociative part, without excluding this possibility. Hence, in SPP at this point: "baby-like voice" rather than "this baby." Exploration of Ineke's power of action regarding the "baby-like voice," of their phenomenal relationship. So far, it seems that, for Ineke, the baby is a scary, most annoying thing. That is, she physically experiences and judges the baby, which reflects a third-person relationship. Exploration and utilization of "scary." Exploration of Ineke's final cause by tapping into her desire to "shake the baby off."	I: I had never contemplated that possibility. I went "How can I react to this remark? What do you mean? Can I talk to it?"
I: (Stares, becomes immobile, then sighs, moves her hands to her face, drops them, sighs again, stares again, shakes her head.) I find it difficult.	TPP: Ineke becomes very emotional. Would this be an instance of her inner "tension?" Might it be that the baby is screaming, right here and now? FPP, QSPP: Empathic feelings. No fear in me to examine the issue, and no fear to empathically stay with Ineke, but a feeling that we can only proceed with much care, since:	
E: Is my question difficult?	SPP: Ineke is in emotional trouble; check if she is still in touch with me and if she is still able to speak to me.	I: Yes. E: What was difficult here is that I proposed a new way of relating that you could not relate to so well. I: Yes. Would one be able to calm that child? Is that possible at all? It only screams! It's something I cannot do. It all happens beyond my control. I cannot influence it. You talked about something that is completely strange to me. What would you want me to do? That can't be. Completely new. Don't come up with a very scary thing like this. I notice how I shook my head at this point. Would you want me to do this, *that fast*? (laughs) E: Gulp! I: Yeah . . . (laughs some more) E: Let's watch where it leads.
I: Yes. (continues to stare) E: Could you perhaps tell me why it is difficult?	SPP: Confirmation that my question is somehow "difficult," and signals that there is something inside that draws a whole lot of attention. SPP: Gentle invitation to stay in contact with me as well.	

I: (stares more, swallows, hands clasped) Yes . . . I . . . (brings her hands to her face again, put them first in front of her mouth and nose, and then moves them to her temples, bending her head down). Hmmm (sighs deeply). Please stop for a while. (moves her tense, stretched hands to and fro) [Ineke's nonverbal stop signal] (Stretches her arms at full lengths, hands up, takes a deep breath, moves her hands to the armrests, moves them back and forth, pushes her hands down, puts both feet on the floor [until this point her lower body had been rigid with her legs crossed, one foot in the air], bends her upper body forward, crosses her hands between her legs, holds them tightly to her trousers, eyes directed to the floor.)	TPP: Significant loss of language, which, along with all nonverbal signs, suggests at least substantial stress. Lowering of mental efficiency. In terms of the hierarchy of action tendencies, engagement in a lower-level action tendency.	
E: Fine, no more questions. You might want to tell yourself that you did well to say stop, to tell me to stop asking questions for a while. And if there is anything you need from me, you can tell me.	FPP, QSPP: sympathy, curiosity, caring. SPP: Full and instant acceptance and reinforcement of Ineke's stop signal.	
I: (rigid posture, shoulders up, breathes from her upper chest)	FPP, QSPP: Glad to have invited her to generate not just a verbal, but also a nonverbal stop signal at the beginning of the SCID-D sessions. SPP: Keep yourself empathically available. TPP: Do not 'save' Ineke. It is important to explore her power to deal with the situation, and to examine what is happening. But that examination cannot be done so far, because of Ineke's stop signal.	
E: Perhaps you may want to breathe a bit more from your stomach.	TPP: Assist her in regulating her emotional reaction. Focus on her difficult, tense breathing. Use her wish to control herself more, without engaging in purging and self-mutilation. Teach her to exhale more. SPP: voice some ideas, but gently, don't be dominant, yet be present.	I: Stomach, *stomach*? What are you talking about! (laughs) Now it's getting very scary. E: The word "stomach" is difficult to handle? I: Yes.

I: (Rubs her feet on the floor, inhales deeply, tense face, inhales again, massages her neck with her right hand, moves her body back and forth in an apparent effort to find a grip, moves her right hand up and down the left lower arm.)		I: The word is hard for an individual with an eating disorder. Dirty, filthy. E: I had not considered that the word "stomach" carried this association, that it might have this load for you. I: I can clearly see how I was caught in my eating disorder in this phase of my life. I notice I had a (fat) stomach; I haven't had that for several years anymore [Ineke's physical appearance and weight are perfectly normal now].
E: Can you get in touch with the chair? Can you feel the floor under your feet?	TPP and SPP: Utilization of her movements.	
I: Yes. (Pulls on the right sleeve with her left hand, bring her hands together again between her legs, shakes her head, then takes the glass in front of her and drinks some water, rubs her face with her right hand.)	TPP and SPP: Some contact. Confirmation.	
E: It seems to me that a lot of your attention is directed toward the inside. You might also want to take a good look around you.	SPP: Careful, egalitarian formulations "it seems that" and "you might." TPP: Invite Ineke to attend to her outer world as well. TPP and SPP: Do not take away her inner attention. The baby might be appalled if I ignored her interests.	
I: Hmm (looks out of the window to her left, moves her body again, touches her chest with her left hand) I'm back again.	TPP: Reorientation. SPP: Reenters contact with me.	I: (laughs)

E: Fine … Could it be important that you tell me about what happened, or would you rather leave the issue alone for a while?	TPP and SPP: It is important to give Ineke a choice. "Leave the issue alone for a while" communicates that the issue will not be "left alone" *forever*. Sensitive formulation: "Could it be important …" "Happened" expresses the past tense.	E: You may want to notice that I offer a choice. I: Yes, very good. Yes, absolutely. You allowed me to look through the window. I have my seat there. And if you hadn't asked, I would decide to look through the window myself. My refuge. The tree. The sky. At these instances I was unable to stay in touch with you. That was too difficult. It was so important that your room had this window, and that there was nature within reach. E: You may hear that I sometimes use phrases like "could it be important to tell me a little bit about …" Prudent phrases including a lot of restrictions. What was it like for you that I use these kinds of formulations, particularly when it comes to taking decisions and making choices? I: Very important. I was not even aware I had choices. And even when you prudently offered choices, I wondered whether I had choices at all. I can see my confusion in the session: "Do I have a choice?" E: I feel it's important for you to learn that you have a choice and that you have choices in your relationship with me. Clinicians may advertently or inadvertently be domineering. I: Yes, I have experienced that many times. E: They may thereby engage in a relationship that has some features of a perpetrator-victim relationship. I: Yes. That's right. Yes, absolutely. E: I describe that, in totalitarian relationships, the dictator as well as the slave have a restricted level and rather small field of consciousness. I: Yes, very narrow. E: Yes. And if one cooperates and offers choices and assigns responsibilities, the involved individuals must raise their level and broaden their field of consciousness. I: Yes, yes. It took a long time in my relationship with you. In my understanding of the time, your slightest leg movement signified that you were a perpetrator too (cf. Chapter 25).

I: (Rubs her face and shakes her head once more.) So much was happening then. It completely floods me. I only feel panic. (Holds her breath)	TPP: Confirmation of the hypothesis that there was inner emotional turmoil that Ineke was hardly able to handle.	
E: Exhale.	SPP: Repetition of a previous suggestion ("breathe more from your stomach"), but now formulated more firmly, because technically judging in the TPP it can be said that she now knows how to act.	
I: (exhales) Not safe.		
E: Not safe. Scary feelings inside? A lot is happening inside?	SPP: Attunement, also by using Ineke's terms "not safe," "scary," and "happening inside" again. TPP: Using different terms is not only completely unnecessary, it would also communicate that my words are *superior* to hers. As if I knew it better. Nonsense!	
I: Yes.	SPP: Consensual confirmation.	
E: Did the screaming start perhaps?	TPP: It seems to be timely to sensitively explore the hypothesis that the inner turmoil concerned or at least included an inner voice screaming.	
I: Yes!	SPP: Ineke confirms.	
E: Screaming.	SPP: I confirm her confirmation.	
I: Yes, and "Stop."	TPP: A new element: "Stop." But the baby did not speak. Who said, "Stop?" Recall that Ineke was so far unable to say the word "Stop."	
E: Stop?	SPP: Ask Ineke.	
I: Yes, stop.	TPP: Again, who says this? SPP: Attunement.	
E: A voice saying stop, you mean?	SPP: Confirmation.	
I: Yes, a voice yelling, "Stop" and "Quit it."		
E: A voice yelling, "Stop" and "Quit it."		
I: Yes.		
E: And is it clear to you what should stop?	TPP: Exploration.	
I: No (shakes her head). E: No hunch about what it might be. I: (shakes her head)	TPP: Ineke does not seem to be in good touch with the "Stop" and "Quit it."	

E: Let me put it this way: Is there something inside that is very young and that screams and something else that is older and that says "Stop" and "Quit it?"	TPP and SPP: Gentle invitation to explore potential differences between the two voices that Ineke heard. I feel entitled to say that the second voice is older because this voice utters words. FPP, QSPP: How hard it must be to hear two loud voices at a time.	
I: (stares ahead, seems absorbed in her inner world, wakes up, bend forwards to me and asks) What did you say?	TPP: It might be that the voices are active, and that this is why Ineke did not hear my question.	[See Ineke's comment below]
E: Could it be that there is something inside that feels very young and that only screams, and that there is also something inside that speaks and yells "Stop" and "Quit it?"	SPP: Repetition of the hypothesis.	
I: Yes, that's what I think (nods affirmatively).	SPP: Support for the hypothesis. TPP: The voices are screaming and yelling. Ineke wants to get rid of them and does not know, let alone understand, the voices. She does not seem to have a clue what are their reasons of existence, their needs and desires, and their histories. Asking about dissociative phenomena triggers them in part. I should not leave these voices alone, but would better serve as a model for careful and stepwise approach, if only because the SCID-D interview should not be a torture for the whole Ineke. It should be a positive experience. Let's strive to increase Ineke's power of action regarding her baby and the older voice. This work may also help me to make a differential diagnosis with respect to psychosis and, more specifically, schizophrenia in that it is commonly far easier to communicate with dissociative parts than with 'voices' in psychosis or schizophrenia.	

E: Would it be a good idea to do a little exercise together?		I: Notice how I bounce back. E: Yes, you seem to become scared. What will happen now? I: First I got scared, but then I realized it was only a *tiny little* test. Not "shall we do *a test?*" That would have been way too much. But *a tiny little test,* well I can do that. You keep it small. So OK. E: There is a lot in words. The trinity (i.e., the present trilogy) starts at an abstract level of analysis, and ends with an analysis of words and the style in which words can be used. [Notice that Ineke heard me saying the word "test," whereas I actually used the word "exercise." Ineke was so scared to be "tested," that she misheard me as we watched the video. Even now that she has become so healthy, that fear reverberates.] I: You said "together." That made all the difference in the world. Mind you, you proposed something that has never ever happened before. Super stressful! It blasts inside. You cannot see that. But I go like a cow. [laughs, but also expresses how scared she was a the time]. But you said, "Shall we explore it together?" Well, OK. And we will not be *doing* it, but we will *explore* a possibility. That makes a huge difference. We will explore it and proceed from there. That's how I heard it. E: Yes, these options were implied.
I: Hmm.	SPP: Ineke does not sound too thrilled.	
E: And see what it would bring?	SPP: Invitation to contemplate that the action might be useful rather than harmful. TPP: Do not allow Ineke to avoid the exercise inasmuch as she can raise a wish to try a new action.	
I: Hmm (concentrated expression).	SPP: Communicates increased interest.	I: I had to really stretch myself as we continued. There were many voices in my head at this point. And I had to listen to you. You said many things, "we'll be exploring this and that," but my head was beyond my control.

E: My idea is that we say that, when there is something very young inside that only screams and when there is something else inside that yells "Stop" and similar things, then there could be difficult things going on. And if that were the case, then we could tell these inner voices that we are starting to grasp something.	SPP: Explanation of the potential new action. I formulate "we" to communicate that Ineke is not alone and that I am willing to assist her. TPP: Set up a new way of relating to the baby and the older voice. Test what its effect would be and how useful the new actions will be to Ineke.	
I: Hmm (continues to concentrate).	SPP: Contemplates the idea.	I: There was that screaming, that "Stop, don't do it, cut it out," and more. And I had to track your words. I had to move forward to even hear you. [this addressed her forward movements, and the accompanying words, "what do you say?"; see above] E: There were more voices than the baby and the voice screaming "Stop, cut it out" at this point? I: Yes, but, oh boy, how could I have said *that*! What I had said was already that much. And there was an extremely loud "NOOO!" Here, in this very episode. And that one overruled everything else. I accepted your invitation, but there was this NOOO. I was in a total conflict. E: Are you aware which part of you shouted no? I: I guess it was Rick. He was a thunderbolt. [The truth was different as Ineke was to find out after the session. See the discussion.]
E: If this fits, we might tell the screaming and the yelling voice that *we are starting to listen, and to understand and to help.* We could make sure that the grown-up Ineke starts to listen and learns how she can help. I: (nods affirmatively) Hmm.	SPP: These sentences address the baby and the older voice. It is a form of "talking through" the adult Ineke. TPP: Include a statement that might serve Ineke's interest: She might be able to do something positive, for herself and for the voices. TPP and SPP: New actions need not be big revolutionary jumps ahead. Smaller steps can be most worthwhile and may provide Ineke with a higher sense of control. SPP: The idea of small steps communicates that I do not expect Ineke to perform miracles. Small steps are more than good enough.	

E: And we could say this together, even if you may find it a bit strange, and track what happens inside. You might tell the voices inside that feel threatened, "OK, I've started to come your way, a little step. I will learn to stop saying "Back off" or do other things to that effect, but move a little closer, to help.	TPP and SPP: Stay with Ineke, do not leave the whole thing up to her. Reach out to the voices, thus speak "inclusively." FPP: This must be a scary thing to do.	I: "I start to come your way." You hear it, "I start to come your way." You mean, I, Ineke, come closer to the parts. But that not the first thing I heard. That was, "I, Ellert starts to come your way, Ineke." E: Ah, that's how you heard it. I: Yes, that how I translated it. I had to tell myself, "No, that's not what he meant, he is not coming closer to me. No? No? No, he is not coming closer." That's what happened. E: I was not aware of this association. But I understand how the sentence can also be heard. I: (laughs)
I: (concentrates, focuses on her inner world, nods) . . . Yes, that a different approach, the world upside down as I see it, yes . . .	TPP: Engages in the action. FPP: It feels good that Ineke dares to do it, feels that she might be able to profit from psychotherapy more than she did so far. But don't rush to conclusions because you want her to be a success, Ellert. *She* must live a desire to achieve changes. She should not get the idea that she must change because *you* want her to.	
E: Now it's important to notice, to feel what is happening inside.	SPP: Focus your attention, Ineke.	
I: (very concentrated on the inner world) . . . If you put it like that, it feels as if . . ., as if . . ., hmm, *that child* (spoken with a touch of depreciation) . . . is *allowed* to exist, that it should not be removed . . . that I am allowed to pay it attention . . . (shakes her head) . . . it feels very strange . . . (shrugs her shoulders) . . . very unreal.	TPP: A flood of new elements. Ineke seems to depreciate "that child"; the theme of allowance pops up again, now in the differentiation of the ability to exist (that child), and Ineke being allowed to pay attention to that child. It is a bit curious that she now talks about "that child" and not about "the baby." SPP: Ineke is communicative, reflective, focused.	I: "If you put it like that," not "if I or we put it like that." E: Right, I also noticed your phrasing. I: To me "if you put it like that" meant "you will be right, thus I must start relating to the voices in a new fashion." I felt, "I have to obey you, let's see if that child might listen. That disturbing nasty child." (laughs) I: I strongly felt it coming that I was going to say "allowed to pay it attention," literally. Bizarre!
E: Yes, I believe you. And what happens now to the screaming?	SPP: Acceptance. TPP and SPP: Test the effect of the action.	
I: I feel that it . . . *pauses* is not the right word . . . yeah, some . . . as if I am . . .		I: (nods several times)
E: Fine, continue . . .		I: How well you encouraged me to continue. You really encouraged me.

I: . . . more involved in it . . . previously it was as if I am that outsider . . .	SPP: Ineke expresses involvement and seems pleased that her action has brought forth something new. TPP: She was an "outsider," not "allowed" and too "scared" to pay attention to her inner vocal and fragile existences, leaving her depersonalized and ignorant.	
E: All right, then you may tell the voices, "OK, I notice a difference." This perhaps opens up a new way of being engaged with myself. I: . . . (continues to be focused inside) . . . yes . . .	TPP and SPP: Utilization of the outcomes so far.	I: The word "open" was very helpful, as was your summary. E: How does a summary like that affect you? I: It communicates that you know how we will proceed. You clarify and provide a new perspective.
E: And you may want to tell the voice yelling "Stop, stop:" "You are *right* . . ." I: Hmm.	SPP: Addressing the verbal voice.	I: (grimaces) That's a big step. That's a really big step. E: Yes. And do you notice how I now address Ineke as the child, not Ineke as the adult. I: Right, you talk to the girl. E: I call addressing more than one part at a time "multispeak." You are sitting there as Ineke, but as an Ineke who encompasses her various parts. I: Absolutely. E: All parts include ears, eyes, and 'I's' (ToT Volume II, chapter 12; Chapters 25–27). I: Yes. E: All parts listen and grasp my words in a particular way. I: Yes. E: And in my view it was very important that they feel and hear that I was addressing all of them. And here, the girl in particular. Here she was: The adult Ineke rejected her, previous therapists had not noticed or ignored her, and that also goes for the other parts. I wanted to reach them, and to tell them something of probable value. I wanted her to know that in my view she was right to say "Stop!" I wanted to reach out to her to set up cooperation (Chapter 22). I: Yes.

		E: But the parts live, so to speak in Flatland. There are things that escape them, that they ignore, or that they regard as insignificant. E: The therapist, thus, has to live in Spaceland to feel into, understand, and reach all. I: Yes. Sure! E: The clinician must sort of create communicative links with all. I: Yes, that's right. E: There is Ineke, the adult woman, a baby, a girl, and possibly more. I thus wanted to set up a relationship with all, so that they can all develop an interest in setting up relationships with each other. That's why I started to apply multispeak in this early phase. I: Yes, and to me it was almost a step too far. At that point I felt to me that you intruded on me. But it may have been necessary. You had to open up the possibilities, and I did not come for no reason. But you did touch something. E: Yes, it was pretty direct. Perhaps I went too fast. That may well be. I: I don't know. Perhaps it was necessary. I am curious to see my reaction. E: I really felt that the girl who was rejected by her parents and by you as well needed to be heard by someone. In this instance I was a bit less concerned with you (as the adult Ineke). I: Yes. E: Let's watch how you react.
E: . . . If bad things are happening, they should stop . . . it's courageous to say "Stop" and "Quit it" . . .	SPP: Affirmation of this voice's wishes. Support of this voice's possible if not probable final cause.	
I: (highly focused inside)		I: Notice how I put my arms against my chest.
E: Perhaps no one listened at the time, but now there is a grown-up Ineke, and if the grown-up Ineke says you're right, you *are* right.	TPP and SPP: Linking Ineke's communications of emotional neglect, emotional abuse, and physical maltreatment, and voicing a hypothesis; indicating that there is something Ineke can now *do*.	

I: (nods repeatedly, sits relatively calmly and immobile) . . . (face grows concerned, however, lifts her right hand) . . . it becomes so tangible . . . and that . . . that feels . . . really scary (body stiffens, right hand stretched) . . . my old way . . . provided less contact . . .	SPP: Communicates mounting tension. Things should not become too tangible, not too real. TPP: Her inner reality may be scary, which provides an impetus to avoid or ignore it.	I: (watches intensely) E: Do you notice your rejecting face? I: (nods) I: Right! *Tangible*, a perfect word. (laughs) I: *Scary* [she said the word before she said it on the tape] (laughs loudly)
E: This new way creates more contact . . . Please experience what happens inside when you use your new way, what happens to the yelling voice?	SPP: Confirming that the new action leads to a new common result, and calling attention to the positive components of the result.	I: Yes . . . E: Here I start to encourage you to enter contact with the girl. I: Yes.
I: (looks up, down, tension drops a bit) . . . as if I can . . . help, as if I can . . . be part of it . . .	SPP: Ineke communicates a new first-person feeling, a new quasi-second person phenomenal judgment, and a new second-person relationship to the baby and the yelling voice.	
E: Fine.		
I: As if I can belong to it after all. I always used to think (Shrugs her shoulders, face showing depreciation, moves her lifted right hand away from her body.) that it was . . .	SPP: Communicates a differentiation of the old and the new, implying a new presentification: I can engage in a different action now.	
		I: Something outside . . . (Spoken before she said it on the video.)
I: . . . something outside of me.		
E: Yes, I think you put it right. It is something that belongs to you after all. You may have needed to believe that it was something outside of you, to stand the hard times. Times in which there cannot only be a screaming baby and someone who yells "Stop" and the like, but also a I who lives daily life, who could not be too close to these scared ways of being. Now you may have reached a time in which the terrible things that happened to you have stopped, a time in which you can return stepwise to your ways of being that have remained behind . . .	TPP and SPP: A communication and a confirmation of an integrative development. Empathizing with and picking up the differentiation of the past and the present. A description of continuing integrative and supportive actions.	I: (nods recurrently as I speak)
E: . . . because they need you.		I: Ohhh. Ohhh! That is quite something you're saying! (grimaces)

I: Yes. Yes ... *that* is ... clear (laughs out the wrong side of her mouth, tenses) ... they jump on me ...	SPP: Ineke communicates that she is not too excited experiencing and knowing how much she is needed.	I: I suddenly become confronted with a major task. Your remark also activates my tendency to please other people: "I am needed, yes. I am needed, so that's what I must and will do. I'll do what you want me to do ..." E: I was not aware at the time that 'being needed' included this particular connotation for you. I realized, however, that I presented a synopsis of the whole therapy. Your diagnosis had become pretty clear to me. I: Yes? E: Sure. I: It had become rather obvious, right? E: Yes. I thus began preparing the therapeutic venture. I: Actually, it had become a therapeutic session. E: Indeed. It became important that you as all parts knew what you were up to. In little steps, yes, but steps in an integrative direction. And if you don't take those steps, things will probably remain unchanged. And you really started to engage in some steps. That was superb.
E: It's not easy. But you may perhaps want to practice the steps we took together today on your own, because they were effective ...	SPP: Empathic expression that the new action is challenging, along with a suggestion that she may want to repeat the action, and this time on her own, which would mean a next step.	
... Would it be OK with you to return to the questions of the interview?	Asking her permission to continue the interview.	I: I went: "Ahh, is that what we're doing? All right, I will readjust myself. Go ahead!" E: I had noticed the mounting tension, and in part for that reason I felt the need to shift the topic. Your videos are so extremely helpful because you are, among other things, so very expressive in a physical sense. Every move you make is full of content and rich in meaning.
I: (adjusts her posture, shows readiness, nods).	SPP: Provides her consent.	
E: Do you ever experience that your body feels strange. I recall we discussed this the last time we met, but would you want to add something?		

I: It's mostly my lower body. [So far, the session has lasted 31 minutes. Hereafter, Ineke gave further positive responses to items addressing depersonalization and derealization. In this context, she reported more instances of dissociative amnesia and confusion regarding the degree of reality of some of her perceptions. That is, she sometimes doubts whether things that happened really happened, even if they were documented. This confusion also happened when she was not tense or emotional. Ineke does not drink alcohol or take drugs. At 36 minutes into the session, I posed the first SCID-D question regarding 'identity confusion':]	TPP: Exploring the background of this response does not seem timely, and it does not seem necessary to make the diagnosis. SPP: Abstaining from further questions regarding strange pelvic feelings implicitly tells Ineke that her well-being is more important than knowing everything about her.	
E: Let's return to questions that address your inner experiences. Do you sometimes feel that there is a struggle inside?		I: (grimaces) Oh. If only because of that word "struggle."
I: (attentive) Hmm. (nods)	SPP: Ineke shows that the question is relevant to her condition.	
E: Could you perhaps describe this struggle?	SPP: "Perhaps" communicates that she is not forced to answer.	
I: For example, it pertains to the screaming and yelling inside. There are . . . it is also about my deceased mother . . . it is as if . . . she is . . . also present (shakes her head, restless legs) . . . here, in my body (kicks her left leg) . . .	SPP: Ineke shows that the issue is highly emotional. The "struggle" is also present in her nonverbal reactions. The kicking leg may indicate anger or frustration. TPP: Could it be that Ineke hears her deceased mother talk to her? Would these be automated recurrent versions of the kind of things her mother told her? Could it perhaps be that the motherly voice is the voice of a controlling EP? The uncompleted sentence "There are . . ." may suggest that more is present inside the baby, the stop-yelling voice, and the mother. FPP, QSPP: How would it be to have a deceased mother inside?	I: (grimaces again, nods several times)

E: What is she doing there . . . in your body?	TPP: Let's ask about the actions of the present mother. SPP: Adoption and utilization of Ineke's terms and descriptions.	
I: (more leg kicking and general restlessness) . . . Preaching . . .	TPP: Does Ineke kick her legs out of anger, or out of some other emotion?	
E: Preaching, hm.	SPP: Adoption of Ineke's word.	
I: Yes.	SPP: Consensus.	
E: She was good at that?	TPP: Continued sensitive exploration.	
I: (nods)	SPP: Affirmation.	
E: Your deceased mother, what is she talking about?	SPP: Continued utilization of Ineke's reactions. The present tense communicates the understanding and acceptance that her deceased mother is not phenomenally dead.	
I: (eyes almost closed) That I should not make a fool of myself. That there are worse things in life.	TPP: Would these be the kind of things her mother said while she was alive?	
E: As we have been talking, did she partake in the conversation?	TPP: Follows up on Ineke's statement that the mother seems to be present, and speaks to her. SPP: Further communication of the understanding that deceased mothers can be phenomenally alive, and that the issue can be discussed.	
I: (nods in silence, tense)	SPP: Consensus.	
E: Hm.	SPP: Affirmation.	
I: I should not make a fool of myself and things like that.	TPP: Another description of what her mother may have told Ineke, probably more than once. FPP, QSPP: What would it be like for a child to hear this kind of aggressive, deprecative talk? And what is it like to continue hearing these words as she is gone?	E: Do you remember this episode? I: Yes. I felt understood by you. That made a major difference. But the mother part in me said, "How do you dare to ask his attention? You don't need it anyone." Here, I receive your attention and understanding, and that is totally forbidden. "Who do you think you are!" I had to earn attention, and even when I had worked hard to deserve some attention, I did not get any. As I was talking to you, I had guilt feelings regarding my mother. Talking about her. Forbidden. E: Does it fit: ignorance, fragility, and control? This internal mother, isn't she about control?

		I: Yes. E: And the little ones, fragile? I: Yes. E: And the interest of not knowing? I: It all fits . . . My leg movements show my anger. I was 35 years old when she died. She told my brother that she dearly loved him, and totally rejected me. She accused me of being a horrible, bad person. I told her a hundred times I would do anything to please her. I could not stop saying that, I became psychotic. The physician gave me an injection to sort of knock me out.
E: How do you deal with that?	FPP, QSPP: How would I have dealt with it?	
I: It's a battle. (moves her right leg) In my way I have forgiven her [for what she did to me] (brisk movement of her left leg).	SPP: Ineke further tells me about the ongoing battle. I sense anger and frustration. TPP: Are her words ("forgiven") and nonverbal actions (kicking) inconsistent, or do they somehow fit together?	[From this point on, Inckc shared several details about her mother. She conveyed that her mother may have had DID. She was relatively OK one moment to become, in a flash of a second and totally unpredictable to Ineke, an enraged individual. As Ineke said, these switches popped up "out of the blue." As we continued to watch the video, Ineke shared some more issues about her mother that are not present in the current text.]
I: But when she was lying on her deathbed, she rose up and pointed her accusative hand and finger at me (Ineke suddenly points with her right hand and finger in front of her, and stretches her left hand in a cramp), although her vertebra were broken due to the bone cancer, with extremely angry eyes . . . (cramping hands entangled) . . . and then I only said, "Tell me what you want me to do, I will do anything, anything for you."	TPP: Ineke does not say it literally, but communicates that her mother accused her in her last minutes once again that she, Ineke, is a bad person, and that she, her mother, will not forgive her for that. A complete role reversal. Ineke is not allowed to exist, because she is inherently bad. Mother told her this until the very last moment.	
And then I turned psychotic . . . but yes, it is as if she still speaks to me in that way, as if it still reverberates . . .	FPP: What a drama, what a disaster. SPP: Small wonder this was too much to take. Small wonder that she became psychotic. TPP: Could this 'psychosis' have been the longer-term activation of an EP? (I knew that Ineke had been admitted to a mental hospital for several months.) SPP: Do not address the psychosis, do not examine its nature right now, because allowing Ineke to tell the story seems much more important.	

E: Hm . . . yes.	SPP: Without interrupting Ineke's flow of words, it feels important to signal that I continue to be with her.	
I: . . . me telling her, "I have forgiven you, forgiven you." But she continues to accuse me, she is still present, also when the little child [in me] yells. It must stop.	SPP and TPP: Ineke could only try to please her mother, because without forgiveness she could not exist, because the mother did not allow her to exist. And the relational mother-daughter drama continues in Ineke's inner phenomenal self and world. The drama must end, but Ineke does not know how to stop it.	
E: But she continues to preach and accuse?	SPP: Communicate the understanding that the drama has not stopped.	
I: Yes.		
E: It [i.e., the motherly voice] sounds so unforgiving. It's never right no matter what you do.		
I: No. As young as I was, whatever I did, it was not right.		
E: Do you ever get angry at her?	SPP: Communicate that anger would be a perfectly normal emotion. FPP: I feel anger regarding her mother. TPP: Take care that your anger, Ellert, does not influence Ineke. If there is anger, it should be her explicit anger, which you can then accept and support.	
I: Sometimes I feel angry, but then there is that big part of me — a part I made really big — that I must forgive her. If I do not do that, then, . . . then . . . I cannot move on. I've put it in a big painting for myself, because otherwise . . . [I cannot live.]	SPP: Yes, she is forced to forgive her mother, because otherwise she cannot exist. TPP: She has probably been unable to put the ongoing drama in words so far. Yet she symbolized the "big piece" in a "big painting," and she did this "for herself" because there was no audience. Nonverbal symbolization is an excellent alternative for and prelude to verbal symbolization that is as of yet unavailable to a person. FPP, QSPP, SPP: How good that she was able to do this for *herself*.	
E: Otherwise you do not know what to do anymore.	SPP: Attunement.	
I: No.	SPP: Consensual acceptance and understanding. We are both moved.	
E: Regarding the struggle inside, does it sometimes also pertain to the question who you really are?	SPP and TPP: It feels and seems timely to continue the SCID-D.	
I: Yes.		
E: Can you describe it?		

I: Yes, sometimes I think there is a twin inside. As if I am a twin sister. As if the other twin *is* OK. It's just me who's failing all the time.	TPP: A new element. A division between an acceptable ANP and an unacceptable one?	
E: And that twin sister is OK. What's good about her?	SPP: Utilization of Ineke's words.	
I: She's my mother's ideal daughter.	TPP: A false self? An ANP who fulfills the role of mother's ideal daughter?	
E: If you allow me to put it this way, and I mean no harm, is this twin of yours perhaps a bit like a puppet on a string ...?	SPP: Sensitive ("I mean no harm"; "a bit like") exploration of the hypothesis.	
I: Yes		
E: ... that precisely did what mother wanted her to do, whereas you sometimes felt something like "but wait a minute, there's also me, the one that I am"?		
I: (Nods all along, her tense hands still entangled.)	TPP and SPP: The hypothesis seems to fit, and there seems to be another inner struggle.	
E: And does your twin sister sometimes tell you what to do and how to do it? "Work yourself to the bone, try harder?"	TPP and SPP: Formulation of this possible struggle.	
I: She's always trying hard to receive approval and acknowledgment.	SPP: Ineke seems to discredit her "twin sister." SPP and TPP: Mind that the "twin sister" may be listening in; make sure you do not join Ineke in her depreciation of a possible second ANP, who strives hard to get at least some acceptance and recognition.	
E: Which is a normal thing to do. Anyone, every child needs approval and acknowledgment. And if that doesn't materialize, then there's a tremendous hunger.	SPP: Empathic communication, focus on need and desire.	
I: Yes, a dry sponge, soaks up every drop.	SPP: Powerful metaphor that reveals a degree of understanding and acceptance of Ineke's primordial need of attachment.	
E: Yes, I get that ...	SPP: Consensus.	
E: Do you ever act as if you are somebody else?	The time seems ripe for a SCID-D item that addresses "identity fragmentation" (a term I do not use because dissociative parts are not totally split and in this sense are not "fragments.").	
I: I sometimes put on a childlike voice.	TPP: Sounds like role-playing. But is it?	

E: Do you do this intentionally or does it happen beyond your control?	TPP: Exploration of the issue.	
I: I find it, uh, hard to make a distinction.	TPP: It could be that my terms were unclear to Ineke.	
E: We sometimes play a role, as in play, quite consciously, quite planned. Some people experience that they do not play a role in this sense, but become influenced by something they cannot resist, by something that determines them against their will. What resembles your experience most?	TPP: Explain a bit more. SPP: Formulate carefully: "We," "some people," "against their will," followed by an open question.	
I: The latter.	SPP: The answer came quick and sounded decisive.	
E: Have other people observed that you sometimes act very differently from your more normal way of being?	TPP and SPP: Sounds like the issue can be explored a bit more.	I: (nods)
I: Sure.		
E: What do they tell you?		
I: I do not tell many people that I receive treatment and that I've been admitted [to a mental hospital], but the individuals I do tell don't understand why.		
They say that I'm always so cheerful and happy.	TPP: Could this pertain to the "twin sister," the ideal person?	
E: Have other individuals addressed you with a different name, other than a nickname?	TPP and SPP: It might be best to move ahead with the SCID-D questions and not to dive into matters too deeply, because the session has already been quite demanding to Ineke.	
I: "Misfit." They said I was the milkman's daughter. I really went with the milkman. I thought that *he* was my father. I did not look like my parents. My hair was very different.	TPP and SPP: An utterly lonely, rejected child looking for a place under the sun. Father pops up for the first time. SPP: It might be better to refrain from exploring the issue at this point given the emotional load of the session so far.	I: (nods)
I always thought I had been adopted.		I: (grimaces)
E: Do you ever find notes you must have written but that you can't explain?	TPP: Continue the interview.	
I: That happens. For example, the suicide note we talked about last time. I recognize the handwriting, but the style can be different. Sometimes the notes are in block letters, but that's not how I write.		

E: And does the writing seem to you to be an adult's hand or is it different?		I: (shakes her head for "no")
I: It can be child-like.	TPP: Could this be the writing of one or more phenomenally young dissociative parts?	
E: Do you recognize it as your writing style?		
I: Yes, but it's the writing style I had as a child. My diary has many pages of it.		
E: And what is the writing about?		
I: I don't really know.	TPP and SPP: This is remarkable. There are "many pages" of writing that she recognizes as her own, but in writing styles that do not fit her current writing. And she does not know what the text is about.	I: The way I read it, I did not take the sentences in.
E: You don't read it?	TPP: How come? SPP: I feel that Ineke would rather not go any deeper into the matter. It might become too confrontational, perhaps. In any case, do not push the issue.	E: I got the impression that you did not take the sentences in. I: No, I did not.
I: I don't know.	SPP: I feel a vague, mounting tension in Ineke. She becomes more withdrawn and evasive. I wonder what is going on.	E: I got the impression that you had become tired, but that there was also something else going on inside you. I: Yes, yes.
[At this point, we had talked for 47 minutes. Skipping some items here, we arrived at the following point:]		
E: Do you ever get instructions to hurt yourself?		
I: Yes, it has to be done, strict instructions that I must obey.	TPP: Who is giving the instructions?	
E: Who gives the instructions?		
I: I can't tell.	SPP: Again, evasiveness. FPP: I feel something's happening that I cannot pinpoint so far. TPP: The theme "father" came up, and from that point onward, Ineke seemed to run in some kind of difficulty. Test a hypothesis: If it's not a dissociative part that imitates mother, then what about father?	
E: Do the instructions perhaps relate to the voice of your mother?	TPP: The question is explorative and very general but it includes a suggestive element.	

I: Don't know.	TPP and SPP: Ineke presents the same kind of tension that she communicated when she was addressing "mother." The reaction pattern does not impress as a result of suggestion.	E: Do you recall what was happening? I: That I do know what was going on? E: In any case that something else than tiredness was going on. I: Yes. I notice I got irritated and slightly turn my body away from you. E: Do you recall what your irritation was about? I: Can I see it again? (we replay the last minute). There were prohibitions related to the abuse, to my father. I had to obey. I knew it, it was my father's voice, not my mother's voice.
E: Is there ever something male-like inside?	SPP: Prudent exploration of an apparently difficult topic.	(Hearing me ask if there was perhaps a male-like voice, Ineke said:) Here you have it. (laughs).
I: (almost closes her eyes, tension mounts considerable, remains silent).		
E: Can you – are you – allowed to say something about it?		I: "Can you and are you allowed to?" That's an excellent way of saying it. Yes. Had you only said "can you," it would not have worked. But "are you allowed to?" communicates your understanding that there can be prohibitions. E: It is a short phrase communicating that I know about controlling parts. I: Yes, yes, yes. "Can you and are you allowed to . . .?" Wow. E: Yes. I: No escape, it had to be done. E: Your reaction is slightly avoidant insofar as you actually know the voice. Considering that a controlling part may regard me as a weak individual, it is important that I show some strength. That's why I don't back off here. I: Yes, that fits.
I: That also relates to pain. Pain, I must have pain, I must mutilate myself.		

E: Who tells you so?	SPP: A more direct question.	E: I do not want a possibly existing male and controlling part to think that I am a coward . . . I: Yes, yes. E: . . . or that I do not appreciate them. I: That they are insignificant. E: In my experience they are controlling, but underlying that power is a major fragility. I: *Absolutely! There are controlling because they are so fragile! That's the point.* E: Yes. And also a lot of ignorance with regard to the actual present. I: (nods intensely) Yes! E: Caught in the past that they experience as the present. I: They are controlling but haven't got a clue about the present. E: Yes. Let's watch what happens next.
I: (sighs, long pause, tense) I think it's a man's voice.		
E: Can you link this voice to somebody you know, such as in the case of your mother? Or is it different?		
I: There are more.	TPP: Further proof that Ineke is not responding to my question if there might be "something male-like inside." She says, with a lot of effort, that there is more than one male voice inside.	E: You're almost trembling. I: Yes. (presses her lips)
E: More. Males?		
I: (nods) Hmm.		
E: What kind of voices are they?		
I: (long pause, coughs, sighs). Men, uh . . . uh . . . who relate to my traumas.	Ineke is in trouble, and gives a clear yet also vague response. She had not said much not much about traumatization by men so far.	E: I had the impression that your 'half-answers' communicated that you were unable to say much more. I: That's right. And I felt your understanding. Your appreciation of the situation was very helpful.
E: Do the voices or powers inside perhaps somehow represent these individuals?	TPP and SPP: Can Ineke make the distinction? Insofar as the male voices involve dissociative parts, it is important to communicate from the start that they have "good reasons" to do whatever they do. If they exist, therapy will have to include these presumably controlling EPs.	E: At the same time, I felt that the controlling voices needed to hear my courage and perseverance. I wanted to reach them because there was so much of your power in that control.
I: Hmm.		

E: Are they perhaps factual representations of these individuals? Or could they also be parts of you that, for some good reason or reasons, do whatever it is that they do?	SPP and TPP: It is important that Ineke makes the distinction, but under pressure she may not always be able to keep up the realization that the male voices concern dissociative parts of her.	E: How do controlling parts react to my statement that they have good reasons for doing what they're doing? I: It reaches and touches them. They certainly hear it. E: What does it mean to them? I: They feel heard, heard. E: I say it to reach out to them, and I mean what I say. I: They feel heard and seen. It does not force them to enter contact with you. But they feel heard and seen. That's enough for the moment. It's a limited communication.
I: I think they're parts of me . . . but when they are so strongly present . . . I have great difficulty grasping they're parts of me.		
E: Hm. In any case, they seem to be really good at imitating these individuals. Do you have any idea why they're doing the things they do?	TPP and SPP: A communication to possibly existing controlling EPs that I am aware that controlling EPs commonly imitate perpetrators. They are in my experience and view not "introjects," but phenomenally younger dissociative parts that demonstrate control, that hide their fragility, and that are stuck in a degree of ignorance, and ignoring.	
I: (sighs deeply, really tense) Hmm.		
E: Do they comment now, perhaps?	SPP: Attunement to Ineke's phenomenal experience.	I: Yes!
I: (inhales deeply) Yes. (Exhales, briefly grins in a stressed kind of way, holds her head in her hands like she did when the baby and the younger child inside started screaming and yelling.)		
E: Can you say what these voices are telling you?		
I: I must shut up.	TPP and SPP: This instruction may relate to Ineke's apprehensive evasion of several of some of my questions.	
E: We could ask them why it is important that you shut up.	SPP: Recurrent empathic statement, that the male voices have a good reason for doing what they are doing.	
I: Because it's a secret.	TPP: Ineke encompasses a "secret."	I: (deep sigh) This was a revelation. Saying that there was a secret was a major step. My body posture! (Imitates her tight body posture in the session.)

E: Hmm. You're not allowed to talk about it.		
I: (nods) Yes. I'm not allowed to talk about the secrets.	TPP: Ineke actually has more than one "secret."	E: You acknowledged that you included secrets. I: Exactly. And still, the truth is still hard to accept. I felt it as I read the preliminary version of the present book. The facts written down in black and white. I 'saw' my father last night, you know. That secret was so awfully strong. E: It was to be the last thing to integrate, acknowledge, accept, and realize in therapy: the reality of 17 years of incest. Your father was your last string to hold on to. A relationship with your mother had proven to be completely impossible. Your family had let you down completely. There had to be somebody. I: Yes. E: Your secret could not possibly be true, because you would have lost your father as well. I: Exactly. E: We dealt with all the maltreatment and neglect that you received from your mother and family. It took us a couple of years. And all the time, you fought to keep the secret. I: Exactly. [We shared more on the theme of incest that will be included in Chapter 34.]
E: Could it be that the male voices expect that you or they will be punished if you break the silence?	TPP and SPP: Careful communication that controlling EPs commonly try to protect the fragile EPs and ANPs, that they are not vicious at heart.	
I: (nods and continues to hold her head between her tight hands).	SPP: Ineke needs support; she is really struggling.	
E: We could say that we understand that it can be too dangerous to talk. Children who are instructed to shut up may believe it is too dangerous to talk.	SPP: "We" communicates that Ineke is not alone, that "we" have a joint understanding of "secrets" and "instructions to shut up." TPP and SPP: Ineke needs more power of action; we can try a small yet most highly significant step. "We" are cooperating, and "you" pose the question to "them."	I: You say "we," right? E: Yes, "we." You were not alone. I: I understand your focus on the controlling voices, because they must be heard. If that does not happen, they're gone. They would feel abandoned. They hope you catch the ball they are throwing.
You know what you might do?		I: Yes, please, I did not know. (laughs)

I: (remains very tense). No. (holds her breath)		
E: You might want to ask them in what year we're living. And you can continue to breathe.		I: That's scary! I: (sighs)
I: (face turns red, transpires) 1970.	TPP: Confirmation of the idea that the male voices may be ignorant regarding the present. FPP and SPP: I feel deep respect for Ineke's courage.	
E: You can tell them in return that you have grown an adult, and that the actual year is 2006, almost 2007. We have advanced some 36 years. You might tell them that you have started to understand that they still live in the most difficult years. Years in which talking about the difficult things was dangerous.	SPP and TPP: Invitation to engage in new actions replacing her passions regarding the male voices.	
I: (breathes faster from her upper chest, and continues to hold her breath)	SPP: Ineke continues to struggle; there will be a fierce inner struggle.	I: Back off, back off! Get lost! That's what they said.
E: You may tell them that you're talking to a person who is not dangerous, who will not punish anyone. Things may look exceptionally scary from the year 1970 for eyes and ears that live in 1970 or so. We may tell the voices or parts of you that they are also important, that they are trying to silence you as a means of saving what can be saved. That was important in 1970.	SPP: I include myself in the interaction. Indirect attunement to, as well as acceptance and appreciation of the male "voices" or "parts" inside.	I: Nuts, nuts, war inside!
I: (Exhales deeply and keeps sighing, more sweating, holds her chest with her right hand, avoids eye contact.)	SPP and TPP: It seems that the struggle continues.	
E: And can you tell me just a little bit about what's happening inside? ... ... Could I tell you what I think is happening? ... Could you look at me for a moment, and notice I'm talking with you? ... Making a little contact with me?	SPP: "Just a little bit" communicates the idea of a small step. TPP: I wonder if it would be better to leave the issue alone for the time being. However, the risk is that the controlling EPs, which I think are the male parts of her, would be regarding me as a weak individual who readily backs off under some pressure, who does not have the power to deal with intense emotional issues, including traumatization by adult men. I thus decided to raise the issue of trust.	E: Having said what I wanted to convey, I return my attention to you more.

I: (Struggles to control her breathing, exhales through her open mouth.)		I: Ohhh. . . . It is of matter of life and death that I start to do this work . . . I have told you my secret. Oohh, what have I done?! What have I done?
E: You know what I think they're saying in return to my words? I may be completely wrong, of course. But what I think is that they are commanding you not to trust me or something similar. Could that be?	SPP: My words and ideas seem to affect the male parts in one way or another.	
I: (Bends forward, holds her head in her hands, head down.)		
E: Whatever they say, I think they are important, too. And I do mean what I say . . .	SPP: I continue to reveal my position.	
I: (struggles)		
E: And you may want to drink some water when you're ready.	TPP and SPP: Utilization of Ineke's previous way of tension reduction.	
I: (Takes the glass with water, holds it with both hands, drinks some, keeps sighing, drinks some more.)		
E: You can tell yourself that there's a lot to learn, and that you can take a step at a time. No one expects more . . . I'm still with you.		
I: (leans back, burps)	SPP: Ineke starts to relax a bit.	I: A burp. How embarrassing! (laughs)
E: That's all right, let it go . . . That's what I say, everything inside you is important. Everyone does his or her utmost. Everyone and everything deserved attention and understanding.	SPP: Attunement, acceptance, multispeak.	E: You had gasped for air, ending up with a stomach stuffed with air. I: Much turmoil inside, what have I done? It is so clear that the work can only be done in steps.
I: (slowly recomposes herself, and receives some emotional support as she does this)		
[From this point in time onward, the session could be completed. Ineke left in a rather silent, grave state of mind and arrived home safely.]		
		E: Your remarks have been so extremely helpful.
		I: Fine. There was such despair. I was amazed that I was able to get home. It was a revelation that I could even continue after such an intense session . . . I always hoped that there would be no one in the house when I returned home. Contact with others after an intense session was simply too much.

The Path So Far

The combined results of the self-reporting questionnaires and the SCID-D interview pointed toward CDID or DID, strongly suggesting the existence of a variety of dissociative parts of her personality that recurrently and powerfully intruded on her (as the predominant ANP). There was a suicidal way of being; a screaming baby, a child – or so it seemed – that yelled "Stop," "Quit it" and the like; a twin sister; the preaching, depreciating, and devaluating 'mother'; adult male voices that included but were not restricted to 'father.' Ineke had no idea or only a very limited comprehension of the nature of the voices, though the twin sister seemed to be an exception in this regard. The intrusions scared and annoyed her, and she had no way of controlling them.

She frequently engaged in passionate substitute actions: overeating, vomiting, mutilating herself, panic attacks, losing concentration, dissociative forgetting, efforts to tend and befriend, that is, to please others on end. She also frequently disconnected herself from her body, leaving her in part physically analgesic and anesthetic. As became apparent in the course of the treatment, her endless walks constituted another means of remaining at a distance from her various fragile EPs (e.g., the yelling child) and controlling EPs ('mother' and 'father'). Ineke's power of action regarding the other ANP (the twin sister) and the EPs was thus very limited.

The amnestic episodes, however, seemed to be relative exceptions, and switching back from full domination by another dissociative part to Ineke as the prime ANP seemed to take far more time and effort than is common for most individuals with DID. Whereas Ineke as the prime ANP was dominant most of the time, she was frequently subject to complex dissociative intrusions. CDID was, therefore, my conservative working hypothesis as her treatment started. I would later change to diagnosis to DID, fully aware that, like all categories, diagnoses are artificial human parsings, replete with fuzzy boundaries that preclude foolproof conclusions regarding borderline cases.

Apart from this, however, there are no major differences between the treatment of CDID and DID. One clinically relevant difference is that the switches in full-blown DID tend to be quite rapid and frequent. Individuals with DID thereby tend to display more directly 'who does what and why.' This circumstance can simplify the clinician's life. The dynamics of individuals with CDID may not always become that clearly exposed. In this disorder, dissociative parts may remain more backstage; they nonetheless communicate their existence sooner or later. And when they do talk to the ANP, the ANP can talk back. And when they talk to the clinician through the ANP, the clinician can talk to them through the ANP in return. Another means of communication with a dissociative part that does not have full control is shared in Chapter 33.

Chapter 35 details that Ineke's personality included more dissociative parts than the ones that appeared to exist or that were alluded to during the two SCID-D interviews. This growing clarity is a common development, particularly when the dissociative disorder is complex. It relates among other things to the overcoming of the phobia that dissociative parts tend to have regarding each other as well as to a growing confidence that the treating clinicians recognize and accept the involved dissociative parts. The development toward ever more clarity of the whole dissociative system also relates to the growing general power of action of patients and to the associated increasing integrative tendencies.

Secrets

Ineke's 'secrets' proved to be an important issue in therapy. But before she was ready and able to specify them, a lot of other therapeutic progress had to be made. This work included developing more power of action regarding her haunting family of origin, which continued to haunt her. One of the breakthrough sessions regarding Ineke's secrets is presented in Chapter 35, where we see that her secrets actually involved affairs her family wanted to keep under the hat as much as she did as the leading ANP and as some but not all EPs.

Epilogue

Three afterthoughts to this chapter. The first concerns Ineke's recent review of our joint venture and of her previous experiences in the domain of psychiatry:

> Meeting a nonauthoritarian clinician with a deep interest in me and in my troubles saved my life. That's the plain truth. Our collaboration stood in full contrast to my previous psychiatric encounters. Amid all the horrors I had lived through and at the time was still experiencing, it was terrible realizing that no one seemed to understand me. I felt so utterly alone in my dealings with psychologists and psychiatrists. None seemed to grasp my troubles, not even during admissions. The clinicians did not *get* it. They displayed a total ignorance of my experiential world and my whole being. They seemed to think I was making a fool of myself. Only two individuals expressed some compassion. Things grew ever worse during the admissions. I put a hot iron against my arm, hid in a laundry room. My self-destructive and suicidal tendencies were intimately related to this utter loneliness and rejection. Prison might have been a better place for me – there no one pretends to offer treatment.

The second matter is that watching the video of the session together was to set the stage for the revelation of a final secret. The third pertains to the topic of dissociative psychosis. In the course of our collaboration, it became apparent that the psychotic episode following the death of her mother had been intimately related to a confused young fragile EP. This 'child' resurfaced during one session and basically stayed in charge for some 2 weeks. The condition necessitated a clinical admission. Chapter 37 details *what* another dissociative part had been doing in the minutes before the 'psychotic' little one popped up; and *what* I said in return and *why*.

Chapter 33

Uncommon Enactive Assessment

Joy . . . is an affect by which the body's power of acting is increased or aided . . . And so . . . joy is directly good . . .
But Melancholy . . . is a sadness, which, insofar as it is related to the body, consists in this, that the body's power of acting is absolutely diminished or restrained. And so . . . it is always evil . . .
Baruch Spinoza (1677a, Part IV, Demonstrations to Propositions 41 and 42, respectively)

Patients can be subjected to circumstances that preclude standard assessment. For example, for a variety of reasons they may be unable to adequately answer diagnosticians' queries. ANPs may not currently have the mental ability to react, or they may be too phobic of their dissociative condition to provide any clarity. Controlling EPs may forbid them to answer questions, as happened to Ineke during the last part of the SCID-D interview (see Chapter 32). These predicaments or still other obstacles challenge the ability and courage of both patients and clinicians to enact an uncommon diagnostic track. Hope for a good result does not exist without the simultaneous fear of failure. Yet nothing else than dedicated courage to act and to cleverly utilize the situation and one's talents can bring forth a favorable development. When beaten paths lead nowhere, react by enacting new ones.

A good dissociation and trauma theory is invaluable when the usual explorative paths fail to result in a fitting analysis of patients' troubles. While the map is not the territory, a good chart can guide a journey through unknown terrain. But no matter how robust and refined a theory may be, it can only fulfill its potential when clinicians know how to read and use it. They must clearly have a fine grasp of both the theory and its implications. They also must have the intellectual capacity and the practical skills to link the theory, the markings on the map, and the problems their patients present.

This chapter provides two examples of uncommon assessment. The first example is spelled out in detail; the other is presented in a much shorter form. Yet both illustrate how a theory can help patients and clinicians to enact uncommon, or perhaps even unprecedented, paths.

Martha

Martha, a 36-year-old married woman, was referred to an outpatient trauma center for the assessment and treatment of frequent seizures. Several physicians had initially suspected temporal lobe epilepsy. This suspicion was raised because some of her seizures included incontinence, tongue-biting, and foaming at the mouth, and because she had a positive reaction to medication (rivotril, depakine). However, the EEG was negative for epilepsy, and the medication effect was short-lived. They, therefore, wondered whether the seizures might involve DSM-IV conversion disorder, more accurately described in ICD-10 (WHO, 1992) as dissociative disorder of movement and sensation. Despite this suspected diagnosis by exclusion of a detected somatic origin, diagnostic uncertainty lingered.

Martha reported chronic parental emotional neglect and abuse from early childhood on. Her parents had maltreated her physically. This history and the lack of common psychological interventions motivated the general practitioner to refer Martha to the trauma center. Her relationships with the various clinicians, including the general practitioner, were quite troubled. She felt misunderstood and mistreated. For example, as she saw it, these professionals had posed an endless series of unhelpful (diagnostic) questions. She also felt that they had not adequately or sensitively dealt with her "attacks." The clinicians' efforts to bring about change had indeed remained fruitless. The "attacks" had actually worsened.

Martha also had frequent seizures in the trauma center. They often happened near the end of her sessions with the psychiatrist and with Jessica, the social psychiatric nurse who treated her. The probability of an attack was highest when a session came to a close.

The seizures had begun in early childhood. Since they had waxed and waned, but they had not been absent for any substantial period of time of her life. Although several physicians had examined her, she did not receive medical treatment until she was 34 years old. Martha appreciated the social psychiatric treatment in the trauma center, which focused on improving her functioning in daily life and also discussed her childhood and ongoing emotional neglect and abuse. However, her seizures continued unabated. Worse, their frequency and duration increased.

Martha, Jessica, and the psychiatrist became desperate. All were deeply concerned because of the futile treatment and the increasingly frequent "attacks." An attack might even last an hour, up to five or even more times a day, and might include foaming. They started with shaking, trembling, or dizziness that turned into paralysis and dropping to the floor. The final stage was total immobility and passivity. Jessica had not observed that Martha lost urine during the attacks. Martha was not allowed to drive a car, and she could hardly go for a walk or go shopping.

The two clinicians stood under tremendous pressure to achieve a favorable result. Other patients were shaken when they found what looked like 'a corpse' in the women's restroom or a corridor of the trauma center. The secretaries complained that Martha recurrently called them in despair or anger, and that she kept them engaged for up to 30 minutes or so. The pressure that Martha exerted on them clearly interfered with their work. The secretaries and other patients were also disturbed when Martha had her attacks in front of the reception desk. "Something had to be done, urgently," they warned.

Jessica and the psychiatrist invited me – I was also working at the center – to talk to Martha. She was apprehensive but also glad to meet me. Jessica was aware of the effectiveness of diagnostic and treatment sessions with several other seizure patients in my practice, and she had shared these facts with Martha. The two were somewhat hopeful and, given the chronicity and severity of the stubborn seizures, at the same time doubtful that assessment and treatment with me would bring produce better results. I for my part was interested in meeting Martha. I felt sorry for her. She had become almost an invalid. I was also interested to see how Martha would react to an approach to assessment and treatment I had developed and successfully applied in other cases of dissociative stupor and dissociative convulsions.

Enactive Assessment: Hypotheses

Since standard assessment had proven ineffective, there was no point in posing more questions of the common kind. So what could be done? Seeking a sensible alternative diagnostic route, I thought it was important to consult the definition of dissociation (Nijenhuis & Van der Hart, 2011a, 2011b; ToT Volume II, Chapter 13) and the theory of structural dissociation of the personality. This definition and theory suggested the following general – and preliminary – hypotheses:

1. If Martha's fainting spells concern dissociative convulsions and stupor, and since dissociative symptoms are per definitionem the manifestation of a dissociation of the personality, she must encompass at least two dissociative subsystems or parts of this whole system.
2. More specifically, there must be at least one ANP and at least one EP. The available data suggested that the demoralized adult Martha constituted an ANP inasmuch as as a whole person Martha would have a dissociative disorder. In this case, there had to be at least one EP.
3. There are negative and positive dissociative symptoms. Fainting can be a negative dissociative symptom inasmuch as it constitutes an avoidance response of the ANP. Fainting can also be a positive symptom inasmuch as it is an intrusion on the ANP originating from the EP's domain. The first possibility does not exclude the second.
4. Since dissociative disorders and intrusions are often trauma-related, it is possible that fainting involves a (re)action pattern in the framework of events that have been traumatic for Martha – and that have been traumatizing for her from an observer's third-person perspective. *Note:* The events involved constitute more than just adverse events inasmuch as they have been a major cause of the dissociation of the personality. Adverse events are traumatic events (in the quasi-second and second-person perspective) and traumatizing events (in the third-person perspective) if and only if they have caused a factual biopsychosocial injury (see ToT Volume I, Chapter 11).

5. Since an individual's personality constitutes an organism-environment system, dissociative parts comprise more than a phenomenal conception of self. They also include a set of phenomenal conceptions of the material and social *umwelt* as well as a phenomenal conception of their relationship to this *umwelt*. This means they have, at least in principle, the power to communicate with this *umwelt*.
6. However, some dissociative parts may lack the power to communicate verbally. In terms of a hierarchy of action tendencies (Van der Hart et al., 2006; see below), they may, for example, be unable to reach the mental level of functioning necessary to the use of language. They may also, or alternatively, be too scared to reveal themselves in a linguistic form. Further, other dissociative parts may keep them from taking the degree of executive control that verbal communication demands. That is why it can be important to invite dissociative parts that remain under these circumstances to use nonverbal means of communication. And that is also why clinicians should engage in relatively simple exchanges with them. They preferably speak a simple and clear language and express themselves in short sentences.
7. Since Martha frequently loses control, it is important to provide her with means of control in the clinical situation. That is, she should best be given a degree of control regarding the clinician's actions that agrees with her need for control.
8. Martha reports chronic and serious emotional neglect and abuse as well as physical maltreatment. Inasmuch as the fainting spells concern positive dissociative symptoms that relate to an EP, these spells may (in part or in full) concern reenactments of traumatizing events that included loss of consciousness.
9. If the fainting spells are the manifestation of temporal lobe epilepsy, there will be no ANP-EP structure in the personality.
10. However, the existence of dissociative convulsions and stupor does not exclude the possible coexistence of temporal lobe epilepsy.

Enactive Assessment: Strategy

The hypotheses and the principles of enactive trauma therapy prompted the following preliminary general plan of action:

1. Attune to Martha's needs, desires, and concepts, verbally and nonverbally.
2. Attune to and utilize her language (i.e., the core terms she uses) and understanding (i.e., the core concepts and relationships between the various core conceptions she uses), including her body language.
3. Strive to establish therapeutic consensus regarding the crucial concerns and seek common goals for the conjoint work.
4. Utilize her disappointment in "the usual methods" by proposing and jointly enacting an uncommon diagnostic and therapeutic path. In this framework, do not start with questions, but rather present a new perspective.

5. Utilize her common experiences and common sense to introduce the notion that individuals can be influenced by inner actions and passions of which they are not the phenomenal agent (as one dissociative part, here ANP). Convey that inner actions can be purposeful and involve a kind of consciousness of their own (as another dissociative part, here as EP). Dreaming might serve as a powerful analogy.
6. Explicitly allow Martha control over the situation. In this framework, use permissive, egalitarian phrases.
7. Inasmuch as this division of her personality exists, allow her control as ANP and as EP in the awareness that ANP and EP will include different needs and desires, hence goals.
8. If she proves to have a dissociative disorder, generate hope that she can, at least in principle, mend her disorder. Since she cannot cure a possible temporal lobe epilepsy, having a dissociative disorder is the better alternative.
9. In order to increase Martha's power of action, encourage interactions between her ANP and EP, which are within their respective reach and which accord with their respective affective interests.
10. In order to strengthen their power of action, foster and encourage the ANP and EP to engage in slightly more advanced action tendencies, inasmuch as these are within their reach, and inasmuch as these actions and their goals appeal to them. The action tendencies involved should substitute for the less efficient actions and passions that characterize the presently demoralized ANP and the isolated EP (if they exist).

The First Session

The left column of Table 33.1 presents a transcript of the very first encounter with Martha. Occasional indications of Martha's nonverbal reactions compliment the verbatim. The right column displays my core second-person perspective phenomenal experiences and judgments as well as my third-person technical judgments. These two perspectives presuppose my first-person perspective and quasi-second-person perspective that, with some exceptions, are not detailed here. Jessica introduced us to each other, opened the session, and remained present during its full duration.

Table 33.1. The first session with Martha

Verbatim transcript with brief descriptions of nonverbal features in parentheses.	Nonexhaustive comments in terms of my various person perspectives. FPP: Occasional indications of my phenomenal experiences, that is, my first-person perspective. QSPP: Indications of my phenomenal judgment of my phenomenal experiences, that is, my quasi-second-person perspective. SPP: My phenomenal judgment of my relational experiences with Martha. TPP: My third-person perspective, that is, my technical ideas and judgments regarding Martha's actions and passions.

J: As we have discussed before, it is important for you, and for us all as well, to examine in greater depth why you sometimes faint. Using common methods, we have tried hard to detect the causes of your fainting. Sadly, our work has remained fruitless in this regard. For example, we have tried to explore whether there are signs or triggers that precede your attacks, but sadly we have been unable to make progress.	SPP: Martha does not know what is going to happen. TPP: The common methods have failed. The application of another "common" approach will thus be useless at best – and insignificant or harmful at worst. The situation calls for an "uncommon" diagnostic track.
M: (nods)	TPP: Martha agrees with Jessica's conclusions.
J: That is why we have asked Ellert to join us and to help us find clues as to what is causing your fainting spells. You have asked what will happen in the session, and I could not answer your question.	TPP: As Jessica frames it, the focus of the session should be on the causes of the spells. I must honor and meet that expectation.
M: (who has been listening attentively) No.	SPP: Martha is engaged and affectively interested.
J: And that is why Ellert can perhaps best respond to your question himself.	TPP: Martha and Jessica expect me to explain the nature of the work that we shall be doing.
M: (Looks at me, out of the corner of her eyes, with an apprehensive, tense, and skeptical smile)	SPP: Martha is tense and skeptical – which is fully understandable under the circumstances. She does not know what is going to happen, and she is uncertain whether the hour will bring more of the same old psychiatric stuff that she has learned to mistrust and despise. I can feel her tension and sympathize with it.
E: Thank you, Jessica, for your clear introduction. And I guess you put it well: You have used all common methods to explore what the fainting is about.	TPP: Utilization of the term "common methods" and recognition that the "common methods" have been useless in her case.
M: (nods)	SPP: Consensus in the sense that Martha and I agree on the statement. "All" communicates that there are no common methods left to be tried.
E: It is not uncommon that the common methods do not work.	SPP: Martha has always been the exception. Other kids and adults laughed at her attacks and teased her over this. But she does not want to be the exception. She wants recognition. The sentence communicates that the lack of treatment response is not her fault. Her condition demands uncommon methods. TPP: The fainting is probably not socially reinforced but has been punished. This suggests that the final cause of the fainting is not any 'attention' she might gain. But it might be, or might include, tension reduction.
M: (listens attentively; nods thoughtfully)	SPP: A feeling of some contact.
E: Some people may have reasons to keep things at a distance, or they cannot get in touch with the core of the matter when the common methods are used. This can apply to fainting as well.	
M: Hmm. (remains highly attentive)	SPP: Martha can accept the idea that she may avoid "things," and that the common methods do not allow phenomenal access to "the heart of the matter." At the least, she does not immediately reject the possibility.
E: This may occur in the case of fainting. I have seen it happen in other individuals in my practice. Individuals may really be unaware as to why certain things happen.	SPP: Another effort to communicate that Martha may not be completely "uncommon," because there are other individuals like her.

M: (shakes her head to indicate that she is unaware of the reasons of her fainting)	SPP: Martha agrees that she does not know the causes of the fainting. This consensus probably strengthens our beginning phenomenal relationship.
E: Professionals tend to ask a lot of questions in these instances, but that doesn't help you to find the answers when you remain unaware of the reasons (of the fainting). And then there may be even smarter colleagues who ask even smarter questions . . .	SPP: I have no desire to discredit colleagues, but want to continue strengthening my phenomenal relationship with Martha. I wish to tell her that I will not be merely posing the common questions. TPP: I do not pose questions at this point; I present ideas.
M: (grins)	SPP: Martha knows that I appreciate what she has been through.
E: . . . that won't help either. But this doesn't mean that the knowledge is unavailable.	SPP: I must come up with an alternative approach. Presentation of a new idea: The knowledge Martha is looking for may be available.
M: (lifts her head and then nods) Hmm.	SPP: Martha's head movement matches the shift in the discourse. She consents that the missing knowledge may be available after all.
E: To explain the issue, may I perhaps refer to dreams. Perhaps you could allow us to talk about dreams for a while . . .	SPP: No questions, I talk about something, about something that Martha did not expect. I do not ask an inquisitive question, but ask her permission in light of her need for control. Talking about dreaming is a move that Martha had not expected. It is an uncommon, new approach that can reassure her that today's approach indeed will be uncommon.
M: (nods)	SPP: She allows me to talk about dreaming.
E: . . . because it might help us to grasp how we might find the causes of the matter (i.e., the fainting fits) after all.	SPP: I do not talk about the fainting for my sake, but for our common purposes. "After all" suggests there is reason for hope after major disappointment and doubt.
M: (nods, but presents a skeptical look, withdraws the edges of her mouth)	SPP: Martha consents, while also displaying reservations.
E: One can ask a person, "Do you sometimes dream at night?" . . .	SPP: A question that Martha can easily answer reduces her uncomfortable tension. It may also distract her a bit from her skeptical feelings. "One can ask a person . . ." is a *truism*, that is, a statement that cannot be denied. A truism introduces a particular idea.
M: Yes. (nods with a relieving laugh)	TPP: Martha laughs. SPP: She feels more relaxed.
E: Of course, I have never met anyone who never dreams. We all dream at times.	SPP: I communicate that Martha is normal in this regard. She is "one of us." And she is a capable person, because she has an answer to the question. "We all dream at times" is another truism.
M: (nods again, laughs)	SPP: Mission accomplished.
E: And then I ask, who dreams? What would you say?	SPP: Another question that is not difficult to answer.
M: I do. (laughs, looks down and then up again)	SPP: Relieved. TPP: Looking down may indicate that she briefly examines herself, and that her "I" includes her whole body.
E: Does that mean that you dream a dream you had planned to dream?	SPP: The question is a bit surprising. It attracts attention and confirms this session is "different." It is not a "common approach." Moreover, the question normalizes Martha, because most normal individuals would deny that they plan their dreams.

M: No. (nonverbal expression of amazement and some confusion)	SPP: Martha seems surprised indeed. Her confusion prompts her to find a resolution.
E: Then who generates dreams? M: (expressed more confusion, and lifts her hands in the air, mouth withdrawn, smiles, then laughs)	SPP: The question increases her confusion. It intensifies her need to find a solution. Laughing reduces the tension a bit. TPP: Manageable confusion tends to activate the exploration action system. It generates a degree of systemic destabilization that opens a door to change.
E: Do you notice how funny this is? Like everyone you say that you dream, but if someone then asks who "creates" the dream, who is behind the kind of story that some dreams are, then you shrug your shoulders.	SPP: The situation is redefined as "funny," which may help to reduce tension more. Martha is "like everyone else." Most people cannot answer the question. TPP: The question is not "this *is* funny" but whether she *notices* that it is funny.
M: Yes. (more laughing)	SPP: More tension reduction. Consensus.
E: And some dreams are a bit story-like and not nonsensical at all.	TPP: Another truism: It is a fact that "some" dreams are a "bit story-like," and that some dreams have "a point." The truism can strengthen a common understanding. It also directs attention to "story" and "sensible." Dreams can be meaningful, and since her fainting spells have been described as dream-like phenomena, her fainting spell may be meaningful.
M: Yes.	SPP: Consensus.
E: And would you say dreams happen inside you? I experience the dream but I do not consciously construct it.	TPP: Truism. Division between the phenomenal, the experiential "I" and something "inside" that is not this "I," but that nonetheless generates a meaningful "story."
M: Yes, you're sleeping and you do not say something like, "Let's have a dream about something (snaps the fingers of her right hand in the air), let me think of a dream." No, it's not like that. (shakes her head) No.	TPP: Martha's phenomenal experience is that she does not generate the dream. SPP: Consensus that our phenomenal "I" is not the mother of the dream.
E: And still something does pop up in us, and it can be sensible, it can have a certain organization. Thus, there must be something inside us that "does" it (i.e., generate the dream).	TPP: A matter of logic. SPP: Communication of the idea that there must be "something inside" her that generates the dream – just as there may be "something inside" that generates the attacks.
M: Yes. (nods)	SPP: Consensus.
E: This common example, thus, gives us reason to think that things can happen inside that we cannot consciously control . . .	SPP: Martha's ignorance regarding the causes of the attacks is "common." She lacks "control," and that lack is common.
M: Yes.	SPP: Consensus.
E: . . . but we can notice that they're happening. This means that there must be something else inside us that sets a dream in motion, and that provides it its form.	SPP: The idea of "something else" that can have goals and that can act pops up again.
M: (nods)	SPP: Consensus.
E: OK. Now I wonder, could your fainting be a bit similar to dreaming?	SPP: Confirmation of the consensual world. TPP: Saying that fainting is "a bit" similar is easier to confirm than saying that fainting is "similar."
You cannot consciously want the dream or stop it . . .	TPP: Another truism.
M: Yes, I think so, yes (thoughtfully).	SPP: Consensus.

E: Something inside you might do it for some good reason.	SPP: "Might" is sufficiently careful. TPP: Organisms comprise final causes. SPP: The presentation of "a good reason" for her debilitating attacks is a surprising move. It raises the question what that "good reason" might be. TPP: The statement is a prompt to activate the exploration action system and its implied attractor: finding an answer to a sensible question. It might also destabilize the fixed belief that the attacks are a mere disturbance.
M: (turns her eyes to the left) Yes, it blocks certain things, I think. As with dreaming, the fainting just happens to me, it simply occurs. Perhaps, consciously or unconsciously (makes quotation marks with her hands in the air) . . . let me put it like this . . . when it comes too close (raises her hands suggesting they carry something from her lap upward, something emotional) . . . that it then shuts something off. Yes, that's what I think.	SPP: Examines her 'inner world.' She links dreaming and fainting, and confirms that they "simply occur." The movement from the height of her lap to the height of her head matches her words that something can "come up." The snapping of the fingers suggests that the "blocking" happens in a split-second. TPP: Her words match the idea of mental avoidance of something threatening inside. It is remarkable that Martha has the ability to generate this psychodynamic idea so quickly. Her action suggests she may be able to profit from psychotherapy after all. SPP: Martha can feel comfortable that she managed to link dreaming and fainting.
E: It can be like that . . .	SPP: Consensus regarding the possibility.
M: (does not seem to listen to my last words; looks at Jessica and says:) I don't know, I'm just saying something. (wipes her hands in the air)	SPP: Voices a reservation. TPP: Why? Did she move ahead too soon, do her words trigger the emotionality inside that can pop up beyond her control?
E: That may be; it sounds like a sensible thought. I have met people who fainted when things started to pop up in them that scared them. Before they could really become consciously aware of something that popped up, they lost consciousness.	SPP: I guess Martha can use some confirmation. I again try to "normalize" her by comparing her case to that of others who were very much like her. TPP: My words are fact based.
M: (nods)	SPP: Consensus.
E: If we would assume that your fainting does not relate to mental causes, that is, that it does not or at least not solely concerns epilepsy, then it would be governed by mental causes. And mental causation is common. Dreaming is also a mental thing.	TPP: Continued linking of dreaming and fainting, now regarding the theme of "mental causation." SPP: Continued normalization, strengthening of the communication that Martha is not some "nutty outlier."
M: Yes. (nods, face serious, focused)	SPP: Consensus, Martha seems to feel a bit reassured.
E: We might add that your fainting is particularly powerful. Your dreams can be pretty powerful, and this fainting also controls you.	TPP: Constructions such as "we might add" are *permissive*. We are not forced to add something, we are free. In SPP the communication is: Your fainting is powerful. "Something inside" can be very powerful, and a lot of power may be needed to control a lot of emotionality.
M: (nods repeatedly)	SPP: A firm consensus.
E: I heard the attacks started when you were 2 years old. M: Yes. (firmly) E: Thus it is something very powerful.	TPP: Statement of a fact. Its implication is that, from her second year of life on, there was a lot of emotionality "inside." SPP: This fact will probably be threatening to Martha.
M: Yes.	SPP: Consensus.

E: What I will be asking is far less powerful.	TPP: It is a fact. SPP: The statement invites a relief: We will not address extreme emotionality in this session.
M: (skeptical look)	SPP: Confusion. Where is this leading, what do you mean?
E: And what do I mean by that? When you have an attack, you drop to the floor.	SPP: Resolution of the tension provided.
M: Yes.	SPP: Consensus.
E: Thus, what may possibly be causing the attacks can control your whole body.	TPP: A fact. SPP: It is powerful.
M: Yes.	SPP: Consensus.
E: And when I say that I will be asking far less, I am only asking for little signals from fingers or the thumb of your left or right hand . . .	SPP: Some relief: Only "little" movements, and only movements of fingers or thumbs. However, why would they move at all? I need to explain this.
M: (skeptical look)	SPP: What are you talking about? Where is this leading? TPP: Confusion invites self-reorganization.
E: . . . because the curious thing is that whatever it is that can generate a fainting spell can listen, it can be conscious.	TPP: A fact. SPP: "Something inside" that is "not-I" can be conscious, that's weird . . .
M: (continues to look skeptical)	SPP: Hence the look.
E: This may initially sound a bit strange, but you might want to return to the dreaming.	SPP: I attune to her skepticism by saying "it may sound strange," not terribly strange but "a bit strange," and only "initially." TPP: The word "initially" may activate the exploration action system; it raises the question about what follows the initial phase?
It takes consciousness to generate a dream . . .	TPP: Statement of a fact. SPP: "Something inside" can be conscious even if you do not know this "something."
M: (looks very surprised)	SPP: Searches her mind.
E: . . . we cannot dream without some form of consciousness.	SPP: Reiteration of the foregoing, with a slight modification: "some form of consciousness."
M: I think so, yes.	SPP: Prudent consensus.
E: If the dream were unconscious, we would not be aware of it.	TPP: Truism, or actually a *tautology*. SPP: Creation of a consensual understanding.
M: No, we wouldn't.	SPP: Acceptance of the idea.
E: So the idea is that you may possess something that has presumably given you the attacks for one or more very good reasons that we do not understand – *yet* – and that has decided not to stop causing these attacks – *yet.*	SPP: A summary of the foregoing, and the suggestion, through the "yet," that the fainting can be understood and that it can be overcome. TPP: Adding the word "yet" gives an *implicit suggestion* that it will become understood and overcome.
M: No. (focused; "no" confirms that the attacks have not stopped so far)	SPP: Consensus.
E: Now I would like to try to talk to that something inside – if it is there at all – not in the form of complete attacks, but in the form of finger signals.	TPP: The idea that the "something inside" can be conscious was needed to conclude that "I can talk to it," and that "if I can talk to it, so can you."
M: (so far she had been sitting with crossed legs. Now she puts both feet on the floor, places her hands on her legs, and gives a tense smile.)	SPP: Martha communicates she is ready to work with finger signals, although she does not know what these are about. She also shows how stressed she feels.

E: Yes, you can sit like that. And what I will be addressing is not your "I," but something inside . . .	TPP: These sentences point out that Martha's phenomenal self is supposed to be passive. She should not do anything. If the whole Martha encompasses another self-conscious center of action, it is this center of action that I invite to respond to the questions.
M: OK . . . (uncertain expression of her face)	SPP: It seems Martha would rather stay in control.
E: . . . and if it exists at all, then I would like it to raise a finger or thumb of the left or the right hand.	TPP: Common instructions regarding *ideomotor finger signals.*
M: (nods, clearly tense)	SPP: She continues to be stressed.
E: Let me first explain how we could do it. One finger or thumb can be used for "Yes," another for "No," and still another for "Stop." And you do not control the movements. All you do is let your hands be. Sort of giving your hands "out of your hands" (the Dutch phrase "handen uit handen geven" stands for giving up control)	TPP: Continued explanations. TPP: Play on the word "hands" to communicate that Martha is invited to let her hands be.
M: OK. (looks even tenser, directs her eyes at Jessica, smiles, and takes a deep breath while returning her gaze to me)	SPP: Martha's tension rises, she looks for Jessica's support. Jessica gives her a friendly smile.
E: You are free to close your eyes or keep them open, whatever you wish. You can tell us what happens, but you can also remain silent.	SPP: There are behaviors Martha *can* control. This freedom seems to reduce her tension a bit. TPP: Whatever she chooses to do, she is cooperating.
M: (nods several times)	
E: Was my explanation sufficiently clear?	SPP: Martha can decide if my explanations were adequate.
M: Yes.	
E: You grasped the ideas, then?	SPP: Martha is a competent person.
M: Yes. Yes.	SPP: She is competent.
E: Excellent.	SPP: Ratification.
M: I find it very scary, though.	SPP: She can put her feelings in words. She is competent but scared.
E: If I were in your chair, I would also have felt quite scared.	SPP: Martha's tension is a common reaction. She and I are both individuals who can be scared under particular circumstances.
M: OK. (relieved)	
E: On the other hand, you might tell yourself, "So far I only have my attacks, and this sounds like something new that could propel me forward."	SPP: I remind her of our *common purpose* and indicate that this uncommon work can bring forth a positive change.
M: Yeah, that's my idea.	SPP: It is important that the work suit "her" idea. TPP: The wording "my idea" indicates personification of the therapeutic venture.
E: And I won't be addressing difficult things inasmuch as the attacks pertain to difficult things.	SPP: This remark may reduce her tension more. TPP: It is generally possible and helpful to balance the assignments during enactive trauma therapy and the traumatized individual's power of action.
M: (nods)	SPP: The remark is welcome.

E: That can be done later, and only if that's what you want.	SPP: The reassurance is: "You will stay in control as much as possible. You make the important decisions when it comes to the difficult themes."
M: OK (nods)	SPP: Martha feels reassured.
E: Let's first see if we can contact what might be giving you the attacks – if it exists at all, for as I presume very good reasons.	SPP: A repetition of phrases and ideas that Martha is already familiar with, and that may give her some hold.
M: Hmm. (nods)	
E: So you can now "give your hands out of your hands" . . .	SPP: Another phrase and idea she already knows. "You can" indicates that she is free to accept or decline the invitation.
M: OK (with another tense smile)	SPP: Same response: Willing but tense.
E: . . . and let us address, sort of together, something inside.	SPP: You are not alone. We'll be doing the work "sort of" together.
M: (laughs) I think I should close my eyes!	TPP: There is no point in sorting out why she feels this need.
E: Feel free to do whatever you wish.	SPP: It is important to reconfirm Martha's freedom.
M: OK. (closes her eyes)	SPP: Consents.
E: Do what makes you feel good, that's fine.	SPP: Reiteration of her freedom. The remark is so general, that she can feel free to do anything she needs and desires. TPP: Her eye closure is defined as a means of accommodation.
M: OK.	SPP: The remark seems welcome.
E: And if you now "give your hands out of your hands," then we can pose that question together: If there is something inside . . . that for good reasons . . . gives the attacks . . . then we ask that something to lift a finger or a thumb to signal it's there. That means, do not give a full attack, but just a tiny bit of it.	TPP: Utilization of something that is already present: her attacks, her experience of a profound and recurrent loss of control. SPP: "A tiny bit of an attack" suggests that the work will not lead to a disaster.
M: (the right index and middle finger lift)	TPP: An ultra fast response. It is interesting that whatever it is about Martha that responded demonstrated freedom: Not one digit moved, but two. Would Martha have responded to my clearly suggestive remarks, or would it be different? Recall that the sociocognitive model of complex dissociation does not explain the phenomenon (see ToT Volume II, Chapter 15). A new neurobiological article involving a comparison of the sociocognitive model of DID and the trauma perspective on DID extends previous findings that the sociocognitive model of complex dissociation does not explain the involved biopsychosocial phenomena (see ToT Volume II). Two new studies point in the same direction (Reinders et al., 2016; Vissia et al., 2016). SPP: Whatever it is that responded to my invitation, it communicates a degree of systemic autonomy.
E: You can remain seated the way you're seated. So tell me, what was that movement like for you?	SPP: Examination of and phenomenal interest in Martha's FPP and QSPP.
M: Not nice. (tense grin)	SPP: Tension. TPP: Why would it be "not nice" for her? It was only two fingers moving.

E: That felt "not nice." What about it was "not nice" for you?	SPP: Acceptance and utilization of Martha's phrase "not nice."
M: It means one does not control one's own body. (speaks fast)	SPP: Martha communicates a felt loss of control of her body. TPP: She formulates "one" and "one's body," rather than "I" and "my body." These formulations may indicate a lack personification. It seems that Martha authentically felt a loss of control that implies a loss of personification. Her phenomenal concept of self "I" became abstract and general ("one"). In her QSPP, "my body" became "one's body."
E: I get what you're saying. Perhaps you can see it this way: "There seems to be something inside me that has things to tell me, and that wants to help me . . . And that help will eventually give me more control than I have ever had before . . ."	SPP: Her gains can perhaps balance her loss of control.
But I also understand that it's not nice when things happen that you did not consciously plan . . .	SPP: Reconfirmation that I accept and understand that her experience was "not nice."
. . . But then again remind yourself that we do not consciously plan our dreams either . . . and we survive that. Let's return to that "something inside" and ask it, "If the signal we noticed means 'Yes,' then please repeat it."	SPP: I basically say: You can deal with this loss of control, and: It is not completely uncommon or new to you. TPP: It is good practice to ask for a confirmation of the finger signals. After all, the movements may have been coincidental even if they did not impress as coincidental.
M: (the right index and middle finger lift again).	TPP: Again, a *fast* reaction. SPP: It suggests a particular eagerness to communicate.
E: Fine, I gather there is something inside Martha that can hear me and that can respond. I now want to ask it to give a signal for "No," so that I know . . .	
M: (Martha's left thumb rises)	SPP: Another quick response.
E: . . . when that something inside that gives the attacks says "No." Please repeat it.	
M: (Martha's left thumb rises again)	SPP: And once again. Why this eagerness? Is there "something inside" Martha that is eager to communicate? TPP: 33 years of waiting to be heard generates a potent urge.
E: That's very fast and clear, excellent.	SPP: Acceptance and confirmation of the competency of what responds.
And because it is important that we can also say "Stop," I now ask the something inside that gives the attacks to give us a signal for "Stop."	TPP: Starting a sentence with "and" can help to generate a flow of ideas and reactions. SPP: "Stop" provides control of the situation. TPP: The provision of a stop signal is important for that reason, particularly when working with traumatized individuals. Traumatization is a major lack of control. Therapy is geared toward restoring their sense of control.
M: (almost instantly, the left index and middle finger lift)	SPP: More eagerness.
E: All right, I will never overlook your "Stop" signal. Please repeat it.	SPP: Communication that "stop" is very important, and that I know and respect that.

M: (quick response)	
E: Fine, that's very clear . . . Thank you very much for talking to me.	SPP: The finger signals are depicted as "talking."
Would you allow me to pose a couple of questions that do not address contents but that, so to speak, address things around it?	SPP: Confirmation of my promise: You can be in charge. I have to ask for permission. SPP: Consistent with my previous words, I offer some protection: We will not talk about "contents" straight away because they might pertain to difficult issues.
M: (yes signal)	
E: Excellent. I presume there is a good reason for the attacks, and that Martha does not know this reason so far. Are these presumptions correct?	
M: (yes signal)	SPP: Confirmation of final cause of the attacks.
E: Martha told me the attacks started when she was 2 years old. This suggests you're very powerful. You do not wane. You persevere. Does this mean that there is something you have to tell Martha?	SPP: Praise for who is responding. My praise is authentic, and it may help to set up a good working relationship.
M: (yes signal)	
E: And have you experienced so far that Martha does not understand what you want to tell her?	SPP: "So far" indirectly points to the possibility that Martha can learn to understand.
M: (yes signal)	TPP: She needs help in this regard.
E: Hm. Then you must feel a bit miserable at times.	SPP: Empathy with her continuing failure to reach Martha.
M: (yes signal)	
E: Yes. Are you glad I'm talking to you?	
M: (yes signal)	SPP: Strengthening of the working relationship.
E: OK. I have the impression that Martha is scared of you.	SPP: Martha may hear that I use her word "scared."
M: (yes signal)	TPP: Whoever is responding knows Martha and knows how she feels.
E: Aha. And can you grasp that she is scared of you?	
M: (yes signal)	
E: Aha. Does it mean that the reasons for the attacks are, so to speak, "not nice"?	SPP: Utilization of "not nice."
M: (yes signal)	
E: Since you continue giving the attacks, I would suspect that, even though it's not nice, that it is important to know what they are about.	SPP: Reconfirmation of the final cause.
M: (yes signal)	
E: You may not know any different solution.	SPP: Sympathy for her limitations.
M: (yes signal)	
E: Could it be that you tell or show Martha a little bit (about the reasons for the attacks) . . .	TPP: Martha may have communicated in the first phase of the session that she faints when something pops up that scares her. I pick up on this idea and start to examine it.
M: (yes signal)	

E: . . . and that, as you do that, Martha mentally leaves?	SPP: Does Martha ignore you?
M: (yes signal)	
E: So that it what Martha is good at, she knows how to run.	SPP: Martha may be listening and she deserves respect, understanding, and praise as well. TPP: It is crucial that clinicians never speak badly of dissociative parts, whether they are activated or deactivated.
M: (yes signal)	
E: And that disturbs you because there's something you have to tell her.	
M: (yes signal)	
E: Yes . . . Could it be that you actually want to tell her everything at once?	TPP: Martha may be leaving because the "something inside" tends to engage in a complete reenactment of traumatizing events.
M: (yes signal)	
E: You try to tell it all at once.	
M: (yes signal)	
E: Could you imagine that that can be too much for Martha?	
M: (no signal)	TPP: One may suspect that Martha is responding to the suggestive quality of at least some of my remarks or questions. Fine. But then how about this "no signal?" It does not fit this explanation at all. SPP: The "something inside" has no sympathy for Martha's mental avoidance and fear.
E: You think she must bear it?	
M: (yes signal)	
E: Do you feel that Martha is more scared than necessary?	
M: (no signal)	
E: Not that. You say, it's really not nice, but Martha has to know.	SPP: The "something inside" communicates her understanding that "what she has to tell Martha" is really "not nice."
M: (yes signal)	
E: Fine, excellent. And that's why you do not leave her alone.	SPP: The "something inside" had no choice: There are things she has to tell Martha, and she only has one tool.
M: (yes signal)	
E: Could I ask if you have a certain sense of age?	SPP: Another polite invitation.
M: (yes signal)	

E: I can ask that. Do you have Martha's age? M: (no signal) E: No. Do you feel older than Martha? M: (no signal) E: No. Do you feel younger than Martha? M: (yes signal) E: Yes. Do you feel a little younger? M: (no signal) E: No. Do you feel like a young adult? M: (no signal) E: Do you feel like an adolescent? M: (no signal) E: Do you perhaps feel like a schoolchild? M: (no signal) E: No. Do you feel like a kindergarten child? M: (no signal) E: Do you feel like a very young child?	SPP: I specify what she confirmed. TPP: Any question implies a suggestion. For example, "Do you feel sad" suggests that the individual may be sad. Any interview or discussion includes suggestive elements. One way to avoid undue suggestion is to "ask in the wrong direction." Thus, here I ask if the "something inside" feels as old as Martha, or even older, although it would be reasonable to assume that she will feel (much) younger given the early onset of the traumatization.
M: (yes signal) E: You feel very young. The attacks started when Martha's body was 2 years old. Do you feel that young perhaps? M: (yes signal)	TPP: It is obvious that, while the inner child may phenomenally feel 2 years of age, she cannot actually 'be' that young. My questions are far too complex for a literal 2-year-old. Apart from this, in later sessions it would appear that the involved dissociative part covered an age range from 2 years to 16 years. Her phenomenal age shifted with the timing of the various traumatizing events she had endured and in which she was still stuck.
E: Aha, so you're feeling still very young … And as to the grounds for the attack, I have understood they are about things that are not nice?	TPP: Exploration of the nature of the traumatizing events. SPP: Utilization of "not nice."
M: (yes signal)	
E: OK. Does something that is "not nice" relate to things in nature, such as thunder and lightning, or to some other thing in nature that can be really scary?	TPP: Again, I make sure that the suggestions "go the wrong way." I address things of nature, traumatization by strangers, etc.
M: (no signal)	
E: Some scary things relate to people. Do the attacks relate to people? M: (yes signal) E: Do they relate to people you do not know well? M: (no signal)	TPP: From the class of nature to the category of people.
E: Do they relate to people you know a bit? M: (no signal) E: Do they relate to people you know well? M: (yes signal) E: Are these persons who do not belong to the family? M: (no signal) E: Do they belong to the family? M: (yes signal)	TPP: From strangers to acquaintances, to family members.

E: Old persons, a grandma or grandpa? M: (no signal) E: They are younger. M: (yes signal) E: Other children in the family? M: (no signal) E: Younger adults like an aunt or uncle? M: (no signal) E: It is about your parents? M: (yes signal) E: About your mother? M: (yes signal) E: Also about your father? M: (yes signal) E: It's about father and mother?	TPP: From elderly family members to children in the family, to one parent, to both parents.
M: (yes signal) E: And is there something father and mother have not done that they should have done? M: (yes signal)	TPP: Martha had reported enduring emotional neglect. SPP: I use a very general description to honor the arrangement that we would not address difficult things in a direct fashion (in this first encounter).
E: Is it also about things they did that they should not have done? M: (yes signal)	SPP: Same comment as immediately above: I give a very general description. TPP: Martha had also reported emotional abuse and physical maltreatment.
M: (yes signal) E: Did they fail to take proper care of a little girl? M: (yes signal)	SPP: I communicate that little girls require and deserve "proper care."
E: The things they should not have done – are these the things parents should not do to a little child? M: (yes signal)	
E: And are these the things Martha does not wish to remember? M: (yes signal)	TPP: I link the traumatic experiences and Martha's motivated mental avoidance of these memories. Martha ignores painful realities.
E: But you say she must know them after all. M: (yes signal) E: Did Martha faint when the parents did things they should not have done? M: (yes signal) E: Did she instantly faint? M: (no signal)	SPP: Reconfirmation of the final cause.
E: First something bad happened, and then she fainted? M: (yes signal)	TPP: I link the maltreatment and the attacks.
E: And was the fainting a way of not knowing, not feeling?	TPP: I link the traumatic events, the seizures, and the final cause of Martha's evasion.
M: (yes signal)	SPP: Consensus.
E: OK, fine, thank you very much for your cooperation so far . . .	SPP: Continuation of a respectful approach.

Could you think of other ways of talking to Martha? Could you imagine a different way of talking to her, so that you can tell her, "Martha, there is something I have to tell you, something you should know?" Could you imagine different ways of talking to her? M: (no signal)	TPP: The "little girl" has a poor sense of control, because she does not reach Martha. She could use more power of action.
E: OK, so fainting is the only thing you know. M: (yes signal)	TPP: She has only one tool.
E: Hmm. If there were different ways of talking to Martha, would you be interested?	SPP: Probing for an interest in extending her power of action.
M: (yes signal)	SPP: She is motivated to extend her action repertoire.
E: I notice you can really work well with the fingers and thumbs. Could you imagine you turn the right hand into a fist? If so, you may make a fist rather than faint to show your presence. M: (fingers start to move) E: Very well, make a fist.	TPP: Utilization of existing tools. The step from moving digits upward to moving them 'inward' so that a fist is formed is not large and may be quite feasible.
M: (makes a fist)	SPP: Mission accomplished.
E: Fine. Now, Martha, please open your eyes. (opens her eyes, looks a bit drowsy) Hi, there you are ... excellent ... take a look at your right hand if you would ... and did you notice that your hand became a fist?	TPP: Martha is about to experience that there is a "little girl" who controls a part of her body in a new way. SPP: Inviting Martha to come forward.
M: (shakes her head)	TPP: It seems Martha had not coupled the right hand/fist to the "something inside" that is actually controlling the hand movements.
E: OK, could you please open your hand, so that it will be like the left?	SPP: The fixed fist demonstrates for Martha that the "little girl" is active and powerful at the present moment.
M: (stretches her left hand, and moves it about, looks at this hand) It doesn't work.	TPP: Her phrase "it does not work" sounds as impersonal as "one's body." The phrase may convey a degree of depersonalization.
E: It doesn't work. Stay calm, you're doing great.	SPP: I accept and confirm her formulation. To balance her failure to open the fist, I commend her for "doing great."
I now invite that "something inside" that previously used fainting to release the right hand. M: (releases the fist)	TPP: Martha and the "little girl" are simultaneously active. We have described this phenomenon as parallel dissociation (Van der Hart et al., 2006). Martha notices that the "little girl" controls her right hand, and that she can respond to requests. SPP: These phenomena may create the idea that there is a reason for her fainting, and that the "little girl" influences the attacks. Martha can also develop the idea that the "little girl" is endowed with consciousness, and that she includes a will. The bottom line of what she can learn is that therapy may work.
E: Very well, fantastic, you're doing so well. Did you notice you are able to show your presence in a new way? M: (yes signal)	SPP: I address the "little girl" again, and invite her to celebrate her new action.
E: Yes. Isn't it ... eh ... exciting to experience that you can do more than you thought you could? M: (yes signal)	SPP: Invitation to engage in a little act of triumph.

E: Could I arrange with you that you will use your fist in the days to come? You can use it in addition to fainting, because Martha needs to be haunted a bit, right? M: (yes signal)	SPP: Extension of our cooperation. The statement that "Martha needs to be haunted a bit" acknowledges that the "little girl" is angry with Martha. The sentence intentionally ends with "right." Little terms like "right" communicate that the addressed individual has a choice. Thus, the "little girl" can feel that she could have said "no." It is easier for us to say "yes" when we feel we could have said "no."
E: Yes. I do not want you to give up the fainting.	SPP: You stay in control. TPP: Do not steal someone's tool, particularly if that tool is the individual's *only* tool.*
I am prepared to help you if you want me to do that.	TPP: By this time, I had decided that Martha's seizures are most likely dissociative, and that she meets the criteria for ICD-10 Dissociative Disorder of Movement and Sensation, more specifically, Dissociative Convulsions. This assessment implies a need and possibility for enactive trauma therapy.
Would you want my help . . . M: (yes signal)	SPP: Hence, my offer.
E: . . . to help you and Martha to overcome the problem. Martha must know there is a problem she cannot solve on her own. M: (yes signal expressing that she agrees with the statement)	SPP: Martha is not stupid or weak, because "she cannot solve the problem on her own."
E: And you impress me so much, you hardly know me, and you already dare to speak to me so clearly. That's really great. You can use your fist, not all the time, but some of the time. And when you use the fist, you make sure that	SPP: Authentic statement based on my FPP experience in the situation, and on the SPP-involved experiences during the unfolding and continuing session.
Martha cannot open her hand, just as you did today. The fist will keep the matter in your hands. You can use your fist to ensure that Martha does not keep running from you and from the things you have to tell her, from the things that need to be resolved, and that we will be working on together.	SPP: Reconfirmation of her increased power of action, and of the fact that therapy is a joint venture.
M: (yes signal)	SPP: Consensus.
E: Excellent. Practice your fist once more so that you are really sure you can do it . . . Imagine once more, you feel: I want to reach Martha, I do not want to be ignored, I show my fist.	TPP: It is important that new actions be practiced more than once. The first time individuals succeed at a new action, they may think the result was unique or coincidental. When they succeed twice, however, they may start believing they can do it. The third time they achieve their aim, they know they have mastered the challenge.

* A scientist was exploring a remote area. After two days, he reached a curious construction. The planks it contained were not neatly sawn, but splintered at their ends. A carpenter was hammering another plank in two pieces. The good man looked exhausted. "You're building a strange house. Are you silly? Why don't you use a saw?" The laborer gave the scientist an annoyed look. "What do you think? That I'm stupid or a mental case? How would *you* build your home, you clever man, if all you possessed is a hammer?"

M: (her head drops to the left, Martha seems to faint, she lies passively in the chair) E: You can show yourself in the fist. You can make her faint. I ask you to refrain from doing that now because it's the fist that needs practicing. I feel you can do that. M: (no reactions)	TPP: Two hypotheses regarding the present fainting are that the "little girl" tests her "old" approach, perhaps because she desires to check if it still works. The other hypothesis is that not this "little girl" but Martha faints now that she knows the new action of the "little girl." Martha may wish to beat this "little girl's" power by fainting before the confrontational fist is formed. Posthoc technical judgment in TPP: The text shows I opted for the first hypothesis. But I had bet on the wrong horse, or so it seems.
E: 2-year-old, please give me a yes signal so that I know you're there. M: (no responses)	FPP, QSPP: Realizing that Martha could remain in this organismic state for a long time, I start to feel uneasy. I must do something to end the fainting, but what? I decided I should first ask whether the "little girl" was still active, although I was aware that a lack of responsiveness could mean several things: The "little girl" and/or the Martha I knew might be inactive.
E: 2-year-old, it seems to me you're using the fainting. That's not forbidden, and you know fainting works . . .	Posthoc technical judgment in TPP: It was perhaps not wrong to make this remark – the wordings were cautious ("it seems to me . . .") – but still I held what I now started to call the "2-year-old" to be responsible for the fainting. But this would not be justified inasmuch as it was the Martha I knew who had "disappeared in fainting."
M: (no responses)	
E: Let time pass by quickly, and go to the concluding phase of the fainting . . .	TPP: I decide to suggest *time acceleration* and am aware the suggestion may fail.
M: (erects her head, puts it on her left shoulder again) E: . . . and then you use your fist . . .	FPP: I am relieved that the idea works.
M: (suddenly makes a fist) E: . . . great, very well done, practice that fist. And you know, that fist is going to draw a whole lot of attention – you can release it now – you know why? M: (no signal) E: Martha is accustomed to the fainting, although she finds it troublesome. But your fist is new and will therefore really be noticed. When you use your fist, Martha will think, "Ah, there is the 2-year-old again." You now get what I mean? M: (yes signal)	Posthoc contemplation in TPP: I could and perhaps should have understood that this quick response indicated that not the "little girl," but the Martha I knew had initiated the fainting spell. What I said was not totally off, but it would have been better to first check *who* had done *what* and *why*. Future work with "the whole Martha" would clarify that both the "little girl" and the "adult Martha" could initiate the fainting attacks.
E: All right. Then use the fist once more. You do not need to practice the fainting anymore, you can already do that very well. Martha, can you please open your eyes for a while? Join us please, I think you can do that. M: (lifts her head from her left shoulder, shakes it a bit, holds her head with her left hand)	Posthoc technical consideration in TPP: Again, inasmuch as the Martha I knew was the cause of the fainting, my correction of the "2-year-old" was a mistake.
E: Is it a bit like waking up?	SPP: Attunement.
M: Yes. E: Fine. And, Martha, please look at your right hand. What does it mean that your right hand has become a fist?	SPP: Consensus.

M: (looks at her right fist). I . . . want it . . . to be like this one (the left hand that she can move freely).	TPP: Martha evades the point of the fist. She wants an easy way out.
E: Shall I tell you? And continue breathing. Can you try to open your right fist?	SPP: I offer support and some assistance.
M: It doesn't work. I want it to be just like the left one (moves the left hand about, looks at the left hand, then to the right hand).	TPP: More evidence that Martha mentally avoids the "2-year-old" and everything this dissociative part of her encompasses.
E: You know why it is like that? M: (shakes her head)	TPP: I direct her attention to the 2-year-old" and her power.
E: You may think, "What a strange doctor, he gives me more symptoms!" M: (laughs)	SPP: A little *playfulness* can alleviate tension. TPP: activation of the action system of play strengthens social bonds, hence our evolving working relationship. SPP: We're enjoying the situation together.
E: Did you track what has happened, the signals in your fingers and all? M: Yes. E: What did you experience? M: . . . eh, . . . yes . . . eh . . . E: What is it about? M: My feelings . . . eh . . . and the fainting . . . a strange experience . . . E: Yes, it is very new, right?	SPP and TPP: Examination of Martha's phenomenal experiences regarding the actions of the "2-year-old" is important. Was she present as the finger signals proceeded? If so, what was it like for her, and what do they mean to her?
M: Yes.	TPP: I could have explored "strange experience" more instead of saying it was a new experience. However, she accepts my reformulation ("strange" → "new").
E: I think you're doing great. What I have understood, and what Jessica has also understood, I guess . . . Jessica: (nods)	TPP: "Understood" implies a focus on cognition rather than on affects.
E: . . . is that you include a part that says, "I've got awful things to tell, awful things have happened, and Martha is scared, she runs away. But I must still tell her what happened."	My phenomenal and technical judgments are that the time has come to formulate several facts about the "2-year-old" and to describe her as a "part."
M: Yes . . .	SPP: Martha accepts my words.
E: Do you know what these things pertain to?	SPP and TPP: It is important that Martha provide her own ideas as much as possible.
M: (her eyes get wet) It is a search for everything that has happened.	TPP: Martha opens up. SPP: Her sorrow shows.
E: What happened when you were 2 years old? (softer voice) M: The maltreatment . . . (stares) E: And do you know who maltreated you? M: My parents. E: That's what 'the fingers' are also saying. I asked whether your parents did not do what they should have done, and whether they did things they should not have done. And the fingers said "Yes."	FPP: I feel along with her, but from the SPP and TPP it seems important that I withhold my sympathy, empathy, and compassion for a while: These affective expressions might interrupt her openness. However, my compassionate tone of voice expresses that I feel along with her during the present and the following sequences.
It seems to me that a part of you has remained stuck in these experiences. I presume she is stuck in these experiences. M: (nods) Yes . . .	TPP: The first time I use the term "part of you." As to timing, the concept of dissociative part is introduced by the time that the existence of this part – a fragile EP – has become undeniably clear.

E: Just like being troubled by recurrent painful dreams, the girl will remain stuck in the painful experiences until you do something about them. And this fainting will return until you meet her to share her terrible experiences. M: (listens attentively)	SPP: I tell Martha the girl will play a major role in her recovery. Martha seems to understand and accept that.
E: The 2-year-old continues to wait until you are ready to stop running away from her.	TPP: Clear directions.
Jessica and I appreciate that you have reasons to run. No one walks happily into a dentist's office. But there are things we can only resolve by owning up to them.	SPP: Sympathy for Martha.
M: (nods) Yes (softly).	SPP: Painful consensus.
E: When very painful things happen to us, a part of us may remain behind. Psychologists use a big word to describe it: a "dissociative part." "Dissociation" means: not incorporated in us. M: (weeps and excuses herself for her tears) ... Please excuse me ... (wipes her tears with her left hand, the right hand is still a fist)	TPP: Decision to offer some explanations that Martha can use. I apply some terms (e.g., "dissociation") she had heard before. SPP: I speak sensitively to stay in affective touch with her. The *psychoeducation* serves to keep Martha focused on the work with the 2-year-old and her painful past.
E: I trust you have every reason to weep. I also feel you have reasons for a little hope. As I also told the 2-year-old, "It is fantastic, you hardly know me, and you still dare to really talk to me."	SPP: I accept her sorrow, and balance her sadness with hope and praise.
It may be the very first time that this part of you has directly talked with anyone. And she can talk, not only through fainting, but also in terms of clear signals. The signals were very clear. So, you could also say, there is reason for hope.	SPP: If I can talk to her, so can you.
M: (as I spoke, Martha was paying close attention while crying softly, tears rolling down her cheeks that she wiped with her left).	SPP: Her emotions felt most sincere. FPP: I felt moved.
E: And there is another reason for hope. Do you know what I have in mind? M: (grins a bit) ... No ...	SPP: The inability to open her fist is utilized as a ground for hope. TPP: Raising a question can generate interest and a focus.

E: Please take a look at your right hand. What does it mean? M: (laughs, moves her left hand about) This one is free! I want . . . eh, . . .	TPP: Enactive trauma therapy, as ever, concerns *making meaning*. TPP: Martha does not seem to know what it means. In SPP, however, I feel she does know what it means, but that she, in her relationship to the 2-year-old, is not thrilled to know it. TPP: Martha tries to avoid entering a new mode of longing and striving. She probably regards the EP as harmful and thus strives to ignore her, perhaps half consciously. She perceived and conceived of the EP as a repeller. However, change involves an extension of her mode space. Overall, therapy must help her to develop a new mode of trajectory. Becoming engaged with the EP and 'her history' and mental contents would better become a systemic attractor (see Chapter 26). This takes the realization that cooperating with the EP serves her better interests, i.e., the healing of Martha as a whole organism-environment system. SPP: I thus felt the need to focus her attention on the young, dissociative part of her to demonstrate that she does not seem to have epilepsy, but a dissociative disorder. This self-reorganization is encouraged whenever my actions destabilize ANP's common mode trajectory regarding the EP and her traumatic memories.
E: I told the 2-year-old, you can show yourself in that hand, and make sure that Martha cannot open her hand, thus showing: "Here I am." And you know what that means?	SPP: Martha's wish to overcome the fainting feels totally authentic. TPP: Inviting the EP to continue clenching her fist perturbs the ANP's system.
M: (shakes her head)	TPP: Martha continues her phobic avoidance of the fragile EP. Creation of some *suspense* to focus Martha's attention.
E: . . . that you do not seem to have epilepsy.	TPP: The existence of the EP and her actions and passions includes most attractive features. SPP: That must feel good.
M: (nods, some tears)	
E: You can resolve the problem. You do not need to faint for the rest of your life. M: I would like that so much. (looks me in the eye, and nods and nods, and then weeps a bit more) E: Can you now open your hand?	The crying moves me in SPP. In TPP, I interpret the crying as a perturbation of Martha's former actions. "Perturbation" here means a disturbance or deviation of a system, state of equilibrium, course, arrangement, motion, process, or action from its regular or normal state or path, caused by an outside influence (cf.www.merriam-webster.com). Being perturbed in this way, Martha may have become more motivated to enter into contact with the EP.
M: (laughs as she shows that she cannot open her hand)	TPP: The ANP is perturbed but struggles to continue her old passion of ignoring the EP.
E: I might offer you a phrase that will cause the hand to relax.	TPP: It seems important to continue throwing sand in that 'old machine' as well as inviting the ANP to engage in a new action.
M: (softly, in tears) OK. E: Shall I tell you? M: (nods)	SPP: I feel that the ANP may be ready for change.

E: If you tell the 2-year-old, "I will listen to you, perhaps not to everything at once, but in manageable steps. If I start to share it with you, will you then please free my right hand?" Did you understand? M: Hmm. (nods and laughs)	TPP: Presentation of a treatment plan in a nutshell. It invites the ANP and the EP to *coordinate* their actions, to *cooperate*, and to *communicate* with one another. SPP: I am aware that these new actions imply an increase of the field of consciousness and the level of consciousness in both dissociative parts, and that this development will involve joy and sorrow. TPP: If the project is to succeed, the new actions should bring more joy than sorrow. They should involve an increase of the whole individual's power of action.
E: Jessica already told me you're a clever woman.	SPP: Martha is "clever" when she understands that the work includes this cooperation and communication.
M: (laughs some more, and we with her) I understand it all right, but I find it strange to talk myself talk like that.	Does she find it strange to talk to the fragile EP, or does her remark rather convey that she is not too thrilled to engage in this cooperation?
E: Yes . . . yes . . . but it's also a chance . . . talking inside may be far more effective than suffering endless attacks. M: (nods) E: You can talk to her. You don't need to . . . M: (laughs)	SPP: Although this approach is demanding, it will be rewarding. TPP: Explain the gain despite the pain. SPP: Consensus.
E: . . . go home with a right fist . . .	TPP: Formulation of the *therapeutic paradox*: Cooperate with the fragile EP, or, as ANP, go home with a frustrated fragile EP that shows her clenched fist. TPP: The ANP's common mode trajectory does not work anymore. She has become destabilized. This destabilization is utilized to foster a new systemic organization.
M: (laughs and hides her face between her left hand) I find it very strange . . . I find it very difficult . . .	TPP: I decide not to explore Martha's feelings, but to keep her focused on the dilemma.
E: The 2-year-old is waiting for you, Martha. She wants to be heard. M: It's hard. E: That part of you cannot solve the issues on her own. She asks you to cooperate with her. M: (sits motionless with her hand hidden in her left hand, her right hand still a fist) E: You can speak with her in external silence, if you prefer.	SPP: I empathize with the needs and desires of the fragile EP, and also phenomenally judge that I must not 'save' Martha as ANP. TPP: Martha starts to seek refuge in her common mode of total ignorance: fainting. Formerly effective passions are rather appealing. They have become overpracticed and thus rather automatic.
M: (head starts to wobble)	TPP: Martha is on the border of fainting.
E: Well. Martha? M: (head continues to wobble) E: You need not go that way . . .	SPP: I try to get Martha's attention.
M: (the right hand relaxes as she faints)	TPP: The ANP has escaped. Maybe the fragile EP can nonetheless make her fist; she may have gained that power of action.
E: This is your old method . . . 2-year-old, make your fist. Use your fist to call on Martha . . . you did it before, so I know you can . . . M: (lies flaccid in the chair, the head hanging on her left shoulder, eyes closed, arms paralyzed, slow breathing)	TPP: Having 'lost' the ANP, address the EP. SPP: Hopefully the little one has not yet become completely deactivated.

E: Come on, 2-year-old, use your fist.	TPP: I must be quick to support the EP, or else we are bound to have another episode of passivity. My action regarding the EP is an instance of '*talking through*.' This is the endeavor to talk to a dissociative part that is presumably present even if subdominant.
M: (fingers start to bend)	FPP: Relief. QSPP: My actions are sufficiently effective. SPP and TPP: The fragile EP does not give up quickly.
E: That's just great. And the more you make the fist, the more Martha wakes up. Martha, wake up. M: (deep sighing) E: Yes, Martha, we're still here.	SPP: Support for the fragile EP. Therapeutic coupling of an observed fact – the formation of the fist – and a suggested effect – Martha's awakening. SPP: Analogy: Martha, you can leave, but your troubles will stay. TPP: 'We' includes the EP.
Well done ... and what did you tell the 2-year-old?	SPP: Support for Martha. TPP: But did she engage in the invited new action?
M: That I really want to solve the problems. That I really want my fist to open. I want to solve the problem but I'm so tired.	TPP: It seems the ANP continued to avoid the hot issue. Her internal struggle eats up energy.
E: I believe you, it was a real strain ... and remember that recognition of the little one will improve your life. She, the girl you were at the time, really needs you.	SPP: Remember the little one, the painful facts of your life, and the probable return on investment in a difficult action.
M: I know that for sure. E: She needs your care and help, and when it comes down to it, you are the only one who can offer it.	SPP: Sounds annoyed that she must attend to the little one. TPP: The ANP got the message, which is in itself a new action.
M: (wipes her tears) ... *Sorry* ... (desperately looks at Jessica) J: (Gently) You can cry ...	TPP: Subsequent sessions clarified that her parents did not allow Martha to cry.
E: (Tenderly) Yes ... M: It makes me so sad. J: Hmm.	SPP: Acceptance of Martha's expressed sadness.
E: What makes you so sad? M: He simply goes his way, and tells me that I deserved the beatings ...	SPP: Confirmation of the sorrow.
E: That does not fit, right? ... No child deserves ...	SPP: I take a compassionate position.
M: Everyone protects him (i.e., her father). Nobody (in the family) wants to talk about it. You can scream from the rooftops, but no one listens. It's just not right. He happily goes his way, and can come and leave with a smile, but then I think, don't you get it, don't you get it? E: OK.	SPP: Martha seems to get in touch with the fragile EP more.
M: I have a problem that I must solve and he acts as if nothing happened or says "I did not mean to do it," but yes, ...	TPP and SPP: My technical and phenomenal judgment is that Martha is annoyed that, in the end, only she can solve the problem. My words may have afforded the action of recalling her father's rejection to take responsibility for his maltreatment.
E: That's a very easy thing to say, right? M: Yes!	SPP: I am on her side.
E: You're not only sad, you're also really angry. M: Yes. Yes.	SPP: Recognition of her complex emotions.

E: For good reasons. We can address all these issues. You can now acknowledge the 2-year-old. You can say, "You exist, and I won't forget you again."	SPP: Do not reject and abandon the fragile EP. Father and mother did that, do not do it yourself. TPP: I *model* the new action for Martha as ANP.
M: When I look at my childhood pictures, and look into those eyes, then I feel "Oh, you poor little girl." E: Yes, from ... M: So little, and already so ...	TPP: Martha engages in the work. SPP: She now empathizes with the little girl she was and becomes compassionate.
E: ... now you can also look inside, each time your hand becomes fixed, you can know, this is my 2-year-old, we have work to do, together, and you may want to say, "I will come your way, I will come your way, I won't leave you alone anymore."	SPP and TPP: Utilization: Looking at the childhood picture turns into looking inside. Next, looking inside turns into talking to the fragile EP, and talking to the EP turns into making a promise.
M: (nods)	SPP: Confirmation.
E: OK?	SPP: Promise again.
M: (nods)	SPP: Reconfirmation.
E: Fine. Can you now open your hand?	SPP: Praise.
M: (opens her right hand, laughs, dries her eyes)	SPP: Mission accomplished; I feel proud of Martha and am happy for her that she managed to take a very significant step. FPP: I feel joy. QSPP: Your personal joy, Ellert, is fine. But remember that your wishes should not be the engine to therapy. The engine should be Martha's needs and desires.
E: The more you are with her, the more you will have a relaxed hand. The more you forget her, the more the fist will become fixed. M: (nods)	TPP: The new actions will be useful, they will bring joy, and this joy will invite and encourage more new actions. Our passions (forgetting, fainting) may include gains, but overall they have become harmful. They now bring more sorrow than joy.
E: You can still faint ...	SPP: We do not take tools from you, but you can decide to use more effective means when they become available to you.
M: I hope not ...	
E: ... but your hand is perhaps a more direct way ... As far as I am concerned we're done for today.	SPP: Fragile EP, you can show yourself in a more direct way.
M: Yes.	SPP: Consensus.
Up to this point, the session had lasted 45 minutes. We made arrangements for some more sessions and started to leave. As we were standing, Martha became dizzy, swayed, and dropped to the floor within 3 seconds. As she was lying on the floor her breathing was initially rapid and shallow, and she was trembling.	TPP: Would the fragile EP perhaps be engaging in an attachment cry? Is she testing her old tool? Would leave-taking afford a reenactment of the traumatic leave-taking from her dying mother (which Jessica had mentioned to me)? There was neither the time to explore these possibilities nor was it the time to do this. Therefore, I decided to contact the fragile EP. Addressing her as "the 2-year-old," I asked her to use "her fist" to show her presence. She responded within 2 minutes, though not consistently – and it took an effort. I reassured her and Martha that we would meet again, that we would do the work, and that it had to be done in steps.

Assessment

The uncommon enactive assessment unveiled that Martha met the criteria for ICD-10 Dissociative Disorder of Movement and Sensation. More specifically her condition involved trauma-related Dissociative Convulsions and Dissociative Stupor.

Sensorimotor dissociative symptoms and disorders concern sensorimotor manifestations of the existence of two or more dissociative subsystems of the personality as a whole organism-environment system. This system incorporates intrinsically related physical, psychological, and psychosociological appearances or properties. Body and mind are not two substances that can be dissociated from each other or that exist in parallel. They are attributes of one substance called Nature or God, Spinoza taught us. Hence, sensorimotor dissociative symptoms and disorders, like cognitive-emotional dissociative symptoms and disorders, are also intrinsically 'mental.' And cognitive-emotional symptoms and disorders, like sensorimotor dissociative symptoms and disorders, are also intrinsically 'physical.' The term 'somatic dissociation' that sometimes appears in the literature does not adequately express this understanding.

Structural Dissociation

The work of the first session revealed that, inasmuch as structure was concerned, Martha's personality included two different conscious and self-conscious subsystems dissociated from each other. Both constituted operationally autonomous centers of action and passion, and both engaged in different action and passions. They also had actions in common such as comprehending Dutch, the ability to relate to someone else, the ability to move the body, and recollecting a number of past events. As applies to all dissociative parts, they were not totally split.

Martha as ANP included a broad set of latent and manifest organismic modes of longing and striving. Some of these were so to speak associated with a 'friendly, reasonably composed adult Martha,' others with a 'hurt, angry, and controlling adult Martha.' As the controlling adult, Martha repeated her complaints on end using basically the same words as if she had not already uttered them before. Operating as this controlling mode of longing and striving, she could hardly be interrupted, let alone stopped. She might put other people under pressure and did not seem to be very aware of the effects this behavior had on others. At these times, Martha almost sounded like an automaton that produced and reproduced the same old passions. The controlling mode of longing and striving was quite different from Martha's presentation as the sympathetic adult. Despite these differences, Martha experienced and knew herself as 'Martha' whether she remained in the sympathetic or in the controlling mode of longing and striving. Because the two were associated with *one* common adult phenomenal conception of self, they involved *two* different modes of longing and striving and did not count as two dissociative parts.

The fragile EP comprised a smaller set of latent and manifest modes of longing and striving. The mode space of this part was more limited than that of the adult Martha. As the treatment proceeded, the little Martha nonetheless covered a substantial number of modes. They mostly pertained to traumatic experiences. Her phenomenal age shifted with the historical timing of the events that had been traumatic for her. It stretched from 2 years to approximately 16 years.

After some 20 sessions, Martha revealed that the misery included recurrent paternal incest as well as sexual abuse by her first boyfriend. In this light, the organization of her personality might have been more complex than the simple division between one ANP and one fragile EP. However, we did not find any evidence of this nature during the full course of her treatment. The organization of one large conscious and self-conscious subsystem of the personality metaphorically referred to as ANP and a smaller conscious and self-conscious structure metaphorically referred to as fragile EP is known as primary structural dissociation of the personality (Van der Hart et al., 2006). In this organization, the ANP commonly encompasses many different modes of longing and striving. It comprises a wide mode space. The mode space of the fragile EP is commonly a far smaller but it often also comprises different modes of longing and striving.

Teleofunctional Dissociation

As ANP, Martha was like any operationally autonomous system primordially affectively interested in the continuation of her existence. 'The sympathetic' Martha was more specifically primarily guided by the needs and desires pertaining to living daily life. 'The hurt and angry' Martha was basically longing for recognition. She strove to achieve it by harping on her – albeit justified – complaints. In both modes, the ANP feared and avoided the singular fragile EP and her world. As this fragile EP, Martha was no less primordially affectively interested in the preservation of her existence. But as this dissociative part, Martha's needs and desires particularly pertained to surviving events that were traumatic to her as well as to meeting acceptance, recognition, and support from ANP and from other people. 'The sympathetic' Martha, 'the hurt and angry Martha,' and the fragile EP were thus guided by different systemic attractors. They had quite different feelings and ideas as to what is useful, harmful, and insignificant.

Dynamic Dissociation

The needs and desires of the ANP and the EP were quite similar in that they both strove to preserve their existence, though their longing and striving were dissimilar or even opposite in other regards. Part of the ANP's affective interest was to ignore or otherwise evade the EP that scared her. She mostly feared and avoided the fragile EP's traumatic memories. She lacked the motivation (will) and power to confront herself with the terrible memories in which the fragile EP was stuck, and she resisted integrating them. The EP, in turn, felt rejected and abandoned by the ANP. However, stuck in traumatic misery and guided by a deep need for recognition and assistance, she could not and did not leave the ANP and the wider phenomenal world alone: The fainting spells had lasted 33 years, and they would probably continue without effective therapy.

As a complex and dynamic organism-environment system, our species includes different levels of action tendencies (Van der Hart et al., 2006, Chapter 9). Action tendencies involve goal-directed, potentially viable, and creative solutions to environmental challenges that have developed out of a long history of evolutionary selection (Buss, 2005). As Van der Hart et al. (2006, p. 3) assert, "[w] tend to think of actions as being carried out or executed. *Action tendencies are not merely propensities to act in certain ways, but involve the complete cycle of action, including latency, readiness, initiation, execution, and completion.*" Beyond a critical degree of activation, action tendencies include perceiving an *umwelt*, sensing physical and affective feelings, developing emotions, phenomenally experiencing and conceiving a self, world, and self as a part of this world, thinking, remembering, and moving in a goal-orienting fashion. They also include particular ways of generating, using, and regulating affects.

A critical feature of action tendencies is that they integrate sensory, perceptual, affective, cognitive, and behavioral actions and their implied contents in a goal-orientated viable and creative fashion. The system's attractors and repellers guide what and how gets integrated and what not. As discussed before, we integrate (very) different 'things' whether we are hungry, sleepy, playful, curious, scared, ashamed, disgusted, angry, caring, or sexually aroused. With shifts in our needs and desires, we enact a partly different self, world, and self as a part of this world. Anyone who reflects on the issue will easily assess this for himself or herself that,

> [w]hen our blood sugar is low and we notice the accompanying sensation of hunger, we become ready to start looking for food. When we perceive a threat cue and feel scared, we are ready to defend ourselves. When we are alone but highly dependent on others, we are ready to cry out for help or support. (Van der Hart et al., 2006, p. 170)

However, despite all variability, we also generate a relatively stable sense of general and personal identity when all goes well.

As an organism-environment system or personality, we encompass various 'levels' of action tendencies. That is, our action tendencies can be more or less complex, hence more or less difficult to achieve. They require more or less mental efficiency (Van der Hart et al. 2006). Mental efficiency involves an ability to raise a certain degree of energy and to invest this energy in the action tendencies required to achieve one's goals. Simple action tendencies do not require much mental efficiency, whereas very complex ones demand high mental efficiency. In this sense, we encompass a hierarchy of action tendencies. To quote Van der Hart et al. (2006, p. 171–172) at length:

> There is substantial contemporary evidence that supports the 19th-century idea (Bain, 1855; Jackson, 1931–1932; Janet, 1926) that the development of our species (phylogeny) and our individual development (ontogeny) involve action tendencies of increasing complexity (e.g., Fuster, 2003). Thus the tendencies range from basic reflexes that are largely autonomatic and rigid, to highly reflective, voluntary, and creative actions. Janet (1926; 1938) conveniently divided them into three main groups – lower, intermediate, and higher action tendencies. Each group includes various sublevels ... The complexity of different action tendencies increased with the number of component actions that we must synthesize (i.e., bind and differentiate), and realize (i.e., personify and presentify). And the more complex an action tendency is, the more complex the perception –motor action cycles it involves.

The following levels of action tendencies can be distinguished:

Lower-level action tendencies
Basic reflexes
Presymbolic regulatory action tendencies
Presymbolic sociopersonal action tendencies
Basic symbolic action tendencies

Intermediate-level action tendencies
Reflexive symbolic action tendencies
Reflective action tendencies

Higher-level action tendencies
Prolonged reflective action tendencies
Experimental action tendencies
Progressive action tendencies

These various action tendencies imply partly different phenomenal experiences and conceptions of self, world, and self as a part of this world. They also comprise particular differences with regard to phenomenal self, time, memory, and regulation. These features are briefly depicted in Figures 33.1 to 33.3.

Martha's fainting spells involved very low-level action tendencies (Van der Hart et al., 2006; see Figures 33.1 and 33.4). They were nonverbal, presymbolic passions involving an all-or-nothing regulation. Martha became dizzy, started to sigh, and rapidly fainted – steps that took only a couple of seconds. Or she did not. The transcript of the first session indicates that as ANP Martha tended to faint rapidly when she became confronted with classically conditioned signs of the EP and this part's affects, thoughts, memories, and behaviors. She had major difficulty exploring the involved fragile EP and her 'contents.' Such exploration implies upholding conditioned phobic flight impulses. Confronted with conditioned signals of the fragile EP and this part's traumatic memories, the ANP typically fainted with very little delay.

Lower Action Tendencies

Type	Self	Time	Memory	Regulation
Basic reflexes Presymbolic regulatory action tendencies Presymbolic sociopersonal action tendencies Basic symbolic action tendencies	*From* an absent phenomenal conception of self (PCS) *to* a mostly bodily PCS *to* a Nonverbal social PCS *to* a PCS that can be verbalized	*From* a minimal *to* a rudimentary *to* an an emergent ability to link a phenomenal present, past, and future *to* an ability to bind and differentiate a phenomenal present, past and future in symbols	*From* procedural memory *to* nonverbal declarative memory *to* emergent narrative declarative memory	*From* all or nothing, explosive actions (approach / avoidance /escape) *to* rudimentary planning of actions *to* social regulation of actions through imitation and cooperation *to* the use of tools, including symbols and an ability to engage in symbolized actions (rituals)

Figure 33.1. Lower-level action tendencies: Types, self, time, memory, and regulation.

Intermediate Action Tendencies

Type	Self	Time	Memory	Regulation
Prereflective symbolic action tendencies Reflective action tendencies	*From* a social to a personal PCS, from being a group member *to* being a phenomenal individual	*From* limited presentification *to* emerging extended presentification	Declarative memory starts to comprise widening stretches of time	*From* actions mediated by fixed schema's and a potent influence of fantasy on perception, affect, thought and behavior *to* actions that are increasingly based on reflection with a growing ability to suspend immediate beliefs and impulses

Figure 33.2. Intermediate-level action tendencies: Types, self, time, memory, and regulation.

Higher Action Tendencies

Type	Self	Time	Memory	Regulation
Prolonged reflective action tendencies Experimental action tendencies Progressive action tendencies	PCS progressively includes reflective ideals that can be symbolized and that increasingly support long-term future action patterns	*From* a solid sense of time and presentification *to* an ever growing sense of the relativity of time, space, and general understanding (e.g., brain, body, Umwelt; matter and mind)	Narrative declarative memory that increasingly serves future actions	*From* actions based on rational and moral principles and actions based on a growing ability to distribute force over a range of actions *to* actions involving a systematized exploration of one's inner and outer world (e.g., conducting experiments), *to* actions based on a comprehension of relativity

Figure 33.3. Higher-level action tendencies: Types, self, time, memory, and regulation.

Lower Action Tendencies in Dissociative Parts

Basic Reflexes
e.g., classically conditioned actions
in Fragile EPs regarding external threat signals, and
in ANPs regarding internal threat signals

Presymbolic Regulatory Action Tendencies
Notably EPs have difficulty waiting before engaging in goal-directed movements. They tend to engage in explosive all or none actions, particularly when they perceive threat signals

Presymbolic Sociopersonal Action Tendencies
e.g., EPs can imitate perpetrators but have difficulty learning from models in the present

Basic Symbolic Action Tendencies
e.g., EPs' use of tools is limited; they may have difficulty waiting for instructions or difficulty following instructions. They may be able to make drawings of traumatic experiences or symbolize these in other nonverbal ways

Basic Forms of Language
e.g., EPs can have limited linguistic skill; they may not be able to verbalize traumatic memories, but may utter some scattered words like "no" or "help" or a short sentence at best

Figure 33.4. Lower-level action tendencies in dissociative parts.

Intermediate Action Tendencies in Dissociative Parts

Prereflective Symbolic Action Tendencies
ANPs are commonly verbal, as are controlling and quite a few fragile EPs. However, they tend to become less verbal, or even loose their verbal skills when they become stressed.
Many ANPs and EPs' thoughts are reflex-like.
For example, EP: I'm in danger; it's my fault; no one will ever like me; all men are evil; you – the clinician – will also abandon me soon.
ANP: When I really think about what happened, I will go mad. It is dangerous to put what happened to me in words.

Reflective Symbolic and Other Action Tendencies
For example, ANP: I have neglected that sad little one inside;
I have now experienced that I can talk to this part of me
Controlling EP: I'm not ony angry. I'm also sad,
and I am not weak when I cry
Fragile EP: I have now experienced that my father does not show up when I tell what he did to me. He is dead.

Figure 33.5. Intermediate-level action tendencies in dissociative parts.

Figure 33.6. Higher-level action tendencies in dissociative parts.

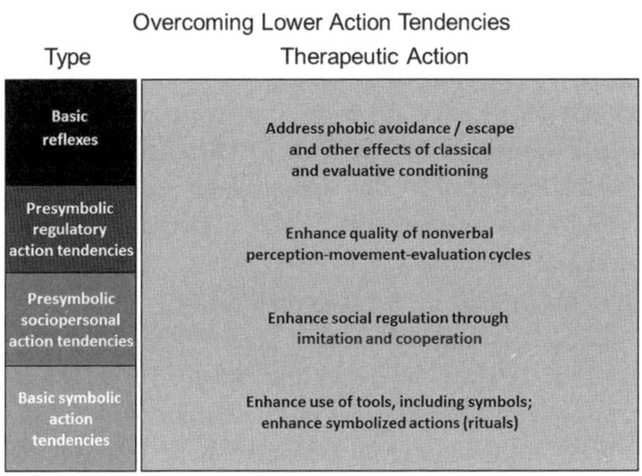

Figure 33.7. Overcoming lower-level action tendencies: General directions.

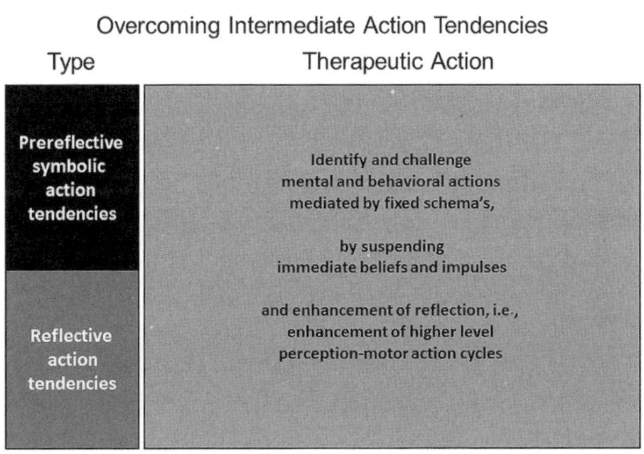

Figure 33.8. Overcoming intermediate-level action tendencies: General directions.

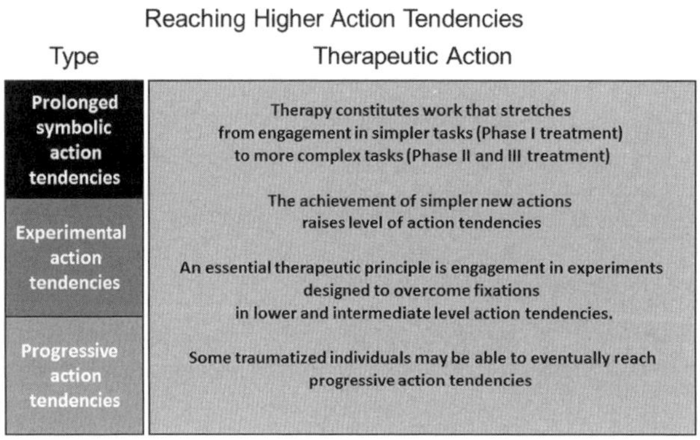

Figure 33.9. Reaching higher-level action tendencies: General directions.

With more therapy sessions, it became apparent that Martha engaged in three main dissociative, part-related mode trajectories. The most prevalent mode trajectories went according to the following pattern:

1. *The ANP is activated.* She is primarily guided by needs and desires of daily life ('The sympathetic Martha') or longs and strives for recognition ('The hurt, angry, and controlling Martha). As this dissociative part, Martha is at the same time repelled by the fragile EP and 'her' traumatic memories.
2. *Reminders of traumatic memories reactivate the fragile EP.* This part is primarily guided by needs and desires of defense and attachment cry that operate as the core attractors of this dissociative subsystem. She is further repelled by the ANP's neglect and rejection as well as other individuals' neglect and rejection.
3. *The fragile EP becomes so strongly activated that she intrudes on the ANP.*
4. *The ANP strives to ignore the EP and the associated traumatic memories.* One strategy of the ANP is to enter the mode that characterizes 'the controlling Martha.' In this mode she keeps on harping about her complaints. She engages in totalitarian passions and thereby restricts and lowers her level and field of consciousness. These alterations of consciousness serve to shut out the EP and this part's pain.
5. *Another evasive mode trajectory is to faint.* This mode transition characterizes 'the sympathetic Martha.' The more the EP becomes activated, and the more the ANP starts to experience the EP and her world, the more the ANP starts to sigh, roll her eyes up, and lower and retract her consciousness. She loses muscle tension and faints within seconds. The eye roll may involve the induction of a self-hypnotic mode.
6. The next stage of the fainting commonly includes vigorous shaking, rapid but superficial breathing, moaning, and uttering an occasional "No!" It seems that the fragile EP reenacts traumatic memories in this phase that the ANP fears, avoids, and resists integrating.
7. *The last stage of the attack* typically comprises immobility, slow breathing, flaccid paralysis, and complete unresponsiveness to the 'external world.'
8. 'The sympathetic Martha' regains consciousness after some 15 to 60 minutes.

Another main trajectory regarding the 'attacks' was that the fragile EP was reenacting loss of consciousness in the context of the traumatization. This loss related to being hit against her head and to being suffocated, in both cases to the point of losing consciousness. A third main trajectory related to the fragile EP's attachment cry. The second and third trajectories are briefly discussed below.

ANP Martha in the Mode of Being Hurt and Angry

In her hurt and angry moods, Martha seemed to reenact the anger she felt against her parents and her family members who were aware of the ongoing traumatization but who did not save her from it. The reenacted anger was also directed toward physicians, psychiatrists, and other professionals who had not or only ineffectively helped her. The professionals included policemen who had not believed her story when she reported the violent rape by her first boyfriend (he had threatened her with a knife during the rape). Martha repetitiously complained that she was not seen, heard, or taken seriously. Her frequent urgent and extensive telephone calls to the Trauma Clinic could be understood as verbal and displaced relational reenactments of this emotional neglect and rejection. In my view, her generally problematic relationships with women more specifically constituted relational reenactments of the chronic emotional neglect by her mother.

Martha expressed her anger in a rather impulsive and all-or-nothing form. Since the expressions were verbal, she could, at least in part, put her strong feelings into words. That is, she managed to express them to a degree in a symbolized form (words are symbols). Her utterances constituted a prereflective symbolic intermediate-level action tendency (see Figure 33.2). It was prereflective because she seemed unable to reflect on it, realize it, and thereby complete the action tendency. When she voiced her rage, she felt strong. However, she tended to faint after some time. When she realized what had happened to her, she wept and felt vulnerable – but never fainted. It actually seemed that her feeling hurt and angry *substituted for* her feeling fragile and hurt. By expressing anger, she could avoid feeling sadness. In this sense her focus on anger substituted for integrating and realizing her sorrow. Her rage involved a means of controlling her fragility.

When feeling hurt and angry, Martha further displayed an unduly restricted field and level of consciousness. In this mood, she largely lost her common feel for social relationships. For example, she displayed little concern for other individual's feelings or thoughts when anger was on her mind. Her utterances were not only repetitious, they were also controlling. That is, she did not reach a level of corporative consciousness or communicative consciousness but remained stuck in efforts at totalitarian control. The 'controlling Martha' commonly calmed down when I first allowed her to express herself, attuned to her using short and simple statements, and showed affective understanding to achieve consensus. Once we had developed a working relationship, sometimes a touch of benign humor might work to wake her up (e.g., "Martha, you must think I am not at my best today; you tell me the same story ten times in a row"). It might also encourage her to look me in the eye while I said something like: "Martha, you are really pissed. I get that. I really get that. Do you get that I get it? I am with you. And are you also with me?" In this fashion I hoped to encourage her to enter a second-person perspective with me, rather than to remain fixed in her first-person and quasi-second person perspectives of feeling terribly hurt, angry, and secretively scared.

When Martha reenacted her anger, she struck me as a depersonalized individual. As she said in the later phase of her treatment,

> I always thought I was going strong when I was angry. I thought I was weak and my life was going awry when I cried. But that's not how it is. It is the other way around: When I dare to feel my pain and express it here with you, I heal.

These reflective symbolic action tendencies tended to emerge when we had tested her reflexive beliefs, and when she had experienced that her former beliefs did not hold. This testing was not 'purely cognitive,' but strongly affectively charged. When we challenged her reflexive beliefs, she would destabilize. It appeared that a degree of destabilization was needed to exert an influence on her fixed ideas. When she became destabilized too soon and too much, she tended to faint or panic and learned nothing. When she remained stable, she also learned nothing or very little. To achieve change, she needed to be sufficiently destabilized to invite a viable and creative self-reorganization.

ANP Martha in the Mode of Being Sympathetic

The 'sympathetic Martha' was sincere, cooperative, and kind. She also had a good sense of humor. As this dissociative part and in this mode, she liked music, loved to sing, dance, and read. She never missed a session but ignored or otherwise avoided pain when she could. In this ignorant mode, she became quite depersonalized. When she did feel and express her sorrow, she impressed me as a very *real* person.

Martha as the Fragile EP

EP's passions were also low-level (substitute action) tendencies. They involved impulsive, nonsymbolized, all-or-nothing reenactments of events that had been traumatic for her and that were traumatic for her still: As the fragile EP, Martha was not oriented to the actual present, but to her phenomenal present that often was the actual past. However, she was social and could learn through instruction and imitation. For example, she could readily communicate using digit-signals. Although the fragile EP understood spoken language very well, she did not speak to me in words, either in the first session or in the whole treatment that eventually encompassed some 70 sessions. However, it would soon appear that she could make drawings as well as write a few words. She could thus engage in simple symbolic action tendencies (drawing, simple language; see Figures 33.1 and 33.4). The fragile EP also grasped language at an intermediate level of action tendencies. These abilities were utilized from the first session. For example, I invited the 'something inside' that appeared to be a young Martha to communicate with me in the form of simple finger signals and to turn the right hand into a fist. In later sessions, the fragile EP proved able to engage with the ANP in an inner dialogue.

As indicated above and as became apparent from the second session on, the fainting was not only a passion of the ANP that substituted for integration of the fragile EP and her horrible 'contents.' The fragile EP might also faint but for a different reason. The fainting concluded the reenactment of physical maltreatment that caused a loss of consciousness: the father's fierce beatings against her head as well as his attempt to suffocate her under a pillow. These reenactments also clearly involved lower-level action tendencies. They were sensorimotor, affective, and behavioral, and they did not include the use of language, at least not prior to the treatment of the involved traumatic memories.

Another reason for the fainting the EP initiated was the wish to stay with individuals she appreciated. As my colleague Jessica had experienced, and as also happened in sessions with me, Martha tended to faint near the end of the sessions or briefly thereafter, albeit while she was still in the building! This pattern could be understood as a cry for attachment from the fragile EP.

Summary of the Core Dynamic of Martha's Modes of Longing and Striving and Dissociative Parts

As the ANP Martha ignored and otherwise avoided the fragile EP and her traumatic memories. The avoidance encompassed low-level action tendencies (i.e., fainting) and intermediate-level action tendencies (i.e., fixed beliefs that integration of the fragile EP and 'her' traumatic memories was awful and dangerous. The fragile EP, however, had the power to intrude on the ANP, albeit originally generally if not solely in the form of nonverbal low-level action tendencies. These intrusions scared the ANP. Since, with the exception of these intrusions, the ANP was largely effective in avoiding the EP, the ANP and EP remained dissociated from each other. Part of Martha's ANP-bound avoidance of the fragile EP was to engage in a hurt, angry, and controlling mode of longing and striving. This mode also involved a quite powerful tendency to reenact traumatic relationships with her parents and other authorities. Engaged in this mode, she was controlling in a way that was not completely unlike the power displays she had observed in the individuals who had hurt her so much.

Phenomenal Dissociation

The ANP and the EP included their own phenomenal conceptions of her self, her *umwelt*, and her self-of-this-world. Phenomenally, the ANP was not the EP, and the EP was not the ANP, just as the phenomenal worlds of the ANP and EP were different. The phenomenal age of the fragile EP and other phenomenal conceptions of her self, her *umwelt*, and her self-of-this-world shifted with the historical timing of the traumatic events. However, the phenomenal conceptions involved were stable in the sense that they remained basically unaltered no matter how often they had been reenacted.

This state of affairs also revealed itself in their different phenomenal conceptions of the relationship with me. When feeling at ease, the ANP's phenomenal idea of her relationship with me was: "You understand and help me. I appreciate that a lot. We get along well with one another. But don't pressure me." When feeling hurt and angry, the ANP's phenomenal idea of the relationship with me was: "Please listen to me; free me from my fainting spells, but do not hurt me; I must talk talk talk – and exert pressure to get your attention. I scream from the rooftops, but nobody listens – you must listen." The EP's version was something like: "Help me! Mommy and Daddy hurt me! No one listens to me or helps me, including the adult one (i.e., ANP). Don't leave me! I'm young, you're older. I want to stay with you. I'm starting to feel you will not beat me, blame me, reject me, or forget me."

A Therapeutic Plan of Action

Given the results of the first session, the following plan of action seemed fitting:

1. Extend the interactions with Martha as ANP and as EP.
2. Do not take sides, do not become, as it were, a part of Martha's system, but at all times treat her whole system, even when speaking to the ANP or the EP in particular. Stay connected with Spaceland, with 'the top of the pyramid,' while visiting Flatland.
3. Define and pursue common goals in steps that the ANP and the EP can manage.
4. Promote interactions between the ANP and the EP within the limits of their respective power of action.
5. Encourage the ANP and the EP to gradually engage in higher levels of action tendencies that increase their power of action and their power to attain common viable and creative goals. For example, encourage the EP to start making drawings of events that were traumatic to her and that relate to loss of consciousness (symbolization through drawing). If this works, invite her to add some words (verbal symbols) to the drawings. If this works, invite the EP to talk to the ANP. Vice versa, stimulate the ANP to use simple and permissive language in interacting with the EP and model this kind of language. For example, do not command, "Close your eyes," but say gently, "You may close your eyes if you wish."
6. Model to the ANP how she can interact with the EP.

7. Help the ANP and the EP to find ways of sharing, symbolizing, and integrating traumatic memories.
8. Do not do the work for the ANP and the EP, but stimulate them to do their own jobs in steps that remain within their reach as therapy progresses. Their successes bring joy and joy increases their power of action, their degree of perfection.
9. In working with the ANP and/or the EP, when attuning to their phenomenal worlds in the second-person perspective, do not lose track of the clinical third-person perspective. Rather, integrate the clinical second-person perspective *and* the clinical third-person perspective.
10. Realize that these two perspectives are grounded in your – the clinician's – first-person and quasi-second-person perspective. Realize that your view is not a view from nowhere, and that it does not reflect 'The Truth.' They involve your personal feelings and ideas as well as your technical ideas.

The Continued Treatment

At the beginning of the second session, I asked if the EP was content that the ANP avoided her less (yes), if she would like to express herself more (yes), and if she was able to make drawings (yes). The EP subsequently drew, in a schoolchild-like fashion, a traumatic scene. As a next step, I asked if she was perhaps also able to write (yes). The ANP experienced the movements involved in the writing but did not experience that she was the agent of these movements. She was quite surprised to see that the EP addressed traumatic memories, and that she had the handwriting of a schoolgirl. In tears, the ANP said that she knew something of the traumatic events – but not everything – and that she had tried to avoid the terrible memories with all her might. The ANP said she felt ashamed and sad that, as she put it, she had abandoned "the little girl." I invited the ANP to check inside where the EP subjectively and phenomenally 'was,' that is, what her current first-person perspective and quasi-second-person perspective were. The ANP found the EP in the house of her parents, while "the little girl" was being physically abused. I suggested that the ANP might want to remove the little girl part of her from that situation and console her. The ANP managed to do this, and she shared the EP's tears. Near the end of the session, I suggested that the EP might want to start exchanging the attacks for "sharing her tears with the ANP."

The Third Session

The ANP shared that she felt much better, almost elated. Sharing the emotional pain with the EP was very difficult, but it also gave her a new perspective. Finally, there was something she could *do* about her debilitating disorder, and it felt good to console the "little girl." In this session, I invited the ANP to interact with the EP verbally, which both parts did well. The ANP was a bit disappointed that the EP did not yet trust her. The EP was quite apprehensive that she (the ANP) would abandon her again.

Invited to share another traumatic memory (the EP said she had many traumatic memories to share), the EP and the ANP synthesized (Van der Hart et al., 2006) how Martha's father had tried to suffocate Martha with a pillow. That is, along with the EP, the ANP experienced and interconnected the various sensations, affects, perceptions, thoughts, and motor actions that constituted the EP's traumatic memory of the event. The synthesis (see Chapter 27) differed from the EP's previous reenactments of the involved event. This time, the ANP shared the recollection of the EP. Together they managed to remain predominantly oriented to the actual present and to put the experience in words – thus to express it mostly in a symbolized form.

Martha lost consciousness at the time, but survived. Later in the session, I suggested that the EP could continue sharing her tears with the ANP as they went home, rather than presenting the ANP with more attacks: This would remind the ANP that the EP needed her recognition and assistance. The suggestion was effective: For the first time, Martha left the session and the Trauma Center without seizures. As ANP, Martha would later report that she had been unable to stop frequent crying spells throughout the week.

The Fourth Session and Beyond

For the purposes of the present chapter, it suffices to mention that over the next couple of sessions, the ANP and the EP synthesized, personified, presentified, symbolized, and realized (Van der Hart et al., 2006) more traumatic memories. That is, they shared more passions in which the EP had been fixated and the ANP had previously fiercely avoided. Passions started to become integrative actions. By the fifth session, the attacks had been reduced to approximately one seizure per week, and their intensity and duration had strongly diminished.

As treatment progressed, Martha realized ever more what had happened to her. As ANP, she knew many, though not all, the facts of the neglect, rejection, maltreatment, and abuse in which she was stuck as EP. However, knowing physical facts demands merely a third-person perspective. Realization, in contrast, is an action that strongly depends on first-person phenomenal experience and quasi-second-person phenomenal judgment. It involves feeling what living the involved event was like (synthesis), and judging, on the basis of this experiencing, that it 'really happened' (presentification), and that it happened to 'me' (personification). Oftentimes, realization also takes the witnessing of one or more second persons. Reality becomes more real in a social frame because we are organism-social environment systems. As Järvilehto (2001c) put it,

> [t]he essential characteristic of the human being is his sociality which means that he is as an individual defined by his social relations. If "social" means cooperation of organism-environ-

> ment systems for a common result, then there is no "sociality" which could exert a causal influence from "outside" on psyche or personality. Thus, human action is not "socially" determined in the sense of causal influence. Sociality is rather one of its basic characteristics. (Järvilehto, 2000a)

Her parents were unavailable as witnesses. Martha's mother had died, but her father was still alive. Using her increasing power of action, she tried hard to share her recollections with him, to express her sorrow during the conversations, and to ask for explanations. He preferred evading the subject, walking away from her, denying even obvious facts, or twisting them. In the end he did admit to some events, but did not take responsibility. He knew what he had done to her, but he did not seem to *realize* it (but see below).

Clinicians can, at least in principle, serve as witnesses, not reflexively, but reflectively (Van der Hart & Nijenhuis, 1999). We examined her memories of events that had been traumatic for her in detail and explored them from various angles, before phenomenally and physically judging that they basically reflected actual events. For example, in one session as ANP Martha was able to share approximately a quarter of all sensations, feelings, desires, perceptions, thoughts, and behaviors that she encompassed as EP regarding the death of her mother. As ANP she had never forgotten the facts. As this part she also knew that her mother was interested in taking her leave from her husband and mostly from Martha's brother, while completely disregarding Martha. She knew that her father had kept her at a distance from the death bed. But the more she as ANP shared EP's phenomenal experiences and judgments, the more the physical facts came to life for her. The more Martha as ANP experienced the facts, the more she was able to phenomenally judge that they "really happened," that her mother had "really" rejected her to her last breath, and that her father had "really" prevented her from approaching her mother. Martha mindfully shared these realizations with me, in tears, but not in terror. As she was almost silently crying, she said, "[f]eeling that it *really* happened, *feeling that* really hurts." In her telling and my empathic listening, and in our consensus that the event had been traumatic, the known facts became socially lived truths.

Associating Mental Phenomena with Tangible Items

Achieving this common result, however, did not come easy. As ANP Martha was so phobic of the fragile EP's trauma-related physical and emotional feelings that she could only approach them in steps. It proved helpful in her therapy – as well as the treatment of many other individuals with a dissociative disorder – to associate mental phenomena with tangible items. I refer to this action as *therapeutic concretization.*

In Martha's case, I first asked her to show how she would hold a little daughter she would like to have had but could not. She dearly held the doll I offered her. Then I asked her to imagine that her daughter had been hurt and to show how she would console her. Martha held the doll even more tenderly. As a next step, I invited her to image that the doll represented little Martha. Martha instantly removed the doll from her body. She initially stretched out her hands that carried 'little Martha.' Soon thereafter she grew so emotional and destabilized that she had to put the doll on the table in front of her.

From this moment onward, we negotiated *how much* of little Martha's feelings and phenomenal realities she, the adult Martha, could take to herself. She settled for 25%. Picking up the doll, she panicked again. I encouraged her to increase the distance between them and to explore the difficulty. It became apparent that the adult Martha had tried to feel "more than 25%." She felt an urge to stretch herself. The passion impressed as a reenactment of her common effort to please her father. He was a demanding person, and when Martha met his expectations and wishes, he would not hit her. I reassured her that in my view 25% was more than enough. Less than 25% would also be fine. The adult Martha had difficulty following this lead. Her tendency to do more than she was up to was strong.

Along the way, I invited Martha to also get in touch with the little one's talents and fine character. Martha shared that she was good at dancing, drawing, and singing. The little Martha was also good-looking, good-natured, and social. Her parents and sister had been far more "stiff and distant." I then suggested that she might ask the little girl what it was like for her to be lying in her – the adult Martha's – arms. The ANP was surprised that the fragile EP was content with the degree of contact that had been achieved. While the ANP was quite stressed, the EP was pretty much relaxed. Utilizing this discrepancy and the ability of dissociative parts to intrude on each other, I proposed that the little one would intrude her feelings of contentment on the adult Martha. She could forward these feelings from her body through adult Martha's hands and arms to the adult's chest and heart. The adult Martha was encouraged to open her body and soul for the incoming sensations and affects. This strategy, which I refer to as *guided therapeutic intrusion*, worked. The emerging joy set the stage for a next action: the synthesis, personification, presentification, symbolization, and realization of another part of the traumatic history that had hitherto still remained dissociated.

In sum: The phasewise elaboration of contacts between dissociative parts, representing 'internal' actions in actions regarding tangible items as well as utilizing dissociative part's ability to intrude on each other were most helpful therapeutic strategies in Martha's treatment. They have also been effective interventions in the treatment of many other patients with a trauma-related dissociative disorder.

The Last Phase of Treatment

Martha's complete treatment encompassed 70 sessions. The penultimate phase focused on the relationship with her father. She struggled to balance, if not to integrate, her needs and desires for his recognition and acceptance of her, her urge to express her anger at him for all he had done to her, and for setting limits on his ongoing intrusive and disrespectful behaviors. It was hard for Martha to come to terms with the in part opposite needs and desires of attachment, defense, self-determination, and viable self-protection.

But she made it. She summoned her father to visit her. She expressed her anger, pain, and sorrow in clear confrontational words, and set limits to his adverse behaviors regarding her. When it became obvious that he refused to take outright responsibility for his actions, she broke off the contact and mourned over the impossibility of having her attachment needs and desires met. In a later phase, she had sporadic contacts with him and sent him home when he ignored or violated the boundaries she had set. Martha experienced and expressed that the development of a positive relationship with both her male psychiatrist and me had served as a supportive solid base for these increasingly powerful actions. Her experience and judgment in this regard met ours.

The final phase of the treatment concerned the relationship with her mother, which Martha had reenacted in recurrent problematic relationships with other women. Gradual realization of the intensity of the emotional neglect and abuse she had received from her mother helped to reduce the relational reenactments. To this end, the ANP needed to completely share the EP's mother-related feelings and memories. Following substantial therapeutic encouragement, Martha dared to meet and accept a female psychiatrist after the male psychiatrist had retired. Experiencing that the 'new' psychiatrist was accepting, respectful, and validating helped Martha to modify her phenomenal conception of women who hold a position of authority.

Epilogue

The therapy came to a close in 2013. Martha had reached complete mental health. All dissociative and other trauma-related symptoms had been resolved. Her life had turned into a good life.

Since that time Martha has been doing very well.

Martha read the verbatim of the first session as well as the present text on the assessment and the treatment in January 2016. In her view, it accurately describes her former condition, history, and treatment. She felt no need to correct a single word. Sure, it had been somewhat confrontational to read the text on her as 'the controlling ANP Martha.' But as she spontaneously and honestly added, "I was like that at times. But I am different now. I now see how limited my perspective was. The various professionals had tried to help me even if their efforts were in vain. But I really needed someone who knew and accepted what my disorder and my life were about. I was lucky I eventually found you and that we managed to cooperate."

To Martha's amazement, her father recently apologized for his wrongdoings, even if he tends to regard his wife as the source of all troubles. He basically started to behave like a good-enough father should. Martha accepted his apologies. They now manage to get along with each other reasonably well. Despite everything, she misses her deceased mother.

Sonja

Assessment is a social action. This does not mean that the patient and the clinician have to *physically* meet as the next brief case example demonstrates.

Sonja (see ToT Volume II, Chapter 12, p. 317, and Chapters 22 and 26 in this volume) had received 5 years of psychotherapy for chronic sexual abuse. While she appreciated the assistance she had received, she continued to experience many symptoms and problems in life. As she told me during our first meeting, the symptoms included "weird things" that neither she nor her therapists had understood very well. A strong, dedicated, and lively woman, Sonja was eager to gain more clarity. Some first diagnostic questions suggested that the peculiar phenomena might be dissociative symptoms. Her high SDQ-20 score of 52 was an indication to administer the SCID-D. Sonja readily consented, and appointments were made.

Much to my surprise, Sonja did not show up for the interview. After half an hour of waiting, I decided to give her a call. She might have forgotten the appointment, or something else might have prevented her coming. When she picked up the phone, she immediately excused herself, and said:

> I feel so ashamed. You know, I had not forgotten the appointment and really wanted to do the interview. It is so important to me. I drove to the building where you are situated. But as I went to open the entrance door, my hand and arm withdrew themselves. My body turned, walked me to my car, got in, and drove me home. And now here I am, at home, whereas I wanted to be with you. You must think I'm completely nuts. I feel so ashamed.

I sympathized with her feelings, and reassured her that there might be a completely sane explanation for her experiences and behaviors. We might as well examine one possibility over the phone, if she wished. Sonja was interested, and asked, "How?"

"Well, there seems to be something about you that can control your body movements while you remain conscious of what happens, right?"

"Right, that's right."

"And if that is right, then it also seems that this 'something' must have a mind of its own – or else it wouldn't be able to drive a car."

"Right again."

"And since it walked and drove you straight home, it clearly had a goal in mind."

"Must be so, I guess."

"If so, we can guess together that it must have a mind or consciousness of its own. Consciousness of itself and of its world"

"Strange!"

"I agree, it may sound strange. But let's see how strange it actually is. If it has a mind and goals of its own, we can guess its goal was to go home rather than visit me."

"But I wanted to be with you."

"Yes, and I wanted to speak with you. And if you perhaps have another mind with its own goals and with its own an ability to control body movements while you remain present, it may not be so hard to speak with it."

"What do you mean?"

"We could do it like this. Which hand is holding the phone?"

"My right hand."

"Your right hand. Fine. Is there something in front of you right now?"

"A table."

"Is it OK with you to put your left hand on the table?"

"OK."

"Now since there seems to be something about you that can move your body to achieve a goal, let's ask it to lift a finger. If it exists at all, that is. If it does not exist, nothing will . . ."

"Oh, my index finger moved."

" . . . happen. Did you move it?"

"No, it moved by itself."

"It moved by itself. Let's ask whether whatever it is that moved you finger is saying 'Yes' by moving your index finger."

"It moved again!"

"Let's ask it to move another finger for 'No.'"

"The middle finger moved."

"Let's ask it to repeat the movement if it uses the middle finger to say 'No.'"

"The middle finger went up again. It's really weird."

"I can understand that it seems weird. It is also true that the reactions have been pretty straightforward so far. Is it OK to continue?"

"Yes."

"If it's OK with you, let's then ask for a finger movement in the left hand to signal 'Stop.'"

"All fingers lift, I cannot control them."

"You cannot control them. Yet they seem to move in a controlled way and not in a random fashion."

"So it seems."

"Let's then ask whatever it is that moves your left digits and hand, if it made sure you're home and not with me."

"The index finger moved."

"It had this goal, or so it seems. Let's further ask if it feels that it is boring to talk with me."

"It says 'No.'"

"That does not seem to be the point. Let's ask if it feels risky to talk with me."

"Yes, the index finger says 'Yes.'"

"Do you have a clue as to why this something might find it risky to talk with me."

"No."

"Since whatever it is that is responding seems willing and able to signal with movements, can it perhaps write?"

"I don't know."

"We can ask. Can you get a sheet of paper and a pencil?"

"There is a notebook here that I can use."

"Excellent, ask along with me if it cares to write."

"The index finger moved."

"Let's ask next if it can write with the left hand."

"It says 'No.'"

"Then please take the phone in your left hand, and hold pencil in your right hand."

"OK."

"OK, then we can ask it to write why it is better for you, Sonja, to be home than to talk with me."

After a brief while Sonja said, "It wrote 'danger.'"

"Hm, it wrote 'danger.'"

"Yes it did."

"Let's ask if it feels it is dangerous to talk with me."

"It writes 'Yes.'"

"Let's ask why."

After some moments of silence, Sonja said, "It's written 'admission' and 'pills.'"

"Were you ever admitted to a mental hospital?"

"Yes, several times."

"And did you get pills there?"

"The index finger moves. I know I got medication for psychosis."

"Were you diagnosed as psychotic?"

"Yes."

"Did you also receive a medication for that diagnosis?"

"Yes."

"Did the medications help you?"

"No, they made matters worse. They knocked me out."

"It might fear that I will admit you to a mental hospital and that I will give you useless or even harmful pills."

"It writes 'Yes.'"

"Hm, it writes 'Yes.' I thank it for that clarification. And I say (in full consonance with my evolving evaluation of Sonja) I will not admit it or you as the whole Sonja to the hospital where I work or anywhere else. I see no reason to do that. I also do not see any reason for medication. Apart from that, I am not allowed to prescribe medication. I'm a psychologist and clinician, not a physician or psychiatrist. I would ask it if it could trust my words?"

"The index and the middle finger moved simultaneously."

"Let's ask if that means "So-so"?"

"The 'Yes' finger lifted."

"OK, then I propose to this something that can move your hand and even your whole body the following: If you do come for the interview, you can sit very close to the door of my room. I will be sitting in the furthest corner away from the door. My room is big, meaning there will be at least five meters between us. If you feel that it's too dangerous to stay, you can run, run to your car, and race home. Apart from this, I repeat: I will not admit you. I will also do my very best to see to it that you do not get any pills. You may talk to me via the fingers, the mouth, or via Sonja. You shall have full control. I want to help you, not control you in any way. Would this be acceptable to you?"

"It's fine with me," Sonja replied.

"I trust that. Does the something inside also accept my proposal? Please ask inside."

"The index finger moves. It feels sort of less tense inside."

"Fine, I will keep my promise."

"OK."

"Does it fit your schedule, Sonja, to meet me next week, same time, same place?"

"It does."

"Fine, I'll see you and the something inside you. You will be welcome. I'm looking forward to your coming."

Sonja came to the appointment at the appointed time. She took a seat close to the door of my office. I sat myself as far away from her and the door as the room permitted. It was not hard to assess Sonja's DID. The Sonja I had met before appeared to be one of several ANPs. The "something" stayed in the background and did not allow Sonja to say much about "it" and several other "things." Still, it became clear that the "something" was a dissociative part. It had sought to prevent a clinical admission, unhelpful medication as well as the assessment of an inaccurate diagnosis. But Sonja also feared the *correct* diagnosis. As described in Chapter 37, there was something about Sonja that intensely feared and hated psychologists, physicians, psychiatrists, and mental hospitals altogether – and for very good reasons.

Conclusion

When the standard assessment of dissociation and trauma is precluded, the assessment must creatively attune to and utilize the potentials and limitations the patient brings to the diagnostic table. Enacting a new diagnostic path does not mean taking a leap in the dark. Clinicians can use their theoretical maps and prior experiences, and the diagnostic dyad can combine these assets with the patient's abilities and understanding. As the two case examples illustrate, the distinctions between assessment and treatment are even less sharp in uncommon forms of enactive assessment of dissociation than they already are in the standard assessment of dissociative disorders.

The uncommon forms can include a measure of suggestion. In fact, this feature may actually be unavoidable. However, clinicians can suggest something else than what they have in mind (e.g., they can ask whether a probable child EP feels older than the ANP). Further, suggestion neither explains dissociative disorders (see ToT Volume II; Vissia et al., 2016) nor does it elucidate why patients resist particular suggestions. Apart from this, enacting a diagnostic path that may include a measure of suggestion is warranted when there are no beaten paths that generally lead to the resolution of urgent diagnostic puzzles and produce common results.

Chapter 34

How Water Beats Rocks and Other Metaphors

If an affect is related to more and different causes which the mind considers together with the affect itself, it is less harmful, we are less acted on by it, and we are affected less toward each cause, than is the case with another, equally great affect, which is related only to one cause, or to fewer causes.
Baruch Spinoza (1677, Part V, Proposition 9)

Imagination is more important than knowledge.
Albert Einstein

My voice will go with you …
Milton Erickson (1982)

Clinicians can adapt their communicative style to the needs and desires of the patient, in order to promote attunement, generate consensus, and foster new actions. They can express themselves in direct or indirect, concrete or metaphorical, and congruent or paradoxical ways. For example, they can tell a patient:

- "It is time to address this painful matter." (direct, concrete, congruent)
- "Is there anything else you wish to say before we will start addressing this painful matter?" (slightly more indirect, but concrete and congruent)
- "The other day, there was a patient who brought up issues of little importance so as to avoid addressing a painful topic." (indirect, but concrete and congruent)
- "Would you like to postpone addressing the hot stuff? Of course, you can. And if you postpone it, how would you feel when the hour is over?" (concrete, but slightly indirect, and slightly paradoxical)
- "I don't want you to start before you're ready." (concrete and direct, but paradoxical inasmuch as the patient is actually ready but feels a strong need for control and would therefore probably resist a congruent remark like "Since you're ready we can start").
- "I doubt if you are ready to address this tough issue. I do not want you to start going there yet." (concrete, more indirect than the above statement, and paradoxical inasmuch as the clinician feels that the patient is ready and wants to address the issue, but expects that the patient will not discuss the issue when the clinician decides it is time).

Clinicians can cast concrete messages in terms of analogies and metaphors. These transformations can prove useful when patients are not ready to receive concrete messages or tend to resist them. Apart from this, some patients are inspired more by analogies and metaphors than by direct statements. It generally holds that these means of communication recognize, support, and strengthen patients' (sense of) self-determination. Further, some patients communicate in analogies and metaphors themselves at times. This may invite clinicians to react in these terms in return.

Patients do not respond passively to clinicians' communications. Inasmuch as they perceive these communications, they synthesize clinicians' ideas in one way or another.[1] They consciously or more unconsciously search and decide how useful the clinicians' words are and what meaning they may have. Enactive trauma therapy holds that clinicians may sometimes engage the patients' exploratory (meaning-making) actions more when they use indirect suggestions rather than direct instructions. As Erickson and Rossi (1979, p. 31) emphasized, "[t]he indirect forms of suggestion are most useful for exploring potentialities and facilitating a patient's natural response tendencies rather than imposing control over behavior." This communicative style perfectly fits the enactive and egalitarian perspective and respects patients' individuality and self-determination that their perpetrators have denied them. They are a most useful means of avoiding a second-person perspective in which clinicians are dominant and patients 'must' follow their leads.

The following case examples illustrate the use of metaphor and some other forms of indirect suggestion. Sonja's controlling EP introduced in the previous chapter had many reservations regarding the treatment. It therefore seemed wise to share the diagnosis, its main features, and its probable (if not practically certain) causes, and its implications for treatment in the form of a metaphor of a river. I chose a natural scene because Sonja loved nature. There are no mountains in The Netherlands, no rocky surfaces where rivers emerge, but several grand rivers (e.g., the Rhine) that cross the country before flowing into the North Sea. My hope was that the tale of the birth and subsequent life of a river would not speak to her life too directly – but directly enough, seeing that rivers were relevant elements of her *umwelt*. The Netherlands is a waterlogged land, and water is for the country both friend and foe (see Chapter 30). These combined features would, I trusted, allow a sufficiently safe and acceptable presentation of the strengths and limitations of rivers.

How Water Beats Rocks[2]

I shared this metaphor with Sonja in the very beginning of her therapy. My comments focus on techniques. The applied techniques include Ericksonian approaches to hypnotherapy that, in my experience and opinion, can be very helpful within and beyond hypnosis.

Some colleagues fear that 'hypnosis' (loosely defined, the organismic mode of high concentration) may suggest factitious dissociative parts and false traumatic memories.

---

1 Prior to any understanding, there must be a perception; one individual may not perceive another individual's communications.

2 The original Dutch text of the metaphor can be found in Nijenhuis (1992).

be reminded that the empirical status of this hypothesis is weak (see ToT Volume II), and that the metaphor basically spoke to phenomena that were already known prior to the session.

The main idea was to enhance Sonja's power of action, to foster her understanding, acceptance, and hope for positive common results. To this end, I offered several ideas about how therapeutic progress could be achieved. For example, the metaphor communicated how useful it is when dissociative parts listen to each other, get to know each other, and learn to appreciate each other more. The metaphor also included the idea of how important it is that dissociative parts learn to cooperate with each other more. Care was taken to express that this work would probably entail hardship. Enactive trauma therapy for chronic abuse is not a walk in the garden; it can be rough and tough going at times. To avoid totalitarianism, I did not want to impose ideas on Sonja, so my aim was to encourage her own search for meaning.

Table 34.1. A river's life

Transcript	Comments
As you are sitting in your chair, leaning against the backrest, you may find pleasure in listening to sounds from nearby or farther away.	The words "sitting" and "leaning" describe factual behaviors to *fixate attention*. The phrase " ... you may find pleasure ..." couples these self-evident facts with a *permissive invitation*. Open-ended *statements* invite individuals to explore themselves. The invitation attunes to Sonja's affects ("pleasure") and ideas. It utilizes what she is already doing (sitting in a chair, leaning, listening to my words). Clinicians gain their patients' attention by focusing on their current behavior and experiences (Erickson, 1958b, 1959). This focusing is the basis of the *utilization* approach (Erickson & Rossi, 1979). Sonja can listen to my words from nearby or from farther away, not listen to my words at all, or listen to other sounds: All options are available, and all are fine. The sentence invites Sonja to examine herself, without defining what she will do or exactly will have to do. And who could even precisely know what an individual will do next? A suggestion ("listen") is coupled to an already exciting action ("leaning"), *creating a network of associations* (Erickson & Rossi, 1979, p. 41). In sum, the opening statements involve a gentle invitation to listen to sounds and to find pleasure therein.
Sometimes relaxing a bit more flows smoothly when there are sounds that rustle, whisper, and gurgle, like the leaves of trees, splashing water of a lake, or a murmuring river.	"... relaxing a bit more ..." is a friendly invitation to deepen her relaxation, without making excessive demands. "A bit more" suffices, and Sonja can decide for herself what constitutes "a bit." There were actually leaves rustling ("sounds from farther away") as the session proceeded. This rustling might help her to bridge listening to natural sounds and listening to my words. The rustling sounds might serve as a natural bridge to the equally peaceful whispering and splashing water of a lake and a river. The effect described is a naturally occurring phenomenon that may provide Sonja with associations that help her to relax a little.

Transcript	Comments
Everything you encompass might listen and wonder, now or later, where all the passing water once emerged and where it has been before.	"All that you encompass . . ." is an example of *multispeak*: All existing and activated dissociative parts are invited to join Sonja, as an ANP, in listening and wondering; "wonder" may serve to raise affective interest; "might listen and wonder" is a permissive formulation of the idea that there is something to listen to and wonder about; "now or later" leaves Sonja the choice as to *when* to listen and wonder (*implied directive*). If she feels that these and other words, phrases, and sentences are of relevance to her, she can synthesize and further act on them. If they do not meet her interests, nothing is lost. Erickson and Rossi (1979, Chapter 2) refer to this type of indirect suggestion as *indirect associative focusing*. "Where all the passing water has been before" asks where she (as any dissociative part) originated and has been before she arrived here.
Have you ever let an image come to your mind of a river's origin, of its source?	*Raising a question without desiring or expecting a verbal response* fixates and directs attention, and it elicits explorative actions (Sternberg, 1975). The metaphor presents ideas, such as portraying Sonja as a river, as an unconscious and conscious mind with an origin.
And have you ever felt it?	". . . felt . . ." directs attention to Sonja's affects and sensations regarding her origins (*ideoaffective and ideosensory focusing*). Images (visual perceptions) and sounds (auditory perceptions) can become linked with physical and emotional feelings. The sentence is an example of *indirect ideodynamic focusing* (Erickson & Rossi, 1979, Chapter 2). It also constitutes a *truism* in that everyone has (had) childhood experiences.
Welling up from the soil, frail and tiny, a rivulet begins to make her way.	"Welling up" and "making" are kinesthetic terms; they emphasize physical "feelings." A frail or fragile rivulet presented in the female form alludes to Sonja as a fetus, baby, and toddler. No matter how tiny, any unfolding organism must find a way, must make meaning, must find a path, must enact a phenomenal self and *umwelt*. This is an undeniable fact that pertains to traumatized individuals as much as to anyone else. Another truism is that any newborn is still frail. Sonja's frailty as a child, thus, was only natural, not a weakness.
Everyone inside can listen and join watching a meandering, agile, and lively creek that is to become a grand river.	"Everyone inside": multispeak; "can": The friendly atmosphere is continued to allow Sonja as any dissociative part to listen, watch, and wonder. Life is portrayed as a capricious movement, but a child will nonetheless become an adult. "Grand" rivers earn respect. There is an impressive future ahead.

Transcript	Comments
Some rivulets have an easy time. They see the light of day where the soil is soft, where drops easily gather, where a riverbed is easily formed.	"Some rivulets" implies that not all tiny evolving rivers have an easy time to enact a phenomenal self and *umwelt*, and to embed in this *umwelt*, to be an inherent part of it. The metaphor refers to injustice. Life more generally is depicted as an integrative development ("drops that gather"). Rivulets are portrayed as acting agents (*going beyond the limits of a class*), which may help Sonja and everything she encompasses to identify with them. The words "light," "soft," and "easily" fit the words "pleasure" and "relaxation." Together these *interspersed words* (Erickson & Rossi, 1979; Haley, 1967) can induce a positive mood. While this *positive set* is good for a start, it is also important to attune to the brutality of Sonja's life.
Other streams are not that lucky and encounter a hard, rocky terrain.	The story, thus, takes a *dramatic turn*, just as adverse events turn the course of one's life. Integration can be hard when life entails adverse events. Some children meet adverse events from early childhood onward – which applied to Sonja. The metaphor communicates that this is not their fault but a matter of bad luck.
They have a hard time collecting the drops of water and keeping them together.	Under these circumstances, integrative actions are hard to achieve.
Notice how a little stream does its utmost to make a riverbed, a place to gain power and to mature.	The little stream is referred to as a "she." While grammatically incorrect, this move may stimulate Sonja to *identify with the struggling rivulet.*
Then she manages to start off, but right away strikes upon a rock that she needs to conquer.	Sonja is depicted as a courageous little girl who gave her best. She achieved some developmental steps, but then finds her way massively blocked. If life is to proceed, potentially or actually traumatizing events need to be " . . . conquered . . . " in one way or another. The *interspersed terms* "hard," "rocky," "trouble," "strikes," "rock," and "conquer" reflect Sonja's world, thus, involve *affective attunement.*
Once upon a time there was a rivulet that began to make its riverbed despite the hard surface. Then she hit upon a big rock that crossed its path.	"Once upon a time" is the classical opening of a fairy tale, and many fairy tales comprise injurious events, presented here as "a big rock." The fairy-tale structure creates a relatively safe distance between the story and the listener. A hypothetical river becomes a tangible river as well as an agent. Sonja is indirectly invited to identify herself to a degree with the unlucky rivulet. "Embedding in a hard surface" obviously stands for a potentially traumatizing milieu. And too much is too much: Her personality became injured, became traumatized.
But now look at how that little wonder beats the strength of the rock. Look at how the water conquered the mighty rock. A rock may be big, but water is clever. Look how the water glides along the boulder, how it eludes the obstacle.	The injured individual is depicted as an intelligent marvel, as an agent who divides and continues as a "dividual" (see ToT Volume I., pp. 67 and 283) to survive. The big rock is now portrayed as an "invasive tower of strength." The sexual abuse connotation is indirectly, yet evidently, addressed. " . . . beats . . . " has a *double meaning: a figural and a literal.* That is, it is acknowledged that Sonja may literally want to crush the invaders.

Transcript	Comments
Doesn't that make you marvel?	Asking a question without expecting or awaiting an explicit answer *elicits attention, stimulates engagement* in the story, and, as mentioned before, *evokes explorative tendencies.* The use of the word "marvel" honors Sonja, values her dissociation, and also communicates acknowledgment and acceptance of her aggressive feelings.
The stream did not need to think twice. One part just slipped to the left and another to the right. And together they outclassed the rock.	Many individuals with dissociative disorders describe their conscious and self-conscious dissociative subsystems as 'parts' of them. This metaphor is used here as it is used in the theory of structural dissociation of the personality. "The stream did not need to think twice" suggests that the reactions are evolutionary prepared, that they are a natural reaction. Presenting the stream as an agent is another example of *depicting an inanimate object as a subject.* It invites Sonja to identity with the stream and to learn about herself in a safe way.
When a terrain is full of huge rocks, the water may repeat its cunning moves. Sometimes the waters will find their own way.	A terrain full of rocks is a clear metaphor for chronic traumatization. Here starts a description of different prototypical dissociative parts (I had already heard about the presence of the classic prototypes).
Circumstances permitting, some streams flow without too much trouble. By watering the plants that line the shores, they enable common life. Other streams encounter rough terrains, causing waterfalls and torrents.	These streams portray ANPs. As ANPs, she could at least continue existing amid all abuse and neglect. One might understand water to represent consciousness and plants to stand for objects of consciousness. Torrents and waterfalls suggest power and depict fragile fight EPs as well as controlling EPs. Their wildness is related to "rough terrain" as a broad metaphor for chronic traumatization. Consciousness does not remain calm when there is great pressure.
The calm waters may hear the wild waters at times, and their roar may impress them.	This sentence communicates that ANPs may be intruded on, or may, more generally, hear the fight and the controlling EPs. "At times" is added to attune to the common fact that the intrusion is intermittent, not chronic. Fragile fight EPs and controlling EPs are encouraged to listen to the ANPs.
You may wonder whether the rough and wild waters also hear the quieter streams? Perhaps not, and perhaps that is also why they may have forgotten that they both flow from one source and therefore belong together, no matter what else happens.	The fight and controlling EPs are reminded that they are part of a wider system no matter how autonomous they may feel. I introduce the powerful parts before the terribly scared and hurt fragile EPs, and the EPs in passive defense. Other parts and at times other individuals as well regard passive defense as a weakness. Focusing on strength prior to weakness presents the patient in a more favorable light.

Transcript	Comments
But, who knows, the wilder waters may have their calmer moments, sooner or later, that allow them to listen more.	Communication between these EPs and ANPs is encouraged and presented as a future task. "Sooner or later" allows the powerful parts involved to decide for themselves when they will start to listen more. "Sooner or later" *covers all possibilities of the class of time* and implicitly suggests that the dissociative parts will start to listen more to each other. Implicit suggestion is an important element of Erickson's approach to therapy. Formulating the issue in the form of a question, I intend to *stimulate self-exploration*.
Or maybe the rivers possess underground connections hidden from eye and ear?	With this sentence I convey that my awareness of the existence of conscious but covert as well as more or less unconscious connections between the various dissociative parts.
There may also be tiny streams that have not managed to leave the mountain range so far.	This is the first direct introduction of the fragile EPs, which may feel injured and which are still caught in 'trauma-land, 'trauma-time,' and a 'trauma-identity' ('Flatland').
They may exist as quiet lakes trying to gather enough water from the source to burst their banks.	"quiet lakes" alludes to the hypoaroused fragile EPs. Some fragile EPs may be gathering enough power to intrude on the ANPs and controlling EPs more. Intrusion is portrayed as something that becomes possible when the quiet lakes "burst their banks."
Or they wait for mountain snow and glaciers to defrost when the first sunbeams of Spring pierce through the clouds at last.	Here I am saying that the development of more positive relationships with others can counter the attachment phobia (warm sunlight). "First" suggests that there will also be "later" sunbeams. "At last" conveys that the development may be more difficult and slower than the patient and the clinician would wish. "Clouds" and "old snow" (see below) stand for traumatic memories. The verb "pierce" has a slightly aggressive tone.
You know, old snow will melt one day.	"one day" is sufficiently vague to fit any developmental pace. "You know" suggests that the patients consciously or unconsciously knows that she can do the work. "old snow" suggests that the patient's traumatic experiences are not fresh; this utilizes the fact that some patches of old snow remain intact for a long time despite rising temperatures in the Spring. However, eventually all snow melts (in The Netherlands in any case!).
The time may have come for the branches that flow from that single source to start to hear each other. The time may have come to recollect their beginnings.	A friendly suggestion: "The time may have come" is different from the strict formulation "the time has come." It necessitates recollecting the beginnings of the dissociation of the personality and the troubles in life this division caused. The sentence fixates attention on change through recollecting traumatic experiences.

Transcript	Comments
If you listen well, that might be the story you hear in the waters.	The EPs entail their traumatic experiences. This is what the ANPs may start to grasp better. The ANPs are encouraged to listen to one another more and particularly to the EPs. "listen" harks back to the opening statements of the session, and "listen well" means that therapy demands the dedicated investment of energy.
The branches may start to realize that the perilous rocks have now been passed, that the streams can bend toward each other more.	The ANPs and the EPs are summoned to presentify the traumatic memories of the EPs. All dissociative parts can in this sense start communicating and cooperating with each other.
After all, all waters stem from that single source, and water is water.	No matter how different the various dissociative parts may be, they belong to one system. "Water is water" is a truism, to be sure; technically it is a tautology. Therapeutically, however, the phrase can help dissociative parts to realize that "after all" that has happened to them during and after the traumatization and the personality divisions, they are nonetheless one. Furthermore, one might also understand the phrase to mean that consciousness as such ("water") cannot be divided (ToT Volume II, Chapter 13).
Streams that have gained the power of action can determine their own course ever more, and they can even decide to unite their forces. They may want to settle their issues with the rocks and other obstacles in ways that used to be utterly unattainable.	It is clear that objects (streams) cannot act. However, as already mentioned above, in terms of metaphors and analogies objects can be given roles of subjects or of agents. We can say, for example, that "the stone feels angry," "the water is clever," or "the lake has deep feelings." Erickson (1966) presented a tomato plant that can feel a kind of comfort, and that can have other dispositions usually available only to subjects. The sentences contain interspersed terms such as "determine," "own course," "decide," "unite," and "settle issues," which support an increase of power of action.
Did you imagine the force of merged waters?	The bundling of forces of the various dissociative parts increases their power of action.
Do you know that bundled water can scrape out, grind, even split stones? The more pressure, the better it works. Imagine split rocks becoming gravel that a grand river washes to the riverbanks and finally into the ocean.	The description includes aggressive connotations. Bundled water, that is, the collaboration of the ANPs and the EPs, can be used to overcome the traumatization. The sentence associates "pressure" (potent affects, collaboration, dedication) and effectiveness.
These images and thoughts and other things can engage everything inside you. They can use them inasmuch as they are useful to them.	Multispeak: The term "useful" *singles out the primordial affective interest of operationally autonomous systems.*
Perhaps that works even better when you doze a bit before you return to the chair that carries you and the ground under your feet.	Together with the previous sentence, the current sentence constitutes a *posthypnotic suggestion.* "Drowse a bit . . ." is what Sonja was already doing. Her factual behavior is linked with the effectiveness of engagement in "these images and thoughts and other things," "the chair that carries you," and "the ground under your feet." This suggests being held by something or someone: This crazy world includes more than misery. The kinesthetic term orients Sonja to her embodiment.

Transcript	Comments
You will receive a tape with these words. You can *listen* to them and *use* them, if you feel like it, and if you have the time.	The fact that Sonja will receive the tape is combined with an extended posthypnotic suggestion. The verbs "listen" and "use" are emphasized. By implying that Sonja decides, she stays in control, it is a *suggestion with an open end* (Erickson & Rossi, 1979, Chapter 2, "2.6): She can listen and use the ideas if they meet her interests and abilities.

Epilogue

Sonja received the tape and used it endlessly. As the main ANP, she said she did not really understand why, but the story somehow intrigued her. She had to return to it time and again. Some of her EPs would tell me at some point that they knew very well why *they* liked the tape so much: They loved to hear stories – no one had ever cared to read Sonja stories, whether in childhood or later. Fight EPs felt recognized given the inclusion of some aggressive elements. Controlling EPs did not trust words (or clinicians) much, but they appreciated the story because it was not "weak" but presented a harsh world that calls for tremendous endurance and strength. Other components they appreciated were control and self-determination.

With adaptations, the metaphor was also used in the treatment of other patients, who generally received it well. It helped them to accept and understand themselves more. Here are some comments:

- "The story expressed that I am normal, that I have a normal reaction to an abnormal world."
- "The image of the rivulets struggling to stay together immediately appealed to the little ones."

The story also provided hope and positive expectations for the future:

- "It was very consoling to hear that the rivulet is not wrong or guilty, but clever."
- One day, the rivulet will become a grand river; something good can come out of me. It gave me hope."

The metaphor broke through isolation and enhanced feelings of togetherness:

- "The silent ones inside had never expected that they had anything to do with the loud ones. The story fostered the realization that they belong together."
- "In the beginning, the loud streams despised the fearful, stupid, silent, and shy little streams. This started to change when it was said that they can recognize each other because despite their differences they all consist of water and all flow from the same source."

Some patients commented that the story had motivated them to return to and integrate traumatic memories:

- "The story clarified that it is necessary to return to the rocks, and that perhaps now, with increased power and joint forces, it is possible to face up to them in a different way. But the work is very difficult and demanding."
- "Various dissociative parts were allowed to link their traumatic experiences to big rocks."

The metaphor has also been used to accompany the fusion of two or more dissociative parts. In these cases, the story had previously been used for the other purposes indicated. In some cases, the patient's two arms and hands were linked to the idea of the dissociative parts to be joined. This application will be discussed in Chapter 37.

Paralinguistics

The above transcript does not include descriptions of paralinguistic components of therapeutic communications. However, these elements are of major importance. A word is a word, like a written (musical) note is ink on paper. But like notes words, phrases, and sentences can be emphasized, suggesting a particular meaning. The ways in which the musical notes are played turn a dry musical score into a musical experience. Words can similarly be spoken in a particular rhythm and pace, and their timing is critical. Some words can be spoken faster and others slower. The first words of a sentence may be spoken in a higher pitch and its later words in a lower tone of voice. The reverse order of emphasis is clearly also possible and exerts a different effect. A further option is to emphasize a particular word by uttering it after a pause. Speaking and playing a musical instrument are not that different. Proper paralinguistics clearly support attunement and therapeutic dancing with the patient more generally. It is hard *not* to move your body or to be moved when the music flows.

Some illustrations of paralinguistic principles may be helpful. Mothers (and fathers) who want their child to relax more tend to speak in a way known as "motherese," which involves the use of rather simple language delivered with a calming, repetitive, wave-like rhythm. I used this phrasing in sentences like, "as you are *sitting* in your chair, *leaning* against the backrest, you may find ... *pleasure* ... in *listening* to sounds ... from nearby or farther away." The sentence was spoken in a soothing, undulating rhythm. The verbs *sitting, leaning, and listening* were slightly emphasized. The word *pleasure* was particularly accentuated.

To augment the relaxing effect, the various phrases were spoken in the rhythm of Sonja's inhalation and exhalation. Relaxation is further stimulated when, as the text proceeds, the clinician speaks less when the patient inhales and more when the patient exhales. This may progress to a phase in which the clinicians begin using less words and uttering those words during later phases of patients' exhalation (" ... a river can relax ..., can relax ..., relax ..."). Speaking words as patient exhales generally invites relaxation. This effect can also be achieved or increased when the words spoken while the patient is exhaling are uttered in a lower pitch and with decreasing speed. Words spoken while the patient inhales generally cause arousal, particularly when they are uttered in a somewhat faster pace.

These various strategies can also be combined as in the sentence: "They can imbue them inasmuch as they are useful to them." The phrase "They can imbue them ..." matched Sonja's inhalation, " ... insofar as ..." accompanied the switch from inhalation to exhalation, and the phrase "... they are useful to them ..." accompanied her exhalation. The pace of the final words was decelerated, and the pitch was lowered.

The emphasis on "... *pleasure* ..." in the third phrase of the first sentence contrasted a bit with the rhythm of the first two phrases. As a result, the emphasized word "... *pleasure* ..." should hopefully draw special attention. The latter effect was further supported and strengthened by inserting brief pauses before and after the word "pleasure." Taken together, the intended goals of the first two phrases were to explicitly attune to Sonja's phenomenal experiences and to implicitly attune to her embodiment (e.g., her breathing pattern). The goal of the strongly emphasized word "... *pleasure* ..." was to invite Sonja to "... find ..." some pleasure and, more specifically, to find pleasure in listening to "... sounds ..."

The opening sentence ("As you are sitting in your chair, leaning against the backrest, you may find pleasure in listening to sounds from nearby or farther away") would have had a different meaning had the emphases been placed on different words. Compare the following phrases:

"As *you* are sitting in your chair ..." or
"As you are sitting in your *chair* ..." or
"As you are sitting in *your* chair ..." or
"As *you* are sitting in *your* chair ..." or
"As you are sitting in your chair ..." (i.e., no particular emphasis on any word at all).

The sentence would also have had a different meaning had the emphasized words not been spoken in a slightly higher pitch than the words that followed, but in a far higher pitch or a lower pitch than the rest of the sentence. The actually applied pitch can be expressed as "As you are (←lower pitch) sitting (←slightly higher pitch) in your chair (←lower pitch), leaning (←slightly higher pitch) against the backrest (←lower pitch), you may find (←lower pitch) pleasure (←slightly higher pitch) in listening to (←lower pitch) sounds (←slightly higher pitch) from nearby or farther away (←lower pitch).[3]

A higher pitched word does not necessarily mean that a word spoken at a lower pitch receives less emphasis. For example, in the sentence "The time may have come for the branches that flow from that single source to make each other's ears, and to recollect their beginnings," the last word "... beginnings ..." was emphasized. To achieve the desired effect, this particular word was spoken in a lower pitch: "... recollect their (slightly higher

3 The backward arrows indicate the emphasis placed on the respective previous word.

pitch) ... beginnings (lower pitch). The difference between an upward and downward directed verbal melody is like the contrast between Chopin's frequent fast and upward melody lines and the solid first eight notes of Beethoven's Fifth with deep emphases on the fourth and the eighth note (Figure 34.1).

Figure 34.1. Chopin and Beethoven.

Years of practice and teaching have taught me that clinicians may speak in a too "flat" manner, and that their timing may be off. The content of their words may be fitting, but a technically correct rendering of the score does not make the music. When clinicians are not communicating engagement in their patients' phenomenal world and affective interests, patients will probably not be moved very much. They may not 'get' the message, or they may feel that the clinician is basically disinterested in them. And they may find the clinician boring in return. Moreover, perpetrators communicate emotional disinterest in their victims' experiences and point of view. This is another reason why technically correct formulations or comments can still miss their target. An emotionally flat style of communication may therefore 'poison' rather than 'nourish' traumatized individuals – or leave the words merely insignificant. Similar unintended effects can ensue when clinicians present new and adequate ideas, but in a phase at which patients are not ready to receive and use them.

As noted before, there is no reality that is meaningful and valuable in and of itself. Meaning and value depend on subjects, and meaning and value can change with time and development. Some children appreciate Maria Callas' rendering of Vicenzo Bellini's *Casta Diva*, but the fact is that most need to mature to hear the beauty of her rendition – and some may never embrace her art. I was moved to read this comment to the YouTube film of her sublime performance in Paris, 1958: "No. Not possible. I am 64, and, though I have very little knowledge of Maria Callas, I have seen this for the first time. I say again, No. I am stunned, frozen to my seat, *awestruck* by her voice, her emotion, her hands, her arms, her shoulders, *her*! I am a fool child, not knowing till now of Maria Callas." One man responded: "I am 67 and I saw her in Genoa, perhaps her last *Tosca*. I was a boy then and the experience is etched on my brain and I will never forget it, ever."

No matter how well meant, how adequate or even brilliant the clinicians' words and ideas may be, they are only wind if patients fail to find meaning and value in them. Statements and questions that are spoken technically correct in terms of a third-person perspective must also fit the phenomenal I (patient)–You (clinician) relationship. If they do not, they are therapeutically inert. Hence, clinicians consider not only how technically correct their words and their paralinguistic and other nonverbal communications are, they also, from their second-person perspective, phenomenally judge how well their communications fit their patients' phenomenal experiences and conceptions. They *care* how well their words enrich their patients' person perspectives.

As remarked above, clinicians' phenomenal judgment depends on their first-person phenomenal experiences and their phenomenal self-judgment in the quasi-second-person perspective. For example, clinicians would better experience and know how they feel and operate in the therapeutic situation and in their life more generally. They are thus challenged to experience how certain or uncertain, joyful or sad, content or frustrated, energetic or exhausted, or patient or impatient they are, both presently and more generally. Their ongoing first-person experiences and quasi-second person judgments affect their second-person perspective regarding their patients. Their patients *feel* this, consciously or unconsciously, in terms of their second-person perspective regarding the clinician. These feelings in patients affect their phenomenal judgments of any moment generated in a session.

Patients' feelings regarding their clinicians are affected by the clinician's attitude, choice of words and images, communicative style, tone of voice, rhythm of speaking, and timing. These feelings are also influenced by their facial expressions and their more general body postures. In this light, an affectively very "flat" presentation impedes a positive therapeutic relationship. Therapy generally works much better when patients and clinicians are socially engaged and effectively communicate this engagement. In physical terms, therapy is far more effective when the action system of social engagement of patients and clinicians as well as the implied ventral vagal nerve are wide awake (see ToT Volume II, Chapter 16). Under the influence of their negative interpersonal experiences in life, patients have likely become hypersensitive to the interpersonal actions and passions of others. To orient themselves, they have become masters of tracking the affects and probable intentions of another person. Such affects and intentions are often expressed in nonverbal and paralinguistic forms more than in spoken words.

In order to become more aware of their own communicative actions and passions, clinicians should videotape some of their sessions with the camera directed at themselves rather than at their patients, or at the very least at their patients and themselves as a dyad.

Clinicians should also practice and track their presentations by speaking to themselves in the mirror or into a camera as if they were talking to a particular patient, just as musicians, painters, and other artists live by the adage: practice, practice, practice. This effort could help them to become more consciously aware of their paralinguistic and other nonverbal expressions as they deliver a metaphor or other some other intervention. As they watch and listen to themselves, clinicians should furthermore from time to time assume the role of the other (i.e., the patient) in order to get an impression of what it is like to be at the receiving end of their own expressions.

Metaphor Construction and Preparation

Therapeutic metaphors require careful preparation. Apart from Erickson's own writings (1980), inspirational sources include Lankton and Lankton's works (1983, 1989). A general framework for metaphor construction is to formulate, in concrete language, (1) the problem that is to be addressed, (2) the common goals of the therapeutic work, and (3) the route that can lead to the realization of these goals.

The next step is to choose the theme of the metaphor. It should preferably fit the affect-laden interests and phenomenal world of the patient rather than those of the clinician. Sonja, for example, loved nature, whereas other patients may be more into music, theater, a particular sport, or a hobby like painting or walking, computers, cars, or engineering. There are also many options within a suitable domain of interest: Nature includes plants, rivers, mountains, islands, trees, animals, and much more.

By applying the chosen theme, each element of the concrete problem, goal, and route is represented in the metaphor. For example, consciousness, life, and development can become depicted in terms of an evolving river. A harsh terrain can stand for an adverse emotional climate. Potentially traumatizing events can be portrayed as big stones, and dissociative parts of the personality as divided streams.

It sometimes happens that a patient, for whatever reason, does not respond favorably to the chosen theme of the metaphor. For example, Sonja might, unbeknownst to me, have negative associations with rivers or water more generally. It is, therefore, a safe strategy – as well as a good exercise in fostering flexibility as clinician – to prepare an alternative metaphor that communicates the same ideas, albeit in terms of a different theme.

Clinicians who are just starting to use metaphors best prepare these in writing. This allows them the time to choose fitting sentences, phrases, and words, and to ponder how they are probably best delivered. First versions can be modified and shortened. For example, reading the text, clinicians may feel that it is too wordy. They may feel it lacks a clear storyline, a plot, or appealing solutions to maintain the patient's interest. Formulating the complete metaphor in writing also allows the clinician to experiment with techniques such as fixating attention, raising interest, using truisms and indirect suggestions, and suggestions with an open ending.

Such detailed and meticulous preparation is, of course, time-consuming. It demands energy and patience. However, the work is worth the investment, in part because, with practice, constructing and delivering a metaphor becomes less challenging. In a way, it is like learning to walk, drive, or ride a bike. In negative terms: no pain, no gain. Phrased more positively with Lao-Tzu, "[d]o the difficult things while they are easy and do the great things while they are small. A journey of a thousand miles must begin with a single step." As always, knowledge is a treasure, but practice is the key to it.

Sleeping Beauty: A Tale for Young Fragile EPs

The following transcript metaphor is offered without further comment. Some readers may find it interesting and worthwhile to explore how a fairy tale can be used as a metaphor for traumatization and its possible consequences.

You know, I guess, the story of Sleeping Beauty. She was the lovely daughter of a King and a Queen. The country inhabited 13 fairies, and all except one were invited to celebrate her birth. Her parents, however, had only 12 golden plates, so that the 13th fairy had to stay at home. The fairies presented the Princess with talents that would make people love her, and that would protect her from harm. As the 11th fairy was pronouncing her wish, the 13th suddenly appeared. Seeking revenge that she had not been invited, she screamed in anger: "One day the Princess shall be pricked by a spindle and shall fall down dead." The fairy that had not yet voiced her wish stood up. Since she could not remove the curse but could only soften it, she spoke: "No, the Princess shall not die, but she will fall into a deep sleep for 100 years."

The King and Queen were determined to prevent the curse placed on their daughter by the spiteful fairy from coming true. They sent out an order that all spindles in the entire Kingdom be burnt. The wishes of the gentle fairy came true: The Princess grew up to be a pretty, sweet, and sensible young girl. Everybody loved her.

One day, the King and Queen had planned to go for a ride. The Princess woke early that morning. Everyone was still asleep, so she wandered about the whole castle. At last, she came to an old tower. There she climbed the winding staircase and reached a little door. Its lock held a rusty key. When she turned it, the door flew open. In the room sat an old woman spinning her flax. She was so deaf that she had failed to hear the command to destroy all spindles in the Kingdom. The Princess wanted to spin too, but the spindle pricked her finger, and she instantly fell into a deep sleep upon a nearby bed. Then the sleep spread and affected the whole castle: the horses, dogs, doves, and flies; the fire in the hearth, and the wind in the trees; the servants, the cook and the kitchen boy, and even the King and the Queen who were preparing themselves for the ride. A hedge of brier roses began to grow up around the castle. Every year it grew higher until at last nothing more could be seen of the castle, not even the flag in the tower.

However, there remained a legend in the Kingdom about the lovely Sleeping Beauty, as the King's daughter came to be called. From time to time Princes came and tried to force their way through the hedge but found it impossible. The thorns, as though alive, grabbed at them and would not let them through.

After many years another Prince came to the country. An old man told him the tale of Sleeping Beauty's castle. He heard that many Princes had tried to make it through the brier hedge. None had succeeded, the old man said. Caught in the hedge, many had perished.

But the young man said, "I am not afraid. I want to reach Sleeping Beauty." The old man did all in his power to persuade him not to go. But the Prince would not listen.

Now the 100 years were just ending. As the Prince approached, the thorns of the hedge turned into beautiful roses. The hedge made way for him of its own accord and let him pass unharmed. In the courtyard, the Prince saw the horses and dogs still sleeping. On the roof sat the sleeping doves with their heads tucked under their wings. When he went into the house, the flies were asleep on the walls and the servants asleep in the halls. Near the throne lay the King and Queen sleeping beside each other. The cook, the kitchen boy, and the kitchen maid all slept with their heads resting on the kitchen table.

The Prince went on farther. At last, he reached the tower and opened the door to the little room where the Princess lay asleep. There she was, looking so beautiful that he could not take his eyes off her. He bent down to kiss her. As his lips touched hers, Sleeping Beauty opened her eyes and smiled up at him. At that moment, everyone and everything in the Kingdom woke up and looked around at each other with astonished eyes. But as life returned to them, they did not realize that they had been sleeping for so many years.

Even today some children are faced with the Sleeping Beauty's fate. Perhaps because of a bad fairy or evil spirit. Pricked by a sharp needle, they fall in a long and deep sleep, and become hidden behind a thorny hedge that scares practically anyone off. After many years only a rumor remains. Some people regard it as a mere myth, saying, "It can't be! Children do not sleep that long, and one cannot stop the world. Leave the story alone."

However, when the time is ripe, an outsider can pass through the hedge unharmed to find the sleeping child. It may be like awakening children or other persons who believe that they only dozed off for a while, and that the world is as it used to be. Isn't it so that long gone times can seem so real and so close? But you can pass through the hedge and notice that the past is ... gone. Would you like to take a good look with me?

The Boxer

Once upon a time there was a girl[4] who experienced bad times. She became so enraged that a part of her only wanted to become a boxer – someone who isn't scared of anything

4 I used the metaphor for a woman with DID.

or anyone. The angry one was not so strong and tough that he could beat mighty and cruel adversaries. Anyone understands this: It takes time and effort to gain power. That's why he[5] practiced the kind of hitting and kicking he knew too well. Standing in front of a mirror he initially saw himself, a hero fighting for the hurt and fragile girl. While boys cannot defeat adults, boys don't give up easily. He practiced and practiced, and practiced some more. Fully absorbed in the action, at some point the girl popped in the mirror. As if by magic he grew convinced that he had hit her and not himself. Wow, that felt good! I can do this! In his triumph, he overlooked how closely the image in the mirror related to him. He also forgot who were his actual foes.

A passerby wondered why the boxer was hitting his reflection. "I'm teaching that silly girl a lesson, can't you see?" The observer gently replied, "You're like a cat fighting his own image in the mirror. You, however, can grasp what a cat cannot. Take a very good look. Aren't you hitting *yourself*?" The boxer ignored this uncomfortable fact. No, no, no, he was strong, the girl was weak. He loved his power as much as he despised her fragility. The outsider got the message. Trying to help the brave boxer, he said, "All that practicing has paid off. You have grown very strong. How about starting to face some new and more challenging opponents?"

While the boxer continued to feel a need to deny his close relationship to the little girl, he gladly agreed that he had gained power. And he did dare to turn his gaze from the mirror to images of brutal times past. His eyes and feelings met a horrible sight: Adults torturing a child. Enraging! Revenge!

But, as the boxer soon wondered, where will I be if I release my anger? Will I lose my power? Will I dissolve?

The outsider reassured him: "All fine boxers are tired after intense battles. All boxers need to reload their batteries. They will probably engage in more clashes before retiring from fighting to do other excellent things. You have trained. You are in superior shape. I guess you have a good chance to win. You can be the little girl's hero now."

The Jigsaw Puzzle

Do you know how jigsaw puzzles are made? It starts with a fine whole image, a thing of beauty, value, and meaning. The whole might be a face or so, with everything it implies. And, then, you know, there may be an awfully sharp punch that splices the whole apart – the face falls apart. Lumping the pieces back together, there it is: the puzzle. It looks pretty messy. Eyes that cannot see so well what happens. No mouth for expressing it. Curious, right, some pieces small, some upside down? It can be hard to believe they all fit together. Do they?

A keen observer may notice several similarities. Some pieces have the same color in common. Some shapes complement each other. A couple of pieces, however, at first sight

5 The controlling EP I tried to reach regarded himself as a boy.

do not seem to belong. Don't they have different colors? Do they belong to the whole bunch at all?

The best thing to do is to start sampling and fitting the easy pieces. Yet at some point, it becomes obvious that all pieces are needed in order to complete the puzzle. The more pieces get connected, the more obvious it becomes what parts are still missing. Have you ever seen a jigsaw puzzle with one part missing? Look at that empty spot. Nothing is more striking than that single hole! A face with a hole in it is not a whole face. The mouth may look weak or the eyes insecure. Put the missing piece in the right place, and a miracle happens. With that one final step everything falls into position. Take the piece away, and the whole becomes obscured again. Put it back in place, and the miracle repeats itself. And you may notice that the piece does not dissolve when it becomes connected. It actually becomes a *crucial* piece of the whole. The more pieces that fit, the more complete the whole becomes.

We can do the puzzle, we can find and explore each piece, and detect where it belongs. We cannot do without a single piece. That also applies to you, or should I say, to you in particular?

The Long Journey, the First Step

A woman lived in the middle of nowhere. She was a kind of shepherd. Some of her animals remained at her house while others joined her on her trips in the vicinity. She worked hard to take care of her possessions. It was a major challenge to earn a decent income, and there were many mouths to feed. The soil was poor so that her cattle, though of strong breeds, looked rather lean. Their fur was not as full and shiny as it might have been.

One day a traveler passed. He spoke of a land of affluence that would welcome her and her herd. The woman listened attentively. But when she understood how long, difficult, and dangerous the road she would have to travel would be, she became disheartened. Many concerns occupied her mind. How about the little ones? Their short legs and fragile bodies might not endure the journey. And how about the older animals? Maybe they were too old and too rigid? Perhaps they had lost interest in change over the years. The woman continued to worry and plug on.

The traveler revisited the place a few years later. "You're still here?" he asked. The woman shared her deep concerns. The voyager nodded, thought hard, and finally said: "You can go, I'm sure. And you can be sure your animals and you yourself will be safe. What is more, you already know it but you do not realize it. Listen, you work hard struggling to survive, you cover many miles every day. Your young animals go along, from here to there and back again. The elderly animals stroll from the stable to the meadow every morning, and from the meadow to the stable at night. The journey to the land of affluence is a big effort, to be sure, but not much more than you and your animals already invest. Stop walking back and forth to your house. Go straight ahead. That's all there is to it. Keep going, every day, one step at a time. Take a step, however small. You can do that now, and again, and again. And when you do that, you will realize, "I'm on my way."

Chapter 35

The Meaning of Sirens

> *... there is no hope without fear ...*
> Baruch Spinoza (1677a, p. 141)

Like life itself, enactive trauma therapy is concerned with meaning-making. In a dissociative context, the more precise formulation regarding meaning would be: "What does what mean to whom, that is, to what dissociative part?" The question can also be posed in terms of actions and passions (or substitute actions): "Who phenomenally perceives and conceives what, and why does this individual or 'dividual' (i.e., dissociative part of an individual) phenomenally perceive and conceive it in this particular way?"

Since subjects and objects exist relative to each other in an ontological as well as an epistemic sense (ToT Volumes I & II, Chapters 24, 25, and 27), there is no objective "truth." An object – which in this context can be anything, including another subject – exists only for a particular subject. It can thus only mean or signify something to that subject. A sign is only a sign when it signals something for someone.

In dissociation, the same subject and object can mean different things to different dissociative parts. Each dissociative part engages in his or her own signification (Chapter 25). For one dissociative part, someone or something may be insignificant, utterly useless; for another, it may be significant in a positive sense and hence useful; and for still another dissociative part it may be significant in a negative sense and hence harmful. Moreover, different dissociative parts may signify an object or constellation of objects as useful, harmful, or insignificant *in their own way*. For example, two EPs may feel that an event is harmful for different reasons.

Recovery from dissociation in trauma implies developing a common phenomenal perception and conception of subjects and objects that one or more dissociative parts signify in their idiosyncratic ways. Signs must become common signs or else the personality remains dissociated. In this light, enactive trauma therapy means progression toward achieving a common phenomenal conception of self, world, and this self's intentionality relationships with this *umwelt*. For a full explanation of the term "phenomenal conception of the intentionality relationship," see ToT Volume II, Chapter 12. A very brief clarification is given in Chapter 24.

In trauma, there is a tendency for dissociative parts to signify themselves, their *umwelt*, and their relationships to this *umwelt* in *excessively rigid* and fixed ways. They tend to signify themselves, other subjects, objects, and dynamic constellations of subjects and objects (i.e., 'events') in a rigid manner. And these ways may not be in their best interests according to someone else's second-person phenomenal judgment or third-person technical judgment – or not anymore. For example, fragile EPs may continue to view themselves as fragile. They commonly quite stubbornly conceive of the past (third-person) world as their present world. In this sense, they may regard individuals as dangerous persons who, in the third-person view, are quite safe. ANPs may feel that contacting fragile and controlling EPs is perilous inasmuch as they remain stuck in their phobia of them.

Many dissociative parts engage in conscious and preconscious actions and passions that effectively keep them at a biopsychosocial distance from one or more other dissociative parts. Inasmuch as this evasion is effective, the phenomenal "contents" of the avoided dissociative parts will not affect the avoidant ones. But this dissociation can be or can become less effective with, among others, time, exhaustion, a change of external circumstances, and therapeutic integrative developments. When the mental avoidance starts to lessen, the meanings one dissociative part assigns to his or her phenomenal self, world, and self as a part of this world can intrude on one or more other dissociative parts.

The scope of these intrusions may be limited. For example, a fragile EP may at some point intrude on an ANP, but the involved ANP may succeed in remaining ignorant of the intrusion as an intrusion of another dissociative part. Also, the ANP may suspect that the intrusion relates to a fragile EP, but nonetheless remains rather ignorant of the phenomenal experiences and conceptions or life world of the involved EP.

Individuals and dissociative parts of individuals make meaning in the context of their primordial affectivity and their implied teleofunctional orientation. That is, their phenomenal conceptions of their self, world, and self-of-this-world are strongly guided by their striving to realize particular goals or final causes. Hence, the question why an individual or dissociative part of an individual makes one meaning rather than another is intimately related to their needs and desires, that is, to their final causes.

WWW: From Symptom to Meaning – Who Does What and Why?

The following extensive case example illustrates these various principles. It exemplifies how Ineke (see Chapter 32), as ANP, entered a session with a debilitating "symptom," how she gradually signified the phenomenon in a new way, and how this new meaning-making resolved the symptom. The case also illustrates that an ANP's new signification affected the other dissociative parts and thereby stimulated them to find new meaning. Since an individual and his or her environment constitute a wholly functional and dynamic organism-environment system, change to one component of the system causes change to other parts of the system.

The work of the session specifically demonstrates how various dissociative parts can be nudged to engage in a common signification in steps. This stepwise approach is helpful when complete confrontations of one dissociative part with the signification of one or more other dissociative parts is, or will probably be, beyond the power of action of the intruded on dissociative part. Under these circumstances, complete confrontations can cause a breakdown, i.e., a decomposition (see Chapter 25) of some kind. This decomposition implies a severe reduction of the intruded on dissociative part's power of action and perhaps a further reduction of other dissociative parts' power of action as well. For example, the patient may be at serious risk of becoming suicidal or 'psychotic' (see below).

Right at the start of one session, after some 5 years of therapy, Ineke – the dominant ANP – shared that she had experienced panic attacks during the past week. The episodes had lasted for hours. They had occurred after ambulances or police cars with howling sirens passed her house. Only long and high-paced walks with her dog could calm her down. She did not know why the sirens scared and confused her so much. All she knew is that they would surely somehow cause another attack in the future. The panic attacks almost completely incapacitated her. Something had to be done about them.

We first discussed a sensible plan of action. Based on previous experiences, we agreed that one or more dissociative parts of her might know something that she as ANP did not know (in part or in full). We also concurred that the intense fear and confusion that she experienced might concern affects of one or more other dissociative parts intruding on her. This agreement was similarly grounded in her prior experiences. We further observed that the matter had become explosive over the last week, though not before this time or at least not as vigorously. This lead us to hypothesize that, inasmuch as the panic attacks related to one or more intruding dissociative parts at all, these parts were in their own way conveying that the time had come to deal with matters that somehow related to sirens.

We decided that it would probably be best to advance with care, given Ineke's limited power of action regarding her EPs and their world, particularly when it came to hints at incestuous sexual abuse. The panic attacks were intense. They occupied her most of the day, precluding daily life activities. These features suggested to us that the matter was excessively emotionally demanding. Previous work with Ineke had taught us that intense emotionality might cause the activation of one or more fragile EPs that can command control for hours or even days on end, making clinical admissions sometimes necessary. In the light of these passions and circumstances, it seemed important to first focus on getting to know the causes of the panic attacks and to keep Ineke as the dominant ANP at a sufficiently secure distance from the involved affects. In other words, we wanted her to start sharing cognitive actions with the dissociative parts that knew about "the sirens," and we wanted to proceed in steps that were within her power of action. We also wanted to help her to approach the EP (or EPs) in a way that would keep her dissociated from their probably fierce emotions. The integration of their affects might follow in a later phase. Since Ineke was good at dissociating knowledge, body sensations, affects, and memories, we concurred that we might utilize her skills in this regard. The session would thus entail integrative actions as well as the strategic utilization of her dissociative skills.

What follows is an integral transcript of the session on the left, with descriptions of some of her nonverbal reactions (Table 35.1). The transcript is accompanied by several comments from my various person perspectives.

Table 35.1. Tracing the meaning of sirens

Transcript I = Ineke E = Ellert Italics express that a word or phrase was paralinguistically emphasized.	Comments. FPP = first-person perspective QSPP = quasi-second-person perspective SPP = second-person perspective TPP = third-person perspective
E: I propose you first ask inside which part or parts might be willing and able to help you *know* what this is all about. So, . . .	TPP: First explore which dissociative parts can be of assistance. SPP: I propose. I do not order. Ineke decides. "first" means, more is to come. The emphasis on "know" means that we do not want to explore affects at this time.
I: Hmm.	SPP: Consensus.
E: . . . it's not going to be about feelings, not about emotions.	TPP: "Feelings" in Dutch can pertain to bodily sensations and to affects.
I: Hmm.	SPP: Consensus.
E: It might be better for you to leave the parts of you that are stuck in painful experiences aside for the time being.	SPP: "For the time being" suggests to the fragile EPs that their body sensations and affects will be addressed later. I wonder whether they will be able to engage in the required action of waiting. They might be too impulsive.
I: (Nods)	SPP: Consensus.
E: Let *knowing* be the first step.	FPP: Being somewhat apprehensive that the fragile EPs might not be able or willing to wait, I feel the need to stipulate again that "knowing" is "the first step," not the last. In my current reflection, I do not know whether the reiteration "Let knowing be the first step" was actually needed. However, as I write these words I recall, and remember recalling then, how difficult and time-consuming the situations had been when the ANP was flooded with intense emotions from the EPs, or when the EPs had taken full control. These incidents prevented me from seeing the next patient twice.
I: Hmm.	SPP: Consensus.
E: It's as if you are looking at something from a distance.	TPP: "Looking at things from a distance" and depersonalization are some of Ineke's dissociative symptoms as ANP. Symptoms are passions or substitute actions that patients enact for good reasons. These substitutes can sometimes be used therapeutically.
I: Hmm.	SPP: Consensus.
E: Almost as if it is happening to somebody else.	TPP: This sentence invites Ineke to use her depersonalization skills to delimit the session to knowing what the sirens mean to (some dissociative parts of) her.

I: (Nods)	SPP: Consensus.
E: You may follow this path, these steps.	SPP: "may" communicates that she, Ineke, decides, whereas I, Ellert, present options and not commands.
I: (nods) E: Fine, then please turn your attention inside and ask who knows something about the issue of the sirens.	SPP: Consensus.
I: (Looks downward, takes a deep breath, readjusts herself in her seat, her hands lie entangled in her lap, keeps her eyes half open, they do not seem to be focused on the room or me, she mostly stares ahead) . . . they are young parts . . . the little . . . the Little Ones . . . (Her tone of voice is relatively high here. Ineke sounds scared).	SPP: Communicates nonverbally that she is starting to engage in explorative actions. Ineke displays a mode shift, that is, a shift of attention and attitude. TPP: "The Little Ones" is the summary label for her several fragile EPs.
E: The Little Ones.	SPP: Attunement through the literal repetition of her words. However, while Ineke spoke the words with reservation and apprehension, in order to communicate reassurance, my tone of voice is affirmative, deeper. I thereby intend to welcome and accept The Little Ones.
I: (Nods)	SPP: Consensus.
E: The Little Ones are scared of sirens.	SPP: Reiteration, and recognition of the fragile EPs' affects.
I: (Nods) Yes.	SPP: Consensus.
E: Who is telling you so? Can you observe the Little Ones yourself, or are one or more other parts helping you?	TPP: Exploration of the current organization of the personality. SPP: The question implicitly suggests that there may be other dissociative parts helping Ineke to stay at an emotional distance. I know from previous work that Ineke's personality encompasses dissociative parts that might be able to help. TPP: It is important that Ineke observes and continues to observe. She wants to alleviate her ignorance of what is going on.
I: (Concentrated. After a while:) The Twins take part in this. (Moves her right arm to the level of her head, and then moves her hand and arm from right to left, back and forth, until she reunites her hands in her lap. Ineke looks concerned.)	TPP: The Twins operate as gatekeepers. They try to separate the world of the ANP from the domains of the various EPs. FPP: It is good that The Twins are involved, but I also realize that their power of action has lessened of late. The fragile EPs do not want to stay secluded in their dreadful phenomenal worlds. They have become more intrusive. I worry that The Twins may not be up to keeping the gate closed to the scared EPs. SPP: Is Ineke communicating nonverbally what is going on right in front of her?
E: Can The Twins help you to detect what the sirens are about? I: (Moves her head up and down again, remains stressed.)	FPP: To repeat, I doubt that The Twins can provide sufficient protection, and I feel that trouble might be on its way.
E: Or could you use some more help?	SPP: "some more help" communicates my appreciation that The Twins are providing help. The phrase also expresses that additional help might be welcome. Since I do not want to insult The Twins, I ask politely.

I: Eh ... It feels like ... The Twins go along with it. (Moves her right hand up and then down.)	TPP: My doubts seem to be justified. SPP: More help is needed. FPP: I'm glad I have been quite careful so far. The hand movements seem to indicate that going "along with it" means getting lost in the intense emotions of The Little Ones.
E: In the fear that rises.	SPP: Attunement.
I: Yes. (Stretches her right and left hand)	SPP: Consensus. TPP: Hypothesis: Ineke stretches her hands and spreads her fingers because she is scared.
E: Yes, this means that there needs to be some filter between you and The Twins ...	SPP: "some filter between" indicates that more protection is needed. Ineke can decide what this "filter" might be.
I: Yes.	SPP: Consensus.
E: ... so that you can observe what the matter is about without getting too emotionally involved.	SPP: Communication of a common purpose. Affirmation of her wishes as ANP.
I: Hmm (Keeps her right hand in a horizontal position and moves it a bit up and down).	TPP: The movement is not new to me. In previous sessions, it accompanied efforts to suppress sensations, affects, thoughts, images, memories, and the like.
E: Who could help you in this regard?	
I: The Observer (Turns her right hand to a vertical plane and moves her right arm and hand up and down). He observes but does not feel.	FPP: I am relieved that The Observer pops up. In previous work, the vertical movement coincided with efforts of some dissociative parts to split two phenomenally experienced and conceived worlds: Controlling EPs to the right side of the ANP's body and world-orientation, and the fragile EPs and their world to the left side of her body. In these situations, the ANP was situated in the middle. TPP: The Observer exerts a dissociated observational function.
E: Yes. Maybe the Observer can observe what engages The Little Ineke's and The Twins, and maybe the Observer only sends you the *images* of what engages, so to speak, little Ineke's?	SPP: "Maybe ... can" communicates respect for Ineke's autonomy. The described idea communicates to Ineke and to the Observer what he might do. "Little Ineke's" expresses that I regard The Little Ones as parts of Ineke. TPP: It is good to remind patients that dissociative parts are parts of a single individual.
I: (Nods. Ineke's right arm and hand are in front of her, at the height of her stomach. She is concentrated, remains silent, and eventually opens her left hand.)	TPP: The opening of the left hand may suggest opening of her "left, traumatic world."
E: And I might add that the images The Observer sends are like images on a DVD. You can have a remote control that allows you to stop the images.	TPP: Extension of ANP's power to stay at a sufficiently safe distance from this emotionality. SPP: Communication of care and the importance of adaptive control.
I: Yes. (Nods, hands move a bit, left hand closed now)	TPP: Closure of her left hand might suggest relative closure of her traumatic world.
E: You can stop them, fast-forward them.	SPP: Practice control.
I: (Concentrated, engaged, nods several times)	SPP: We are working on a common goal.
E: And you can zoom them out, let them disappear in the background. That might also be possible.	SPP and TPP: More options to consider and practice.

I: (Moves her right hand back and forth; she sometimes closes her eyes for a brief while.) I see myself lying in a child's bed, [I am] little.	TPP: The movements from the right to the left seem to express that Ineke sees images passing in front of her eyes. Her open eyes neither seem to notice me nor my office. The sirens could be related to early childhood experiences. SPP: "I see myself" conveys that Ineke is observing herself from a distance.
E: In a child's bed, little.	SPP: Attunement.
I: Yes. (Nods)	SPP: Consensus.
E: And can you bear this, or are the images still too near?	TPP: Checking Ineke's synthetic capacity. SPP: Reminder that control and keeping sufficient distance are pivotal.
I: It is good to have the ability to put them at a distance (Keeps her right hand vertically erect next to her right shoulder. Ineke sometimes moves the hand at this height, from right to left, and back again. Then she keeps it erect again, to the right side of her. Meanwhile, Ineke does not engage in eye contact with me. She spreads and stretches the fingers of her left hand at the level of her stomach. It seems she is getting quite tense).	SPP: Yes, she really needs this control. TPP: I wonder what the arm and hand movements (from right to left and vice versa) mean. FPP: The lack of eye contact worries me, because I have experienced that Ineke can disappear in her inner phenomenal world, a world in which I can no longer reach her. In these circumstances she may start to take my words for commands from perpetrators. She may even start to regard me as a dangerous person, if not as an outright perpetrator.
E: You may want to test the stop, pause, and fast-forward buttons.	SPP: Test your control now that tension mounts.
I: Hmm. (Is silent, bends her head to the left at some point and then bends it to the right; her left hand remains stretched in a horizontal plane.)	TPP: There is something happening that unnerves Ineke. It would seem to be important to check what it might be. Why this head movement to the left? Prior experiences have taught us that there are controlling EPs who can interfere with explorative work. The left hand may communicate that the fragile EPs are opening up despite their tension.
E: And do all other parts agree with our approach? I think, for example, of Rick and The Reconciler?	SPP: Explore your inner world. Recognize that there may be known or unknown dissociative parts that object.
I: (Remains almost immobile, after a delay:) I have not been concerned with that. (Moves her right arm and hand back and forth)	TPP: Ineke seems to explore the possibility that there is disagreement among the dissociative parts. Previous work has frequently revealed such struggles.
E: It would be better to ask. All parts of you count and all should have their say.	SPP: Clear, direct stimulation to engage in the action. Recognition of all dissociative parts that may currently be active.
I: Yes. (Remains silent for a considerable time; closes and opens her left hand) The exploration troubles The Reconciler . . . But he realizes its importance.	SPP: Consensus. TPP: The Reconciler is ambivalent. From previous work we know that he is loyal to the parents (Father was still alive at the time of this session, Mother had died). Whereas he is mainly guided by the action system of attachment, his ambivalence suggests that he is no longer totally dominated by the need for attachment to the parents. Opening and closing her left hand might express the need and difficulty to open a painful world.

E: Hmm. How good of him to realize that. I: (continued to move her right hand back and forth; her left hand is closed)	SPP: Praise for The Reconciler. Joy increases the power of action.
E: What troubles him in particular?	SPP: Attunement to The Reconciler's concerns.
I: . . . That the images will probably become ever clearer. (Opens and stretches and spreads the fingers of her left hand.)	TPP: I interpret this as follows: The Reconciler fears that the images might reveal something that is at odds with his attachment interests. However, he also understands now that this something needs to be clarified. The left hand might express the opening of the fragile EPs' realities.
E: Hmm . . . He understands it is important to examine the images. But he also finds it a burden.	SPP: Attunement.
I: Yes.	SPP: Consensus.
E: What does he need [in order to bear the work]? The same distance from the images that you are keeping, so that like you he – so to speak – will not plunge into the affects?	SPP: Communication that The Reconciler includes needs and wishes, that these strivings count, and that I have no wish to flood him with affects he may not be able to bear.
I: Yes, that we stay together. (The positions of the right and left hand are as before.	TPP: The Reconciler seems to need Ineke's help. Although I know him as a powerful controlling EP, he may be less powerful than his passionate power displays suggest.
E: He and you must stay together . . . [You should] not abandon him.	SPP: Affirmation of The Reconciler's and Ineke's common desires.
I: (Nods) Yes. (Nods again) E: OK.	SPP: Consensus. FPP: It feels good that The Reconciler has advanced to the position that perhaps not everything can be reconciled, that secure attachment to the parents was and – as far as the father is concerned – is still unattainable. TPP: He may be on his way to engaging in the action of misachievement.
I: I should not choose sides. (Slowly lowers her right hand and puts it on her right leg, which is crossed over her left leg.)	TPP: Hypothesis: The Reconciler feels that Ineke should not turn herself against him in favor of The Little Ones. He also seems to hold that Ineke should not reject her parents, at least not in all regards, and not at all cost. The movement of the right hand could suggest: Let's remain peaceful with each other.
E: And that is fine with you?	TPP: Exploration of a possible conflict of interests.
I: (Stretches her right hand again) . . . It puts me in a dilemma, now. (Moves her stretched right hand upward.)	SPP: There is a dilemma. TPP: The upward right hand seems to communicate that there is something of importance at this side of her body and head.
E: What dilemma?	SPP: Attunement, exploration.

I: (Moves her right arm and hand upward to the level of her head and moves them from left to right.) . . . I would like him to be at a greater distance from me . . . so that his voice does not affect me so much, does not influence me so strongly. (Moves her left hand up and down and moves the fingers of this hand. The right hand stays up.) That I can act according to my own conscience. (Moves her right hand down and turns it from a vertical position to a horizontal position.)	TPP: Ineke hears The Reconciler, who speaks to her from the right. He intrudes on her. There is a disagreement between Ineke and The Reconciler. Ineke does not want to act according to anyone else's conscience. The Reconciler, in contrast, feels the need to accept and incorporate the parent's morals. Here we have a conflict between the attachment system (attachment cry, 'tend and befriend' parents) and the social dominance system (personal autonomy). The pattern suggests 'disorganized' attachment that, in the view of Van der Hart, Steele, and me (Van der Hart et al., 2006), rather comprises dissociative attachment.
E: And what is The Reconciler's conscience like?	TPP: Exploration of The Reconciler's conscience and thereby perhaps also of the family's conscience. SPP: I communicate that the Reconciler's conscience also counts. FPP and QSPP: Remember, you do not want to fight with the Reconciler's conscience if this happens to reflect the morals of the traumatizing family. Like Ineke, you, Ellert, should not "take sides." You will not help Ineke to solve the conflict of interests (attachment, fitting in the family) and personal autonomy by expressing yourself or letting yourself be guided by the anger you feel regarding her traumatizing milieu. Anger is a passion. Be guided more by the love of reason. Do not want *anything* from Ineke. It is up to her to decide what she needs and desires and does. *Being clinicians, they should not want anything from their patients.*
I: (Instantly moves her right arm and hand from left to right in a horizontal plane at the level of her stomach) "That everything will turn out well, that everything is not true." (Moves both hands, hands stretched, fingers spread, in front of her stomach, hands erect. Then she moves her right arm and hand upward again to the right side of her head, some 10 cm from her head.)	TPP: The Reconciler reveals his typical actions. The various movements express suppression (right horizontal arm and hand that push something down), and reconciliatory actions (right horizontal arm and hand that seem to iron out particular things). They also seem to involve an effort to divide (vertical movements). The Reconciler seems to display how Ineke as a child had to hope that the problems would be resolved sooner or later.
E: I guess this means that, for his sake, the exploration should proceed slowly.	SPP: "I guess . . ." expresses that I do not have access to 'The Truth.'
I: Yes. (Closes and half opens her left hand.)	SPP: Consensus. TPP: The opening and closing of the left hand suggests again that it expresses the opening and closing of painful world of the fragile Little Ones. They seem to be situated on the left-hand side of Ineke's body and *umwelt*.
E: Let's decide that The Reconciler can also say "Stop," that he can also say that he cannot bear it.	SPP: It is a proposition, not a command. SPP: Reconciler, I respect you and feel that you deserve control.
I: (nods)	SPP: Accepts.
E: And we also consider his view that it is important to learn to realize what simply happened.	SPP: Acknowledgment of his ambivalent needs and desires that include the exploration of the Little One's world.

I: (Opens her left hand, spreads and stretches her fingers. She turns her head to the left, brings it back to the middle, moves it again to the left, and finally takes it back to the middle where it stays for the time being.)	TPP: Again that movement of her head to the left. Twice even. What does it mean?
E: And The Reconciler now knows that Ineke is not a little girl anymore but a grown-up woman who lives on her own. You may want to remind him of these facts.	TPP: Controlling EPs like The Reconciler tend to be confused in time. They are thereby also confused regarding the actual age of ANPs. He used to think that Ineke is a little girl. He continues to be confused even when his ideas regarding time, place, and age are corrected. SPP: "may want" allows Ineke to decide.
I: (Nods several times) . . . Yes, I think he often thinks I am still that little girl. (Nods)	TPP: Hypothesis substantiated.
E: Because The Reconciler is able to observe images you might as well send him images or pictures showing that you are an adult woman, and that you have your own home.	TPP: Utilization of The Reconciler's ability to see images (e.g., images stemming "from the left"). My encouragement to interact with him serves integrative purposes.
I: (Nods). That I can decide for myself.	TPP: It implies an increase of Ineke's power of action and a lessening of determination by the parents' morals, that is, reduction of external influences. Her passions start to become actions. SPP: Strong affirmation of this success.
E: Yes, yes. I: (Nods several times, right arm up, left hand open in front of her stomach.)	SPP: Consensus. The open left hand suggests more openness to a likely very painful past.
E: That you are stronger, older, receive support. I think The Reconciler has remained stuck in a time in which you had to rely on yourself. It is important that he knows you are a grown-up, independent, and stronger now, with good female and male friends.	SPP: I stimulate Ineke to share these social facts with The Reconciler. In doing so, I also remind Ineke as ANP of the progress she has made since childhood.
I: (Concentrating in silence) . . . that family is not all. That's what he thinks [that the family of origin is all], that I must return [to that family].	TPP: The remarks seem to help her to become less dependent on her family. They are at least consistent with her evolving realization that she has become more independent, and that she has gathered relationships with other significant others. The remarks, in any case, support the idea of diminishing dependency on individuals who traumatized her and who, in a certain sense, still traumatize her (for example, in the form of ongoing intrusive actions).
E: Yes, Reconciler, that applies to *a child*. You are absolutely right, that is how it is *for a child*.	SPP: I address The Reconciler *directly*. I agree with him that, for a child, the family of origin means everything. TPP: The idea is to strengthen our relationship, and thereby to support his growing trust in me. SPP: "for a child" implicitly conveys the idea that the family need not be everything for an adult.

I: (Nods as I speak, right arm and hand still erect next to her head, fingers spread.)	TPP: The tense right hand may communicate that The Reconciler continues to be stressed. He could use more support as well as some more time to reflect. Reflection may be a difficult action for him. He seems to be mostly caught in prereflective symbolic action tendencies (see Chapter 33). The next step in his evolution would be to engage in more reflective symbolic action tendencies at the intermediate level (see Chapter 33).
E: For a child the family is all. But not for an adult woman who is confronted with a family that hurts.	SPP: Invitation to reflect.
I: . . . and The Reconciler always tries to persuade me that those people are not my parents, that they [i.e., the real parents] are good people, that *I am bad*, that *I am a naughty dirty girl*! (Raises her voice, her whole body tenses) . . . *I* . . . (Keeps her breath when she does not speak.)	TPP: Ineke shares how the Reconciler tries to reconcile, how he speaks to her. Saying that Ineke was to blame, I presume, reveals the parents' morals. Imitation is a lower-level action tendency. (Distressed) children need little power of action to imitate (see, among others, Chapter 23), and when the stress and the interests are high, reflection becomes a very difficult action.
E: Yes, that's what he had to tell you, Ineke. You detect this fact once more. This is The Reconciler's way of enabling you to live in that family. I: It is as if he does not want to accept, and that he cannot believe that I *am* an adult now.	
E: Yes, show him and tell him, "You may find it hard to accept, you may think it is a pitfall." But you tell and calm him saying "I am really an adult now, and I am not dependent on these individuals anymore. Mother has died . . ."	TPP: The Reconciler's passions have become very rigid. He also seems to fear that accepting Ineke's current age and life conditions might be a pitfall. Traumatized children have often been fooled to believe in appealing ideas and thoughts that were offered but then crushed (e.g., "If you do this for me, then, you will get a present." But the presents never came or turn out to be other traumatizing events). SPP: I mostly urge Ineke to reassure him. He, so to speak, lives with her, not with me.
I: *She belongs to the sirens.* (Spoken in a very decisive tone of voice.)	TPP: A sudden switch in mode. It is true that I referred to her mother. However, that reference in itself does not explain Ineke's realization that her mother belongs to the sirens. SPP: I feel she expresses a readiness to move on. The Reconciler may also express that he has become sufficiently convinced that Ineke has matured.
E: Mother belongs to the sirens.	SPP: Attunement, using Ineke's words.
I: They both belong to the sirens.	SPP: Correction. It's more complicated.
E: Mother and Father both belong to the sirens.	SPP: Attunement.
I: Yes.	SPP: Consensus.
E: You and The Reconciler can observe the images. You have the remote control. And do not go any faster than either of you can cope with . . .	SPP: I suggest that the two parts can proceed with caution, and that each part's interests and power of action deserve consideration. I do not take sides.
I: (As we speak, Ineke moves her right arm back and forth to the right side of her body.)	TPP: What would this recurrent movement entail?

E: It's better to go too slow than too fast . . . And then you may recount in words what you observe regarding Father and Mother and the sirens.	SPP: "Recount in words" conveys the idea that her nonverbal expressions are a way of storytelling. TPP: Nonverbal (re)actions and passions are lower-level action tendencies. The invitation to express herself in words more involves an encouragement to engage in symbolic action tendencies (Chapter 33). Recounting a past inhibits the tendency to reenact it. One might also express the issue in terms of the brain, that is, under the attribute of matter: Expressing oneself linguistically engages neocortical brain structures more (prefrontal and temporal). Nonverbal reenactments are associated more with an activation of midbrain structures such as the basal ganglia and amygdala as well as the brain stem (see ToT Volume II, Chapters 17–18).
I: (Continues to make the described movements, opening and closing her left hand. Moves her head to the left and brings it back to the middle.)	TPP: No words so far. Yet, Ineke is engaged in the work. I continue to wonder about the head movements.
E: Do you see images?	SPP: Attunement.
I: Yes. (Spoken with a pinched-off voice, sighs.) E: You may share the images with me. Otherwise, it is as if you are on a lonely island. But we are together, you know.	SPP: Consensus. Becomes more stressed. I feel a need to prevent Ineke from disappearing in a reenactment. She needs to stay in touch with me. TPP: Our contact implies the social engagement action system, which can help to reduce emotional reactions.
I: (Her breathing becomes heavier. She moves her left hand upward on the left side of her body.)	TPP: Activates the sympathetic nervous system more. It becomes even more probable that Ineke as ANP, together with the Little Ones and still other dissociative parts, start to reenact a traumatizing event.
E: Please take a look at me, Ineke. And Reconciler, you can also glance at me and realize "Wait a minute, Ellert wasn't there but he's here."	SPP: Decision to instruct Ineke as ANP and her other parts, notably The Reconciler, to attend to my presence. TPP: Seeing me could help her differentiate the actual, third-person present and the phenomenal, first-person past. This may allow her to regulate her affects more. The differentiation involves the action of presentification.
I: (Struggles, sighs, moans, and then briefly looks at me.) E: Yes, take a look, I'm sitting with you. I: (Continues to struggle, eyes closed.) . . .	TPP: It is somehow very difficult for Ineke to look at me. One hypothesis that crosses my mind is that she, under the influence of her various EPs, starts to take me for someone else. Maybe she has started to incorporate me into the framework of her past (reenactment of events that were traumatic for her). However, she would better incorporate this past in the confines of the present (i.e., engage in the action of presentification).
I: . . . The Reconciler tells me that what I see is not true.	TPP: Ineke and The Reconciler see images, most probably images of the past. He tells her that the images do not reflect actual events. This suggests he is reengaging in his old task of denying lived facts.
E: That is what The Reconciler is saying here and now?	SPP: Attunement.
I: (Nods)	SPP: Affirmation.

E: Ah, that's his old task. Take him by the hand, and tell The Reconciler, "OK, this is your old task, this is what you had to do over and over."	SPP: Consensus. Instruction to talk to The Reconciler while engaging in the action of presentification.
I: (More struggling)	TPP: It is hard.
E: Ineke, it is a bit complex, but you are, so to speak, looking in three directions: You notice what happened in your childhood; you also observe what The Reconciler had to do over and over; and you see me sitting here with you, and I see you sitting here in your chair with me.	SPP: Acknowledgment that the challenge is complex. TPP: Detailing and encouraging three simultaneous actions. SPP: I stress and thereby hope to maintain our therapeutic cooperation and communication.
I: (Sighing, sweating, moves her right arm downward as if this hand tries to cover something up.)	SPP: Ineke and The Reconciler are struggling with each other. TPP: A display and to some degree a reenactment of an intense attachment problem, of a conflict Ineke has been unable to resolve so far.
E: What do you observe over there that, according to The Reconciler, is not true?	TPP: Another invitation to tell me in words what ANP and the Reconciler as controlling EP observe – images that they phenomenally conceive in two opposite ways. It is a struggle of realization. SPP: Choice of words: "observe" to assist Ineke in maintaining an emotional distance regarding the images.
I: (First she moves her right arm again, up and down. Then she moves her right hand from the far right against the right side of her head. In the act her head bends to the far left and down) ... being hit very hard against my head ... because I cry so loudly.	TPP: Moving her right arm and hand up and down seems to express the effort to split off the painful past. Moving her head from the right to the left suggests she was hit on the right side of her head. SPP: Excellent that Ineke could also put the hitting in words. TPP: The present tense remark that she cries "so loudly" suggests how close she is to a full reenactment. The statement also raises the question why she was crying so loudly (see the section 'Phases of Healing' below).
E: Hmm ... OK ... and that is what your right hand is showing, that hitting ... or it is doing or showing something else ...?	SPP: Attunement and careful examination: I am not saying that the right hand portrays the hitting; the motor action might mean other things.
I: (Moves her right hand faster in the indicated manner, clearly showing a hitting movement. She next moves her right arm and hand from right to left in front of her head, as she had done when she reported seeing images.)	TPP: No words this time, yet a rather clear confirmation that the movements express hitting and her reactions to the hitting.
E: What is your hand doing? Look at it, Ineke, your hand is moving back and forth (from her right side, in front of her face, to the left, and back again).	SPP: Directing Ineke's attention to these recurrent movements.
I: Many images ... many images (tense voice) E: Images that pass? I: (Continues to move her right arm) ... and a door that squeaks very loudly, hinges that squeak intensely (stressed voice, makes grimaces) ... and then ... E: Hmm ...	TPP: Starts using words again in the present tense. Expresses intense reactions to the squeaking sound. Hypothesis: The sirens might be analogous to the shrieking hinges that seem to signal deep trouble for Ineke.

I: (Imitates heavy beating on her head with her right arm and hand, tilts her head briskly to the left in the act) . . . hitting against my head . . . (repeats the movement while she holds her left hand at a slight distance from the left side of her head) . . .	TPP: This time the hitting and tilting seem more like demonstrations than reenactments. That is, the movements now have an as-if quality. Ineke also manages to express herself in a few words. She is making advancements regarding symbolization of a traumatic experience and memory.
E: Where were you hit? I: Against my head and ear (repeats the above movements) . . . E: There, against your ear? I: Yes. E: And who hit you, Father or Mother? I: (makes grimaces, sighs) . . . My mother . . .	SPP: Asking for the details, I try to stimulate Ineke to put the traumatic experience in words. TPP: Words distance us from our immediate experiences. They are symbols that represent our experiences. They are not the experiences themselves.
E: Your mother hit you? You cried loudly for some reason and Mother hit you?	SPP: To keep us oriented on common goals, I give a brief summary of what Ineke had shown and said.
I: Yes (exhales) . . .	SPP: Affirmation.
E: OK, is The Reconciler with you? I: (Shakes her head, not as a response to my question but as an apparent means of shaking off sensations of her head. Ineke holds and strokes her right ear) . . .	SPP: Include the Reconciler. He will be inclined to deny the story. TPP: Back to the conflict.
E: Can he stand this?	SPP: Sympathy for The Reconciler.
I: (Whispers, fast, irritated) *This is not your mother, this is not your mother,* (then louder) this is *not* your mother.	TPP: Denial of an obvious fact. It sounds like The Reconciliator has taken executive control.
E: Go slowly, it is time to go slowly, let him say what he has to say. I: (Moves her right and left arm up and down, turns her head back and forth.)	SPP: Do not fight with The Reconciler, Ineke. In my FPP and QSPP, do not fight with him yourself, Ellert. TPP: Let The Reconciler communicate his old task and his way of performing it.
E: No need to fight his words. You can notice his task. Can you grasp it?	SPP: Focus on an *affective understanding* his passions. TPP: Stay at the top of the pyramid.
I: Yeah, but he always confuses me . . .	TPP: Ineke understands The Reconciler.
E: I get that. On the other hand, as Ineke you can realize that you have developed a part of you in your childhood that could not realize the facts. Can you grasp that? I: Hmm. (still quite tense) E: That reality was unlivable for you as a child.	SPP: Acceptance and invitation to grasp The Reconciler's roots.
I: *Yeees.*	SPP: Powerful affirmation.
E: What you're learning is not just what happened, but also what The Reconciler had to do over and over. I: (Her heavy breathing lessens a bit). E: The little girl who was hit by her mother, that awfully squeaking door, and, on the other hand, The Reconciler who had to save what can be saved, who had to say "This is not your mother. Your mother does not do such things."	TPP: I put my understanding into words.

I: (Stops moving her arms and head; nods.) E: He now simply repeats what he had to do over and over. He shows what he had to do during your childhood.	SPP: We seem to have reached a consensual understanding, a common result. Things start to gain meaning. They seem to fit because Ineke calms down.
I: (Becomes calmer. Suddenly:) . . . It's getting dark now (calmer, softer voice).	TPP: It so often happens in trauma work that the achievement of one thing almost instantaneously leads to the expression of another thing. *The completion and result of one action is the prelude to another.*
E: Dark? I: It's getting dark (both arms up). E: Yes . . . I: A squeaking tone through my ears, a very loud squeaking tone in my head. (right arm and hand move from right to left, several times; tense, very emotional voice.) E: There is squeaking in your head?	TPP: Why? What is Ineke expressing or perhaps reenacting now? It seems important to track her moves.
I: Loud squeaking, in my ear, and then . . . completely black. E: A squeaking door, your Mother who hits you, squeaking in your ear and head, and then it gets dark . . .	TPP: The hinges were squeaking, and following the hitting, the squeaking was also in her head. Does darkness mean that Ineke was knocked unconscious?
E: I now say "Stop the images, there is no need to go any further."	TPP: Since Ineke commonly needs time to calm down after intense work, it is important to start concluding our sessions in due time, so that she can go home safely. SPP: Ineke has booked progression. She is at the border of her integrative capacity. I therefore decide to communicate that I do not expect her to access more images that beset The Little Ones.
E: . . . Just one question. The squeaking of the door and the squeaking in your ear, do these sounds relate to the sirens, or is it something else? I: It is the danger that . . . that . . . there is hitting . . . very hard hitting . . . and then the very loud tone in my ear . . . very loud . . . (very emotional) E: Yes, do I get it right that the sirens remind you of the squeaking of the hinges and the squeaking in your right ear from when Mother hit you?	SPP and TPP: Is this why the sirens upset you so much? Is this an answer to the question that we set out with?
I: Yes! (Grimaces, keeps both hands in the air and moves them in the air, fingers stretched.)	SPP: Affirmation.
E: Enough images for today. Stop the images now. Thank the Twins. Tell the Little Ones that we will be returning to the events later. Enough for now. You can address The Reconciler and tell him, "Reconciler, perhaps you do not need to repeat your former actions anymore."	TPP: Remain at the 'top of the pyramid' and include all participating parts. SPP: Be respectful and thankful to them all. Meet the fragile EPs in their need to be heard. Create new actions for The Reconciler.

I: (Rapid breathing, tense face and body) And now Rick pops up and says, "*You see, you see, I was right, I was right, you see!*" (speaks quickly, hyperaroused). E: He says he was right? I: Hmm. (very stressed) E: In what way was Rick right? I: That it *did* happen . . . E: That it did happen. Rick has always said that it *did* happen?	TPP: There is another issue popping up. SPP: Rick overrules the idea to conclude the session; he feels a need to express his point of view. TPP: He used to be a fight-like fragile EP. SPP: He used to be rather mistrustful and uncooperative, but this attitude has changed more recently, in part following my consistent appreciation of him and of the goals he tried to attain.
I: Yes. And The Reconciler always denied it. That makes Rick very angry. E: Yes, Rick, we understand that that [The Reconciler's denial] makes you angry. Do you understand that The Reconciler *had* to do his job? I: (Moans, breathes heavily.)	TPP: It seems important to reduce the tension between Rick and The Reconciler regarding the question of what really happened. SPP: I address Rick directly. SPP: This is going to be a confrontation. Rick is very emotional and could thus use Ineke's (as ANP) support if not lead. It also seems that The Reconciler feels he must continue his work.
E: Ineke, I suggest you relieve The Reconciler of his task. I: (Struggles)	SPP: Encouraging Ineke to alleviate The Reconciler from his assignment. This might help to reduce the conflict among the various parts regarding the truth.
E: You can make this decision. You can tell him, "Thank you very much for all the years of hard work. I'm an adult now, and I'm stronger, so you do not need to deny the facts anymore. I can deal with them, you do not need to distort them." You can decide to tell him that.	SPP: You decide; you are in charge. TPP and SPP: Ineke engages in the work.
I: (More concentrated, starts to move her previously stretched hand right hand in circles.) . . . And now comes, "You are my sweet little girl, my sweet little girl . . ." E: Hm. I: You are my sweet little girl, you are my sweet little girl . . . E: Who says that, Ineke? I: The Consoler, The Consoler. The Reconciler also belongs to it and the . . .	TPP: A new element emerges. The issue is complicated. I know the repetitive phrases as the kind of things The Consoler – another male controlling EP that exists in proximity to The Reconciler – typically utters. The sentences concern the phrases Father uttered in the context of sexual abuse. Some of her dissociative parts were relatively clear that there had been massive sexual abuse. However, as ANP Ineke has so far been completely unable to consider the issue. So far in therapy, she had used her power of action to integrate ever more components of the emotional neglect, emotional abuse, and physical maltreatment. If The Consoler also belongs to the sirens, then in what way?
E: The Consoler and The Reconciler are close to each other?	TPP: Assessment of the current relationship between the two. SPP: Show an interest in the Consoler as well.
I: (Continues to turn her right hand in circles) . . . yes, and the 4-year-old and the 6-year-old, they too . . . hmm (exhales with major tension) . . .	TPP: These are fragile EPs that, as has been clearly hinted at in previous sessions, relate to the onset of sexual abuse by her father.
E: Fine, well, if I were you, Ineke, I would say to these others parts, "Next time we will also listen to you. We cannot do everything on one day." Tell them, "Enough for the day, we've done enough and discovered enough. It's a lot as it is."	SPP: My effort to communicate, first, that we can address the issue in the next session, and, second, that it is better not to stretch the various dissociative parts' limits.
I: *Yeess.* (Stops turning her right hand in circles, leaves her left hand open.)	SPP: Ineke applauds the idea that we do not need to consider The Consoler's issues until the next session.

E: I tell all [parts] from my chair, "We are doing this work, this difficult work, in steps. Nobody reaches Paris [the city of light, a metaphor we used before] in a single day. I: (Continues to breath heavily) E: We're making a journey. Each time we take one step more.	SPP: An effort to address all dissociative parts and to reiterate the idea that our work is a long journey that will bring matters to light in feasible steps.
I: [I want to] fly for a while. E: Flying away from that house, right? I: (Nods) E: Time and again there had to be an Ineke who could survive an extremely painful reality. I: Last night, I could do it again. E: You could do it again. I: Yes. (Sighs, moves her hands in circles on either side of her head.)	SPP: Good, Ineke is using a very old fantasy that can calm her down. In fact, the involved flying is more like lucid dreaming than fantasizing.
E: Reconciler, have you heard from Ineke that you no longer need to continue that difficult work, that Ineke is strong enough now?	SPP: I return to the idea that Ineke can relieve The Reconciler of his old assignment.
I: . . . that I do not need to feel so guilty . . .	TPP: It seems that Ineke starts to follow her own conscience.
E: No.	SPP: I support her view.
I: . . . that I consider this true.	TPP: The whole sequence (crying, hitting, loss of consciousness, etc.) becomes Ineke's phenomenal conception of what happened to her as a young child.
E: Yes.	SPP: Affirmation.
I: This is . . . this is . . . what . . . happened . . . how . . . how . . . *so* . . . (Ineke as ANP is very engaged, very emotional.)	SPP: Ineke starts to own her truth, with every bit of energy and dedication. TPP: Her language sounds a bit disorganized, a bit childlike perhaps, but the meaning of her words is clear.
E: I hear you say, *so* . . . I: This is how it was . . .	SPP: Attunement; making myself present as a witness.
E: Take The Reconciler by his hand and tell him . . .	SPP: Attunement. TPP: Involve The Reconciler. It is important that he joins Ineke in the evolving realization.
I: This is how it was. Sooo horrible . . .	SPP: Starts to formulate a grammatically more correct sentence.
E: This is your reality.	SPP: I paraphrase her communication.
I: *This is my truth . . . this is my truth!* (Both hands at the level of her chest, moves them, back and forth, in a parallel fashion, as she also moves her upper body in a rhythm.)	SPP as well as TPP: An act of realization as well as an expression of the need and desire to follow her own conscience. Ineke frees herself from the morals of the family of her origin. TPP: There is a balance between the left and right arm and hand, suggesting growing internal balance.
E: "This is my truth" . . . this is what I clearly hear you saying. I: Yes!	SPP: Affirmation.

E: Make sure that The Reconciler stays present . . . You can tell him, "Boy, you have done well. Don't deny the facts anymore." Reassure him that you can bear your own truth.	SPP: The Reconciler should preferably be present so that he can notice that Ineke can indeed accept and live her truth.
I: (Stops the swaying and reaches her right arm and hand out to the lower right frontal side of her, as if holding the hand of a child.)	SPP: Ineke seems to reach out to The Reconciler. It is remarkable that she finds him at the level of the seat of her chair. I wonder whether this height suggests that he is subjectively not that tall, perhaps even only a child.
E: Yes, hold him.	SPP: Attunement.
I: . . . Yes, he must be part of this! (in a pinched off voice)	SPP: Consensus.
E: Yes. That's what I also say from my chair. Reconciler you belong to this . . .	SPP: I also address The Reconciler directly.
I: Er, yes . . .	SPP: Ineke's affirmation.
E: . . . You have done great work . . . I: Yeah . . . E: . . . work that was absolutely needed. But now Ineke has matured . . .	SPP: Praise for The Reconciler to communicate my understanding and appreciation of his goals and work.
I: Yes . . . (Brings her now clenched right fist toward her stomach.)	SPP: Consensus.
E: . . . And now there is room for other work, and there is ample work to do. You won't be unemployed.	TPP: Dissociative parts should not be left without a task or goal, or else they may feel they will be useless or that they will "die."
I: (Moves her right fist from her stomach to the right side.)	SPP: It feels like Ineke places The Reconciler next to her.
E: Good . . . and now you can take a rest, together, you can tell each other, "We've done enough for the day . . ."	SPP: I address all dissociative parts.
I: (Exhales, starts to become calmer.) E: ". . . we have managed to cooperate . . . that's very good, that's a real achievement. Now is the time for a break, for *rest* . . ."	
I: . . . being allowed to fly beyond it . . .	
E: Yes, of course. Use you flying skills. You can fly away from that place for a while.	
I: (Her arms and hands "fly.") . . . Yes.	SPP: There seems to be a growing feeling among the various parts that the session can be concluded. I speak slowly and rhythmically, and emphasize the word "rest" to guide and support relaxation.
E: After all, in real time, we have already flown away from that time and place, over the years . . . I: (Moves her head to relax her should and neck.)	SPP: "We" suggests togetherness. We are together in a different time and place. Utilization of the image of "flying."
E: . . . because how many years ago did this happen, Ineke?	SPP: Fostering presentification.
I: . . . ah . . . I think . . . 45 years . . .? E: . . . 45 years ago . . . I: . . . bizarre . . .	SPP: Ineke sounds surprised. She did not realize the major gap in time.

E: It sounds a bit bizarre. I: Yes. E: Yes . . . but you can see it this way . . . I: It's as if it's happening now.	SPP: "It sounds bizarre . . ." conveys acceptance of her experience, and it also modifies her judgment.
E: It seems to you as if it is happening now, that is how it feels to you, that is how you experience it . . . and the clock and calendar say it happened 45 years ago. A half of a human lifetime ago.	TPP: Traumatic memories are generally more or less timeless. SPP: "It seems to you as if . . ." communicates acceptance of her sense of time, and also corrects her judgment. I encourage her to presentify the memory.
I: (Nods)	SPP: Consensus.
E: You are safe now.	SPP: Encouragement to "be" in the present. Siren-like sounds do not need to disturb Ineke so much anymore.
I: Yes, that's what the sirens wanted to tell me . . . when I heard them pass [her house] . . . that's how it was . . .	TPP: Therapy is about new meaning-making. Sirens as objects, however, do not "want" anything. Objects do not include wishes, but individuals or "dividuals" (that is, dissociative parts; see ToT Volume I) do.
E: That's how it was. Yes, the Little Ones intrude on you with their memories . . . their experiences . . .	SPP: Ineke expresses that the sirens carried this meaning for her, and I link the sirens and the intentions of The Little Ones.
I: Yes (sighs) E: . . . to tell you how things were. I: The sound, *sooo* piercing, piercing everything else.	SPP: Consensus.
E: Piercing your head . . . I: Yes. E: It must have screeched in your head. I: Yes! E: And isn't that what happens when someone hits you hard on your head and ears?	SPP: Continuation of the common understanding. SPP: You had a normal response to an abnormal event.
I: Yeah.	SPP: Consensual reality.
E: All right. That's how things were, there and then, in a remote past. And Reconciler, you can join Ineke as she flies away, though not away from her truth . . . I: . . . no, distance . . . E: . . . distancing yourself from your intense feelings . . . I: . . . yeah . . . E: That's fine. I: (Lets her hands face and approach each other in front of her, her face grows calmer, more composed.)	SPP: Keeping The Reconciler aboard, and reminding Ineke to make sure he does not get lost. The instruction to not fly away from the truth reminds The Reconciler that his old task is over.
E: Yes, very good. I: (Lets the fingers from her right and left hand touch each other.) E: We can start to close the session . . . I: (Separates her hands.)	TPP: It is important to allow patients time to recover and to attune to their pace.
E: You can be a little bit proud of yourselves. You've made it together, as a group.	SPP: The success is a group achievement. Let all dissociative parts be part of the feeling of accomplishment.

I: (Exhales several times, moves her open right hand back and forth in the direction of the open, somewhat moving left hand.) E: Together …	SPP: The approaching hands express a degree of togetherness. SPP and TPP: I am phenomenally and technically aware that the right side (Reconciler, Consoler) and the middle (Ineke as ANP, The Twins) "are really getting in touch with" the left side (The Little Ones – including the 4-year-old and the 6-year-old – and Rick). This implies open access to the fragile EPs' physical and emotional feelings. FPP: Should I allow this degree of integration, or would it be better to block it? I decide to follow Ineke's track but am on guard.
I: Yes. (Moves her right hand close to her left hand. Her hands express renewed tension as they come close. Then the movement is interrupted) … *not* … *not* … (Her hands circle around each other, when they touch each other, Ineke startles, and withdraws her right hand in a defensive reflex, as if in shock.)	SPP: The "hands" communicate a wish to be very close, to unite. It may be that Ineke as ANP wants to take care of The Little Ones. However, the growing tension suggests that this degree of integration is a bridge too far at this point. The right finger and the middle finger touching, really touching the left fingers is too scary. TPP: The defensive reflex could well be ANP's conditioned reaction to getting in touch with more than *knowing* what happened?
I: Yes … *no consoling now* … (hands move to her head, in parallel, brisk movements, very stressed) … *not that* … *but, but* (raises her voice, speaks quickly in a higher pitch) *I want to tell them they have done the right things* … E: Right. I: … *but, but, no* … *no* … *no consoling now* (hands up, wide apart in the air, almost in a panic) E: No, no consoling. Tell The Consoler, ah, wait a minute, not those things now … P: No, no, [we are] good, all right, but no, no consoling. (Hands move wildly in the air; Ineke is still on the border of panic.)	SPP: Ineke as ANP is in trouble. SPP and TPP combined: She wants to be in touch with her various dissociative parts that "… they have done the right things …" However, the implied intimacy is too much. I hypothesize that the action involves consoling her other parts. But consoling reminds her of her father's 'consoling' ("You are my sweet little girl"). As could be strongly suspected and as would prove to be the case, Father's consolation was the (common) overture to sexual abuse. See the discussion.
E: Yes, I get it. Take a good look at me, take a good look.	
I: (Heavy breathing again, arms move restlessly, panics) … *ooohhh* …	FPP, QSPP, and SPP: I feel it is important that Ineke gets in touch with me more, and that she needs to get an idea about what real consolation is like. TPP: She is on the break of a reenactment of her father's "consoling." The situation calls for activation of the social engagement system and its implied power to influence strong affects. But Ineke must not socially engage with her father (The Reconciler) and must not "console" (The Consoler) the Little Ones and Rick, because these passions imply the defense action system.
E: Take a look at me, please. P: (Breathes fast, sighs, hands make imploring movements.) E: You and all the parts. All together now, take a look, then I can tell you something. I: (Hyperventilates, holds the right armrest with her right hand and then the left armrest with her left hand, struggles to find some support.)	SPP and TPP: I decide to be directive. No permissive formulations now, but clear instructions. Ineke needs this guidance. SPP and TPP: Include all activated dissociative parts.

E: Not like Father's consoling . . .	SPP: Attunement. I try to help Ineke to differentiate between Father's consoling and real consoling.
I: (vigorously shakes her head)	SPP: Consensus.
E: Look at me for a while. You are seated on your side of the table, I am sitting here and remain seated here. Take a look and listen, and then I simply say, "It was terrible, really terrible, nobody is allowed to do this to a child."	TPP: It seems possible that Ineke is engaging in a relational reenactment with me. That is, she may perceive and conceive me as a father-like individual. My words of consolation and my understanding of her affects, including the affects involved in Mother's physical and emotional abuse, may alarm her in some regards. My words may sound like consolation, but consolation is dreadful. SPP: Clear instructions to perceive and conceive of the actual present. Differentiation of Ineke's father and me. I take a clear relational position, also regarding her father. "To do this to a child" is intentionally formulated broadly. Ineke can complete what "this" pertains to.
I: (Glances at me, with great difficulty, shakes her head for "No.")	SPP: Consensus.
E: Very sad, very sad (compassionate). I: (Starts to calm down, slowly.) E: And Consoler, listen to how I do it (i.e., calming and consoling the whole Ineke) . . . You can apply it if you wish . . . You can all realize that nobody's allowed to do this to a child. Consoler, you may console the way I do it.	SPP: Real consolation. SPP: My words seem to assist Ineke. TPP: The Consoler could use a modeling of adequate consolation. SPP: Friendly and permissive invitation to follow my lead.
I: (Gasps for air as I speak, but slows down her rate of breathing, her breathing jolts.)	SPP: The Consoler and other parts seem to respond.
E: Does my style appeal to you?	SPP: I address the Consoler directly.
I: (Nods)	SPP: Affirmation. Consensus that consoling can be different.
E: Then we can say once more, in concert, "What happened was horrible. Nobody is allowed to do that to a child."	TPP: Social engagement action system. SPP: Let's console together. Acknowledgment of the traumatization.
I: (Calmer now, shakes her head for "No," holds her hands still tight to the armrests.) No.	SPP: Consensus.
E: And anybody who does it nonetheless is guilty of maltreatment. I: (Exhales and calms down more.)	SPP: A clear formulation that perpetrators are guilty, not their victims.
E: That's how it is . . . Can The Consoler hear this . . . and can he take it in?	SPP: I foster realization.
I: (Nods)	SPP: Consensus.
E: That's how you can do it. We all learn new things, and so do you, Consoler. The Reconciler learns to do things differently, so Consoler you can learn to do things differently, too. Little Ones, we start to see and understand more.	SPP: I continue to address the Consoler directly, but also address the other dissociative parts to substantiate that "we all learn new things." "We" includes me. I am not them, but I join them in certain regards.
I: Not: "naughty little girl."	TPP: A possible hint at sexual abuse.

E: No, "not naughty little girl." Not at all. No, more something like: "Oh, you little girl, how much pain did you have to endure, how scared and confused you must have been."	TPP and SPP combined: Without detailing the deeper meaning of the phrase – a phrase that her father used – I agree with Ineke and every part she comprises, that the phrase does not apply. I offer an alternative phrase.
I: Yes, and *no* consoling! (firmly) . . . Not . . .	SPP: Acceptance and consensus.
E: No, no consoling in that way. That consoling belongs to your father, and that way isn't consoling at all, right?	SPP: Differentiation of consoling.
I: No. (Makes suppressing movements with her right hand, sighs).	SPP: Consensus.
E: How terrible that was.	SPP: More real consolation.
I: And that it is *true* [i.e., that it really happened]. E: And that it is true. I: That is very . . . dreadful . . . E: Very dreadful. Yes. I: Beyond comprehension.	SPP and TPP: Ineke differentiates the terrible events as such and the fact that they are true. That is, she expresses, most adequately, that knowing the facts and realizing them are two different things. SPP: I hear this as: "I am beginning to realize what happened to me, but how can I comprehend that my parents neglected, maltreated, and abused me so systematically and for so long?"
E: Beyond comprehension that parents do things like that.	FPP and QSPP: What is it like to a child and experience this? How would my life have turned out had the chronic traumatization happened to me? Also, I do *not really phenomenally* understand why parents do such things, how they systematically strive to ruin the life of their child. Technical understanding (in TPP) and phenomenal understanding (in QSPP and SPP) are very different things.
I: (Shakes her head.)	SPP: Consensus.
E: No . . . All right. You [i.e., all parts] can meet each other at this point. I: (Deep sigh)	SPP: Inclusion of all parts. I am with the whole Ineke, and her dissociative parts can be with each other.
E: Very, very dreadful that this happened.	SPP: Reiteration, more consolation through sympathy.
I: Yes . . . (Moves her right hand again in the direction of her left hand, in an explorative fashion, then moves them up, each hand to its own side of her head.)	SPP: Affirmation, acceptance, consensus.
. . . That . . . that . . . in whatever way . . . things will turn out all right.	SPP: I hear her saying: "I do not quite know how I can resolve the problems, how I can ever comprehend what my parents did to me. But somehow there is a way out of this misery."
E: Yes, they will. You are well underway. Again, enough for the day, you are well underway, and every journey takes breaks. For now, take a break. I: Yes, time for some flying. (Moves her hands gently in the air.)	SPP: Affirmation that there is a way out. And she is *underway*: utilization of Ineke's term "way." Associating "way" and "journey" and "break." SPP: Ineke can distance herself a bit and for the time being from her inner emotional turmoil.
E: Yes. [I switch the camera off] Close the session for yourself.	SPP: Acceptance and affirmation, and stimulation of autonomy: Ineke closes the session for herself.
I: (Exhales, slows down her breathing, takes her head in her hands, and calms herself. Ineke leaves the session recomposed.)	

Discussion

Ineke entered the session engulfed by decomposing panic attacks that she, as ANP, did not understand. What did they mean? This much she knew: Sirens somehow elicited them. But it was not until the week preceding the session that the sounds had become a real problem to her. Why? She had heard squealing sirens of passing ambulances, police cars, and fire engines all her life and had not totally panicked then. So why this change? What did it mean?

The question '*w*ho does *w*hat and *w*hy?' (www) often helps to orient the search for meaning when patients with a dissociative disorder present with symptoms they do not fully grasp. This therapeutic 'internet' may not work as fast as machines like Google, but it can certainly guide and accelerate the endeavor. The www capitalizes on the insight that in dissociative disorders many symptoms relate to actions or passions of dissociative parts that they engage in to achieve their particular aims. The dissociative parts being intruded on may not know the answers to the www questions, but the intruding parts can generally provide them quite readily.

The Making of New Meaning

In order to search for meaning, we used Ineke's dissociative skills and dissociative parts to advance in steps. I offered the notions of looking at images from an emotional distance, of using a remote control, and of receiving assistance from dissociative parts that could protect Ineke as ANP from the involved fragile EPs' physical and emotional affections. Ineke as ANP put the first two ideas into practice. She detected that the sirens were intimately related to The Little Ones, and she secured help from The Twins and The Observer. I modeled welcoming and appreciating these various dissociative parts, and Ineke worked with them. The Twins were willing to help but seemed insufficiently able to keep the images at a distance. Observing the images, they started to synthesize traumatic sensations and emotional affections as well and got lost in the phenomenal selves and worlds of The Little Ones. The Observer seemed better able to delimit the synthesis of the traumatizing event to visual images.

Whereas The Little Ones were able to show their phenomenal realities as images, they were unable to presentify them on their own. Showing images is a lower-level action tendency that involves a far lower action tendency than putting a most painful experience in words, let alone recounting past traumatic experiences and events from the perspective of the actual present. The fragile EPs involved synthesized and personified crying in Ineke's bed in her children's bedroom, squeaking sounds from the hinges, observing Father and Mother entering the room, Mother hitting her hard against the right side of her head, screaming sounds in her head, and a world getting dark (i.e., losing consciousness).

The Little Ones seemed eager to show and share their phenomenal realities. However,

The Reconciler more generally feared synthesizing the reality of the hitting and the paternal maltreatment and abuse. He felt the actual truth should not become a phenomenal truth because it would definitively ruin any hope of a secure relationship with the parents. A controlling EP, The Reconciler had to deny The Little Ones' phenomenal realities, leaving Ineke as ANP squeezed in the middle. He had to avoid the decomposition and the sorrow that the involved realization would imply (in his view). One of his strategies to achieve this aim was to simply deny the events. Another method he used was bombarding Ineke with remarks that the maltreating adults were not her real father and mother.

The Little Ones (fragile EPs) and Rick (a fight, but no less fragile EP) wished that the other dissociative parts would also acknowledge and accept the reality of the traumatization, and would help to free them from their horrific *umwelt*. These needs and desires clearly conflicted with those of The Reconciler, whose job it was to generate a phenomenal conception of the family members that allowed him and Ineke as ANP to live with them. Whereas he seemed to be a powerful part, the work of the session had revealed that his phenomenal conception of self included the idea of being a fragile boy. The Reconciler tried to control his world, but he also felt vulnerable. More than controlling and feeling fragile, he was also ignorant in the sense that his phenomenal self, world, and self-of-that-world pertained to realities that had actually (i.e., in the third-person perspective) ceased to be.

Dissociative Attachment

A major part of the work of the session involved overcoming dissociative attachment patterns. To achieve this aim, Ineke's needs and desires to heal and her ability to reach higher-level action tendencies were paramount. The required higher-level actions included mindfully knowing, experiencing, and accepting a most painful reality. It more generally demanded consistent engagement in the therapy as a long-term project directed toward integration and realization. However, the plights of the Reconciler and the struggles of the Consoler jeopardized Ineke's ability to engage in these difficult higher-level actions.

In prior therapeutic work, I had encouraged Ineke to accept and take care of her various fragile EPs. She understood quite well that it was her task to engage in this work. Whereas she was willing to meet her fragile EPs, she feared and detested their intense hunger for care. She was also afraid of their body sensations, affects, thoughts, and memories.

A gradual and systematic approach was called for. Breaking down old fences between the fragile EPs (The Baby, The 4-Year-Old, The 6-Year-Old, the approximately 12-year-old Suicidal One) and the ANPs (Ineke and The Twins) enabled the fragile EPs to intrude on the ANPs more. This progression may explain why sirens started to have an effect on Ineke as they had not had before. Sirens may have reactivated the fragile EPs involved. However, Ineke was at the time probably able to keep the involved EPs at bay using various substitute actions (passions), which included bingeing and throwing up, self-mutilation, numbing physical and emotional feelings, and occasional complete switching. These switches sometimes manifested as psychotic-like presentations involving young fragile EPs and suicidal acts.

The gradual opening of the old solid borders between these various primordially operationally autonomous systems activated the controlling EPs. Inasmuch as the ANPs had stayed at a safe phenomenal distance from the fragile EPs, Ineke as a whole individual had managed to maintain the status quo, albeit with difficulty. Hoping for acceptance and love, she continued to interact with the traumatizing family. She adapted herself extensively to the family's needs and desires, and remained sufficiently depersonalized and derealized to enable these interactions. Previous clinicians had not recognized her dissociative condition, so that their therapies did not present a major danger. This composition of forces changed with the present therapy, which fully recognized, acknowledged, and utilized her dissociative condition. And when the therapy began to move in a direction that scared the controlling EPs, they were activated. The Reconciler and The Consoler felt that the other dissociative parts should remain loyal to the family of origin. They also felt that hope for a better life was futile: Such hope, a dangerous idea, had to be crushed.

This dynamic between controlling EPs, fragile EPs, and ANPs is a classic pattern in dissociative disorders. Controlling EPs resist attachment relationships and reject hope. Stuck in a phenomenal traumatic world, fragile EPs want to be saved. ANPs, scared of an extremely painful reality, are motivated to ignore EPs and continue to adapt to an impossible world. The growing contacts between ANPs and fragile EPs alarm the controlling EPs, which then try to block this development. This dynamic explains why controlling EPs generally pop up in therapy the more fragile EPs and ANP engage in mutually integrative actions replacing their old passions. This dynamic will become even clearer in Chapter 37.

Phases of Healing

The Consoler emerged almost instantaneously once the ANPs (Ineke as ANP and the Twins) and the Reconciler started to cooperate more and make new meaning. At some point in the session, Ineke as ANP developed and personified a new phenomenal truth and morality regarding the traumatization ("This is my truth") the Reconciler was able to leave intact. Shortly thereafter The Consoler became strongly activated. In trauma therapy, it often happens that the moment one common goal is achieved the next issue emerges – a classic pattern. It is as if the whole organism-environment system, the whole unity of an individual's body and conscious and unconscious mind, 'knows' how to heal. My long-term experiences with severely traumatized individuals have actually convinced me that this knowing is not an "as if." It is real. The tendency toward integration can be compared to the healing of a physical wound. The comparison should not be surprising if it is considered that the body and the mind are attributes of one substance.

Considered under the attribute of matter, wound healing entails three major dynamic phases that may (but need not) proceed in a linear fashion: "[I]t is 'critical to remember that wound healing is not linear and often wounds can progress both forwards and back through the phases depending upon intrinsic and extrinsic forces at work' within the patient" (http://www.clinimed.co.uk/wound-care/education/wound-essentials/phases-of-wound-healing.aspx). The phases are described as inflammation, proliferation, and maturation. In the *inflammation phase* we find, among other things, bleeding, the contraction of blood vessels, clotting, and the dilation of blood vessels allowing the arrival of essential cells at the site of the injury (for example, antibodies, white blood cells, and growth factors). The *proliferation phase* involves, among other things, the rebuilding of the wound with new granulation tissue and the formation of epithelia cells that resurface the wound. Once the wound has closed, the final *maturation phase* follows which provides a network of connective tissue. Cellular activity regresses, and the number of blood vessels in the area of the healing wound decreases.

Considered under the attribute of mind, traumatization brings forth a mental wound that includes a division of the personality. Its healing can also be described in terms of phases. Here, too, it is "critical to remember that wound healing is not linear and often wounds can progress both forwards and back through the phases depending upon intrinsic and extrinsic forces at work ..." within the organism-environment system (Hutchinson, 1992) (see http://www.clinimed.co.uk/would-care/education.aspx on the phases of wound healing).

The dissociation of the system is analogous to inflammations. For example, newly developing EPs tend to intrude on newly developing ANPs in the form of nightmares and flashbacks. The dissociation of the personality settles and can become chronic when ANPs learn to avoid EPs and their 'contents.' Under these circumstances, the proliferation phase prevents the emergence of the maturation phase. The wound remains open in that the EPs do not disappear but remain intact. Some do not mature and others emancipate, for example, in the context of ongoing traumatization. All EPs can occasionally become reactivated and reenact their phenomenal self, world, and self as a part of this lived *umwelt.* They remain unduly ignorant of factual progressions, such as the flow of actual time, and of possible progressions, such as ANPs' developments and the termination of the traumatization. The open wound eventually exhausts the whole system. As a result, many if not all dissociative parts sooner or later become demoralized.

Enactive trauma therapy represents the attempt to reach the maturation phase of wound healing. To this end, the development goes back to the inflammation phase. Wound healing is stimulated through metaphorical examination and a cleaning of the cell structure, supportive stitching, and interventions that counter the inflammations. This work can lead to a renewed proliferation phase, involving among other things a reorganization of the personality. Moving "forward and backward," the maturation phase can eventually be reached. Inflammations are checked, the open wound closes, and eventually a scar develops.

The appearance of The Consoler, following the moment The Reconciler's concerns had sufficiently been met, was indeed a progressive healing step that started with a regression to the inflammation phase. It turned out to be the overture to a phase in therapy in which Ineke as ANP became confronted with a phenomenal history of 17 years of paternal sexual abuse that, in her and my best estimation, also constituted an actual reality. A question the above session left unanswered was why Ineke has been crying so loudly in her bed. Ineke recently told me that she remembered only crying out of utter despair. She had longed for affectionate nearness and had feared it at the same time. These contrary longings became reinforced with each new traumatic experience.

It was important that Ineke as ANP did not touch The Little Ones in the session, neither figuratively (mental synthesis) nor literally (her right hand touching her left hand). The Little Ones included the traumatic memories of the onset of the sexual abuse and hence all involved sensorimotor, perceptual, and affective nonsymbolized passions. Ineke as ANP did not have the power to integrate these traumatic memories at this stage of her progression. That is, she was not ready to accept the horrible memories. A confrontation with the reality of the massive sexual abuse would have decomposed her rather than have composed her at a higher level of integration. For example, it might have caused another suicidal or "psychotic" episode, that is, a long-term reactivation of a fragile EP. Chapter 38 shows that this hypothesis was well founded. Yet, as a whole system, she did communicate in the above session that the theme of "consolation" would be the next issue to address. In this sense, I encouraged Ineke as a whole system to engage in adequate consolation. But she did not know, at least not as The Consoler, what this action entails and what it feels like to be properly consoled. I thus acted as a model in this respect. Directly addressing all involved dissociative parts, I reassured them that the issue of "consolation" would eventually be addressed. I also emphasized that I did not belong to the family that put Ineke under extreme pressure to keep her mind and mouth shut.

Embodiment

The transcript includes descriptions of Ineke's physical reactions and movements. Even if they are but an approximation of the richness of her actual physical displays, they may serve to communicate how intensely dissociative parts are embodied. Dissociative parts generate their own phenomenal experiences and conceptions of self, of their *umwelt*, and how they are a part of this whole phenomenal world. These experiences and conceptions are deeply embodied (as neuroimaging also demonstrates with respect to the dissociative part-dependent functioning of the brain; see ToT Volume II, Chapters 17 and 18). The embodiment of Ineke as ANP was directly observable. When EPs take full control, as happened during the nightly suicidal episode described in Chapter 32, their embodiment also lies within direct sight of a knowledgeable observer. This may apply as well to an intruding (other) ANP. An expert observer can sometimes also rather clearly detect the embodiment of dissociative parts that intrude on the ANP, which, these intrusions aside, exerts executive control. I was thus able to observe some elements of the embodiment of The Little Ones, The Twins, The Observer, The Reconciler, The Consoler, and Rick. And this embodiment was very real to Ineke as ANP. For example, the right hand touching the left hand comprised Ineke as ANP getting in emotional and sensory touch with The Little Ones. The ANP was in part embodied in the right hand, and The Little Ones were associated with her left hand. When Ineke as ANP reached figuratively out to The Reconciler in an effort to stay in touch with him, she extended her right hand not at the level of an adult's hand, but at the height of a child's or teenager's physical hand.

Observations like these have inspired me to utilize 'the body' ever more in trauma therapy. For example, one dissociative part can be asked to connect herself, her whole being with one hand of the body. Once she has managed to do this, another dissociative part can be asked to connect her being, her predominant sensations, feelings, desires, hopes, thoughts, and memories with the other hand. Inasmuch as the two parts are willing and able to meet, they can move the two hands at their own pace in the other's direction. When they touch, they will get in literal and figurative touch with each other's being. Full encounters may still be beyond the involved dissociative parts power of action and will to engage in this action. In this case, the clinician can offer the idea that only two fingers meet. For example, the fingers that entail and can bridge body sensations can contact each other, but not the fingers that are associated with other phenomenal experiences or conceptions such as particular emotions. Other 'finger-contacts' can be added when the encounter of the first two fingers has brought joy and increases the involved dissociative parts' power of action. And if two hands or even two fingers meeting is too demanding, it is quite possible to restrict the intensity of the encounter by placing a thicker or thinner object between the two hands or fingers, say a cushion or a cloth. For example, it may be suggested that this object filters out 95% of the involved EP's physical feelings, emotions, thoughts, or memories. When the 'receiving' dissociative part(s) can synthesize and personify 5% of the contacted dissociative part's or parts' mental and behavioral contents, the 'receiving' part or parts may be ready to synthesize and personify, say, 10%. And when the involved part or parts have experienced that they can proceed from 0% to 10%, they may be ready to move from 10% to 20%, and so on.

Some clinicians may find it hard to believe how real the dissociative parts' embodiment is to these parts. Clinicians may struggle to accept that fragile child EPs really are convinced they are small, and that these dissociative parts cannot grasp they are part of an adult's body (and mind). Many individuals with dissociative disorder have met clinicians who in friendly or not-so-friendly words ordered them to quit "the nonsense" (i.e., dissociative phenomena the involved clinicians do not regard as real or authentic). And when this command leads nowhere – I have never experienced that such commands, in fact, do work – the clinical relationship suffers and the therapy more often than not gets completely bogged down.

It is far better to attune to phenomenal experiences and conceptions of the dissociative parts and to generate a 'phenomenal consensus' in these various regards. The term phenomenal consensus expresses that the clinician continues to believe that, say, the small fragile EP constitutes a part of an adult's body and mind, while also accepting the phenomenal experiences and conceptions of the involved fragile EP. The transcript of the session illustrates this attitude with regard to each and every dissociative part – and to Ineke as a whole person. Successful attunement and consensus building provides joy. This agreement and joy increase the patients' power of action and offer opportunities for further advancements that may finally entail successful maturation.

Ineke overcame her DID including the dissociative psychotic episodes after 7 years of treatment with me. Two clinical admissions aside, she attended weekly sessions and never missed one. In exceptional cases, there were some brief messaging contacts. With one exception described in Chapter 38, she did not engage in suicidal thoughts leading to suicidal actions. Her self-mutilation basically stopped from the beginning phase of her treatment.

A Brutal Confession, the Unveiling of a Final Secret, and the Right to Exist

As stated in Chapter 32, Ineke and I met again in January 2016 to watch the video of the second assessment session and to gather her first-person comments on its contents and on her evaluation of my role during this session and our collaboration in general. Ineke shared and displayed her mental health. She was well up to watching the session and to discussing many more emotional issues regarding her traumatic and more general history, dissociative disorder, clinical experiences including several misadventures and ineffective venture as well as the successes.

Among other things, we considered the veracity of the incestuous abuse once more that her family continues to ignore to this day. Ineke recounted that, by the time her father somehow suspected that the treatment would include a consideration of incest, he had paid her a visit. He urged her to sign a document he had prepared involving a very formal statement that he had never touched her in an "indecent or inappropriate" way. At the time, Ineke's power of action did not suffice to refuse his commands. So, after 3 hours of intense pressure, she gave in. On the next day and thereafter, her father triumphantly spread the good news to the extended family – and no one posed any questions. When discussing the issue, however, Ineke posed the crucial question: "Why would an innocent father go to such lengths if the daughter neither accuses him in person nor talks about incest to family members?"

As reported before, when he was dying her father evaded Ineke's prudent invitations to discuss her recollections of incest. She had had to run from the situation in despair. Taking her leave, Father had kissed her on the mouth and had worked his tongue inside her during the act. As Ineke now sees it, the weird brutal action made sense after all. The wordless act had been a confession.

The day after our meeting Ineke wrote she had kept a final secret; she could not withhold anymore or else the present book would not include the full truth about her. And that should not happen, she added. She said she had a dissociative part that she had not been allowed to mention or show before. She feared that going against this prohibition would end in severe punishment, and that it would result in the loss of an essential part of her. I invited her to share the issues with me, if she felt like it.

Upon accepting the offer, Ineke accurately reminded me that during our meeting and thereafter in an email, she had expressed her intense longing to have substitute parents. The confession had stirred up the previously secretive part. He felt betrayed. Enraged and scared, he intruded on Ineke. Ineke felt his emotions, heard his screaming, and started to misconceive her partner as a perpetrator. She went back and forth between her needs and desires and those of the previously secretive but now strongly intruding part. My advice was to list and juxtapose the concerns of each position.

The part wrote things like, "You [Ineke] betray me, you abandon me, you need someone and that someone is me, you know that you can only exist through me, how much louder must I shout, I am the only one who can protect you, NOOOO, NOOOO, NOOOOO!!!!!!" [i.e., stay loyal to me]. Ineke tried to reassure him that she would not leave him, that it seemed he and she were both confused, that she would like to console him and lessen his fear, but that she was uncertain how to do that.

Ineke asked for some more advice. I wrote: "Could it be that his fear is a reenactment of your fear of punishment as a child? The fear of your father's revenge for disclosing secrets and attaching to others than him? Could it be that this part strives to help you synthesize how much your father's threats scared you at the time? Ineke's next email contained one word: "Yessss." My reaction was this: "In that case, I would say, 'experience the fear, don't fight it. Thank the part for having carried the heavy load and tell yourself: This fear I am feeling now is my old fear, it has been that bad, how dreadful to have frightened a child so badly.' Something like this?"

Ineke replied (I am abbreviating her message a bit), "I am starting to understand why the part has become so active. The publication of the book, my role in it . . . I hardly dare to say it, but how fortunate that I do not need to be sooo scared of him (i.e., her father) anymore. He is dead. The part communicated that I was only entitled to exist through him. Without the NOOOO!!! [i.e., without the denial of the incest], NO EXISTENCE!!! This part screamed even louder than the screaming baby and the sirens, that I have no chance but to obey. I am now starting to understand it all. As I watched the video, I felt, no, I heard him scream, but was not permitted to tell you. When my hands were at my head in the video, he was so very present."

"What a magnificent step, Ineke," I wrote back. "Yes, I feel free, really free. My remaining wish is to externalize this loud nooo that has ruled my life. To let it out at a safe place in nature, preferably with you, to leave it behind me." A few weeks later, with my modest support, Ineke let her nooo go free.

Chapter 36

Hand in Hand

The force and growth of any passion, and its perseverance in existing, are not defined by the power by which we strive to persevere in existing, but by the power of an external cause compared with our own.

The force of any passion, or affect, can surpass the other actions, or *power of a man, so that the affect stubbornly clings to the man.*

An affect cannot be restrained or taken away except by an affect opposite to and stronger than the affect to be restrained.
Baruch Spinoza (1677a, Part IV, Propositions 5, 6, and 7)

In order to heal, ANPs must overcome their phobia of EPs. The more they overcome this phobia, the more ANPs and EPs can coordinate their actions, cooperate, and communicate. This coordination, cooperation, and communication (Chapter 22) are necessary in order to help ANPs overcome their phobia of the traumatic memories in which EPs are stuck.

It sometimes happens that an ANP cannot raise the mental level to engage in this integrative work just yet, while one or more EPs strongly intrude on him or her. It may also be that an ANP phenomenally experiences an inability to 'reach' or 'find' the intruding EP(s). One explanation for this phenomenon is that the involved ANP preconsciously avoids the EP(s) (see ToT Volume II, Chapter 19). Under these circumstances, clinicians can first help such ANPs to raise their mental energy and efficiency – their power of action – until they obtain the power and courage to start addressing the EP(s). However, this strategy generally takes time, and time can be a scarce commodity when the intrusions are debilitating.

In such circumstances, clinicians may decide to work directly with the involved EP(s), to meet the needs and desires of EP(s) within limits, and to help them overcome their load to a degree that allows the ANP(s) to contact and work with the EP(s) after all. For example, let an EP comprise passions that an ANP finds extremely scary or otherwise intimidating. Say the ANP's fear (and perhaps disgust or hatred) of the EP amounts to 9 on a scale of 1 to 10. Let it also be the case that the ANP can cope with these emotions at a level of 7. Under these conditions, the ANP will become decomposed when she enters in direct and full contact with the EP. Clinicians may propose a restricted form of interaction or indirect contact with the EP, but ANP may resist these suggestions. Now if the clinician's work with the EP reduces the EP's load from 9 to 7, *then* the ANP may succeed in interacting and working with the EP.

The present chapter illustrates this therapeutic strategy. The case also exemplifies that psychotherapy cannot or need not always remain limited to verbal exchanges. In a monistic Spinozean philosophical frame, the mental implies the physical as much as the physical implies the mental. The straightforward implication of this philosophical position is that psychotherapy involves the body as much as the mind, just as body-oriented therapies involve the mind as much as the body. In this general sense, any strict division of psychotherapy and body therapy is nonsensical.

In my view and experience, psychotherapy can also effectively and safely include limited forms of physical contact if the patient is not affected by mere words, and if particular restrictions are carefully met. Sometimes a single touch conveys more than a thousand words, and sometimes there are no words that can express what even minimal forms of touch communicate. The growing realization that we are inescapably embodied should thus modify the division of (trauma) therapy in two parts, that is, in psychotherapy and in body-oriented therapy.

Trauma clinicians should better realize what it is like for a child to be raised in a world without a caring touch, in a world in which their body was unwelcome, beaten, kicked, depreciated, ridiculed, exposed, abused, invaded. They should better strive to imagine what such treatment means. Not all clinicians are sufficiently mindful in this regard.

For example, some trauma clinicians use the phrase 'a safe place.' In doing so they seem to assume that the patient has experienced and knows what 'safety' is, and that the word carries a positive meaning for patients. But many chronically traumatized individuals have never been touched in a safe way and to many the word 'safe' has no experiential meaning. And what if perpetrators initially asserted that their victims were 'safe' with them, but subsequently abused them? In these cases, the word 'safe' likely signals or refers to the ones who suffered.

An ANP may have some understanding of 'safety' and have experienced some safe touch. But what about the EPs the ANP avoids, which are stuck in trauma-time and trauma-land in which their body is neglected, maltreated, or abused? How should these dissociative parts know what physical safety and more general physical well-being are even like? One might counter that ANPs can offer EPs such positive experiences. If this works, that strategy is fine. But what if the involved ANP is depersonalized and more or less sensory anesthetic, phobic of body sensations, or terrified to get in literal and figurative touch with the EP of concern? The ANP's depersonalized, anesthetic, and rejecting touch, or – in the worst case (that alas not seldom applies) – total physical and affective rejection may foremost reinforce the EP's negative physical and emotional experiences. The ANP may thereby confirm if not strengthen the EP's phenomenal conceptions such as "I am dirty; despicable; fat; a whore; a big hole; a nobody; a thing."

The idea that mere words can heal chronically traumatized individuals who have never experienced physical and emotional safety may be simply an illusion. The common goals of enactive trauma therapy thus often include helping the patient, as any dissociative part, to gain positive sensorimotor experiences. In some cases, this work involves new kinds of contact among the various dissociative parts, notably ANP(s) and EP(s). It may also include degrees of touch with partners, children, and friends that the patient can experience as 'safe.' They may even learn to enjoy these experiences. In some cases, the clinician may also have an active, albeit quite limited, role.

The present chapter provides two illustrations. The first involves a session in which an EP and I held each other's right hands, and engaged in mutual movements of the right hand and arm. The second case involves a far briefer description of how an ANP learned to hold an EP that the ANP feared.

Agnes

Agnes (52 years, married, three adult children) had many somatic complaints and symptoms. The presence and severity of her sensorimotor and cognitive-emotional dissociative symptoms as well as the structure of her dissociative personality justified the diagnosis of CDID. The disorder had developed in the context of chronic emotional neglect and abuse by her father, mother, and brother. Her father had also abused her sexually from early childhood through early adulthood and had exploited her as a child prostitute to serve his 'friends.'

The treatment was effective. However, it was complex, and the pace of recovery was relatively slow, mostly because of the recurrent physical diseases of Agnes and her husband as well as the fact that the core family and most members of the wider family completely rejected Agnes – and her husband too.

The general approach to treatment was to encourage Agnes as ANP under my guidance to meet, recognize, and cooperate with her various EPs. The strategy was effective in many cases, but not in all. One exception was her inability to set up cooperation with one very dominant controlling EP that remained loyal to the family. Another limitation of Agnes as ANP was her inability to reach and affect some of her fragile EPs.

The session described below involves an illustration of the latter problem. At some point, Agnes as ANP was unable to move her upper right arm; it seemed glued to the right side of her chest. She could, however, sometimes move and use her right lower arm and hand, whereas at other times her lower arm became pushed against the front part of her chest, and her right hand became a fist. Therapy had taught Agnes to explore her inner world when she experienced such sensorimotor intrusions. The action generally brought her into contact with one or more EPs, and she might succeed in recognizing and gradually cooperating with the involved parts.

In the present case, Agnes as ANP had detected on her own that the fixed right arm and hand related to one of her fearful fragile and childlike EPs. Whereas she succeeded in talking to the dissociative part, she did not manage to influence this part's actions or passions: The motor inhibitions continued. Talking to the ANP, I became phenomenally (second-person perspective) and technically (third-person perspective) convinced that the involved ANP and fragile EP were incapable of achieving advancements together. I decided to guide the ANP's communications with the EP, but this assistance did not work either. We thus felt that I might better meet and work with the fragile EP before the ANP interacted with the EP more. The ANP and EP consented to this plan of action.

The transcript illustrates how clinicians can work with a scared fragile EP and how the problem of a fragile EP can be pinpointed. It also conveys how physical touch and movement can be used to achieve common goals that may be far harder or even impossible to reach by exclusively verbal means. The text further exemplifies the use of Erickson's (1966) so-called interspersal technique, the idea being that one or more words can be interspersed within a sentence to focus on particular aspects of patients' experiences and to facilitate their associations, explorations, and other actions that may be therapeutically useful. The italicized words that appear in the left column indicate slightly or more strongly emphasized and interspersed words. These emphases were placed using a lower or occasionally higher pitch, by inserting pauses before the word or phrase was uttered, and/or by slowing down the pace of speaking. For example, in the sentence: "You may want to experience what it is like to *lower your shoulders a bit*, as if they're *sluggish* and *heavy* . . . you can *let go* a little . . .," the italicized words were slightly emphasized. They thereby gently summoned Agnes as the EP to lower her shoulders and relax them a bit more rather than instructing, let alone commanding, her to do that. Interspersed words can sometimes also be meaningful and useful to a patient when they are not somehow emphasized. However, music played with delicate intonation and feeling generally entices far more than a flat rendering. And, ". . . intonation is not a single system of contours and levels, but the product of the interaction of features from different prosodic systems – *tone, pitch-range, loudness, rhythmicality* and *tempo* in particular" (Crystal, 1975, p. 11).

As always, and as indicated before, the choice of words and phrases is important. For example, it is generally much more helpful to use patients' phenomenal conceptions, rather than to reformulate in terms that (in the third-person perspective) may be technically correct, but that make little phenomenal sense to them. The transcript (Table 36.1) illustrates the frequent adoption and use of Agnes' phenomenal conceptions.

Table 36.1. Freeing a fixed arm

Transcript of the session inasmuch as it involved an activated fragile EP with the identity of a young girl. A = Agnes as a fragile EP E = Ellert	Comments FPP = first-person perspective QSPP = quasi-second-person perspective SPP = second-person perspective TPP = third-person perspective
A: (Breathes intermittently with her right arm against the right side of her chest and lap. Her face is tense and she bites her lower lip. When her EPs are activated, Agnes typically sits with her eyes closed. This also applies to the present session.)	Agnes is present as a fragile EP. She gives her permission to film the session. I install the camera.
E: Very well . . . If it's ok, I'm going to *sit* with you.	TPP: I explain what I'm doing so that Agnes as the present EP will know what is happening. Moving forward, I check whether the EP will allow me to sit rather close – which is needed given the interventions I have in mind. SPP: I express that I fully accept this part's presence. I slightly emphasize "sit" to communicate that I will basically be at her side rather than doing anything, that is, something that would scare her.
A: (Continues the above behaviors, but she does not engage in some kind of mammalian defensive action as I approach her.)	TPP: nonverbal feedback that my nearness does not seem to scare Agnes.
E: Let's start doing the exercise we discussed a minute ago. You feel that removing your arm from [the rest of] your body leaves your body *unprotected*?	TPP: I formulate the problem and test the stated hypothesis: The fixed arm may be a reenactment of a defensive maneuver. The fact that the EP shows up in the therapy and reenacts this defensive pattern may also be a communication that it is time to address the issues involved, which could pertain to traumatic experiences/memories.
A: (Nods several times) E: . . . and then it feels like you're in great *danger*.	SPP: Consensus.
A: (Nods several times more; remains tense.)	SPP: Consensus.
E: And now we want to *figure out* whether that holds *really* true or not.	SPP: Reiteration of the common goal. TPP: "that" stands for 'removal of her arm will be dangerous.' We will test a rather reflexive belief.
A: When I do that it's as if my body is *naked*.	TPP: The implication is that, if she removes her arm from her chest, Agnes will feel as if she is sitting naked in front of me. The italics in Agnes' sentences indicate her emphases.
E: Yes, as if it is *naked*.	SPP: Affirmation through literal repetition of Agnes' phrase. TPP: As always, it is important to attune to and use the patient's formulations and conceptions.
A: (Nods) E: *Unprotected*.	SPP: Consensus.
A: (Nods) Yes.	SPP: We agree that the crucial point in nakedness is being unprotected.

E: Did you learn to keep your arm close to your body when you were with your father, to *protect yourself*?	TPP: This remark reiterates what Agnes had told me as ANP.
A: Yes. (bends her lower right arm from her lap to the front of her chest. The upper arm stays in the same position as before. Her breathing and face remain tense.)	SPP: Affirmation. TPP: Agnes seems to reenact how she tried to protect herself when her father attacked her physically and sexually.
E: Yes. Do you *often* keep your arm and hand against your chest?	TPP: Knowing that her father had physically maltreated and sexually abused Agnes from early childhood to early adulthood, this question communicates to her as the EP that I am very aware of the chronicity of the traumatization. Using the past tense, Agnes is encouraged to engage in presentification of the horrors she lived.
A: Yes. (Nods, her mouth and face as tense as before.)	SPP: Affirmation.
E: How did you move your arm and hand *precisely*? A: (Brings her arm and hand again from the lap to her chest, and turns her hand in a fist.)	TPP: With this question, Agnes is invited to express her defensive movements in more detail. The deliberate action may help her to presentify the past more. Asking patients to slow down, interrupt, or minimally modify reenactments can help to break their rather automatized character and increase the patient's conscious awareness of what they are doing. It destabilizes the reenactment; it can be like inserting little sand in an old machine.
E: And then it *got fixed* [in that position]?	TPP: Continued fostering of presentification.
A: Yes.	SPP: Affirmation.
E: It is as if your arm and hand are still fixed, *right*?	TPP: The past and the present are linked.
A: Yes. (Nods) Almost *rooted.*	SPP: With "almost rooted" Agnes communicates the chronicity of the traumatization and her physical defense.
E: *Almost* rooted. Now let's go ahead and see if we can *change* this a bit – if *you* can change it. You *don't have to* change it, but you're *allowed to* do it if *you wish.* You can decide for *yourself.*	SPP: Agnes decides, her autonomy is recognized.
A: (Nods)	SPP: Agnes consents.
E: My hand is right in front of you. If you stretch your arm and hand out a bit, you'll *meet my hand.*	TPP: I open my hand in front of Agnes, but do not enter her body space. If she wants to take my up on my invitation, she must move toward my hand.
A: (Stretches out her right hand and fingers, while her left hand holds her right hand, but then releases it.)	TPP: Agnes shows she wishes to take my hand, but that she feels a need to be very careful.
E: Yes, fine, *reach out* and you'll meet my hand.	SPP: Communication that her careful approach is fine. "Meet" suggests coordination and cooperation.

A: (Bends her chest forward, but her right arm stays put against her chest.)	TPP: Agnes shows the ambivalence. She wants to take my hand – and she wants to protect herself from the physical and sexual attack she fears. The ambivalence is probably in part a reenactment of her disorganized attachment to her father. The ambivalence involved continues to reflect a conflict between her needs and desires for attachment as well as her needs and desires for defense.
E: And you bend forward and *that's fine*, and you can also let your arm become *ever so slightly* removed from your body.	TPP: "ever so slightly" is an application of the *principle of minimal change*. This principle contains the idea that a minimal change is commonly achievable but still constitutes a change. And by simply repeating little steps, one can eventually take a big step. A dripping tap fills a bucket sooner than most people think.
A: (bends even more forward, but keeps her right arm tight against her chest) Ahh . . . *no* . . . E: That's exactly what you want to learn, right? . . . You can *move a bit more* in my direction if you *wish*. A: Ahh . . . (sighs)	TPP: Agnes does not know how to resolve the conflict between attachment and defense.
E: All right, and *feel* what it is like, . . . yes, *feel* what it is like.	SPP and TPP: The interest is in her phenomenal experience.
A: (Moves her chest and right arm forward again, without removing her arm from her chest.)	TPP: Repeated nonverbal communication that she does not dare to test the possibility that releasing the fixed arm will be safe even while sitting with me.
E: And you're bending *your whole body* forward, right? Yes, it may feel that that is the best you can do right now.	SPP: Attunement.
A: (Sighs again in an intermittent fashion) *Yeees.* (takes my open, upward facing hand.)	SPP: Powerful affirmation and implied consensus. TPP: Taking my hand is a completely new action.
E: Yes, and feel what it is like to *feel my hand* . . . A: It is *cold*!	TPP: It is important that Agnes explore that interpersonal touch can be secure. SPP: Her hand feels reasonably calm, and her touch is neither firm nor weak.
E: Yes, my hand is colder than yours, *I feel that as well.*	SPP: Affirmation and expression of a common experience.
A: Yes.	SPP: Affirmation and consensus.
E: And what is it like in *other* regards?	TPP: The recurrent use of the phrase "What is it like" intentionally communicates a major interest in her experiential world, in her first-person perspective. "in *other* regards" suggests that there is more that Agnes can experience. The touch may have a deeper meaning.
A: I don't know what your hand is going to *do*.	TPP: Agnes seems to regard my hand as a body part with a will of its own. This dissociative understanding may reflect her abundant abhorrent sensorimotor experiences. Her words may also express that she tends to regard her father's body and that of other abusers as collections of unpredictable body parts.
E: Hm, yes, you do not know what my hand is going to *do*.	SPP: Consensus.

A: *No* (wrinkles up her whole face) No . . .	SPP: Affirmation.
E: *My hand* belongs to *me*, *completely* . . . A: Yes . . .?	TPP: A communication that I personify my hand. SPP: Invitation to experience and synthesize "Ellert" and "hand" so that she will hold "Ellert's hand." SPP: Agnes sounds surprised.
E: Yes, it does. *My hand* belongs to *my voice*. It *completely* belongs to *me* . . .	
A: Yes?	SPP: More surprise. TPP: The hypothesis that Agnes experiences other individuals as a collection of minded and dangerous body parts seems to fit.
E: Yes, and how do I *sound*? A: (Very stressed, wrinkled up face again, breathing continues to be quite superficial.) . . . *Quiet* . . .	SPP: Invitation to elaborate on her synthesis.
E: I sound *quiet* . . . *Fine*.	SPP: Intentional use of Agnes' word "quiet."
A: Yes . . . (Face and body show exhaustion) . . . ahh, . . . my arm is getting *so tired*.	TPP: Shifting her attention to her exhaustion, Agnes may implicitly communicate that she is ready for the next move.
E: Yes, *so tired* . . . Would you like to move your body back a bit, so that your back is leaning against the back of the chair?	TPP: The idea is to utilize her exhaustion and to respond to her implicit suggestion that she is ready for the next step.
A: Yes, but then *my arm will become detached from my body, uh* . . .	SPP: Agnes reminds herself (and me) that she continues to believe that this move is dangerous.
E: Yes, you might move your body *just a little bit*, only *a little bit back* to notice what that is like, *notice* whether you are in danger. Just a centimeter or less. A: (Very tense, but moves her chest back a bit.)	SPP: Invitation to test her phenomenal conception and her old fixed idea, applying the principle of minimal change.
E: Your arm becomes removed a bit [from your chest], *very well*, very well. Be *curious*, *notice* what this is like, *notice* whether there is real danger. A: (Moves her chest from right to left and back again in a jerky way, breathes intermittently.)	TPP: Phrases like "be curious" are used to activate the exploration action system and to place less emphasis on the defense action system. SPP: "Notice what this is like" serves to encourage Agnes to explore her phenomenal experiences.
E: You do not need to go any further if you do not *want* to . . . First, examine what this is like . . . *Hear* how my voice sounds . . . *Notice* how you can experience *me as a whole person* through *your* hand . . . A: (Continues to explore, while she also continues to support her right elbow with her left hand . . . releases a deep sigh . . . brings her right arm back to the right side of her chest.)	SPP: Agnes, not I, is the one who is in control. TPP: Emphasis is on careful and mindful exploration as well as on the importance of synthesizing me as "a whole person" and her hand as *her* hand.
E: What is it like? Did any bad things happen? A: (Still tense; shakes her head.) No. E: Does my hand *feel quiet*? Is my voice as *quiet* as before? A: (Nods). Yes.	SPP: The focus on Agnes' experiences and the results of her new action. TPP: Therapeutic experiential hypothesis-testing.
E: Let's try again. A *little bit*, a centimeter or so.	TPP: Application of the principle that new actions need repetition to settle. SPP: "A little bit" once more communicates the principle of minimal change.

A: (Moves her right arm forward again, her upper body makes jerky movements, her right hand lies in my right hand, as before, Agnes keeps her right hand, and thereby mine as well, at the height of her chest.)	TPP: Agnes makes advances and regulates the position of our hands. She is struggling to control the situation, while experimenting all the while.
E: Your arm is separated a little bit from your body, right? A: Yes. E: And *feel* what is happening ... notice what is happening.	SPP: Drawing attention to the result of her new action and its consequences.
A: It *hurts* ... E: Yes, your muscles move your arm back and forth at the same time. They withdraw and want to give space [for new movements].	TPP: It was clear to me that she meant that her muscles were hurting, not the fact that we were holding each other's hands.
A: Also *here.* (Points with her left hand to her right shoulder.)	SPP: Confirmation that her muscles are hurting, not the new action as such.
E: You may want to give your muscles a chance to *learn*, and you can *track what happens.* A: (Moves her right arm a bit more forward.)	SPP: The focus is on the development of new actions and their useful and safe results.
E: You are very *courageous* ... very courageous ... well done ... and *what happens* now that your arm is a bit removed from your body?	SPP: Supporting the new actions through praise.
A: (her right arm and hand shake; she shakes her head) A bit uncertain. (feeble voice) E: (I physically go along with every move she makes.) A bit uncertain, right? A: (Moves her right arm more forward so that it now really detached from her chest.)	TPP: Although Agnes still feels a bit uncertain, she makes major advances.
E: Your arm simply wants to shake. *Feel* what that is like, and *feel free* to go along with the shaking. That's perfectly okay. A: (Her arm continues to shake.)	TPP: Agnes' hand is described as a body with a will of its own. The idea is to encourage her to let the shaking occur, to not fight it.
E: I propose that you give your arm ample space to tremble, let it *simply move.*	SPP: "I propose that ..." means Agnes does not need to do what I say. The emphasis is on her liberty.
A: (Removes her arm ever further from her chest; the shaking intensifies; our hands are joined as before.)	TPP: Agnes continues to experiment.
E: Wow, notice what it's *doing* [removing the arm from her body], really, you're so courageous! And let it *move.* Your arm had *almost* grown onto your body. And it seems you're learning how *it is detaching itself* again ...	SPP: Communication of pleasant surprise. Her former words are utilized: "... *almost* grown to your body ..." and the emphasis, as before, is on "almost." Another emphasis is on detachment.
A: (Continues to practice; becomes calmer, her face grows less tense.)	TPP: Evidence that the new action is becoming less stressful. SPP: Agnes starts to feel a little safer.
E: ... and that *you're safe* ... you can take everything in, that we're in *this room*, the way I am *talking* with you, that you are *safe here*, you could *take this all in* ... A: (The trembling lessens, she brings her left hand to her head, sighs.)	SPP: Emphasis on the positive common results and on the integration of these new actions and its useful results. TPP: I can safely use the word 'safe' now that Agnes has experienced what safety is.

E: . . . and it seems that your hand *is calming down.* A: (her right arm has stopped trembling) I feel light in my head. E: Yes, do you know why? A: (Shakes her head) E: It might be because you have been breathing deeply and quickly. You might be hyperventilating. You know what that is? A: (Shakes her head) E: Sort of taking in more air than you need and breathing out too little. A: (relaxes her right arm and hand, and brings them to the right lower side of her body, takes my hand along, while she now breathes more slowly and calmly) Hmm.	TPP: The shaking and trembling hand is described as an autonomous subject, because this may fit her current experience best.
E: *Excellent.* And *what is it like*? Is it dangerous?	SPP: Another question to focus Agnes' attention on the results of her new action.
A: (Softly shakes her head.) No (Her voice is tense, however.).	SPP: Some realization that the present differs from the past.
E: No danger . . . and your arm becomes *quiet* . . . and there is *no danger.*	SPP: Fostering of presentification.
A: (firmer:) *No.* (Shakes her head several times, tears roll down from her closed eyes.)	TPP: Realization proceeds.
E: It touches you a bit.	SPP: Attunement.
A: *Ye-es.* (with a sigh)	SPP: Affirmation.
E: And it *is* touching . . . hmm . . . it is *touching.*	SPP: Affirmation and communicating consensual experience. TPP: The term 'touch' is used in a triple sense: We are literally in touch with each other through our joined right hands, we are emotionally in touch, and the results of the new action are touching. We have achieved a common result.
A: (another sigh)	SPP: Affirmation.
E: Your arm can *change* . . . *you can change* . . . you can *learn* . . . things that looked so scary just 10 minutes ago . . .	TPP: These remarks have the structure of posthypnotic suggestions.
A: But you don't *do* anything [bad things, such as hit or abuse me]. E: You're learning that there are people who don't do anything [bad] . . . allowing you to *change your body* . . . hmm	SPP: Agnes succeeds in distinguishing me from her father and other abusive individuals she met in life.
A: *How is that possible?* E: Not everyone is like Daddy . . . not everyone is like him . . .	SPP: Agnes is really surprised.
A: (sighs)	SPP: The sigh seems to express acceptance.

E: OK . . . let your arm *relax*, let it go *loose* from your body. What is it like to have *a relaxed arm* . . .? *Notice* (I move her relaxed hand and arm a bit around in the space in front of her body, and she lets me, no resistances.). Will you allow me to *do this*?	SPP: I utilize the growing confidence by gently moving Agnes' hands through the air a bit, but emphasize that she retains control.
A: (Nods twice)	SPP: Agnes allows me to move her right arm a bit.
E: You can feel the difference. (More guided movements, using more space.) What is it like to have a *free arm*?	SPP: The focus is on having an arm that she can move freely because there is no need to keep it fixed to her chest.
A: (Becomes tenser, shakes her head, intermittent breathing.) You're not *going to hit* [me], are you? (Speaks quickly)	SPP: Agnes does not feel completely safe, though.
E: *Nooo*, not at all. You may as well *guide my hand* and move it about. As if my hand floats in the air, like in a carousel. A: (Really tense now, continues to speak fast.) That's the beginning of *hitting*, right?	SPP: Reassurance, in part by allowing her to move my hand again. A carousel may have some positive connotations for Agnes. TPP: My movements operate as a conditioned signal for Agnes. Moving her arm confronts her with past terror.
E: No, no, no, this is not the beginning of hitting at all, do it if you please, *take my hand with you*, just as you did a little while ago . . . A: (Intermittent tense breathing, her upper body shakes, but her right arm and hand remain relaxed.)	SPP: Reassurance and reiteration of my invitation to move my hand as she pleases.
E: Move my hand about for a while . . . fine . . . take it along . . . *you can steer*, I'm happy to follow your lead.	SPP: The emphasis is on Agnes' control of the situation.
A: *No, no* (with her left hand in front of her mouth), it's *impossible*. E: You have felt more than once that some things are impossible. But things can appear to be *different* [when you examine them]. Give it a try!	TPP: Agnes cannot believe that the results of our joint actions are real. What happens does not fit her phenomenal conception of the world.
A: But, but, then you, *you must do what I want you to do*, that's *impossible*!	SPP: Agnes has never experienced before that she can define what other individuals have to do.
E: It *is* possible. You can try and . . . *experience it for yourself* . . .	SPP: Invitation to continue the action and to test its results.
A: (Intermittent breathing, holds her left arm in front of her chest, tense voice, speaks quickly, face wrinkled.) It will make me sick if I *have to do it*.	TPP: Like many other chronically traumatized individuals, Agnes tends to feel that she is obliged to do what others want her to do.

E: Well, no, you *don't* have to do it. Here, sitting with me and talking to me, there is never anything that you *have* to do. You are *allowed* to do things if you *feel like* doing them. *You can decide*, you can decide *for yourself.* A: (Stressed all over her body, except her right hand and arm; she starts to move my hand about in front of her body.) E: *Very well.* A: (Moves my hand and arm in various directions.) E: You're *doing* it . . . you're really *doing* it . . . A: (Holds her left hand in front of her mouth, sighs, several times, keeps moving our right hands and arms about.)	SPP: Communicates that I do not belong to the ones who wish to dominate her. Rather, I stress her freedom, her basic right to self-determination.
E: You can do it . . . *you can do things* in this world . . . you can do things in the world with *your body* . . . and it works out *fine.*	TPP: This statement generalizes the present common results. It has the form of a posthypnotic suggestion.
A: (Calms down, exhales more, relaxes her face.) *Yeah.*	SPP: Confirmation.
E: And *notice* my *quiet voice.* Notice there is *no danger.* A: No, right? (Continues to move our connected right hands and arms; her face shows surprise.)	SPP: Time and again, the focus is on Agnes' experiences. Only *her* experiences can convince her that the present is not a copy of the horrible past.
E: You're *doing* it.	SPP: In my communications, I also emphasize doing (i.e., acting).
A: Yes, yes I *did*, right? (Expresses relief and interest.)	SPP: Consensus.
E: Yes . . . A: (stretches her right arm at full lengths to the right space in front of her) Now my arm is very far away! E: Yes, very far, right. A: (moves our hands and arms more to the left). E: You're *really doing* it.	SPP: Confirmation.
A: (Hand in front of her mouth, giggles) *Yes* . . .	TPP: The giggling is a component of her act of triumph. Triumph brings joy that increases the power of action as well as replaces sorrow. Joy confirms change for the better. Finding pleasure in experimenting belongs to the action system of play.
E: You're taking my hand on a little trip. A: (Continues) Ohh. Ye-es. (Giggles more, starts to enjoy the exercise.)	SPP: Resonating her pleasure, I talk about a little trip and share her joy.
E: My hand is *happy* to go with yours. A: Yeah . . . E: Do you notice that? A: *Yes.* (Continues moving, more rapidly now.) Yeah . . .	SPP: I portray my hand as a positive subject.
E: Isn't this *funny*? A: Yes (Left hand in front of her mouth again, smiles.) *Yes* . . . (laughs)	TPP: Emphasis on terms like 'happy' and 'funny' fit the action system of play.
E: (I laugh with her.) A nice little game, right?	FPP and QSPP: I get carried away a bit under the influence of my activated action system of play. I forget that sexual abusive individuals often use phrases like ". . . nice little game . . ."
A: (Tenses up instantly.)	TPP: Agnes is startled.

E: Fine, it's OK. But that word scares you, right?	FPP and QSPP: I feel bad that I made a mistake. SPP: I try to calm and console her and to resonate with her fear.
A: Yes, yes, but you're not scared now? E: No. I am simply Ellert, not your Daddy.	SPP and TPP: Still a bit confused, the statement that "I am simply . . . etc." did not fit well, although it may have helped Agnes to understand that I had no wish to engage in her father's games. I thought that Agnes feared that I might play vicious 'little games' with her. In hindsight, she was rather concerned that I, being the one who 'had to follow' her movements, was scared.
A: You do not need to keep your arm against your body?	SPP: Agnes stays more focused than I did. To reiterate, it seems that she puts herself in my position, identified with me from her life world, and thus wondered whether I, like her, was terribly scared that someone else – here Agnes – was controlling my arm.
E: No, no, no. That's what you thought? You're thinking "Ah, I take Ellert's hand along," and "Now he cannot keep his arm to his chest?"	SPP: I put the idea in words. FPP and QSPP: I experience that my confusion and shame settle a bit.
A: Yes. (Continues moving our right hand and arm)	TPP: It seems like we're back on track.
E: There is no need to do that [keeping my arm against my chest], you're not hurting me. A: That's *not* what I want. (calmer)	SPP: Confirmation, consolation, and reassurance. Agnes learns that her body can gradually become a resource, rather than a constant source of trouble.
E: Sure, *I know*, and I do not want to hurt *you*. Perhaps you can continue to *learn* that I do not want to hurt you. You can notice that, *using your body*.	SPP: Acceptance.
A: (Nods, face and body calm, except her shoulders) E: You have pulled your shoulders up. A: Yes, and it is *hurting* here. (Touches her upper right arm with her left hand.)	TPP: This clearly noticeable fact probably carries meaning.
E: You may want to experience what it is like to *lower your shoulders a bit*, as if they're *sluggish* and *heavy* . . . you can *let go* a little . . . A: (Moves her right shoulder about and lowers it a bit.) Like this . . .	TPP: The invitation to slightly lower her shoulders may have come a bit early. I could have explored its goals, its teleofunctional role first.
E: Yeah, *like this* . . . that's different . . . how's this? A: It doesn't feel comfortable.	TPP: Agnes responds nonetheless.
E: Not comfortable? You have to *get used to it*? Just give your shoulders a chance. A: It feels so *tight* here. (Left hand touches the right side of her neck.) E: Yes, your muscles are accustomed to being tense.	TPP: Again, it might have been better to examine the purpose of the behavior. People do things for a reason.
A: Yes, *one must raise one's shoulders.*	TPP: Here Agnes starts to share *why* she is raising her shoulders.
E: You must raise your shoulders, you say? Why's that? To protect your head?	TPP: I might have left out the remark that she may want to protect her head. The simple and open question ". . . Why's that . . .?" would have sufficed.
A: (Does not move.) That's what needs to be done. E: Why's that?	TPP: Agnes starts to clarify.

A: It *looks better.*	TPP: I wonder who says so?
E: Ah, not in my eyes.	SPP: I try to reassure her. However, in TPP, it might have been better to say: "In what regard?" It is not wrong to say "not in my eyes" but the remark misses the point that it is not very relevant for Agnes how I phenomenally judge her posture. The point is why she feels, as the involved EP, that it looks better to pull up her shoulders.
A: If you raise your shoulders, you're stronger. You're *stronger* then.	TPP: Here is the point: She feels stronger.
E: That's what you had to do when you were with your father? Strong, you're your shoulders up, like a soldier? A: Yes . . . *Prepare for the attack.* E: Ah-ha. But, you know what, here you can *act differently.* Here you can do what is more *natural. Relax* your muscles. No need to spend energy lifting your shoulders here.	SPP and TPP: We're back on track. A lack of attunement can happen and is not necessarily detrimental, whereas a continuing lack of attunement, that is, misattunement without repair is harmful.
A: More like this . . . *soooo* . . . (drops her shoulders, the right more than the left one) E: Like a well-fed, sleepy baby. They *relax.* And you can be like that. And notice that you're *safe* here. A: Yes. (relaxes the right shoulder some more) E: Your right hand and arm have become *relaxed* already.	TPP: Agnes responds.
A: It is *so tired* . . . E: Yes, when we use our muscles a lot, they grow *tired.*	TPP: The more Agnes experiences she is safe, the more she can allow herself to feel tired.
A: (Nods several times) E: Fine. And I guess your right shoulder will also be tired. A: (Nods) Very, very tired.	SPP: Consensus.
E: Very, *very tired.* And I guess there may be *many more muscles* of your body that are very, very tired.	SPP: Attunement, consensus. TPP: Generalization: many muscles will be tired: Agnes had many physical complaints that might in part be related to continuous stress reactions.
A: (Nods several times, looks calm.)	SPP: We agree.
E: And when they know they are *safe,* they can *relax and rest.*	TPP: Muscles are described as subjects that can relax and rest. The net effect may be that Agnes hears: "I can relax and rest now that I am safe at last."
A: But if you relax your muscles that means you don't *control* them.	SPP and TPP: Agnes continues to express how important it is for her to control herself as much as possible. TPP: Agnes voices a conflict: She wishes to relax, but she fears that relaxation implies a loss of control.
E: You cannot control the muscles of your right arm right now? A: He is *so tired.* E: Yes, *so tired.* A: . . . that you hardly feel him, and then you *cannot control him* . . .	SPP: Attunement.

E: In closing our meeting, you can steer my hand through the air once more. (We still hold each other's hands.) And notice you can *control* your *relaxed* right arm and hand. You can *do that.* A: (Moves our right hands through the air.)	SSP: Appreciating Agnes' need for control, it may be valuable for her to experience that relaxation is not incompatible with control.
E: Experience your *control.* You had the idea that you could not control a relaxed arm and hand, *but you can.*	SPP: Ratification of her experience.
A: Yes. (Moves my right hand to the right frontal side of her, smiles) To that side. E: Yes, to that side. A: Far removed from me. E: Far removed from you ... A bit more in your direction won't work for you?	SPP: Agreement.
A: (Shakes her head, presses her lips.)	
E: You're sure?	
A: (Moves her hand slightly in her direction, and then keeps it at a distance of some 20 centimeters in front of her stomach.) Not any further than this.	TPP: Agnes sets a clear limit. SPP: She will feel scared.
E: That's perfectly OK. *You steer.* A: Yes, it shouldn't come any closer. E: You feel it should not come any closer. A: Yes, otherwise your hand would be closer to me. E: And if you do not want that, that is *perfectly fine.*	SPP: Total acceptance of her limit setting. TPP: Refers to my hand as an "... it ..." SPP: Acceptance of her limit. FPP: I do not experience any wish to come closer. In fact, I do not experience any wish apart from the wish to help Agnes achieve the results she is after.
A: I know you won't do anything [bad], but I don't dare it [to keep your hand a little closer].	TPP: Knowing and realizing something are very different matters.
E: That's fine. A: I *don't dare to trust* you [that much] (almost weeps) ... That's *terrible*, right?	SPP: Full acceptance.
E: No, *not at all.* You have already done so much for yourself today. More than enough.	SPP: It is not terrible that Agnes does not fully trust me. TPP: The issue of trust needs more work, but Agnes needs to rest before the theme of trust can be addressed.
A: (weeps) But I hate myself for it. E: Shall we talk about this next time?	TPP: Self-blame and self-hate are related topics that needs to be addressed but not now.
A: (Nods while weeping)	SPP: Acceptance.
E: For now, you came take home the thought: "*I can change*, I can even change things and ideas that have been fixed for years and years.	TPP: Remarks that can operate as posthypnotic suggestions. 'Fixed' has a literal and metaphorical meaning.
A: (weeps, left hand in front of her mouth). You aren't *angry* at me, are you?	TPP: Another instance of insecure attachment: Agnes is scared that her lack of total trust in me will make me angry.

E: No, not at all. Listen to my voice. Do I sound angry? A: (Shakes her head) E: Does my hand feel angry? A: (Shakes her head) E: Fine. I feel we can *cooperate very well.* A: (weeps) E: Fine, take everything you've learned today with you. And remember: "Wait a minute, *there's more* I can and want *to learn.*" A: (Nods fiercely)	SPP: I stimulate Agnes to explore my mood by attending to easily accessible features of my behavior.
E: "I've come as far as I've come today." And you're doing *great*... Just great... You can *surprise yourself*... And be a little sad that there's still more for you to learn. A: *Yeah*...	SPP: Recognition and acceptance of her achievements and her sadness. "... You can surprise yourself..." harks back to the surprising changes. This means: "Do not judge too soon that some new action is unachievable."
E: *Relax.* Perhaps you can use the energy of your sorrow to *create a plan* how you want to *take another step forward* the next time we meet.	TPP: "Negative energy" can be turned in "positive energy."
A: (sighs, with relief)	SPP: Acceptance.
E: If I have been able to change this, *there's more I can change.*	TPP: An idea presented as a posthypnotic suggestion. SPP: Raising Agnes' interest in further change.
A: (relaxes more) I can learn those other things as well? E: Yes, *certainly*! I'm amazed how much you learned today. A: (deep sigh)	SPP: I feel she is interested.
E: (I sigh with her.) Very well, take your relaxed hand, arm, and shoulder with you.	TPP: Agnes will evidently take her whole body with her, but the crux of the 'posthypnotic suggestion' is "... your *relaxed* hand, arm, and shoulder..."
A: (Moves our hands and arms some more.)	SPP: Through our physical link, I can immediately feel that Agnes is *freely* moving her and my right arm. What an accomplishment!
E: *Great*... And you can release our hands when you're ready. A: Yes. (releases our hands, her face and body are relaxed) (At this point, the session continued with an invited return to Agnes as ANP)	SPP: I communicate that Agnes is in control.

Through the work of the present session, Agnes overcame her fixated right arm and the result was definitive. The next step in her therapy was to encourage Agnes as ANP to integrate the involved EP's traumatic memories regarding sexual abuse by her father more.

Physical Contact Between Patients and Clinicians

Ethical psychotherapy codes tend to forbid direct physical contact between patients and psychotherapists. This prescription is grounded in the belief that these contacts may provoke or strengthen unhealthy forms of dependency, unilateral or bilateral sexual feelings, or other unhealthy relationships between psychotherapists and their patients. However, there are serious reasons to call for a reconsideration of the rule that psychotherapeutic interventions should not include physical components.

Factual Considerations

It is a fact that clinicians engage in two kinds of physical contact with their patients: direct and indirect. Shaking hands is an example: When shaking their patients' hand in greeting, clinicians clearly engage in a direct form of physical contact. The ethics of psychotherapy do not forbid this action. While this form of direct touch may seem innocuous, it might not be so innocent or insignificant. For example, when clinicians initiate the action, they may not check whether their patients actually want to shake hands at all, or what particular *kind of* handshake their patients prefer. Patients may find that the clinician's grip is too strong or too weak, too dominant or too submissive. They may also experience that the clinician's arm and hand are invading their phenomenal body territory. Some clinicians habitually make sure (consciously or unconsciously) that their hand is on top. They also express relational dominance when they define the amplitude and pace of the shaking.

Shaking hands is clearly associated with direct physical contact. But the *absence of direct physical contact does not mean the absence of physical affections.* Clinicians and patients entertain physical contact, no matter what. For example, some clinicians habitually stand with their legs spread wide while shaking their patients' hand. Their gaze is direct and their body is 'open' in a way that some traumatized individuals find uncomfortable if not distressing or alarming. Other clinicians exhibit far less eye contact and show a body posture that some traumatized individuals or dissociative parts of them may experience as too 'closed' or too 'absent' for comfort.

Clinicians clearly have to take some position and make some movements during sessions. Sometimes they bend forward and show an open or concerned face to show interest or concern. They may try to cheer the patient up by speaking with a light tone of voice or by putting on a happy face. They may try to maintain a 'neutral' posture and a 'neutral' face to present (what they consider) a 'professional' attitude. However, the meaning of these communications is not defined by their good intentions but by the way a particular patient or dissociative part perceives and conceives the involved movements and expressions. The patient as a whole or a dissociative part may consciously or preconsciously experience and judge that the clinicians' face is too happy, too evaluative, too intrusive, or too neutral – and likely react accordingly. ANPs and fragile EPs have quite different reactions to facial expressions that they consciously and preconsciously perceive (see ToT Volume II, Chapter 18).

Psychotherapists and other clinicians may not or do not sufficiently notice how their postures and movements affect patients. They may not be accustomed or trained to attend to and closely track patients' physical expressions, and some patients express their affective reactions only minimally. Clinicians may also be so focused on trying to understand their patients' problems or utterances that they miss their patients' nonverbal and paralinguistic reactions. By bending forward out of interest, engagement, or concern, they may overlook that some patients withdraw their mouth or hands, move their head slightly backward, freeze their facial musculature, start to breathe from their upper chest more, swallow, or start to speak in a higher pitch, or with more difficulty.

Further, some clinicians fail to be consciously aware of their own characteristic postures, movements, manner of speaking, tone of voice, etc., and how these nonverbal and paralinguistic features affect their patients. Some male clinicians tend to sit with spread legs in front of their patients and appear to be quite unaware of this habit. While they commonly do not intend to present sexual signs, their posture may scare some patients or dissociative parts, particularly those who have been sexually abused. Some clinicians who tend to gesticulate a lot may not observe or realize how their rather sudden or expressive movements can startle their patients, particularly those who have been physically abused. For example, as the involved EP, Agnes even feared that my *slowly* moving hand might involve the start of hitting.

A further observation and common knowledge is that, like other individuals, clinicians are not always in control and aware of their nonverbal and paralinguistic expressions. Their face and tone of voice tend to be in constant flux; they express themselves affectively in ways they do not or not fully control, notice, or acknowledge. Like anyone else, clinicians are primordially affective and embodied. For whatever reasons, some clinicians long and strive to hide their affects. As mentioned above, some wish or were taught to remain 'neutral.' Such clinicians would better realize that it is nearly impossible to hide pleasure, concern, fear, annoyance, anger, disgust, shame, disinterest, fatigue, and pain, and other emotions and states.

Furthermore, as mentioned before, clinicians' affections and modes of longing and striving do not 'inform' their patients. Their patients rather attach a particular meaning to their involved observations, consciously or unconsciously. Like clinicians, patients signify themselves and their world at all times. *There is no neutrality in life*. Moreover, most chronically traumatized individuals have learned to meticulously track and sensitively read other people's intentions and affections. Under the guidance of the defense, attachment, social engagement, and social dominance action systems, they have learned to detect signs of impending rejection, maltreatment, and abuse, as early and as accurately as possible. And since each dissociative part co-constitutes his or her *umwelt*, each part will tend to perceive and conceive a different world. A single look, a single move or touch from the clinician affords multiple sensations, affects, thoughts, and behaviors in a dissociative individual.

Empirical Considerations

An empirical reason for reconsidering ethical codes regarding touch is that particular kinds of limited physical contact between patients and clinicians can be effective and efficient. Sensorimotor approaches to trauma therapy demonstrate the issue (e.g., Levine, 1997, 2010; Ogden, Minton, & Pain, 2006). The transcript quoted above also testifies to the efficacy of psychotherapeutic interventions that include a limited form of physical contact. The intervention was actually stimulated by favorable experiences with other fragile EPs, which were fixed in sensorimotor reenactments of traumatizing events.

Hand-to-hand contacts can serve several objectives. For example, they can provide an opportunity for patients to experience that not all hands want to grab, hit, or sexually arouse them. This limited form of physical contact can also be a means for patients to explore, experience, and know what safe touch is and feels like. As with Agnes, I have also used hand-to-hand contacts to allow patients to control the movements of my hands, that is, to control *me*.

Another example may be found in a woman with DID who was flooded with images of blood, of huge mouths that wanted to eat her, and of shapes that chased her, everywhere. This apparent psychotic phase had been going for 2 weeks when she arrived at the next session with me. She reported as a leading ANP that antipsychotic medication and support from a psychiatric nurse had been fruitless, as had her own efforts to reach the EPs that might be related to the images and the associated intense fear. The psychotic phenomena had been and continued to be so intense that all dissociative parts including the presenting ANP were totally confused and unable to assess what was real and what was imagined. Our best hypothesis was that the psychosis related to Fred, a male EP who had surfaced in the previous session. Since neither the presenting ANP nor any other dissociative part had managed to reach him, we decided that I would invite him to come forward and talk to me.

The plan worked. As Fred came forward, he instantly ran to a corner of my room. He yelled that there was blood all over the place. Men with big mouths were chasing him. He repeatedly ordered me to send them off. Noticing my videocamera, he asked what I wanted to do with the recording. He was convinced I would sell it, but recurrently added, "I will not undress." When I tried to reassure him, Fred repeated that the people he saw would have to go. I asked him to point them out to me.

"There, and there, and there. Your mouth is also huge."

I invited him to come a little closer to examine the proportions of my mouth.

"No, no!"

Saying I would like to help him, I slowly went over to him while keeping my hands at my back to communicate I had no intentions of harming him. Standing near a scared Fred, I measured the width of my mouth with a finger and the thumb of my right hand. Having shown the small gap between my fingers, I gently took his right hand with my left hand to physically assess the measure of the gap for himself. As a next step, I brought the small gap back to my mouth to demonstrate that my mouth was not any bigger than the gap he had seen and felt for himself.

Fred reacted: "I think everyone wants to kill me. They will eat me. They want to grab me, they put pills and more pills in my mouth. And continue and continue."

"Why would they want to do that?"

"They want to kill me."

"You're scared to death they will kill you."

"Yes."

"And now you're scared I also want to kill you."

"Yes."

"Please take my hands and feel if they want to grab and kill you."

"No . . .!"

"Please allow me to help you a bit."

I took his right hand again and brought it in the direction of my right hand.

"Please feel if there is anything they want to do."

"They may want to hit me."

"Test whether my hand wants to hit. Feel free to check."

Fred touched my hand. After a while, he said, "No."

"No, and it is fine with me that you guide my hand. Take my hand and put it somewhere where you want it to be."

Fred put it at the height of my shoulders.

"And if you want to alter the position, now or later, you can do that. That's fine with me."

"It can't be, it can't be!"

"I think it can, please notice, Fred."

"I can hardly believe it."

"You can hardly believe it. What would you need to believe it just a little bit more?"

Fred placed my hand higher up.

"What do you observe?"

"I'm scared you will bring me around."

We explored the issue, while my right hand stayed where Fred had put it. Fred related how a group of men had drugged him and persuaded him to seriously hurt other children. There had been no way to escape. Fred had screamed they should better kill him. But they did not do that. Totally confused and drugged, Fred had done things to other children that had caused a lot of blood. The more he managed to put the awful events in words, the more the hallucinations and fears began to lift. He eventually cried bitterly, and I supported him.

Fred's fear that the men would come to punish him for telling and crying constituted a final issue in the session. I proposed to check whether the men were indeed coming to get him and opened the door. Fred shivered all over. I reported there was nobody in the corridor. Fred was not convinced that he was safe, so we checked the world beyond the therapy room together, hand in hand. This helped.

Fred felt sad but calmed down. He agreed to retreat to a sufficiently restful place inside where he could stay until the next session. I suggested he might want to take the positive experiences of the session including the lessened fear with him. Thereupon, the leading ANP was invited to come forward. We shared the essence of the session. Then the patient could go home recomposed.

Hand-to-hand contact can also give patients a chance to experience that they can push someone else's hand back and thus exert an influence on another person (Ogden et al., 2006). Another method is to hold hands during deep and terribly painful mourning. Some patients have never been supported in this way before.

A related, potentially helpful form of direct physical contact is holding a still hand on the patient's back to facilitate and support crying. This intervention accompanied the work with a controlling EP of an adult woman with DID who presented himself as a cool, strong guy. He also felt deeply hurt and fragile but tried to hide these feelings to keep up a strong face. The controlling EP reported how several fragile child EPs had been severely physically abused and raped. He believed that the sexual abuse had not happened to him. However, he had observed the recurrent rapes from a distance. The sight had been most distressing. And he had been severely beaten and choked to unconsciousness by the mother's partner. The mother had been drunk when the physical abuse occurred and had not come to his aid. The controlling EP had focused on escaping. When he was on the verge of crying in the session, but remained stuck in this phase, the supportive and accepting hand of a female co-clinician on his back was most helpful to get his mourning started. As he said later: "In the beginning, it was scary to have that hand on my back, but then . . ., then . . . . . . [long pause]" – "What did you feel then?" – ". . . then . . . I felt . . . *I am not totally alone* . . . not a drunken mother . . ."

Crying against the clinician's shoulder for some time while mourning over excessively painful traumatic memories may occasionally also be helpful. The large majority of patients does not need or desire this form of physical contact to integrate traumatic memories. But a few do, or else they remain stuck in their horrors. In such instances, I take particular care that only our shoulders meet, and that my hand on the patient's back remains immobile. In all cases, this degree of supportive physical contact supports the mourning and strengthens the clinical working relationship. I have never experienced negative outcomes or negative side effects.

In Agnes' case, and in other similar cases, I did not offer my hand to establish a working relationship with the involved fragile EP or other dissociative part or parts. The intervention was rather utilized for purposes that were far more difficult or impossible to overcome with mere verbal exchanges. For several reasons, it is important that clinicians refrain from contacting EPs and setting up a working relationship with them through direct physical contact. Clinicians cannot know in advance what meaning the physical contact will have for a dissociative part they do not know well. Further, the dissociative part involved must get to know the clinician and the nature and context of their restricted physical interaction with the clinician before they will be able to decide for themselves whether they want this form of contact at all. I left it up to Agnes' EP whether there should be some restricted physical contact between her and me, and for how long. This contact was not established to serve my personal interests, but only those of the patient. That is how things should be in therapy.

Sometimes it is necessary to physically discourage or inhibit hand and arm movements. Some dissociative parts wish to have quick sex to control a man who, as she fears, might otherwise rape her. One dissociative part in a patient reached out to grab my genitals while making sexual movements for this reason. It was clearly important to stop her action. More than this, it was important to stop her actions in a manner that would not shame her, so that she would continue to communicate her full acceptance and understanding. I gently but also firmly took the patient's hand, looked her in the eye, and told her with a compassionate voice, "I guess I know what you want to do, and why. Doing what you want to do has probably helped you when times were hard. But we can be peacefully together without sex. You will notice this as we let time pass." The patient struggled to control the situation along the well-paved route and started to plead to have sex. "It will be really quick." I continued my verbal and nonverbal actions until the patient calmed down. Blocking her former defensive action initially destabilized the involved dissociative part, but eventually resulted in self-reorganization.

Theoretical Considerations

There are also some theoretical grounds for reconsidering the role of the body in psychotherapy. Psychotherapists and other clinicians and patients are, like anyone else, embodied and environmentally embedded organism-environment systems per their very nature (see ToT Volumes I & II as well as Chapters 24, 25, 27, and 29). And since consciousness basically involves noticing physical affections (see Chapter 29), patients and clinicians cannot but affect each other, mentally *and* physically, with or without direct physical contact.

This conclusion is fully Spinozean in nature, as the following formulations and propositions demonstrate (1677a, Part II; see also Chapter 29). A basic formulation is that "the idea which constitutes the essence of the mind involves the existence of the body so long as the body itself exists" (p. 77). Our mind exists inasmuch as our body exists, and our mind knows our body. However, this knowledge is limited, because *[t]he human mind does not know the human body itself, nor does it know that it exists, except through ideas of affections by which the body is affected* (Proposition 19). While our awareness and knowledge of our body are certainly limited, it is not poor: *The idea that constitutes the formal being* [esse] *of the human mind is not simple but composed of a great many ideas* (Part II, Proposition 15). Further, we do not only experience and know affections of our body; we can also develop ideas or conceptions (synonyms) of the involved physical affections and perceive these conceptions. As

Spinoza proposed, *[t]he human mind can perceive not only the affections of the body, but also the ideas of these affections* (Proposition 22). But our perceptions of our ideas of our physical affections are incomplete and imperfect: *The mind does not know itself, except insofar as it perceives the ideas of the affections of the body* (Proposition 23).

The implication of these various propositions is that the more we learn to perceive and conceive of the affections of our body, the more we get to know ourselves. This knowledge increases our power of action. What is more, per Proposition 26, *[t]he human mind does not perceive any body as actually existing, except through the ideas of the affections of its own body*. Hence, we feel and know other individuals including their sensations, affects, etc., through our own body, and the more sensitive we are, the more we tend to feel, know, and understand. And the more ideas we develop, the higher our power of action will be with respect to ourselves, other individuals, and objects.

Adherence to Spinoza's insights implies the realization that the distinction between the mental and the physical is largely artificial. Psychotherapy, then, is a professional meeting of two living bodies that are, within limits, conscious of themselves and of each other. It is an encounter of two organism-environment systems, of two embodied and environmentally embedded individuals who, if all is well, strive to realize at least some common goals. (They also respectively entertain goals they do not have in common. For example, clinicians clearly strive to earn an income, and they may seek to fulfill an ambition.) Since matter and mind are attributes of one substance, and since subjects who strive to achieve common goals essentially affect each other, psychotherapy implies 'body therapy,' just as body-oriented therapies imply psychotherapy.

This realization has far-reaching consequences for the training, guidance, and work of trauma clinicians and clinicians more generally as well as for the rules that guide any kind of clinical contact and venture. A more or less categorical prohibition of touch in psychotherapy is not helpful, and it does not prevent transgressions, as ample sad evidence has demonstrated. Apart from this, it does not teach us under what circumstances what kinds of direct and indirect physical contact in (trauma) therapy can, in fact, be effective and appropriate.

New Rules and Training

To safeguard the patient, the clinician, and the patient-clinician dyad, new rules regarding indirect and direct physical touch must be determined. One general sensible rule would be that the decision to use a limited form of direct physical contact in psychotherapy should serve clear therapeutic goals. It should also be completely consensual and under the control of the patient. And it should, and in my experience can, remain quite limited. In some cases, the safety of the situation can be guaranteed by the presence of a colleague. It is also possible to include a body-oriented clinician who can execute body-infused interventions that would not otherwise fit the patient-psychotherapist collaboration.

Another new rule can be that clinicians must be trained and educated regarding their body and its role in therapy. They should be helped to develop a higher level of conscious awareness of their body, their body movements, and their physical actions and passions as well as just how these features affect their patients. This includes characteristic postures, eye and other movements, facial expressions, ways of using their hands, manner of walking, speaking, and looking at patients.

By way of illustration, clinicians can be helped to detect how they tend to extend a hand to their patients and how it affects various individuals and their dissociative parts. It is also very useful for them to learn a variety of handshaking styles, concentrating on the variable outcomes with different individuals and dissociative parts. Clinicians who wish to communicate an egalitarian attitude may reach out to present their hand while keeping their hand in a vertical position. Turning the back of their hand to the floor (showing open palms) commonly creates a different reaction than turning the back of the hand upward (suggesting dominance). Clinicians may also learn to reach out slowly enough for patients to track the clinicians' action and to freely respond to it. For example, clinicians can learn to detect the importance of giving patients time and the opportunity to refuse to take the reached out hand. This also goes for allowing patients the opportunity to prevent the clinician's hand from coming any closer to them. Clinicians can also experiment with the results of different kinds of pressure and shaking.

Clinicians should also be trained to raise their consciousness about how open or closed body postures affect their patients. For example, as they approach traumatized individuals, they learn to notice that it can make a major difference whether they stand in front of the patient with their legs spread a bit and their lower body part in full sight (e.g., uncovered by one of their hands) or whether they stand with other lower body parts turned a bit sideways, with one leg before the other, and with one hand held placed gently in front of the lower body region. As remarked above, this also goes for sitting with spread legs or crossed legs. Generally speaking, chronically traumatized individuals respond better when clinicians keep their lower body parts 'closed' (e.g., crossed legs, perhaps with one hand lying loosely in their lap), but keep their upper body parts and face more 'open.' Female clinicians should be assisted to realize that breasts can signal danger, disgust, or both to patients who have been sexually abused by women.

Videos of the patient-clinician dyad are an excellent means for raising clinicians' level of consciousness concerning how their physical actions affect their patients and how their patients physically affect them. Videos allow clinicians and their coaches, supervisors, team members, and trainers to observe all verbal, paralinguistic, and nonverbal expressions in detail, and to evaluate how the mixture seems to affect their patients. They allow modifications of some of the clinician's actions and can help to delimit the clinician's passions including 'countertransferential' reactions.

Clinicians are best trained to track and evaluate their feelings while engaging in some form of physical contact with a patient. They can also be taught to ask themselves questions like: "Would I feel like engaging in the present physical contact if I were to find the patient physically unattractive?" "Would I feel comfortable with this contact if other people were watching?" "Would I engage in the action if the patient were of a sex and sexual orientation that does not appeal to me sexually?" Clinicians may determine they would not be inclined to engage in the physical contact with an individual they find physically or sexually unattractive; they may detect that they would rather not want to be observed by others as they engage in the act. If that is the case, they should probably conclude that something is wrong, which should keep them from the involved action altogether, or they could discuss the issue with a supervisor.

The approaches to physical contact between patients and clinicians described may turn out to be more effective than simply forbidding clinicians to touch their patients in any way and under all circumstance. It might even prevent some clinicians from abusing patients emotionally, physically, and sexually.

Exceptional Clinical Situations that Crucially Involve the Body

Sometimes patients engage in rather extreme physical actions. For example, one patient with CDID suddenly and unexpectedly clung to me while leaving a session. As she did this, I felt that freeing myself from her embrace with force would be rude, so I decided to turn my body by 90 degrees, so that only the left side of my body was in direct contact with the patient's body. Then I talked to her for a while, accepting her need for comfort. Then, as gently as I could, I said that it would be better to distance ourselves a bit more; in doing this I tried to avoid shaming the patient. The situation worked out fine and had no negative consequences.

Other exceptional situations can practically force clinicians to use some degree of physical force. This happened once to me with Ineke (see Chapters 32 and 35). One day she walked into the session as a very irritated and suicidal EP. As this part she expressed that all parts wanted to die, and that she therefore wanted to end treatment with me on the spot. She referred to our arrangement regarding suicide. The principle I adhered to in her case, and one that I adhere to, in general, is the recognition that patients have the right to end their life. On the other hand, therapy is a vote for life, not a choice against it. Although suicide and therapy are antithetical endeavors, suicidal wishes can be fully understandable and should be discussed extensively in therapy. But patients who have committed themselves to therapy and its goals are thus not entitled to commit suicide for the duration of the treatment.

Before ending the treatment, the patient should discuss her suicidal wish and decision with the therapist first. She should bring up the subject at the start of a session, not at the end and not on the phone or in a written communication. Each and every part of the patient should have his or her say, since suicidal parts that end the patient's life become homicidal when one or more dissociative parts want to continue living. If a patient as a whole wants to end her life, and if she has discussed the issue with the therapist in sufficient depth, then she has the right to end the treatment contract and to do thereafter whatever she wants to do. In this case, the clinician should instantly inform the general practitioner and the originally referring individual or institute that the treatment has ended and why.

As the suicidal part, Ineke angrily expressed that she was aware of the above arrangement, and that she had met the requirements: All parts wanted to die, and she had informed me in person at the start of the session. Then she got up and rushed for the door. This left me about 2 seconds to decide how to react. My gut feeling told me that she would absolutely carry through with it, and that it would be totally wrong to let her leave in this mode of longing and striving. My intuition and instantaneous reflection left me no other choice but to grab Ineke, who was already halfway the door. We fought. She yelled at me, and I forcefully uttered that she had crossed the therapeutic boundaries. I needed every bit of muscle strength I had to drag her back to her chair. Once she was more or less seated again, Ineke yelled at me some more, looking scornfully the whole time. Then the suicidal part suddenly disappeared and a confused 4-year-old fragile EP took her place.

This fragile EP stayed in executive control despite my efforts to reactivate the ANP. This circumstance necessitated a clinical admission. I informed the staff about the diagnosis, the treatment, and Ineke's present condition. We continued the weekly therapy sessions. It took approximately 2 weeks before Ineke resurfaced as the ANP.

Another totally unexpected situation arose when an EP of a patient with DID suddenly took full executive control. Within a second, she had taken off her T-shirt, which left her sitting there in a quite revealing bra. As this part, the patient expressed that she knew what all men want, and that she was very good at it. She could not wait to get things going. I pointed out that I did not want to have sex with her, and that our meeting was not at all about having sex together. I added that I would like to hear why she felt and acted the way she did, how she had learned to act in this way, etc. As I talked to her, I made sure to focus on her face and not on the rest of her body, which avoided shaming her, and our understanding grew. The part disappeared as suddenly as she had emerged, leaving the main ANP sitting in her chair partly undressed. I said: "... I can see you're shocked. Nothing bad has happened, but what occurred did surprise me. Why don't you start dressing again and I'll tell you what happened and why." Then I gave her the details of the impulsive action and shared my understanding of it. The patient (as the predominant ANP) took it well. Once things had returned to a calmer situation, I also mentioned that I would discuss with my team how clinicians should best act in a situation like this, and that I would also like to hear her opinion. The patient was content with my approach, as was the team. The team decided that the (e.g., male) clinician should best walk out of the room, saying that he will return with a (e.g., female) colleague, if the situation cannot be quickly resolved in some other way. Alternatively, the clinician could call a colleague. The basic idea is to communicate to (the dissociative part of) the patient that therapy is in principle a confidential collaboration between two individuals, but that under a few, rather exceptional circumstances, the therapist will (be entitled to) get help from one or more colleagues.

Conclusion

Individuals affect each other mentally and physically, both with and without direct physical contact. Clinicians are consciously aware of this and apply this knowledge to themselves and their interactions with all patients from the very moment they meet. One complication is that the various dissociative parts can have different perceptions and conceptions with respect to other people's nonverbal (and verbal) presentations, so that clinicians may need to somewhat adapt their presentations with regard to different dissociative parts. Clinicians' training and supervision should communicate these facts. Their education should help them to become consciously aware of their nonverbal and paralinguistic presentations and the effects thereof. It should also help them to vary these expressions. Raising their consciousness of their own physical affections and of those of their patients increases their power of action. Clinicians including psychotherapists should thus become experts at noticing and tracking their patients' and their own nonverbal and paralinguistic actions and passions, and at reflecting on how these patterns affect the two parties. They should pay attention to their own and their patients' body and physical affections as much as to their own and their patients' emotional affections and thoughts.

Chapter 37

Sympathy for The Devil

> *A true knowledge of good and evil cannot check any emotion by virtue of being true, but only in so far as it is considered as an emotion.*
>
> *Insofar as men are torn by affects which are passions, they can be contrary to one another.*
>
> *He who lives according to the guidance of reason strives, as far as he can, to repay the other's hate, anger, and disdain toward him with love, or nobility.*
> Spinoza (1677, Part IV, Propositions 14, 34, and 46)

Readers are already acquainted with Sonja. Many physicians and the mental healthcare system, in general, were well aware of the multiproblem family in which she grew up. The medical files on the family grew to be voluminous. Still, professionals did not know, consider, or explore the extremity of Sonja's and her sisters' chronic traumatization. Not by far.

Dissociative Amnesia and Dissociative Hypermnesia

Clinicians whose help Sonja had sought out as an adult remained ignorant of significant portions of her terrible history. This relative unawareness was related to the fact that they had overlooked or ignored her DID. In hindsight, they had attended only to Sonja as the main ANP. However, as this ANP Sonja had managed to largely avoid the EPs, who were stuck in horrors she was consciously unable or unwilling to recollect. Because the clinicians had not assessed the DID, they had also failed to attend to the involved EPs. This circumstance reinforced mistrust of adults of these and other EPs, particularly of individuals in positions of authority.

Following her assessment (see Chapter 32), and in accordance with the principles of phase-oriented treatment of chronic traumatization and dissociation (e.g., Van der Hart et al., 2006), we encountered more than 20 dissociative parts. Many had become very elaborate in the course of 17 years of emotional neglect, emotional abuse, physical maltreatment, and sexual harassment and abuse. Sonja was an energetic and dedicated person who worked extremely hard. She showed a remarkable motivation and capacity to learn. She also proved to be creative. For example, once a few other ANPs and several fragile EPs had appeared in our sessions and in daily life, she crafted figures to represent the parts; she added each of them to a miniature world that reflected Sonja's whole personality and gave each dissociative part (i.e., each figure) his or her proper place in this overarching system. An important feature of this miniature world was that the positions of the figures were not static but dynamic, that is, the figures could move about within this world in accordance with the particular goal or goals they wanted to achieve. They could also take new positions in keeping with their therapeutic progression.

At my invitation, Sonja as the main ANP also set up a place within her inner world where all *unveiled* dissociative parts could meet on a daily basis. I suggested they would preferably convene first thing in the morning to discuss the plans for the day. Another goal was their becoming ever more acquainted among themselves. The various parts thus learned why each had evolved and what each had tried to achieve. I encouraged them to explicitly value each other for their hard work in the understanding that each had contributed to their joint preservation.

As we got acquainted with ever more dissociative parts, their features, and their memories, Sonja's history became more complete. The present chapter describes a portion of this development, including the synthesis, personification, presentification, symbolization, and realization of several traumatic memories. Prior to the three sessions presented and discussed, Sonja had told me that her mother used her three daughters as prostitutes. For Sonja, the eldest child, the sexual misery started when she was 6 years old. The clientele encompassed some 50 men. Sonja often took the abuse to protect her younger sisters. Her mother punished her severely when she started to resist the forced prostitution as a young adolescent. One of the mother's bizarre means of controlling Sonja was to lock her in a small barn for days, naked, and without food or drink. Sonja as ANP had only a superficial recollection of this horror prior to her therapy with me. Several fragile EPs, however, knew the facts all too well. They mostly recalled them in the form of vivid traumatic memories (i.e., sensomotoric and affectively charged reenactments; see ToT Volume I, Chapter 11 for a definition of 'traumatic memory').

The reactivated EPs involved sometimes intruded on Sonja as the main ANP. For example, when I inquired about positive sensorimotor dissociative symptoms in the assessment phase, Sonja told me that she sometimes experienced "lumps" on her body. She shivered intensely as she related that they sometimes *moved*. Through several fragile EPs Sonja as the main ANP detected in therapy what these mobile lumps were all about: traumatic memories of rats crawling over her body when she was locked in the barn. The EPs had noticed them upon awakening from sleep.

Here is another illustration of combined dissociative amnesia for Sonja as the main ANP and dissociative hypermnesia for fragile or controlling EPs. After approximately 1 year of treatment, Sonja reported the inability to remember what she had done or what had happened during parts of many Wednesday mornings. Whereas she had ignored this circumstance for many years, for some reason she had recently become more consciously aware of the selective amnesia. Seeking to resolve the issue, I asked if perhaps one of her parts might know what had happened during the time that Sonja as the main ANP was amnestic. A fragile EP made herself known and shared that a particular man came to

Sonja's house every Wednesday morning. His arrival activated this particular EP, which knew very well why the man came. She took care of the sexual business. The man had started to abuse her when Sonja was 12 years old and had since never ceased 'visiting' her.

To stop this sexual abuse, I invited the fragile EP and Sonja as the amnestic ANP to share its facts as well as the physical and emotional feelings the traumatization entailed. This made it possible to start training the two parts to resist the man. Several other EPs who also wanted to put an end to the sexual encounters took part in the training, which included the following steps:

1. Sonja was invited to draw a circle on the floor of the therapy room. We agreed that the area within the circle would represent her physical and emotional space. I was to 'attack' this space with increasing vigor, but would under no circumstance touch her body.
2. The first attack consisted of a ball that I rolled rather gently toward Sonja's circle. The first time she froze, and the ball entered her domain. Over time and with encouragement to stop the ball with her best foot, she managed to defend her territory.
3. The second type of attack repeated the first, but now I kicked the ball with more force. Sonja froze again, but with practice she succeeded in kicking the ball back.
4. The third type of attack involved a big ball that I pushed. With more practice, Sonja managed to stop it too.
5. The fourth attack did not involve an invading ball, but me, who threatened to cross the circle's border. I looked her in the eye but held my hands at my back and kept my mouth shut. Sonja succeeded here as well after a few rounds.
6. In the fifth and last round, I made every attempt to enter the circle, not by using physical force, but by using persuasion and threat. Sonja needed much encouragement and support, and after several rounds, she managed to resist me.

This training took up two sessions. The next time, the man came, Sonja and the participating EPs told the man to go and to leave for good. They also told him that he had to confess to the abuse in the presence of her husband and her best friend, or else she would report him to the police. The man came and confessed. Sonja reported him anyway. Curiously no legal action was taken against him. There was "a lack of evidence." Sonja, her husband, and her friend were all very disappointed. However, Sonja refrained from appealing in order to save energy and time for her therapy.

Meeting The Helper

As therapy progressed, Sonja as the main ANP developed an ever better relationship with The Helper. The Helper had taken the abuse by Sonja's stepfather as well as the traumatic pregnancy, the traumatic childbirth, and the motherhood of the daughter. She regarded herself as the true mother of two more children that Sonja and her husband had gotten.

In full contrast, Sonja as the main ANP did not appreciate that she had children. Sure, she knew that there were three children living with her and her husband, but she did not feel or acknowledge that they were *her* children. Sonja further thought that raising children was peanuts. To her, children basically raise themselves. This idea did not seem to be coincidental seeing that Sonja had had to raise herself. She displayed a 'belle indifference' in some regards. Dissociative amnesia for matters that related to the children was one of them.

At some point, Sonja wanted to fuse with The Helper. By this time, she knew that the children were indeed her children, but still it did not feel that way at all. Sonja as the main ANP thought that the fusion would be fun; she resisted the realization that the fusion implied the complete sharing of all matters concerning the then 22-year-old daughter and the two adolescent sons. More than once Sonja had used her decisiveness and energetic power to confront herself with difficult matters. Faced with fears, she tended to bravely confront them rather than avoid them, once she had set her mind to it. My prior experiences with Sonja had thus taught me that it was wiser to go along with her therapy-related modes of longing and striving than to utter reservations.

So, I did not interfere with her fusion wish. To limit the flood of emotions I anticipated, I did suggest that Sonja might want to "link everything that you are, your needs, wishes, feelings, thoughts, fantasies, memories, and behaviors with the hand of the body that fits you best." Exploring the issue, Sonja felt that it would be the right hand. Next, she was given time to "establish the links." After a minute or two, Sonja reported that she had created the connections.

In a next step, I invited The Helper to connect her complete being with the left hand. Mediated by the action system of caretaking, The Helper was quite concerned that Sonja might not be up to a full confrontation with her – The Helper's – being (i.e., with The Helper's phenomenal self and world). After discussing the issue, we decided that we would stop the confrontation if Sonja started to decompensate under the pressure. We further agreed that the two hands might meet in steps. Contact between the right and left thumbs might represent cognitive transfer, and contact between the index fingers the sharing of previously dissociated sensorimotor phenomena. Contact between the right and left middle fingers, ring fingers, and little fingers might stand for the sharing of emotions, memories, and behaviors, respectively. Full contact of the right and the left hand entailed full contact between Sonja's and The Helper's being. Placing folded hands on her stomach would accompany and symbolize their complete fusion.

The leading third-person principle of the session was to assist Sonja as the main ANP to absorb The Helper's past and present life into herself – within the limits of her present integrative capacity. The more and the more intense the thumbs, fingers, and full hands met, the more Sonja indeed synthesized and personified The Helper's phenomenal self, world, and self-of-this-world. And the more Sonja as the main ANP entered The Helper's recollections of traumatizing events (stepfather's rapes, the traumatic pregnancy, and childbirth), the more she struggled to stay oriented to the present in terms of time, place, and her adult identity. I escorted her on this journey with care and patience. I suggested they might want to go slowly with the confrontation, to proceed at a fitting pace, taking all the time necessary. Meanwhile, I helped Sonja as the ANP to stay in contact with her present environment, including me as her clinician. I also encouraged her to put the traumatic experiences and events into words as they emerged. This symbolization could generate a certain distance between these experiences and memories and would thereby help to prevent Sonja from slipping into a full reenactment of the involved experience and events. She struggled but succeeded: *luctor et emergo.*

Sonja synthesized and personified how she had been barely 16 years old and 9 months pregnant, feeling extremely big. She also experienced with intense emotions how she had been taken to a hospital where labor had been induced with the help of a massive amount of hormones. She subsequently synthesized, personified as well as presentified The Helper's former fixed idea that "he (i.e., the stepfather) had it put it (i.e., the embryo) there (i.e., in her womb), so that's where it belongs (forever)." As she continued the integrative work, Sonja relived birth cramps, reexperienced how physicians and nurses were "pulling and pushing" on her body. She gasped for air at times and breathed heavily throughout. The moment the daughter was about to be born, The Helper's fixed idea got broken: "Ohhhh my God ... oh my God." And when the child actually entered Sonja's brutal world, Sonja burst out into tears upon realizing, "The child is mine ... she is *really mine* ... oh." From this intensely emotional phase onward, Sonja started to calm down. After some 15 minutes of settling herself into her new phenomenal and physical reality, she was able to go home while staying in close contact with The Helper.

The next session Sonja as the ANP related that major changes had occurred. Returning home, she had hugged her daughter Alien together with The Helper. Until that moment, Alien had only experienced The Helper's somewhat coarse touch. This relative insensitivity was a manifestation of The Helper's moderate physical and affective anesthesia. While she really cared for Alien, The Helper *had needed to be* more or less anesthetic – or else she could not have withstood the harsh realities of Sonja's life. Following the integration of The Helper's load, however, normal sensitivity returned. Thus, hugging Alien for the first time as the combined Sonja as the main ANP and The Helper, Alien spontaneously uttered, "Mommy, this is the first time you've really *touched* me!" We are all deeply moved.

Sonja also related that The Helper and she had constantly been in close touch with each other. It felt good to her, she was elated. With the lifting of her dissociative amnesia with respect to everything that concerned Alien, Sonja had no difficulty integrating the existence the two children she and her husband had gotten. She was further surprised to notice how much time and effort it takes to raise children: "What an immense job it is!" she said. She was also shocked to notice the extent of her prior selective dissociative amnesia with regard to the rearing and taking care of her children: "Every time something regarding the children popped up, I left in a split second. I now feel and notice how it worked. Unbelievable."

Meeting The Devil

Sonja revealed how she and The Helper had come very close. In her steadfast style, she wanted to go ahead with their fusion. I asked if all parts of her agreed. She mumbled there was some "noise in her head," but she did not want to be concerned with that. Without awaiting my consent, she brought her hands together again. However, within a couple of seconds, the hands were torn apart and held wide apart. Her whole body was spitting fire, I was told:

"But *I* don't want this!!"
"You don't want this."
"No!"
"Who is telling me this?"
"I'm *The Devil.*"
"Pleased to meet you, Devil."
"I don't want them to get together."
"You don't want them to get together."
"No!"
"What is the very good reason you don't want that?"

The Devil's first reactions to this inquiry started to reveal that she had major issues regarding children and mothers. She claimed that Sonja's mother was *not her* mother, and that Sonja's children were *not her* children (Table 37.1):

Table 37.1. First encounter with The Devil

Transcript D = The Devil E = Ellert Italics express that a word or phrase was emphasized.	Selective comments FPP = first-person perspective QSPP = quasi-second-person perspective SPP = second-person perspective TPP = third-person perspective Sonja: Remarks that Sonja made as we reviewed the video of the session that took place in 1995 some 20 years later.
D: (Looks me straight in the eye throughout. Continuously wrenches the right ankle of her jeans with both hands. Sometimes a bit less and sometimes with full force and sometimes, so to speak, with her complete body. By the end of the sessions, the right ankle had become totally scraped. Speaks decisively most of the time.)	TPP: Generally, The Devil's actions, feelings, and thoughts are totalitarian in nature. Consistent with the theoretical reflections contained in this volume, totalitarian operations involve a limited level of consciousness. My general approach is to raise this level by inviting the patient to engage in a corporative relationship. This relationship is built on my respect for her abilities and goals, and on showing that she can prudently start to respect my actions both as a professional and as a human being. My next aim is to strive for a communicative relationship, once we have managed to achieve a level of consciousness that comes with a corporative relationship (see Chapter 22).

D: (Referring to Sonja's mother.) That woman is not my mother. I did not experience being born from her.	TPP: The Devil must have a good reason to deny that Sonja's mother is also her mother. SPP: It feels like The Devil was absolutely convinced that the woman was not her mother.
E: I did not experience my being born from my mother either. But that does not mean she's not my mother. D: I was not born from that woman.	TPP: Third person does not affect The Devil. It is better to stop using logic. The denial will probably be affectively motivated.
E: You don't want her to be your mother. D: No.	TPP: I try to become attuned to The Devil's affective interests and to slightly reframe her expressions.
E: You don't want to know anything about mothers and children. D: No. E: And that's why you don't want to have any business with Sonja and the children. D: Right. I have no children and I don't want any children. (speaks quickly) E: Because you're very angry at a woman who was around and who was in charge.	SPP: I continue to attune to her phenomenal self and world to achieve a common result: an understanding of The Devil's core issues.
D: Not in charge of me. I was always in charge. E: Really? D: Yes. E: When you were present, you were in control. D: Yes.	TPP: Being in control seems to be a core motive. Acknowledging that Sonja's mother is also her mother, and that she has children including a child stemming from an act of incest would imply acknowledging that she, The Devil, was and is not in substantial control of her life. The Devil's communicative style suggests that she follows negative totalitarian power models. It is important to exchange this style for a more positive power model that is less totalitarian. Perhaps The Devil can learn from my firm but fair style. Moreover, controlling EPs have no respect for weak individuals. I should thus be rather direct and powerful in my interactions with The Devil. Better to "speak her language."
E: *But you were not always present.* D: No. (Briskly shakes her head.) E: Why weren't you always present?	TPP: A confrontation with a painful truth.
D: Because there are the others, too. Because *they are always there*! (angry) E: Yes.	TPP: The others = the other dissociative parts.
D: *I don't want that! I* want to be present, *always.*	TPP: There is a fight going on among the various dissociative parts for control.
E: You want to be always present and you always want to be the way you are.	SPP: Attunement.
D: Exactly! (loud)	SPP: Consensus.
E: If that would work, there wouldn't be any problem.	SPP: Continued attunement.
D: No! (loud)	SPP: Consensus again. TPP: "No" means that there would not be a problem if she –The Devil – were always in full control.
E: Hm. And now the trouble is that things are not the way you want them to be.	SPP: Attunement as well as a demonstration that I am not afraid to speak the truth.

D: Yes. Things are changing. *They're becoming different. Much different.* And you are to blame! (Moves her head forward in my direction.)	SPP: Consensus. TPP: The Devil makes some grammatical mistakes.
E: Hm. And that's what makes you angry.	SPP: Attunement.
D: Yes, but if you're not around, I'm in total control. Then I can tell them to do whatever I want.	SPP: The Devil displays her negative power.
E: But you still allow the body to show up here (i.e., in the sessions)?	TPP: I pinpoint an obvious truth that The Devil ignores. I do not wish to "beat" The Devil, but to show her that I can also be powerful, and powerful in a fair way.
D: I can't always prevent that. If it were up to me, we wouldn't be here. I did not want to come here at all. (speaks quickly)	TPP: It is excellent that The Devil can admit her limitations.
E: And tell me . . . ah . . . doesn't that . . . ah . . . mean that . . . ah . . . your power is *limited*?	SPP: I strive to set up an empathic confrontation (Chu, 1992), a little bit in the style of Inspector Columbo.
D: Kind of true, yes. (A softer tone of voice)	SPP and TPP: It is important to notice that The Devil *does not act out: She is honestly confronted with a painful truth.* I have often experienced that controlling EPs do not act out when they are empathically and sensitively confronted. Many clinicians tend to be rather scared of controlling EPs. They commonly fear that these parts will act out on *them* when they speak firmly according to the facts. When these parts sense the clinician's fear, they tend to loathe them more and may start to act out more.
E: That's not nice, but kind of true. D: (Stares ahead; mumbles some unclear words.)	SPP: Empathic reaction using The Devil's phrase "kind of true." TPP: My empathic confrontation with a painful fact has "thrown sand in her well-oiled totalitarian machine." As mentioned before, destabilization of well-oiled but dysfunctional modes of longing in striving is often needed to achieve true change. It serves to invite the autonomous systems that dissociative parts and traumatized individuals as a whole are to reorganize themselves.
E: Are you scared that the others will send you away? That they don't want you? D: . . . I won't allow that. E: All right, I believe you. But aren't you a little scared of it? D: Who could send me away? E: Well, if the others [i.e., the other dissociative parts] gain power . . .	SPP: Was it perhaps not so clever to suggest that The Devil might be *scared* of something? If she is scared of something and admits it, she does not meet the demands of her controlling role. Devils aren't supposed to be scared of anything. SPP and TPP: On the other hand, it may not have been so bad to communicate that I am aware that controlling EPs secretly feel fragile.
D: Then you get through to them less and less! E: Then you get through to them less and less. Then you can impose your will on the others less and less, then there will be even less personal space for you – and that's not a good thing.	TPP: The Devil again agrees that her power is limited. SPP: The Devil feels a loss of power, and I know she feels and resents it. SPP: Empathic attunement to The Devil's interests.
D: No!	SPP: Consensus.

E: What do you want to do with your personal space? D: (pauses) . . . Simply . . . when I get mad . . . E: Getting mad? D: Yes. E: At whom in particular? D: (pauses, softly) . . . everyone . . . E: Everyone. D: (softly) Yes. E: All your life? D: Yes. (firmly)	TPP: This question addresses The Devil's core affective interests. FPP, QSPP, and SPP: *I* experience and communicate *my* interest in *her* primary affectivity.
E: . . . getting mad . . . that's the whole point of your life . . . D: (pauses) . . . something like that. E: Something like that. Something unlike that as well?	SPP: Attunement utilizing The Devil's own words.
D: Yes, when I get very angry! E: What do you do when you get very angry? D: Then I hit them. E: And who are they? D: Everyone. E: Everyone. Have all people hurt you?	TPP: Either angry or very angry: The Devil is, so to speak, one-dimensional.
D: Most of them. E: Many people. D: Yes.	TPP: The Devil does not deny that she was abused. Many controlling EPs, however, deny that they were abused or maltreated.
E: Has someone ever treated you properly?	SPP: I communicate that, in my view, The Devil deserves to be treated "properly."
D: Me? No! Such people do not exist. E: Such people do not exist. D: No.	TPP: The Devil's phenomenal world only includes villains. I am among them.
E: There have never been people who *listened to you*?	SPP and TPP: In the interest of setting up a good working relationship with The Devil, I intentionally use the term "listen." Good people listen to one another.
D: No, there are no good people. E: That's your experience.	TPP: Again, the statement includes me.
D: Yes.	SPP: Consensus.
E: What would make a good person? D: (surprised) What would make a good person? E: Yes.	TPP: When trying to set up this working alliance, it would be helpful to know what kind of person The Devil might accept.
D: One cannot *make* a person! E: Of course. What I mean is, what is the mark of a good person?	TPP: The Devil takes my expression literally.
D: If they simply accept the way I am. E: Angry. D: Yes!	SPP: It feels like The Devil is "opening the door of her house" a bit. I can listen, and I can accept that she is angry.
E: I fully accept that you're angry. D: Simply *so* . . . (Wrenches the ankle firmly.)	SPP: Empathic attunement.

E: Simply *so* angry. And probably much angrier than you're showing here. D: (Impulsively wrenches the ankle even more firmly.) Yes!!	FPP and SPP: Sympathy for her anger. TPP: Trying to communicate real understanding it can be useful to use hyperboles. I am not saying that my sentence exaggerates The Devil's rage, but it does pinpoint that the degree of anger she displays in the session is a mild version of her anger. SPP and TPP: The Devil confirms my hypothesis. This encourages me to invite The Devil to cooperate with me to achieve common goals. Sonja: I understand what you were trying to achieve. Whatever I said as The Devil, you did not turn angry. You remained calm, fair, direct, and dedicated. You did not start to yell at me. You acted so differently from what I had been accustomed to all my life, including in psychiatry. And you made me think. That made a difference.
E: Yes. So extremely angry . . . Has anyone ever offered you help to deal with that anger? D: . . . . . . No! E: Would you accept it if someone were to offer you help?	SPP: Testing whether The Devil can accept an offer to help her. Can she accept that she, despite her power, could use some help? The Devil must feel very alone. TPP: Helping and being helped involves a corporative relationship. FPP: I feel so sorry for her.
D: . . . How?	TPP: The Devil reflects! So far, she has been rather reflexive (i.e., impulsive). Now she poses a question and shows an interest in a corporative relationship.
E: We would have to discuss that, but the whole thing starts with accepting your anger. D: (listens) E: Being angry at all people who have hurt you so much. And there have been many.	SPP and TPP: I sense a chance to reach The Devil. I instantly strive to utilize her present ability to reflect. FPP and SPP: I sympathize with her rage.
D: (Intense wrenching, bends forward in the act.)	SPP: The Devil displays her anger as well as the ability to restrain herself. For example, she wants to hit people, but she does not hit me. FPP, QSPP, and SPP: The Devil's anger does not scare me.
E: Angry inside because you are not in full charge of the others as you would so much like to be; angry at the other parts because they do not accept you, because they try to isolate or ignore you; and because they are scared of your extreme anger . . . Could that be it? D: (More intense wrenching) . . . I don't know.	SPP: I add "could that be it" to show that I do not want to control her. I do not want to talk over her head. TPP: The enactive trauma clinician should not dictate, should not be a totalitarian controller.
E: Or do I say stupid and weird things?	SPP: I say this to communicate my willingness to hear and accept her phenomenal judgment of me, and to express that she probably does not think highly of me. The Devil has listened to me for quite a while. She has already granted me a lot. SPP and TPP: By downgrading myself a bit, I upgrade her. I told her some things and she listened. Now she can, as she probably sees it, get even with me. This creates a kind of symmetry in our relationship. It is a relationship of give and take.
D: In my view you're a prick anyway. E: Hm.	SPP: And she rejects me. That does not bother me. She surely has a reason.
D: I've always felt that way.	SPP: The Devil is totally honest.

E: Right, that's how you feel. And why?	SPP: I accept her rejection and value her honesty. I also show an interest in the reason why she rejects me.
D: That's just how I feel. All that dicking and messing around. E: All that dicking and messing around, all those words.	TPP: I hypothesize that "dicking and messing around" refers to *talking*, and that The Devil deeply mistrusts words. She may also feel that there is no power in words, in mere talk. SPP: Attunement. I utilize her words.
D: Exactly!	SPP: Consensus.
E: Yes. D: You stir everything up. E: Yes. D: When they've been here, they . . . . . . that's what they've always done. (intense wrenching, hisses) E: Then they've gained power against you.	SPP: Ratification of our consensus.
D: (Looks downward, and then back at me.)	SPP: It feels like she is looking for help, though she cannot directly ask for help. TPP: Longing for help and asking for it are contrary modes of longing and striving for individuals whose primary affect is a need and desire for autonomy. The Devil is in conflict with her contrary needs and desires and does not know where to go.
E: Would you want to cooperate with me?	SPP: I utilize her confusion but offer an escape route. Rather than offering help, I invite The Devil to cooperate. TPP: Cooperation involves a symmetrical power relationship. A relationship of a helper and someone being helped involves a corporative level of consciousness. However, it also has a touch of a dominant (helper)-subdominant (the one being helped) pattern that The Devil probably cannot or does not dare to accept.
D: Pss. (hisses, casts a denigrating glance, then looks away, starts to sit on her lower legs and feet) . . . No . . . no . . . why?	TPP: The Devil rejects cooperation. It seems she clings to being dominant and controlling.
E: What I notice is that you find it hard to manage your totally understandable anger. It seems you do not know how to move. You are terribly pissed. Of course. And I guess you will remain stuck and suffocate in your anger the more the other parts reject you . . . Could that be the case?	SPP: While she does not accept the offer, she still asks why cooperation might be useful. It feels like she does not completely reject the idea. I thus continue my invitation and explain why, in my view, cooperating with me might be more useful than rejecting me. TPP: Asking The Devil if my reasoning might make sense, we may reach a consensus that helps to set up a corporative relationship.
D: That could be, yes.	SPP and TPP: Consensus.
E: Yes.	SPP and TPP: Affirmation.
D: And *so what*?	TPP: The Devil strives to maintain her autonomy.

E: My offer is to assist you with all that anger, to find ways to release that anger in useful ways.	SPP: I hope that my firmness can correct The Devil's idea that there is no power in words, that I am not just "dicking and messing around." FPP: I feel sorry for her that she is caught in such a dilemma. How awful it must be, and how awful it must have been for her as a child to need such major help and to be consistently denied this help. What a cruel world! She had to fight for autonomy all by herself in a world that gave her no chance to influence her fate.
D: (Listens, sighs, straightens her right ankle, looks down, then up, out of a window. Looks at a painting on the wall. She orients herself. Does not look at me anymore. Pauses.)	SPP: It feels like The Devil is contemplating risking a more symmetrical relationship against the odds.
E: That's my offer.	SPP: I hope my consistency persuades The Devil to take a step. SPP and TPP: Cooperation is unknown territory for her. It is an unknown action, and its outcome is exceptionally uncertain.
D: Hm. E: You know what, I would not want to isolate you.	SPP: She seems to be making a move. SPP: I utilize her "hm" as well as my feelings of sympathy for her. FPP: I feel a need and desire to help.
D: (Turns her attention back to me.) And then how . . . ah . . . did you think . . . you could . . . *do that?* . . . If you would simply tell the others to stop (doing their new things) . . . Things were OK . . .	SPP: The Devil takes a step. TPP: She briefly engages in a new mode of longing and striving, but quickly shifts to her old mode of longing and striving for autonomy. The Devil is very keen on persevering in her existence; she is a real autonomous system.
E: You know I don't think things were OK. D: *No, things were OK.* (Very angry. Stands up)	TPP: It is important to raise The Devil's level and field of consciousness. SPP: She needs my fair and consistent firmness. She must experience that I am trustworthy. FPP: I find no pleasure in opposing The Devil. I would be far easier to agree that, "things were OK." But this agreement would be at odds with the facts, and we must face reality.
E: What I have in mind is that there have been individuals who have hurt you very much. That's why you're angry. OK?	SPP: I try to avoid being overly dominant by saying what "I have in mind." The statement respects that The Devil may have different things in mind. SPP: I fully understand and accept her rage. FPP and QSPP: How angry would I be if people had treated me like that?
D: (Listens attentively.) E: Why is it bad to hurt others so much? Why? It's bad because the people were not concerned with your feelings and interests at all. Not concerned with your pain, disgust, your shame, your anger. They did not leave you alone. Right?	TPP: The Devil closely attends to my words, and it seems my solid approach is useful to her. SPP: I feel myself into The Devil's position, and use my first-person feelings to voice my understanding of her as well as my sympathy for her.
D: Hmm.	SPP: Consensus. SPP and TPP: Continue the action. The Devil does not deny her fragility.

E: These people did not show any respect for boundaries. They continued on and on with their vicious deeds. And the more they maltreated and abused you, the angrier you got. And the less the others [i.e., dissociative parts] managed to defend themselves, the more anger you had to carry with you. D: (Listens attentively as I speak.)	TPP: It is important to include the dynamics between the controlling EP and the others, that is, the fragile EPs and the ANPs.
E: Was it like that? D: Hmm. E: Yes? D: Yes.	TPP: "Was it like that?" invites The Devil to take an explicit position. SPP: Continue to strive for the achievement of a common result: the determination of a horrible reality. Also: she is allowed to disagree.
E: Thus, if what you regard as the stupid parts inside did not do anything, you had to take care of business. D: (continues to listen with her full attention) E: Was it like that?	SPP and TPP: It is always wrong for clinicians to speak badly of (other) dissociative parts. That is why it is important to use conditional phrases like "what you regard as stupid parts" when one or more dissociative parts depreciate one or more other dissociative parts.
D: Yes. But I don't want to do that anymore! (angry)	SPP: Consensus. The Devil wants a change! But she has no idea how to achieve it.
E: Sure, you're right.	SPP: Full acceptance.
D: I simply want to be *me, just me.*	TPP: The Devil expresses her need and desire for autonomy in no uncertain words. She is really convinced that she is a true person, not a dissociative part of a wider system.
E: Fine. And, I repeat, what has made you so angry is that other persons have not abided by the common rules that should guide us: *You are you*, and nobody is allowed to grab you. That's not right. Right?	SPP: Attuning to her need and desire for autonomy, I phrase "you are you."
D: That is how things should be.	SPP: Consensus.
E: That is how things should have been. And because they were not like that, things were not right. Now we can try to do the right things. I want to cooperate with you, and that means that we abide by the rules: I am not allowed to grab you and you are not allowed to grab me. D: I know that. (speaks rather calmly) E: Or else we would be doing the same bad things that all those brutal people did to you. D: But I would really like to do those things.	SPP: Affirmation of our consensus. TPP: "Right" operates as a bridge between agreement and justice. SPP: "We can try to do the right things" presupposes that we will cooperate. TPP: It is important to state clear boundaries in straightforward terms. Sonja: I recall that we made that agreement.
E: Of course you would! When we are that angry, we feel an urge to do such things. I can easily understand that! And yet it's not allowed. Or else we act like the individuals who hurt us.	SPP: Full understanding and affective acceptance.
D: And then who is doing the right thing? (angry) *What do you know about right and wrong?!* (shouts). ***What do you know about right and wrong!*** (Shouts even louder)	All person perspectives: Indeed, what do I know about living in Sonja's world? How can I really feel and judge what it is like to be her?
E: I know that what is not right is what crosses the boundaries of your will.	SPP and TPP: I have in mind that The Devil's boundaries have been brutally crossed, and that she crosses the boundaries of the other dissociative parts. It is clearly not right to cross someone else's boundaries.

D: *But this* [i.e., what was happening between The Devil, the other parts, and me] *is something I don't want either.* (Bends forward, stretches out her hand to display "this.")	SPP and TPP: Did I cross her boundaries?
E: Hm ... OK ... but ... ah ... we have a problem here ... inasmuch as there are other parts of the whole Sonja who *do want* these kinds of changes.	FPP: Confusion! Help! QSPP: Do my actions and words cross her boundaries? SPP: Felt like we were on the track together. I had not expected The Devil's "attack." TPP: In hindsight, I am tempted to believe that my confusion lowered my level of consciousness. My stumbling reflects my disappearance in Flatland. I needed some time to get back to Spaceland, back to the "top of the pyramid." Being in Spaceland again, I reintegrated the various interests of Sonja as a whole system. It easily happens that clinicians lose the perspective of Spaceland when they intensely interact with one dissociative part. They may start to restrict their field of consciousness under these circumstances and start to interact with a dissociative part as if that dissociative part were not a part of a whole person that comprises several dissociative parts and a host of modes of longing and striving. The risk is falling into the trap of *pars pro toto.*
D: Yes, and that is exactly what you stir up, and then they get together, and then they become one big bunch. (angry)	TPP: The Devil confirms my previous hypothesis that the other dissociative parts are excluding her. In any case, this is how The Devil sees it.
E: And it seems you are not part of this development. But that's not the idea.	SPP: Get her onboard!
D: But I ... I ... don't want to be part of it. (hisses several times) E: How about the rest of the bunch growing so strong that they can get angry with persons who do not abide by the rules. How about their growing so strong that they can take actions themselves? In this case, you would not have to carry even more rage. D: That's impossible. Impossible. Can't be. E: That can't be? D: No, can't be.	SPP and TPP: The Devil does not want to be excluded, but she does not want to accept the other dissociative parts either. She does not want the others to become stronger because she does not approve of their methods. She is still clueless as to how to solve the problem. I must show her that cooperating with the other dissociative parts can be quite useful to her.
E: That's not what I am observing. I am observing that Sonja and the others *do* get stronger and *do* put up boundaries more.	TPP: The Devil continues to regard the other dissociative parts as weaklings.
D: That's what I meant to say. But you don't get that. That goody-goody. That stupid bitching they're doing. All day long. Running their mouth. Man! Come on! E: What would you rather do?	SPP: Firm and fair opposition.

D: Pound away! Pound away, just like that, instantly.	TPP: The Devil continues to feel that there no power lies in words. She only knows and trusts the power of physical actions. She copies negative totalitarian power models, that is, individuals who control the world by engaging in physical actions. These impulsive actions are low-level action tendencies (Van der Hart et al., 2006; Chapter 33). It is important to invite The Devil to reflect more, also when she becomes emotional. Relatively simple reflection involves an intermediate-level action tendency (Chapter 33).
E: You'd pound them away, and then what? D: What do I care. E: Then you'd be going to prison, and then you're sitting in your cell and then what? D: And then what? E: Then what? D: Nothing, then there's nothing. E: Then there's nothing, just sitting in your cell. D: So what, one day you get out of the cell. E: Yes? D: Absolutely, yes. Have you ever been in a cell? E: In a cell? No.	SPP: I invite The Devil to consider the consequences of physical aggression.
D: I have, and I know you get released one day. E: How long would that take? D: Maybe a week, a month, or perhaps even a year. But one day you get released.	SPP and TPP: She has been in a prison cell? I did not know that. What does she mean? FPP: Slightly shocked. SPP: It seems best to follow The Devil's lead and see where we end up.
E: And do you want to throw away your life for that? D: If I could take out one of them, yes. E: Really? D: Yes! E: Hm. In that case you do . . . D: . . . not abide by the rules. (spoken in a derogative way) E: Right. D: But there are so many prohibitions – there is so much that one should not do. E: Do you feel our world should continue like this? D: But everyone trespasses the rules.	SPP: "Throw away" fits The Devil's tendency to engage in physical actions.
E: Do you feel that's the right way? D: That's a different matter. E: OK. Shall we try to act responsibly, and nonetheless allow for your anger? And nonetheless, make sure that you do not need to carry even more rage around with you? And make sure that what you regard as the sissies can carry and cope with intense anger? D: That's impossible. E: You feel that's impossible. You cannot imagine that things can change? You actually said that things *are* changing.	TPP: I try to raise The Devil's level of consciousness. She manages to make a distinction between what people do and what they are not supposed to do. SPP: We agree that it is wrong to trespass boundaries. I reinvite her to find different solutions in cooperation with me.

D: I don't want to be part of that bunch. Let them stay as stupid as they are. E: . . . stupid as they are? D: Yes. E: Wouldn't you rather want them to become stronger and act on their anger within fitting boundaries? D: No! E: You don't want that? D: No. E: You want to continue carrying that rage? D: No. E: Then what *do* you want? D: Nothing. E: But the world keeps on turning. D: Hm. E: More rage would not be a good thing?	TPP: The Devil is still caught in her old phenomenal conceptions of self, world, and self as a part of this world.
D: No. (becomes quite sulky. Stops wrenching her jeans. Seems to reflect a bit) E: I'm offering my help. I'm here to cooperate with you.	SPP: Now it feels like The Devil is confused.
D: (remains sulky, mumbles, and then, all of a sudden:) Then, how . . . uh . . . had you wanted to do that? E: You suffocate in your anger. No space for anything else. I would want to look together with you for ways that reduce your rage.	FPP: Relief. SPP: The Devil shows an interest. TPP: The Devil manages to reflect a bit.
D: And then how had you figured to do that?	SPP: More interest.
E: We would have to discuss that. That's why we need to cooperate.	SPP: Reiteration of my proposal to cooperate.
D: And who else should be part of this? E: Other parts of the whole Sonja that can help. D: And then? E: Then you will get more space and energy for doing other things. Then there will be less internal divisions and struggles. Less loss of energy in continuing anger.	TPP: It seems that The Devil expects that other parts or perhaps other people will have to be involved.
D: And whom will you inform about this in the external world? E: As far as I am concerned, no one. Would anyone in the external world need to be told? D: No!! E: No!	SPP: Does she want to tell me something about people in the external world?
D: But that's what they do? Everyone does that. E: Everyone? D: Yes, everyone talks.	SPP and TPP: Another reason to hate talking?
E: Everyone talks? D: Yes. E: Who is 'everyone'?	SPP: What does she mean? TPP: It might be that The Devil wants to tell me something of importance. SPP: Let's continue to explore the issue following The Devil's lead as closely as possible.

D: Everyone who gets involved. She tells everyone. E: When she's in a supermarket, she tells others? D: When you're that angry? Yes. E: When you're so angry? D: Yes. E: And who is this "she?" D:	SPP and TPP: Who is "she?"
E: The mother?	TPP: I hypothesize The Devil is talking about mother, the woman she cannot accept as her mother.
D: (Stares, wrenches her right ankle.) E: Who is "she?"	SPP: I have a strong feeling that The Devil is starting to cooperate with me, and that she is starting to unveil more about why she resents the mother and talking. The Devil avoids answering my question. TPP: I take this avoidance as a cautious confirmation of my hypothesis. FPP: I feel important things are about to happen.
D: And then everybody says that I'm unmanageable, uneducable, and God knows what else. So it does not change one iota.	TPP: Hypothesis: Talking does not change one iota.
E: And in what year are you living? D: Why do you care? E: I care. D: I don't. E: What's the present year? D: Now? E: Yes. D: . . . at some point, it is 1965, and then all of a sudden it's 1985, and then again 1970.	TPP: The Devil is not actually in prison. If she has been in a prison at all, this must have happened in an earlier time. I may start to understand her more when we explore the issues of her phenomenal time and place. Controlling EPs tend to be more or less ignorant regarding the present.
E: Time jumps back and forth for you? Should it stay that way? Or could you use some change? D: It's always been like this. E: That can be hard on you. You tell me mother gossips about you in the supermarket.	TPP: I try to integrate the capriciousness of The Devils' orientation in time and place, and the theme of change.
D: Yes, that's what she does. E: I believe you. Do you still live with Mother? D: No. E: Where do you live? D: In the prison. E: In the prison? D: Yes. E: You're in prison now? D: Yes. I'll be returning to my cell soon. I now have some time off.	TPP: Confirmation of the hypothesis that The Devil is talking about (her) mother. From here things become clearer. The Devil is convinced that she is living in a different city, that she carries Sonja's maiden name (Klomp), and that she does not know Sonja Bartelds. Her phenomenal self, world, and self-of-this-world also prove resistant in light of contrary evidence. Her conceptions remain fully intact until she starts to trust me enough to share her history with me. She has the idea that she is staying in a prison in a different city. She thinks I'm nuts. The third-person physical facts I present do not correspond with her phenomenal realities.
The following text involves a selection of the things The Devil and I actually said during the remainder of the session. The Devil declared things like: D: I know where I live! I know my name! . . . D: . . . I'm 14 years old . . .. D: . . . I do not have the body of an adult woman . . .	

D: . . . I do not know whose bag this is. It's not mine . . .	TPP: Sonja had brought a bag to the session.
D: . . . You have put me in prison. I had to tell everything, now I've told you everything, and now I am stranded in prison . . .	TPP: The Devil believes that I am a prison psychologist, that I have previously enticed her to *talk* to me, and that this led to her 'incarceration.' The Devil reenacts her time in "prison." This prison was an observational closed ward for – as it was seen at the time –"unmanageable" adolescent girls.
E: . . . Do you want me to help you get out of prison? Would you dare to trust me just enough to cooperate so that we can get you out of your prison? . . . D: I'm leaving. I do not want to talk to you anymore. It does not help me at all. E: Do you want to cooperate with me to gain your freedom?	SPP: I felt that The Devil might be affectively interested in getting out of her prison. "Trust me just enough" appreciates that she feels she can hardly trust me, if at all.
D: It's impossible. You have decided that I have to go to Zetten. If you can reverse your decision, then it's fine with me. E: I cannot reverse the decision. But I can help you understand that the Zetten things have already happened . . . E: . . . I am asking you to consider that I am not talking nonsense. It seems to me you are confused in time, I do not find pleasure in telling you that . . . E: . . . I can also tell you it's not your fault. You think that Zetten is something awful still to come, and I know Zetten has already happened . . .	TPP: "Zetten" refers to the village that is home to a mental hospital. Sonja was referred to this hospital. I knew that "Zetten" had a bad reputation, in part because of the application of an extreme behavioristic regime and abuse of institutional power. But for the most part, "Zetten" earned its infamous reputation from the fact that Dr. Finkensieper, the psychiatrist in charge of the hospital, was accused of and convicted of sexually abusing several admitted disturbed and in many cases chronically traumatized adolescent girls under his care. He also entertained sexual relations with former patients. He was sent to prison for 6 years in 1990.
E: . . . Other parts inside know this. They can tell you that Zetten has already happened . . .	TPP: It is important to include the other dissociative parts. They are aware of different phenomenal realities.
D: Hmm. E: You may want to come and sit with me. I propose we try a little cooperation. Let's try to detect that more has happened than you know. Do you dare to take this step? D: And what if you are right? E: We could then take the next step to help you overcome terrible things that happened to you. D: It is not my fault that I am in prison. E: I believe you.	TPP: At this point, The Devil is sitting on the floor in a corner of the room. SPP: Excellent, she is contemplating that I may not be talking nonsense. It feels like The Devil has become a bit more accessible.
D: I landed here because I talked once. And now you want me to talk again. How can I do that?	SPP: It is dangerous to talk!
E: I promise you will not return to a prison cell or to Zetten.	TPP: I knew that Sonja had been admitted to Zetten when she was 14 to 15 years old.
D: You dare to make promises! If it isn't the case, then I will return and beat you up. E: You're not allowed to beat me up. D: But I will do that.	SPP: I mostly hear this as "I cannot take another deception."
E: In my reality, you will never go to Zetten again. I am totally confident of that. But as I see it, you are confused about a couple of things, and it would help if you could accept that.	SPP: It does not feel right to fight over the boundaries at this point. TPP: It is more important to help her start engaging in the act of presentification.

A little later, and in steps I mentioned that: E: I want to help to resolve the confusion. We can examine together whether your reality holds, does not hold, or does not hold in some regards. What confuses you is what is and what has been. You have already told me that for you time jumps from one year to another. Sometimes the gaps cover many years. When you are in 1965 the world must look different than when you are in 1985. And in my reality, it is currently 1995. Cooperation means learning. Would you like to hear from other parts in what year we are presently? D: No, I do not have to see that. E: Do you want to hear from other parts that you do not need to go to Zetten? D: (Deep sigh, long pause.) E: Shall we grant other parts a chance to tell you if it's true? D: Hmm. E: Is that OK? D: Well, let them do that. (Returns to her seat.) E: Fine, please be seated and let's ask Sonja or The Helper or both to tell The Devil that she will not have to go or return to Zetten. D: (Listens silently and relatively calmly, no more wrenching.)	
E: You only need to listen. I do not need to tell you that you do not need to go or return to Zetten. Other parts know it.	SPP: It feels like The Devil is ready to start listening to the other parts more. She seems ready to explore that listening to them can be useful. I have listened to her, and she has listened to me. TPP: Listening to each other involves a step toward a communicative level of consciousness.

Completion of the Session

The Devil started to listen to the other parts, particularly to the ANPs. They told her that "Zetten" had happened to the adolescent Sonja. The Devil had a hard time believing this. She continued to be apprehensive that she was being tricked. So how could the session be completed in a sufficiently satisfactory manner? Considering The Devil's competitiveness and need for relational control, I proposed a bet. I felt that a bet might serve as a suitable sublimation of her wish to beat others, literally. Now she would get the chance to beat me figuratively. My bet was that she would not return to a cell, but that she could go home with Sonja as ANP, The Helper, and other parts. My bet was also that she would be welcome to attend another session with me. Her bet was that these claims would not materialize.

As The Devil left the therapy room, she did not take the bag with her. Sonja returned some 15 minutes later. She wondered if she had forgotten to bring her bag along. It contained, among other things, her car keys.

The Next Session

Sonja looked bewildered as I came into the waiting room a week later. By the looks of it, The Devil was present but not just that. Contrary to Sonja's usual sporty outfits, she wore a short skirt, a feminine blouse, and high heels. The Devil's brisk way of moving failed to help her control them. She struggled and stumbled, but at some point, the movements became delicate and actually quite seductive. A funny and sad sight. When I inquired what was going on, The Devil complained that The Lady tried to take full executive control. As she volunteered, The Lady used "the silly garments" and her elegant moves and looks to achieve her task: controlling men through quick and effective sex that she initiated and defined. I told The Lady that it was a pleasure to meet her and that there was no need to take charge. As I continued, I felt at ease in The Devil's company, and it was important that The Devil would notice that she was not in a prison cell. Once The Lady hesitantly withdrew herself, The Devil paced up and down my room, bursting with energy and apprehension. It seemed important to offer her a chance to invest a part of this organismic energy in a physical activity. I thus invited her to a firm walk. The Devil strongly doubted that I really intended to go on a walk with her. Since there seemed to be little point in convincing her with words, I walked out the door of my room, saying, "Let's go!" I took the lead, walked down the corridor, descended the stairs, and passed the entrance of the outpatient clinic. The Devil followed my trail, stumbling as well. It was a rainy day in autumn. Wet mud surrounded the new building. The Devil suddenly kicked off the high heels and stepped into the sludge. She sank in it to the ankles, but managed to grab the piece of wood she had spotted, and swayed her weapon wildly in the air. "Come one, let's walk." Without waiting for her answer, I crossed the street to reach a wooded area. We continued at a fast pace. Continuing to swing her stick, The Devil shared the story of her life in a voice. At times she was screaming at the top of her lungs.

As mentioned before, several of Sonja's dissociative parts had told me that her mother had used her daughters as prostitutes. As the eldest child, Sonja often took the abuse to protect her sisters. Mother strictly forbade Sonja to speak about this form and other forms of chronic traumatization with anyone. For years she was too scared to oppose her mother. Going against her mother resulted in extreme punishments.

During our high-paced walk, The Devil shared traumatizing experiences and events with me that I had not heard about from Sonja's other dissociative parts. She – The Devil – came into existence when Sonja became a despondent adolescent. The Devil found the courage to talk to the family physician. When this plea for help was fruitless, she informed the police. The investigation that followed was way too superficial to yield any result. Several EPs related that the authorities had actually *ignored* or disbelieved their revelations of extreme ongoing abuse and maltreatment (see below).

The lack of any assistance and understanding from family members or authorities turned her utterly despondent and furious. When The Devil became suicidal, she was sent to an observational psychiatric institution – her prison. From there she was transferred to The Heldring Foundation in Zetten (see the transcript above for more details on this institution), an orthopedagogic institution for girls that, as it was said or believed, were exceptionally hard to *control.* That's where The Devil was "incarcerated." She was frequently put in an isolation chamber for 'trespassing.' Like the other girls, she was subjected to silly and harsh if not sadistic 'behavior therapeutic' rules and practices. It had been documented that this 'therapeutic regime' was invented for the workers' ease and other needs and desires more than for the girls' sake. At times The Devil was summoned to visit Dr. Finkensieper. He abused her sexually more than once.

The Devil's testimony lasted the full hour. I listened and bore witness to her detailed traumatic memories. Near the end of our up-tempo walking session, The Devil calmed down. She went home much relieved and feeling confident I was not her prison psychologist, but a sincerely interested and compassionate professional. In the following session we discussed which dissociative parts would need to synthesize, personify, presentify, symbolize, and realize The Devil's traumatic memories. We also developed ideas how these integrative actions could proceed. We decided to use a large psychomotor therapy room to grant Sonja the space she needed. The dissociative parts to be involved in this were to be represented by small figures. Sonja felt this would help her to hold a grip on them. She represented the main perpetrators in the form of black stuffed balls and placed the various figures on a bench. Under the leadership of The Devil, the group shared the rage. While I had never heard a person uttering fury any louder, the shouting did not imply a loss of control. Sonja knew very well what she was doing, and the words she directed at the perpetrators were clear and on target. I bore witness to an outburst of Sonja's emotions and expressions which lasted approximately 30 minutes. Relieved and content with their actions, the group of parts then went home. In the following session, The Devil fused with several other parts that included Sonja as ANP.

From Totalitarian to Communicative-Egalitarian Relationships

The two transcripts illustrate a part of Sonja's development. Caught in a malignant totalitarian *umwelt*, and under the influence of a strong will to survive it, she divided her personality into several parts. Dissociative parts such as Sonja as the leading ANP and The Helper more or less operated as a corporate institution. Sonja ran the household, enjoyed being her husband's partner, and held a job she enjoyed and that provided an income. The Helper, on the other hand, was not concerned with these matters that much: She operated as the mother of three children, and some other parts also operated in daily life. While The Lady navigated around potentially abusive men, she also wanted to have fun. She hated The Helper's unappealing garments. The Helper wore wide coats to drag stuffed animals of the child EPs and other stuff of the actual children around. She needed a big car. The Lady liked proper fashion. Fancying a sports-car, she intentionally crashed The Helper's ugly vehicle. Although the parts of daily life were competing for 'body time' and struggling to get their needs and desires met, they also took care of some of the various wills that basically comprises any individual. In this sense, they were more or less organized like corporate task sharing: "You take care of this, I'll take care of that."

The Devil had learned to mistrust such corporative forms of cooperation. Influenced by all the negative power displays that characterized her *umwelt*, she made sure that the will and power to influence her fate remained intact as much as possible. None of Sonja's perpetrators or partners in crime had managed to control her. The Devil had in this sense succeeded in her mission.

The Devil had also become deeply hurt. Her powerful presentation notwithstanding, she was also rather fragile, and in several regards quite ignorant. She felt scared, lonely, overburdened, though she tried to hide or ignore this. The Devil was further confused as to time, place, identity, and the present, third-person world in general. Stuck in a brutal and traumatizing life, she knew or trusted only totalitarian control, which, however, isolated her from those parts of Sonja that increasingly engaged in corporative relationships.

In this order of things, The Devil had to oppose the next advancement: the rapidly evolving communicative and egalitarian relationship of Sonja as the leading ANP and Sonja as The Helper. This mode of operation had to be crushed. It was unknown and deeply mistrusted. On top of that, it involved increasingly higher levels and broader fields of consciousness. She did not want to be part of this "crowd" because this development would inevitably lead to the synthesis, personification, presentification, and realization of Sonja's traumas. How could The Devil follow this route to pain, weakness, dependency, and words?

She needed a new perspective; she needed to detect that there can be power in words, and that at least some clinicians are consistently courageous, understanding, and caring, not just regarding 'sissies,' but regarding inner commanders no less. I thus had to be strong and sensitive, persistent and flexible, talking and moving. I had to be attuned, build a consensus, and invite new actions, not once but recurrently. As applies to all dissociative parts, she had to resignify her phenomenal self and *umwelt*, and both her experienced and conceived relationships of this self and this *umwelt*. This meant discovering that her former repellers might become attractors, and that the former insignificants might actually be useful (significant-good) or harmful (significant-bad).

The Devil and the other parts were magnificent. Together they followed the route to growing communication and egalitarianism with all its implied pros and cons. The work with Sonja as the leading ANP, The Helper, The Devil, The Lady, and still others was clearly important in itself. It also constituted a model for the integration of other traumatic memories and the eventual fusion of the associated dissociative parts. As Sonja experienced time and again, we learned that this integration can be very painful at times, but that the suffering does not last that long. She once compared it to serious surgery: It is profound and not without risks, but when it's over, it's over.

The work with The Devil and related dissociative parts included some not altogether common interventions, some of which addressed her embodiment. The Devil was so restless during the second session in which she was dominant that it seemed best to apply her energy to firm walking. She had used it herself in the first sessions for wrenching and eventually ripping her jeans. At the beginning of the second session, she picked up a stick and used it to control some of her rage. I supported the actions, among others things by keeping up a high pace and remaining attuned to her loud words (e.g., "I really hear your rage. You can let me hear all of it. Use your words, tell me in your way, I'm here").

Sonja's Body and Mind

Sonja presented a number of curious phenomena that raise intriguing questions regarding the relationship of body and mind. With the deepening of our relationship, Sonja dared to talk about some extraordinary physical phenomena. Shame and the idea that nobody would believe her had long kept her from talking about these things with others. One resulting phenomenon was that the size of her feet and her bra size were constantly and significantly changing. One week they might be as much as two sizes smaller or larger than the week before or after. Her weight also shifted profoundly within a week or within a few days. Garments that had fit her perfectly when she bought them might not fit at all several days later. The assistants in the shops where she liked to buy her shoes and clothes were confused more than once. As the treatment progressed, she realized that the physical shifts related to mental shifts, that is, they related to the respective dominance of various dissociative parts. My research mind told me that it would be important to study these kinds of phenomena, if only because several other patients with DID reported similar dissociative-part-dependent physical shifts.

But there was more. When the therapy had become focused on the integration of traumatic memories, one day Sonja unexpectedly gave me a call. A strange thing had happened: A clearly visible and significant scar involving white epithelium had spontaneously burst open and had started to bleed. This had occurred while she, in the presence of her husband, had started to recollect the traumatic origin of the wound. Her husband would later testify that Sonja had not cut or scratched herself. Sonja felt ashamed, she said. I tried to comfort her by voicing acceptance, compassion, and interest. When she came to the next session, she showed me the wound, now healing, which clearly followed the shape of the scar. I had seen the scar before, but we had not discussed or even mentioned it before. And even, this time, we did not talk about it for long. Sonja shared with me the traumatic childhood memory involved, and we marveled a bit how the body and the mind are related. The wound healed without complication in 2 weeks. But now the scar that had been with Sonja for several decades was gone as well – and gone for good. Sonja's mind healed, and so did her body.

Therapeutic Exposure from an Enactive Perspective

Several studies suggest that imaginary exposure to traumatic memories can be an effective treatment for individuals with PTSD. Positive effects have also been achieved in individuals with significant comorbidity. Inspired by the findings, some cognitive behavior therapists feel that approaches to the treatment if individuals with complex dissociative disorders such as the ones described in *The Haunted Self* and the present book are needlessly complex. Van Minnen (2012), for example, proposed that imaginary exposure should also be the treatment of choice – and sufficient – for this population.

Van Minnen (2012) thinks such exposure leads patients to experience that they need not avoid their traumatic memories because they do not pose an actual danger. To make her point, she compares the exposure to stepping in a bath blindfolded, not knowing if the water contains creepy animals such as snakes or harmless rubber duckies. The procedure is bound to trigger fear, but sooner or later one discovers that the traumatic memories are not scary abhorrent beasts but only innocuous toys.

The idea that traumatized individuals are scared of their traumatic memories, and the idea that some measure of exposure to these memories can be an effective intervention is not new. It actually dates back to the work of Pierre Janet, who proposed the concept and term "phobia of traumatic memories." In trauma-related dissociation of the personality, the traumatic memories are intimately associated with EPs that ANPs have come to fear, detest, and ignore or otherwise avoid. Rejected EPs, in turn, become scared of ANPs. This led me to propose the concept and term "phobia of dissociative parts" (Nijenhuis, 1994b). Traumatic memories and many hyperaroused EPs reveal threatening sensorimotor features as well as strong affects that ANPs long and strive to avoid. These sensations, movements, and affects do not exist in themselves but are tied to sensorimotor and affectively charged actions, or, in the terms of the present book, to passions.

In a series of publications, Van der Hart, Steele, and I (Steele, Van der Hart, & Nijenhuis, 2005; Van der Hart, Nijenhuis, & Steele, 2005; Van der Hart et al., 2006) introduced the concept and term "phobia of trauma-derived mental actions and contents." Considering that chronically traumatized individuals (or at least as some of their dissociative parts) tend to fear, detest, and avoid attachment needs and desires and relationships, we also proposed the concept and term "trauma-related phobia of attachment." We also proposed that trauma therapy, including the treatment of complex dissociative disorders, is best geared toward overcoming these various phobias, though not exclusively. For example, it may also be necessary to develop efficient ways to deal with intense affects to replace the patients' substitute actions.

So far, so good. But what exactly *is* 'exposure'? Many clinicians seem to adhere to philosophical realism, which holds that there are experiencing and knowing 'subjective' individuals living in an 'objective' world. And this 'objective' world contains Truths. Hence, there is a system separate from subjects. The domain of the subjective is seen as another system. Subjects may (within limits) know Truths, and some (e.g., scientists) know it better than other (less educated and less smart) folks. Some (i.e., clinicians) know the Truth that traumatic memories are like innocuous rubber duckies. Less fortunate others (i.e., phobic patients) are confused when they experience them and regard them as exceptionally harmful. To educate the ignorant and the confused, the wiser clinicians thus do best to expose them to the rubber duckies. This leads patients to experience and detect the world of Truth.

Exposure is sometimes cast in terms of a stimulus-response or stimulus-stimulus psychology.[1] This is seen as confronting traumatized individuals with a set of classically conditioned stimuli (= the traumatic memories), which more or less automatically trigger a set of conditioned emotional and cognitive responses (= fear), which in turn cause conditioned avoidance responses (i.e., ways of avoiding traumatic memories). From this perspective, confrontations with the rubber duckies as conditioned stimuli lead to fear reduction and cognitive modifications, especially the more the individual experiences the Truth that the traumatic memories are more harmless than harmful.

My text, however, takes the position that subject and objects exist relative to each other. Subjects should not be seen as the more or less passive recipients of an objectively existing world, but rather to experience and know objects, *the subject must engage in an action*. We only have sensations, affective feelings, emotions, perceptions, thoughts (conceptions), memories, and fantasies, and we only move when we also engage in the actions of sensing, emoting, thinking, remembering, etc. There is no pregiven world. There are no 'stimuli' that exist or even could exist on their own. As Zhuang Zi taught us, the world and I are one. Conscious and self-conscious subjects are phenomenal subjects, and the world and the truth represent their phenomenal and physical world and truth.

Exposure, then, is not something 'done' to an individual, and it is not about cognizing the Truth. We only confront ourselves with something (a feeling, a memory, etc.) when we engage in an action. In itself exposure is nothing, and one subject cannot 'expose' another subject to anything inasmuch as this other individual does not engage in some kind of action. Enactive trauma therapy thus holds that subjects enact their phenomenal self, their phenomenal world, and the relationships of this self and this world. Nobody can act for somebody else, and nothing can do something in and of itself. It can also be said like this: 'Hetero-exposure' or 'thing-exposure' exists only for exposed subjects inasmuch as subjects expose themselves. In this sense, any exposure is self-exposure.

The next step would be to say that memories including traumatic memories do not exist as some kind of memory traces that individuals 'find' or stumble upon (Braude, 1995, 2006; Bursen, 1978; Heil, 1978). As Braude, Bursen, and Heil explain, memory trace theory is a confused theory indeed. Recollecting the past in one way or another is a mental action. In dissociative disorders, different dissociative parts tend to recollect the past in different ways. For example, Martha from Chapter 33 knew most of what had happened to her, but she knew it only in a depersonalized and derealized way. Not the Little Martha. She was stuck in the sensorimotor and affectively charged experience that traumatic memories per definitionem are. As the leading ANP, Ineke (Chapters 32 and 35) did not

1 I do not discuss here the latter variation of learning theory.

recollect chronic childhood incest, though as The Reconciler she knew it but refused to acknowledge it. As The Consoler she also knew it, but regarded the whole thing as benign. She believed that father loved her. As Rick, she knew that the incest was real, and as The Little Ones and several other EPs she suffered immensely. As one ANP and as The Devil, Sonja did not know she had children, but as The Helper she knew it only too well. When Ineke as the leading ANP got to experience and know some exceptionally painful components of her phenomenal world, she turned psychotic.

To repeat: Exposure is exposure inasmuch as individuals or dissociative parts of individuals engage in particular actions. Inasmuch as the integration of traumatic memories is a common goal, enactive trauma therapy is an endeavor to help patients to engage in integrative actions. However, integration is not the result of a single action; it encompasses synthesis, personification, presentification, symbolization, and realization (see also Van der Hart et al., 2006) – and engagement in one action does not imply engagement in all others. For example, fragile EPs recurrently synthesize and personify particular traumatic memories. They recurrently expose themselves to traumatizing events. But they do not (or insufficiently) presentify, symbolize, and realize them. The self-exposure involved in the synthesis and personification of EPs which do not include a degree of presentification and realization is not therapeutic at all. Often, this presentification is possible only when a dissociative part has participated in the self-exposure and has the mental level to engage in the actions of presentification and realization with or without clinical assistance. For example, as the leading ANP, Sonja was initially only able to synthesize, personify, presentify, symbolize, and realize the fact that she had children after previous work with me and with my assistance. With more experience, she, The Helper, and her various EPs started to integrate traumatic memories in 'sessions' she organized with these various parts, which they performed together without any help from me or anyone else.

Further, self-exposure plus engagement in integrative actions it is not an all-or-nothing affair: It comes in degrees. This feature can be and often must be utilized in therapy. Many individuals with complex dissociative disorders can at some point in therapy expose themselves to a portion of a traumatic memory, or to a portion of all traumatic memories they possess. That is, they can synthesize, personify, presentify, symbolize, and realize some of them, but not all of them. For example, Ineke did great work in the session described in Chapter 35. She gave all she had to give at that point in her development. However, the integration of the incest had only just begun. Martha learned to integrate the traumatic memories associated with Little Martha in steps that involved increasing degrees of 'contact' with the The Little One (that was somewhat concretized in the form of a doll she held more or less close to her).

Clinicians should thus try to help their patients to find an optimal balance between the 'self-exposure actions' involved in the integration of traumatic memories and their present capacity to engage in these actions (e.g., Kluft, 2013; Van der Hart et al., 2006). Some patients may be too avoidant of their traumatic memories; they are probably capable of more integrative actions than they dare or wish to engage in. I have also met patients who demand too much in this regard: They want to do more and do more quickly than they are up to. This overenthusiasm and overdedication tends to cause decompensations, some of which can be serious. A not so serious effect in Martha's treatment was that she lost consciousness when she pushed herself too hard. Some clinicians avoid inviting and encouraging traumatized individuals to engage in integrative actions. Some demand more than patients can manage or wish to do, which can also lead to decompensations.

Considering that exposure to traumatic memories always means self-exposure, there is no exposure inasmuch as patients or dissociative parts of them do not engage in the action of recollecting these memories. Van Minnen says that the phase-oriented approach to the treatment of complex trauma-related dissociation is far too complex and quite unnecessary. A former DID patient I had accompanied on her road to full recovery firmly disagreed. As she said,

"Ellert, you were unable to
- expose me to traumatic memories that I, as the major ANP, did not recollect;
- know that I encompassed EPs to the extent that I did not show or report them because of my major phobia of the diagnosis;
- expose me to my traumatic memories as long as I denied my diagnosis;
- expose me to traumatic memories while I was exceptionally phobic of my EPs;
- ethically expose me to my traumatic memories before examining if they might pertain to real events or to my confused mind;
- expose me to the traumatic memories before I had learned to trust you, to understand myself more, to trust my EPs, to collaborate with them rather than to fight them;
- expose me to the traumatic memories when my controlling EPs and suicidal EPs acted out on you in sessions;
- expose me to the traumatic memories inasmuch as I struggled with a major phobia of attachment and detachment."

Her objections are also my objections. Phase-oriented enactive trauma therapy does not constitute a waste of time and effort. Rather than a needlessly complex venture, it proposes a stepwise approach to overcoming, among other things, intense phobias of attachment and detachment, of trauma-bound mental and behavioral actions and implied contents, of dissociative parts, and of traumatic memories. This work involves a tremendous amount of self-exposure. Sitting with someone in a room for hours, talking about their most feared, detested, and shameful realities, exposes one to multiple situations that many chronically traumatized individuals have experienced, perceived, and conceived of as dangerous.

Enactive trauma therapy involves helping chronically traumatized individuals to achieve other common results as well. These include raising the level of consciousness and broadening the field of consciousness of the patient as a whole as well as of each and every dissociative part they may encompass. The venture commonly also includes raising the level of action tendencies that the patients can engage in. In the most general sense, it is the endeavor to make sense of the nearly incomprehensible. It is about finding meaning in life following the gruesome cruelty that in many cases was inflicted by the very individuals who should have provided love and care. Some third persons feel that nonintegrated recollections of this life can be rightfully compared to a collection of rubber duckies. First persons and compassionate second persons are bound to disagree.

Twenty Years Later: Sonja's Reactions to Watching The Devil

Sonja overcame her DID and other symptoms of traumatization in 4 years of treatment with me. She worked exceptionally hard and received full support from her understanding and accepting husband. The therapy was terminated some 20 years ago. Now an integrated whole, she has remained in perfect health from that time to this day.

As mentioned above, I recently invited Sonja to watch the videos of the two sessions presented in this chapter to hear her comments on her experiences and my contributions. She was very willing and able, if only to be of help to clinicians who may find it difficult to handle very powerful dissociative parts. Here are some more statements regarding the video of The Devil; this seems to me to be a proper way to complete *The Trinity of Trauma*.

> "It was very important that you were not scared of me as The Devil. It is crucial to continue reaching out to a part like her and to resist becoming intimidated. You dared to say that her power was limited. Wow! Sure, she was powerful but she was also scared, and there was a lot she did not know or understand."

> "Your consistent kindness, calmness, and respect for me as a whole person and for each and every dissociative part I encompassed were crucial. And you recognized that parts have perfect reasons for doing what they are doing. I had never been treated and understood in this way – not at home and not in psychiatry. Promises made were always promises broken. Psychiatrists tend to be dominant personalities: Some are outright domineering, and a few are outright abusive. Dr. Finkensieper was one of the latter. Several other staff members in Zetten were also extremely controlling [like this psychiatrist's severe transgressions another documented fact]. One woman forced me to do the dishes of a whole department several times at night, although everything was in perfect order after the first round. She just *enjoyed* exercising her power. Like her, several other staff members accused me of violating the rules. I was punished a lot. But they knew or could have easily known that their accusations were often unjustified. Apart from this, I became hostile. I fought to keep at least some feeling of self-respect. Another reason for my being belligerent was to make sure that I landed in the seclusion room. It was a safe haven from Dr. Finkensieper. I stayed in that room for weeks more than once, and I did not mind it at all. Neither my mother, my family of origin, nor Zetten managed to break my will."

> "At times, The Devil took your words literally, which created confusion. It was helpful that you understood her mistakes without shaming her, and that you offered clarifications. People sometimes misunderstood my utterances. For example, I often said that things were one big

clique. People thought I was talking about external things or affairs, but I was also describing a tremendous inner struggle, and that struggle included The Devil. You always asked what I meant, you did not jump to conclusions."

"When you invited me to cooperate, it sounded attractive and at the same time very scary. I had experienced such cooperation in the past as dangerous. Nobody had ever done something for nothing. There was always a price to pay. So I was very skeptical. I wondered what kind of 'cooperation' you had in mind. And what would you want me to pay in return? I was not aware of fair cooperation. Cooperation always meant abuse to me."

"When I would look out the window during a session, or mumble and mutter, I was contemplating what to do. Of course, I wanted help, but I had never actually received help or understanding from anyone, so what was I to make of your offers? At some point in the session, hope arose that change might be possible after all. But hope was a dangerous thing. As a child, I had still hope. One day I fled to my grand(step)mother. I liked her. When I told her about the ongoing abuse and the abusers, I did not realize I was talking about her son. So what did she do? Together with the vicar, she took me back home. She told him what I had told her. I screamed and screamed when they left, because I knew how badly I would be punished for my revelations. They must have heard me screaming. Yes, they heard me. If I could not even trust a vicar, who could I trust? From that day I swore I would never go into a church again. What went on in the church was absolute nonsense. Many individuals become deeply hurt in the name of the church."

"The more people crushed my hopes, the more hope became an utterly dangerous thing to me. And the more dangerous it became, the more I merely wanted to survive. In the background there was the faint thought that maybe, maybe, one day my misery will end. Maybe. But this was not the same as hope. It was just a mere thought. I had abandoned hope."

"I feel strong now and can defend myself. Recently, someone I knew rather well made inappropriate sexual advances. I had never expected him to do that. But I stood firm and sent him off, straight away and for good. But it really hurts when people do that."

"Now I feel that pain. I did not feel it then (as Sonja, the main ANP). My pain disappeared in all parts (fragile and controlling EPs). I now instantly feel the pain and the sadness and can deal with it. When I have done that, the emotions are over and done with. My old life was like one big chest of drawers: Every time something dreadful happened, I put it in a drawer. Then it was gone – or so I (erroneously) assumed. The drawers were my dissociative parts (EPs). I am still fond of drawers, though!" (laughs)

"Whenever I became sulky during a session, as The Devil I knew you were right. But I was so enraged that there was no room to admit it. I did not want to acknowledge it. I was looking for a reason to resist cooperation even if there was none."

"Several of my dissociative parts tried to navigate difficult situations by talking. Watching the video I realize how important The Helper was. She had to find a middle road. The Devil as an exceptionally strong part of me mistrusted words. And then there was the Sonja who engaged in talking and talking to handle tough situations. What a struggle to find a way to live! Small wonder I was deadly tired at night."

"When my mother was dying, I wrote her a letter to ask if there was anything she wanted to tell me before she passed away. I actually sent her three letters. But she never answered them."

"I have come to realize a lot. My mother's intellect was very limited. It was normal to maltreat children, physically and emotionally, in the world into which she had been born and raised and in which she continued to live. The sexual boundaries were very weak if not completely missing. I strongly suspect my mother was also sexually abused as a child. She and several other families I've known have remained caught in that vicious world. But with me the cycle of traumatization stopped. And for that I am very proud of myself."

Chapter 38

222 Propositions Regarding Enactivism and Enactive Trauma Therapy

The only thing necessary for the triumph of evil is for good men to do nothing.
Edmund Burke (1729–1797)

This closing chapter summarizes the major points of Volume III. It has two parts: enactivism and enactive trauma therapy. The obvious link between the two is that enactive trauma therapy is based on enactivism. A number of perspectives call themselves 'enactive.' The version that grounds enactive trauma therapy involves, or in my view fits, the following propositions. They are to be understood in close connection with the propositions formulated in ToT Volumes I and II, Chapter 21. Some of these are actually included in the present set summarizing the Volume III.

Enactivism

Primordial Affectivity

1. Any living organism longs and strives to preserve its own existence.
2. Any living organism is primarily and affectively interested in itself.
3. This affectivity guides the organism's behavior and cognition.

Mind and Matter

4. All living organisms are physical as well as mental systems.
5. As detailed in ToT Volumes I and II, mind and matter are two different properties of one substance or system: nature. The one does not cause the other. Rather, they involve different ways of conceiving a living biopsychosocial system as a unity.

Relativity of Subject and Object; Meaning Making

6. Machines and parts of machines (e.g., bolts, bearings, wheels) can perfectly exist in an environmental void. Any organism, however, exists, and can only exist, in an environment that meets the organism's basic needs. Organisms are dynamic organism-environment systems. They include two features that machines lack: person perspectives and any interest in the continuation of their existence.
7. There are neither objects nor events without sentient and knowing subjects, and there are no subjects without a material and social world. Subjects and objects are co-occurrent, co-constitutive, and co-dependent. That is, there is a relativity of subjects and objects.
8. An organism's 'self,' 'world,' and couplings of this self and world are not pregiven. Each and every living organism must and does bring forth a conception of self, a conception of the world or *umwelt*, and a conception of relationships of this self and *umwelt* in ongoing embodied, world-oriented, and experience-based actions. The term 'enaction' stands for this recurrent generation.
9. Nothing has meaning in and of itself. Meaning is not pregiven. Organisms long and strive to create meaning.
10. Meaning making is primarily an affective affair. As stated above, affective interests guide cognition. Affectless cognition does not cause affects.
11. Meaning making primarily involves experiencing and judging what is useful, harmful, or insignificant.
12. What is useful to an organism operates as a systemic attractor.
13. What is harmful to an organism operates as a systemic repeller.
14. Anything that strengthens the organism's internal and external relationships is useful to an organism. Anything that decomposes these relationships is harmful (death being the extreme state). Anything that does not affect the relationships is insignificant.
15. Living well means experiencing and differentiating between what is useful, harmful, and insignificant as well as succeeding in gaining the useful, in avoiding or escaping from the harmful, and abandoning the useless. Gaining the useful brings joy; confrontations with the harmful cause sorrow.

Morality

16. Good and bad are not pregiven. Morality follows affects but does not cause them.
17. Organisms consider good to be what is useful, bad to be what is harmful, and meaningless to be what is neither useful nor harmful.

Organism-Environment Systems and Operationally Autonomous Systems

18. Organisms neither consist of nor experience and know a 'separate' self and a 'separate' world. Rather, ontologically, affectively, and epistemically speaking, they constitute

organism-environment systems. The boundaries between what constitutes an individual organism and what constitutes its environment are very fuzzy (e.g., human bodies include millions of bacteria, without which they could not live).

19. Organisms are also operationally autonomous systems in the sense that they long and strive to preserve their existence, distinguish between their self and not-self, and generate couplings between their self and not-self.
20. There is a knotty dialectic: Organisms are operationally autonomous systems and at the same time organism-environment systems. Through ongoing action, they bring forth a self. By enacting this self, they also enact a not-self, an *umwelt* as well as borders between and couplings of this self and this *umwelt* (without which no organism/self can exist).

Embrained, Embodied, Embedded

21. Like many other organisms, (human) individuals are embrained. However, (human) experience, knowledge, and behavior cannot in any way be reduced to their brain. Organisms consist of more than their brains (or 'brain-substitutes').
22. Like other organisms, (human) individuals are embodied and environmentally embedded. Organisms, that is, consist of more than their body.
23. Life involves intrinsic relationships between the brain (or 'brain-substitute'), the body, and the environment. 'Intrinsic' means: One component does not exist on its own and hence cannot operate without the other components.

Mental and Phenomenal Systems

24. All living organisms are mental systems, because they have an interest in themselves and their world. Living organisms *feel*.
25. Some organisms are also phenomenal systems. Phenomenal systems are systems that experience and know what it is like to have experiences and to know themselves, their *umwelt*, and the phenomenally experienced and conceived relationships of their phenomenal self and *umwelt*. Phenomenal systems feel that they feel and know that they know.

Needs and Desires

26. There is no substantial difference between needs and desires. The only difference is that needs are unconscious and desires are conscious.
27. Needs and desires manifest themselves in modes of longing and striving.

28. The more complex an organism is, the more needs and desires it encompasses and the wider its mode space will be.
29. Needs and desires can be compatible or even synergistic. They can also be incompatible and contrary.

Modes of Longing and Striving

30. Particularly complex organisms can include contrary modes of longing and striving. Opposite modes manifest themselves as ambivalences and polyvalences or as conflicts.
31. Each mode of longing and striving comprises and organizes its own perceptions, sensations, affective feelings, thoughts (i.e., conceptions), fantasies, memories, behaviors, and, in a general sense, meanings.
32. Each mode of longing and striving comprises and organizes one or more particular syntheses of perceptions, sensations, affective feelings, etc.
33. Healthy individuals largely integrate, and thus basically overcome, their ambivalences or polyvalences. They largely integrate the various implied modes of longing and striving.

Integration: Synthesis, Personification, Presentification, Symbolization, and Realization

34. To become a personal experience, an organism must personify its synthesis.
35. To become a normal explicit memory, an organism must presentify its synthesis such that it is experienced and known as an experience and as an event that pertains to its chronological and phenomenal past. In this case, the chronological (third-person) and the phenomenal (first-person) past correspond.
36. Further, the organism must integrate its synthesis of the past with one or more other syntheses that bring forth the present such that its synthesis of 'the present' is experienced and known as something that is more real than its synthesis of 'the past.'
37. To become an image of the future, an organism must presentify its synthesis such that it is experienced and known as a synthesis pertaining to the future.
38. Further, its synthesis of the future must be integrated with one or more other syntheses of 'the present' such that the synthesis of 'the present' is experienced and known as something that is more real than its synthesis of 'the past.'
39. Healthy individuals largely enact viable syntheses, and personify as well as presentify their syntheses.
40. Healthy individuals can also largely symbolize and realize their personified and presentified experiences.

41. The adequate integration of various particular modes of longing and striving is beyond reach in pathology, as may be the adequate synthesis, personification, presentification, symbolization, and realization of each separate mode of longing and striving.
42. A lack of synthesis manifests itself in negative phenomena such as anesthesia, analgesia, unduly selective perception, and emotional numbing. 'Negative' stands for 'something absent that would better be present.'
43. A lack of personification manifests itself in the negative phenomenon of depersonalization.
44. A lack of presentification manifests itself in a confusion of the present, past, and future.
45. A lack of realization manifests itself in the negative phenomenon of derealization as well as the more general phenomenon in misjudging the implications of experiences, events, and facts. In these cases, individuals do not (sufficiently) heed the implications of experiences, events, and facts.

Integrative Limitations, Adverse Events, and Traumatic and Traumatizing Events

46. In the framework of the relativity of subjects and objects, pathology emerges from and involves an undue limitation of the power of action.
47. Patients engage in passions the more they are dominated by external causes. They engage in actions the more they operate according to their personal causes.
48. Patients engage in passions or substitute actions the more they are unable to engage in more efficient but generally more difficult actions.
49. Adverse events challenge the will and ability of individuals to integrate the involved experiences and facts.
50. Integrating (recurrent) adverse events saves mental health but may demand a high to exceptionally high power of action.
51. The inability to integrate adverse experiences and events turns these experiences and events into traumatic experiences and traumatic events in the first-person, quasi-second-person, and second-person perspective. This inability turns adverse experiences and events in traumatizing experiences and events in the third-person perspective.
52. Synthesizing, personifying, presentifying, symbolizing and realizing, that is, fully integrating chronic adverse events and their consequences, is an extremely demanding and complex action.
53. The difficulty increases and may reach its summit when parents or other significant others on which the individual is dependent neglect, maltreat, abuse, or otherwise hurt the involved individual.
54. A common conflict lies between attaching to and defending oneself against significant others.

55. Individuals who consist of contrary needs and desires may alternate between these different needs and desires – or do not know where to go.
56. Individuals who consist of contrary needs and desires may (but need not) be dissociative operationally autonomous and dissociative organism-environment systems.
57. Individuals who consist of contrary or otherwise incompatible needs and desires may associate the involved modes of longing and striving with one phenomenal experience and conception of self, world, and self as a part of this world. These individuals comprise a conflicted but not dissociative operationally autonomous organism-environment system.

Dissociation in Trauma and Dissociative Subsystems

58. Individuals who consist of contrary needs and desires that they associate with a different phenomenal self, phenomenal *umwelt*, and phenomenal self-*umwelt* borders and couplings are dissociative systems. These individuals consist of a dissociative organism-environment system including plural phenomenal experiences and conceptions of self, *umwelt*, and relationships of this self and *umwelt*.
59. Dissociative subsystems or 'parts' of the personality are embrained, embodied, and environmentally embedded.
60. Dissociative parts are primarily need and desire (or will).
61. Dissociative parts constitute operationally autonomous systems.
62. Dissociative parts are conscious and self-conscious subsystems.
63. Dissociation of the personality involves an initial decomposition and subsequent recomposition of the personality in two or more dissociative parts inasmuch as the original personality *a priori* constituted a largely integrated organism-environment system.
64. Dissociation of the personality involves a composition of two or more dissociative parts inasmuch as the original personality did not *a priori* comprise a largely integrated organism-environment system.
65. This recomposition or composition involves a particular structural dissociation of the personality (i.e., a division of a unitary system into dissociative subsystems).
66. Structural dissociation can follow when an individual experiences and knows one or more events that are so averse to the involved individual that he or she does not succeed in integrating (i.e., synthesizing, personifying, etc.) the event(s) in the framework of one phenomenal self, world, and self as a part of this world.
67. Dissociative subsystems are commonly not fully split. Rather, they maintain more or less extensive and dynamic relationships with one another. This collection of relationships can be addressed as the dynamic dissociation of the personality.
68. Dissociative parts involve their own phenomenal experiences, thoughts, and behaviors. The term phenomenal dissociation of the personality captures this feature.

69. Dissociative parts involve their own goals. This dissociative part-dependent goal-orientation is what the term teleological dissociation of the personality intends.
70. Each dissociative part basically longs and strives to persevere in its existence in his or her own way.
71. Some dissociative parts may be suicidal. The longing and striving to end their life commonly involves a longing and striving to find rest. Some imagine a (better) afterlife. The large majority of dissociative parts do not seem to seek nothingness.

Prototypical Dissociative Parts

72. Dissociation of the personality is an ongoing creative act.
73. Each dissociative part exists and continues to exist by virtue of ongoing creative actions or passions. They cease to exist when the involved actions or passions are discontinued.
74. It is theoretically, scientifically, and clinically useful to distinguish between prototypical dissociative parts.
75. Distinguishing between prototypical dissociative parts allows theoreticians, scientists, and clinicians to know, analyze, study, and appreciate these types as well as the derivatives.
76. ANPs primarily long and strive to achieve interests of daily life. In this sense, they avoid or try to escape from being in touch with the affective, cognitive, and behavioral domains of fragile EPs and controlling EPs.
77. ANPs tend to be primarily guided by action systems for functioning in daily life and by the implied systemic attractors and repellers.
78. ANPs tend to encompass a variety of actual and latent modes of longing and striving.
79. Fragile EPs primarily long and strive to preserve their existence in the light of perceived and conceived actual, potential, or imagined threats to their existence.
80. Fragile EPs tend to be primarily guided by the mammalian action system of defense or the action system of attachment cry, and by the implied systemic attractors and repellers.
81. Fragile EPs commonly include several modes of longing and striving, but their mode space tends to be smaller than the mode space of ANPs.
82. Prototypical controlling EPs primarily long and strive to exert the power to dominate others so as to control their (i.e., the involved controlling EP's) fate.
83. Controlling EPs tend to be primarily guided by the action system of self-determination/social dominance, and by the implied systemic attractors and repellers.
84. To achieve their goals, controlling EPs tend to imitate some of the actions and passions of perpetrators. That is, they imitate negative power models.
85. Controlling EPs commonly include several modes of longing and striving, but their mode space tends to be smaller than the mode space of ANPs.

86. Stating that ANPs, fragile EPs, and controlling EPs are prototypes means that traumatized individuals can consist of other kinds of dissociative parts.
87. The prototypical primary dissociation is the development and maintenance of one ANP and one fragile EP.
88. In prototypical secondary dissociation of the personality, there is one ANP and more than one EP. The EPs may include apart from one or more fragile EPs one or more controlling EPs.
89. Prototypical tertiary dissociation of the personality comprises more than one ANP and more than one EP.

Dissociative Parts and Consciousness

90. The level of consciousness and the field of consciousness depend on the type of social relationship.
91. The level of consciousness and the field of consciousness tend to be rather low in totalitarian relationships. They are commonly higher and broader in corporate relationships and reach their summit in communicative, egalitarian relationships.
92. Dissociative parts display a particular level and field of consciousness and self-consciousness.
93. Dissociative parts that relate to other individuals and to other dissociative parts in totalitarian ways tend to have a rather low and restricted consciousness, particularly when they feel that their self-determination is being threatened.
94. Controlling EPs commonly mistrust a subdued clinician and oppose a domineering one.
95. They tend to value and learn from clinicians who are transparent, courageous, fair, challenging, and consistent. They appreciate and learn from clinicians who understand the importance of self-determination in the face of chronic traumatization that leaves children almost powerless. They appreciate and can learn to cooperate and communicate with clinicians who present positive power models.
96. Fragile EPs tend to act like slaves. They appreciate clinicians who can grasp and respect their fragility and their need for defensive control and attachment cry.
97. ANPs may achieve a higher level of consciousness and a broader field of consciousness. This consciousness is associated with cooperative relationships with other individuals or other dissociative parts who are also able to engage in a form of cooperation.
98. Some ANPs can reach a communicative level and field of consciousness when they feel relatively safe and competent.
99. ANPs value clinicians who can grasp and respect the importance of daily life needs and desires, and who offer cooperation and open communication.

Enactive Trauma Therapy

100. Enactive trauma therapy is an egalitarian, cooperative, and communicative venture.
101. In the most general sense, it involves helping patients to bring forth a more viable phenomenal self and *umwelt* as well as more viable couplings of and distinctions between this self and *umwelt.*
102. In many regards, the venture is a movement from recurrent reenactments of traumatizing events and relationships to enactments of a more viable mental and phenomenal self, *umwelt* as well as couplings and distinctions of this self and this *umwelt.*

Enactive Trauma Clinicians

103. Like other individuals, clinicians are embrained, embodied, environmentally embedded, and primarily affective.
104. Enactive trauma clinicians long and strive to be maximally communicative in their relationships with themselves, with their patients at large, and with their patients' dissociative parts.
105. Realizing that "evil begins when you start to treat people as things" (Terry Pratchett, *I Shall Wear Midnight*), enactive trauma clinicians eschew mere engagement in a third-person perspective regarding their patients. They long and strive to continually experience, know, and integrate their first-person, quasi-second-person, second-person, and third-person perspectives in the clinical situation.
106. They regard and respect patients and their dissociative parts as individuals and 'dividuals' (ToT Volumes I & II) who want to raise their power of action. They do not regard them as individuals and 'dividuals' who wish to depend on them, who are powerless, who make their life miserable, or who otherwise frustrate their intentions.
107. Clinicians long and strive to raise their patients' level and field of consciousness inasmuch as these progressions fit the patients' needs and desires.
108. Enactive trauma clinicians as professionals long and strive to coach their patients as a unity as well as their dissociative parts toward the achievement of the patients' viable therapeutic goals.
109. Enactive trauma clinicians as private persons may want many things regarding their patients as a unity and their dissociative parts. Ideally, they experience and know these personal needs and desires, but withhold them inasmuch as these wills are harmful, useless, or otherwise irrelevant with respect to the patients' viable treatment goals.
110. If clinicians do not withhold their personal needs and desires in the sense of #109, they engage in 'countertransferential' actions, substitute actions, or more generally passions. Such enactments may involve clinicians' reenactments of relational or other issues they have yet to resolve.

Egalitarianism

111. Enactive trauma therapy comprises the egalitarian collaboration of a patient and a clinician as two primarily affective organism-environment systems.
112. This collaboration involves participatory sense-making.
113. The domain of treatment is the *umwelt* the two individuals have in common. Without a common *umwelt,* there can be no treatment.
114. Enactive trauma clinicians long and strive to achieve this common *umwelt.*
115. They do not dictate what their patients should perceive, sense, feel, think, remember, and do. Rather, they invite and encourage their patients as a unity and their dissociative parts to explore new viable actions. Viable actions maximize the achievement of the useful and minimize the reception of the harmful and the insignificant, or are steps toward these goals.
116. Enactive trauma clinicians comprehend and appreciate that all dissociative parts long and strive to achieve their goals. In this sense, they treat all dissociative parts equally and with deep respect.
117. Enactive trauma clinicians work hard, but make sure they do not work harder than their patients.
118. Milton Erickson's egalitarian and most creative (hypno)therapeutic style and techniques beautifully fit the egalitarian enactive approach to trauma therapy.
119. Erickson's use of analogy and metaphor also exquisitely fits enactive trauma therapy.

Goals

120. The therapy is guided by a longing and striving to achieve common results. Without such longing and striving to achieve common results, there can be no viable or adequate treatment.
121. The final common result is ideally the complete healing of the patient, that is, the full restoration of the patient's wholeness or health.
122. Viable and adequate treatment goals pertain to the patient's longing to engage in more useful and efficient actions. These actions generally replace substitute actions and passions.
123. Viable and adequate treatment goals per session stem from the longings and strivings to engage in actions that, in the best clinical assessment, are useful to patients and within their present or potential reach. A useful opening statement is, therefore, "What do you want to achieve in the present session?" (This sentence is generally far better suited than asking how the patient's week has been.)
124. At some point in time, the treatment goals can include the longing and striving to integrate, symbolize, and realize the patient's traumatic past.

125. Clinicians should not lightheartedly allow patients to set their goals too high or carelessly allow that the longings and strivings of patients are not ambitious enough.

Attunement, Consensus Building, and Leading

126. Enactive trauma therapy is like dancing. It takes pacing, attunement, timing, sensitivity to balance, movement and rhythm, courage as well as a reciprocal ability and willingness to follow sensible leads and to lead adequate strivings.
127. Enactive trauma clinicians should long and strive to become attuned to the phenomenal experiences (first-person perspective), phenomenal judgments (quasi-second-person perspective and second-person perspective), and physical judgments (third-person perspective) of patients and their dissociative parts.
128. Attunement communicates a deep affective interest in patients both as a unity and as any dissociative part, that is, in their phenomenal experience and conception of self, of their *umwelt*, and of their couplings of self and *umwelt*.
129. Successful attunement leads to a consensual world, to a common *umwelt*. This *umwelt* is an enacted therapeutic domain ratified explicitly by the patient and the clinician (e.g., clinician: "This is how it feels"; patient: "Yes, this is how it feels"; clinician: "Hmm, this is how it feels").
130. Many chronically traumatized individuals have never or seldom experienced benign affect-laden interest from significant others; they have never or seldom experienced a common benign and mindful *umwelt*.
131. Attunement and the generation of a consensual understanding also build, ratify, and intensify the clinical relationship and bond.
132. Receiving such interest raises the consciousness and power of action of patients and their dissociative parts, and with it their capacity for change.
133. The clinical longing and striving to achieve attunement, consensus, and the development of new viable actions is a continuous matter that is applied to all dissociative parts.
134. Higher levels of consciousness and interpersonal relatedness intensify the physical and emotional feelings of ANPs and open the door to the EPs and to traumatic memories that ANPs typically fear and despise.
135. An intensification of the clinical relationship and bond may scare controlling EPs who have sworn to be independent of everyone and to never trust an adult again.
136. Enactive trauma clinicians should appreciate and handle this double therapeutic paradox (#134, #135) with care.
137. Many clinicians rush to take the lead before ample time has been taken to become attuned to the patient or dissociative part and to develop a consensual *umwelt*. This haste is often counterproductive in the treatment of chronically traumatized individuals.
138. It is generally wise to work within the limits of the power of action of patients (or their dissociative parts) and then to extend their power of action from this basis.

139. The general third-person clinical principle is to invite, encourage, assist, model, and coach patients in the direction of ever more integrative actions (synthesis, personification, presentification, symbolization, and realization).
140. This work involves the enactment of a more or less new phenomenal self and *umwelt*, and more or less new couplings of this self and this *umwelt*.
141. One element in the enactive approach to trauma therapy is Erickson's principle of utilization, which involves utilizing available actions for therapeutic purposes rather than trying to engender actions that are strange to the patient. The motto is to utilize 'what is already there' rather than striving to achieve 'what is not there.'
142. Enactive trauma clinicians treat the whole patient, that is, the whole structural, dynamic, phenomenal, and teleological system of dissociative parts. They engage in work with one or more dissociative parts only according to the ongoing appreciation that the parts are parts of a dissociative whole.

Enactive Trauma Therapy: Healing Steps

143. Healing involves the gradual or sudden increase of the patient's power of action.
144. Healing involves the present engagement in actions that are more useful (or less harmful or insignificant) than the inefficient, insignificant, or harmful actions, substitute actions, or passions they replace.
145. Patients or a particular dissociative part of them can sometimes be too impulsive, reflex-like, thoughtless, inconsiderate, and blind to better options. In that case, their development progresses from lower-level action tendencies to higher-level action tendencies. For example, clinicians may invite and encourage patients who reenact or tend to reenact traumatizing events or relationships in sensorimotor, strongly affect-laden, and behavioral ways to make a drawing of the traumatizing events. They can ask them to add a few spoken and written words to the drawing. Then they can ask them to describe what happened in affectively lived words and what the experience was like and what it meant to them. Finally, they can invite and encourage patients to put the whole event in lived and reflected words.
146. In other cases, patients may engage in action tendencies that are too complex, too advanced relative to the demands of the situation. For example, some traumatized individuals or dissociative parts of them deeply contemplate engaging in a behavioral action or taking a decision, whereas actual engagement in the action or taking a quick decision would be far more useful. In this case, they are too reflective.
147. It is often better to aspire to a minimal or modest degree of change than to go for major steps when the patient's capacity for change is low. Major goals can commonly be achieved by a series of minor steps ("You have taken a step. Great. You can do it. When you take a similar step, you will have achieved twice as much. And when you can take these two steps, you can take four.").

148. The principle of minimal change involved is grounded in the simple fact that a change is a change and that many small changes make a big change.

Embodiment and the Body in Trauma Therapy

149. Since patients and clinicians are embodied, their common environment profoundly includes their bodies.
150. The absence of direct physical contact between patients and clinicians does not exclude indirect physical contacts. On the contrary, given embodiment and the unity of individuals as matter and as mind, any common environment necessarily implies some physical contact between patients' and clinicians' bodies.
151. In this light, the question is not whether treatment includes the body, but *how*.
152. Limited forms of direct physical contact between patients and clinicians can sometimes be most useful. These contacts may generate results that other interventions cannot achieve or cannot achieve as effectively and efficiently.
153. Given the above, there is an urgent need for new rules regarding direct and indirect physical contact in trauma therapy.
154. Clinicians need to be educated and trained regarding indirect and direct physical contact in treatment.

Who Does What and Why?

155. A general clinical concern in enactive trauma therapy is the question "Who does what and why?"
156. This concern pertains to any dissociative part.
157. Any dissociative part engages in mental and/or behavioral actions or passions for one or more good reasons. Enactive trauma clinicians show a primary affect-laden interest in the final causes of individuals and their dissociative parts in the wider frame of dynamic causality (i.e., the collective material, efficient, formal, and final causality).
158. Intrusions in dissociative disorders are nothing else than mental and behavioral actions or passions of one or more dissociative parts and their implied contents that affect one or more other dissociative parts.
159. It is therapeutically useful for intruded on dissociative parts to explore what other dissociative parts intrude on them and why.

Pointland, Lineland, Flatland, and Spaceland

160. Traumatized individuals and their dissociative parts tend to live in 'Flatland' in at least some crucial regards. Some are citizens of 'Lineland,' and an occasional dissociative part may be the sole inhabitant of 'Pointland.'

161. Clinicians ideally reside and remain footed in 'Spaceland.'
162. Clinicians are and should at all times stay, so to speak, 'Spacelanders' while working with 'Flatlanders,' 'Linelanders,' or 'Pointlanders.' They invite, encourage, and coach 'Pointlanders' to migrate to 'Lineland,' 'Linelanders' to move to 'Flatland,' and 'Flatlanders' to become citizens of 'Spaceland.'
163. While clinicians work with entities of lower dimensional complexity, they stay in intense touch with the virtues of 'Spaceland.' On their travels to lower dimensional domains, they constantly view the venture from the top of the pyramid, observe the whole pyramid, and stay in permanent touch with this 3-D world.

Phobias

164. Patients with dissociative disorders may have a phobia of the diagnosis.
165. Dissociative parts may have a phobia of trauma-related actions and contents (e.g., phobias of trauma-related affects, physical feelings, thoughts, and behaviors).
166. Some dissociative parts have a phobia of attachment, and some a phobia of detachment. Some include combinations of the two.
167. Dissociative parts tend to have a phobia of each other.
168. ANPs and controlling EPs tend to have a phobia of the traumatic memories of fragile EPs.
169. Phobias can be overcome by synthesizing, personifying, presentifying, contextualizing, symbolizing, and realizing the feared and/or despised and avoided mental contents.
170. These various actions succeed only inasmuch as they are within the phobic will and power of action of the individual or dissociative part.
171. The involved phobias can and commonly are best overcome in steps.
172. To this end, clinicians help their patients as unities and as their dissociative parts to understand how they can engage in feared, despised, and avoided mental and behavioral actions in steps. All sorts of 'imaginary filters' can be most useful (e.g., sensory, perceptual, affective, and cognitive 'filters').
173. Rational understanding does not correct problematic affects. An affect can only be changed by an affect opposite to and more powerful than the affect to be overcome or eliminated.
174. Integration, symbolization, and realization of traumatic experiences and events are affect-laden actions that can eliminate trauma-related affects and other affects inasmuch as they are stronger than the problematic affects.
175. A powerful therapeutic alliance affectively boosts the power of these healing actions. In some cases, these healing actions are beyond reach without this alliance.

Imaginal Exposure

176. The therapeutic technique known as (imaginal) 'exposure' involves exposure only inasmuch as patients engage in actions that bring forth the feared, despised, and avoided.
177. Clinicians cannot expose their patients to anything. Only patients can expose themselves to something. Exposure is always self-exposure involving a relativity of subjects and objects.
178. Imaginal exposure does not serve as a sufficient instrument in the treatment of dissociative disorders inasmuch as the treatment does not engage dissociative parts that, so to speak, contain the traumatic contents, and inasmuch as the dissociative parts to be exposed and the dissociative parts that contain the 'phobic contents' do not have contact and cooperate with each other.
179. When these conditions are not met, the phenomenal selves, *umwelten*, and relationships between the involved selves and *umwelten* do not become phenomenal realities to the to be 'exposed' dissociative parts.
180. Sitting with an adult and clinical professional in a secluded room and engaging in a close relationship with this adult commonly implies self-exposure with respect to the phobias of attachment, detachment, and the diagnosis dissociative disorder.
181. Engagement in the treatment of a dissociative disorder commonly implies self-exposure to trauma-related mental contents and behaviors.
182. Engagement in the treatment of a dissociative disorder commonly implies self-exposure of one dissociative part to one or more other dissociative parts.
183. Engagement in the treatment of a dissociative disorder commonly implies self-exposure to traumatic memories.
184. Living with a dissociative disorder commonly includes self-exposure to interpersonal relationships (many patients entertain such relationships) as well as dissociative symptoms and intrusions that relate to other dissociative parts and to traumatic memories.
185. This self-exposure (see #182) is not therapeutic, inasmuch as it involves trauma-related affects that are stronger than contrary affects such as the affect of feeling safe in the actual present situation (see #173).

Concretizations

186. Given low or modest levels of action tendencies, it is often worthwhile to put abstract phenomena and principles in a concretized form.
187. One concretization is to represent dissociative parts in the form of symbols, like little wooden figures of various shapes, natural stones, dolls, or other fitting objects.
188. The advantage of this type of concretization over drawings of dissociative parts is

that the representations of the dissociative parts can be moved in particular ways to symbolize their reciprocal relationships as well as desirable changes of these relationships. Drawings are static; movable objects can be dynamic.

189. Another concretization is inviting a dissociative part to connect his or her being and features with one hand, and to invite other dissociative parts to link his or her being with another hand. The dissociative parts can then be invited to move their hands in ways that display their intentions and actions regarding each other. Approach can symbolize interpart approach, touching two figures prudent interpart contacts, and distancing interpart avoidance or escape. A piece of cloth or some other suitable object between the two hands can represent some kind of filtered contact between two parts.
190. Clinicians can suggest that useful feelings, thoughts, etc., of one part can stream from one part into another part when the two hands meet. This willful 'intrusion' involves utilizing the ability of dissociative parts to intrude on each other (see #141).
191. Therapeutic sessions may start by putting the representations of dissociative parts on the table in the therapy room in a way that displays their positions and present dynamics. It becomes much harder to avoid other dissociative parts when their concrete representations and the relationships among them are displayed on the table.
192. Clinicians can next ask the involved group of dissociative parts to express what kind of change they would want to achieve, for example, by indicating moves of the represented dissociative parts.

Overcoming the Trinity of Trauma in Psychiatry, Psychology, and Psychotherapy

193. The healthcare system at large continues to misunderstand, underdiagnose, misdiagnose, undertreat, or mistreat chronically traumatized individuals.
194. The existence of chronic traumatization and the complex problems of chronically traumatized individuals are considered to be threatening by a substantial number of healthcare professionals.
195. Fragile healthcare providers prefer to ignore or emotionally control chronically traumatized individuals rather than to adequately treat them.
196. Ignorance involves disinterest or low interest in relevant research findings and disinterest in education in trauma and trauma-related dissociation of the personality. Ignoring these topics and other forms of avoidance include transferring chronically traumatized individuals to 'specialists,' failure to screen for trauma and dissociation, failure to use self-report questionnaires to assess dissociative symptoms, and failure to administer semistructured interviews to assess dissociative disorders. It also involves uncritically accepting prejudices and distortions regarding trauma, traumatized individuals, individuals with dissociative disorders, the veracity of traumatic

memories, the nature of phase-oriented trauma therapy, and the actions of trauma therapists.

197. Emotional control includes believing that these patients cannot be helped, that they are manipulative, that they report false memories, that dissociative disorders, in fact, do not exist. Other forms of emotional control take the form of claiming that colleagues who diagnose and treat dissociative disorders are suggesting these conditions – and to attack, depreciate, or ridicule them.
198. Inasmuch as these conditions apply, the professionals involved would be better off overcoming their ignorance, fragility, and control by raising their power of action regarding chronic traumatization and its consequences. This takes systematic education, training, professional guidelines and rules, coaching, and experiencing diagnostic and treatment successes.
199. At the most general level, it means realizing that professional ignorance and emotional control of chronic childhood traumatization and its consequences are contributing to its perseverance and hence to anyone's fragility.
200. The education of clinicians and scientists working in the field of healthcare and disorders should include providing profound knowledge and expertise regarding chronic traumatization and dissociation.

Society and Chronic Childhood Traumatization

201. Societies are urgently challenged to rid themselves of the monster of chronic child sexual abuse, physical and emotional maltreatment, and emotional neglect.
202. To date, not a single society has achieved this goal to any satisfactory degree.
203. Societal ignorance and emotional control regarding chronic traumatization and dissociation are common passionate substitutes for adequate integrative social action.
204. These passions constitute low-level and short-sighted efforts to manage societal fragility because they strongly contribute to its maintenance.
205. For example, emotional control such as demanding preventive measures or accusing healthcare professionals of failing chronically traumatized individuals (commonly children) come to the limelight only when severe cases of chronic childhood traumatization reach the social media. Control efforts commonly include short-lived upheaval and emotional discussions, which generate at best insufficiently integrative and temporary actions that tend to bear little lasting fruit.
206. Like traumatized individuals who are clinically challenged to raise their mental and behavioral level, society is challenged to dare to feel and know the nature and severity of the problem of chronic traumatization and dissociation – and not for a day, but forever.
207. Societies need to synthesize the problem, that is, to come to feel and know its existence and the deep problems it presents. Next, they are to personify it, that is, to

appreciate that the problem concerns all of society. Then, societies are challenged to presentify it, which means learning to appreciate the harmful short-term and long-term effects of continued societal ignorance and emotional control of the problems at hand. In presentification, this appreciation is grounded in past experiences regarding trauma, trauma prevention, and trauma therapy, and reflective imagination of future consequences of societal actions or the lack of it. To reflect on the issue, society must symbolize it, which involves putting painful facts into words or other clear symbols that, at the highest level, take the form of sophisticated trauma theories and hypotheses derived from the formulations. The final and most difficult step is to realize the facts of chronic childhood traumatization and its consequences for present and future generations. Realization means more than acknowledging; it involves a deep appreciation of the problems involved, implying the development, execution, and permanent continuation of effective and efficient action to delimit their occurrence and their consequences.

208. Societies should free themselves from their self-chosen seclusion in Pointland, Lineland, or Flatland regarding chronic traumatization and dissociation and finally reach and settle in Spaceland.
209. Societies can and should influence the quality and quantity of healthcare provided for chronic traumatization and dissociation. These aims can be achieved only through dedicated and lasting actions, including, to name but a few, fostering the recognition of the painful problems under consideration, setting and maintaining higher standards of care, generously investing in the education and training of professionals (physicians, teachers, psychiatrists, psychologists, psychotherapists, scientists, judges, attorneys, police) regarding chronic traumatization and trauma-related dissociation, generous and recurrent investment in the early assessment and treatment as well as scientific study of chronic traumatization, and inclusion of healed traumatized individuals in the healthcare system to educate professionals and to coach other traumatized individuals.
210. These and related actions cannot be reached by a one-off effort. They must be an ongoing concern. Otherwise, gains will soon evaporate in the heat of the trinity of trauma: ignorance, fragility, and control.
211. The power of the parents and families of origin regarding their children is broad, but in far too many cases this power takes the form of malevolent control.
212. Societies that seriously care about their children, the future generations, and society as a whole cannot condone the criminal acts involved. Viable checks on parental/familial power must be found, particularly if one wishes to prevent the controlling institutes from becoming a power structure of its own. And remember: power corrupts. However, it should also be clear that the absence of checks on parental and familial power in the past clearly demonstrated the terrible consequences that can have for many individuals, families, larger social groups, and society at large. The result includes intense personal suffering, high crime rates, a rise in substance abuse,

suicidality, relational problems, general occupational underachievement, and intergenerational transmission of childhood traumatization.

213. There is thus a profound need to reconsider the way in which children are raised as well as reconsider the all too often unchecked rights of parents regarding their children.
214. Such reconsideration will trigger an ongoing societal discussion as well as high levels of action tendencies, which in turn demands high levels of social communication. Solutions cannot be found at the mere corporate level of consciousness.
215. The populace should demand this discussion and engage in it. Governments should foster and enable it, and take serious and lasting heed of its common results.
216. The discussion should reflect the fact that, according to the principles of democracy, any one power needs to be controlled by another power.
217. Self-centered natural rights of individuals and self-centered societal interests run parallel: Social cooperation and open communication lie in the best interest of each individual and of all of society. But there is also a difference: Social relations go beyond the individual, but there is no social system beyond human societies. Societies are thus challenged to oblige themselves to counter the drama of chronic childhood traumatization. One way to do this is to formulate and pass proper laws that – in negative terms – forbids society and its citizens to ignore or emotionally control the problem. Positively speaking, this law should obligate society to permanently acknowledge and counter chronic childhood traumatization.
218. This said, it is important to realize that societies are made up of human beings, and that "the world is a dangerous place, not because of the people who are evil, but because of the people who don't do anything about it" (Albert Einstein).
219. Because "[t]he evil that is in the world almost always comes from ignorance ..." (Albert Camus), the first action of good people is to turn their ignorance of pain into knowledge.
220. The second and far more difficult action is for good people to realize the implications of that knowledge.
221. Realizing the existence and implications of child abuse and neglect is an extremely demanding and long-lasting action.
222. To quote Spinoza: Excellent actions are as difficult as they are rare.

Appendix 1

Some Notes on the Efficacy of Enactive Trauma Therapy

'Dissociation,' dissociative disorders, and the treatment of these conditions are starting to attract more attention in the trauma field. This is certainly a useful and significant-good development. But there is also a harmful and significant-bad issue that hinders the field, though the problem and its ramifications presently have not warranted full recognition. Instead, they are basically ignored or in any case insufficiently realized.

Defining and Using the Concept of 'Dissociation' in Contradictory Ways

The difficulty lies in a fundamental and ongoing confusion with regard to the domain of 'dissociation.' In some regards today the construct is defined in overly broad and in other regards in overly restrictive ways (see ToT, Volumes I and II, particularly Chapter 13 and 14). This creates ongoing confusion of tongues.

For example, many studies on PTSD have now discovered that individuals who 'dissociate' can have a different reaction to PTSD treatment than individuals who do not 'dissociate.' In these studies, dissociation is not comprehended as a division of the personality, but merely captures depersonalization and derealization. These negative symptoms may, but certainly need not, be associated with a division of the personality into two or more conscious (sub)systems. Examples include Bae, Kim, and Park (2016), Bennett, Modrowski, Kerig, and Chaplo (2015), Halvorsen, Stenmark, Neuner, and Nordahl (2014), Van Minnen, Zoellner, Harned, and Mills (2015), and Wolf, Lunney, and Schnurr (2016).

A *minimum* requirement of conceptualizations and theories is that they be *internally consistent*. Concepts and theories should not include or imply contradictions, or else they become useless-insignificant. However, lack of internal consistency and its implied contradictions exist with regard to the most definitions and applications of 'dissociation' (see Nijenhuis, 2014b, 2015a, 2015b, 2015c). For example, either one recognizes the existence of negative and positive dissociative symptoms, or one delimits the domain of dissociative symptoms to negative or positive dissociative symptoms. But one cannot constrain the domain to negative dissociative symptoms in some instances (evidently implying the exclusion of positive dissociative symptoms) and include positive dissociative symptoms in other instances. Doing so implies internal inconsistency, which basically puts an end to any concept. DSM-5 distinguishes between a dissociative subtype of PTSD and a classic form of PTSD. The latter involves recurrent hyperaroused reenactments of traumatic memories, not commonly leading to the integration of the involved sensorimotor and affect-laden experiences. The classic form would not be dissociative. However, at other places the DSM-5 states that there are positive dissociative symptoms. The involved conceptual internal inconsistency is not unique to DSM-5, but can be observed in the general field of trauma.

Dissociative Disorders Require a Specific Kind of Treatment

Keeping these conceptual problems regarding the conceptual domains of dissociation and dissociative disorders in mind, it can be said that complex dissociative disorders including DID are valid and quite prevalent disorders amenable to psychotherapy (Dorahy et al., 2014). Collective clinical expertise now exists in the form of treatment guidelines (International Society for the Study of Trauma and Dissociation, 2011). Several experts have detailed their extensive clinical experiences in articles, chapters, and books. While their approaches differ in some regards, the commonalities outweigh their differences. All recommend a phase-oriented integrative approach that includes working with the dissociative parts of the personality, and all report this treatment and its treatment components to be generally effective (e.g., Boon, Steele, Van der Hart, 2011; Chefetz, 2015; Chu, 1998; Ellason & Ross, 1997; Courtois & Ford, 2009; Howell, 2005; Huber, 1995, 2003; Kluft, 1984a, 1996, 2013; Pearlman & Courtois, 2005; Putnam, 1989, 1992, 1993, 1997; Ross, 1989, 1997; Van der Hart et al., 2006). This phasic approach essentially dates back to the work of 19th-century pioneers and to the brilliance of Pierre Janet in particular.

As reviewed in ToT, Volume I, Chapter 6, and Volume II, Chapter 15, research findings are consonant (and hence supportive) of these collective experiences. For example, we are beginning to receive confirmation that patients with these disorders have a suboptimal response to standard exposure-based treatments for PTSD, resulting in high levels of attrition from this kind of treatment (Brand, Lanius, Vermetten, Loewenstein, & Spiegel, 2012). Vice versa, several naturalistic studies and open trials show that it pays to specifically address the patients' trauma-based dissociative phenomena. Patients who received this treatment start to function better, and their dissociative symptoms become reduced (Brand et al., 2012).

Emerging scientific work is now confirming clinical expertise that a phase-oriented integration-focused approach to treatment is generally helpful (Brand, Classen, McNary, & Zaveri, 2009b; Brand & Stadnik, 2013; Brand et al., 2012; Brand, Loewenstein, & Spiegel, 2014; Myrick et al., 2012; Myrick, Brand, & Putnam, 2013). This approach to the treatment of complex dissociative disorders generates pre/post effect sizes that are comparable to pre/post effect sizes in treatment studies of complex PTSD (Brand et al., 2009a, 2009b). It generally leads to decreased symptoms of dissociation, depression, PTSD, distress, suicidality, and self-mutilation. Using a prospective, naturalistic design, Brand and Stadnik (2013) found that a reduction in dissociative symptoms in patients with complex dissociative disorders was related to a decrease in the overall severity of posttraumatic stress and distress symptoms. Controlled for the length of time for follow-up, the length of time practicing therapy, and the length of time treating dissociative patients, initial severity of dissociation predicted change in dissociative symptoms at 30 months. Other studies also suggest that the severity of dissociative symptoms, including sensorimotor dissociative symptoms is negatively associated with treatment outcome (Jepsen, Langeland, & Heir, 2014).

Research also confirms the general clinical experience that young adults generally improve faster than older adults (Myrick et al., 2012), as do those with less initial dissociative symptoms and other pathological alterations of consciousness (Brand & Stadnik, 2013), fewer current stressors, and less revictimization (Myrick et al., 2013). Revictimization tended to decrease over the 30 months in Myrick et al.'s (2013) study.

Useful (Significant-Good) and Harmful (Significant-Bad) or Useless (Insignificant) Treatment of Complex Dissociative Disorders

The prospective *Treatment of Patients with Dissociative Disorders (TOP DD) Study* (Brand & Loewenstein, 2014) documents positive effects from an integrative trauma treatment that includes therapeutic engagement with dissociative parts of the personality. This treatment is associated with a decrease in dissociative symptoms and phenomena.

The findings of the study fully contrast with the predictions of the iatrogenic model of DID (ToT Volume II, Chapter 15). Because severe symptomatology and impairment are associated with DID, iatrogenic harm may come from depriving DID patients of treatment that targets DID symptomatology. There is no clinical evidence or research demonstrating that dismissing the diagnosis, or ignoring or rejecting dissociative parts of the personality, is in any way therapeutic. Many patients, including Ineke, Martha, and Sonja in this volume experienced and reported that this diagnostic flaw and treatment actually only makes matters worse. Reviewing the literature on DID treatment, Brand et al. (2014) found that poor outcome is related to treatment that does not include direct engagement with dissociative parts of the personality. In contrast, phase-oriented, trauma-focused psychotherapy for DID is associated with significant-good and useful improvements.

Further, claims that DID treatment is harmful are based on anecdotal cases, opinion pieces, and reports of damage that are not substantiated in the scientific literature. These claims are also grounded in misrepresentations of the data as well as misunderstandings about DID treatment and the phenomenology of DID. The findings lead Brand et al. (2014, p. 169) to warn that "[g]iven the severe symptomatology and disability associated with DID, iatrogenic harm is far more likely to come from depriving DID patients of treatment that is consistent with expert consensus, treatment guidelines, and current research."

Community Therapists and Expert Therapists of Complex Dissociative Disorders: What Do They Do?

A recent study showed that community therapists of individuals with CDID and DID tend to apply several interventions that expert therapists recommend (Myrick, Chasson, Lanius, Leventhal, & Brand, 2015). These include helping patients to handle strong affects and dissociation-focused interventions. However, experts focus more on relational interventions, education, grounding and containment skills, and stabilizing patients after re-victimization by alleged perpetrators. Enactive trauma therapy includes all of these.

Clinicians working with chronically traumatized and highly dissociative patients should realize the impact of the therapeutic alliance (Cronin, Brand, & Mattanah, 2014) as well as the importance of the patients' first-person and second-person perspectives. Patient-rated therapeutic alliance predicted better treatment outcomes, and predicted these results better than therapist-ratings of the therapeutic alliance (Cronin et al., 2014). Further, the effect sizes regarding developing and maintaining a strong therapeutic alliance were stronger for patients with CDID and DID than the effect sizes regarding these variables found for many other patient groups.

Controlled Group Comparison Outcome Studies and Their Limitations

There are no randomized controlled clinical trials (RCT) or less stringent controlled clinical trials of phase-oriented treatment of complex dissociative disorders, let alone of the present more specifically enactive approach. Does this mean that this approach to trauma therapy is not evidence based and therefore unscientific? Several issues deserve consideration.

RCTs and less stringent groupwise treatment efficacy studies are clearly worthwhile. But they also include serious limitations. One restriction is that their results involve averaged group scores that may mask differences between patients. Further, established effects need not also be clinically relevant changes. The trials are further generally quite time-limited and focus on a limited set of variables. However, the treatment of complex cases generally demands a long-term approach and includes a host of variables that may affect change. For example, the treatment of individuals with DID takes on average 8 years. These circumstances practically exclude the possibility of controlled studies of the full treatment, evidently including RCTs.

Moreover, patients with complex dissociative disorders are commonly excluded from RCTs and other controlled groupwise treatment efficacy studies. This particularly applies to dissociative patients who are recurrently suicidal, psychotic, or occasionally psychotic, or patients who severely mutilate themselves. In all trials I am aware of, complex dissociative disorders are nowhere considered as a differential *main* diagnosis, if a differential diagnosis at all. Inasmuch as 'dissociation' is considered, it is quite often seen as (co-morbid) symptoms. Moreover, in these cases 'dissociation' tends to be defined (if it is defined at all) as lowering the level of consciousness and retraction of the field of consciousness. Quite often the term only stands for depersonalization and derealization (two phenomena that are not specific to dissociative disorders). In these studies 'dissociation' is not comprehended as positive symptoms nor as a structural, dynamic, phenomenological, and teleological dissociation of the personality.

Single-Case Studies

Repeated single-case studies need not be any less scientific than randomized clinical trials (Schubert, 2011). This particularly applies when multiple-case studies are compared to one another (Yin, 2003). *They may, in fact, constitute the only way to evaluate the efficacy of assessment and treatment strategies and interventions in complex clinical situations.*

There is another important reason why carefully executed multiple-case studies can be most helpful. As Lazarus (1991, p. 29) explains, "[t]he basic arena of analysis for the study of emotion process is the person-environment relationship. The basic unit of this relationship is an adaptational encounter or episode." Whatever actions and passions a clinician may engage in, they will only be significant to a patient inasmuch as the patient perceives, hence experiences and understands them, and regards them as useful or harmful (cf. Schubert, 2011, p. 363). Only when these conditions are fulfilled can the actions and passions of clinicians potentially affect their patients' further actions and passions. If and to what degree the actions and passions of clinicians influence their patients also depends on the degree to which patients remain in a stable systemic state, and how willing and open they are to develop new actions (e.g., Clarkin & Levy, 2003; Grawe, 2004). The actions and passions of a clinician do not or hardly perturb (i.e., affect, destabilize) the patient as a whole system or a dissociative subsystem of the patient when the patient's systemic stability is high, and when his or her motivation for change is low. But the less stable systemic stability of the whole patient or a dissociative part is, and the higher the patient's need and desire to achieve change, the more the clinician's action may influence the patient. This influence is clearly also dependent on the degree to which the clinician's actions meet the goals that the patient strives to achieve. The more the patient and the clinician strive for a common goal, the more effective the clinician's interventions tend to be.

There is indeed mounting evidence that change is related to systemic instability (e.g., Schiepek, 2011; Schubert, 2011). Personality disorders involve high systemic stability and count as unfavorable predictors of therapeutic change, particularly when the patient's personal and interpersonal competencies are low. Further, there can be therapeutic changes that *precede* the application of therapeutic techniques such as 'exposure' or 'cognitive restructuring' of 'irrational beliefs.' These so-called 'sudden changes' or 'early rapid responses to treatment interventions' have been clinically observed as well as documented in single-case studies (e.g., Goodridge & Hardy, 2009; Haas, Hill, Lambert, & Morell, 2002; Hayes & Strauss, 1998; Ilardi & Craighead, 1994; Lambert, 2005; Lutz, Bachmann, Tschitsaz, Smart, & Lambert, 2007; Lutz et al., 2013; Schiepek, 2011; Wilson, 1998).

In a considerable number of cases sudden gains and sudden losses in psychotherapy, including trauma therapy, suggest that change may be a nonlinear systemic development (Aderka, Appelbaum-Namdar, Shafran, & Gilboa-Schechtman, 2011; Doane, Feeny & Zoellner, 2010; Kelly, Rizvi, Monson, & Resick, 2009; Konig, Karl, Rosner, & Butollo, 2014; Kruger et al., 2014; Lutz et al., 2013). Scientists and clinicians may be tempted to ascribe these effects to the application of specific interventions. However, meta-analyses suggest that specific treatment interventions do not explain more than 1% to 15% of the variance of treatment outcome (e.g., Lambert & Ogles, 2004). Further, several time-series analysis in single-case studies have demonstrated that therapeutic changes (such as symptom reduction) may actually *precede* specific interventions such as 'exposure.' In these studies, the changes relate rather to systemic destabilization, motivation to achieve change, the quality of the patient-clinician relationship, the clinician's attunement to the patient, the creation of hope that change is within reach, and other 'nonspecific' treatment factors. Sudden changes preceding specific treatment interventions and treatment outcome variance that seem attributable to 'nonspecific' treatment factors are consistent with the idea that therapeutic change may involve systemic self-reorganization of the patient as an organism-environment system.

Multiple Cases Studies of the Treatment of Complex Dissociative Disorders

There are no 'evidence-based' treatment protocols available for the problems individuals with complex forms of psychopathology present: There is no evidence from RCT's or other controlled studies. And in light of the above, it is rather unlikely that such evidence can be generated at all (I am not talking about the effects of specific interventions). So what should clinicians do? When there is no path to follow, they must be inventive (Chapter 30). This does not mean they are clueless. There are reasonable theories and years of clinical expertise to guide them. Further, positive outcomes of a particular path in one case can usefully inspire the approach in a similar case. The treatment of Martha's recurrent loss of consciousness was strongly inspired by previous results in other cases (Chapter 33).

Taken together, the above considerations call for multiple-case studies of the treatment of complex dissociative disorders. Experts have in fact developed their understanding and treatment of complex dissociative disorders more or less on this basis. Their work lacked scientific precision, no doubt, but it was not unsystematic either. And it involved a major amount of solid clinical evidence. If I am permitted to use my own case, a rough estimate reveals that I have worked with complex dissociative patients for more than 30,000 hours in the last 33 years, and that I have coached colleagues in numerous hours as well. My clinical actions did not involve trial and error, but comprised ongoing and systematic reflection at the level of each separate patient and of traumatized patients in general. I also worked to incorporate the expertise of leaders in the field as well as lessons from evolving biopsychosocial research. In the large majority of cases, the harvest was rich. The health that Agnes, Ineke, Martha, and Sonja achieved was not exceptional.

The degree of reflection and systematic actions involved does not fully meet the ambitions of a trauma treatment that wants to be both clinically wise and scientifically supported. It does not exhaust the options either. The ongoing work on the methodology of multiple-case studies can be well applied to the phase-oriented treatment of complex dissociative disorders and to enactive trauma therapy as a specific version of this general approach.

Appendix 2

The Need for and the Utility of Minimal Constraints on the Concept of Dissociative Parts

Ross[1] (2014a) feels that the theory of structural dissociation of the personality (TSDP) includes several unresolved problems. In his view, one of these is that minimal constraints on the concept of dissociative parts are irrelevant. He does not see the "logical, philosophical or theoretical necessity of setting a threshold" (p. 287). Nor does he see the "clinical utility" (p. 287). Ross wonders (p. 287) "[w]hy can't some dissociated compartments hold full EPs or ANPs, some partial or near-threshold EPs, and others just a memory without there being a full EP?" Considering that the concept of dissociative parts of the personality is a core feature of TSDP, it seems important to provide a substantial part of my rejoinder (Nijenhuis, 2015c) here:

A quick initial answer to Ross' point of view is that judging the degree to which some structure qualifies as a full, partial, or rudimentary ANP or EP is possible only when the core features of prototypical ANPs and EPs have been identified and defined. Without these characterizations and formulations, judging the degree to which a subsystem of an individual's personality qualifies as a particular prototypical part of the personality is impossible.

Before turning to the minimal constraints on the concept of dissociative parts, let me discuss the general need for constraints on concepts.

Concepts are Artificial Constructs

To begin with, no concept exists separately from knowing individuals. Any concept out there is necessarily a human, and hence an artificial, construction. Nature can be parsed in countless ways, but all parsing is relevant to a particular human interest, and a particular parsing can be more or less helpful to achieving a set goal (Braude, 1995; Spinoza, 1677a; Wittgenstein, 1953). For example, there are no naturally given distinctions between what is and what is not a 'game' (Wittgenstein, 1953) or how one comprehends the word 'man.' As Spinoza (1677a, p. 56) observes,

1 The complete article (Nijenhuis, 2015c) is available at www.enijenhuis.nl

> ... notions are not formed by all [men] in the same way, but vary from one to another, in accordance with what the body has more often been affected by, and what the mind imagines or recollects more easily. For example, those who have more often regarded men's stature with wonder will understand by the word man an animal of erect stature. But those who have been accustomed to consider something else, will form another common image of men – for example, that man is an animal capable of laughter, or a featherless biped, or a rational animal.

Along a dimension of temperature, H2O can be experienced and conceptualized as ice or snow, water, and water vapor, but the boundaries between these different concepts are fuzzy. We have no difficulty experiencing and knowing H2O at a temperature of -10 °C as ice (hard matter), and H2O at a temperature of + 10 °C as water (fluid), but we can have difficulty saying whether there is watery ice or icy water at temperatures around 0 °C. Similar problems regarding H2O include the boundaries of the concepts of rain, drizzle, fog, and damp. And there are many different kinds of snow and ice. Further, we are able to distinguish between delicate shades of a color as we perceive them, but we may not (be able to) have clear concepts of, say, blue 'shade 1003' and blue 'shade 1004.' That is, we cannot precisely differentiate and think about these shades of blue in the absence of their physical appearance.

These examples may suffice to indicate that the difficulty of defining a sharp lower bound of the concept of dissociative parts of the personality is not a weakness in the TSDP. Rather, boundary problems pertain to any concept, to any theoretical construct that aims to capture natural phenomena and positions on a quantitative continuum. Quantitative dimensions tend to include boundary problems between nearby yet different prototypes (Rosch, 1977). Further, quantitative differences can imply qualitative shifts, including shifts that are of practical, clinical, theoretical, scientific, or other relevance. It is often useful, and sometimes even life-saving, to distinguish between these different qualities. Any car driver would prefer to know whether a road is dry, wet, or frozen, or realize how near cold rain can be to becoming a glaze.

Unbounded and overgeneralized concepts are necessarily indistinct, blurry, and vague. For example, a term such as 'thing' can stand for practically any object, the term 'one' covers all individuals, and the term 'they' is sometimes used in a similar way in spoken language (e.g., "Give me that thing," "One should be modest," and in reference to an indistinct group of individuals such as a peoples at large "They cannot be trusted"). Such unbounded and overgeneralized words are theoretically, clinically, and scientifically useless. Solid theoretical, clinical, and scientific terms and concepts should thus be as clear and distinct as possible, and they should fit their intended use. The concepts of dissociation, dissociative part, and dissociative disorder are no exceptions to these requirements.

Ross (2013, 2014a), as well as Schimmenti and Caretti (2014)[2], feel that dissociation is a core feature of many mental disorders – or, in any case, of far more disorders than are

2 Schimmenti and Caretti's comments on my article "Ten Reasons for Conceiving and Classifying Posttraumatic Stress Disorder as a Dissociative Disorder" is also available at www.enijenhuis.nl

judged to be dissociative in DSM-IV, ICD-10, or TSDP. Unless they would mean that any mental disorder essentially involves a dissociation of the personality – in which case the term dissociation is basically a synonym for the term psychopathology – they too will need to set a boundary on the(ir) concepts of dissociation, dissociative part of the personality, and dissociative disorder. My discussants may prefer more liberal concepts than the ones TSDP proposes, but their versions need boundaries just the same. Without clear and bounded concepts of dissociation, dissociative parts, and dissociative disorders, we cannot assess what phenomena count as instances of these phenomena and constructs. For example, without this clarity, it is impossible to judge with any reasonable precision which individuals have a dissociative disorder, which are false positives, or which have some other (nondissociative) mental disorder, or what structures count as a dissociative part, what structure includes some but not all core features of a dissociative part, and what structures do not constitute a dissociative part at all.

Integrative Limitations

The concept of integrative limitations requires a clear and distinct concept of integration. Merriam-Webster Online defines integration as "the combining and coordinating of separate parts or elements into a unified whole." Perfect integration pertains to Nature as a whole, or, if one prefers, to God. As Spinoza put it, "[a] substance which is absolutely infinite is indivisible" (1677a, Part I, Propositions 13; see also Proposition 12). Even mentally very healthy human beings fall seriously short of this excellence. Integrative limitations are, in fact, ubiquitous and manifold in mental health and psychopathology. To single out one integrative challenge, like individuals with a mental disorder, mentally healthy individuals experience ambivalences, or rather 'polyvalences.' We all struggle with different interests at times: "Shall I postpone this tedious assignment, or shall I do it right now to get it over with? Shall I enjoy another glass of wine or mind my responsibilities as a driver? Shall I marry someone, postpone my decision, or just stay single?" These common integrative problems can often be comprehended in terms of conflicts between different desires or responsibilities, as conflicts between different wills or duties. As applies to any integrative problem, the recognition and fulfillment of one particular will (i.e., one 'element') does not annihilate the existence of one or more different wills (i.e., other 'elements').

Integrative problems such as conflicts between various wills become more intense and elaborate in mental disorders. Often one has become unduly and chronically dominant. For example, agoraphobia involves a conflict between the defense action system ("It is dangerous to be in the street, I'd better stay at home") and some other action systems such as exploration ("It is interesting to buy fashionable clothes, mine have become outdated and worn"), social engagement ("It is fun to meet friends in a bar") and play ("It would be great to attend a live performance of the Concertgebouw Orchestra," or "I would love to play tennis today"). In agoraphobia the defense system wins at the expense of the interests of other action systems, as it does in several other mental disorders (e.g., obsessive-compulsive disorder, anorexia, avoidant personality disorder).

Conflicts of will also characterize what some call 'ego-states' and 'ego-state disorders' (e.g., Phillips, 1993; Phillips & Frederick, 1995; Watkins & Watkins, 1997) as well as what Kellogg and Young (2006) call different 'modi.' An ego-state is defined as "an organized system of behavior and experience whose elements are bound together by some common principle" (Watkins, 1991, p. 233). This formulation is so broad that it is hard to imagine what behavioral and mental state would *not* count as an ego-state. For example, one may wonder what distinguishes an outspoken mood from an ego-state. Further, it is not clear if, or in what sense, ego-states and modi are different, and what their respective conceptual lower and upper bounds are. Modi, thus, stretch from innate and universal to dissociative parts in DID. Individuals with bipolar mood disorder also display a lack of integration. They shift between different ways of being that involve not just different moods, but also shifts in will that do not become integrated. Being euphoric, they do not or insufficiently integrate their previous existence as a deeply depressed individual; being depressed, they lose their elated existence.

Whereas common and many pathological conflicts involve integrative problems, regarding any conflict as an instance of dissociation would generate a huge as well as indistinct category. If the term 'dissociation' were to stand for any lack of integration, it would be most unclear what phenomenon or construct a clinician, scientist, or theoretician has in mind when he or she says that "John dissociates," "Jane is dissociated," "dissociation is a mental defense," etc. Equating any kind of integrative problem/deficit and dissociation would miss important phenomenological, theoretical, clinical, and empirical differences between, on the one hand, common or more pathological conflicts, mood swings, modi, and ego-states, and, on the other hand, dissociation of the personality involving two or more dissociative parts, each with their own phenomenal conceptions of self, world, and self-of-the-world.

Because there are important phenomenal, theoretical, clinical and scientific/empirical differences between dissociative parts of the personality and other human integrative limitations or imperfections, making these distinctions serves phenomenological, theoretical, clinical, and scientific/empirical interests.

Phenomenological Interests

Experiencing a conflict between two wills that an individual regards as his or her own is phenomenologically very different from experiencing a conflict between an ANP and a fragile EP or between a fragile EP and a controlling EP – or being flooded by feelings, thoughts, images, or behaviors that stem from one or more dissociative parts than the engulfed dissociative part is now aware of. At best dissociative parts relate to each other in a second-person perspective (e.g., I [ANP] – You [fragile EP]). But they may also, unilaterally or bilaterally, relate to each other in third-person perspective (e.g., I [ANP] – a screaming voice [fragile EP's voice]). They may not relate to each other at all (e.g., an ANP that is not aware of the existence of a fragile EP, whereas this EP may or may not be unaware of ANP). The latter condition involves, so to speak, a zero-person perspective (e.g., ANP-?). For example, an ANP may experience major gaps in time without a clue as to what happened during this episode, and why.

Clinical Interests

Clinically, the existence of a dissociation of the personality implies particular symptoms. These symptoms are dissociative symptoms, because they are manifestations of the existence of this particular organization of the personality. This organization and these dissociative symptoms require clinical interventions that do not fit common ambivalences, mood disorders, mood shifts, modi, ego-states, or would-be dissociative parts in false-positive cases of dissociative disorder. Given the clinical interest of fostering integrative actions, clinicians are ill advised to regard and treat all kinds of integrative problems or deficits as a dissociation of the personality, as something that implies the existence of dissociative parts. Failure to distinguish between ubiquitous conflicts, mood shifts, modi and the like, and dissociative parts that per our definition include their own phenomenal conceptions of self, world, and self-of-the-world has more than once resulted in ineffective, if not bad therapy. For example, treating an individual with borderline personality disorder as if he or she were a case of dissociative identity disorder tends to obstruct rather than foster integrative actions.

Scientific/Empirical Interests

The distinction between dissociative parts and conflicts, mood shifts, modi, and ego-states is also of scientific interest. For example, TSDP holds that individuals experiencing common intrapersonal conflicts and individuals encompassing two or more dissociative parts of the personality have different patterns of brain activity. To test this hypothesis, scientists must know which individuals do and do not encompass dissociative parts (i.e., prototypical parts such as an ANP, a hyperaroused fragile EP engaging in flight and freezing, a fragile, hypoaroused EP engaging in tonic immobility). They must also have a clinical and theoretical idea of the biopsychosocial features of each of these prototypical dissociative parts. Further they must know how various dissociative parts and individuals who are or may be involved in common or pathological intrapersonal conflicts but who do not encompass such dissociative parts are different in at least some crucial regards. Equipped with this knowledge, we have been able to study the features of authentic ANPs and fragile, hyperaroused EPs, and we have succeeded in showing that mentally healthy individuals as well as actors and high and low fantasy-prone individuals, have very different supraliminal and subliminal reactions to particular experimental stimuli (e.g., trauma scripts, neutral and angry facial expressions). Another example is that, according to TSDP, dissociative parts and manifestations of dissociative parts (i.e., dissociative symptoms) are bound to have different correlates and causes than phenomena such as absorption, imaginative involvement, a retracted field of consciousness, and low levels of consciousness. If the term "dissociation" captures any integrative problem or deficit, it is practically impossible to say what hypotheses or statements like "dissociation is correlated with adverse events" or "dissociation is caused by adverse events" actually mean.

Empirically speaking, dissociative symptoms – i.e., symptoms of the existence of a dissociation of the personality – are characteristic of individuals with a dissociative disorder, but not of individuals with a mental disorder that does not involve a dissociation of the personality as defined in TSDP (Van der Hart et al., 2006), and as formulated by Nijenhuis and Van der Hart (2011a, 2011b). For example, bipolar mood disorder is not associated with sensorimotor dissociative symptoms (Nijenhuis et al., 1997, 1999); it demands a different kind of treatment than dissociative disorders. Borderline personality disorder that is not comorbid with a dissociative disorder (Korzekwa, Dell, Links, Thabane, & Fougere, 2009), restrictive anorexia (Waller et al., 2003), major depressive episode (Sar, Kundakci, Kiziltan, Bakim, & Bozkurt, 2000), and anxiety disorders (Nijenhuis et al., 1996, Sar et al., 2000) are not associated with significant somatoform dissociative symptoms either.

These few examples may suffice to demonstrate that there are important phenomenal, theoretical, clinical, and scientific/empirical differences between dissociative parts of the personality and other human integrative limitations. This proposition raises the following question: In what way or ways the concepts of dissociation, dissociative symptoms, dissociative parts, and dissociative disorders can be discriminated from other integrative limitations? According to our definition of dissociation (Nijenhuis & Van der Hart 2011a, 2011b; Nijenhuis 2015a, 2015b) and TSDP (Van der Hart et al., 2006), ambivalences, polyvalences, mood shifts, modi, and ego-states do not qualify as dissociative parts of an individual's personality. Hence, their existence does not justify the classification of individuals with these integrative limitations as bona fide cases of dissociative disorder. Individuals who experience and display these phenomena (e.g., common conflicts or mood shifts), however, still personify their different ways of being, that is, they still link them with, and embed them in, an overarching phenomenal conception of self, world, and self-as-a-part-of-the-world. For example, although different ego-states and modi are conscious and self-conscious structures, and although they can include considerable shifts in the individual's conception of self, world, and this self-as-a-part-of-that-world, the whole organism-environment system that comprises the individual still associates these different conceptions to one overarching conception of self (e.g., "I am John"). As one of his ego-states, John thus may want to continue smoking, but as a different ego-state he wants to quit this addiction. But John regards both states as his own. They are both part of his identity, even if he may not welcome his different states and the wishes, feelings, thoughts, wills, and actions these states include.

In contrast to Ross, Schimmenti and Caretti, I thus hold that different kinds and different degrees of integrative deficiency constitute quantitatively and qualitatively different phenomena. That said, it is valuable to recognize that conceptual distinctions between prototypical dissociative parts of the personality and other structures such as different moods, modi, and ego-states do not exclude the existence of particular commonalities and similarities between them. This overlap can be an inspiration to apply some of the insights with respect to dissociative parts to these other structures. In this vein, I have described that with respect to chronic childhood abuse, maltreatment, and neglect perpetrators, their partners in crime (e.g., family members who are aware of the ongoing traumatization), psychologists, psychiatrists, and people at large can function in alternating ways that can be described as apparently normal, fragile emotional, and controlling emotional (ToT, Volume II, Chapter 20). For example, perpetrators such as child abusers can present themselves and be seen by others as normal. However, their normality is only apparent; hence, they act in an ANP-like way of being and functioning. When abusing a child, they are clearly emotional controlling (controlling EP-like), and when accused of abusing the child, they act as if they were the victim, functioning in a fragile EP-like mode.[3] In some regards, it may be worthwhile to describe and comprehend Young's modi and ego-states in terms of ANP-like, fragile EP-like, and controlling EP-like ways of being and functioning. However, it is confusing to address individuals or groups of individuals who do not meet the full criteria of dissociative parts and who do not have a dissociative disorder as 'ANP,' 'fragile EP,' or 'controlling EP.' The point is that there are not just a few commonalities between dissociative part-like ways of being and functioning and real dissociative parts, but also *significant differences*. Overestimating the commonalities and underestimating the differences necessarily has serious clinical, theoretical, and empirical consequences.

Dissociative Parts and Minimal Constraints on Consciousness

Having detailed that worthwhile concepts imply artificial boundaries, that conceptual boundaries are relative to their intended use, and that there are differences between dissociation/dissociative parts and other kinds of integrative limitations or deficits, I now turn to Ross' question regarding the boundaries of dissociative parts in TSDP. Dissociative parts in TSDP are defined as conscious subsystems of an individual's personality. This feature distinguishes these subsystems from other subsystems that make up an individual, and that may not be well integrated. For example, an individual's personality as a whole organism-envi-

3 If their personality is dissociated, perpetrators or other individuals such as their partners in crime clearly do not function in ANP-like and EP-like ways of being, but include actual ANPs and EPs.

ronment system encompasses a host of subsystems such as cells, synapses, neural networks, organs, the blood circulation system, the sympathetic nervous system, the ventral vagal parasympathetic system, the dorsal vagal parasympathetic nervous system, etc.

To illustrate the idea of a rudimentary EP, here is a short description of Rita (pseudonym), a young woman with recurrent nightmares and related dissociative episodes. She said: "I do not have a clue as to what the nightmares are about. When I have them, I'm terribly scared, but don't know why. Something is coming at me, something bangs against my head, and it feels as if I'm about to die. The last thing I know is that my body rises and screams. Then I find myself back in the living or in the streets. My friend tells me I then rush out of the bed, bump against the furniture, and stumble down the stairs. I'm not aware of what I'm doing, but eventually find myself back in the living room or sometimes even in the street." Fearing the nightmares, Rita had developed a phobia of sleep and major sleep deprivation, which exhausted her and made her constantly irritated: She lost her job. Apart from being deadly tired and irritated, Rita also met the criteria for depersonalization disorder. We decided to examine what or who was scream, rushing out of the bed, running down the stairs – who was controlling her body and behavior during the nightly episodes. Since whatever or whomever it was had taken full control over her consciousness and behavior, 'it' might react to Rita's and my questions using particular fingers or thumbs as signals for 'Yes,' 'No,' 'Stop,' and 'Don't know.' It appeared that 'it' was a single fragile EP that regarded herself as 3 years old. As ANP, Rita knew she had experienced a car accident when she was 3 years old. However, she did not feel that this incident was associated with her nightmares at all (see Nijenhuis, 2015a). But it was. As this EP, Rita seemed hardly, if at all, aware that during the nightly dissociative episodes she was reexperiencing and reenacting the accident. The EP's phenomenal conception of self, world, and self-as-a-part-of-the-world were focused on this one traumatizing event. Her experiences and conceptions did not include much more than experiences and ideas of being a child playing with a ball, of noticing that a car is coming at her, of being utterly scared, of falling, of receiving a blow against her head, of hurting, of the world turning dark. As this EP, Rita was not in touch with her other existence as ANP – or else she would have experienced and known that she had in fact survived the accident, that she had grown to become an adult, etc. As the depersonalized ANP she initially resisted integrating "the child" and the accident in which this EP was stuck. Once this EP and the ANP's mental avoidance and hate of the EP and the traumatic experience in which this EP was fixed had been detected, it appeared that the patient had PTSD (a constellation of negative and positive dissociative symptoms in proximate association with a nonintegrated and recurrently reenacted traumatizing event).

Since, according to TSDP, the lower boundary of the concept of dissociative parts is that they are conscious structures, determining rudimentary and more evolved dissociative parts calls for formulating the minimal constraints on the concept of consciousness. In this regard, I follow Metzinger's (2003) idea that the limits are global availability, phenomenal now, and transparency.

- *Global Availability:* There is a World. From a phenomenological perspective, the concept of global availability involves the notion that the contents of states of consciousness do not stand alone, but are found and integrated into a single phenomenal world. It consists of at least several connected but differentiated components that are unified in a whole. A conceived world, in this sense, involves a highest-order situational context in which the individual embeds the phenomenal contents of his or her different conscious states. The contents of these states can be globally available to them in a variety of ways. A somewhat crude classification is that the involved contents can be globally available for guided attention, cognitive reference, and control of behavioral action. In some cases, phenomenal contents exist less in the form of explicit phenomenal concepts (i.e., as contents one can think and categorize) than as phenomenal presentata, that is, as experiences.
  Dissociative parts meet this criterion. They live in a world they experience and conceive, and they embed their experiences and conceptions in this global, highest-order frame. For example, Rita's fragile EP experienced and knew herself as a particular child, as a girl, as her parent's daughter, as someone living in a particular house. She knew what balls and cars are, what playing is like. She experienced and knew that she was playing, that cars can be dangerous objects, and that a particular car approached her, overtook her, and hit her. She also experienced intense fear and pain with respect to these events. The fragile EP also experienced and knew that the accident was an inherent part of her life.
- *Phenomenal Now:* This World is Now. Whatever we experience, we experience it *now*. This now is not some formal now or a now shared among different individuals. Rather, it constitutes our subjectively experienced present, our phenomenal now. The phenomenal now generally encompasses a couple of seconds, and it may be displaced in 'objective' (clock) time. Clinical observations strongly suggest that all dissociative parts of the personality experience their living in a present, and that all naively believe that their sense of the present – their phenomenal now – is equal to the actual now. For example, during her reenactments, the fragile EP presented above lived the phenomenal now of the accident. Her very limited existence beyond the accident also included a phenomenal now, such as experiencing that she was talking (with finger signals) with another person (i.e., with me as the clinician who invited her to respond to simple questions with finger signals for 'Yes,' 'No,' 'Don't know,' and 'Stop').
- *Phenomenal Presentata:* Dissociative parts sometimes merely have experiences and implicit conceptions (i.e., phenomenal presentata) when they, for adaptive reasons, would better also know explicit conceptions. This deficiency exists, for example, when they reexperience traumatizing events. Dissociative parts that are fixated in these events do not recall these events as autobiographical, narrative memories, that is, as simulations of the past. Rather, they experience and know reactivated traumatic memories as phenomenal presentata occurring in their phenomenal now. Reenactments of traumatic memories – one might also say, reactivated traumatic memories – are not like common

autobiographical memories. They are not symbolized and explicit personal narratives pertaining to phenomenal past events. They are iconic, involuntary, mostly nonverbal sensorimotor and in many cases highly affectively charged experiences that are insufficiently condensed in time (Janet, 1928a; Nijenhuis 2015a, 2015b; Van der Hart et al., 2006; Van der Kolk & Van der Hart, 1989). Some reenactments, however, do not involve hyperarousal but hypoarousal. To the degree that traumatic memories involve phenomenal presentata, they are commonly unavailable for cognitive control. This implies that dissociative parts with such memories have very little cognitive control over them. To repeat, they do not conceive of the horrific past as the past (or as having 'passed'). As they reenact their traumatic memories, they live this third-person past in the mode of their first-person present.

- *Transparency:* This World Is. Individuals do not necessarily have introspective, epistemic access to their mental actions that generate their phenomenal states, i.e., through introspection. Lack of this introspective access is known as an autoepistemic limitation. It is an absolute limitation to knowing how mental states are generated (Northoff, 2003). Somewhat counterintuitively, the autoepistemic limitation is also known as transparency (McGinn, 1989, Metzinger, 2003). Because of this transparency, conscious beings experience the world and themselves as given, real, and undoubtedly existing (Metzinger, 2003) to the degree that they are not depersonalized, perceive their environment in an unreal fashion (i.e., derealization), or emotionally or physically numb (degrees of experienced and perceived reality is also a useful constraint on the concept of consciousness and self-consciousness; see ToT, Volume I, Chapter 12). For example, as the fragile child EP that recurrently reenacted the car accident Rita undoubtedly felt: "I exist, there is a world, I am part of that world, and the world is the way I experience and conceive it."

Minimal Constraints on Self-Consciousness: Phenomenal Self-Conception and Phenomenal Conception of an Intentionality Relationship

According to Metzinger (2003), a conscious system becomes a self-conscious system when an information-processing system develops a phenomenal self-model under the transparency constraint. For a variety of reasons, I disagree that human beings 'process' (objectively existing, subject-independent) 'information.' For example, the concept of 'information' does not explain meaning, ownership, and agency (DiPaolo et al., 2010; Hutto & Myin, 2013; Nijenhuis, 2015a, 2015b; Thompson, 2007). We are not some fancy computer; we are organism-environment systems that actively and – dreamless sleeping aside – continuously make meaning and continuously create a sense of ownership and agency. Any individual, whether awake or dreaming, continuously conceives of himself or herself phenomenally, that is, creates a phenomenal conception of self (PCS) rather than modeling "something" that exists separately from him or her. We do not craft a model of ourselves as a kind of thing in itself, some model of the 'real thing' we 'actually are.' Rather, our 'I' is the one we experience and conceive we are. Without these actions, we would not phenomenally 'have' or 'be' an 'I.'

In this sense, each dissociative part of the personality generates his or her own PCS when they are awake or dreaming. The PCS of each dissociative part may have particular features in common with the PCS some other dissociative part generates, but it also differs from this other PCS in one or more crucial respects.

Individuals and dissociative parts of individuals commonly also generate a phenomenal conception of another individual or group of individuals, one or more other dissociative parts, and one or more objects, events, and, more generally, of the global world as they experience and know it. When individuals or dissociative parts of an individual who generate a PCS are also consciously aware of and relate to another subject, a group of subjects, an object, or a constellation of objects in a particular way, they can be said to engage in a phenomenal conception of an intentionality[4] relationship (PCIR), that is, of the particular way in which they relate their experience and idea of who they are with their experience and idea of what they are conscious of – and that they do not regard as a part of themselves. These are phenomenal and intentional 'I-You' and 'I-object' relationships, respectively. To the degree to which two or more dissociative parts are at least slightly consciously aware of each other, each will experience and think "I'm me, I'm not the other."

According to Metzinger (2003), we require the first-person perspective for the phenomenal experience of being someone, for controlling our actions, for becoming the object of our own attention, and for cognitive self-reference. This perspectivalness is also needed for creating a link between ourselves as a phenomenal subject and the phenomenal world. When this link exists, we can appreciate that we are acting and experiencing subjects of the world as we experience and know it. Dissociative parts meet this criterion. Their PCS and PCIR essentially encompass this perspectivalness. A dissociative part that is awake or dreaming can thus be defined as a subsystem of an organism-environment system that meets the requirements of global availability, phenomenal now, transparency, and, perspectivalness. They continuously generate their own PCS and associated set of PCIR. These involve their different person perspectives: first-person ('I,' phenomenal experience), quasi-second-person ('I-me, myself, mine' relationships involving phenomenal judgment), second-person ('I-You' phenomenal relationships), and third-person ('I-object' physical relationships).

---

4 Every mental act has a mental content, and this content pertains to a perceived and conceived 'object.' Every perception, belief, desire, etc., has an object that it is about: the perceived, the believed, the wanted (see http://en.wikipedia.org/wiki/Intentionality). This 'aboutness' is what the philosophical term 'intentionality' stands for. It stems from the Latin *intendere*, which once referred to drawing a bow and aiming at a target. As Thompson (2007) holds, in phenomenology consciousness is seen as intentional by 'aiming toward' something beyond itself.

Dissociative Parts Need Not Be Verbal

The constraints of TSDP on the concept of dissociative parts do not include the requirement that dissociative parts have their own explicit conceptions of self, world, and self-as-part-of-the world. For example, some EPs are unable to speak, articulate their identity, or tell how they differ from other dissociative parts. Their PCS and PCIR can remain nonverbal. Nonverbal perspectivalness is in itself all but abnormal, as it can also apply to mentally healthy individuals. For example, preverbal children certainly generate a PCS and PCIR, that is, a point of view involving a phenomenal subject-subject and/or subject-object relationship. Even prenatal twins seem to be focused first on their own developing body, and only later (i.e., from the 11th week of gestation on, and increasingly more between the 11th and 18th week of gestation) do they also direct their attention toward the twin brother or twin sister (Castiello et al., 2010). They also seem to relate differently to the twin and the uterine wall, which might be an early form of subject-other subject versus subject-object distinction. Our earliest memories are not cognitive, but experiential and embodied. In the words of Krueger (2010, pp. 66–70),

> ... fundamental affective structures ... scaffold basic forms of social understanding, support the emergence of sensorimotor skills enabling this basic understanding, and ... motivate our most fundamental sense of self. [Hence,]... why not speak of our earliest intersubjective engagements as involving a kind of affect-laden, but nonconceptual (i.e., nonrepresentational) understanding? ... even our earliest interactions are bathed in feeling – that is, exquisitely tuned feeling-relations that attune us to others in fundamental ways, and which provide the inter-corporeal scaffolding both supporting and motivating the growth of our capacities and competencies for social engagement as well as the development of our sense of self.

PCSs are strongly body-oriented, perhaps because the body is a steady frame of reference (Metzinger, 2003). As Spinoza (1677a) stated: "The human mind does not know the human body itself, nor does it know that the body exists, except through the ideas of affections by which the body is affected" (Spinoza, 1677a, Part II, propositions 19–29). Consciousness starts with sensing, and subsequently perceiving and conceiving of the living body when the body is affected by some cause. Cognition is grounded in experience; cognition does not cause experience. Schopenhauer (1819, 1844) would agree: The will becomes a motive for the intellect; the will precedes the intellect. Spinoza continues in proposition 26 to say that objects ("external bodies") appear for us when they affect our body, and when we, as a whole organism, notice that affection:

> The human mind does not perceive any external body as actually existing, except through the ideas of the affections of its own body. Demonstration: If the human body is not affected by an external body in any way, then the idea of the human body, that is the human mind, is also not affected in any way by the idea of the existence of that body, in other words, it does not perceive the existence of that external body in any way.

Minimal Dissociative Parts, Minimal Contents

The existence of a dissociative part may be limited to a traumatic experience/traumatic memory or even to a particular element or phase of the traumatic experience/traumatic memory. Reactivation of this part, then, implies a reenactment of the involved traumatizing event. Even this kind of reenactment includes a particular PCS and (set of) PCIR. Such EPs reenact a particular subject-object relationship, often without knowing that they are reenacting it. Although EPs experience themselves, their world, and themselves-as-a-part-of-that-world as given, and although most experience themselves as undoubtedly existing and real, this does not imply that they can verbalize and reflect on their PCS and PCIR. Their level of mental efficiency may not enable them to engage in these verbal and reflective actions. Dissociative parts that cannot verbalize or reflect on their PCS and PCIR may, however, still (be able to) engage in self- and world-oriented conceptual actions, however implicit these conceptions may remain in some cases. Clinicians who have observed traumatic reenactments can testify that even nonverbal EPs engaging in reflex-like actions generate a PCS and set of PCIR. They experience and conceive of an 'I,' particular objects (and, perhaps, other subjects), this 'I' as related to these objects and subjects in the framework of a particular event, global world, and phenomenal Now. These clinicians may have seen, for example, how individuals who reenact a traumatic memory ward off perceived threat, how they tremble and hide, cover their head or eyes, scream perhaps, how they flee, freeze, fight, or play dead.

To Have an Autobiographical Memory, Someone Must Remember and Personify It

I agree with Schimmenti and Caretti (2015) that individuals can become classically conditioned with regard to previously more or less neutral cues that signal or refer to the traumatizing event. This signal, referential, and evaluative learning is in fact an explicit component of TSDP (Nijenhuis et al., 2002; Van der Hart et al., 2006). However, I disagree with Ross (2014a) and with Schimmenti and Caretti (2015) that traumatic memories can be just 'memories' (e.g., mere implicit, procedural structures)[5]. Rare exceptions aside involving a temporary loss of any phenomenal conception of self (for an example, see Nijenhuis, 2015a, 2015b), traumatic reenactments do not exist in an impersonal void, but are associated with someone who reenacts, with someone whose reenactment it is. Reenacted traumatic memories, thus, concern someone's experiences and actions. They include at least a minimal experience (i.e., a presentatum) and minimal PCS (i.e., a conception of self). For example, triggered by a classically conditioned cue, say a knife, a

---

5 The presumed existence of memory traces is a most problematic idea (e.g., Braude, 1995, 2006; Bursen, 1978; Heil, 1978).

reenacting patient may as an EP writhe in pain and scream: "Don't hurt me." To the degree that the patient as a whole individual does not synthesize, personify, and presentify the reenactment, the subsystem of the patient who does not integrate the reenactment (e.g., an ANP) remains dissociated from the subsystem of the patient that engages and commonly recurrently reengages in the reenactment (i.e., an EP). The involved subsystems of an individual's personality qualify as dissociative parts precisely because they meet the criteria of global world, phenomenal Now, transparency, and perspectivalness: They generate a PCS as well as a more or less limited set of PCIR when they are reactivated. When latent dissociative subsystems of the individual's personality become manifest, they thus start and continue to engage in actions that include the actions of being an 'I' as a part of a 'world.'

Assessment of Dissociative Disorders and the Accessibility and Assessability of Dissociative Parts

Ross is concerned that it may be impossible to assess the existence of a dissociative part. This difficulty can certainly exist in some cases or phases of treatment. In certain cases, the existence of dissociative parts is not instantly noticeable. However, the inherent difficulty in assessing the formal cause of trauma (i.e., a particular organization of the personality as an organism-environment system) does not mean that this organization does not exist, and that this organization cannot be assessed at a later point in time. In the case of Rita given above, it took therapeutic work to discover the existence of a child EP and to get in touch with this part. Does this mean that clinicians cannot assess the existence of a dissociative disorder in cases involving dissociative parts that they – the clinicians – have not formally met? I think not, at least not in any absolute sense. Clinicians often provisionally diagnose dissociative disorders on the basis of a constellation of dissociative symptoms (see below). They do not need to instantly know the formal cause of the patient's condition, that is, the dissociation of his or her personality, but may presume its existence given the symptoms. Similarly, diagnostic instruments for dissociative disorders assess a constellation of symptoms rather than dissociative parts, although it is diagnostically most helpful to become acquainted with two or more dissociative parts. For example, dissociative disorders of movement and sensation in ICD-10 (WHO, 1992), such as dissociative stupor and dissociative convulsions, are diagnosed on the basis of dissociative symptoms. DSM-5's Chronic and Recurrent Syndromes of Mixed Dissociative Symptoms (CRSMDS)[6] – the former DSM-IV example 1 of Dissociative Disorder Not Otherwise

6 CRSMDS is another one of those 'not otherwise specified' (NOS) diagnoses in DSM-5. The proposal of the Dissociative Disorders Advisory Committee for ICD-11 is to lift this dissociative disorder, which may be the most prevalent of all dissociative disorders, from an NOS status to a regular diagnosis under the name of Complex Dissociative Intrusion Disorder (CDID; Nijenhuis et al., 2014).

Specified – are also diagnosed on the basis of a constellation of dissociative symptoms rather than on the assessment of a dissociative organization of the personality.

This diagnostic practice is not at odds with TSDP because, according to our definition of dissociation in trauma, dissociation of the personality manifests in positive and negative cognitive-emotional (psychoform) and sensorimotor (somatoform) dissociative symptoms (Nijenhuis & Van der Hart, 2011a; Van der Hart et al., 2006). These symptoms suggest an underlying dissociation of the personality. It is more the rule than the exception that this organization, this formal causality of the disorder, becomes clear(er) only with treatment. This is why in many cases dissociative disorders can only be provisionally diagnosed. The disorder becomes formalized following the consistent observation of one or more dissociative parts. Because of this observation the clinician can conclude that the one who came to assessment and treatment is also a dissociative part of the individual and not the complete person. For example, certainly not all dissociative parts in individuals with DID present themselves during clinical assessment, and in some cases the existence of dissociative parts can initially only be suspected. Many individuals with CRSMDS typically do not directly present dissociative parts during assessment apart from an ANP who presents dissociative symptoms. This ANP may report and show intrusions (e.g., hearing child-like voices) of what later appears to involve EPs. But the existence of EPs can often only be suspected in a diagnostic phase.

Detecting the existence of dissociative parts may in some cases take time, sometimes even a lot of time. To illustrate: A woman with depersonalization disorder did not seem to encompass dissociative parts. Her condition was hard to treat. After 4 years of uselessly trying to lessen her depersonalization symptoms, it became apparent that she included a child EP who was stuck in a singular rape by her father. When the ANP integrated the traumatic memory and the associated fragile EP, her otherwise intractable depersonalization disorder swiftly and fully remitted. With this work it became clear how much she had previously been functioning as an ANP. From being an individual with a distant and quite superficial presentation, she turned into a warmhearted, differentiated woman. Other patients with depersonalization disorder do not encompass dissociative parts, so that, according to TSDP and Nijenhuis and Van der Hart's (2011a) definition of dissociation in trauma, they do not have a dissociative disorder. The condition of these individuals rather involves a persistent, unduly low level of personification of personal experiences, not a dissociation of the personality.

Detection of Rudimentary EPs in PTSD (and Other Dissociative Disorders)

Ross asks how a rudimentary EP can be detected in PTSD. As mentioned above, dissociative parts do not need or be able to verbally express themselves as subsystems involving their own person perspectives. However, the presence of these person perspectives can be assessed with a reasonable degree of certainty by preferably consistent and recurrent clinical observation and by the use of deductive logic that runs as follows: PTSD includes negative and positive symptoms. Formulated in PTSD Criterion B in the DSM-5, the positive symptoms are intrusion phenomena, stemming from one or more conscious and self-conscious subsystems of the patient's personality, because traumatic memories (as well as autobiographical, narrative memories) do not exist in a personal void. To remember an autobiographical experience and event, an individual must engage in an action, that is, in the act of recollecting a portion of his or her personal past. No action, no memory. A memory is thus always someone's memory. A traumatic reenactment is not a common autobiographical memory, but someone's sensorimotor, cognitive-emotional, and behavioral reenactment. The reenacting subsystem or subsystems are conscious and self-conscious, because they meet the minimal criteria of consciousness as well as include PCS and PCIR that are not or not sufficiently shared by one or more other conscious and self-conscious subsystems of the patient. This lack of integration of the individual's personality can be logically deduced from the fact that PTSD patients temporarily, and more or less completely, lose their PCS and global world (i.e., a large coherent set of PCIR) that pertain to their present life (i.e., orientation in time and place, idea of personal age, other features of their present identity, relationships), and replace it by a different PCS and set of PCIR. This PCS and these PCIR make up the traumatic reenactment. They involve an orientation in time, space, identity, relationships with objects and other subjects that are phenomenally present, but that are, in the second-person and third-person perspective of observers, not actually present. In that sense, the PCS and set of PCIR that make up the reenactment are hallucinatory. Observers are generally able to notice that someone is engaging in a more or less complete reenactment. The 'one' who reenacts and who intrudes on the PTSD patient's current existence (i.e., his or her current PCS, globally available current world – his or her coherent set of current PCIR– and phenomenal Now that match the third-person present) is clearly a conscious and self-conscious existence oriented to and stuck in the traumatic past (i.e., in 'trauma-time'). The intruding 'one' is clearly dissociated from the individual's present existence, from the 'one' that is intruded upon. If the intruding part were integrated with the patient's conscious and self-conscious present existence, the reenactment would stop; if it were integrated, the intruding and intruded on parts would know and realize that they are safe, that the thing happened in the past, that objects and subjects that were once dangerous are no longer present or dangerous. But reenactments and intruding reenactments do not lead to this integration for the duration of the disorder. This lack of integration and the continued existence of two (or more) conscious and self-conscious subsystems is the core problem of PTSD as well as of all other dissociative trauma-related disorders.

The following example serves to demonstrate the point. The focus is on a shift in the patient's second-person and third-person perspective regarding individuals and objects that once presented a major threat, but that, in the eye of third persons, are no longer threatening.

> A married couple was severely tortured for hours by two burglars who wore helmets. As ANP, the husband knew that policemen who ride a motorbike and for that reason wear a helmet are generally trustworthy (present PCS and globally available world). As ANP, he thus did not have an abnormal reaction to policemen. However, when stopped by a helmeted policeman while driving his car, the sight of a helmeted head that looked at him through the side window of his car (a set of classically conditioned stimuli) instantly took him back to the past that then became his phenomenal present. This reorientation implied the regeneration of a former first-, quasi-second-, and second-person perspective as well as a former goal-orientation regarding helmeted men (fragile EP; flee when you can). The reactivation of the fragile EP went along with the loss of the PCS and set of PCIR that marked the ANP. As the fragile EP, the patient perceived the policeman as one of his torturers and felt his very life was at stake (reactivation of a former second-person perspective regarding his and his wife's torturers; loss of the second-person perspective regarding a policeman). He panicked and pushed the throttle (behavioral reenactment; flight fitted the third-person past, but not the third-person present). A dangerous pursuit followed that culminated in an upsetting arrest. The patient did not integrate the fragile EP and this part's horrible experiences as ANP during or following the event, so that his PTSD persisted (cf. Nijenhuis, 2015b).

By affectively attuning to their patients and by carefully observing them, clinicians can, at least in principle, phenomenally judge in second-person perspective (I, clinician – You, patient) and physically judge in the third-person perspective (I, clinician – the patient as an object of my study), that the patient encompasses two or more conscious and self-conscious subsystems. Although talking with an EP assists them in reaching this conclusion, verbal exchanges with an EP are not the only way to phenomenally and physically judge that the patient includes more than one conscious and self-conscious subsystem (in the above example, one ANP and one fragile EP). The clinician can ask the PTSD patient what (s)he experienced during the reenactment. When the patient does not recollect the reenactment, the clinician receives a first indication that the 'one' who does not recollect it might constitute an ANP. The patient may alternatively have had the feeling that (s)he was being intruded on by a traumatic memory, and/or that not (s)he but 'something inside' was reenacting past horror. This lack of personification is another powerful indication that an EP is reenacting the traumatic experience, and that an ANP does not or insufficiently personify the reenactment. In sum, clinicians can commonly examine and judge the features of the reenactment with their patients as it happens as well as *de post facto*.

Following some further reactions to criticisms of the theory of dissociation of the personality in trauma, I concluded that "whatever limitations or flaws [the theory] may include, they do not pertain to this theory's lower bound of the concept of dissociative parts of the personality. The criterion that dissociative parts include their own at least rudimentary phenomenal experience and conception of self is a clear and distinct idea that, in a prototypical sense, distinguishes these parts from other insufficiently or imperfectly integrated subsystems of an individual's personality" (Nijenhuis, 2015c, p. 82).

Appendix 3

The Somatoform Dissociation Questionnaire (SDQ-20)

The SDQ-20 (Nijenhuis, Spinhoven, Van Dyck, Van der Hart, & Vanderlinden, 1996) evaluates the severity of somatoform or sensorimotor dissociative symptoms. The items of the instrument were specifically constructed to measure sensorimotor manifestations of dissociation of the personality. They were derived from a pool of 75 items describing clinically observed sensorimotor dissociative symptoms that in clinical settings had appeared upon reactivation of particular dissociative parts of the personality and that could not be medically explained. The items pertain to negative (e.g., analgesia) and positive (e.g., site-specific pain) dissociative phenomena.

Scoring

The range of possible scores per item on the SDQ-20 runs from 1 (*absent*) to 5 (*very severe*). The minimum score is thus 20, and the maximum score is 100. The respondent is also asked to indicate whether a physician has connected the symptom or bodily experience with a physical disease. In our SDQ studies, we did not adjust the item scores when the physical disease was indicated, as such indications often did not seem to be accurate. For example, the respondent might interpret "hyperventilation" as a physical disease. We, therefore, suggest that the item scores not be adjusted for indicated physical disease when the SDQ-20 (or SDQ-5, see Appendix 4) is used for research purposes. However, in clinical practice one may wish to adjust the relevant item score to "1" when physical disease is indicated, the medical diagnosis has been checked with the physician who assigned it, and this diagnosis seems valid.

Scalability

Mokken scale analysis showed that the 20 items are strongly scalable (Nijenhuis et al., 1996: Loevinger coefficient of homogeneity H = .50; Nijenhuis et al., 1998a: 0.56). The items met the assumptions of single and double monotonicity. —In a replication study (Nijenhuis et al., 1998a), one item (Mokken coefficient of homogeneity = 0.28) failed to reach the lower bound (≥ 0.30), though its exclusion only marginally affected the Loevinger coefficient of homogeneity (increasing to 0.58). The Mokken coefficients of homogeneity of the other items ranged from 0.40 to 0.63.

Reliability

The internal consistency of the SDQ–20 is excellent (Nijenhuis et al., 1996, Cronbach's α 0.95; Nijenhuis et al., 1998a: .96). The test–retest reliability is satisfactory (Sar et al., 2000).

Relationship with Demographic Characteristics

We did not find indications that SDQ-20 scores are affected by age or sex.

Convergent Validity

We found (Nijenhuis et al., 1996) the intercorrelations between the SDQ-20 score and the Dissociation Questionnaire (DIS-Q; Vanderlinden, 1993) total score as well as three of the four factor scores to be high ($.71 < r < .76$, $p < .0001$). The DIS-Q evaluates the severity of cognitive-emotional dissociative symptoms. The intercorrelation with the absorption scale was more moderate ($r = .46$, $p < .0001$). In a replication study (Nijenhuis et al., 1998a), the intercorrelation between the SDQ–20 and the DIS-Q total score was $r = .82$, and the correlations between the SDQ and the four DIS-Q factor scores were as follows: identity fragmentation factor $r = .81$; loss of control, $r = .72$; amnesia, $r = .80$; absorption $r = .60$.

In yet another study (Nijenhuis et al., 1997b), an intercorrelation of $r = .85$ was assessed with the Dissociative Experiences Scale (DES; Bernstein & Putnam, 1986) in psychiatric patients. Nijenhuis, Van der Hart, and Kruger (2002) and Sar et al. (2000) also found a strong association between the SDQ-20 and the DES in psychiatric patients, as did Van Duijl, Nijenhuis, Komproe, Gernaat, and de Jong, (2010) in Ugandan patients with spirit possession disorder, and Nijenhuis et al. (2003) in women with chronic pelvic pain.

These results strongly support the convergent validity of the SDQ-20. More data supporting the convergent validity of the SDQ-20 can be found in ToT Volumes I & II.

Discriminant Validity

The distribution of SDQ-20 scores for individuals with different mental disorders and mental healthy individuals is presented in ToT Volume I, Chapter 6, Table 6.1. Roughly speaking, DID is associated with mean SDQ-20 scores between 50 and 60, suggesting severe sensorimotor dissociative symptoms. CDID, in turn, is associated with mean scores between 40 and 50, indicating marked sensorimotor dissociation. Mean scores between 30 and 40, representing a significant degree of sensorimotor dissociative symptoms, were documented in patients with PTSD, DSM-IV conversion disorder (DSM-IV, APA, 1994)/dissociative disorders of movement and sensation (ICD-10, WHO, 1992), including pseudoepilepsy (labeled dissociative convulsions in ICD-10), and patients with eating disorders, particularly those who report traumatization. Patients with other mental disorders tend to have scores below 30, as do individuals in the general population.

In one study (Nijenhuis et al., 1999), we found that the SDQ-20 discriminates between (1) Dissociative Identity Disorder, (2) Dissociative Disorder NOS, (3) Somatoform Disorders, and (4) other psychiatric diagnostic categories, including bipolar mood disorder. The differences between (1) DID, (2) DDNOS, (3) somatoform disorders, and (4) other psychiatric disorders remained statistically significant after controlling for general psychopathology as assessed with the SCL-90-R (Derogatis, 1992; Nijenhuis et al., 1999). Sensorimotor dissociation thus differs from general psychopathology.

Construct Validity

The SDQ-20 scores were best predicted by self-reported physical and sexual traumatization in patients with dissociative disorders and psychiatric controls (Nijenhuis et al., 1998b), even after statistically controlling for self-reported emotional traumatization (emotional neglect and emotional abuse). These traumatization scores were composed of four factors, i.e., presence of trauma, duration of trauma, relationship to the perpetrator, and subjectively rated impact of trauma. Self-reported traumatization in the developmental period 0–6 years best predicted somatoform dissociation.

Sensorimotor dissociation was strongly associated with reported exposure to potentially traumatizing events, notably cumulative trauma reporting and bodily threat from a person in a range of other studies, even after statistically controlling for self-reported emotional neglect and emotional abuse (Nijenhuis et al., 1998b; Nijenhuis, Van Engen, Kusters, & Van der Hart, 2001; Nijenhuis et al., 2003; Nijenhuis, Van der Hart, & Kruger, 2002; Waller et al., 2000). Physical abuse was associated with more somatoform dissociative symptoms in patients with DSM-IV conversion disorder, described in ICD-10 as dissociative disorders of movement and sensation (Roelofs, Keijsers, Hoogduin, Naring, & Moene, 2002). Conjointly, these studies demonstrate consistent associations between somatoform dissociation and reported cumulative traumatization and threat from a person to the integrity of the body and life in clinical and nonclinical samples, and in samples from different cultures.

More data supporting the convergent validity of the SDQ-20 can be found in ToT Volumes I & II.

Screening Capacity

The cutoff value for the SDQ-20 in the screening for DSM-IV dissociative disorders is > 28. The SDQ-20 performs equally well as the DES and the Multidimensional Inventory of Dissociation (MID; Dell, 2006; Somer & Dell, 2005) in the screening for DSM-IV dissociative disorders (Müller et al., 2013). Because the SDQ-20 includes the smallest number of items of these three self-reporting instruments, it is a very efficient screener.

SDQ-20 scores are correlated with scores for psychoform or cognitive-emotional dissociative symptoms as well as with reported and documented adverse events (ToT Volume II, Chapter 15, Table 15.1.). The associations were found for various diagnostic groups.

The SDQ-20 has now been translated into various languages. They are available for the public on www.enijenhuis.nl. This website also offers several studies on the SDQ-20 for those who have requested and received free membership.

S. D. Q.-20

This questionnaire asks about different physical symptoms or body experiences, which you may have had either briefly or for a longer time. Please indicate to what extent these experiences apply to you **in the past year**.

For each statement, please circle the number in the first column that best applies to YOU.

The possibilities are:
1 = this applies to me NOT AT ALL
2 = this applies to me A LITTLE
3 = this applies to me MODERATELY
4 = this applies to me QUITE A BIT
5 = this applies to me EXTREMELY

If a symptom or experience applies to you, please indicate whether a **physician** has connected it with a **physical disease**. Indicate this by circling the word YES or NO in the column "Is the physical cause known?"

If you wrote YES, please write the physical cause (if you know it) on the line.

Example:

	Extent to which the symptom or experience applies to you	Is the physical cause cause known?
Sometimes: My teeth chatter	1 2 3 4 5	No Yes, namely . . .
I have cramps in my calves	1 2 3 4 5	No Yes, namely . . .

If you circled 1 in the first column (i.e., This applies to me NOT AT ALL), you do NOT have to respond to the question about whether the physical cause is known.

On the other hand, if you circle 2, 3, 4, or 5, you MUST circle No or YES in the "Is the physical cause known?" column.

Please do not skip any of the 20 questions.

Thank you for your cooperation.

Legend:
1 = this applies to me NOT AT ALL
2 = this applies to me A LITTLE
3 = this applies to me MODERATELY
4 = this applies to me QUITE A BIT
5 = this applies to me EXTREMELY

	Extent to which the symptom or experience applies to you	Is the physical cause known?
Sometimes:		
1. I have trouble urinating	1 2 3 4 5	No Yes, namely . . .
2. I dislike tastes that I usually like (women: at times OTHER THAN during pregnancy or monthly periods)	1 2 3 4 5	No Yes, namely . . .
3. I hear sounds from nearby as if they were coming from far away	1 2 3 4 5	No Yes, namely . . .
4. I have pain while urinating	1 2 3 4 5	No Yes, namely . . .
5. My body, or a part of it, feels numb	1 2 3 4 5	No Yes, namely . . .
6. People and things look bigger than usual	1 2 3 4 5	No Yes, namely . . .
7. I have an attack that resembles an epileptic seizure	1 2 3 4 5	No Yes, namely . . .
8. My body, or a part of it, is insensitive to pain	1 2 3 4 5	No Yes, namely . . .
9. I dislike smells that I usually like	1 2 3 4 5	No Yes, namely . . .
10. I feel pain in my genitals (at times OTHER THAN during sexual intercourse)	1 2 3 4 5	No Yes, namely . . .
11. I cannot hear for a while (as if I were deaf)	1 2 3 4 5	No Yes, namely . . .
12. I cannot see for a while (as if I were blind)	1 2 3 4 5	No Yes, namely . . .
13. I see things around me differently than usual (for example, as if looking through a tunnel or seeing merely a part of an object)	1 2 3 4 5	No Yes, namely . . .
14. I am able to smell much BETTER or WORSE than I usually do (even though I do NOT have a cold)	1 2 3 4 5	No Yes, namely . . .
15. It is as if my body, or a part of it, has disappeared	1 2 3 4 5	No Yes, namely . . .
16. I cannot swallow, or can swallow only with great effort	1 2 3 4 5	No Yes, namely . . .
17. I cannot sleep for nights on end, but remain very active during daytime	1 2 3 4 5	No Yes, namely . . .
18. I cannot speak (or only with great effort) or I can only whisper	1 2 3 4 5	No Yes, namely . . .
19. I am paralyzed for a while	1 2 3 4 5	No Yes, namely . . .
20. I grow stiff for a while	1 2 3 4 5	No Yes, namely . . .

Before continuing, please check that you have responded to all 20 statements.

You are asked to fill in and place an X beside what applies to you.

21. Age:	... years
22. Sex:	... female ... male
23. Marital status:	... single ... married ... living together ... divorced ... widower/widow
24. Education:	... number of years
25. Date:	....
26. Name:	....

Thank you very much for your cooperation.

Appendix 4

The Somatoform Dissociation Questionnaire (SDQ-5)

The 5-item SDQ-5 was derived from the SDQ-20 and includes the items 4, 8, 13, 15, and 18. These 5 items as a group best discriminated between patients with dissociative disorders and nondissociative psychiatric comparison patients (Nijenhuis et al., 1997b, 1998a). The range of possible scores per item on the SDQ-5 is 1 (*absent*) to 5 (*very severe*). The minimum score is thus 5, and the maximum score is 25.

Sensitivity and specificity were high, positive predictive value corrected for the prevalence of dissociative disorders (rated at 10% among psychiatric patients) was satisfactory, and the prevalence-corrected negative predictive value was excellent. In a study of three independent samples, we found that a score of ≥ 8 yielded the optimal balance between sensitivity and specificity. Among all patients of these samples, only one patient who did not have dissociative disorder obtained a score ≥ 11.

Compared with the Dissociative Experiences Scale (DES; Bernstein & Putnam, 1986) as a screening instrument for dissociative disorder (Draijer & Boon, 1993), the SDQ-5 did at least equally well. According to the results of three samples we studied, 43–84% of the respondents who obtain a score of ≥ 8 would have dissociative disorder. If one were to assume that the prevalence of dissociative disorders among psychiatric outpatients is 5%, one in two patients with above-cutoff scores would have one of the DSM-IV dissociative disorders.

The SDQ-5 was more sensitive than the DES in assessing dissociative pathology among patients with somatoform disorders. About two-thirds of them passed the SDQ-5 cutoff, while a quarter passed the DES cutoff. Many somatoform disorder patients thus seem to experience substantial sensorimotor dissociative symptoms, while a minority experiences considerable cognitive-emotional dissociative symptoms.

A third of the 50 eating disorder patients we studied obtained above cutoff SDQ-5 scores. None of the bipolar mood disorder patients passed this value, as did very few of a mixed comparison group, which mainly included anxiety disorders, depression, and adjustment disorder.

Patients who obtain SDQ-5 scores ≥ 8 should be interviewed using the Structured Clinical Interview for DSM-IV Dissociative Disorders (SCID-D; Steinberg et al., 1993) or the Dissociative Disorders Interview Schedule (DDIS; Ross et al., 1990) in order to assess or exclude DSM-IV dissociative disorder. The SDQ-5 performed less well in a sample of Turkish psychiatric patients (Sar et al., 2000). In this sample, the sensitivity and specificity of the SDQ-20 were more satisfactory. At the optimal cutoff of 35, and corrected for a prevalence of DSM-IV dissociative disorders (estimated at 10%), the sensitivity was 0.45 and the specificity 0.98. The sensitivity and specificity of the DES at a cutoff of 25 were very similar. In Dutch/Flemish samples, the discriminating power of the SDQ-20 was slightly less, compared to this power of the SDQ-5 (Nijenhuis et al., 1997b).

In clinical practice, it is efficient to administer the SDQ-20, and then calculate the SDQ-20 as well as the SDQ-5 scores.

S. D. Q.-5

This questionnaire asks about different physical symptoms or body experiences, which you may have had either briefly or for a longer time. Please indicate to what extent these experiences apply to you **in the past year.**

For each statement, please circle the number in the first column that best applies to YOU.

The possibilities are:
1 = this applies to me NOT AT ALL
2 = this applies to me A LITTLE
3 = this applies to me MODERATELY
4 = this applies to me QUITE A BIT
5 = this applics to me EXTREMELY

If a symptom or experience applies to you, please indicate whether a **physician** has connected it with a **physical disease.** Indicate this by circling the word YES or NO in the column "Is the physical cause known?"

If you wrote YES, please write the physical cause (if you know it) on the line.

Example:

	Extent to which the symptom or experience applies to you	Is the physical cause cause known?
Sometimes: My teeth chatter	1 2 3 4 5	No Yes, namely . . .
I have cramps in my calves	1 2 3 4 5	No Yes, namely . . .

If you circled 1 in the first column (i.e., This applies to me NOT AT ALL), you do NOT have to respond to the question about whether the physical cause is known.

On the other hand, if you circle 2, 3, 4, or 5, you MUST circle No or YES in the "Is the physical cause known?" column.

Please do not skip any of the 5 questions.

Thank you for your cooperation.

Legend:
1 = this applies to me NOT AT ALL
2 = this applies to me A LITTLE
3 = this applies to me MODERATELY
4 = this applies to me QUITE A BIT
5 = this applies to me EXTREMELY

	Extent to which the symptom or experience applies to you	Is the physical cause known?
Sometimes:		
1. I have pain while urinating	1 2 3 4 5	No Yes, namely . . .
2. My body, or a part of it, is insensitive to pain	1 2 3 4 5	No Yes, namely . . .
3. I see things around me differently than usual (for example, as if looking through a tunnel or seeing merely a part of an object)	1 2 3 4 5	No Yes, namely . . .
4. It is as if my body, or a part of it, has disappeared	1 2 3 4 5	No Yes, namely . . .
5. I cannot speak (or only with great effort) or I can only whisper	1 2 3 4 5	No Yes, namely . . .

Before continuing, will you please check whether you have responded to all 5 statements?

You are asked to fill in and place an X beside what applies to you.

6. Age:	. . . years
7. Sex:	. . . female . . . male
8. Marital status:	. . . single . . . married . . . living together . . . divorced . . . widower/widow
9. Education:	. . . number of years
10. Date:	. . . .
11. Name:	. . . .

Thank you very much for your cooperation.

Appendix 5

The Traumatic Experiences Checklist (TEC)

Systematic assessment of a wide range of potentially traumatizing events is often inherent and mandatory in trauma research, though it remains a relatively neglected area in clinical practice (Carlson, 1997). Highly vulnerable individuals should not be exposed to self-report trauma questionnaires or untimely trauma interviews. However, assessment of trauma history, even if stressful, is appreciated by most patients and rewarding to clinicians (Walker et al., 1997).

Given the limits in time and funding, conducting extensive trauma interviews may remain beyond reach in many research studies – and beyond routine application in most clinical settings. Administration of retrospective self-report questionnaires, on the other hand, can be an acceptable, efficient, and cost-effective alternative. Moreover, some patients may be less inhibited to report potentially traumatizing events on self-report measures than in the context of face-to-face trauma interviews (Carlson, 1997). For practical purposes, as a first step it is advisable to assess recalled adverse events using self-report instruments and subsequently to conduct adverse event interviews with patients who have high scores and who can emotionally cope with detailed interview items (Carlson, 1997).

The Traumatic Experiences Checklist (TEC; Nijenhuis et al., 1999) is a reliable and valid self-report instrument that can be used in both clinical practice and research. This questionnaire was developed in the context of a research study that aimed to assess the correlations among a wide range of reported adverse experiences, including emotional neglect and emotional abuse, sensorimotor as well as cognitive-emotional manifestations of dissociation (Nijenhuis et al., 1998b). Consistent with the wording of the DSM-IV (American Psychiatric Association, 1994) criterion A of posttraumatic stress disorder (PTSD), the self-report measures that were available at the time (e.g., Trauma Assessment for Adults, Resnick, 1996; the Trauma History Questionnaire, Green, 1996; and the Traumatic Stress Schedule, Norris, 1990) do not include items that assess emotional neglect and emotional abuse. Other self-report questionnaires, such as the Childhood Trauma Questionnaire (Bernstein et al., 1994) include items that assess emotional neglect and abuse, but do not address potentially traumatizing events that may happen to adults. Some studies have suggested that adult psychopathology may be related to a pathogenic family structure rather than to adverse events such as physical and sexual abuse per se

(Fromuth, 1986; Nash et al., 1993). Thus the TEC includes items that address emotional neglect, emotional abuse, parentification, and extraordinary family burdens, such as poverty, psychiatric illness, alcoholism, or drug addiction of one or both parents.

The TEC involves items that assess events that are not necessarily traumatizing to every individual, as is true for any self-report trauma questionnaire. At the same time, experiences that are not traumatic to most individuals can be quite traumatic to others.

The psychometric characteristics of the TEC are good to excellent (Nijenhuis et al., 1999; Schumacher et al., 2011). Various scores can be calculated using a manual scoring form (included below). For research purposes, a syntax is available at www.enijenhuis.nl.

T. E. C.

People may experience a variety of traumatic experiences during their life. We would like to know three things: (1) Whether you have experienced any of the following 29 events? (2) How old were you when they happened? (3) How much of an impact did these experiences have on you?

1) In the *first column* (i.e., Did this happen to you?), indicate whether you had each of the 29 experiences by circling YES or NO.
2) For each experience where you circled YES, *in the second column* (i.e., Age) list your age when it happened. If it happened more than once, list ALL of the ages when this happened to you. If it happened over many years (e.g., age 7–12), list the age range (i.e., age 7–12).
3) In the *final column* (i.e., How much of an impact did this have on you?), indicate the impact by circling the appropriate number: 1, 2, 3, 4, or 5.

Legend:
1 = none
2 = a little bit
3 = a moderate amount
4 = quite a bit
5 = an extreme amount

Example:

Experience	Did this happen to you?	Age	How much of an impact did this have on you?
You were teased	No Yes	...	1 2 3 4 5

Thank you for your cooperation.

Legend:
1 = none
2 = a little bit
3 = a moderate amount
4 = quite a bit
5 = an extreme amount

Experience	Did this happen to you?	Age	How much of an impact did this have on you?
1. Having to look after your parents and/or brothers and sisters when you were a child	No Yes	...	1 2 3 4 5
2. Family problems (e.g., parent with alcohol or psychiatric problems, poverty)	No Yes	...	1 2 3 4 5
3. Loss of a family member (brother, sister, parent) when you were a CHILD	No Yes	...	1 2 3 4 5
4. Loss of a family member (child or partner) when you were an ADULT	No Yes	...	1 2 3 4 5
5. Serious bodily injury (e.g., loss of a limb, mutilation, burns)	No Yes	...	1 2 3 4 5
6. Threat to life from illness, an operation, or an accident	No Yes	...	1 2 3 4 5
7. Divorce of your parents	No Yes	...	1 2 3 4 5
8. Your own divorce	No Yes	...	1 2 3 4 5
9. Threat to life from another person (e.g., during a crime)	No Yes	...	1 2 3 4 5
10. Intense pain (e.g., from an injury or surgery)	No Yes	...	1 2 3 4 5
11. War-time experiences (e.g., imprisonment, loss of relatives, deprivation, injury)	No Yes	...	1 2 3 4 5
12. Second generation war victim (wartime experiences of parents or close relatives)	No Yes	...	1 2 3 4 5
13. Witnessing others undergo trauma	No Yes	...	1 2 3 4 5
14. Emotional neglect (e.g., being left alone, insufficient affection) by your parents, brothers or sisters	No Yes	...	1 2 3 4 5
15. Emotional neglect by more distant members of your family (e.g., uncles, aunts, nephews, nieces, grandparents)	No Yes	...	1 2 3 4 5
16. Emotional neglect by nonfamily members (e.g., neighbors, friends, stepparents, teachers)	No Yes	...	1 2 3 4 5
17. Emotional abuse (e.g., being belittled, teased, called names, threatened verbally, or unjustly punished) by your parents, brothers or sisters	No Yes	...	1 2 3 4 5
18. Emotional abuse by more distant members of your family	No Yes	...	1 2 3 4 5
19. Emotional abuse by nonfamily members	No Yes	...	1 2 3 4 5
20. Physical abuse (e.g., being hit, tortured, or wounded) by your parents, brothers, or sisters	No Yes	...	1 2 3 4 5
21. Physical abuse by more distant members of your family	No Yes	...	1 2 3 4 5

Experience	Did this happen to you?	Age	How much of an impact did this have on you?
22. Physical abuse by nonfamily members	No Yes	...	1 2 3 4 5
23. Bizarre punishment. If applicable, please describe:	No Yes	...	1 2 3 4 5
24. Sexual harassment (acts of a sexual nature that DO NOT involve physical contact) by your parents, brothers, or sisters	No Yes	...	1 2 3 4 5
25. Sexual harassment by more distant members of your family	No Yes	...	1 2 3 4 5
26. Sexual harassment by nonfamily members	No Yes	...	1 2 3 4 5
27. Sexual abuse (unwanted sexual acts involving physical contact) by your parents, brothers, or sisters	No Yes	...	1 2 3 4 5
28. Sexual abuse by more distant members of your family	No Yes	...	1 2 3 4 5
29. Sexual abuse by nonfamily members	No Yes	...	1 2 3 4 5

30. If you were mistreated or abused, how many people did this to you?

A) Emotional maltreatment (if you answered YES to any of the questions 11–16)
Numbers of persons: ...

B) Physical maltreatment (if you answered YES to any of the questions 17–19)
Number of persons: ...

C) Sexual harassment (if you answered YES to any of the questions 20–22)
Number of persons: ...

D) Sexual abuse (if you answered YES to any of the questions 23–25)
Number of persons: ...

31. Please describe your relationship with each person mentioned in your answer to question 30 (e.g., father, brother, friend, teacher, stranger, etc.), and add if the person(s) was (were) at least 4 years older than you at the time when the experience(s) occurred. For example, write "friend (–)" if this friend was less than 4 years older than you. Write "uncle (+)" if this uncle was more than 4 years older than you.

A) Emotional neglect ...

B) Emotional abuse ...

C) Physical abuse ...

D) Sexual harassment . . .
E) Sexual abuse . . .
32. Please describe any OTHER traumatic events that had an impact on you.

33. If you have answered YES to any of the questions 1–29, how much support did you receive afterward? (give the number of the question and the level of support)	
Question number	Level of support (0 = none, 1 = Some, 2 = Good)
. . .	. . .
. . .	. . .
. . .	. . .
. . .	. . .

You are asked to fill in and place an X beside what applies to you.

34. Age:	. . . years
35. Sex:	. . . female . . . male
36. Marital status:	. . . single . . . married . . . living together . . . divorced . . . widower/widow
37. Education:	. . . number of years
38. Today's date:	. . ./. . ./. . .
39. Name:	. . . .

Thank you very much for your cooperation.

Scoring Form Traumatic Experiences Checklist (TEC)

I. TEC total score: summated item scores
0 = absent
1 = present

Item	
1	0 – 1
2	0 – 1
3	0 – 1
4	0 – 1
5	0 – 1
6	0 – 1
7	0 – 1
8	0 – 1
9	0 – 1
10	0 – 1
11	0 – 1
12	0 – 1
13	0 – 1
14	0 – 1
15	0 – 1
16	0 – 1
17	0 – 1
18	0 – 1
19	0 – 1
20	0 – 1
21	0 – 1
22	0 – 1
23	0 – 1
24	0 – 1
25	0 – 1
26	0 – 1
27	0 – 1
28	0 – 1
29	0 – 1

TEC total score presence reported potentially traumatizing experiences:

Σ item (1–29) = (range 0–29)

II. TEC Developmental Level Composite Score per Trauma Area and Trauma Area Composite Scores

EMOTIONAL NEGLECT					
Items 14, 15, 16	Presence 0 (absent) 1 (present)	Duration 0 (< 1 year) 1 (> 1 year)	Relationship to perpetrator(s) 0 = nonfamily, or family if not: 1 = parents, brothers, sisters	Subjective response 0 (1 or 2) 1 (3, 4, or 5)	Developmental level composite score
0–6 years					(0–4)
7–12 years					(0–4)
13–18 years					(0–4)
				composite score emotional neglect →	(0–12)

EMOTIONAL ABUSE					
Items 17, 18, 19	Presence 0 (absent) 1 (present)	Duration 0 (< 1 year) 1 (> 1 year)	Relationship to perpetrator(s) 0 = nonfamily, or family if not: 1 = parents, brothers, sisters	Subjective response 0 (1 or 2) 1 (3, 4, or 5)	Developmental level composite score
0–6 years					(0–4)
7–12 years					(0–4)
13–18 years					(0–4)
				Composite score emotional abuse →	(0–12)

THREAT FROM A PERSON TO THE INTEGRITY OF THE BODY (1): PHYSICAL ABUSE					
Items 20, 21, 22	Presence 0 (absent) 1 (present)	Duration 0 (< 1 year) 1 (> 1 year)	Relationship to perpetrator(s) 0 = nonfamily, or family if not: 1 = parents, brothers, sisters	Subjective response 0 (1 or 2) 1 (3, 4, or 5)	Developmental level composite score
0–6 years					(0–4)
7–12 years					(0–4)
13–18 years					(0–4)
				Composite score bodily threat 1 →	(0–12)

THREAT FROM A PERSON TO THE INTEGRITY OF THE BODY (2): THREAT TO LIFE, PAIN, BIZARRE PUNISHMENT

Items 9, 10, 23	Presence 0 (absent) 1 (present)	Duration 0 (< 1 year) 1 (> 1 year)	Subjective response 0 (1 or 2) 1 (3, 4, or 5)	Developmental level composite score
0–6 years				(0–3)
7–12 years				(0–3)
13–18 years				(0–3)
			Composite score bodily threat 2 →	(0–9)

BODILY THREAT TOTAL SCORE: SUMMATED COMPOSITES BODILY THREAT 1 & 2: (0–21)

SEXUAL HARASSMENT

Items 24, 25, 26	Presence 0 (absent) 1 (present)	Duration 0 (< 1 year) 1 (> 1 year)	Relationship to perpetrator(s) 0 = nonfamily, or family if not: 1 = parents, brothers, sisters	Subjective response 0 (1 or 2) 1 (3, 4, or 5)	Developmental level composite score
0 – 6 years					(0–4)
7 – 12 years					(0–4)
13 – 18 years					(0–4)
				Composite score sexual harass-ment →	(0–12)

SEXUAL ABUSE

Items 27, 28, 29	Presence 0 (absent) 1 (present)	Duration 0 (< 1 year) 1 (> 1 year)	Relationship to perpetrator(s) 0 = nonfamily, or family if not: 1 = parents, brothers, sisters	Subjective response 0 (1 or 2) 1 (3, 4, or 5)	Developmental level composite score
0 – 6 years					(0–4)
7 – 12 years					(0–4)
13 – 18 years					(0–4)
				Composite score sexual abuse →	(0–12)

III. Developmental Level Total Composite Scores and Total Trauma Composite Score

Developmental level	Emotional neglect Developmental composite score	Emotional abuse Developmental composite score	Bodily threat Developmental composite score	Sexual harassment Developmental composite score	Sexual abuse Developmental composite score	Developmental level total Trauma composite score
0–6 years	(0–4)	(0–4)	(0–7)	(0–4)	(0–4)	(0–23)
7–12 years	(0–4)	(0–4)	(0–7)	(0–4)	(0–4)	(0–23)
13–18 years	(0–4)	(0–4)	(0–7)	(0–4)	(0–4)	(0–23)
					Total trauma composite score	(0–69)

References

Aanes, S., Bjuland, K. J., Skranes, J., & Lohaugen, G. C. (2015). Memory function and hippocampal volumes in preterm born very-low-birth-weight (VLBW) young adults. *Neuroimage, 105*, 76–83.

Abbott, E. A. (1884/1992). *Flatland: A romance in many dimensions*. New York: Dover Thrift Edition.

Abdollahi, F., Abhari, F. R., Delavar, M. A., & Charati, J. Y. (2015). Physical violence against pregnant women by an intimate partner, and adverse pregnancy outcomes in Mazandaran Province, Iran. *Journal of Family and Community Medicine, 22*(1), 13–18.

Aderka, I. M., Appelbaum-Namdar, E., Shafran, N., & Gilboa-Schechtman, E. (2011). Sudden gains in prolonged exposure for children and adolescents with posttraumatic stress disorder. *Journal of Consulting and Clinical Psychology, 79*, 441–446.

Alhusen, J. L., Ray, E., Sharps, P., & Bullock, L. (2015). Intimate partner violence during pregnancy: Maternal and neonatal outcomes. *Journal of Women's Health, 24*(1), 100–106.

Allen, J. G., & Coyne, L. (1995). Dissociation and vulnerability to psychotic experience: The Dissociative Experiences Scale and the MMPI-2. *Journal of Nervous and Mental Disease, 183*, 615–622.

Al-Qahtani, N. H. (2005). Foetal response to music and voice. *Australian and New Zealand Journal of Obstetrics and Gynaecology, 45*, 414–417.

American Psychiatric Association (APA). (1980). *Diagnostic and statistical manual of mental disorders III*. Washington, DC: Author.

American Psychiatric Association (APA). (1987). *Diagnostic and statistical manual of mental disorders III – revised edition*. Washington, DC: Author.

American Psychiatric Association (APA). (1994). *Diagnostic and statistical manual of mental disorders IV*. Washington, DC: Author.

American Psychiatric Association (APA). (2013). *Diagnostic and statistical manual of mental disorders, 5th edition (DSM-5)*. Washington, DC: Author.

Anderson, A. L., & Thomason, M. E. (2013). Functional plasticity before the cradle: A review of neural functional imaging in the human fetus. *Neuroscience and Biobehavioral Reviews, 37*(9 Pt B), 2220–2232.

Anderson, M. C. (2005). The role of inhibitory control in forgetting unwanted memories: A consideration of three methods. In N. Ohta, C. MacLeod, & B. Uttl (Eds.), *Dynamic cognitive processes* (pp. 159–189). Tokyo: Springer-Verlag.

Anderson, M. C., & Green, C. (2001). Suppressing unwanted memories by executive control. *Nature, 410*, 366–369.

Anderson, M. C., & Huddleston, E. (2012). Towards a cognitive and neurobiological model of motivated forgetting. *Nebraska Symposium on Motivation, 58*, 53–120.

Anderson, M. C., Reinholz, J., Kuhl, B. A., & Mayr, U. (2011). Intentional suppression of unwanted memories grows more difficult as we age. *Psychology and Aging, 26*, 397–405.

Andrews, P. W., Gangestad, S. W., & Matthews, D. (2002). Adaptationism: How to carry out an exaptationist program. *Behavioral and Brain Sciences, 25*, 489–504; 504–553.

Appelfeld, A. (1994). *Beyond despair*. New York: Fromm International.

Asling-Monemi, K., Naved, R. T., & Persson, L. A. (2009). Violence against women and the risk of fetal and early childhood growth impairment: A cohort study in rural Bangladesh. *Archives of Disease in Childhood, 94,* 775–779.

Bae, H., Kim, D., & Park, Y. C. (2016). Dissociation predicts treatment response in eye-movement desensitization and reprocessing for posttraumatic stress disorder. *Journal of Trauma and Dissociation, 17*(1), 112–130.

Bain, A. (1855). *The senses and the intellect.* London: Parker.

Barbaras, R. (1999). *Le désir et la distance.* Paris: Vrin. English translation by P. B. Milan, Desire and distance: Introduction to a phenomenology of perception. Stanford: Stanford University Press.

Bateson, G. (1972). *Steps toward an ecology of mind.* New York: Ballantine Books.

Bedau, M. A. (1997). Weak emergence. In J. Tomberlin (Ed.), *Philosophical perspectives, Volume 11: Mind, causation, and world* (pp. 375–399). Malden: Blackwell.

Beeghly, M., & Tronick, E. (2011). Early resilience in the context of parent-infant relationships: A social developmental perspective. *Current Problems in Pediatric and Adolescent Health Care, 41,* 197–201.

Bennett, D. C., Modrowski, C. A., Kerig, P. K., & Chaplo, S. D. (2015). Investigating the dissociative subtype of posttraumatic stress disorder in a sample of traumatized detained youth. *Psychological Trauma, 7,* 465–472.

Bergman, K., Sarkar, P., Glover, V., & O'Connor, T. G. (2008). Quality of child-parent attachment moderates the impact of antenatal stress on child fearfulness. *Journal of Child Psychology and Psychiatry, 49,* 1089–1098.

Bergman, K., Sarkar, P., Glover, V., & O'Connor, T. G. (2010). Maternal prenatal cortisol and infant cognitive development: Moderation by infant-mother attachment. *Biological Psychiatry, 67,* 1026–1032.

Bergson, H. (1911). *Matter and memory.* Translated by N. M. Paul & W. S. Palmer. London/New York: George Allen/Macmillan.

Bernstein, E. M., & Putnam, F. W. (1986). Development, reliability, and validity of a dissociation scale. *Journal of Nervous and Mental Disease, 174,* 727–735.

Bernstein, D. P., Fink, L., Handelsman, L., Foote, J., Lovejoy, M., Wenzel, K., . . . Ruggiero, J. (1994). Initial reliability and validity of a new retrospective measure of child abuse and neglect. *American Journal of Psychiatry, 151,* 1132–1136.

Bhide, P. G. (2009). Dopamine, cocaine and the development of cerebral cortical cytoarchitecture: A review of current concepts. *Seminars in Cell & Developmental Biology, 20,* 395–402.

Bijker, E. W. (1996). History and heritage in coastal engineering in the Netherlands. In N. C. Kraus (Ed.), *History and heritage of coastal engineering* (pp. 390–412). New York: American Society of Civil Engineers.

Bitbol, M. (2008). Is consciousness primary? *NeuroQuantology, 6,* 53–72.

Bliss, E. L. (1986). *Multiple personality, allied disorders, and hypnosis.* New York: Oxford University Press.

Block, N. (1996). How can we find the neural correlate of consciousness? *Trends in Neuroscience, 19,* 456–459.

Block, N. (2005). Two neural correlates of consciousness. *Trends in Cognitive Sciences, 9*(2), 46–52.

Block, N. (2007). Consciousness, accessibility, and the mesh between psychology and neuroscience. *Behavioral Brain Sciences, 30,* 481–499; 499–548.

Bohm, D., & Hiley, B. J. (1993). *The undivided universe: An ontological interpretation of quantum theory.* London/New York: Routledge.

Bolles, R. C. (1970). Species-specific defense reactions and avoidance learning. *Psychological Review, 71,* 32–48.

Bolles, R. C. F., & Fanselow, M. S. (1980). A perceptual-defensive-recuperative model of fear and pain. *Behavioral Brain Sciences, 3,* 291–301.

Boon, S., Steele, K., & Van der Hart, O. (2011). *Coping with trauma-related dissociation.* New York: Norton.

Bowlby, J. (1969). *Attachment and loss, Vol. I: Attachment.* New York: Basic Books.

Bowlby, J. (1973). *Attachment and loss, Vol. II: Separation: Anxiety and anger.* New York: Basic Books.

Bowlby, J. (1980). *Attachment and loss, Vol. III: Loss: Sadness and depression.* New York: Basic Books.

Brand, B. L., Classen, C. C., Lanius, R., Loewenstein, R., McNary, S., Pain, C., & Putnam, F. W. (2009a). A naturalistic study of dissociative identity disorder and dissociative disorder not otherwise specified patients treated by community clinicians. *Psychological Trauma: Theory, Research, Practice, and Policy, 1,* 153–171.

Brand, B. L., Classen, C. C., McNary, S. W., & Zaveri, P. (2009b). A review of dissociative disorders treatment studies. *Journal of Nervous and Mental Disease, 197,* 646–654.

Brand, B. L., Lanius, R., Vermetten, E., Loewenstein, R. J., & Spiegel, D. (2012). Where are we going? An update on assessment, treatment, and neurobiological research in dissociative disorders as we move toward the DSM-5. *Journal of Trauma and Dissociation, 13*(1), 9–31.

Brand, B., & Loewenstein, R. J. (2014). Does phasic trauma treatment make patients with dissociative identity disorder treatment more dissociative? *Journal of Trauma and Dissociation, 15*(1), 52–65.

Brand, B. L., Loewenstein, R. J., & Spiegel, D. (2014). Dispelling myths about dissociative identity disorder treatment: An empirically based approach. *Psychiatry, 77,* 169–189.

Brand, B. L., & Stadnik, R. (2013). What contributes to predicting change in the treatment of dissociation: Initial levels of dissociation, PTSD, or overall distress? *Journal of Trauma and Dissociation, 14,* 328–341.

Braude, S. E. (1995). *First person plural: Multiple personality and the philosophy of mind.* Lanham: Rowman and Littlefield.

Braude, S. E. (2006). Memory without a trace. *European Journal of Parapsychology 21,* 182–202.

Brazelton, T. B., Tronick, E., Adamson, L., Als, H., & Wise, S. (1975). Early mother-infant reciprocity. *Ciba Foundation Symposium, 33,* 137–154.

Brezinka, C., Lechner, T., & Stephan, K. (1997). The fetus and noise. *Gynäkologisch-geburtshilfliche Rundschau, 37*(3), 119–129.

Brende, J. O. (1984). The psychophysiologic manifestations of dissociation: Electrodermal responses in a multiple personality patient. *Psychiatric Clinics of North America, 7*(1), 41–50.

Briquet, P. (1859). *Traité clinique et thérapeutique de l'hystérie, Tome I* [Clinical and therapeutic treatise on hysteria, Vol. 1]. Paris: J-B Baillière et Fils.

Bursen, H. A. (1978). *Dismantling the memory machine: A philosophical investigation of machine theories of memory.* Dordrecht, The Netherlands: D. Reidel.

Buss, C., Davis, E. P., Hobel, C. J., & Sandman, C. A. (2011). Maternal pregnancy-specific anxiety is associated with child executive function at 6–9 years of age. *Stress, 14,* 665–676.

Buss, C., Davis, E. P., Muftuler, L. T., Head, K., & Sandman, C. A. (2010). High pregnancy anxiety during mid-gestation is associated with decreased gray matter density in 6–9-year-old children. *Psychoneuroendocrinology, 35*(1), 141–153.

Buss, C., Entringer, S., Swanson, J. M., & Wadhwa, P. D. (2012). The role of stress in brain development: The gestational environment's long-term effects on the brain. *Cerebrum, 2012,* 4.

Buss, D. M. (2005), *The handbook of evolutionary psychology.* New York: Wiley.

Bijker, E. W. (1996). History and heritage of coastal engineering in the Netherlands. In N. C. Kraus (Ed.), *History and heritage of coastal engineering: A collection of papers on the history of coastal engineering in countries hosting the International Coastal Engineering Conference 1950–1996* (pp. 390–412). New York: American Society of Civil Engineers.

Carlson, E. B. (1997). *Trauma assessments: A clinician's guide.* New York: Guilford.

Castañeda, C. (1970). *The teachings of Don Juan: A Yaqui way of knowledge.* London: Penguin.

Castiello, U., Becchio, C., Zoia, S., Nelini, C., Sartori, L., Blason, L., . . . Gallese, V. (2010). Wired to be social: The ontogeny of human interaction. *PLoS One, 5*(10), e13199.

Castoriadis, C. (1987). *The imaginary institution of society.* Cambridge: MIT.

Chalmers, D. J. (2008). Strong and weak emergence. In P. Clayton & P. Davies (Eds.), *The re-emergence of emergence: The emergentist hypothesis from science to religion.* Oxford: Oxford University Press.

Chefetz, R. (2015). *Intensive psychotherapy for persistent dissociative processes: The fear of feeling real.* New York: Norton.

Cheng, D., Schwarz, E. B., Douglas, E., & Horon, I. (2009). Unintended pregnancy and associated maternal preconception, prenatal and postpartum behaviors. *Contraception, 79,* 194–198.

Christian, L. M., Franco, A., Glaser, R., & Iams, J. D. (2009). Depressive symptoms are associated with elevated serum proinflammatory cytokines among pregnant women. *Brain, Behavior, and Immunity, 23,* 750–754.

Chu, J. A. (1992). Empathic confrontation in the treatment of childhood abuse survivors, including a tribute to the legacy of Dr. David Caul. *Dissociation, 5,* 98–103.

Chu, J. A. (1998). *Rebuilding shattered lives: The responsible treatment of complex posttraumatic and dissociative disorders.* New York: Wiley.

Clark, A. (2001). *Mindware.* Cambridge: MIT.

Clarke, D. M., & Kissane, D. W. (2002). Demoralization: Its phenomenology and importance. *Australian and New Zealand Journal Psychiatry, 36,* 733–742.

Clarkin, J. F., & Levy, K. N. (2003). The influence of client variables on psychotherapy. In M. Lambert (Ed.), *Handbook of psychotherapy and behavior change* (5th ed., pp. 194–226). New York: Wiley.

Class, Q. A., Buss, C., Davis, E. P., Gierczak, M., Pattillo, C., Chicz-DeMet, A., & Sandman, C. A. (2008). Low levels of corticotropin-releasing hormone during early pregnancy are associated with precocious maturation of the human fetus. *Developmental Neuroscience, 30,* 419–426.

Cleveland, L. M., Minter, M. L., Cobb, K. A., Scott, A. A., & German, V. F. (2008). Lead hazards for pregnant women and children, Part 1: Immigrants and the poor shoulder most of the burden of lead exposure in this country. *American Journal of Nursing, 108*(10), 40–49; 50.

Colombetti, G. (2014). *The feeling body: Affective science meets the enactive mind.* Cambridge, MA: MIT.

Cooley, C. H. (1968). The social self: In the meanings of "I." In C. Gordon & K. J. Gergen (Eds.), *The self in social interaction. Volume I, Classic and contemporary perspectives* (pp. 87–91). New York: Wiley. [Reprinted from *Human nature and the social order.* New York: Charles Scribner & Sons, 1902, pp. 143–141, 144–153, and 155–157.]

Coons, P. M. (1984). The differential diagnosis of multiple personality: A comprehensive review. *Psychiatric Clinics of North America, 7*(1), 51–67.

Cosmelli, D., & Thompson, E. (2010). Embodiment or enactment? Reflections on the bodily basis of consciousness. In J. Stewart, O. Gapenne, & E. D. Di Paolo (Eds.), *Enaction: Toward a new paradigm for cognitive sciences* (pp. 361–385). Cambridge, MA: MIT.

Cosmelli, D., & Thompson, E. (2010). Embodiment or envatment? Reflections on the bodily basis of consciousness. In J. Stewart, O. Gapenne, & E. di Paolo (Eds.), *Enaction: Toward a new paradigm for cognitive science* (pp. 361–385). Cambridge, MA: MIT.

Courtois, C. A., & Ford, J. D. (2009). *Treating complex traumatic stress disorders: An evidence-based guide.* New York: Guilford.

Coussons-Read, M. E., Okun, M. L., Schmitt, M. P., & Giese, S. (2005). Prenatal stress alters cytokine levels in a manner that may endanger human pregnancy. *Psychosomatic Medicine, 67,* 625–631.

Coxe, R., & Holmes, W. (2009). A comparison of two groups of sex offenders identified as high risk and low risk on the Static-99. *Journal of Child Sexual Abuse, 18,* 137–153.

Crisp, P. (1983). Object relations and multiple personality: An exploration of the literature. *Psychoanalytic Review, 70,* 221–234.

Cronin, E., Brand, B.L., & Mattanah, J.F. (2014). The impact of the therapeutic alliance on treatment outcome in patients with dissociative disorders. *European Journal of Psychotraumatology, 5.*

Crowley, M.S., & Seery, B.L. (2001). Exploring the multiplicity of childhood sexual abuse with a focus on polyincestuous contexts of abuse. *Journal of Child Sexual Abuse, 10*(4), 91–110.

Crystal, D. (1975). Prosodic features and linguistic theory. In *The English tone of voice: Essays in intonation, prosody and paralanguage.* London: Edward Arnold.

Dalenberg, C.J. (2000). *Countertransference and the treatment of trauma.* Washington DC: American Psychological Association

D'Angelo, D.V., Gilbert, B.C., Rochat, R.W., Santelli, J.S., & Herold, J.M. (2004). Differences between mistimed and unwanted pregnancies among women who have live births. *Perspectives on Sexual and Reproductive Health, 36,* 192–197.

Davidson, R.J., Jackson, D.C., & Kalin, N.H. (2000). Emotion, plasticity, context, and regulation: Perspectives from affective neuroscience. *Psychological Bulletin, 126,* 890–909.

Davis, E.P., Glynn, L.M., Dunkel Schetter, C., Hobel, C., Chicz-Demet, A., & Sandman, C.A. (2005). Corticotropin-releasing hormone during pregnancy is associated with infant temperament. *Developmental Neuroscience, 27,* 299–305.

Davis, E.P., Glynn, L.M., Schetter, C.D., Hobel, C., Chicz-Demet, A., & Sandman, C.A. (2007). Prenatal exposure to maternal depression and cortisol influences infant temperament. *Journal of the American Academy of Child and Adolescent Psychiatry, 46,* 737–746.

Davis, E.P., & Sandman, C.A. (2010). The timing of prenatal exposure to maternal cortisol and psychosocial stress is associated with human infant cognitive development. *Child Development, 81*(1), 131–148.

De Jaegher, H., & Di Paolo, E. (2007). Participatory sense-making: An enactive approach to cognition. *Phenomenology and the Cognitive Sciences, 6,* 485–507.

De Jaegher, H., Di Paolo, E., & Gallagher, S. (2010). Can social interaction constitute social cognition? *Trends in Cognitive Sciences, 14,* 441–447.

Deleuze, G. (1988). *Spinoza: Practical philosophy* (transl. R. Hurley.). San Francisco: City Lights Books.

Del Giudice, M., Ellis, B.J., & Shirtcliff, E.A. (2011). The adaptive calibration model of stress responsivity. *Neuroscience and Biobehavioral Reviews, 35,* 1562–1592.

Dell, P.F. (2006). The multidimensional inventory of dissociation (MID): A comprehensive measure of pathological dissociation. *Journal of Trauma and Dissociation, 7,* 77–106.

Demos, E.V. (Ed.). (1995). *Exploring affect: The selected writings of Sylvan S. Tomkins.* Cambridge, UK: Cambridge University Press.

Dennett, D. (1988). *Quining qualia.* Retrieved from http://www.fflch.usp.br/df/opessoa/Dennett-Quining-Qualia.pdf

Derogatis, L.R. (1992). *SCL-90-R administration, scoring and procedures manual II.* Towson, MD: Clinical Psychometric Research, Inc.

Descartes, R. (1637). *Discourse on the method of rightly conducting one's reason and seeking truth in the sciences* (transl. J. Bennett, 2007). Retrieved from http://www.earlymoderntexts.com/pdfs/descartes1637

Di Paolo, E.A. (2009). Extended life. *Topoi, 28*(9), 9–21.

Di Paolo, E.A., De Jaegher, H., & Rhohde, M. (2010). Horizons for the enactive mind: Values, social interaction, and play. In J. Stewart, O. Gapenne, & E.A. Di Paolo (Eds.), *Enaction: Toward a new paradigm for cognitive science* (pp. 33–87). Cambridge, MA: MIT.

Doane, L.S., Feeny, N.C., & Zoellner, L.A. (2010). A preliminary investigation of sudden gains in exposure therapy for PTSD. *Behavior Research & Therapy, 48,* 555–560.

Donalek, J.G. (2001). First incest disclosure. *Issues in Mental Health Nursing, 22,* 573–591.

Dorahy, M.J., Brand, B.L., Sar, V., Kruger, C., Stavropoulos, P., Martinez-Taboas, A., ... Middleton, W.

(2014). Dissociative identity disorder: An empirical overview. *Australian and New Zealand Journal of Psychiatry, 48,* 402–417.

Dorahy, M. J., Shannon, C., Seagar, L., Corr, M., Stewart, K., Hanna, D., . . . Middleton, W. (2009). Auditory hallucinations in dissociative identity disorder and schizophrenia with and without a childhood trauma history: Similarities and differences. *Journal of Nervous and Mental Disease, 197,* 892–898.

Draijer, N., & Boon, S. (1993). The validation of the Dissociative Experiences Scale against the criterion of the SCID–D, using receiver operating characteristics (ROC) analysis. *Dissociation, 6,* 28–38.

Eich, E. (1995). Mood as a mediator of place dependent memory. *Journal of Experimental Psychology. General, 124,* 293–308.

Eich, E., Macaulay, D., & Ryan, L. (1994). Mood dependent memory for events of the personal past. *Journal of Experimental Psychology. General, 123,* 201–215.

Ellason, J. W., & Ross, C. A. (1997). Two-year follow-up of inpatients with dissociative identity disorder. *American Journal of Psychiatry, 154,* 832–839.

Ellenberger, H. F. (1970). *The discovery of the unconsciousness: The history and evolution of dynamic psychiatry.* New York: Basic Books.

El Marroun, H., White, T., Verhulst, F. C., & Tiemeier, H. (2014). Maternal use of antidepressant or anxiolytic medication during pregnancy and childhood neurodevelopmental outcomes: A systematic review. *European Child and Adolescent Psychiatry, 23,* 973–992.

Entringer, S., Buss, C., Andersen, J., Chicz-Demet, A., & Wadhwa, P. D. (2011). Ecological momentary assessment of maternal cortisol profiles over a multiple-day period predicts the length of human gestation. *Psychosomatic Medicine, 73,* 469–474.

Entringer, S., Epel, E. S., Lin, J., Buss, C., Shahbaba, B., Blackburn, E. H., . . . Wadhwa, P. D. (2013). Maternal psychosocial stress during pregnancy is associated with newborn leukocyte telomere length. *American Journal of Obstetrics and Gynecology, 208,* e131-e137.

Erickson, M. H. (1958a). Pediatric hypnotherapy. *American Journal of Clinical Hypnosis, 1,* 25–29.

Erickson, M. H. (1958b). Naturalistic techniques of hypnosis. *American Journal of Clinical Hypnosis, 1,* 3–8.

Erickson, M. H. (1959). Further techniques of hypnosis: Utilization techniques. *American Journal of Clinical Hypnosis, 3,* 3–21.

Erickson, M. H. (1966). The interspersal hypnotic technique for symptoms correction and pain control. *American Journal of Clinical Hypnosis, 3,* 198–209.

Erickson, M. H. (1980). *The collected papers of Milton H. Erickson on hypnosis. Volume I: The nature of hypnosis and suggestion; Volume II: Hypnotic alterations of sensory, perceptual, and psychophysiological processes; Volume III: Hypnotic investigation of psychodynamic processes; Volume IV: Innovative hypnotherapy* (ed. E. L. Rossi). New York: Irvington.

Erickson, M. H. (1982). *My voice will go with you: The teaching tales of Milton H. Erickson.* (ed. with commentary Sidney Rosen). New York: Norton.

Erickson, M. H., & Rossi, E. L. (1979). *Hypnosis: An exploratory casebook.* New York: Irvington. Available at http://codenlp.ru/books/hypnotherapy.pdf

Fanselow, M. S., & Lester, L. S. (1988). A functional behavioristic approach to aversively motivated behavior: Predatory imminence as a determinant of the topography of defensive behavior. In R. S. Bolles & M. D. Beecher (Eds.), *Evolution and learning* (pp. 185–212). Hillsdale, NJ: Erlbaum.

Flinn, M. V., Nepomnaschy, P. A., Muehlenbein, M. P., & Ponzi, D. (2011). Evolutionary functions of early social modulation of hypothalamic-pituitary-adrenal axis development in humans. *Neuroscience and Biobehavioral Reviews, 35,* 1611–1629.

Fonagy, P., Gergely, G., Jurist, E. L., & Target, M. (2002). *Affect regulation, mentalization, and the development of the self.* New York: Other Press.

Foote, B., & Park, J. (2008). Dissociative identity disorder and schizophrenia: Differential diagnosis and theoretical issues. *Current Psychiatry Reports, 10,* 217–222.

Frank J. (1968). The role of hope in psychotherapy. *International Journal of Psychiatry, 5,* 383–395.

Fromuth, M. E. (1986). The relationship of childhood sexual abuse with later psychological and sexual adjustment in a sample of college women. *Child Abuse and Neglect, 10,* 5–15.

Fuchs, T., & De Jaeger, H. (2010). Nonrepresentational subjectivity. In T. Fuchs, H. C. Sattel, & P. Henningsen (Eds.), *The embodied self: Dimensions, coherence and disorders* (pp. 203–214). Stuttgart: Schattauer.

Fuster, J. M. (2003). *Cortex and mind: Unifying cognition.* New York: Oxford University Press.

Gallagher, M., & Chiba, A. A. (1996). The amygdala and emotion. *Current Opinions in Neurobiology, 6,* 221–227.

Gallagher, S., & Zahavi, D. (2008). *The phenomenological mind: An introduction to philosophy of mind and cognitive science.* London/New York: Routledge

Garcia, J. (1981). Tilting at the paper mills of academia. *American Psychologist, 36,* 149–158.

Garrett, D. (1999). Teleology in Spinoza and early modern rationalism. In R. J. Gennaro & C. Huenemann (Eds.), *New essays on the rationalists* (pp. 310–335). New York: Oxford University Press.

Garrett, D. (2002). Spinoza's conatus argument. In O. Koistinen & J. Biro (Eds.), *Spinoza: Metaphysical themes* (pp. 127–158). New York: Oxford.

Gelinas, D. J. (1983). The persisting negative effects of incest. *Psychiatry, 46,* 312–332.

Gentry, J., & Bailey, B. A. (2014). Psychological intimate partner violence during pregnancy and birth outcomes: Threat of violence versus other verbal and emotional abuse. *Violence Victims, 29,* 383–392.

Gibson, J. J. (1977). The theory of affordances. In R. Shaw & J. Bransford (Eds.), *Perceiving, acting, and knowing* (pp. 67–82). Hoboken, NJ: Wiley.

Gibson, J. J. (1979). *The ecological approach to visual perception.* Boston: Houghton Mifflin.

Gonzalez-Alzaga, B., Lacasana, M., Aguilar-Garduno, C., Rodriguez-Barranco, M., Ballester, F., Rebagliato, M., & Hernandez, A. F. (2014). A systematic review of neurodevelopmental effects of prenatal and postnatal organophosphate pesticide exposure. *Toxicology Letters, 230,* 104–121.

Goodridge, D., & Hardy, G. E. (2009). Patterns of change in psychotherapy: An investigation of sudden gains in cognitive therapy using the assimilation model. *Psychotherapy Research, 19*(1), 114–123.

Gottlob, L. R., Golding, J. M., & Hauselt, W. J. (2006). Directed forgetting of a single item. *The Journal of General Psychology, 133,* 67–80.

Grawe, K. (2004). *Neuropsychotherapie* [Neuropsychotherapy]. Göttingen: Hogrefe.

Green, B. L. (1996). Trauma History Questionnaire. In B. H. Stamm (Ed.), *Measurement of stress, trauma, and adaptation* (pp. 366–369). Lutherville, MD: Sidran.

Haas, E., Hill, R., Lambert, M. J., Morell, B. (2002). Do early responders to psychotherapy maintain treatment gains? *Journal of Clinical Psychology, 58,* 1157–1172.

Haley, J. (Ed.). (1967). *Advanced techniques of hypnosis and therapy: Selected papers of Milton H. Erickson.* New York: Grune & Stratton.

Halvorsen, J. O., Stenmark, H., Neuner, F., & Nordahl, H. M. (2014). Does dissociation moderate treatment outcomes of narrative exposure therapy for PTSD? A secondary analysis from a randomized controlled clinical trial. *Behavior Research and Therapy, 57,* 21–28.

Han, A., & Stewart, D. E. (2014). Maternal and fetal outcomes of intimate partner violence associated with pregnancy in the Latin American and Caribbean region. *International Journal of Gynaecology and Obstetrics, 124*(1), 6–11.

Hanson, R. K., & Morton-Bourgon, K. E. (2005). The characteristics of persistent sexual offenders: A meta-analysis of recidivism studies. *Journal of Consulting and Clinical Psychology, 73,* 1154–1163.

Harkins, L., Howard, P., Barnett, G., Wakeling, H., & Miles, C. (2015). Relationships between denial, risk, and recidivism in sexual offenders. *Archives of Sexual Behavior, 44*(1), 157–166.

Hart, S. (2011). *The impact of attachment.* New York: Norton.

Hayes, A.M., & Strauss, J.L. (1998). Dynamic systems theory as a paradigm for the study of change in psychotherapy: An application to cognitive therapy for depression. *Journal of Clinical and Consulting Psychology, 66,* 939–947.

Heil, J. (1978). Traces of things past. *Philosophy of Science 45,* 60–67.

Helps, A. (1868). *Realmah.* London: Macmillan.

Hilgard, E.R. (1977). *Divided consciousness: Multiple controls in human thought and action.* New York: Wiley.

Hodgson, G.M., & Knudson, T. (2010). *Darwin's conjecture: The search for general principles of social and economic evolution.* Chicago: The University of Chicago Press.

Hofmann, S.G. (2005). Perception of control over anxiety mediates the relation between catastrophic thinking and social anxiety in social phobia. *Behaviour Research and Therapy, 43,* 885–895.

Howell, E. (2005). *The dissociative mind.* Mahwah, NJ: Analytic Press.

Huber, M. (1995). *Multiple Persönlichkeiten: Überlebenden extremer Gewalt* [Multiple personalities: Survivors of extreme violence]. Frankfurt a. M.: Fischer.

Huber, M. (2003). *Wege der Traumabehandlung: Trauma und Traumabehandlung, Teil 2* [Trauma treatment: Trauma and trauma treatment, Part 2]. Paderborn: Junfermann.

Hurley, S.L. (1998). *Consciousness in action.* London: Harvard University Press.

Husserl, E. (1954/1970). *The crisis of European sciences and transcendental phenomenology: An introduction to phenomenological philosophy.* Evanston, IN: Northwestern University Press. (Posthumous German publication, *Die Krisis der europäischen Wissenschaften und die transzendentale Phänomenologie: Eine Einleitung in die phänomenologische Philosophie,* W. Biemel (Ed.). (1954). The Hague: Martinus Nijhoff).

Husserl, E. (2000). *Logical investigations I-II* (transl. J.N. Findley). London: Routledge.

Hutchinson, J. (1992). *The wound programme.* Dundee: Centre for Medical Education.

Hutto, D.D., & Myin, E. (2013). *Radicalizing enactivism: Basic minds without content.* Cambridge, MA: MIT.

Ilardi, S.S., & Craighead, W.E. (1994). The role of non-specific factors in cognitive-behavior therapy for depression. *Clinical Psychology Research and Practice, 1,* 138–156.

International Society for the Study of Trauma and Dissociation. (2011). Guidelines for treating dissociative identity disorder in adults, third revision. *Journal of Trauma and Dissociation, 12,* 115–187.

Jackson, J.H. (1931–1932). *Selected writings of John Hughlings Jackson (Vols. 1–2).* London: Milford.

Janet, P. (1889). *L'automatisme psychologique: Essai de psychologie expérimentale sur les formes inférieures de l'activité humaine* [Psychological automatism: An experimental psychological essay on the inferior forms of human action]. Paris: Felix Alcan; Paris, Société Pierre Janet/Payot, 1973.

Janet, P. (1893). *L'état mental des hystériques: Les stigmates mentaux.* Paris: Rueff & Cie. (English translation *The mental state of hystericals* (2nd ed.). Paris: Félix Alcan. Reprint: Lafitte Reprints, Marseilles, 1983).

Janet, P. (1901/1977). *The mental state of hystericals: A study of mental stigmata and mental accidents* (edited and with prefaces by D.N. Robinson). Washington, DC: University Publications of America.

Janet, P. (1903). *Les obsessions et la psychasthénie, Vol. 1.* [Obsessions and psychasthenia]. Paris: Félix Alcan.

Janet, P. (1907). *The major symptoms of hysteria.* London/New York: Macmillan.

Janet, P. (1909). Problèmes psychologiques de l'émotion [Psychological problems of emotion]. *Revue Neurologique, 17,* 1551–1687.

Janet, P. (1925). *Psychological healing.* New York: Macmillan. (Original work published as Les médications psychologiques. (1919). Paris: Félix Alcan).

Janet, P. (1926). *Les stades de l'évolution psychologique et le rôle de la faiblesse dans le fonctionnement de l'esprit* [Stages of psychological evolution and the role of weakness in the functioning of the mind]. Paris: A. Chahine.

Janet, P. (1927). La peur de l'action: Les terminaisons de l'action; Les échecs and les triomphes [The fear of action: The completion of actions; Misachievements and triumphs]. *Revue Philosophique de la France et de l'Etranger, 104,* 5–21.

Janet, P. (1928a). *L'evolution de la mémoire et de la notion du temps* [The evolution of memory and of the notion of time]. Paris: A. Chahine.

Janet, P. (1928b). *De l'angoisse à l'extase, Vol. 2, Les sentiments fondamentaux* [From agony to ecstasy, Vol. 2: The fundamental feelings]. Paris: F. Alcan.

Janet, P. (1932). On memories which are too real. In C. MacFie Campbell (Ed.), *Problems of personality* (pp. 141–150). New York: Harcourt, Brace.

Janet, P. (1938). *La psychologie de la conduite* [The psychology of action]. In H. Wallon (Ed.), *Encyclopédie Française* (pp. 808–11–808–16). Paris: Société de Gestion de l'Encyclopédie Française.

Jardri, R., Houfflin-Debarge, V., Delion, P., Pruvo, J. P., Thomas, P., & Pins, D. (2012). Assessing fetal response to maternal speech using a noninvasive functional brain imaging technique. *International Journal of Developmental Neuroscience, 30,* 159–161.

Järvilehto, T. (1998a). The theory of the organism-environment system: I. Description of the theory. *Integrative Physiological and Behavioural Sciences, 33,* 321–334.

Järvilehto, T. (1998b). The theory of the organism-environment system: II. Significance of nervous activity in the organism-environment system. *Integrative Physiological and Behavioural Sciences, 33,* 335–342; 343.

Järvilehto, T. (1999a). The theory of the organism-environment system: III. Role of efferent influences on receptors in the formation of knowledge. *Integrative Physiological and Behavioural Sciences, 34,* 90–100.

Järvilehto, T. (1999b). Is radical constructivism radical enough? *Karl Jaspers Forum,* commentary 14 from September 28. Retrieved from http://oulu.academia.edu/TimoJ%C3%A4rvilehto

Järvilehto, T. (2000a). Theory of the organism-environment system: IV. The problem on mental activity and consciousness. *Integrative Physiological and Behavioural Sciences, 35,* 35–57.

Järvilehto, T. (2000b). Consciousness as cooperation. *Advances in Mind Body Medicine, 16,* 89–92; 97–101.

Järvilehto, T. (2000c). Feeling as knowing. *Consciousness & Emotion, 1*(2), 53–65.

Järvilehto, T. (2001a). Feeling as knowing: Part 2. Emotion, consciousness, and brain activity. *Consciousness & Emotion, 2*(1), 75–102.

Järvilehto, T. (2001b, July). *Machines as part of human consciousness and culture.* Paper presented at an International Symposium Machine Consciousness, Jyvaskyla, Finland.

Järvilehto, T. (2001c, September). *Philosophical problems in neuroscience and psychophysiology.* Seminar on "Perils and prospects of the new brain sciences." Stockholm. See http://www.academia.edu/4661624/Philosophical_problems_in_neuroscience_and_psychophysiology

Järvilehto, T. (2004). Consciousness and the ultimate essence of matter. *NeuroQuantology, 3,* 210–218.

Jepsen, E. K., Langeland, W., & Heir, T. (2014). Early traumatized inpatients high in psychoform and somatoform dissociation: Characteristics and treatment response. *Journal of Trauma and Dissociation, 15,* 572–587.

Johansson, B., Wedenberg, E., & Westin, B. (1992). Fetal heart rate response to acoustic stimulation in relation to fetal development and hearing impairment. *Acta Obstetrica and Gynecologica Scandinavica, 71,* 610–615.

Jonas, H. (1966). *The phenomenon of life: Towards a philosophical biology.* New York: Harper and Row.

Jonas, H. (1973). *Organismus und Freiheit: Ansätze zu einer philosophischen Biologie* [Organism and freedom: Toward a philosophical biology]. Göttingen: Vandenhoeck & Ruprecht. (New edition (1994): *Das Prinzip Leben.* Frankfurt am Main und Leipzig: Insel.)

Jonas, H. (1992). *Philosophische Untersuchungen und metaphysische Vermutungen* [Philosophical investigations and metaphysical presumptions]. Frankfurt a. M. and Leipzig: Insel.

Kant, I. (1781/1998). *Critique of pure reason*. Cambridge, MA: Cambridge University Press.

Kant, I. (1910). Quoted in Weber and Varela, 2002: *The critique of judgement* is quoted (as KdU hereinafter) according to Vol. V of the Preußische Akademie-Ausgabe (Akad.-A.), Berlin 1910ff., with section and page (The Akademie pagination appears also in the margin of, for example, the J. C. Meredith (Oxford 1928) translation of the *Critique of Judgment*).

Kellogg, S. H., & Young, J. E. (2006). Schema therapy for borderline personality disorder. *Journal of Clinical Psychology 62*, 4, 445–458.

Kelly, K. A., Rizvi, S. L., Monson, C. M., & Resick, P. A. (2009). The impact of sudden gains in cognitive behavioral therapy for posttraumatic stress disorder. *Journal of Traumatic Stress, 22*, 287–293.

Kelso, J. A. S., & Kay, B. A. (1987). Information and control: A macroscopic analysis of perception-action coupling. In H. H. Heuer & A. F. Sanders (Eds.), *Perspectives on perception and action* (pp. 3–32). Hillsdale, NJ: Erlbaum.

Kierkegaard, S. (1843/1987). *Either/or. Part II.* (transl. H. V. Hong & E. H. Hong). Princeton: Princeton University Press.

Kluft, R. P. (1984a). Treatment of multiple personality disorder: A study of 33 cases. *Psychiatric Clinics of North America, 7*(1), 9–29.

Kluft, R. P. (Ed.). (1984b). *Childhood antecedents of multiple personality.* Washington, DC: American Psychiatric Press.

Kluft, R. P. (1987). First-rank symptoms as a diagnostic clue to multiple personality disorder. *American Journal of Psychiatry, 144*, 293- 298.

Kluft, R. P. (Ed.). (1990a). *Incest-related syndromes of adult psychopathology*. Washington: American Psychiatric Press.

Kluft R. P. (1990b). The slow leak technique. In C. D. Hammond (Ed.), *Handbook of hypnotic suggestions* (pp. 529–530). New York: Norton.

Kluft, R. P. (1996). Treating the traumatic memories of patients with dissociative identity disorder. *American Journal of Psychiatry, 153*(Suppl 7), 103–110.

Kluft, R. P. (2013). *Shelter from the storm: Processing the traumatic memories of DID/DDNOS patients with the fractionated abreaction technique.* Charleston, SC: CreateSpace.

Kluft, R. P., & Fine, C. (Eds.). (1993). *Clinical perspectives on multiple personality disorder*. Washington, DC: American Psychiatric Press

Koerbagh, A. (1668/2011). *A light shining in dark places, to shed light on matters of theology and religion* (ed. and transl. M. Wielema). Leiden: Brill.

Konig, J., Karl, R., Rosner, R., & Butollo, W. (2014). Sudden gains in two psychotherapies for posttraumatic stress disorder. *Behavior Research and Therapy, 60*, 15–22.

Korzekwa, M. I., Dell, P. F., Links, P. S., Thabane, L., & Fougere, P. (2009). Dissociation in borderline personality disorder: A detailed look. *Journal of Trauma Dissociation, 10*, 346–367.

Krueger, J. (2010). Comment: Radical enactivism and inter-corporeal affectivity. In T. Fuchs, H. C. Sattel, & P. Henningsen (Eds.), *The embodied self: Dimensions, coherence and disorders* (pp. 43–65). Stuttgart: Schattauer.

Kruger, A., Ehring, T., Priebe, K., Dyer, A. S., Steil, R., & Bohus, M. (2014). Sudden losses and sudden gains during a DBT-PTSD treatment for posttraumatic stress disorder following childhood sexual abuse. *European Journal of Psychotraumatology, 5*.

Kull, K. (2000). An introduction to phytosemiotics: Semiotic botany and vegetative sign systems. *Sign Systems Studies, 28*, 326–350.

Laddis, A., & Dell, P. F. (2012). Dissociation and psychosis in dissociative identity disorder and schizophrenia. *Journal of Trauma & Dissociation, 13*, 397–413.

Lagercrantz, H., & Changeux, J. P. (2009). The emergence of human consciousness: From fetal to neonatal life. *Pediatric Research, 65*, 255–260.

Lambert, M. J. (2005). Early response in psychotherapy: Further evidence of the importance of common factors rather than "placebo effects." *Journal of Clinical Psychology, 61*, 855–869.

Lambert, M. J., & Ogles, B. M. (2004). The efficacy and effectiveness of psychotherapy. In M. J. Lambert (Ed.), *Handbook of psychotherapy and behavior change* (pp. 139–193). New York: Wiley.

Lankton, C. H., & Lankton, S. R. (1989). *Tales of enchantment: Goal-directed metaphors for adults and children in therapy.* New York: Brunner/Mazel.

Lankton, S. R., & Lankton, C. H. (1983). *The answer within: A clinical framework of Ericksonian hypnotherapy.* New York: Brunner/Mazel.

Lao Tzu. (2009). *Tao te ching: A book about the way and the power of the way.* (Translated by U. K. Le Guin with the assistance of J. P. Seaton.) Boston: Shambhala.

Lazarus, R. S. (1991). *Emotion and adaptation.* Oxford, New York: Oxford University Press.

LeDoux, J. E. (2002). *Synaptic self: How our brains become who we are.* New York: Viking Penguin.

Lee, G. Y., & Kisilevsky, B. S. (2014). Fetuses respond to father's voice but prefer mother's voice after birth. *Developmental Psychobiology, 56*(1), 1–11.

Leeuwenburg, B. (2013). *Het noodlot van een ketter: Adriaan Koerbagh 1633–1669* [The fate of a heretic: Adriaan Koerbagh 1633–1669]. Nijmegen: Vantilt.

Levine, P. A. (2010). *In an unspoken voice: How the body releases trauma and restores goodness.* Berkeley: North Atlantic Books.

Levine, P. A., & Frederick, A. (1997). *Waking the tiger: Healing trauma.* Berkeley: North Atlantic Books.

Lewis, M. D. (2005). Bridging emotion theory and neurobiology through dynamic systems modeling. *Behavioral and Brain Sciences, 28*, 169–194; 194–245.

Lindquist, K. A., Wager, T. D., Kober, H., Bliss-Moreau, E., & Barrett, L. F. (2012). The brain basis of emotion: A meta-analytic review. *Behavioral and Brain Sciences, 35*, 121–143.

Liotti, G. (1999). Disorganization of attachment as a model for understanding dissociative psychopathology. In J. Solomon & C. George (Eds.), *Disorganization of attachment* (pp. 297–317). New York: Guilford.

Liotti, G. (2004). Trauma, dissociation and disorganized attachment: Three strands of a single braid. *Psychotherapy: Theory, Research, Practice and Training, 41*, 472–486.

Liotti, G. (2006). A model of dissociation based on attachment theory and research. *Journal of Trauma & Dissociation, 7*(4), 55–73.

Liotti, G. (in press a). The multimotivational approach to attachment informed psychotherapy: A clinical illustration. *Psychoanalytic Inquiry, 37*(5).

Liotti, G. (in press b). Conflicts between motivational systems related to attachment trauma: Key to understanding the intrafamily relationship between abused children and their abusers. *Journal of Trauma and Dissociation.*

Llinas, R. R. (2001). *I of the vortex: From neurons to self.* Cambridge, MA: MIT.

Llinas, R. R., & Roy, S. (2009). The "prediction imperative" as the basis for self-awareness. *Philosophical Transactions of the Royal Society B Biological Sciences, 364*(1521), 1301–1307.

Lorentzen, E., Nilsen, H., & Traeen, B. (2008). Will it never end? The narratives of incest victims on the termination of sexual abuse. *Journal of Sex Research, 45*, 164–174.

Lubek, I., & Apfelbaum, E. (1987). Neo-behaviorism and the Garcia-effect: A social psychology science approach to the history of a paradigm clash. In M. Ash & W. Woodward (Eds.), *Psychology in twentieth century thought and society* (pp. 59–91). Cambridge: Cambridge University Press.

Ludwig, A. M. (1983). The psychobiological function of dissociation. *American Journal of Clinical Hypnosis, 26,* 93–99.

Ludwig, A. M., Brandsma, J. M., Wilbur, C. B., Bendtfelt, F., & Jameson, H. (1972). The objective study of multiple personality disorder. *Archives of General Psychiatry, 26,* 298–310.

Lutz, W., Bachmann, F., Tschitsaz, A., Smart, D. W., & Lambert, M. J. (2007). Zeitliche und sequentielle Muster von nonlinearen Veränderungen im Therapieverlauf: Das Phänomen der Sudden Gains und Sudden Losses in ihrem Kontext [Chronological and sequential patterns of nonlinear changes in the course of therapy: The phenomenon of sudden gains and sudden losses in their context]. *Zeitschrift für Klinische Psychologie und Psychotherapie, 36,* 261–269.

Lutz, W., Ehrlich, T., Rubel, J., Hallwachs, N., Rottger, M. A., Jorasz, C., . . . Tschitsaz-Stucki, A. (2013). The ups and downs of psychotherapy: Sudden gains and sudden losses identified with session reports. *Psychotherapy Research, 23*(1), 14–24.

Machado, A. (2003). *Border of a dream: Selected poems.* Port Townsend, WA: Copper Canyon.

Maturana, H. R. (1980). Biology of cognition. In H. R. Maturana & F. J. Varela (Eds.), *Autopoiesis and cognition: The realization of the living* (pp. 5–58). Dordrecht, The Netherlands: D. Reidel.

Maturana, H. R., & Varela, F. J. (1980). *Autopoiesis and cognition: The realization of the living.* Dordrecht, The Netherlands: D. Reidel.

McGinn, C. (1989). *Mental content.* Oxford: Blackwell.

Mead, G. H. (1934). *Mind, self, and society.* Chicago: Chicago University Press.

Mead, G. H. (1968). The genesis of the self. In C. Gordon & K. J. Gergen (Eds.), *The self in social interaction. Volume I, Classic and contemporary perspectives* (pp. 51–59). New York: Wiley. (Reprinted from The genesis of the self and social control. *International Journal of Ethics, XXXV, April 1925, 3,* 251–273.)

Merleau-Ponty, M. (1945/1962). *Phenomenology of perception.* London: Routledge & Kegan. (Translation of *Phénomenologie de la perception.* Paris: Éditions Gallimard).

Mesulam, M. M. (1981). Dissociative states with abnormal temporal lobe EEG: Multiple personality and the illusion of possession. *Archives of Neurology, 38,* 176–181.

Metzinger T (2003). *Being no one: The self-model theory of subjectivity.* Cambridge, MA: MIT.

Micali, N., & Treasure, J. (2009). Biological effects of a maternal ED on pregnancy and foetal development: A review. *European Eating Disorder Review, 17,* 448–454.

Monk, C., Georgieff, M. K., & Osterholm, E. A. (2013). Research review: Maternal prenatal distress and poor nutrition – Mutually influencing risk factors affecting infant neurocognitive development. *Journal of Child Psychology and Psychiatry, 54,* 115–130.

Monk, R. (1991). *Ludwig Wittgenstein: The duty of genius.* London: Vintage Books.

Müller-Pfeiffer, C., Rufibach, K., Wyss, D., Perron, N., Pitman, R., & Rufer, M. (2013). Screening for dissociative disorders in psychiatric out- and daycare patients. *Journal of Psychopathology and Behavioral Assessment, 35,* 592–602.

Mulgan, G. (2006). *Because you're worth it.* Retrieved from http://www.theguardian.com/commentisfree/2006/jun/12/becauseyoureworthit

Myrick, A. C., Brand, B. L., McNary, S. W., Classen, C. C., Lanius, R., Loewenstein, R. J., & Putnam, F. W. (2012). An exploration of young adults' progress in treatment for dissociative disorder. *Journal of Trauma and Dissociation, 13,* 582–595.

Myrick, A. C., Brand, B. L., & Putnam, F. W. (2013). For better or worse: The role of revictimization and stress in the course of treatment for dissociative disorders. *Journal of Trauma and Dissociation, 14,* 375–389.

Myrick, A. C., Chasson, G. S., Lanius, R. A., Leventhal, B., & Brand, B. L. (2015). Treatment of complex dissociative disorders: A comparison of interventions reported by community therapists versus those recommended by experts. *Journal of Trauma and Dissociation, 16*(1), 51–67.

Nagel, T. (1979). What is it like to be a bat? In T. Nagel, *Mortal Questions* (pp. 165–180). New York: Cambridge University Press.

Nash, M. R., Hulsey, T. L., Sexton, M. C., Harralson, T. L., & Lambert, W. (1993). Long-term sequelae of childhood sexual abuse: Perceived family environment, psychopathology, and dissociation. *Journal of Consulting and Clinical Psychology, 61,* 276–283.

Nemiah, J. C. (1981). Dissociative disorders. In A. M. Freeman & H. I. Kaplan (Eds.), *Comprehensive textbook on psychiatry, Third edition.* Baltimore: Williams & Wilkins.

Nijenhuis, E. R. S. (1992). Hoe water wint van steen: Een metaforisch verhaal voor mensen met een ernstige dissociatieve stoornis [How water beats rocks: A metaphorical story for subjects with complex dissociative disorders]. *Hypnotherapie, 13*(4), *57–66.*

Nijenhuis, E. R. S. (1994a). Doornroosje en andere verhalen voor dissociatieve patiënten en therapeuten [The Sleeping Beauty and other stories for patients with dissociative disorders and for their clinicians]. *Hypnotherapie,* 15(3), 54–59.

Nijenhuis, E. R. S. (1994b). *Dissociatieve stoornissen en psychotrauma* [Dissociative disorders and psychological trauma]. Houten, The Netherlands: Bohn Stafleu Van Loghum.

Nijenhuis, E. R. S. (1999/2004). *Somatoform dissociation: Phenomena, measurement, and theoretical issues.* Assen, The Netherlands: KoninklijkeVan Gorcum, 1999 (Reprint New York: Norton).

Nijenhuis, E. R. S. (2014a). Ten reasons for conceiving and classifying posttraumatic stress disorder as a dissociative disorder. *Psichiatria e Psicoterapia 33,* 74–106.

Nijenhuis, E. R. S. (2014b). Dissociation in the DSM-5: Your view s'il vous plait, Docteur Janet? *Journal of Trauma & Dissociation, 15,* 245–253.

Nijenhuis, E. R. S. (2015a). Volume I: The evolving concept of trauma. In E. R. S. Nijenhuis, *The trinity of trauma: Ignorance, fragility, and control. The evolving concept of trauma/The concept and facts of dissociation in trauma* (pp. 2–274). Göttingen: Vandenhoeck & Ruprecht.

Nijenhuis, E. R. S. (2015b). Volume II: The concept and facts of dissociation in trauma. In E. R. S. Nijenhuis, *The trinity of trauma: Ignorance, fragility, and control. The evolving concept of trauma/The concept and facts of dissociation in trauma* (pp. 276–552) Göttingen: Vandenhoeck & Ruprecht.

Nijenhuis, E. R. S. (2015c). Boundaries on the concepts of dissociation and dissociative parts of the personality: Required and viable. *Psichiatria e Psicoterapia 34,* 1, 55–85.

Nijenhuis, E. R. S., & Den Boer, J. A. (2009). Psychobiology of traumatization and trauma-related structural dissociation of the personality. In P. F. Dell & J. A. O'Neil (Eds.), *Dissociation and the dissociative disorders: DSM-V and beyond* (pp. 337–367). New York: Routledge.

Nijenhuis, E. R. S., Lewis-Fernandez, R., Moskowitz, A., & Moreira-Almeida, A. (2014, September). *Proposals and evidence for the ICD-11 classification of dissociative disorders.* World Health Organization, ICD-11 Symposium Series, World Congress of Psychiatry, Madrid.

Nijenhuis, E. R. S., Spinhoven, P., Van Dyck, R., Van der Hart, O., de Graaf, A. M. J., & Knoppert, E. A. M. (1997a). Dissociative pathology discriminates between bipolar mood disorder and dissociative disorder (letter). *British Journal of Psychiatry 170,* 581.

Nijenhuis, E. R. S., Spinhoven, P., Van Dyck, R., Van der Hart, O., & Vanderlinden, J. (1997b). The development of the Somatoform Dissociation Questionnaire (SDQ-5) as a screening instrument for dissociative disorders. *Acta Psychiatrica Scandinavica, 96,* 311–318.

Nijenhuis, E. R. S., Spinhoven, P., Van Dyck, R., Van der Hart, O., & Vanderlinden, J. (1996). The development and the psychometric characteristics of the Somatoform Dissociation Questionnaire (SDQ-20). *Journal of Nervous and Mental Disease 184,* 688–694.

Nijenhuis, E. R. S., Spinhoven, P., Van Dyck, R., Van der Hart, O., & Vanderlinden, J. (1998a). Psychometric characteristics of the Somatoform Dissociation Questionnaire: A replication study. *Psychotherapy & Psychosomatics, 67,* 17–23.

Nijenhuis, E. R. S., Spinhoven, P., Van Dyck, R., Van der Hart, O., & Vanderlinden, J. (1998b). Degree of somatoform and psychological dissociation in dissociative disorder is correlated with reported trauma. *Journal of Traumatic Stress, 11,* 711–730.

Nijenhuis, E. R. S., Spinhoven, P., Van Dyck, R., Van der Hart, O., Chatrou, M., Moene, F. & Vanderlinden, J. (1999). Somatoform dissociation discriminates among diagnostic groups over and above general psychopathology. *Australian and New Zealand Journal of Psychiatry, 33,* 512–520.

Nijenhuis, E. R. S., & Van der Hart, O. (1999). Somatoform dissociative phenomena: A Janetian perspective. In J. M. Goodwin & R. Attias (Eds.), *Splintered reflections: Images of the body in trauma* (pp. 89–127). New York: Basic Books.

Nijenhuis, E. R. S., & Van der Hart, O. (2011a). Dissociation in trauma: A new definition and comparison with previous formulations. *Journal of Trauma & Dissociation, 12,* 416–445.

Nijenhuis, E. R. S., & Van der Hart, O. (2011b). Defining dissociation in trauma. *Journal of Trauma and Dissociation, 12,* 469–473.

Nijenhuis, E. R. S., Van der Hart, O., & Kruger, K. (2002). The psychometric characteristics of the Traumatic Experiences Questionnaire (TEC): First findings among psychiatric outpatients. *Clinical Psychology and Psychotherapy, 9,* 200–210.

Nijenhuis, E. R. S., Van der Hart, O., & Steele, K. (2002). The emerging psychobiology of trauma-related dissociation and dissociative disorders. In H. D'Haenen, J. A. Den Boer, & P. Willner (Eds.), *Biological psychiatry* (pp. 1079–1098). London: Wiley.

Nijenhuis, E. R. S., Van Dyck, R., Spinhoven, P., Van der Hart, O., Chatrou, M., Vanderlinden, J., & Moene, F. (1999). Somatoform dissociation discriminates between diagnostic categories over and above general psychopathology. *Australian and New Zealand Journal of Psychiatry 33,* 512–520.

Nijenhuis, E. R. S., Van Dyck, R., Ter Kuile, M. M., Mourits, M. J. E., Spinhoven, P., & Van der Hart, O. (2003). Evidence for associations among somatoform dissociation, psychological dissociation and reported trauma in patients with chronic pelvic pain. *Journal of Psychosomatic Obstetrics and Gynecology, 24,* 87–98.

Nijenhuis, E. R. S., Van Engen, A., Kusters, I., & Van der Hart, O. (2001). Peritraumatic somatoform and psychological dissociation in relation to recall of childhood sexual abuse. *Journal of Trauma and Dissociation, 2,* 49–68.

Noë, A. (2009). *Out of our heads.* New York: Hill and Wang.

Norris, F. H. (1990). Screening for traumatic stress: A scale of use in the general population. *Journal of Applied Social Psychology, 20,* 1704–1718.

Northoff, G. (2003). *Philosophy of the brain: The brain problem.* Amsterdam/Philadelphia: John Benjamins.

Northoff, G. (2014a). *Minding the brain: A guide to philosophy and neuroscience.* London: Palgrave Macmillan.

Northoff, G. (2014b). *Unlocking the brain. Volume II. Consciousness.* New York: Oxford University Press.

Nunes, K. L., Hanson, R. K., Firestone, P., Moulden, H. M., Greenberg, D. M., & Bradford, J. M. (2007). Denial predicts recidivism for some sexual offenders. *Sexual Abuse: A Journal of Research and Treatment, 19,* 91–105

Nunes, K. L., & Jung, S. (2013). Are cognitive distortions associated with denial and minimization among sex offenders? *Sexual Abuse, 25,* 166–188.

O'Connor, T. G., Bergman, K., Sarkar, P., & Glover, V. (2013). Prenatal cortisol exposure predicts infant cortisol response to acute stress. *Developmental Psychobiology, 55,* 145–155.

Ogden, P., Minton, K., & Pain, C. (2006). *Trauma and the body: A sensorimotor approach to psychotherapy.* New York: Norton.

Öhman, A., & Mineka, S. (2001). Fears, phobias, and preparedness: Toward an evolved module of fear and fear learning. *Psychology Review, 108,* 483–522.

Overmier, J. B., & Murison, R. (2005). Trauma and resulting sensitization effects are modulated by psychological factors. *Psychoneuroendocrinology, 30*, 965–973.

Overton, W. (2015). Processes, relations, and relational-developmental-systems. In R. M. Lerner (Ed.), *Handbook of child psychology and developmental science* (7th ed., Kindle edition, pp. 1–54). Hoboken: Wiley.

Oyama, S. (2000). *The ontogeny of information: Developmental systems and evolution* (2nd ed.). Durham, NC: Duke University.

Panksepp, J. (1998). *Affective neuroscience: The foundations of human and animal emotions.* New York: Oxford University Press.

Panksepp, J., & Biven, L. (2012). *The archeology of mind: Neuroevolutionary origins of human emotions.* New York: Norton.

Pearlman, L. A., & Courtois, C. A. (2005). Clinical applications of the attachment framework: Relational treatment of complex trauma. *Journal of Traumatic Stress, 18*, 449–459.

Pechtel, P., & Pizzagalli, D. A. (2011). Effects of early life stress on cognitive and affective function: an integrated review of human literature. *Psychopharmacology, 214*(1), 55–70.

Peirce, C. S. (1978). *Collected papers, Vol. II. Elements of logic* (ed. C. Hartshorne & P. Weiss). Cambridge, MA: Belknap.

Pessoa, L. (2008). On the relationship between emotion and cognition. *Nature Reviews Neuroscience, 9*, 148–158.

Pessoa, L. (2010). Emotion and cognition and the amygdala: From "what is it?" to "what's to be done?" *Neuropsychologia, 48*, 3416–3429.

Pessoa, L. (2012). Beyond brain regions: Network perspective of cognition-emotion interactions. *Behavior and Brain Sciences, 35*, 158–159.

Phillips, M. (1993). The use of ego-state therapy in the treatment of posttraumatic stress-disorder. *American Journal of Clinical Hypnosis 35*, 241–249.

Phillips, M., & Frederick, C. (1995). *Healing the divided self: Clinical and Ericksonian hypnotherapy traumatic and dissociative conditions.* New York: Norton.

Picciolini, O., Porro, M., Meazza, A., Gianni, M. L., Rivoli, C., Lucco, G., . . . Mosca, F. (2014). Early exposure to maternal voice: Effects on preterm infants development. *Early Human Development, 90*, 287–292.

Pisoni, C., Garofoli, F., Tzialla, C., Orcesi, S., Spinillo, A., Politi, P., . . . Stronati, M. (2014). Risk and protective factors in maternal-fetal attachment development. *Early Human Development, 90*(Suppl 2), S45–S46.

Pliny. (1949–1954). *Pliny's natural history.* Transl. by H. Rackham, W. H. S. Jones, & D. E. Eichholz and taken from the 10 volume edition published by Harvard University Press and William Heineman, London.

Pluess, M., & Belsky, J. (2011). Prenatal programming of postnatal plasticity? *Development and Psychopathology, 23*(1), 29–38.

Plumb, T. N., Cullen, P. K., & Minor, T. R. (2015). Parameters of hormetic stress and resilience to trauma in rats. *Stress, 18*(1), 88–95.

Polderman, T. J., Benyamin, B., de Leeuw, C. A., Sullivan, P. F., van Bochoven, A., Visscher, P. M., & Posthuma, D. (2015). Meta-analysis of the heritability of human traits based on fifty years of twin studies. *Nature Genetics, 7*, 702–709.

Pryce, C. R., Azzinnari, D., Spinelli, S., Seifritz, E., Tegethoff, M., & Meinlschmidt, G. (2011). Helplessness: A systematic translational review of theory and evidence for its relevance to understanding and treating depression. *Pharmacology and Therapeutics, 132*, 242–267.

Protevi, J. (Ed.). (2006). Enaction. In *A dictionary of continental philosophy* (pp. 169–170). New Haven: Yale University Press.

Putnam, F. W. (1984a). The psychophysiological investigations of multiple personality disorder: A review. *Psychiatric Clinics of North America, 7,* 31–41.

Putnam, F. W. (1984b). The study of multiple personality disorder: General strategies and practical considerations. *Psychiatric Annals, 14,* 58–62.

Putnam, F. W. (1989). *Diagnosis and treatment of multiple personality disorder.* New York: Guilford.

Putnam, F. W. (1992). Using hypnosis for therapeutic abreactions. *Psychiatric Medicine, 10*(1), 51–65.

Putnam, F. W. (1993). Dissociative disorders in children: Behavioral profiles and problems. *Child Abuse and Neglect, 17*(1), 39–45.

Putnam, F. W. (1997). *Dissociation in children and adolescents: A developmental perspective.* New York: Guilford.

Putnam, F. W., Guroff, J. J., Silberman, E. K, Barban, L., & Post, R. N. (1986). The clinical phenomenology of multiple personality disorder: A review of 100 recent cases. *Journal of Clinical Psychiatry, 47,* 285–293.

Rand, K., & Lahav, A. (2014). Maternal sounds elicit lower heart rate in preterm newborns in the first month of life. *Early Human Development, 90,* 679–683.

Redfield, J. (1993). *The Celestine prophecy.* New York: Warner Books.

Reinders, A. A. T. S., Nijenhuis, E. R. S., Quak, J., Korf, J., Paans, A. M. J., Haaksma, J., . . . Den Boer, J. (2006). Psychobiological characteristics of dissociative Identity disorder: A symptom provocation study. *Biological Psychiatry, 60,* 730–740.

Reinders, A. A. T. S., Willemsen, A. T. M., Vos, H. P. J., Den Boer, J. A., & Nijenhuis, E. R. S. (2012). Fact or factitious? A psychobiological study of authentic and simulated dissociative identity states. *PLoS ONE, 7*(6), e39279.

Reinders, A. A. T. S., Willemsen, A. T., Vissia, E. M., Vos, H. P., Den Boer, J. A., & Nijenhuis, E. R. (2016). The psychobiology of authentic and simulated dissociative personality states: The full monty. *Journal of Nervous and Mental Disease, 204,* 445–457.

Remarque, E. M. (1929). *Im Westen nichts Neues.* Berlin: Ullstein. (English translation, *All Quiet on the Western Front,* New York: Ballantine, 1982.)

Resnick, H. (1996). Psychometric review of the Trauma Assessment for Adults (TAA). In B. H. Stamm (Ed.), *Measurement of stress, trauma, and adaptation* (pp. 362–365). Lutherville, MD: Sidran.

Rizzolatti, G., Cattaneo, L., Fabbri-Destro, M., & Rozzi, S. (2014). Cortical mechanisms underlying the organization of goal-directed actions and mirror neuron-based action understanding. *Physiology Reviews, 94,* 655–706.

Roelofs, K., Keijsers, G. P., Hoogduin, K. A., Naring, G. W., & Moene, F. C. (2002). Childhood abuse in patients with conversion disorder. *American Journal of Psychiatry, 159,* 1908–1913.

Rofé, Y., & Rofé, Y. (2013). Conversion disorder: A review through the prism of the rational-choice theory of neurosis. *Europe's Journal of Psychology, 9*(4).

Rosch, E. (1977). Human categorization. In N. Warren (Ed.), *Advances in cross-cultural psychology* (Vol. 1, pp. 1–49). London: Academic Press.

Rosenbaum, M., & Weaver, G. M. (1980). Dissociated state: Status of a case after 38 years. *Journal of Nervous and Mental Disease, 168,* 597–603.

Ross, C. A. (1989). *Multiple personality disorder: Diagnosis, clinical features, and treatment.* New York: Wiley.

Ross, C. A. (1997). *Dissociative identity disorder: Diagnosis, clinical features, and treatment of multiple personality.* New York: Wiley.

Ross, C. A. (2013). *Structural dissociation: A proposed modification of the theory.* Richardson, TX: Manitou Communications.

Ross, C. A. (2014a). Unresolved problems in the theory of structural dissociation. *Psichiatria e Psicoterapia, 33,* 285–292.

Ross, C. A. (2014b). Biology and genetics in DSM-5. *Ethical Human Psychology and Psychiatry, 15*, 195–198.

Ross, C. A. (2014c). The equal environments assumption in schizophrenia genetics. *Psychosis, 6*, 189–191.

Ross, C. A., Heber, S., & Anderson, G. (1990). The Dissociative Disorders Interview Schedule. *American Journal of Psychiatry, 147*, 1698–1699.

Ross, C. A., Miller, S. D., Reagor, P., Bjornson, L., Fraser, G. A., & Anderson, G. (1990). Schneiderian symptoms in multiple personality disorder and schizophrenia. *Comprehensive Psychiatry, 31*, 111–118.

Ross, C. A., Norton, G. R., & Wozney, K. (1989). Multiple personality disorder: An analysis of 236 cases. *Canadian Journal of Psychiatry, 34*, 413–418.

Runes, D. D. (1951). *Spinoza dictionary.* New York: The Philosophical Library.

Sandman, C. A., Davis, E. P., Buss, C., & Glynn, L. M. (2011). Prenatal programming of human neurological function. *International Journal of Peptides, 2011*, 1–9.

Sar, V., Kundakçi, T., Kiziltan, E., Bakim, B., & Bozkurt, O. (2000). Differentiating dissociative disorders from other diagnostic groups through somatoform dissociation in Turkey. *Journal of Trauma and Dissociation 1*(4), 67–80.

Schenk, L., & Bear, D. (1981). Multiple personality and related dissociative phenomena in patients with temporal lobe epilepsy. *American Journal of Psychiatry, 138*, 1311–1316.

Schiepek, G. (2011). Der psychotherapeutische Prozess: Einblicke in die Selbstorganisation bio-psycho-sozialer Systeme [The psychotherapeutic process: Insights into the self-organization of bio-psycho-social systems]. In C. Schubert (Ed.), *Psychoneuroimmunologie und Psychotherapie* (pp. 353–373). Stuttgart: Schattauer.

Schimmenti, A., & Caretti, V. (2014). Dissociation as a transdiagnostic construct. A commentary on Ellert R. S. Nijenhuis' paper "Ten reasons for conceiving and classifying posttraumatic stress disorder as a dissociative disorder." *Psichiatria e Psicoterapia 33*(1), 74–106.

Schlotz, W., Godfrey, K. M., & Phillips, D. I. (2014). Prenatal origins of temperament: Fetal growth, brain structure, and inhibitory control in adolescence. *PLoS One, 9*(5), e96715.

Schlumpf, Y. R., Nijenhuis, E. R. S., Chalavi, S., Weder, E. V., Zimmermann, E., Luechinger, R., & Jäncke, L. (2013). Dissociative-part dependent biopsychosocial reactions to backward masked angry and neutral faces: An fMRI study of dissociative identity disorder. *Neuroimage: Clinical, 3*, 54–64.

Schneider, K. (1959). *Clinical psychopathology.* New York: Grune and Stratton.

Schopenhauer, A. (1819/1958). *The world as will and representation, Vol. I* (transl. R.Burdon, H. Haldane, & J. Kemp). Clinton, MA: The Falcon's Wing.

Schopenhauer, A. (1844/1958). *The world as will and representation, Vol. II* (transl. R.Burdon, H. Haldane, & J. Kemp). Clinton, MA: The Falcon's Wing.

Schopenhauer, A. (1889/2007). *On the fourfold root of the principle of sufficient reason* (transl. K. Hillebrand). New York: Cosimo.

Schubert, C. (2011). *Soziopsychoimmunologie: Integration von Dynamik und subjektiver Bedeutung in die Psychoimmunologie* [Sociopsychoimmunology: Integration of dynamics and subjective meaning in psychoimmunology]. In C. Schubert (Ed.), *Psychoneuroimmunologie und Psychotherapie* (pp. 374–405). Stuttgart: Schattauer.

Schumacher, E. F. (1973). *Small is beautiful.* London: Blond & Briggs.

Schumacher, E. F. (1999). *Small is beautiful: Economics as if people mattered: 25 years later . . . with commentaries.* Vancouver: Hartley & Marks.

Schumacher S., Martin-Soelch C., Rufer M., Pazhenkottil A. P., Wirtz G., Fuhrhans C., Hindermann E., & Mueller-Pfeiffer C. (2011). Psychometric characteristics of the German adaptation of the traumatic experiences checklist (TEC). *Psychological Trauma: Theory, Research, Practice, and Policy, 4*, 338–346.

Schutter, D. J., & Van Honk, J. (2005). The cerebellum on the rise in human emotion. *Cerebellum, 4*, 290–294.

Schutter, D. J., & Van Honk, J. (2006). An electrophysiological link between the cerebellum, cognition and emotion: Frontal theta EEG activity to single-pulse cerebellar TMS. *Neuroimage, 33,* 1227–1231.

Schutter, D. J., & Van Honk, J. (2009). The cerebellum in emotion regulation: A repetitive transcranial magnetic stimulation study. *Cerebellum, 8*(1), 28–34.

Sego, S. A., Golding, J. M., & Gottlob, L. R. (2006). Directed forgetting in older adults using the item and list methods. *Neuropsychology, development, and cognition. Section B, Aging, neuropsychology and cognition, 13*(1), 95–114.

Seidmann, S., Schlumpf, Y. R., & Jäncke, L. (2014). *When one look is all it takes: A single-case eye-tracking study in a patient with dissociative identity disorder, a simulant, and healthy controls.* Master thesis, University of Zurich, Philosophical Faculty.

Sender, R., Fuchs, S., & Milo, R. (2016). Are we really vastly outnumbered? Revisiting the ratio of bacterial to host cells in humans. *Cell, 164,* 337–340.

Shvil, E., Rusch, H. L., Sullivan, G. M., & Neria, Y. (2013). Neural, psychophysiological, and behavioral markers of fear processing in PTSD: A review of the literature. *Current Psychiatry Reports, 15,* 358–367.

Somer, E., & Dell, P. F. (2005). Development of the Hebrew-Multidimensional Inventory of Dissociation (H-MID): A valid and reliable measure of pathological dissociation. *Journal of Trauma and Dissociation, 6*(1), 31–53.

Spät, P. (2009–2010). *Panpsychismus: Ein Lösungsvorschlag zum Leib-Seele-Problem* [Panpsychism: A proposed solution to the body-mind problem]. Dissertation, Albert-Ludwigs-Universität, Freiburg.

Spiegel, D. (1984). Multiple personality as a posttraumatic stress disorder. *Psychiatric Clinics of North America, 7*(1), 101–110.

Spinoza, B. (1677a). *Ethics* (transl. and ed. E. Curley). London: Penguin.

Spinoza, B. (1677b). *De Nagelate Schriften van B. d. S.* [The posthumus writings of B. d. S.]. Amsterdam: Rieuwertsz.

Steele, K., Van der Hart, O., & Nijenhuis, E. R. S. (2005). Phase-oriented treatment of structural dissociation in complex traumatization: Overcoming trauma-related phobias. *Journal of Trauma and Dissociation, 6*(3), 11–53.

Steinberg M. (2000). Advances in the clinical assessment of dissociation. The SCID-D-R. *Bulletin of the Menninger Clinic, 64,* 146–63.

Steinberg, M., Cicchetti, D., Buchanan, J., Rakfeldt, J., & Rounsaville, B. (1994). Distinguishing between multiple personality disorder (dissociative identity disorder) and schizophrenia using the Structured Clinical Interview for DSM-IV Dissociative Disorders. *Journal of Nervous and Mental Disease, 182,* 495–502.

Steinberg, M., Cichetti, D. V., Buchanan, J., Hall, P., & Rounsaville, B. (1993). Clinical assessment of dissociative symptoms and disorders: The Structured Clinical Interview for DSM–IV Dissociative Disorders. *Dissociation, 6,* 3–16.

Steingard, S., & Frankel, F. H. (1985). Dissociation and psychotic symptoms. *American Journal of Psychiatry, 142,* 953–955.

Sternberg, S. (1975). Memory scanning: New findings and current controversies. *Quarterly Journal of Experimental Psychology, 22,* 1–32.

Swaab, D. (2010). *Wij zijn ons brein* [We are our brain]. Amsterdam: Uitgeverij Contact.

Swanson, J. D., & Wadhwa, P. M. (2008). Developmental origins of child mental health disorders. *Journal of Child Psychology and Psychiatry, 49,* 1009–1019.

Taft, A. J., Powell, R. L., & Watson, L. F. (2015). The impact of violence against women on reproductive health and child mortality in Timor-Leste. *Australian and New Zealand Journal of Public Health, 39,* 177–181.

Thelen, E. (2005). Dynamic systems theory and the complexity of change. *Psychoanalytic Dialogues, 15,* 255–283. Nonlinear systems theory and psychoanalysis: Symposium in honor of Emmanuel Ghent.

Thelen, E., & Smith, L. B. (1994). *A dynamic systems approach to the development of perception and action.* Cambridge: MIT.

Thompson, E. (2007). *Mind in life: Biology, phenomenology, and the sciences of mind.* Cambridge, MA: Belknap Harvard.

Thompson, E. (2011a). Précis of *Mind in life: Biology, phenomenology, and the sciences of mind. Journal of Consciousness Studies, 18,* 10–22.

Thompson, E. (2011b). Reply to commentaries. *Journal of Consciousness Studies, 18,* 176–223.

Thompson, E., Lutz, A., & Cosmelli, D. (2005). Neurophenomenology: An introduction for neurophilosophers. In A. Brook, & K. Akins (Eds.), *Cognition and the neuroscience movement* (pp. 40–97). New York: Cambridge University Press.

Thompson, E., & Zahavi, D. (2007). Philosophical issues: Phenomenology. In P. D. Zelazo, M. Moscovitch, & E. Thompson (Eds.), *The Cambridge handbook of consciousness* (pp. 67–87). Cambridge: Cambridge University Press.

Timberlake, W. (1993). Behavior systems and reinforcement: An integrative approach. *Journal of Experimental Analysis of Behavior, 60*(1), 105–128.

Timberlake, W., & Lucas, G. A. (1989). Behavior systems and learning: From misbehavior to general principles. In S. B. Klein, & R. R. Mowrer (Eds.), *Contemporary learning theories* (pp. 237–275). Hillsdale, NY: Erlbaum.

Trevarthen, C., & Aitken, K. J. (2001). Infant intersubjectivity: Research, theory, and clinical applications. *Journal of Child Psychology and Psychiatry, 42*(1), 3–48.

Tronick, E. Z. (1989). Emotions and emotional communication in infants. *American Psychologist, 44,* 112–119.

Tronick, E. (2006). The inherent stress of normal daily life and social interaction leads to the development of coping and resilience, and variation in resilience in infants and young children: Comments on the papers of Suomi and Klebanov & Brooks-Gunn. *Annals of The New York Academy of Sciences, 1094,* 83–104.

Tronick, E., & Beeghly, M. (2011). Infants' meaning-making and the development of mental health problems. *American Psychologist, 66,* 107–119.

Tronick, E. Z., & Cohn, J. F. (1989). Infant-mother face-to-face interaction: Age and gender differences in coordination and the occurrence of miscoordination. *Child Development, 60*(1), 85–92.

Tronick, E., & Reck, C. (2009). Infants of depressed mothers. *Harvard Review of Psychiatry, 17,* 147–156.

Turvey, M. T., & Shaw, R. E. (1999). Ecological foundations of cognition. I. Symmetry and specificity of animal-environment systems. *Journal of Consciousness Studies, 6,* 95–110.

Van der Hart, O., & Friedman, B. (1989). A reader's guide to Pierre Janet on dissociation: A neglected intellectual heritage. *Dissociation, 2,* 3–16.

Van der Hart, O., & Nijenhuis, E. R. S. (1999). Bearing witness to uncorroborated trauma: The clinician's development of reflective belief. *Professional Psychology: Research and Practice, 30,* 37–44.

Van der Hart, O., & Nijenhuis, E. R. S. (2008). Dissociative disorders. In P. H. Blaney, & T. Millon (Eds), *Oxford textbook of psychopathology* (2nd ed., pp. 452–481). New York, Oxford: Oxford University Press.

Van der Hart, O., Nijenhuis, E. R. S., & Steele, K. (2005). Dissociation: An insufficiently recognized major feature of complex posttraumatic stress disorder. *Journal of Traumatic Stress, 18,* 413–424.

Van der Hart, O., Nijenhuis, E. R. S., & Steele, K. (2006). *The haunted self: Structural dissociation and the treatment of chronic traumatization.* New York: Norton.

Van der Hart, O., Van Dijke, A., Van Son, M., & Steele, K. (2000). Somatoform dissociation in traumatized World War I combat soldiers: A neglected clinical heritage. *Journal of Trauma and Dissociation, 1*(4), 33–66.

Van der Kolk, B. A., & Van der Hart, O. (1989). Pierre Janet and the breakdown of adaptation in psychological trauma. *American Journal of Psychiatry, 146,* 1530–1540.

Vanderlinden, J. (1993). *Dissociative experiences, trauma, and hypnosis.* Delft: Eburon.

Van Duijl, M., Nijenhuis, E., Komproe, I. H., Gernaat, H. B. & de Jong, J. T. (2010). Dissociative symptoms and reported trauma among patients with spirit possession and matched healthy controls in Uganda. *Culture, Medicine, and Psychiatry, 34,* 380–400.

Van Minnen, A. (2012, November). *"Ik ben niet bang voor de boze badeend . . . ik ben niet bang, ik ben niet bang . . ."* [I am not scared of the bad rubber duck . . . I am not scared, I am not scared]. Keynote at the Fall Conference of the Vereniging voor Gedragstherapie en Cognitieve Therapie, Veldhoven, The Netherlands.

Van Minnen, A., Zoellner, L. A., Harned, M. S., & Mills, K. (2015). Changes in comorbid conditions after prolonged exposure for PTSD: A literature review. *Current Psychiatry Reports, 17,* 549.

Van Reijen, M. (2013). *Spinoza in bedrijf: Van passie naar actie.* [Spinoza in operation: From passion to action.] Zoetermeer, The Netherlands: Uitgeverij Klement.

Van Schie, K., Geraerts, E., & Anderson, M. C. (2013). Emotional and nonemotional memories are suppressible under direct suppression instructions. *Cognition & Emotion, 27,* 1122–1131.

Varela, F. J. (1979). *Principles of biological autonomy.* New York: Elsevier.

Varela, F. J. (1988). The creative circle: Sketches on the natural history of circularity. In P. Watzlawick (Ed.), *L'invention de la réalité* [The invented reality] (pp. 329–347). Paris: Editions du Seuil. (Original publication: *The invented reality: Contributions to constructivism* (pp. 309–325). New York: W. W. Norton, 1984. Available at http://cepa.info/2089)

Varela, F. J. (1991). Organism: A meshwork of selfless selves. In A. Tauber (Ed.), *Organism and the origin of self* (pp. 79–107). Dordrecht, The Netherlands: Kluwer.

Varela, F. J. (1992). *Autopoiesis and a biology of intentionality.* Paris: Ecole Polytechnique. Retrieved from ftp://ftp.eeng.dcu.ie/pub/alife/bmcm9401/varela.pdf. Also in B. McMullin & N. Murphy (Eds.), *Proceedings of Autopoiesis and Perception, ESPRIT BRA 3352,* Dublin City University.

Varela, F. J. (1996). Neurophenomenology: A methodological remedy for the hard problem. *Journal of Consciousness Studies, 3,* 330–349.

Varela, F. J. (1997). Patterns of life: Intertwining identity and cognition. *Brain and Cognition, 34,* 72–87.

Varela, F. J., & Bourgine, P. (Eds.). (1991). *Towards a practice of autonomous systems.* Cambridge MA: MIT.

Varela, F. J., Thompson, E., & Rosch, E. (1991). *The embodied mind: Cognitive science and human experience.* Cambridge, MA: MIT.

Vas, J. P. (2013). Tones and being tuned: Suggestions for the common origins of music therapy and hypnotherapy. *Psychiatrica Hungarica, 28,* 159–164.

Vissia, E. M. Giesen, M. E., Chalavi, S., Nijenhuis, E. R. S., Draijer, N., Brand, B. L., & Reinders, A. A. T. S. (2016). Is it trauma or fantasy based? Comparing dissociative identity disorder, posttraumatic stress disorder, simulators, and controls. *Acta Psychiatrica Scandinavica, 134,* 111–128.

Voegtline, K. M., Costigan, K. A., Pater, H. A., & DiPietro, J. A. (2013). Near-term fetal response to maternal spoken voice. *Infant Behavior Development, 36,* 526–533.

Von Uexküll, J. (1934/2010). *A foray into the worlds of animals and humans: With a theory of meaning* (transl. J. D. O'Neill). Minneapolis, MN: University of Minnesota Press.

Walker, E. A., Newman, E., Koss, M., & Bernstein, D. (1997). Does the study of victimization revictimize the victims? *Psychiatry and Primary Care, 19,* 403–410.

Waller, G., Babbs, M., Wright, F., Potterton, C., Meyer, C., & Leung, N. (2003). Somatoform dissociation in eating disordered patients. *Behavior Research and Therapy, 41,* 619–627.

Waller, G., Hamilton, K., Elliott, P., Lewendon, J., Stopa, L., Waters, A., . . . Chalkey, J. (2000). Somatoform dissociation, psychological dissociation and specific forms of trauma. *Journal of Trauma and Dissociation, 1,* 81–98.

Watkins, H. H. (1991). Ego-state therapy: An overview. *American Journal of Clinical Hypnosis 35,* 232–240.

Watkins, J. G., & Watkins, H. H. (1997). *Ego states: Theory and therapy.* Norton, New York.

Weaver, J. (2010, December 23). Social before birth: Twin first interact with each other as fetuses. *Scientific American.* Retrieved from http://www.scientificamerican.com/article/social-before-birth/

Weber, A. (2002a). The "surplus of meaning": Biosemiotic aspects in Francisco J. Varela's philosophy of cognition. *Cybernetics & Human Knowing, 9*(2), 11–29.

Weber, A. (2002b). Feeling the signs: Organic experience, intrinsic teleology and the origins of meaning in the biological philosophy of Hans Jonas and Susanne K. Langer. *Sign System Studies, 30*(1), 183–200.

Weber, A. (2010). The book of desire: Toward a biological poetics. *Biosemiotics, 4,* 149–170.

Weber, A. (2014). *Alles fühlt: Mensch, Natur und die Revolution der Lebenswissenschaften* [Everything feels: Man, nature and the revolution of the life sciences]. Klein Jasedow, Germany: Thinkoya.

Weber, A., & Varela, F. J. (2002). Life after Kant: Natural purposes and the autopoietic foundations of biological individuality. *Phenomenology and the Cognitive Sciences, 1,* 97–125.

Weber, M. (1904/1949). Objectivity in social science and social policy. In E. A. Shils & H. A. Finch (Eds. and Trans.), *The methodology of the social sciences* (pp. 49–112). New York: Free Press.

Weinberg, M. K., & Tronick, E. Z. (1996). Infant affective reactions to the resumption of maternal interaction after the still-face. *Child Development, 67,* 905–914.

Wellman, C. L., Cullen, M.-J., & Pelleymounter, M.-A. (1998). Effects of controllability of stress on hippocampal pharmacology. *Psychobiology, 26,* 65–72.

White, K., Lehman, D. R., Hemphill, K. J., Mandel, D. R., & Lehman, A. M. (2006). Causal attributions, perceived control, and psychological adjustment: A study of chronic fatigue syndrome. *Journal of Applied Social Psychology, 36,* 75–99.

Wielema, M. (2003). Adriaan Koerbagh: Biblical criticism and enlightenment. In W. van Bunge (Ed.), *The early enlightenment in the Dutch Republic 1650–1750* (pp. 61–80). Leiden: Brill.

Williams, J. H., & Ross, L. (2007). Consequences of prenatal toxin exposure for mental health in children and adolescents: A systematic review. *European Child and Adolescent Psychiatry, 16,* 243–253.

Williamson, O. E. (1995). Hierarchies, markets and power in the economy: An economic perspective. *Industrial and Corporate Change, 4*(1), 21–49.

Wittgenstein, L. (1953). *Philosophical investigations.* MacMillan, New York.

Wolf, E. J., Lunney, C. A., & Schnurr, P. P. (2016). The influence of the dissociative subtype of posttraumatic stress disorder on treatment efficacy in female veterans and active duty service members. *Journal of Consulting and Clinical Psychology, 84*(1), 95–100.

Wordsworth. W. (1807). *Ode: Imitation of immortality from recollections of early childhood.* Available at http://www.bartleby.com/101/536.html

World Health Organization. (1992). *ICD-10. The ICD-10 classification of mental and behavioral disorders: Clinical descriptions and diagnostic guidelines.* Geneva, Switzerland: Author.

Wu-Chi, L. (1990). *An introduction to Chinese literature.* Westport: Greenwood Press.

Zhou, S., Rosenthal, D. G., Sherman, S., Zelikoff, J., Gordon, T., & Weitzman, M. (2014). Physical, behavioral, and cognitive effects of prenatal tobacco and postnatal secondhand smoke exposure. *Current Problems in Pediatric Adolescent Health Care, 44,* 219–241.

Zhuang Zi. (2008). *The wisdom of Zhuang Zi on Daoism.* Translated with annotations and commentaries by Chung Wu. New York: Peter Lang.

Zoia, S., Blason, L., D'Ottavio, G., Bulgheroni, M., Pezzetta, E., Scabar, A., & Castiello, U. (2007). Evidence of early development of action planning in the human foetus: A kinematic study. *Experimental Brain Research, 176,* 217–226.

Author Index

Subject Index